Lovecraft and a World in Transition

The Hippocampus Press Library of Criticism

S. T. Joshi, *Primal Sources: Essays on H. P. Lovecraft* (2003)
S. T. Joshi, *The Evolution of the Weird Tale* (2004)
Robert H. Waugh, *The Monster in the Mirror: Looking for H. P. Lovecraft* (2006)
Scott Connors, ed., *The Freedom of Fantastic Things: Selected Criticism on Clark Ashton Smith* (2006)
Ben Szumskyj, ed., *Two-Gun Bob: A Centennial Study of Robert E. Howard* (2006)
S. T. Joshi and Rosemary Pardoe, ed., *Warnings to the Curious: A Sheaf of Criticism on M. R. James* (2007)
S. T. Joshi, *Classics and Contemporaries: Some Notes on Horror Fiction* (2009)
Kenneth W. Faig, Jr., *The Unknown Lovecraft* (2009)
Massimo Berruti, *Dim-Remembered Stories: A Critical Study of R. H. Barlow* (2010)
Gary William Crawford, Jim Rockhill, and Brian J. Showers, ed., *Reflections in a Glass Darkly: Essays on J. Sheridan Le Fanu* (2011)
Robert H. Waugh, *A Monster of Voices: Speaking for H. P. Lovecraft* (2011)
Donald Sidney-Fryer, *The Golden State Phantasticks: The California Romantics and Related Subjects* (2012)
William F. Nolan, *Nolan on Bradbury: Sixty Years of Writing about the Master of Science Fiction* (2013)
Steven J. Mariconda, *H. P. Lovecraft: Art, Artifact, and Reality* (2013)
S. T. Joshi, *Unutterable Horror: A History of Supernatural Fiction* (2014)
Massimo Berruti, S. T. Joshi, and Sam Gafford, ed., *William Hope Hodgson: Voices from the Borderland* (2014)
Lovecraft Annual (2007–)
Dead Reckonings (2007–)

LOVECRAFT
AND A WORLD IN TRANSITION

Collected Essays on H. P. Lovecraft

S. T. Joshi

Hippocampus Press
New York

Copyright © 2014 Hippocampus Press
Works by S. T. Joshi © 2014 by S. T. Joshi

Published by Hippocampus Press
P.O. Box 641, New York, NY 10156.
http://www.hippocampuspress.com

All rights reserved.
No part of this work may be reproduced in any form or by any means without the written permission of the publisher.

Cover photograph of H. P. Lovecraft courtesy of Dan Lorraine. A cropped version of this image appeared with "The Phenomenon of HPL" by Helen V. Wesson in the *Fossil*, 55, No. 154 (July 1957). The photograph is published here for the first time, with the entire image intact.

Cover design by Jessica Forsythe.
Back cover photo by Emily Marija Kurmis.
Hippocampus Press logo designed by Anastasia Damianakos.

First Paperback Edition
1 3 5 7 9 8 6 4 2

ISBN 978-1-61498-105-3

Contents

Introduction 7
I. Biographical Studies 11
    Lovecraft and *Weird Tales* 13
    Further Notes on Lovecraft and Music 22
    Lovecraft's Library 27
    Lovecraft's Revisions: How Much of Them Did He Write? 31
    Lovecraft and His Wife 46
    Lovecraft and the Films of His Day 49
    The Rationale of Lovecraft's Pseudonyms 53
    Lovecraft and the Munsey Magazines 62
    Barbarism vs. Civilization: Robert E. Howard and H. P. Lovecraft in Their Correspondence 73
II. Philosophical Studies 97
    The Political and Economic Thought of H. P. Lovecraft 99
    "Reality" and Knowledge: Some Notes on Lovecraft's Aesthetic ... 105
    In Defence of Dagon and Lovecraft's Philosophy 115
    Lovecraft's Alien Civilisations: A Political Interpretation 122
    Lovecraft and a World in Transition 144
    Lovecraft and the "Big Issue" 157
    H. P. Lovecraft: The Fiction of Materialism 160
    Lovecraft and Religion 182
    Time, Space, and Natural Law: Science and Pseudo-Science in Lovecraft 191
III. Thematic and Textual Studies 217
    Autobiography in Lovecraft 219
    Lovecraft's Other Planets 232
    Textual Problems in Lovecraft 243
    The Structure of Lovecraft's Longer Narratives 258
    The Dream World and the Real World in Lovecraft 275
    Topical References in Lovecraft 289
    Humour and Satire in Lovecraft 308
    A Guide to the Lovecraft Fiction Manuscripts at the John Hay Library 322

IV. Studies of Individual Works 341
Who Wrote "The Mound"? 343
On "The Book" 347
On "Polaris" 352
On "The Tree on the Hill" 357
Lovecraft and the *Regnum Congo* 362
The Sources for "From Beyond" 367
On "The Descendant" 372
What Happens in "Arthur Jermyn" 375
"The Tree" and Ancient History 378
Lovecraft and Dunsany's *Chronicles of Rodriguez* 383
Some Sources for "The Mound" and *At the Mountains of Madness* 388
The Case of Charles Dexter Ward 393
Excised Passages from "The Thing on the Doorstep" 410

V. On Lovecraft's Essays, Poetry, and Letters 417
"History of the *Necronomicon*" 419
"Supernatural Horror in Literature" 422
Two Spurious Lovecraft Poems 437
A Look at Lovecraft's Letters 440
Lovecraft's Fantastic Poetry..453
Lovecraft, Regner Lodbrog, and Olaus Wormius......................465
Lovecraft's Essays...473

VI. On Lovecraft's Legacy and Influence 499
The Development of Lovecraftian Studies: 1971–1982...........501
R. H. Barlow and the Recognition of H. P. Lovecraft..............539
A Literary Tutelage: Robert Bloch and H. P. Lovecraft...........548
Passing the Torch: H. P. Lovecraft and Fritz Leiber 566
Lovecraft at Last...579
The Cthulhu Mythos 585
The Recognition of H. P. Lovecraft, 1937–2013......................616

Sources 621
Index.. 625

Introduction

There is a certain posthumous feeling to this volume, but the plain fact of the matter is that I am not likely to write many more critical essays on Lovecraft of the sort contained here, so it struck me as useful to gather my widely scattered essays for whatever value they may have.

It will be noted that the essays range from as early as 1978 (when I was twenty) to 2009. Read chronologically, they would perhaps reveal some facts about their author's intellectual development, if that were of any interest to anyone. Since it is clearly not, I have decided upon a broadly thematic arrangement that collects essays of approximately the same general subject, even at the risk of a certain amount of repetition. I have resisted the temptation to revise the essays significantly, although I have updated most of the citations.

It should be evident from my overall work on Lovecraft—which includes such book-length works as *H. P. Lovecraft: The Decline of the West* (1990), *H. P. Lovecraft: A Life* (1996; revised as *I Am Providence: The Life and Times of H. P. Lovecraft* [2010]) and *The Rise and Fall of the Cthulhu Mythos* (2008)—that my general concerns with Lovecraft focus on (a) the critical analysis of his work; (b) the philosophical thought that underlies much of his writing; (c) other bodies of work (essays, poetry, letters) aside from the fiction that tends to garner most of the attention among readers and critics; (d) the facts of his biography and the relation of his life to his work; and (e) his influence upon subsequent writers. The six section divisions of this book reflect these interests.

I began my study of Lovecraft as early as 1975, when, as an eager teenager just about to enter my senior year of high school, I embarked upon the grandiose plan of assembling an anthology of Lovecraft criticism—the volume that eventually became *H. P. Lovecraft: Four Decades of Criticism* (1980). It was around that time that I came into contact with many of the leading scholars and critics of that period—Dirk W. Mosig, R. Alain Everts, David E. Schultz, J. Vernon Shea, and others. Mosig in particular guided my understanding of Lovecraft for at least the next three years, and I gained considerable benefit from my association with Schultz, Donald R. Burleson, Peter Cannon, Marc A. Michaud, Will Murray, and—a bit later—Robert M. Price and Steven J. Mariconda. My entry into Brown University in 1976 materially aided my work, by allowing me constant access to Lovecraft's papers and manuscripts and to a wondrous array of writings by and about him.

My focus at that time, aside from the *Four Decades*, was the compilation of a bibliography of Lovecraft (published by Kent State University Press in 1981); but I also embarked tentatively on critical and philosophical analysis, the first results of which were the early essays "Autobiography in Lovecraft" and "'Reality' and Knowledge." With Mosig's abrupt departure from the field around 1978, Burleson, Schultz, I, and others were forced to take over the reins of Lovecraft scholarship. I contributed a short monograph on Lovecraft to the Starmont Reader's Guides series in 1982; Burleson wrote *H. P. Lovecraft: A Critical Study* (1983); Peter Cannon eventually wrote a fine monograph for Twayne's United States Authors Series (1989). My establishment of *Lovecraft Studies* (1979f.) helped foster much scholarship, as did other publications by Michaud's Necronomicon Press.

As the centennial of Lovecraft's life approached in 1990, I felt the need to undertake a more ambitious philosophical study of Lovecraft, so I wrote *H. P. Lovecraft: The Decline of the West*. This was one of several books that appeared around this time, all centred around the H. P. Lovecraft Centennial Conference at Brown University (August 17–19, 1990). By this time I had written the bulk of the essays in this book; several of those that date to the 1990s were in fact introductions to editions of works by or about Lovecraft.

Much as I had sought to evade it, the task of writing a new biography to supersede L. Sprague de Camp's *Lovecraft: A Biography* (1975) seemed to fall to me, so I wrote the book in 1993–95. It was unable to find a haven with a commercial or academic publisher, and Necronomicon Press did me the great favour of issuing it in 1996; but it had to appear abridged (about one-third of the text had to be omitted). Nevertheless, the book was on the whole well received. It also signalled, perhaps understandably, the effective end of my critical/philosophical/biographical work on Lovecraft. I had pretty much said all that I wished to say, and felt it was time to leave it to others to contribute work of a different sort or work that probed the issues I myself had treated in a more searching way. This work has happily been done by such scholars as Robert H. Waugh, J.-M. Rajala, Gavin Callaghan, and others. Even the demise of *Lovecraft Studies* (eventually replaced by the *Lovecraft Annual*, just as Hippocampus Press has replaced Necronomicon Press as the publisher of record for Lovecraft studies) did not stem the tide, and it seems in no danger of abating.

My interests shifted to broader studies in weird fiction as a whole, as testified by *The Weird Tale* (1990), *The Modern Weird Tale* (2001), *The Evolution of the Weird Tale* (2004), and, most recently, *Unutterable Horror: A History of Supernatural Fiction* (2012). It will be evident that my admiration for Lovecraft's own theoretical writings on weird fiction—scattered as many of them are in letters—deeply infuse these works; and it is also evident that this interest has led me to study Lovecraft's influence on other writers, as my essays on Bloch and Leiber, as well as the *Rise and Fall*, attest.

This book does not of course include every scrap of material I have ever written on Lovecraft: some inferior or ephemeral essays have been omitted, and none of the work I wrote for the *New Lovecraft Collector* (1993-99) has been included. My reviews of works by and about Lovecraft were included in *Classics and Contemporaries* (2009) and are not reprinted here. Anyone wishing to see all my writings on Lovecraft can check the bibliography on my website (www.stjoshi.org).

I trust that the essays included here still have some value, if only because they are rooted in a careful study of the facts of Lovecraft's biography, the specific details of his texts, and a broad understanding of his place in the history of weird fiction. None of them claims to be comprehensive, and several of them have sparked rebuttals or qualifications whose validity I am entirely prepared to acknowledge. As the end result of decades of scholarship—apart from my editorial, bibliographical, and other work—I hope they will remain relevant in the years to come.

—S. T. JOSHI

Seattle, Washington

Abbreviations

AT	*The Ancient Track: Complete Poetical Works* (2nd ed. Hippocampus Press, 2013)
CE	*Collected Essays* (Hippocampus Press, 2004-06; 5 vols.)
ES	*Essential Solitude: The Letters of H. P. Lovecraft and August Derleth* (Hippocampus Press, 2008; 2 vols.)
HPL	H. P. Lovecraft
JHL	John Hay Library, Brown University
D	*Dagon and Other Macabre Tales* (Arkham House, 1986)
DH	*The Dunwich Horror and Others* (Arkham House, 1984)
HM	*The Horror in the Museum and Other Revisions* (Arkham House, 1989)
MM	*At the Mountains of Madness and Other Novels* (Arkham House, 1985)
MW	*Miscellaneous Writings* (Arkham House, 1995)
OFF	*O Fortunate Floridian! H. P. Lovecraft's Letters to R. H. Barlow* (University of Tampa Press, 2007)
SL	*Selected Letters* (Arkham House, 1965-76; 5 vols.)

I. Biographical Studies

Lovecraft and *Weird Tales*

In the days of Senf's covers, monthly Jules de Grandins, Henry S. Whitehead and Dunwich Horrors, into Rankin's era with his clouded, evil, misty illustrations, bursting into Howard's pulsating epics, Depression days and bi-monthly issues—terrible time of famine—and so on into the present day. *Per ardua ad astra!*" So one reader (Reginald A. Pryke in the October 1937 issue) saw the development of *Weird Tales* and its minor if distinctive place in American civilisation. In spite of the reams of drivel and hackwork that cluttered every issue, in spite of its rejecting the best tales of Lovecraft, Whitehead, Moore, and other serious fantaisistes, in spite of the shaky financial foundations on which it managed to run for an astonishing thirty years, the "unique magazine" has remained exactly that to its current followers (whose number is now far greater than its original readership), and in spite of all shall always have a small place in the study of history and letters; for among its achievements can be named two in particular: its enlivening the confused third and fourth decades of this century with its familiar red covers, thereby becoming an authentic element of American popular culture; and its publishing many of the important works of Howard Phillips Lovecraft, now universally acknowledged as the twentieth century's premier fantaisiste and a figure of growing importance in world literature.

But it would be an error to say that these blessings are unmixed, as it would be presumptuous to assume that Lovecraft would never have reached his present status in weird fiction had he never appeared in *Weird Tales*. Second-guessing history is a tricky proposition for the historian or critic, but in this case some hypotheses can be made on certain effects that *Weird Tales* had on Lovecraft's writing—effects that, had he never submitted there, might not have occurred.

Lovecraft was the first to admit that his habit of writing specifically for *Weird Tales* resulted in a corrupting of his style so that it became more explicit, less suggestive, and more "pulpish." Despite his statements that he never wrote with a particular audience in mind, we have other remarks that attest to his desire to cater to the readership of the magazine—or, at any rate, to gain some needed revenue by placing tales there.[1] By the time Lovecraft realised the results of this cheapening effect, it was too late. It is clear that such tales as "The Horror at Red Hook," with its hackneyed use of traditional occultism, and "The Dunwich Horror," with its naive confrontation of good vs. evil (Armitage vs. Whateley), were written with *Weird Tales* in mind. Whether Lovecraft could have retained the subtlety of "The Music of Erich Zann" or the delicate prose-poetry of "The Quest of Iranon" in his later years is open to question, since regardless of *Weird Tales* he seemed to be moving toward the cosmic horror of *At the Mountains of Madness* in the course of his development as a weird writer. If it is true, as H. Warner Munn remarked in the magazine's letter column, "The Eyrie" (March 1925), that *Weird Tales* "discovered" Lovecraft, then it must be noted (as Lovecraft often did) that in its discovery it produced a writer significantly different from the one who, from 1917 to 1923, was writing solely for "self-expression" and publishing solely in amateur journals.

But *Weird Tales* affected Lovecraft's writing in another way, through its repeated and capricious rejections of his best tales. Ever sensitive to criticism, Lovecraft could not fail to be bothered when his tales were rejected, not on lack of merit, but on their failure to conform to the artificial and hackneyed standards of *Weird Tales* and other pulps. It is ironic, however, that some of his rejected stories were, when later accepted and published, praised more highly than those that editor Farnsworth Wright considered more in tune with *Weird Tales*' audience. Wright knew that Lovecraft was a powerfully original writer, but he made the mistake of underestimating the intelligence and tastes of his readership: like the Valetudinarian of Addison (*Spectator*, 29 March 1711) who was so concerned about his health that he became the more ill, Wright was so hesitant to inflict his public with work that departed from the conventional ghost story or "scientifiction" tale (or, as Lovecraft more aptly termed it, "boys' wild west stuff given an interplanetary setting, with handsome young space-pilots instead of cowboys and sheriffs, and 'Martians' and 'moon-men' instead of Indians and outlaws" [*SL* 5.302–3]) that he dared not publish such tales as "The Call of Cthulhu" or "Through the Gates of the Silver Key" without first rejecting them. It is chilling to read Lovecraft's remark that the rejection of *At the Mountains of Madness* by Wright "did more than anything else to end my effective fictional career" (*SL* 5.224).

Wright, however, was not the only one who underestimated his readership: it must be admitted that Lovecraft may have done so as well. When he called the *Weird Tales* audience a "herd of crude and unimaginative illiterates" (*SL* 4.53) he

---

1. "I shall [soon] devote myself to the composition of more stories to submit to *Weird Tales*" (*SL* 2.37).

seemed not to consider the numerous readers who, in "The Eyrie," praised Lovecraft's own tales and analysed the sources of their horror quite ably. Indeed, as time passed his views became more and more jaundiced, to such a degree that in 1935 he felt obliged to let loose this jeremiad:

> [Pulp magazine editors] aim to please the very lowest grade of readers—probably because these constitute a large numerical majority. When you glance at the advertisements in these cheap magazines (& they wouldn't continue to be inserted if they weren't answered) you can see what a hopelessly vulgar & stupid rabble comprise the bulk of the clientele. These yaps & nitwits probably can't grasp anything even remotely approaching subtlety. *Suggestion*—the most artistic way to present any marvellous event—means absolutely nothing to them. One has to draw a full diagram & drive the idea into their heads with a hammer before they "get" it.[2]

While it cannot be denied that many readers were puerile and had undeveloped tastes in weird fiction (the inane praises of such hacks as E. Hoffmann Price, Edmond Hamilton, Seabury Quinn, and others prove it), there were a good many others whose levels of appreciation were somewhat higher. Lovecraft himself had an inkling of this when he tried to plead with Wright that the "Eyrie-bombarding proletariat" (*SL* 4.322) was not representative of the total readership of the magazine; but this had little effect on Wright, who told Lovecraft "that his index to popular whim is, almost exclusively, the flood of semi-illiterate Eyrie mail which pours in upon him" (*SL* 3.194). A number of current critics have deemed Farnsworth Wright a capable editor; but to hold such an opinion is to ignore his treatment of the writer who, aside from being the most important contributor to the magazine, is now largely responsible for the continuing consideration of the magazine at all. Wright, it is true, managed to keep *Weird Tales* on its feet through the Depression; but it was at the expense of rejecting the best work of its best writers and publishing torrents of pulpish hackwork whose permanent inhumation can only be a blessing to weird fiction.

Who read *Weird Tales* and why? It is an interesting social commentary that a number of them turned to the "unique magazine" simply to escape the "mass of literary farce that we are treated to in the other magazines" ("The Eyrie," August 1929). Lovecraft too recognised that the material published in what H. Warner Munn ("The Eyrie," March 1925) called the "ultraconservative" magazines was becoming "increasingly lifeless, sterile, mannered, preoccupied with form, and obviously linked with obsolescent attitudes and interests and per-

---

2. HPL to Duane W. Rimel, 16 April 1935 (ms., JHL).

spectives" (*SL* 5.399). Both *Weird Tales* and the "ultraconservatives" represented two sides of the cultural havoc of American (and European) civilisation between the two World Wars: the latter opted for a blind return to conventionalism, while the former chose imaginative (or sometimes not so imaginative) escape from the hideous realities of Al Capone and the Great Depression. *Weird Tales* was still serving this function in the late 1930s, as a comment in "The Eyrie" of June 1937 (which almost anticipates the decade of the 1950s and Joe McCarthy) shows: "In these days of stark realism of wars and rumors of wars, of cracked politics and politicians, of 200% Americans and enemies that bore from within, it was more than relief to turn to a Lovecraft story."

Here is only one reader of many who identified Lovecraft with *Weird Tales*. Donald A. Wollheim (October 1937) did the same when he said that Lovecraft's myth-cycle (particularly such elements as the *Necronomicon*) "was one of the factors contributing to the making of WT's vivid and unique personality." It is a delicate question whether Lovecraft or such other writers as Seabury Quinn or Edmond Hamilton were actually the most "popular" contributors to the magazine. To be sure, these latter writers, experienced and businesslike pulpsters that they were, contributed far more voluminously to *Weird Tales* than Lovecraft; but readers were constantly clamouring for the latter's work (especially in the 1930s, when the relative sparsity of his original fiction, as well as his reluctance to submit to the magazine and risk additional rejections, caused Wright to appease readers with the feeble expedient of reprinting earlier tales by Lovecraft), and I think it can safely be said that even the magazine's cruder readers recognised that Lovecraft was on a higher plane than Quinn or Hamilton.

Nor was it the case (as with other such accidentally popular geniuses as Beethoven, Virgil, and Shakespeare) that readers failed to appreciate Lovecraft's true merits and enjoyed him for some coincidentally appealing feature of his work. In several letters to "The Eyrie" (many from Lovecraft's own correspondents) we note a vague and confused awareness of the philosophical bases of his work; a few of the letters, indeed, may represent some of the more astute early vignettes of Lovecraft criticism. Robert E. Howard, even before he began corresponding with the Providence writer, grasped that his "range is cosmic" (May 1928); and while we may smile at his remark that Lovecraft "touches peaks in his tales which no modern or ancient writer has ever hinted," we nonetheless must be impressed at Howard's perception of the central doctrine of Lovecraft's work (expressed by Lovecraft himself in his letter to Farnsworth Wright of 5 July 1927, published in the February 1928 issue of *Weird Tales*). A good number of readers were captivated by Lovecraft's polished, erudite, and slightly archaic style, and Ray Cummings expressed the feelings of many when he said, "Never have I encountered any purer, more beautiful diction. [His tales] sing; the true poetry of prose" (June 1926). Harold Farnese maintained that Lovecraft's "weird and eldritch atmosphere has yet to be equalled by other writers" (August 1931), while a comment by E. Hoffmann Price hints at a major philosophical concept in Lovecraft's later work:

> In his utter unreality and impossibility, he is like a non-Euclidean geometer who, though working on physically impossible axioms, reasons truly from them and produces theorems, and subsequent Q.E.D.'s, which are as true as if they actually were true; or as one who reasons of the inconceivable fourth dimension and by self-consistent hypotheses and logic deals logically with impossibility. (April 1926)

The "self-consistency" that Price notes is equivalent, more or less, to what Lovecraft felt must now be the basis for true fantasy: "The time has come when the normal revolt against time, space, and matter must assume a form not overtly incompatible with what is known of reality—when it must be gratified by images forming *supplements* rather than *contradictions* to the visible and mensurable universe" (SL 3.295-96).

Not all of Lovecraft's fans in "The Eyrie," however, were so astute. Several writers (despite their assertions that they had read Shakespeare and other such writers) confirmed Lovecraft's opinion of their "semiilliteracy"—or, at any rate, their lack of judgment—by proclaiming him and *Weird Tales* among the best works in world literature. We know through Lovecraft's letters that he censured many of his younger correspondents (R. H. Barlow, J. Vernon Shea, Willis Conover) for holding such views as "*Weird Tales* is the best magazine ever published" (October 1926) or that "Lovecraft is as great a writer as ever lived" (June 1929) or that "The Outsider" is "the greatest weird story ever written" (September 1931). And we can only laugh at the puerility of J. Wasso (February 1930), who wished to form an H. P. Lovecraft fan club. These opinions reflect the difference between true critical appreciation and that immature adulation which regrettably casts a dubious shadow on the author himself. Indeed, it may have been precisely such remarks that caused Edmund Wilson, in 1945, to condemn "the Lovecraft cult" as "on even a more infantile level than the Baker Street Irregulars and the cult of Sherlock Holmes" (Wilson 49). Lovecraft has had to wait too long to escape the pathetic talons of fandom.

Not only was Lovecraft praised to the skies in *Weird Tales*, but many championed his poorer stories—"The Hound," "The Lurking Fear," "The Horror at Red Hook." The phenomenal response to "The Dunwich Horror" is a virtual index to its (unconscious) conformity to pulp standards. Still more amusing are those fans who were so taken with Lovecraft that they (unconsciously?) imitated his erudite writing style when writing their letters:

"The Dunwich Horror" transported me, upon the wings of imagination, to the uttermost depths of vast caverns in the bowels of the earth—caverns which are swept by foul, moaning winds laden with the breath of the grave and which contain cosmic cesspools wherein the corruption, filth and evil of millions of centuries have accumulated; from there I traveled, in an instant, to far-off worlds or places where only a brief glimpse of unnamable horrors and formless, space-filling alien entities send me scurrying and screaming (mentally) with terror back to my warm fireside. (April 1930)

Then there were the truly eccentric readers whose minds were somehow ignited by Lovecraft's tales: one tells us that "The Outsider" is a true story founded on an incident in Germany; another notes some mysterious essays on Shakespeare written by Lovecraft during his involvement with amateur journalism; yet another, quoting Ibsen in the process, wishes the *Necronomicon* to be serialised in *Weird Tales*.

This brings up one of the more amusing aspects of Lovecraft's popularity in *Weird Tales*: the remarkably widespread belief that the *Necronomicon* was an actual book, and that his myth-cycle of Cthulhu and Yog-Sothoth had an actual basis in fact or was an authentic cycle of folklore. The hoax was obviously aided by Lovecraft's correspondents, who in their own tales used these very elements as if out of a common pool of esoteric knowledge. Indeed, virtually all of his newer correspondents—Derleth, Conover, Howard, Shea, Rimel, and others—had to be disabused as to the reality of the myth-cycle. The game was of course carried on after Lovecraft's death: in one of the most famous letters in "The Eyrie," one J. H. Stewart, Jr, tells how Manly Wade Wellman nearly stumbled upon a copy of the *Necronomicon* in a bookstore presided over by an ancient crone (July 1952).

What is also interesting is the use of the term "Elder Gods" by readers to describe the gods of Lovecraft's mythos. It was, of course, August Derleth who, after Lovecraft's death (and initially in the story "The Return of Hastur"), launched his own myth-cycle where "Elder Gods" battled the "Great Old Ones" in a puerile struggle of good vs. evil. Derleth, indeed, took every opportunity to foster his myth-cycle and to claim that it represented the development of the mythos as Lovecraft himself would have done had he lived (cf. his letter in the May 1941 issue). The "Elder Gods" have no existence in Lovecraft's tales (certainly not the all-powerful one that Derleth gave them), and even in "The Strange High House in the Mist" there are mentions only of strange, unexplained entities called "Elder Ones." *Weird Tales* readers seem to have confused them with the Great Old Ones (Cthulhu, Nyarlathotep, Yog-Sothoth, et al.), for Bernard Austin Dwyer (June 1930) makes reference to "Other Gods in the Elder World." Another writer, B. M. Reynolds (October 1936), mentions the Elder Gods themselves—this being the earliest mention of them in a quasi-Derlethian sense that I have found. Robert Leonard Russell makes note of "Cthulhu, Azathoth and the other Elder Gods" (August 1937), and Jacques Bergier speaks of Lovecraft's "cycle of the Elder Gods and strange civilisations" (September 1937). It is tempting to wonder whether these mentions in any way helped to shape Derleth's perverted conception of Lovecraft's myth-cycle.

The facility with which many readers noticed the Lovecraftian flavour of some of his revisions published in *Weird Tales* is striking. Hazel Heald's tales in particular were called out for mention, one reader soberly informing us that "Even Lovecraft . . . could hardly . . . have surpassed the grotesque scene" that served as the climax to "The Horror in the Museum" (May 1934). Aside from Heald, this "female Lovecraft" (June 1935), William Lumley's "The Diary of Alonzo Typer" was praised, Paul S. Smith claiming that Lumley had a fair chance of being "a worthy successor to the late master" (August 1938). Lovecraft himself wryly remarked that "some of my revision clients congratulate *themselves* when the readers praise stories (like 'The Last Test', 'The Curse of Yig', 'The Horror in the Museum', 'Winged Death', etc.) that *I* wrote" (*SL* 4.394).

Not all readers expressed favourable views, of course: despite the obviously sensible policy that only letters of praise were allowed, in the main, to appear in "The Eyrie," some dissenting letters emerged; interestingly, these came largely during the editorships of Edwin Baird (1923-24) and Dorothy McIlwraith (1940-54), and their absence during Wright's tenure can only be another sign of his paranoiac insecurity. Toward the latter days of the magazine, when the end was perhaps visible, there flared up a minor debate about Lovecraft's worth as a writer which is interesting not so much for the arguments expressed (being on both sides basically subjective and irrelevant), but for the fact that a majority of adverse critics have taken precisely the view here adopted by Joseph V. Wilcox, who put forth the claim that Lovecraft's style was "turgid"[3] and not suitable for the weird tale.

The number of Lovecraft's correspondents who wrote letters praising him in "The Eyrie" (many of these letters appearing before their writers even began corresponding with him) is interesting. These included not merely his fellow fantaisistes—Derleth, Munn, Wandrei (although only after Lovecraft's demise), Bloch, Kuttner, Price, Clark Ashton Smith, and others—but associates only marginally involved in weird fiction—James F. Morton, Harold S. Farnese, J. Vernon Shea, Bernard Austin Dwyer, Paul J. Campbell, and the like. Several

---

3. This curiously is echoed by the classical scholar and critic Gilbert Highet in his idiosyncratic snipe at HPL in *A Clerk of Oxenford* (New York: Oxford University Press, 1954), 9.

writers, in fact, became associates of Lovecraft through "The Eyrie" itself—Derleth, Howard, and perhaps Jacques Bergier. On the other hand, it is odd that such colleagues as Frank Belknap Long, Robert H. Barlow, and others, who were both Lovecraft's close friends and significantly involved in either *Weird Tales* itself or fantasy fandom, never sent letters to "The Eyrie"—or, at any rate, never had them published.

Lovecraft's death in March 1937 produced the most overwhelming tide of letters of comment ever found in "The Eyrie," and far exceeded the amount for other such deceased writers as Robert E. Howard or Henry S. Whitehead. A great many of Lovecraft's correspondents, from those who had known him in the 1920s (Smith) to those who had corresponded with him only a few months before his death (Robert A. W. Lowndes, Earl Peirce), sent letters of regret, while other associates (particularly Henry George Weiss and Kenneth Sterling) extolled him as a great writer, thinker, and epistolarian. Those who had known Lovecraft only through his work were as moved by his death as they had been by his stories: "I feel," writes Robert Leonard Russell, "as will many other readers of *Weird Tales*, that I have lost a real friend" (August 1937). But Lovecraft's work by no means stopped appearing upon his demise: many tales previously rejected were now printed, and when these ran out poems were used to satiate the readers' demands. But, as L. Sprague de Camp (435) has pointed out, Lovecraft's death, so closely following that of Robert E. Howard and the virtual surcease of Clark Ashton Smith's fictional output, dealt a fatal blow to *Weird Tales*, caused it to lose much of its "vivid and unique personality," and heralded a death that, though staved off for some seventeen years, was as inevitable as Lovecraft's own. There were still, under the none too competent guidance of Dorothy McIlwraith, some fine writers appearing in its pages—Bloch, Bradbury, Wellman, and others—but the lack of any writer of the stature of a Lovecraft or a Howard, plus the rising competition of the science fiction magazines and the emergence of the paperback book as an alternative to the pulp magazine, ensured *Weird Tales*' collapse. In its decline "The Eyrie" too dwindled from the lively readers' column of the 1920s and 1930s to the dry editorial ramblings of the 1940s and 1950s. From a full 160 pages to a small digest size—such was the ignominious end of a magazine that had seen in its pages the work of Lovecraft, Whitehead, Smith, Long, Wandrei, Bloch, and so many of the most important figures in modern weird fiction; but perhaps it could have met no other fate, for it was very much a product of its time, very much a part of the Roaring Twenties and Depression Thirties from which it had sprung.

It is needless to say that both Lovecraft and *Weird Tales* would have been very different without each other; but whether for better or for worse, their fortuitous joining helped to bring about what is probably the finest weird fiction that the twentieth century has ever seen. In view of this, the crudities and absurdities of *Weird Tales* become trivial, just as refulgent gold outshines its dross.

Works Cited

de Camp, L. Sprague. *Lovecraft: A Biography*. Garden City, NY: Doubleday, 1975.

Wilson, Edmund. "Tales of the Marvellous and the Ridiculous." 1945. Rpt. in S. T. Joshi, ed. *H. P. Lovecraft: Four Decades of Criticism*. Athens: Ohio University Press, 1980. 46–49.

Further Notes on Lovecraft and Music

If we must admit that Lovecraft's musical taste was rudimentary in the extreme, we can also agree with August Derleth ("Lovecraft and Music") that Lovecraft was at times too self-deprecatory about his own reactions to classical music. Some of his random remarks, however, can shed additional light not only upon his own involvement with music, but with certain points in the history of music and musicology itself.

Lovecraft tells us that he began taking violin lessons at the age of seven: "I was so exact in time and tune, and showed such a semi-professional precision and flourish in my crude attempts, that my plea for a violin was granted when I was seven years of age" (SL 1.29). Lovecraft's sound rhythmical sense—which allowed him, so early as the age of two, to be able to "repeat any poem of simple sort with unfaltering cadence" (SL 1.32), and which, of course, led to his later efforts at poetry[1]—could have carried him far in music, but the drudgery of practicing played havoc on his nerves and he was forced to give up the violin at the age of nine.

Just before the end of his "career," however, he gave "a public recital at which I played a solo from Mozart before an audience of considerable size" (SL 1.30). What was the piece in question? Mozart wrote no works for unaccompanied violin—such as Bach's six sonatas and partitas, BWV 1001-06—so that one assumes that Lovecraft played one of Mozart's sonatas for violin and piano, with his instructor, a Mrs. Wilhelm Nauck, accompanying on the piano. If this assumption is correct, then we may be limited to some of Mozart's very early—and very easy—sonatas, e.g. K. 6-15 (where the keyboard part is actually substantially more difficult than the violin part). These ten sonatas were written between 1762 and 1764, when Mozart was between the ages of six and eight. Among even this group we can eliminate some of the harder sonatas (K. 11-15) as being well beyond the capabilities of a violinist of two years' experience: these sonatas involve such relatively advanced techniques (which one encounters only after about five to seven years of playing) as rapid string-

---

1. It is suggestive that his first extant poem, "The Poem of Ulysses" (8 November 1897), also dates to the year when he began the violin.

crossings, triple—or even quadruple—stops (although usually on open strings), rapid succession of trills, tremolos, shifts into second or third position (rarely beyond), and the like. Moreover, many of the later sonatas are in "flat" keys (works in "sharp" keys are much easier to play on the violin than works in "flat" keys). Indeed, it may be that Lovecraft played one movement (probably the slow movement or the minuet, since even the allegros of the early sonatas are demanding to a very inexperienced player) of the sonata in C, K. 6, in D, K. 7, or in B-flat, K. 8. Lovecraft's description of a "solo *from* Mozart" implies only part of a work rather than a complete work.

Nevertheless, this accomplishment of Lovecraft's is a fairly impressive one. Most violinists of that age nowadays are not given any works in the standard repertoire to play, but are rather fed on workbooks by such instructors as Applebaum, Sevcik, and the like. Either such workbooks did not exist in Lovecraft's day, or his instructor felt that Lovecraft was advanced enough to venture into the performance of actual classics. He need not have learned to read music—probably he did not—since the notes in his part could be designated by "coding" the proper fingerings on the proper strings. Nevertheless, any boy who could play anything of Mozart's after two years at the violin merits our praise.

The broader question as to why Lovecraft was given Mozart and not some other composer to play leads us centrally into Lovecraft's whole attitude toward the appreciation of music. We know that his taste in music (as in other arts) was *associative*; that is, he enjoyed a work of music because it triggered mental associations and memories in him. "Whenever I seem to appreciate a strain of music, it is purely through association—never intrinsically. To me, *Tipperary* or *Rule, Britannia* has infinitely more emotional appeal than any creation of Liszt, Beethoven or Wagner" (SL 3.221). Now there is nothing wrong with this sort of appreciation, as long as one realizes (as Lovecraft did) that this music is not of the highest aesthetic calibre. But if we accept this associational appreciation of music in Lovecraft, we are led to a further question: Why did he not appreciate the music of that eighteenth century to which he felt such close aesthetic and emotional ties?

I refer, of course, to the music of the Baroque era (now dated to ca. 1580–1730, although individual Baroque composers lived on into the 1760s), now enjoying an astonishing revival in our own time. Lovecraft must have been aware at least partially of this branch of music: he could hardly have failed to notice Addison's vicious and vengeful attacks on Italian opera in general and Handel in particular (*Spectator* nos. 5, 18, 28, 29, 31);[2] or Bos-

---

2. Addison's attacks are, incidentally, probably due more to envy than to anything else: he had written the libretto to Thomas Clayton's opera *Rosamond* (1707), which had failed miserably; shortly thereafter Handel introduced Italian opera to England

well's fervent appreciation of Handel in the *Life of Johnson*. And what is more, he would surely have appreciated the thorough Englishness of Purcell—as in *Dido and Aeneas* (1689), with its classical theme, or *King Arthur* (1691), its libretto written by John Dryden—or of Handel himself, whose *Water Musick* (1717) and *Musick for the Royal Fireworks* (1749) ought to have made an impression on Lovecraft. Indeed, Lovecraft tells us that his favorite classical music is "conventional grand opera . . . and Dick Wagner" (*SL* 3.342), which indicates his fondness for the "blood-and-thunder" type of music replete with trumpets, horns, tympani, and the like—just the thing we find in the *Fireworks Musick*.

The reason that Lovecraft seems not to have enjoyed these examples of late Baroque music is that he probably never heard them; and he never heard them because in his day much of Baroque music was appreciated almost solely, if at all, by specialists. It should be noted that Baroque music became almost wholly forgotten around 1750 (earlier in Italy and France), the Rococo and Classical periods with their fundamentally different psychological and philosophical bases being ushered in by J. C. Bach, Haydn, and Mozart. Indeed, it was the lot of Vivaldi (1678–1741) to become old-fashioned in his own time, so that he died a pauper's death in Vienna. Bach, too, was censured for his over-attention to complex counterpoint (recall Mozart's championing the superiority of monophony: "Melody is the very essence of music"), although Handel (1685–1759) had a better time in a musically backward England. In any case, the resurrection of Baroque music was begun by Mendelssohn in his revival of Bach's *St. Matthew Passion* in 1829 (of a piece with this is Beethoven's reverence for Handel and Brahms's edition of the harpsichord works of Couperin), but even then Baroque music was slow to recover. Vivaldi, indeed, was completely unknown until a few decades ago—before then he was known, if at all, not as the Father of the Concerto, but as an obscure and mediocre Italian, some of whose violin concerti Bach had inexplicably chosen to transcribe for keyboard. Although fourteen collections of Vivaldi's work had been published in his lifetime (one—Op. 13—probably spurious; see Selfridge-Field 229; Talbot 132f.), the bulk of his work lay in manuscript for 200 years and was discovered only in the early decades of the century (see Kolneder 2f. for a vivid account of the discovery of these manuscripts). His instrumental work began to be published, performed, and recorded only in the late 1940s and following, and the Istituto Italiano Antonio Vivaldi only completed its publication of the "Complete Instrumental Works" (in 530 volumes; they are not complete) in 1972. Appreciation for Handel has always lingered after a fashion among the British—but he was known almost exclu-

---

with *Rinaldo* (1711), an instant success.

sively for *Messiah* (not a work to interest the atheistic Lovecraft in spite of its exquisite music) and other oratorios. (Many of his countless operas have even yet not been revived.)

Lovecraft unconsciously gives us an indication of the knowledge of Baroque music in his time when he speaks in passing of "the music of Handel, Bach and Beethoven" (*SL* 5.395). Bach and Handel were long regarded (and by laymen still are) as the sole pinnacles of the Baroque, while the whole Italian tradition from Monteverdi to Vivaldi—from which both Bach and Handel drew much of their inspiration and technique—was forgotten. Indeed, we can now finally return to the question of why Lovecraft was given Mozart instead of some other composer to play on the violin. Nowadays young pupils are usually given Baroque music—Vivaldi, Corelli, Telemann, Handel, etc.—because of its technical simplicity. Such music was, of course, unavailable to Lovecraft, and Mozart was not merely the simplest of composers whom he could play, but was virtually the oldest composer in the regular concert repertoire. (We must also remember that chamber orchestras and the use of "authentic" or original instrumentation was unheard of until the 1950s.)

If idle speculation of this sort has any value, then one may with fair confidence say that Lovecraft would have enjoyed some of the eighteenth-century music of the late Baroque, simply through its ability to conduct him imaginatively to the century of Pope and Johnson. (It is interesting to note, however, that Johnson shared Lovecraft's coldness to music.) Since Lovecraft seemed more attuned to vocal music than to instrumental—although of Wagner's he singles out the "Ride of the Valkyries," and Alfred Galpin records that Lovecraft was strongly affected by Chopin's instrumental work—he might well have enjoyed the more "dramatic" of Handel's oratorios (*Judas Maccabaeus, Jephtha, Samson*, etc.; even *Israel in Egypt*, which is not strictly dramatic, employing charming word-painting and monumental choral effects), some of the Baroque operas in English (Blow's *Venus and Adonis*, Purcell, Handel's *Acis and Galatea*, with libretto by John Gay and additions from Pope, Dryden, and others), or such things as Handel's *Anthems for the Coronation of George II* (in one of which the choir bursts forth with "God Save the King! Long Live the King!"), or some of Vivaldi's more fiery concerti. Lovecraft was so thorough a student of the eighteenth century that it is a tragedy that he did not expand his appreciation to the domain of music.

We may also remark of some early works of music which incorporated elements of fantasy or even horror; from the daemonic *Toccata and Fugue in D minor* and *Chromatic Fantasy and Fugue* of Bach to Tartini's *Devil's Trill Sonata* (whose final cadenza has something of the cosmic) to Vivaldi's *Concerto "Funebre"* (RV 579) to some chilling works of Corelli's (e.g., Op. IV, No. 1, third movement; Op. VI, No. 4, second movement) which seem to suggest the resolute marching of the dead. Programme music in general—whose very principle is to suggest extra-musical ideas—was essentially a child of the Baroque, and would surely have appealed to Lovecraft's visual imagination. Some of Vivaldi's programmatic works are marvellously evocative: note the two different concerti entitled "Night" (RV 439 and 501), the *Four Seasons* (with movements depicting such things as the nightmare of a drunken shepherd, the buzzing of bees in summer, the icy chill of winter, etc.), and the like. Nor can we ignore such later works as Beethoven's *Wellington's Victory Overture*, which incorporates the British national anthem.

The times were, however, against the possibility of Lovecraft's learning to appreciate Baroque music, and even if he had lived into the 'forties and 'fifties it is unlikely that his musical taste would have changed. But Lovecraft's relative blind spot in music need not be censured too strongly; he himself expressed it best when he said:

> Of course—if everybody were theoretically perfect in mental and emotional balance and sensitiveness, we would all be responsive to every form of art just as soon as education opened up our channels of perception and recognition. But the human race simply isn't built that way. We are for the most part imperfect chance products of varied evolutionary conditions, so that any one of us must be content with only part of the aesthetic responsiveness which an ideally perfect human being would possess. Some, of course, are lucky enough to possess a much wider range than others . . . but nobody is 100% responsive to all the aesthetic stimuli which exist. (SL 5.96)

Works Cited

Derleth, August. "Lovecraft and Music." *Utopia* No. 1 (May 1945): 3–7. *Romantist* 4–5 (1980–81): 45–47.

Kolneder, Walter. *Antonio Vivaldi: His Life and Work.* Tr. Bill Hopkins. London: Faber & Faber, 1970.

Selfridge-Field, Eleanor. *Venetian Instrumental Music from Gabrieli to Vivaldi.* New York: Praeger, 1975.

Talbot, Michael. *Vivaldi.* London: J. M. Dent, 1978.

Lovecraft's Library

The reasons for studying H. P. Lovecraft's personal library may not be immediately evident to the casual reader. To be sure, there is some intrinsic curiosity value in knowing that he owned a 1567 black-letter edition of Ovid, or a complete file of *Weird Tales, The Fantasy Fan,* and other now fabulously rare journals of fantasy fiction, or several issues of *The Rhode Island Almanac,* by a writer (or, rather, a series of writers) disguised by the classic Augustan pseudonym of Isaac Bickerstaff, a pseudonym once used by Lovecraft himself.[1] And yet, a listing of Lovecraft's library is far more than a farrago of *curiosa;* for Lovecraft, like Samuel Johnson (to mention only one other whose library has been catalogued), was so thoroughly a man of letters that his library—not greatly distinguished from a bibliophilic point of view— was an essential part of his life and thought: it shaped his intellectual growth; it was one of his most prized possessions; it was a storehouse of ideas that found expression in all phases of his literary work. To understand the man, we must first understand his books.

Amidst the glaring and outré covers that adorn the paperbound editions of his stories—now distributed in the millions of copies throughout the world—it is often forgotten that Providence-born Howard Phillips Lovecraft did far more than write the greatest horror fiction since Poe. Poems, essays, and particularly letters would occupy a far greater proportion of his collected writings than his admittedly great fiction; indeed, his letters may perhaps be his greatest achievement, so full as they are of a stupefyingly diverse erudition. If nothing else, he wrote more letters than almost anyone in the twentieth century and, perhaps, in all literary history: an estimated 80,000 letters emerged from his pen, although probably fewer than 10,000 now survive. The letters alone may confirm that Lovecraft, aside from being Rhode Island's greatest native writer, might occupy—or come to occupy—a significant place in modern intellectual history. That he was, intellectually, highly gifted is beyond doubt: from the age of four to his death at forty-six he was an omniv-

---

1. In HPL's debate with the astrologer J. F. Hartmann in the Providence *Evening News,* September–December 1914 (cf. *SL* 1.4–5); now rpt. in *CE* 3.

orous reader, thus abundantly making up for the missed opportunity (because of poor health) of attending Brown University. Fittingly for a man who had not the world but the cosmos for his subject of study, his reading tastes were bewilderingly wide, and his library in large measure reflects the *crème de la crème* of his readings—those books that he was satisfied not merely with reading, but with owning.

It is therefore regrettable that a complete listing of Lovecraft's library is not available to us; instead, fewer than 1000 of his 1500 or so volumes have hitherto been located and catalogued. Though it is possible to estimate the nature of the missing portions of the library, and though certain areas have surely been catalogued with comparative thoroughness, there is nonetheless little chance that these lacunae will ever be filled. To begin with, it seems that many of Lovecraft's volumes on science and philosophy are absent from the present list: of the books by Darwin, Haeckel, Huxley, Margaret Murray, and many others to which Lovecraft frequently referred in his letters there is hardly a trace (possibly he consulted many of these only in libraries); nor do we find much by Santayana, Bertrand Russell, Hobbes, Spinoza, and the other thinkers whom Lovecraft admired. Volumes of history—especially modern history—seem, too, in rather short supply.

But on the positive side we are aware of a great many volumes that Lovecraft often proclaimed often to be dear to his heart. In particular we note the profusion of Greek and Latin classics, books on ancient history and civilisation, English poetry and belles lettres (particularly of the eighteenth century), New England history and antiquities, and—most important of all to the literary scholar—his holdings of weird fiction, which may be considered virtually complete thanks to the availability of a list in Lovecraft's own hand—"Weird &c. Items in Library of H. P. Lovecraft"—which he prepared late in life, evidently "for the benefit of distant members of the 'weird fiction gang' [i.e., his literary correspondents] who wish to borrow spectral volumes not obtainable in their home-town bibliothecae" (SL 5.243-44).

Lovecraft's poverty precluded extensive campaigns of book-buying, and a good many of the volumes in his library—particularly those of eighteenth- and early nineteenth-century imprint—were holdovers from his family library. This may explain the profusion of works by Dickens, Thackeray (who "induceth drowsiness" [SL 1.73] in Lovecraft), Jane Austen, and others (in particular the totally un-Lovecraftian romances of Mrs Mulock) in which he found little interest. Many other volumes—beginning, perhaps, with the presentation of Lang's *Arabian Nights* by his mother in 1898—were gifts, as the inscriptions on the volumes by Donald Wandrei, Walter J. Coates, Samuel Loveman, and others testify. A small number must have been acquired gratis as a consequence of Lovecraft's being a contributor to the volume: thus we find the Christine Campbell Thomson anthologies published by Selwyn & Blount, Hammett's *Creeps by Night*, Harré's *Beware After Dark!*, and others. But a substantial residue was purchased by Lovecraft himself, either upon publication or through used-book stores, where, as he remarked, "one can obtain astonishing bargains" (*SL* 2.287).

In many ways Lovecraft's library was an enviable one. He possessed a remarkable collection of Augustan and early Romantic poetry, encompassing both the great—Keats, Shelley, Coleridge, Thomson, Gray—and the near-great—Shenstone, Beattie, Trumbull, Crabbe. His statement that "I picked up my peculiar style from Addison, Steele, Johnson, and Gibbon" (*SL* 1.11) is confirmed by his significant holdings of these and other eighteenth-century masters of English prose.

Although Lovecraft knew a smattering of many tongues—though not, as Zealia Bishop would have us believe, of African dialects!—he could read only English and Latin fluently; so that what volumes of French, Italian, German, and Greek literature he owned were almost exclusively in translation. (His possession of Baudelaire's *Lettres* in French was the result of a gift.) Moreover, many of his Latin volumes were in translation or in bilingual editions with interlinear translations (a technique upon which Latinists now look with horror). Needless to say, he owned those celebrated translations of the Latin and Greek classics which have in turn themselves become classics—Dryden's *Aeneid*, Pope's *Odyssey* and *Iliad*, Garth's Ovid, Dryden's Plutarch (revised by Clough), Chapman's *Hymns of Homer*, Murphy's Tacitus, and the like. His volumes on ancient history and civilisation were largely high-school or college textbooks, some rather shoddy and most now outdated; but Lovecraft never claimed to be a specialist, and his knowledge in this field, as in so many others, was admirable for a layman.

The few science books in his library of whose existence we know—largely astronomy, biology, and chemistry—are almost without exception textbooks or general, non-technical manuals. Lovecraft's disinclination for mathematics prevented him from penetrating the mysteries of astronomy and physics as deeply as he would have liked; perhaps a fortunate circumstance, else we might have seen competent if dry astronomy volumes from him rather than the brilliant weird fiction by which he is now achieving a tardy if universal fame. It was, in fact, precisely because Lovecraft did not become a specialist in any single field that he could coordinate his multifarious knowledge and distil it into his fiction and essays: without being a geologist he could write such a convincing narrative as *At the Mountains of Madness*; without being a specialist in New England history, he could pen such a tale as *The Case of Charles Dexter*

Ward. But had he been a scholar either in one field or the other, we might perhaps never have seen one or the other of these tales. True enough, his knowledge can be picked apart and criticised by any specialist; but could that specialist boast the catholicity of taste, the inveterate curiosity in so many academic fields, and the impressive integration of this knowledge into a single and coherent philosophy such as Lovecraft achieved? Although the concept of the Renaissance man may be becoming increasingly obsolete with the bewildering expansion of knowledge in all fields, it is hard to doubt that Lovecraft was the latest to attempt and, perhaps, to succeed in filling that role.

But there was perhaps one field in which Lovecraft could justifiably claim authority—weird fiction; for it is the belief of many that Lovecraft's essay on "Supernatural Horror in Literature" is the finest study of its kind, providing not only a succinct history of the genre from antiquity to the present, but also guidelines toward its aesthetic bases and a defence of its worth as a literary form. Lovecraft not only read all types of weird literature, from the best to the worst, but sought to establish a collection encompassing his personal favourites in the field. It is not surprising that Dunsany, Machen, Poe, Shiel, Bierce, Hawthorne, Blackwood, and others who significantly influenced Lovecraft's own writings are heavily represented in his library; but these are just the tip of the iceberg of his holdings. Such tantalisingly obscure volumes as Leonard Cline's *The Dark Chamber,* J. Provand Webster's *The Oracle of Baal,* Henri Béraud's *Lazarus,* James De Mille's *A Strange Manuscript Found in a Copper Cylinder,* and others filled his shelves; and their perusal might unearth literary influences hitherto unknown to scholars.

Lovecraft the *littérateur,* then, cannot be separated from his library; it was as integral to his being as the New England landscape he adored. That Lovecraft would "part with all my furniture and squat and sleep on the floor before I'd let go of the 1500 or so books I possess" (*SL* 2.287) is eloquent enough testimony to a man for whom books were, not an evasion from the "real" world, but the essence of that real world itself: reality may comprise not only the prosiness of daily existence, but the thoughts of the great minds that have, perhaps more than the conquests of war or the complexities of political manoeuvring, shaped our civilisation. It is this reality that Lovecraft devoted a lifetime in seeking.

Lovecraft's Revisions: How Much of Them Did He Write?

One of August Derleth's few intelligent statements was when he said, in connexion with the "best" of Lovecraft's revisions, that they "are certainly good enough to stand among Lovecraft's [original] stories—and why not?—since Lovecraft wrote most of what is memorable in them!" (*HM* [1970 ed.] xiii). This is clearly the case, and in many instances the term "ghostwritten" would seem to apply better than "revised." Lovecraft's only officially ghostwritten tale was "Under the Pyramids" for Harry Houdini, and the others were at least nominally based upon actual drafts or at worst plot-germs by the nominal authors. And yet it can in no way be stated categorically that Lovecraft's revisions and collaborations are entirely or (in a few cases) even largely his: in those few instances where we have the original drafts of tales subsequently revised by Lovecraft, we learn that his role in the various works differed widely; and this conclusion is supported—in the overwhelming majority of tales for which we do not know exactly the nucleus from which Lovecraft began—by testimony from his letters and (although this is always a dangerous instrument) internal evidence. It will be our purpose here to ascertain the precise degree of Lovecraft's role in all the stories that are deemed either revisions or collaborations; such a determination being not only important in itself but vital to our ability to use the respective tales more accurately to shed light upon Lovecraft's other stories and his work and thought as a whole. We shall try to proceed in a roughly chronological sequence, although at times it will be more convenient to consider together all the stories written for a single revision-client.

The Winifred V. Jackson collaborations

It is fairly clear from Lovecraft's correspondence that nearly all the writing and much of the conception for "The Green Meadow" (1918 or 1919) and "The Crawling Chaos" (1921) came from Lovecraft. He remarks that "in prose technique she [Jackson] fails, hence can utilise *story* ideas only in collaboration with some technician" (*SL* 1.136). Lovecraft goes on to remark that "the opening paragraph of 'The Green Meadow' was written from my own dream" (SL 1.116)—this refers not to the "Introductory Note" to the tale (which, though signed "E. N. B.–L. T., Jr." [= Elizabeth Neville Berkeley and Lewis Theobald, Jr., the pseudonyms of the two authors], is surely by Lovecraft—see SL 1.136: "I . . . supplied the quasi-realistic . . . introduction"), but the first paragraph of the tale proper. The rest of the tale is equally Lovecraftian in prose style, although apparently the end of the story incorporates some ideas by Jackson.

Lovecraft remarks of "The Crawling Chaos" that "I took the title . . . from my Nyarlathotep sketch (now repudiated) because I liked the sound of it" (OFF 191). It must then date after the prose-poem "Nyarlathotep" (December 1920), although Lovecraft notes his projected work on the collaboration so early as May 1920 (SL 1.116). Like its predecessor, this tale was almost certainly written entirely by Lovecraft and was based upon dreams by Lovecraft and Miss Jackson that happened roughly to coincide. (I suspect that Lovecraft may have exaggerated the degree of similarity when he mentions the matter in his letters.) It is almost universally acknowledged that these two tales are some of Lovecraft's worst, even among the revisions.

"Poetry and the Gods" (with Anna Helen Crofts)

In its one appearance in Lovecraft's lifetime (*United Amateur*, September 1920) this tale was signed "Anna Helen Crofts and Henry Paget-Lowe." The fact that Crofts is listed first does not necessarily mean that she contributed more to the work than Lovecraft, since Lovecraft would out of courtesy have allowed the name of his female collaborator to be listed first. I have not been able to find out much about Crofts save that she was a real person (some have believed her to be a pseudonym of W. V. Jackson or someone else), an amateur writer residing in the far northwestern corner of Massachusetts. She is mentioned in no correspondence by Lovecraft seen by me. The bulk of the tale—with its heavy reliance on classical mythology—is almost certainly Lovecraft's. The examples of "free verse" included in the tale were once conjectured to be by Crofts, but it has recently been discovered that they are from an actual published work: "Sky Lotus" by Elizabeth Jane Coatsworth, published in *Asia* (August 1919). De Camp (134) curiously remarks of this tale that "the prose has a feminine ring foreign to Lovecraft"—inspired, one suspects, by nothing more than the fact that a woman is the central character (this may indeed have been Crofts's addition or the nucleus from which Lovecraft worked). The prose style is, however, no more "feminine" than that of Lovecraft's other quasi-Dunsanian tales.

The Sonia Greene revisions

Lovecraft never speaks explicity of his work on the two stories by Sonia H. Greene (Davis), but Davis does. In her memoir she notes that the idea for "The Horror at Martin's Beach" (1922) was suggested by a visit taken by her and Lovecraft to Magnolia, Massachusetts; this must have taken place in June 1922 (see SL 1.185). Davis records that she "sat up and wrote the general outline which he [Lovecraft] later revised and edited" (19). This procedure follows that of several of Lovecraft's lesser revisions, where he would work from a pre-existing draft by another writer. One supposes that Lovecraft retained a certain amount of prose by Davis.

"Four O'Clock" (1922) is an entirely different case. Davis[1] writes that this tale was written only at the suggestion of Lovecraft, hence probably contains almost no Lovecraftian prose or Lovecraftian content. A few random phrases appear to be Lovecraftian, and once the word "burden" [= message or import; cf. "The Cats" (1925): "Yelling the burden of Pluto's red rune"] is used—a very Lovecraftian usage. Lovecraft may then have touched up the prose of this tale, but as its content seems to owe nothing to Lovecraft it had best be regarded as not belonging at all to the Lovecraft corpus.

The C. M. Eddy revisions

Many are unaware that Lovecraft revised at least four tales for C. M. Eddy, Jr, his early associate in Providence. The first appears to be the deservedly forgotten "Ashes" (Weird Tales, March 1924); and if Lovecraft himself (SL 1.257) had not mentioned that he had "corrected" this work, no one would ever have detected a Lovecraftian element in it. This is evidently the first of the revisions, and the one in which Lovecraft had the least hand; unfortunately, he does seem to have had a small hand in it, perhaps contributing random snatches of prose. It is a pointless and hackneyed tale with a nauseating romantic element that, by the standards of 1923, might almost have been termed pornographic.

"The Ghost-Eater" (1923) seems to be largely Lovecraft's—the opening scene is very reminiscent of "The Picture in the House" (1920) —but the concluding dialogue might perhaps be Eddy's, as well as the rather naive and conventional plot.

"The Loved Dead" (1923), certainly the most enjoyable of the Eddy revisions, seems to bear many Lovecraftian touches, but Lovecraft probably merely added or corrected passages from a pre-existing draft by Eddy (who was, or tried to be, an independent writer). Some of the prose is reminiscent of "The

---

1. Letter to Winfield Townley Scott, 11 December 1948 (ms., JHL).

Hound" (1922), but this may be Eddy's own work, since he had read that tale in ms. (see *SL* 1.254, 292). The mention of "Phlegethon," however, emphatically betrays Lovecraft's hand, since he noted this term—one of the five rivers in Hades—in the commonplace book and used it in "The Other Gods" (1921).

"Deaf, Dumb and Blind" (1924) is probably another tale whose idea (rather vaguely and nebulously expressed) was Eddy's but much of whose prose—especially the actual diary of the deaf, dumb, and blind man—is Lovecraft's: the diary bears such references as "Ocypetian fumes," "Cabirian orgies," and "soul-sickening Saturnalia" which I doubt whether Eddy could have come up with.

In general these tales were probably all conceived by Eddy, and Lovecraft probably added few details of plot (the relative shortness and insubstantiality of the tales may confirm this) but revised or wrote much of the actual prose. His contribution in all the tales can be rated at slightly more than 50%.

"Under the Pyramids" (with Harry Houdini)

This is, as mentioned, Lovecraft's only authentic ghostwriting effort, but as Houdini provided at least a certain nucleus of the plot (see *SL* 1.312f.) it was therefore composed very much like Lovecraft's other revisions. Needless to say, the development of the plot and the entire writing is Lovecraft's, and this tale comes the closest of all the revisions (save, perhaps, "The Mound") to being regarded as his own work. Its foreign genesis, however (Lovecraft may never have written such a tale about Egypt on his own initiation, much less made Houdini himself the actual narrator of the tale), must nonetheless compel us to segregate it, however lightly, from Lovecraft's original fiction.

"Two Black Bottles" (with Wilfred B. Talman)

The rather complicated and unpleasant history of this tale's revision (Talman apparently resented the extent to which Lovecraft made emendations to his draft) have been recorded both by Lovecraft (*SL* 2.61-62, 72) and—briefly—by Talman ("The Normal Lovecraft"). Talman recently told Dirk W. Mosig that Lovecraft in the end supplied only the colloquial dialogue for the tale; this remark is suspect both because there seem to be other random paragraphs that are Lovecraft's (as, indeed, is implied in *SL* 2.61) and because some of the dialogue is not in fact similar to the other uses of dialect found in Lovecraft's own work (although this tale is admittedly set, apparently, somewhere in New York State and not in New England). I suspect that Talman rejected many of Lovecraft's suggestions and additions and reinstated his own prose. Lovecraft's hand in the tale may then amount to no more than 30%.

The Adolphe de Castro revisions

It has now become very easy to ascertain precisely the degree of Lovecraft's revision of the two tales by Adolphe de Castro—"The Last Test" and "The Electric Executioner"—known to have been revised by Lovecraft. De Castro's own versions of these two tales were published in a collection of his stories, *In the Confessional and the Following* (New York & San Francisco: Western Authors' Publishing Association, May 1893; as by Gustav Adolf Danziger). These texts shed much light on Lovecraft's revisions of tales that, although in the horror genre, were not of compelling interest to him. Lovecraft frankly remarked, after reading the original versions of the tales, that de Castro's "fiction is unspeakable" (*SL* 2.207) and notes that he spent a full month (presumably in late 1927) working on the revision of a tale that de Castro had called "A Sacrifice to Science" and which Lovecraft retitled "Clarendon's Last Test" (the published title, "The Last Test," may have been an alteration made by Farnsworth Wright for its appearance in *Weird Tales*). In the end all Lovecraft has done for both tales is merely to rewrite them (in the revised versions the prose is Lovecraft's from beginning to end) but retain quite faithfully the plot-lines and even certain small particulars.

In "Clarendon's Last Test" Lovecraft preserved the California setting (de Castro himself had spent much time on the West Coast), the characters (although the names of some have been changed), and the thread of the plot; but—aside from replacing the nebulously depicted assistant of Dr Clarendon ("Dr Clinton" in de Castro) named Mort with the evil Atlantean magus Surama—he has added much better motivation for the characters and in general fleshed them out. Both this tale and "The Electric Executioner" contain some frivolous references to Cthulhu, Yog-Sothoth, and the like, and Lovecraft is probably merely having some fun to ease the drudgery of revision. He has made this tale about half again as long as de Castro's original, although he remarked of the latter that "I nearly exploded over the dragging monotony of [the] silly thing" (*SL* 2.207). Lovecraft's own version is not without monotony and prolixity of its own, but is still a vast improvement over de Castro's version.

Lovecraft made fewer alterations with "The Electric Executioner" ("The Automatic Executioner" in de Castro), and has again followed the plot-line exactly. Amusingly, in redrawing the character of the mad inventor Feldon, Lovecraft has modelled the figure upon an eccentric (and much more harmless) character whom he encountered in 1929 on a train ride from New York to Washington (see "Travels in the Provinces of America" [1929], *CE* 4.34). Otherwise the plots of the two versions are identical, down to the baffling conclusion and the hint about "astral bodies." Both the Aztec exclamations and the references to the creatures of Lovecraft's myth-cycle were added by Lovecraft.

Lovecraft remarks, however, in November 1930 that "I did accidentally land . . . three tales of Old Dolph's" (SL 3.204)—but what could this third tale be? De Castro only published "The Last Test" and "The Electric Executioner" in *Weird Tales,* and no other published versions of his work have come to light. It appears, then, that we are here dealing with a "lost" Lovecraft revision. It is likely that this tale, while perhaps accepted by *Weird Tales* or some other periodical, was in fact never published (or, rather, republished), and that it has now perished. (I think it is unlikely that Lovecraft merely arranged for the publication of a tale by de Castro without revising it: he remarks at one point that "His yarns haven't even the start of anything truly weird" [SL 5.208], and elsewhere states that "I've revised several tales for de Castro" [SL 5.44], and one assumes that "several" refers to more than two.)

The Zealia Bishop revisions

By all accounts the three tales revised for Zealia Bishop—"The Curse of Yig" (1928), "The Mound" (1929-30), and "Medusa's Coil" (1930)—are the best of the revisions and collaborations, and (save for the confused "Medusa's Coil") can stand comparison with Lovecraft's own work. One would accordingly expect to find much original work by Lovecraft in them, and such is indeed the case. Lovecraft has written at length in his letters about the writing of "The Curse of Yig" (see especially SL 2.232-33), and we need cite only the following: "By the way—if you want to see a new story [in the new *Weird Tales*] which is practically mine, read 'The Curse of Yig'. . . . This specimen is wellnigh a piece of original composition on my part, since all I had to go by was a synopsis of notes describing a pioneer couple, the attack on the husband by snakes, the bursting of his corpse in the dark, and the subsequent madness of the wife. All the plot and motivation . . . are my own—I invented the snakegod, the curse, the prologue and epilogue, the point about the identity of the corpse, and the monstrously suggestive aftermath" (SL 3.29-30). It certainly appears that Lovecraft was proud of this tale—perhaps even more so than some of his original works.

"The Mound" is no less clear-cut. As shown in my article, "Who Wrote 'The Mound'?," Bishop's plot-germ was (in the words of R. H. Barlow) roughly as follows: "There is an Indian mound near here, which is haunted by a headless ghost. Sometimes it is a woman." This brilliant tale can take its place next to any of Lovecraft's longer narratives in its vast scope and rich texture.

One would like to think that "Medusa's Coil" owes a little more—at least in plot—to Bishop, for in its anomalous plethora of supernatural phenomena it presents a confused scenario impossible to harmonise into an unified whole. Unfortunately, Bishop seems to have had as little to do with this story as with the others (one might suppose that she provided a plot-germ about a modern-day Medusa, but this would probably be all); and the tale is one of the most disappointing of Lovecraft's lengthier efforts. Lovecraft rarely refers to the revision in his letters, although it seems to be alluded to in this reference: "one of my revision jobs is giving me fairly good practice in weird plot-weaving."[2] The date of this letter (August 1930) does not quite fit, since Lovecraft elsewhere remarks that "I did most of the job [on "Medusa's Coil"] in Richmond on one of my trips—afternoon after afternoon in Maymont Park" (*OFF* 276), and he visited Richmond in May 1930 (*SL* 3.149f.). Still, if Lovecraft did "weave the plot" of this tale, he did so singularly badly; and perhaps he realised this, for in 1934 he remarked of the tale (still unpublished): "It isn't much of a story anyhow. . . . I wouldn't give a dime for it myself" (*OFF* 143).

It is to be noted that both "The Mound" and "Medusa's Coil" were significantly adulterated by the hand of August Derleth, who—finding these manuscripts still unpublished after Lovecraft's death—decided to "touch them up" for a pulp market. Corrected texts now appear in the revised edition of *HM*.

The Henry S. Whitehead collaborations

I maintain that Lovecraft's role in the two tales written with Henry S. Whitehead—"The Trap" and "Bothon"—differs considerably. Of "The Trap" Lovecraft states to R. H. Barlow (*OFF* 24) that he wrote the entire central portion of the tale (i.e., the section where the young boy enters the strange-dimensioned mirror-world), although I think it is likely that the last three-fourths of the tale is written by Lovecraft. It is somewhat peculiar that Whitehead, a distinguished writer in his own right, would allow a tale in which he had so little a hand, both in conception and in writing, to be published under his name; but perhaps Lovecraft refused co-authorship.

That Lovecraft had a hand in "Bothon" (published in *West India Lights*) was deduced by William Fulwiler, who noted that Lovecraft's references to a tale called "The Bruise" must refer to "Bothon." But while Fulwiler is convinced that at least the latter half of the tale (i.e., the Mu-narrative) is actually written by Lovecraft, I feel—and only internal evidence can be a guide—that there is actually no Lovecraft prose in the story. It is very obvious that Lovecraft had a hand in mapping out the Mu-narrative (certain obviously Lovecraftian place-names would alone confirm this), but I cannot be convinced that he actually wrote any portion of the story. The references to it in Lovecraft's letters need imply nothing more than that he provided only a sort of

---

2. HPL to Clark Ashton Smith, [6 August 1930] (ms., JHL). The date of the letter is conjectural.

synopsis of the Mu-narrative which Whitehead could have written up. Indeed, Lovecraft notes that an earlier version of the tale (where Mu is not involved) had been rejected by *Strange Tales* (SL 4.37), and all that he says is that the new ending was "suggested and mapped out by myself" (SL 4.127). But whether or not Lovecraft wrote any part of the tale, it is clear that much of the plot is his, and this tale can still be classified as a legitimate collaboration.

"Through the Gates of the Silver Key" (with E. Hoffmann Price)

This is one collaboration where we can tell precisely what portions have been contributed by the respective collaborators; for Price's original typescript of his continuation of "The Silver Key" (which he called "The Lord of Illusion") still survives and was published in 1982. This 22-page draft is of course enormously enlightening for the genesis of the tale, and Lovecraft has managed to maintain far more of Price's language and conception than Price himself has led us to believe. Lovecraft did not, as in many other cases, merely make his additions and corrections upon Price's draft, but wrote the whole tale over again in pencil, and the opening scene in New Orleans is extensively elaborated by Lovecraft.

Price then prepared a typescript of Lovecraft's pencil draft and—aside from making many mistakes and misreadings in the process—wilfully altered a few passages throughout the text (particularly Lovecraft's citations of the *Necronomicon*). Price further added marginal notes and queries about the appropriateness of some words and phrases (as, indeed, Lovecraft had done extensively on Price's "Lord of Illusion"), and Lovecraft must have modified these passages and instructed Price to make a new draft for submission.

This latter draft does not survive, but revisions of select passages—clearly Lovecraft's—duly appear in the published version (*Weird Tales*, July 1934).

In short, although much of the language of the tale is Lovecraft's, much of the conception is correspondingly Price's, and this tale can be regarded as a true collaboration.

The Hazel Heald revisions

Of the five tales by Hazel Heald revised by Lovecraft there can be question of Lovecraft's involvement only in one—"The Man of Stone" (1932), evidently the earliest of the revisions. No manuscripts of any of these tales—either by Heald or by Lovecraft—have come to light, and references in the letters are comparatively sparse. I have found no allusion to "The Man of Stone" in Lovecraft's correspondence, but Heald's own comment may be illuminating: "Lovecraft helped me on this story as much as on the others, and did actually rewrite paragraphs" (quoted in Derleth's note to "The Man of Stone," *HM*

[1970 ed.] 270). The first part of the sentence is suspect, but the second allows us to infer both that Heald made a draft of the tale herself and that Lovecraft merely corrected or added to it. If anything we can be certain that the diary of "Mad Dan" is Lovecraft's, since it contains references to the *Book of Eibon*, R'lyeh, Shub-Niggurath, etc. There is even one sentence—"They must think I'm deaf, dumb, and blind!"—that may wryly refer to the C. M. Eddy revision of a decade before.

For the other tales I suspect that Heald only provided synopses, and several of these tales are close to original fiction on Lovecraft's part. Lovecraft admits as much in reference to "The Horror in the Museum" (1932), which is "a piece which I 'ghost-wrote' for a client from a synopsis so poor that I wellnigh discarded it. . . . [It] is virtually my own work" (SL 4.229). It is all the more amusing when we learn of one *Weird Tales* reader's reaction to the tale: "Even Lovecraft . . . could hardly, I suspect, have surpassed the grotesque scene in which the other-dimensioned shambler leaps out at the hero" (Joshi, *Weird Writer* 77).

"Winged Death" (1932) is not so fine a story—perhaps because it adds nothing to Lovecraft's myth-cycle (as many of the other revisions do) and is a simple tale of a murderer paying the consequences of his crime—and Lovecraft admitted that it "was nothing to run a temperature over. . . . My share in it is something like 90 to 95%" (SL 4.403). Again a synopsis by Heald seems to be suggested.

"Out of the Aeons" (1933) is probably the best of the Heald revisions and can actually take a place next to Lovecraft's own tales. There can be no question of Lovecraft's authorship from start to finish, and he is explicit on the point: "I should say I *did* have a hand in it. . . . I wrote the damn thing! . . . But it's really foolish to attempt jobs so extensive, when with the same amount of work one could write an acknowledged story of one's own. This is the last collaboration of the sort I shall ever attempt" (SL 5.130). One is even hard put to ascertain what sort of synopsis Heald could have provided for the tale: surely she could not have contributed even the idea of the sub-narrative about Mu, and probably she had a vague conception about a mummy coming to life in a museum.

"The Horror in the Burying-Ground" (1933/34/35) is a rather slight but still entertaining tale, and again the entire conception and execution must be Lovecraft's. The New England backwoods dialect used in the story is very reminiscent of "The Dunwich Horror," as is the very opening of the tale ("When the state highway to Rutland is closed, travellers are forced to take the Stillwater road past Swamp Hollow"; cf. "The Dunwich Horror": "When a traveller in north central Massachusetts takes the wrong fork at the junction of the Aylesbury pike just beyond Dean's Corners he comes upon a lonely and curious country"). Again, the nucleus of the plot—the strange pseudo-embalming fluid used by the village undertaker—is likely to have been the extent of Heald's involvement in the tale.

The Duane W. Rimel revisions

These revisions are among the most recent to come to light; their very discovery was a collaborative effort between Will Murray, Robert M. Price, and myself. The first of these revisions appears to be the sonnet series "Dreams of Yith." In R. H. Barlow's bound copy of the *Fantasy Fan* (where the sonnets appeared in the issues for July and September 1934) there is tipped in a small sheet of paper containing two versions of the first sonnet of the series, the one apparently Rimel's original and the other evidently Lovecraft's revised version. Both versions are in Lovecraft's handwriting. One supposes that many of the ten sonnets of the cycle were revised by Lovecraft, as suggested by his letter to Rimel of 13 May 1934: "Your new series of verses sounds highly interesting, and both Barlow and I went over the enclosed specimen with minute attention and sincere appreciation. . . . At the moment I can't get time to give a detailed exposition of this matter, but I'll enclose the rough draught with notes, plus a finished version" (ms., JHL). This same letter contains a reference to a story by Rimel: "I read your 'Tree on the Hill' with great interest, and believe it truly captures the essence of the weird. I like it exceedingly despite a certain cumbrousness and tendency toward anticlimax in the later parts. I've made a few emendations which you may find helpful, and have tried a bit of strengthening toward the end." This makes it clear that Lovecraft completely rewrote the ending of the story (Section III) and made revisions to earlier portions; I am not prepared to believe, however, with Robert M. Price that Lovecraft also completely rewrote Section II, although it is obvious enough that the quotation from the mythical *Chronicle of Nath* in this section is from Lovecraft's pen.

A few months later Lovecraft announces having revised another tale by Rimel, which the latter had called "The Sorcery of Alfred": "Very glad to see the new tale—which reminds me somewhat of Dunsany. I'm returning it with a few changes which I think would help somewhat. . . . I've taken the liberty of changing the name of the hero—since the common English name of *Alfred* hardly fits in with the fabulous setting. . . . Hope you'll find *Aphlar* suitable as a successor."[3] "The Sorcery of Aphlar" is very slight, but has some echoes of Lovecraft's early Dunsanian fantasies.

---

3. HPL to Duane W. Rimel, 23 July 1934 (ms., JHL).

At least one further tale of Rimel's was revised by Lovecraft: "The Disinterment," published in *Weird Tales* for January 1937. In a letter to Rimel, HPL notes: "First of all, let me congratulate you on the story. Really, it's *splendid*—one of your best so far! The suspense & atmosphere of dread are admirable, & the scenes are very vividly managed.... I've gone over the MS. very carefully with a view to improving the smoothness of the prose style—& I hope you'll find the slight verbal changes acceptable."[4] Rimel has maintained that the story is largely his, but it contains characteristic usages pointing clearly to Lovecraft's authorship (or revision) of a substantial portion of it.

Curiously enough, as with the de Castro corpus, there seems also to be a "lost" Rimel revision. In Lovecraft's so-called "Death Diary" for 28 January 1937 he writes laconically: "Finish Rimel revision" (*CE* 5.241). What could it be? It appears to be a story titled "From the Sea," which Lovecraft returned to Rimel in mid-February "with such minor changes as I think are needed."[5] The story was apparently never published and presumably does not now survive. However minor the revisions, it is the last piece of fiction on which Lovecraft worked.

The R. H. Barlow collaborations

The earliest of Lovecraft's revisions of the stories of R. H. Barlow have only recently come to light. They are two very short sketches, "The Slaying of the Monster" (February 1933) and "The Hoard of the Wizard-Beast" (December 1933). When the stories were first published, the manuscripts—Barlow's typescripts with Lovecraft's revisions—were also printed, allowing us to gauge precisely the degree of Lovecraft's revision of them. Lovecraft also discusses at length his work on these tales in letters to Barlow (see *OFF* 51 and 90).

Barlow's typed draft of "The Battle That Ended the Century" (1934) survives; indeed, all Lovecraft has done is to correct and add to it in pen. The foundation of the story, then, is Barlow's, and it must be said that some of the funniest parts are his and not Lovecraft's; the latter, however, provided the comical parodies of names (Frank Chimesleep Short for Frank Belknap Long) which Barlow had left unchanged. Apparently it was Lovecraft's own oversight not to alter Otis Adelbert Kline's name, although he tried to rectify this by remarking to correspondents on this oversight and suggesting "Oatmeal Addlepate Crime." Lovecraft's role in this work, then, is no more than about 35 to 40%.

In "'Till A' the Seas'" (1935) Lovecraft has again merely written corrections and additions in pen on a typed draft by Barlow (one page is reprinted in facsimile in *HM* [1970 ed.] 98). The revisions are very heavy at the beginning,

---

4. HPL to Duane W. Rimel, 28 September 1935 (ms., JHL).
5. HPL to Duane W. Rimel, [20 February 1937] (ms., JHL).

less so in the middle (the narrative about Ull, the last surviving human) and become heavy again at the end, including one long insert about the cosmic futility of mankind. Lovecraft's role can be roughly estimated at 50%.

In "Collapsing Cosmoses" (1935) Lovecraft and Barlow wrote about every other paragraph. Barlow actually ended up writing a little more than Lovecraft, and several of the better jokes are his. Here is, certainly, one exception to the rule that Lovecraft wrote the best portions of his revisions and collaborations!

I initially believed that Lovecraft wrote virtually the whole of "The Night Ocean" (1936), but further evidence has since forced me to retract the statement. Most important is the passage in Lovecraft's letter to Hyman Bradofsky (4 November 1936; ms.) which led Dirk W. Mosig to discover Lovecraft's hand in the tale: "Sorry 'The Night Ocean' is such a mess. Did Barlow send you the mere rough draught which I corrected? I assumed he would prepare another copy, for I ripped the text to pieces in spots." This passage alone reveals that Lovecraft was working on a draft by Barlow, and only rewrote the text "in spots." I reached this conclusion indirectly by examining Barlow's earlier tale, "A Dim-Remembered Story" (published in the *Californian* for Summer 1936). This tale reveals such a significant advance upon Barlow's previous—and very crude—fiction that one must credit Barlow with making great strides as a fictionist; and this tale bears no trace whatever of Lovecraft's revisory hand (nor would Lovecraft have praised it as highly as he did had he had much of a hand in it). "A Dim-Remembered Story" is obviously influenced by Lovecraft—as can be seen simply in Barlow's ingenious use of Lovecraft's "unexplainable couplet," "That is not dead . . .," as chapter headings for the four sections of the tale—but I maintain that Lovecraft had nothing to do with the conception or writing of the work. Lovecraft moreover wrote to Duane Rimel that "The Night Ocean" itself was "one of the most artistic weird tales I've ever read,"[6] and this sort of praise would be uncharacteristic if Lovecraft had written the bulk of the story. But the discovery of Barlow's typescript, with Lovecraft's revisions, puts the matter to rest, and Lovecraft's contribution can be considered to amount to no more than 10%. One can only wonder what sort of fictionist Barlow would have become had he continued to produce work of this calibre.

"The Challenge from Beyond"

This hardly needs comment, but is included for the sake of completeness. Of course Lovecraft wrote only his portion of the round-robin tale, and naturally had to use the characters and settings of the two episodes preceding his. The complications involved in the setting up of the sequence of writing (see *SL* 5.199f.) need not concern us here.

---

6. HPL to Duane W. Rimel, 20 February 1937 (ms., JHL).

"The Diary of Alonzo Typer" (with William Lumley)

Lovecraft actually alludes to this tale as a collaboration ("my sympathy for old Bill Lumley has caused me to break my new anti-collaboration rule and fix up a tale of his" [OFF 299]), and we are in an unique position to understand the nature of this collaboration; for—as in "Through the Gates of the Silver Key"— both Lumley's original (handwritten) draft (the title is his) and Lovecraft's handwritten text—a complete rewriting—still survive. Lumley's draft—now printed in *Medusa's Coil and Others* (2012)—is a confused, ungrammatical, incoherent, and unintentionally hilarious attempt at a story, and one supposes that Lovecraft took sympathy for Lumley's complete incompetency at fiction-writing. He has, however, retained random phrases from the original, and the general setting—a man who comes to an abandoned house and meets strange horrors—is Lumley's. Lumley alludes to Yian-Ho (which he presumably derived from "Through the Gates of the Silver Key"), while the *Book of Hidden Things* and the *Seven Lost Signs of Terror* are also the work of Lovecraft's occultist friend. Lovecraft has added the "Editor's Note" heading the tale, the whole business with Adriaen Sleght and Claes van der Heyl, and—unfortunately—the ludicrous ending where Alonzo Typer continues writing in his diary as he is dragged away by some nameless abomination.

"In the Walls of Eryx" (with Kenneth Sterling)

All that survives (aside from the published versions) is a typescript (presumably by Sterling, since the typewriter face is otherwise unrecognisable to me) and some carbons of it. I have been told by Dirk W. Mosig (who questioned Sterling on the matter) that the idea for the invisible maze was Sterling's, but probably the development as well as the entire writing of the tale were Lovecraft's. Certainty on the matter is difficult, as few other early examples of Sterling's fiction seem to survive for purposes of comparison. The conventional idea of using Venus as a setting may also be Sterling's. The in-jokes (farnoth-flies = Farnsworth Wright) may have been simultaneously devised by Sterling and Lovecraft, since Lovecraft would probably not have introduced them on his own initiative without Sterling's approval. Sterling lived for a time in Providence, and the two probably conferred frequently on the details of the story much as Lovecraft and Barlow did on "The Battle That Ended the Century" and "Collapsing Cosmoses."

In conclusion, some general remarks about Lovecraft's revisions are in order. We have noted that the role played by his collaborators or clients differs widely; but in nearly every case the actual genesis, nucleus, or idea for the story is not Lovecraft's. If nothing else, the collaborators provided a plot-germ which he later developed; even if, in some cases, that plot-germ was only two short sentences and led to a 25,000-word story ("The Mound"). In many instances (particularly in early revisions, but also in such late tales as "Through the Gates of the Silver Key," "The Diary of Alonzo Typer," and "The Night Ocean") an actual draft—coherent or otherwise—was provided by the collaborator, and Lovecraft either wrote his corrections directly upon it or rewrote it entirely (while still retaining at least a few phrases from the original). Not infrequently there is far more of the original retained than one might initially have supposed, and all credit for the excellencies of a particular tale must not be indiscriminately attributed to Lovecraft. In several cases the title, the general setting, characters, and other formal details were provided by the collaborator, although in nearly every case the development and motivation were supplied by Lovecraft. The external origin of the settings of many of the revisions accounts for the very diverse locales we find in them: both the de Castro tales (and presumably the lost third one) are set in California or Mexico, an area well known to de Castro but not to Lovecraft— and both tales have their fictional time-reference in the 1880s and 1890s, since the original tales were set in this period. Of the Oklahoma setting used in the Zealia Bishop tales Lovecraft remarks to Bishop: "For geographical atmosphere and colour I had of course to rely wholly on your answers to my questionnaire, plus such printed descriptions of Oklahoma as I could find. I hope very much that I have avoided grave errors" (SL 2.232). Lovecraft, of course, in his original work would have set a tale only in a locale familiar to him either by direct acquaintance (New England) or by extensive research (Antarctica, England). It therefore becomes a matter of conjecture who was responsible for the fictional New England towns created in the C. M. Eddy revisions, since both the collaborators were natives of Providence and Eddy at the time may actually have known New England better than Lovecraft (the former frequently took the latter upon various tours to places Lovecraft had never before seen). The New York State setting of "The Diary of Alonzo Typer" does not, however, owe anything to Lumley (although he was a resident of Buffalo), and all the geogrpahical and ethnographic data in the tale are due to Lovecraft's own researches (begun in the late 1920s) in the history of New York State—researches inspired, at least as far as the Dutch element is concerned, by Wilfred B. Talman.

Another telling distinction between the revisions and Lovecraft's original work is their general shoddiness of writing. From the manuscripts which survive we can determine that Lovecraft took much less care in the diction, construction, and general execution of the revisions, even those which he wrote from mere plot-germs or synopses; hence the thematic incoherence of "Medusa's Coil," certain structural awkwardnesses in "The Mound," the laborious and pretentious "Editor's Notes" in "The Green Meadow" and "The Diary of Alonzo Typer," and the occasional looseness and colloquialism of language found in even the best of the revisions. Lovecraft is certainly not to be blamed for this, since the revisions (not the official collaborations) would not bear his name, and since—however much enjoyment he may have derived in writing some of them—they were generally a business venture whose financial returns were slight in comparison to his original fiction: for "The Curse of Yig" he charged Bishop $17.50 (SL 2.233), when an original work of equal length would have garnered him at least $90.00 from *Weird Tales*. There was then virtually no incentive for Lovecraft to expend great care in the tales, and he is in fact to be praised not merely for his remarkable generosity to his clients but for the trouble he took in making some of his lengthier revisions into really substantial and even brilliant weird tales.

And brilliant some of them certainly are: "Under the Pyramids," "The Curse of Yig," "The Mound," "Out of the Aeons," and a few others need fear no comparison from even the best of Lovecraft's original work, and several of the later revisions add significantly to the Lovecraft Mythos. Many of these tales are still underrated even by Lovecraft scholars; but once we take into consideration the differing levels of involvement of his collaborators, even the purists among us can find not only enjoyment but substantial edification from these works. They are an unique body of work—I know of no other writer who engaged in precisely this sort of activity—and they ought to be appreciated as such.

Works Cited

Barlow, R. H. *The Hoard of the Wizard-Beast and One Other*. West Warwick, RI: Necronomicon Press, 1994.

Davis, Sonia H. *The Private Life of H. P. Lovecraft*. Ed. S. T. Joshi. 1985. Rev. ed. West Warwick, RI: Necronomicon Press, 1992.

De Camp, L. Sprague. *Lovecraft: A Biography*. Garden City, NY: Doubleday, 1975.

Fulwiler, William. "Mu in 'Bothon' and 'Out of the Eons.'" *Crypt of Cthulhu* No. 11 (Candlemas 1983): 20-24.

Joshi, S. T., ed. *A Weird Writer in Our Midst: Early Criticism of H. P. Lovecraft*. New York: Hippocampus Press, 2010.

Price, E. Hoffmann. "The Lord of Illusion." *Crypt of Cthulhu* No. 10 (1982): 47-56.

Lovecraft and His Wife

Of H. P. Lovecraft and Sonia H. Greene (later Davis) Maurice Lévy wrote: "It is hard to imagine a couple more ill-matched." After all things are considered, this statement must be regarded as fundamentally true. This is not the place for any detailed examination of why Lovecraft, after thirty-four years of bachelorhood, decided to marry, move to New York, and then separate from his wife after two years to return in relief to his native Providence. But we may note that Lovecraft himself wavered between citing the cause of the marriage's failure as "98% financial" (SL 3.262)—a cause perhaps unjustly ridiculed by his critics—and a broader view of the matter:

> And yet I didn't find matrimony such a bugbear as one might imagine. With a wife of the same temperament as my mother and aunts, I would probably have been able to reconstruct a type of domestic life not unlike that of Angell St. days, even though I would have had a different status in the household hierarchy. But years brought out basic and essential diversities in reactions to the various landmarks of the time-stream, and antipodal ambitions and conceptions of value in planning a fixed joint milieu. It was the clash of the abstract-traditional-individual-retrospective-Apollonian aesthetic with the concrete-emotional-present-dwelling-social-ethical-Dionysian aesthetic; and amidst this, the originally fancied congeniality, based on a shared disillusion, philosophic bent, and sensitiveness to beauty, waged a losing struggle. (SL 3.8)

To this assessment very little really need be added; although a reading between the lines of Sonia Davis's memoir of Lovecraft, published in unabridged form as *The Private Life of H. P. Lovecraft* (1985), will allow one to develop the picture in considerable detail.

What we are faced with is a couple, both of whom were of comparatively advanced age for a marriage—Lovecraft at thirty-four, Sonia at forty-one and herself a widow—and who were both headstrong and independent people unwilling or unable to compromise because they in fact did not have a sufficient ground of common understanding. Sonia in her memoir constantly emphasises how she gave way to Howard on many points so as to help him eradicate his "complexes"; and the latent resentment she must have felt at so doing is not difficult to detect. Conversely, it is clear that she was not satisfied with certain of Lovecraft's views and habits, and strove to change them without, apparently, even considering what the psychological effect would be on him; and Lovecraft himself must have felt a certain resentment at being forced suddenly to give up cherished codes of behaviour because his wife did not sympathise with them. So simple a thing as the choice of Lovecraft's clothing—Sonia being irritated at his old suit, hat, and even billfold, and he complaining that the new suit Sonia had picked out for him was "entirely too stylish"—has all the makings of an episode out of a situation comedy, but is in fact a clear and almost tragic example of a fundamental difference of temperament: to Lovecraft a suit of an old cut and style was genuinely in keeping with his code of gentility, whereas to Sonia—who in her millinery trade had to keep up with the latest fashion—such attire must have been almost an embarrassment. Neither party was "wrong" for adopting the view they did; there was simply no meeting-ground for such a cavernous difference of taste.

The extent to which Sonia harps upon money matters in her memoir may in part be justified—she was clearly trying to set the record straight and correct the inadequacies of previous treatments, especially by W. Paul Cook—but also underscores another point of tension which Lovecraft was perhaps reluctant to mention to his correspondents. For a full two years—from 1924 to 1926—Lovecraft was essentially supported financially by his wife and, to a much lesser degree, his aunts. He had virtually no independent income, and his bootless efforts to find employment in New York are poignantly chronicled in his letters of the period. Such a state of affairs must have been galling to one of Lovecraft's aristocratic lineage. Lovecraft was in an extremely ticklish position: he saw clearly that Sonia cared deeply for him, to the point of showering money in his direction; how then to extricate himself from a situation which was obviously unsatisfactory to both parties? Recall that Sonia and Howard lived together for only ten months—March through December 1924; after that point Sonia had to take various jobs out of state, and cohabitation occurred only sporadically and temporarily. Sonia's idea to live in Providence with Howard and set up a shop there was met with firm resistance on the part of Lovecraft's aunts: in Sonia's laconic words, "neither they nor Howard could afford to have Howard's wife working for a living in Providence." That pungent word-play on "afford"—referring not to money but to social standing—is revealing. This is an attitude which many in our day find hard to understand, especially as nowadays it is almost essential for both husband and wife to work to bring in an adequate income; but in the 1920s in New England the Puritan-Victorian tradition—call it "shabby gentility" if you will, but it is no less real for that—had not died out, and the response of Howard and his aunts is a perfectly comprehensible one. Again the great gulf of differing temperaments faces us.

But if the problems facing the marriage—the extreme difference of attitudes obscured by some superficial common interests; the pressure of Lovecraft's moving to New York and trying to find work; the financial difficulties brought on by the collapse of Sonia's millinery business and her shuttling across the country from one job to another—almost doomed the marriage to failure, then perhaps there is still truth to W. Paul Cook's statement (although he meant something rather different by it) that Lovecraft "had been tried in the fire and come out pure gold." What his marriage and his whole New York episode did was to give Lovecraft a healthy dose of reality: the reality of conjugal life, of living in the big city, of getting a job. To this extent Sonia did relieve some of Lovecraft's "complexes" by forcing him to come to terms with life. Lovecraft had indeed been abnormally sheltered as a child, an adolescent, and a young man; his attitudes before marriage bore all the traces of cocksure dogmatism spawned from sequestration, bookishness, and ignorance of the world. When he fled precipitately back to Providence in 1926, it was not to bury himself away once again, but to establish a safe haven for himself so that he could examine and confront the world with philosophic calm. It was then that Lovecraft began his great travels, from Quebec to Key West; then that he wrote his maturest fiction, from "The Call of Cthulhu" to "The Shadow out of Time"; then that he began actually thinking about the state of the nation and the world, converting to socialism and FDR's New Deal. In this development Sonia certainly helped, even if indirectly; and we must be grateful to her for writing this invaluable memoir, filled with charming and touching anecdotes of Lovecraft the lover and husband which only she could have provided. Rambling, confused, repetitious, and in part incoherent as it is, it has no replacement.

Lovecraft and the Films of His Day

H. P. Lovecraft's opinion of film was not high. This fact should not be surprising: to one so devoted to the written word, the crude films of Lovecraft's early years could only engender a shudder of disgust. Moreover, his first love in the performing arts was drama, and on the whole he preferred the stage to the cinema. He wrote in 1934:

> I first saw a play at the age of 6. Later, when the cinema appeared as a separate institution (it had been part of the Keith vaudeville since 1898 or 1899), I attended it often with other fellows, but never took it seriously. By the time of the first cinema shows (March 1906, in Providence) I knew too much of literature and drama not to recognise the utter and unrelieved hokum of the moving picture. (SL 4.355)

Lovecraft was, however, a little disingenuous here, because his early letters actually testify to a considerable enjoyment of the films of the 1910s and 1920s—not merely horror or fantasy films, which he might be expected to enjoy, but comedies and melodramas as well. In 1915 he actually wrote a poem to Charlie Chaplin ("To Charlie of the Comics"), and in a later letter compares the merits of Chaplin and Douglas Fairbanks (SL 1.50–51). At this time he declared himself "a devotee of the motion picture," remarking that "Some modern films are really worth seeing, though when I first knew moving pictures their only value was to destroy time" (SL 1.18).

In 1917 occurred a peculiar episode. Lovecraft went to see a film, *The Image-Maker of Thebes*,[1] at Fay's Theatre in Providence. The theatre was offering a prize of $25 for the best review of the film, and Lovecraft decided to participate. He found the film very poor: ". . . a rough-hewn amateurish affair dealing with reincarnation in a pitifully feeble and hackneyed manner, containing not the slightest subtlety or technical skill in plot, directing, or setting" (SL 1.42–43). His review was very harsh, and yet it won the prize! Regrettably, the

---

1. For further information on this film, see John T. Soister, *American Silent Horror, Science Fiction and Fantasy Feature Films, 1913–1929* (Jefferson, NC: McFarland, 2012), 293–94.

review was never published, and now appears to be lost.[2] It perhaps constitutes the only instance of film criticism by Lovecraft!

By 1919 Lovecraft was professing that "I formerly attended the cinema quite frequently, but it is beginning to bore me" (SL 1.89). Nevertheless, he saw D. W. Griffith's *The Birth of a Nation* (1915) both as a stage play[3] and as a film (SL 1.89), and also read the book on which they were based, Thomas Dixon's *The Clansman* (1905). It must be admitted that Lovecraft's enjoyment of this film about the Ku Klux Klan in the years following the Civil War may well have stemmed from his agreement with the film's racialist bias.

The Image-Maker of Thebes may not have been the first "weird" or supernatural film Lovecraft saw; he earlier notes seeing the film version (1915) of George du Maurier's novel *Trilby*, although he remarks that "it seemed incomplete to me because I have seen the actual play, and have attached so much importance to the deep, fiendishly insinuating *voice* of Svengali" (SL 1.18). A later letter is very harsh concerning some of the great horror films of the day:

> As a thorough soporific I recommend the average popularly "horrible" play or cinema or radio dialogue. They are all the same—flat, hackneyed, synthetic, essentially atmosphereless jumbles of conventional shrieks and mutterings and superficial, mechanical situations. *The Bat* made me drowse back in the early 1920's—and last year an alleged *Frankenstein* on the screen *would* have made me drowse had not a posthumous sympathy for poor Mrs. Shelley made me see red instead. Ugh! And the screen *Dracula* in 1931—I saw the beginning of that in Miami, Fla.—but couldn't bear to watch it drag to its full term of dreariness, hence walked out into the fragrant tropic moonlight! (SL 4.154-55)

To those who have come to regard these films as "classics" in their own right, it must be remembered that the film medium was still new and unrecognised in Lovecraft's day, and that it had scarcely begun to show the subtlety and profundity of later works; as an aesthetic medium it was decidedly inferior to literature, and Lovecraft's response is by no means unusual or unexpected. It is from this perspective that we must interpret his comparison of the film version of Gustav Meyrink's *The Golem* with the original novel. Of the book he stated that it was "the most magnificent weird thing I've come across in aeons! The cinema of identical title in 1921 was a mere substitute using the name—with nothing of the novel in it" (SL 5.138). And yet, Lovecraft did find praise for the film version of *The Invisible Man* (1933): "Surprisingly good—might easily have been absurd, yet succeeded in being genuinely

---

2. Some years ago Marc A. Michaud and I attempted to locate the files of Fay's Theatre in Providence, but were unsuccessful.

3. See "In a Major Key" (*Conservative*, July 1915); rpt. in CE 1.57.

sinister" (SL 4.362). In an unpublished letter to August Derleth, Lovecraft says that he wanted to see the bizarre *Cabinet of Dr. Caligari* (1921), but never did so.[4] And let us not forget his enthusiasm at seeing *The Phantom of the Opera* (1925) in New York:

> ... what a spectacle it was!! It was about a *presence* haunting the great Paris opera house ... but was developed so slowly that I actually fell asleep several times during the first part. Then the second part began—horror lifted its grisly visage—& I could not have been made drowsy by all the opiates under heaven! Ugh!!! The *face* that was revealed when the mask was pulled off ... & the nameless legion of *things* that cloudily appeared beside & behind the owner of that face when the mob chased him into the river at last![5]

His diary reports a viewing of *The Lost World* (an adaptation of the Conan Doyle novel) on 6 October 1925, but there is no corresponding letter testifying to his reaction to this remarkable film, a landmark in the use of special effects in its depiction of dinosaurs in South America. One would like to think he would have appreciated the nightmarish futuristic visions of Fritz Lang's *Metropolis*, since they coincide so starkly with Lovecraft's own foreboding prophecies of a future controlled by soulless machines.

Perhaps Lovecraft did not approach films in the proper light, especially films that adapted existing literary works. He seems to have believed that the sole criterion of excellence in such works was the faithfulness of their adaptation of the original text. But a "film adaptation" is very much an adaptation—a transference of moods, images, and effects from one medium to another. Many have asserted that Lovecraft's own tales are "unadaptable" to film or any other medium; and in a sense that is true, if one assumes that such an adaptation will mechanically duplicate the effect of the written word on to the screen. Such an undertaking is futile from the start.

An entirely different type of film that Lovecraft found very stimulating was the historical film, especially those set in his beloved eighteenth century. In 1921 he noted that he had seen both the stage and the cinema version of *David Garrick*, based on a play by T. W. Robertson.[6] Of the cinema version Lovecraft remarks: "This was one of the finest scenic productions I ever saw—the eighteenth century and Dr. Johnson's day mirrored without flaw or anachronism. In

---

4. "Too bad we both missed 'Dr. Caligari,' for it was by all accounts the best fantastic cinema ever produced." HPL to August Derleth, 16 December 1926 (*ES* 56).

5. HPL to Lillian D. Clark, 18 September 1925 (ms., JHL).

6. There were several film versions of this play: one in 1912, two in 1913, one in 1916, and one in 1928. HPL could have seen any of the first four. The play dates to 1864.

matters of scenery the moving picture can of course leave the stage far behind; though this hardly atones for the lack of sound and colour" (SL 1.127). Late in life Lovecraft saw several films of this kind. Interestingly, he enjoyed Cecil B. DeMille's *Cleopatra* (1934), stating that it "had excellent Roman scenes" (SL 5.100); evidently the daringly scanty attire worn by Claudette Colbert did not offend his usually prudish sensibilities.

But the historical film that Lovecraft enjoyed above all others was *Berkeley Square* (1933), based on a play by John Balderston. This film is a sort of historical fantasy in which a man of the twentieth century somehow merges his personality with that of his eighteenth-century ancestor. Lovecraft saw the film four times in late 1933 and praised it highly, largely because it echoed some of his deepest sentiments:

> It is the most weirdly perfect embodiment of my own moods and pseudo-memories that I have ever seen—for all my life I have felt as if I might wake up out of this dream of an idiotic Victorian age and insane jazz age into the reality of 1760 or 1770 or 1780 . . . the age of the white steeples and fanlighted doorways of the ancient hill, and of the long-s'd books of the old dark attic trunk-room at 454 Angell St. God Save the King! (SL 4.364)

In a recent article[7] Darrell Schweitzer argues for the possible influence of this film on Lovecraft's own time-travel story, "The Shadow out of Time" (1934–35).

But a much earlier influence of film upon Lovecraft's stories can be cited. In the prose-poem "Nyarlathotep" (1920) the mysterious Egyptian figure of the title presents strange pictures "shadowed on a screen." In a letter describing the dream that inspired the story, Lovecraft remarks that among the exhibitions in Nyarlathotep's presentation was "a horrible—possibly prophetic—cinema reel" (SL 1.161). This is certainly the earliest use of explicit film imagery in Lovecraft; and his later stories show many signs of such imagery. The whole issue of Lovecraft and movies has yet to be explored in detail; but in spite of his generally low opinion of the films of his day, it can be argued that film played no insignificant role in his life. May we not, then, expect that someday film makers will repay the favour by producing an adaptation of Lovecraft's work that is worthy of the name?

---

7. "H. P. Lovecraft's Favorite Movie," *Lovecraft Studies* Nos. 19/20 (Fall 1989): 23–25, 27.

The Rationale of Lovecraft's Pseudonyms

Much has been written on the identification of Lovecraft's pseudonymous publication of stories, poems, articles, and letters, but surprisingly little attention has been paid to the more essential matter of *why* Lovecraft used pseudonyms at all or why he used any given pseudonym for a given publication. The work of Robert H. Barlow, Willametta Keffer, George T. Wetzel, and several others had already resulted, by the 1950s, in the identification of the overwhelming bulk of Lovecraft's pseudonyms, although a few new ones came to light as recently as a few years ago; but I have yet to find any discussion of the rationale of his pseudonyms.

In the first place, attention should be paid as to which works appeared pseudonymously. It is significant that only two of Lovecraft's original works of fiction did not appear under his own name: the humorous tale "A Reminiscence of Dr. Samuel Johnson" (1917) and the prose-poem "Ex Oblivione." The significance of this, however, may not be entirely obvious, because the fact of his use of pseudonyms for various works must be conjoined with the fact that virtually all his pseudonymous appearances were in the amateur press, the most notable exceptions being his early letters and articles for Providence *Evening News* (under the "Isaac Bickerstaffe, Jr." pseudonym), for which he is not likely to have received payment. What this means is that Lovecraft virtually stopped using pseudonyms at the very time he ceased his extensive contributions to the amateur press—roughly 1923—and turned to professional publications. It is very likely that a strong impetus for his use of pseudonyms was the very quantity of his amateur writing, especially poetry: it seems clear that, his modesty being what it was, he did not wish to give the appearance of flooding certain amateur journals with his own work.

Which amateur journals received Lovecraft's pseudonymous contributions? There were a good many, but chief among them was the *Tryout*, in which a large proportion of his poetry was published. Only three items in Lovecraft's own amateur journal, the *Conservative*, were published pseudonymously: "Ye Ballade of Patrick von Flynn," "Inspiration" (both as by "Lewis Theobald, Jun."), and "The Unknown" (for which see below). The majority of Lovecraft's pieces in the *Conservative* (essays and editorials for the most part) either appeared under his own name or were unsigned—although in the latter case there was no especial secret as to his authorship. Other amateur journals such as the *United Amateur,* the *Silver Clarion,* and the *Wolverine* also received a fair number of Lovecraft's pseudonymous pieces.

This finally gets me back to the issue of why pseudonyms were used largely for poetry and not for stories or essays. It should not be assumed that Lovecraft used pseudonyms simply for works he did not value or whose authorship he did not wish to acknowledge. Firstly, such pseudonyms as "Ward Phillips" and "Henry Paget-Lowe" are scarcely very concealing, and it seems likely that most amateurs also knew of the "Lewis Theobald, Jun." pseudonym, which is by far the most extensively used. (It is under this pseudonym that Lovecraft's two collaborations with Winifred Jackson, "The Green Meadow" and "The Crawling Chaos," appeared; Jackson herself used her well-known pseudonym, "Elizabeth Berkeley.") Secondly, it became somewhat awkward for Lovecraft to publish his stories pseudonymously, since his first published amateur story, "The Alchemist" (*United Amateur,* November 1916), was his "credential" (i.e., a work that established his literary capability) for joining the United Amateur Press Association. The only odd thing is that this credential took so long in being published, since Lovecraft had joined the U.A.P.A. early in 1914 and had contributed voluminously over the next two and a half years. (Most credentials were published immediately upon a member's joining the association.) Then, when "The Tomb" was published in the *Vagrant* (November 1919), it was prefaced by an article by W. Paul Cook, "Howard P. Lovecraft's Fiction," which established Lovecraft in the amateur press as a fiction writer of note.

It is still a little puzzling that more essays did not appear pseudonymously, but it is interesting to see exactly what types of essays did so appear. The three most extensively used pseudonyms for Lovecraft's nonfiction are Isaac Bickerstaffe, Jr., El Imparcial, and Zoilus. The last is the easiest to deal with, since I have determined that, of the five Zoilus columns published in the *Wolverine* from 1921 to 1923, four are by Lovecraft and the other by Alfred Galpin. The name Zoilus needs no explanation, as it refers to the Greek critic of the fourth century B.C. who harshly criticised the Homeric poems. And yet, the Zoilus columns themselves are not especially harsh or polemical, and in fact one of them (by Lovecraft) is a paean to the amateur poet Lilian Middleton.

Willametta Keffer first tentatively identified El Imparcial as a Lovecraft pseudonym (Keffer 83). August Derleth doubted the attribution on the flimsy ground that "it is not the kind of pen-name HPL would normally have selected," whatever that is supposed to mean. But Keffer was right, and to date seven pieces by El Imparcial have been discovered, all of which concern amateur journalism. Keffer located four of them, and I admit with some embarrassment that one of these—an article on Winifred Jackson—eluded my notice and failed to be incorporated in my bibliography of Lovecraft.

The Isacc Bickerstaffe, Jr. pseudonym does not require much elaboration, either, since Lovecraft himself provides a good account of it (see *SL* 1.4–5). He unearthed this Augustan pseudonym—used by both Jonathan Swift and Joseph Addison—to satirise the hapless astrologer J. F. Hartmann in the pages of the Providence *Evening News*. In addition to the three articles (actually two articles and a letter) published under this pseudonym, Lovecraft also wrote several articles attacking Hartmann under his own name, creating the impression that there were actually three individuals involved in the whole astrology controversy. Hartmann, clearly, never saw through the ploy, for in one of his responses he notes querulously: "Two recent articles in these columns, by an enemy falsely posing as an astrologer, are real 'gibberish,' the kind which our critic [i.e., Lovecraft] does not criticise."[1]

It is clear, then, that Lovecraft restricted his pseudonymous appearances of essays to very specific types: articles on amateur journalism (El Imparcial), attacks on astrology (Isaac Bickerstaffe, Jr.), a critical column under what is essentially a "house name" (Zoilus), and the like. Two items—"The Trip of Theobald" (1927), relating Lovecraft's visits to various New England sites in 1927, and "The Convention" (1930), an account of the 1930 N.A.P.A. convention in Boston—appeared in the *Tryout* as by "Theobald"; the very use of this laconic surname for what are clearly very autobiographical pieces indicates the degree to which Theobald was identified—and known by amateur readers to be identified—with Lovecraft. "Cats and Dogs" appeared posthumously in *Leaves* as by "Lewis Theobald, Jun.," but this was obviously R. H. Barlow's doing, as the manuscript is unsigned.

Lovecraft, accordingly, restricted his pseudonyms largely for poetry, and again I maintain that it was largely the sheer volume of poetry that he was writing at this time (1914–23) that largely spurred his use of pseudonyms, not some belief on his part that his poetry was inferior or embarrassing. We can, however, refine this idea still further by examining exactly which pseudonyms Lovecraft used for which poems.

Some pseudonyms—used for only one or two appearances—are easily dispensed with. The manuscript of the poem "Life's Mystery" was signed L. Phillips Howard; this fatuously bombastic poem was followed by a satirical response, "On Mr. L. Phillips Howard's Profound Poem Entitled 'Life's Mystery.'" I have no idea when this poem was written; it could conceivably be yet another attack on T. S. Eliot's *The Waste Land*, billed by its proponents as "a

---

1. J. F. Hartmann, "A Defense of Astrology" (14 December 1914), rpt. in *CE* 3.344–48.

poem of profound significance," sparking Lovecraft's response in "Waste Paper," subtitled "A Poem of Profound Insignificance."

The pseudonym Alexander Ferguson Blair, used for the poem "North and South Britons" (1919), was identified by Tom Collins in *A Winter Wish*. No doubt Lovecraft wished to create the impression that this poem, urging unity of feeling between England and Scotland, was written by a Scotsman. No other work has been discovered under this pseudonym. Other pseudonyms were also used only once for various poems: Jeremy Bishop for the nasty satire "Medusa: A Portrait" (although the typescript bears the pseudonym "Theobaldus Senectissimus, Gent."); John J. Jones for the self-parody "The Dead Bookworm"; Richard Raleigh for "To a Youth" (a poem about Alfred Galpin); and Albert Frederick Willie for the parody, "Nathicana." Of the Richard Raleigh pseudonym Lovecraft states on a typescript of "To a Youth" (JHL): "How is this for an Elizabethan pseudonym?" HPL refers to the celebrated Elizabethan courtier Sir Walter Ralegh (whose name was formerly spelled "Raleigh"). Albert Frederick Willie is, in its first two names, an allusion to Alfred Galpin, and in its last name to Galpin's mother's maiden name, Willy. Galpin and Lovecraft actually cowrote the poem. The pseudonym Michael Ormonde O'Reilly was used when Lovecraft allowed his juvenile poem "To Pan" to appear in the *Tryout* for April 1919. This issue of the *Tryout* contained two other juvenile poems (all from *Poemata Minora, Volume II*, 1902), each printed under a pseudonym: "To the Old Pagan Religion" (as by Ames Dorrance Rowley) and "Ode to Selene or Diana" (as by Edward Softly). Still more curiously, the three poems were printed under titles different from those in the *Poemata* manuscript—"Pan," "The Last Pagan Speaks," and "To Selene." I imagine these titles changes were Lovecraft's.

Lawrence Appleton is again a transparent pseudonym. The two poems written under this pseudonym—"Hylas and Myrrha: A Tale" and "Myrrha and Strephon"—are among many directed toward Alfred Galpin, specifically relating to his various romantic involvements with girls in his hometown of Appleton, Wisconsin (all the "Damon and Delia" poems, as well as the play *Alfredo*, are on this subject). The Appleton surname clearly relates to Galpin's town of residence, while Lawrence refers to Lawrence College (now Lawrence University) in Appleton, which Galpin attended.

Wetzel speculated, somewhat laboriously, on the "Archibald Maynwaring" pseudonym, but failed to note the obvious origin of the name: Arthur Mainwaring, an obscure Augustan poet who translated a portion of "Garth's Ovid" (i.e., Ovid's *Metamorphoses* translated under the editorship of Sir Samuel Garth), which Lovecraft read as a boy. The three poems published under this pseudonym are all rather innocuous: a harmless pastoral poem,

"The Pensive Swain"; a poem on the shared birthday of Alfred Galpin and Margaret Abraham, "To the Eighth of November"; and, somewhat curiously, an explicitly religious poem entitled "Wisdom" (with the subtitle "The 28th or 'Gold-Miner's Chapter of Job, paraphrased from a literal translation of the original Hebrew text, supplied by Dr. S. Hall Young"). This poem appeared in the *Silver Clarion*, a journal known for its somewhat naive piety, and praised by Lovecraft as such (see his brief article "Comment" in the *Silver Clarion*, June 1918). The poem concludes:

> "Behold," He cries unto the mortal throng,
> "This is the Wisdom ye have sought so long:
> To reverence the Lord, and leave the paths of wrong!"

Henry Paget-Lowe, author of "On Religion," would certainly not have approved something like this! One can only imagine that Lovecraft wished to supply John Milton Samples, editor of the journal, with some copy to fill up his pages. It should be noted that the three "Archibald Maynwaring" poems all appeared in October or November 1919.

Humphry Littlewit, Esq. is somewhat of a curiosity. The name seems designed to be self-parodic or self-deprecating, but the three works for which this name was used are not exactly of this sort. To be sure, "A Reminiscence of Dr. Samuel Johnson" (1917) was written with tongue in cheek, and was in part intended as a send-up of Lovecraft's already well-known pose of extreme age and of his old-fashioned writing style ("Tho' many of my readers have at times observ'd and remark'd a Sort of antique Flow in my Stile of Writing . . ."); but what are we to make of the fact that the manuscript of "Waste Paper," Lovecraft's hilarious parody of T. S. Eliot, also bears this pseudonym? (I cannot imagine that the published version of the poem, in some still unlocated Providence newspaper, bore the pseudonym as well, although it may well have appeared anonymously.) This poem is certainly not a *self*-parody by any stretch of the imagination. But the most curious instance is the series of poems appearing under the title "Perverted Poesie or Modern Metre." This cycle is very early, dating possibly to 1914, and appeared posthumously in the amateur journal *The O-Wash-Ta-Nong*, edited by Lovecraft's old-time amateur colleague George W. Macauley; either Macauley or one of his associates must have worked from a manuscript supplied by Lovecraft. But what is most bizarre is that, of the four poems in the cycle—"The Introduction," "Unda, or, The Bride of the Sea," "The Peace Advocate," and "A Summer Sunset and Evening"—two had already appeared in Lovecraft's lifetime under pseudonyms other than "Humphry Littlewit, Esq." "Unda" appeared in 1916 as by "Lewis Theobald, Jr.," and "The Peace Advocate" appeared in the *Tryout* for May 1917—under the name "Elizabeth Berkeley"! This was the second instance of a Lovecraft poem appearing under the pseudonym of Winifred Jackson, the other being the weird poem "The Unknown" (*Conservative*, October 1916); he explains in a letter that this occurred "in an effort to mystify the [amateur] public by having widely dissimilar work from the same nominal hand."[2] These poems, again, are not *self*-parodic, although they are certainly parodies—of the mawkishly romantic love lyrics of the Lord Byron or Thomas Moore type ("Unda"), of pacifism ("The Peace Advocate"), and of the vapid pastoral elegy ("A Summer Sunset and Evening").

Ames Dorrance Rowley is the one pseudonym of Lovecraft's that is meant as a parody of *someone else*—in this case, the amateur poet James Laurence Crowley. One would imagine that the poems appearing under this name would somehow be parodies of poems by Crowley, or at least of Crowley's manner, but I am not entirely convinced that this is the case. Certainly it is not the case for the juvenile poem "To the Old Pagan Religion" (published as "The Last Pagan Speaks"). Of the three other poems, perhaps only "Laeta; a Lament" can be considered a genuine parody of Crowley. It rather resembles "Unda, or, The Bride of the Sea" in tone:

> How sad droop the willows by Zulal's fair side,
> Where so lately I stray'd with my raven-hair'd bride:
> Ev'ry light-floating lily, each flow'r on the shore,
> Folds in sorrow since Laeta can see them no more!

The two other poems are both militaristic—"To Maj.-Gen. Omar Bundy, U.S.A." and "The Volunteer." I would certainly like to think that these are somehow parodic, but the sad fact is that they do not seem to be. Here is the final stanza of the former:

> So ever shine COLUMBIA'S brave,
>   First in the fray, unconquer'd still;
> Whose glories echo o'er the wave,
>   And ev'ry land triumphant fill!

The tone of these poems is scarcely different from that of such windy (but seriously intended) patriotic effusions as "An American to Mother England" or "Britannia Victura."

Among the most extensively used of Lovecraft's pseudonyms are Henry Paget-Lowe, Ward Phillips, Edward Softly, and Lewis Theobald, Jun. Of these, the easiest to deal with is Henry Paget-Lowe. I have already remarked how transparent the pseudonym is, and I cannot imagine that any amateur

---

2. HPL to the Gallomo, 12 September 1921; *Letters to Alfred Galpin* (New York: Hippocampus Press, 2003), 108.

could have failed to recognise it. It is strange that all five works written with this pseudonym appeared in 1920. "Poetry and the Gods," a tale with Anna Helen Crofts (not a pseudonym), is one of his few collaborative stories to appear pseudonymously. Of the four poems, two are innocuous paeans to seasons ("January" and "October"), one a neo-classic spasm ("On a Grecian Colonnade in a Park"—whose title, but nothing else, is obviously derived from Keats's "Ode on a Grecian Urn"), and one rather biting satire, "On Religion." Regardless of the merits of these poems, they were all clearly intended seriously and not self-parodically.

Ward Phillips is also scarcely much of a disguise, and it is under this name that Lovecraft's one original *weird* tale—the prose-poem "Ex Oblivione"—appeared. But it is of note that a good many of Lovecraft's very powerful weird *poems* also appeared under this pseudonym—"Astrophobos," "Bells," "The City," "A Cycle of Verse," "The Eidolon," and "The House." Other works by Ward Phillips are highly personal tributes to friends ("To Mr. Hoag, on His Ninetieth Birthday"; "In Memoriam: J. E. T. D.," an elegy to the deceased amateur Jennie E. T. Dowe; "Sir Thomas Tryout," on the death of C. W. Smith's cat) and a poignant philosophical poem ("Ambition"). As with Humphry Littlewit, Esq., the *name* "Ward Phillips" is somewhat self-parodic (recall the obviously parodic figure of that name in "Through the Gates of the Silver Key"), but the works appearing under the name are not.

The Edward Softly pseudonym derives from Joseph Addison's *The Tatler* No. 163 (25 April 1710), where a sentimental poem is attributed to one "Ned Softly." Accordingly, the pseudonym is used for a number of Lovecraft's parodic pastorals satirising Alfred Galpin's youthful love affairs ("Chloris and Damon," "Damon and Delia, a Pastoral," "The Dream" [subtitled: "Respectfully Dedicated to Master Consul Hasting," a Galpin pseudonym], and "To Delia, Avoiding Damon"). Otherwise it was used for a humorous poem about C. W. Smith ("Tryout's Lament for the Vanished Spider") and a perfectly pleasant little Christmas poem ("Christmas," an 8-line lyric not to be confused with the interminable 327-line "Old Christmas").

Lewis Theobald, Jun. is the most difficult of Lovecraft's pseudonyms to categorise, as it seems to have been used for a bewildering variety of works—essays, story collaborations, and poems alike. We have already remarked on the essays ("The Trip of Theobald" and "The Convention") and the collaborations ("The Green Meadow" and "The Crawling Chaos"), and also on the fact that the name seems to have become known very early on in the amateur world as a Lovecraft pseudonym: an unsigned "biography" of Theobald appeared in the "News Notes" section of the *United Amateur* for March 1918 (it was likely written by Verna McGeoch, Official Editor of the U.A.P.A. at the time). I am not sure that the origin of the *name* Lewis Theobald, Jun. has any particular bearing on the works published under that name. As is well known (see Boerem), the name derives from a celebrated eighteenth-century poet and critic (whose edition of Shakespeare [1733] is still highly regarded) who had the misfortune of earning the wrath of Alexander Pope (he severely—and rightly—criticised the errors in Pope's own 1725 edition of Shakespeare) and was accordingly pilloried in the first version of Pope's *Dunciad* (1728). But Lovecraft seems to have adopted the name, at least initially, as a sort of half-parodic reference to his own eighteenth-century inclinations and to the acknowledged mediocrity of his archaic poetry. But the name was used so frequently, from 1916 onward, that its original meaning and purpose seem to have been lost, and it became simply another Lovecraft alter ego like Henry Paget-Lowe and Ward Phillips.

If anything, the bulk of the Lewis Theobald, Jun. poems are humorous and mildly satiric, many directed at his own colleagues. Here again we have a number of poems about Galpin ("Damon—a Monody," "To Alfred Galpin, Esq.," "To Damon," "To Mr. Galpin, upon His 20th Birthday"), not all of which are by any means satirical; a number of parodies of or poems about Rheinhart Kleiner ("Cindy: Scrub-Lady in a State Street Skyscraper," "To Mistress Sophia Simple, Queen of the Cinema," "To Phillis," "To Rheinhart Kleiner, Esq., upon His Town Fables and Elegies");[3] a satire of both Kleiner and George Julian Houtain ("Ex-Poet's Reply"); a parody of a poem by Olive G. Owen ("The Nymph's Reply to the Modern Business Man"); more general parodies of romantic poetry ("The Poet of Passion," "The Poet's Rash Excuse," "Unda, or, The Bride of the Sea"); poems about Frank Belknap Long ("To Endymion") and Maurice W. Moe ("On the Return of Maurice Winter Moe, Esq., to the Pedagogical Profession"); and two birthday poems to Jonathan E. Hoag. All these poems are lighthearted and somewhat frivolous, but they are not all sharp satires, although "Ye Ballade of Patrick von Flynn" and, perhaps, "Monody on the Late King Alcohol" are. On the other hand, Lewis Theobald, Jun. was used for some undoubtedly serious and even some very touching poems, including the exquisite "Sunset," the pensive "Brotherhood," "Inspiration," and "Sonnet on Myself," and two weird poems, "The Rutted Road" and—surprisingly late—"The Wood" (1929). It becomes evident, therefore, that this pseudonym was not used in any systematic way save perhaps for poems that perhaps had some special personal significance to Lovecraft.

---

3. It should be pointed out that HPL's letter to Alfred Galpin (21 August 1918; *Letters to Alfred Galpin*, 25–34) contains a number of parodies of poems by Kleiner, under such pseudonyms as "Kleinhart Reiner," "Edvardus Softleius," "Anacreon Microcephalos," and (my favourite) "A. Saphead."

In 1927 Lovecraft made an odd statement about pseudonyms in a letter to Zealia Bishop. "No one can advise another regarding the choice of a nom de guerre, since only one's self can fully grasp all the sentimentally associative factors concerned. . . . For my part, I have always used my own name as a matter of course—for sheer lack of any reason to use any other—except for hack work too poor to be acknowledged" (SL 2.161–62). This last sentence is clearly false: however little Lovecraft valued his early poems later on in life, he would never have wished to repudiate such things as "A Cycle of Verse" or "The House" (which was written about the same house in Providence that served as the setting for "The Shunned House"), or in any case would never have dismissed this material as "hack work." Still, it is evident that Lovecraft became increasingly disinclined to use pseudonyms, as they tended to violate his notions of writing as pure self-expression: "My only general objection to pseudonyms is that they tend to imply a sort of self-consciousness or self-dramatisation on the user's part, which is somewhat foreign to the process of impersonal, disinterested artistic creation. They imply that the user stands off and thinks of himself as an author, instead of being so wrapped up in his aesthetic vision that he never regards himself as a person at all" (SL 2.162). And yet, Lovecraft's early use of pseudonyms for a wide array of works—poetry, essays, fiction, collaborations, and even letters—points not merely to a tremendous fecundity in writing but to a careful awareness of the purpose and direction of a given work, whereby the use of a pseudonym enhances its general atmosphere and conveys a certain knowing wink to those readers who are in on the joke. The fact that so many of his pseudonyms—Isaac Bickerstaffe, Jr., Humphry Littlewit, Esq., Archibald Maynwaring, Lewis Theobald, Jun.—hark back to the eighteenth century once more emphasises the spiritual affinity to the Augustans that Lovecraft claimed from very early youth. It was that affinity which led him to write, in his best poetry, some of the most pungent satire and parody of his period, under pseudonyms that betrayed rather than concealed his authorship.

Works Cited

Boerem, R. "The First Lewis Theobald." In Darrell Schweitzer, ed. *Essays Lovecraftian* (1976); rev. ed. as *Discovering H. P. Lovecraft*. Mercer Island, WA: Starmont House, 1987. 42–46.

Derleth, August. "New HPL Pseudonyms Rejected by Derleth." *Fossil* No. 159 (October 1958): 90.

Keffer, Willametta. "Howard P(seudonym) Lovecraft: The Many Names of HPL." *Fossil* No. 158 (July 1958): 82–84.

Wetzel, George T. "The Pseudonymous Lovecraft." *Xenophile* 3, No. 4 (November 1976): 3–5, 73.

Lovecraft and the Munsey Magazines

Lovecraft's relations with the Munsey magazines have always been fraught with confusion, largely because the exact number and content of his letters to the various magazines were never precisely known; but now that the biographical and bibliographical conundrums surrounding this matter have been solved, we are in a better position to clarify a significant chapter in Lovecraft's early life.

When we read, in his letter to the *All-Story* for 7 March 1914 that Lovecraft had "read every number of your magazine since its beginning in January, 1905," we are taken aback both by the voluminous amount of early pulp fiction he must already have absorbed and by the fact that in later years he would actually conceal this absorption. As early as 1916 he was prevaricating in a letter: "In 1913 I had formed the reprehensible habit of picking up cheap magazines like *The Argosy* to divert my mind from the tedium of reality" (*SL* 1.41). This is one of the few instances where Lovecraft actually lies about himself; no doubt he was already embarrassed at this literary slumming, given that he was then attempting to establish himself as a classicist of the purest sort.

What is more remarkable, the *Argosy* and *All-Story* were by no means the only magazines of this kind that Lovecraft was reading. *The Rhode Island Journal of Astronomy* for 27 September 1903 cites an article in the October *Munsey's Magazine,* so he must have read at least some issues of that journal. In later years other admissions begin to filter through, almost in spite of himself: he read Street & Smith's *Popular Magazine* around 1905-10;[1] he read the entirety of the *Railroad Man's Magazine* (1906-13);[2] he began reading the *Black Cat* around 1904.[3]

What, exactly, was the fascination of these magazines? In 1905 Lovecraft had already gained most of the interests that would persist throughout his life: antiquarianism; chemistry; astronomy; classical literature; Augustan poet-

---

1. HPL to Richard F. Searight, 26 September 1935; *Letters to Richard F. Searight* (West Warwick, RI: Necronomicon Press, 1992), 64.
2. HPL to Richard F. Searight, 16 April 1935; *Letters to Richard F. Searight,* 54.
3. HPL to R. H. Barlow, 14 April 1932 (OFF 29).

ry; and, of course, weird fiction. But he had by no means read all the standard weird fiction that had been written up to that time, and would be surprisingly late in discovering some of the great weird writers of the later nineteenth and early twentieth centuries. Of course, his discovery of Poe at the age of eight (as well as his concurrent reading of dime and nickel novels) had turned his creative energies definitively toward weird fiction; but he would discover Ambrose Bierce and Lord Dunsany only in 1919, Arthur Machen in 1923, Algernon Blackwood and M. R. James in 1924, and Robert W. Chambers in 1927. Accordingly, Lovecraft had little access to *recent* weird writing, and it was this void that the Munsey magazines filled: "In general . . . the Munsey publications did more to publish weird fiction than any other magazine enterprise of the early 20th century."[4] So Lovecraft put up with the vast array of mediocrity in these magazines for the few weird nuggets they contained.

The convoluted history of the various Munsey magazines can be encapsulated briefly here. The *Argosy* began as the *Golden Argosy* in 1882, changing to the *Argosy* in 1888; it had started out as a weekly, became a monthly in 1894, and reverted to a weekly on 6 October 1917. It continued publication until 1948. The *All-Story* began as a monthly in 1905, became the *All-Story Weekly* on 7 March 1914, merged with the *Cavalier* to become the *All-Story Cavalier Weekly* on 16 May 1914, reverted to the *All-Story Weekly* on 15 May 1915, and merged with the *Argosy* to become the *Argosy All-Story Weekly* on 24 July 1920. The editor of the *All-Story* during its entire run was Robert H. Davis. The *Argosy*'s editor during the period of Lovecraft's letters was Matthew White, Jr, although Lovecraft in letters mentions a T. N. Metcalf, who was perhaps a sub-editor or editor of the letter column, entitled "The Log-Book."

Lovecraft's first published letter to the Munsey magazines—discovered only recently—appeared in the *Argosy* for November 1911 (it is identified as by "H. P. L. of Providence, Rhode Island"). "The Log-Book" had only been established in February 1911, and letters were slow to appear; but by the end of the year many readers from around the country had begun to write in, being initially identified only by initials and city of residence. Lovecraft's letter in the September 1913 issue speaks of having "been guilty of an inch or two in the Log-Book," and the letter of November 1911—praising, of all people, Albert Payson Terhune, the future creator of Lassie—is the only one prior to 1913 that can be attributed to him. It may also have been at this time that Lovecraft wrote an effusive poem, "To Mr. Terhune, on His Historical Fiction," which, although specifically addressed to the editor of the *Argosy*, was not published there.

---

4. HPL to R. H. Barlow, 31 March 1932 (OFF 28).

His next published letter, appearing in the 8 February 1913 issue of the *All-Story Cavalier*, is a praiseworthy comment on Irvin S. Cobb's magnificent tale of a half-man, half-fish hybrid, "Fishhead." It is my feeling that this powerful tale lodged in Lovecraft's mind and would form a significant influence on "The Shadow over Innsmouth" (1931), which similarly treats of the union of fish and human beings. In the fall of that year Lovecraft's letter-writing campaign shifts to the *Argosy*; but at the moment I wish to return to the letter of 1914 that I have already quoted, a letter of close to 2000 words, taking up nearly two full printed pages. It is a sort of grand summation of everything he liked in the magazine and an encapsulation of what he thought the magazine stood for. Scorning the plea of one G. W. F. of Dundee, Scotland, for more "probable" stories, Lovecraft declaims:

> If, in fact, man is unable to create living beings out of inorganic matter, to hypnotise beasts of the forest to do his will, to swing from tree to tree with the apes of the African jungle, to restore to life the mummified corpses of the Pharaohs and the Incas, or to explore the atmosphere of Venus and the deserts of Mars, permit us, at least, in fancy, to witness these miracles, and to satisfy that craving for the unknown, the weird, and the impossible which exists in every active human brain.

That last statement is certainly a little sanguine: if everyone had a craving for the unknown, then weird fiction would not be as unrecognised a literary mode as it is. But the catalogue presented above is not only a series of synopses of some of the celebrated tales published in the *All-Story* but, in several instances, a selection of plot-elements that Lovecraft himself would use in his own later work.

There follow paeans to many of the *All-Story*'s most popular writers. Who is first to be named? "At or near the head of your list of writers Edgar Rice Burroughs undoubtedly stands." Lovecraft goes on to single out *Tarzan of the Apes* (October 1912), *The Gods of Mars* (January–May 1913), and *Warlord of Mars* (December 1913–March 1914), although it is typical that while praising these stories he takes care to point out astronomical and other errors in the works. Later in life Lovecraft seemed embarrassed at his juvenile (or not so juvenile: he was twenty-three when he wrote this letter) fondness for Burroughs, and he sought to distance himself from the creator of Tarzan. In 1929, when urging a correspondent not to yield to the temptations of the market and write hackwork, he lumps Burroughs with Edgar A. Guest and Harold Bell Wright as examples of the fact that "the veriest idiot and ignoramus can sometimes bring down fame on a luck-shot" (*SL* 2.325). Not long thereafter, in saying that "I shall sooner or later get around to the interplanetary field myself," he adds explicitly: "you may depend upon it that I shall not choose Edmond Hamilton, Ray Cummings, or Edgar Rice Burroughs as my model!" (*SL* 3.88). This gives no indication of how much he had enjoyed the John Carter Martian novels fifteen years before.

In his letter Lovecraft goes on to praise many other writers, few of whom are of any note—William Patterson White, Lee Robinet, William Tillinghast Eldridge, William Loren Curtiss, Donald Francis McGrew, and others. A later letter (published in the *All-Story Cavalier Weekly* for 15 August 1914) praises George Allan England, Albert Payson Terhune, and Zane Grey. What is remarkable is that most of these writers did not even write weird fiction: Zane Grey, of course, was the legendary Western writer; Terhune became famous for dog stories; McGrew was an adventure writer whose "red-blooded" stories met with Lovecraft's thunderous approval; and he even liked the many humorous tales in the magazine. This means that Lovecraft read each issue—sometimes 192 pages, sometimes 240 pages—from cover to cover, month after month or even (when it changed to a weekly) week after week. This is an appalling amount of popular fiction for anyone to read, and in fact it contravened the purpose of the magazines, which was that each member of the family would read only those stories or those types of stories that were of interest to him or her.[5] One begins to develop the impression that Lovecraft was compulsive in whatever he did: his discovery of classical antiquity led him to write paraphrases of the *Odyssey, Iliad,* and other works; his discovery of chemistry led him to launch a *daily* scientific paper; his discovery of astronomy led him to publish a weekly paper for years; and now his discovery of pulp fiction caused him to be a voracious reader of both the good and the bad, both the work that appealed to his special tastes and the work that did not.

It is possible that the *All-Story* published this long letter in its issue of 7 March 1914 because Lovecraft himself had become, after a fashion, a celebrity in the entire Munsey chain. This had come about in a very odd way. Lovecraft, reading everything the *Argosy* put in front of him, found some material less appealing to his fastidious taste than others. It is, then, no surprise that a popular *Argosy* writer named Fred Jackson would be blasted by Lovecraft in the issue for September 1913. Jackson had become an *Argosy* staple, and two of his short novels had appeared complete in recent issues, "The First Law" in April 1913 and "The Third Act" in June 1913. This really was an unprecedented amount of space to give to a single author, and the subject-matter of these works was not of a kind to sit well with Lovecraft. "The First

---

5. See Will Murray, "Lovecraft and the Pulp Magazine Tradition," in *An Epicure in the Terrible,* ed. David E. Schultz and S. T. Joshi (1991; New York: Hippocampus Press, 2011), 103.

Law" is an unbelievably sappy, melodramatic, and verbose story of an opera singer; here is a sample:

> She struggled against him fiercely, her whole being outraged, but he was by far the stronger. He held her fast, and his lips touched her ear, her throat, her chin, and eyes, and at last crushed her mouth until she gasped for breath.
>
> Then he drew back and she lay passive in his arms, trembling, terrified at the madness that possessed her. It was as though he had awakened some sleeping demon—a creature unknown to her, a creature thirsty for his kisses, aching for his embrace.

Jackson would probably have made a good Harlequin romance writer today.

What is frequently overlooked is that Lovecraft's tirade was not inspired merely by the unwonted dominance of Jackson in the pages of *Argosy* but by a letter purportedly attacking him in the July 1913 issue. This letter—by one F. V. Bennett of Hanover, Illinois—is, however, so illiterate that Lovecraft believed it to be a sort of self-parody designed indirectly to praise Jackson. Lovecraft's own letter in the September 1913 issue could hardly be taken as a self-parody. He expresses the opinion that Bennett's letter "is in reality a sly attempt at augmenting the fame of your contributor, Fred Jackson," and continues:

> To the eye of a disinterested observer it appears as though an effort were being made forcibly to obtrude Mr. Jackson upon the reading public by an unexampled campaign of advertising, and by the selection for publication in the Log-Book of those letters wherein he receives the greatest amount of adulation.

There is something to be said for this, too: the Log-Book of the previous several issues had been filled with praise for Jackson, many of them from men, curiously enough. Of course, Lovecraft overlooks the possibility that Jackson really was popular with *Argosy* readers; or, rather, overlooks the undoubted fact that most of the magazine's readers had very lax literary standards and were only interested in cheap entertainment. Lovecraft, indeed, does not claim that Jackson's novels "are wholly wanting in merit," noting a little dryly that "There is a numerous set of people whose chief literary delight is obtained in the following of imaginary nymphs and swains through the labyrinthine paths of amorous adventure"; but he strenuously objects to the dominance of such work in the *Argosy*. And it is a fact, maintains Lovecraft, that Jackson is simply a bad writer.

The response to this letter is not likely to have been predicted either by Lovecraft or by Matthew White, Jr. The November 1913 issue contained several more letters on Jackson: one by the redoubtable F. V. Bennett, just as illiterate as its predecessor and evidently unaware that Lovecraft had ranked him as a Jackson supporter; one, by "E. F. W. C." of Paris, Kentucky, attacking Jackson but not alluding to Lovecraft; and two others specifically supporting Jackson and attacking Lovecraft and Bennett. One of these, by T. P. Crean of Syracuse, New York, claims:

> I am still puzzling over H. P. Lovecraft's letter. I can understand how the brilliant F. V. Bennett cannot go Jackson's stories. But Mr. Lovecraft, from his letter, should be able to tell a good story when he reads one. I am personally of the opinion that this letter was merely to display to THE ARGOSY world his vocabulary . . .

This is a refrain that would frequently be rung in the entire controversy.

The affair, however, might not have taken the peculiar turn it did had not the other letter, by John Russell of Tampa, Florida, been written *in verse*. Lovecraft describes it as "a piece of tetrameter verse . . . which had in it so much native wit, that I resolved to answer it" (*SL* 1.41). Sure enough, he responded in the January 1914 issue with a verse epistle of his own in what he fancied was the manner of Pope's *Dunciad*. In fact, it is a very clever poem, and reveals that penchant for stinging satire which would be one of the few virtues of his poetic output. The manuscript of the poem is headed "Ad Criticos" ("To [my] critics") (with the subtitle "Liber Primus," probably inserted at a later date as Lovecraft continued to add to the cycle). He praises Russell for his cleverness and wit, and then proceeds to take his other enemies to task. He concludes the poem by comparing the present time to "Charles the Second's vulgar age," when "Gross Wycherley and Dryden soil'd the stage."

But before Lovecraft's verse letter was printed, he was ferociously assailed in the December 1913 issue. Some of the titles which the editor affixed to the letters give some idea of the outrage Lovecraft had provoked: "Challenge to Lovecraft"; "Virginia *vs.* Providence"; "Elmira *vs.* Providence"; "Bomb for Lovecraft." Two letters did take Lovecraft's side, however; they were each headed "Agrees with Lovecraft."

In a "Liber Secundus" published in the February 1914 *Argosy* Lovecraft takes potshots at these new opponents. The tone of this poem is much sharper than that of its predecessor. Lovecraft was, of course, in a position of overwhelming intellectual superiority to most of his victims, and sometimes it seems as if he is shooting fish in a barrel; but the satire is nonetheless withering for all that. In this issue he begins to gather both friends and enemies—mostly the latter. One of the staunchest of the former is no other than F. V. Bennett, who had unwittingly begun the controversy. Now becoming literate (or having his letter corrected of spelling mistakes and of erroneous or absent punctuation), he writes, "well, shake, H.P.L.," and claims that "we started the ball that called a halt to the rush of Jackson soft stuff." This remark seems to be confirmed by an editor's note in the issue: "I can promise that you won't get too much Jackson in 1914." This does not mean, of course, that readers would get *no* Jackson: another short novel, "Ambushed" (a mystery story with a romance element), had already appeared in the October 1913 issue, and "Winged Feet" was published in February 1914; but after this there was nothing until "The Marriage Auction" in January 1915. Thereafter, however, Jackson returns with a vengeance: "Red Robin" appeared in July 1915, "The Diamond Necklace" in October and November 1915, "Where's the Woman?" from 6 October to 3 November 1917, and "A Woman's Prey" in 24 November 1917; "Young Blood" appeared serially in *Munsey's* beginning in October 1917. In this sense it could hardly be said that Lovecraft and his supporters had helped to effect any sort of change in the *Argosy's* editorial policy; the fact is that, as various editor's notes make clear, Jackson finally ceased to appear in the Munsey magazines because he decided to take up the writing of plays, and in fact gained considerable success at this new career.

Lovecraft continued to be raked over the coals in succeeding issues, himself adding only a "Correction" of a printing error in his first "Ad Criticos" poem. But something strange now happens: no more replies by Lovecraft himself are published in the *Argosy* until October 1914. There are two further books of "Ad Criticos": did he not submit them for publication? or were they not accepted? The latter seems unlikely, since an editorial note at the end of "Correction for Lovecraft" declares: "You are always welcome in the Log-Book."

By summer the controversy had begun to die down. An editorial note in the May 1914 issue declares that "The same old warfare over Jackson is going on, in prose and verse," and this issue does indeed contain a number of poems attacking Lovecraft. But with Lovecraft himself not replying (or, at least, with his replies not being printed), the debate had little to feed itself upon. The unpublished "Liber Quartus" of "Ad Criticos" does take up some of these attacks, but of course it did not see the dignity of print at the time.

The controversy came to an end in the October 1914 issue. An entire section of "The Log-Book" bears the heading "Fred Jackson, Pro and Con"; inevitably, the "Jackson Boosters" outnumber the "Jackson Knockers." None of the former addresses Lovecraft specifically, but of the latter the loyal F. V. Bennett stands up for his mentor. But the most interesting item is a poem headed "The Critics' Farewell" and bearing both Lovecraft's and Russell's names. They did not actually collaborate on the poem; rather, Lovecraft wrote the first part (headed "The End of the Jackson War") and Russell wrote the second (headed "Our Apology to E. M. W."); Lovecraft's, naturally, is in heroic couplets, and Russell's is in very racy and irregular anapaests. Lovecraft notes that this truce was made at the insistence of T. N. Metcalf, who "intimated that the poet's war must soon end, since correspondents were complaining of the prominence of our verses in their beloved magazine" (*SL* 1.42).

We now come to the two most curious items in this entire matter. A letter by one "Augustus T. Swift" of Providence, Rhode Island, appeared in the *Argosy* for 15 November 1919, and another by the same author in the issue for 22 May 1920. Augustus T. Swift has been assumed to be a pseudonym of Lovecraft's; the letters were first attributed to him in the early fan magazine *Golden Atom*, whose editor Larry Farsaci reprinted these letters (along with the one in the *All-Story Cavalier* for 15 August 1914) in the issue for December 1940. By what authority did Farsaci make this attribution? It seems as if he did so purely by conjecture—in other words, by the mere fact that the letters were written from Providence. But was Lovecraft the only reader of *Argosy* (or the only one who wrote letters to the editor) in the city of Providence? A simple examination of the Providence city directory for 1919–20 establishes that there was a real individual named Augustus T. Swift living at 122 Rochambeau Avenue in Providence. It is manifestly clear that these two letters are not by Lovecraft at all.

It should have occurred to Farsaci, or to many later scholars who have blithely attributed these letters to Lovecraft, that there are some very bizarre features to them. In the first there occur such utterly non-Lovecraftian usages as "snappy," "a bang-up good story," and (in reference to Francis Stevens's *Citadel of Fear*) the comment that it "would make *one amazing moving-picture drama.*" Would Lovecraft really have said such a thing? But the second letter is even more odd; it concludes with the remarkable assertion (concerning a short story about whaling): "Being a native of New Bedford, Massachusetts, and having heard whale-ship talk from infancy, I followed the detailed descriptions of polar scenes with unusual interest." This sentence alone should have raised suspicions, but it does not appear to have done so.

All that remains here is to ascertain the exact chain of events which led to the attribution of these letters to Lovecraft. As I have stated, Farsaci seems to be the culprit here. R. H. Barlow, in his article on "Pseudonyms of Lovecraft" (*Acolyte*, Summer 1943), makes no mention of the Augustus T. Swift "pseudonym"; but it is picked up by Ray H. Zorn in the *Lovecraft Collector* for January 1949 (surely on the basis of the reprinting of the letters in *Golden Atom*), and subsequently in the bibliographies of Wetzel (1955), Chalker (1966), and, it must be admitted, Joshi (1981). As in so many other instances, a massive house of cards has been built up on evidence that could have been demolished in a moment. That demolition has now occurred, and these works should be definitively banished from the Lovecraft corpus.

Some further consequences follow upon the spuriousness of these letters. Although Lovecraft admits to reading A. Merritt's "The Moon Pool" in the *All-*

Story for 22 June 1918, there is now no evidence that he read the *Argosy* at all after 1914, or that he read and enjoyed the work of Francis Stevens (which is praised in the Augustus T. Swift letters), although it is conceivable that he might have. Stevens's novels *The Citadel of Fear* and *Claimed* have been reprinted in paperback, with blurbs from Augustus T. Swift attributed to Lovecraft! One hopes this sort of thing will not occur again.

It is worth reflecting on what the whole *Argosy/All-Story* battle over Fred Jackson meant to Lovecraft. In a sense we owe thanks to Mr Jackson (or perhaps F. V. Bennett) for making the rest of Lovecraft's career possible, for there is no telling how long he would have continued to vegetate in the increasingly hothouse atmosphere of 598 Angell Street, where he had lived alone with his mother since 1904 and where he dwelt in hermitry after a "nervous breakdown" that cut short his high school career and prevented his attending college. Lovecraft had no job, was only toying with chemistry and astronomy, was living with a mother who was steadily losing her mental stability, was writing random undistinguished bits of verse about his native region, and was devouring the Munsey magazines but had no thought of contributing any fiction to them or to any other market. But Jackson's work so irritated him that he emerged from his cloister at least to the extent of bombarding letters to the magazines in question. While it was John Russell who initiated the practice of writing in verse, Lovecraft found it a golden opportunity to adapt his beloved Augustan satire against a very modern target.

Lovecraft seems to have responded reasonably well to the abuse with which he was bombarded, although it is evident that at least a few items—especially by Russell—irritated and perhaps even wounded him. Possibly he ceased to submit his work to the *Argosy* after the first few items because he felt the cause was hopeless: it was obvious that he was not changing very many people's minds, and was only irritating many loyal readers. Some of the responses to Lovecraft are surprisingly bitter and hostile, suggesting—whimsically, one hopes—that physical violence be done to the opponent of the beloved Fred Jackson.

The curious thing about the responses to Lovecraft is that many readers took offence at his mere voicing of criticism of Jackson, as if such a thing were in itself somehow off-limits. Some of these comments were on target—those that maintain that the *Argosy* was not published exclusively for one reader's benefit, or that no one is under the obligation to read the magazine—but many readers expressed indignation at the mere levelling of criticism of any kind. The slang terms used to designate this adverse criticism—to "knock" or "kick"—are inherently pejorative, and were interpreted as a sort of personal failing, as if Lovecraft were a misanthrope who could not say anything good about anyone.

One also wonders whether Lovecraft would have engendered the response that he did had he attacked any other writer but Fred Jackson. It certainly appears as if Jackson had a very loyal following both in the *Cavalier* and in the *Argosy*; and I repeat my amazement at the number of men who seemed genuinely to enjoy his love stories. Here again some of the personal attacks are interesting: Lovecraft as the crusty bachelor, as one who has been jilted and is therefore hostile to any expressions of tender emotion, as a cynic who scorns the romantic element in life. Some of these accusations are, indeed, on the mark, but they are irrelevant to the issue of the actual merits of Jackson as a writer; and here Lovecraft is surely correct in declaring Jackson to be sentimental, stylistically careless, and catering rather calculatingly to the expectations of his audience. But Jackson's defenders were on the whole so pathetically ill-educated that they could not even begin to make the fundamental critical distinction between a story that they happened to like and a story that had genuine literary substance. Of course, Jackson's attackers were by and large not much better in this regard.

The ramifications of this entire episode, for Lovecraft, go far beyond the exchange of abuse on a mediocre and insignificant writer. It was, perhaps, the first occasion when he encountered opinions radically different from his own, and coming from a group of people very different (and, quite honestly, quite inferior) in education, culture, and socioeconomic status from his. Although he does not seem to have had much respect for many of his opponents—except, again, Russell—and indeed seems to have had a fairly easy time dynamiting their positions, he would later find such differences of opinion among his friends, colleagues, and correspondents invaluable in shaking him out of his certitudes and broadening his perspective.

What is one to make of Lovecraft's voluminous reading of the Munsey magazines at all? They were certainly not the high literature that he customarily read, and he slogged through an enormous quantity of rubbish to unearth the few flawed gems that he found imaginatively stimulating. But Lovecraft clearly had such a thirst for the weird that he would go to any lengths to come upon it; we can see this same phenomenon in his later reading of *Weird Tales*, *Amazing Stories*, and the other pulps that emerged in the 1920s and 1930s for a shorter or longer period. Most of them he would drop after an issue or two, realising that they were hopelessly conventional and formulaic; but *Weird Tales* he read to the end, commenting charitably on those few tales (mostly by his own colleagues) that marginally elevated themselves from the general standard of mediocrity. At the same time, however, Lovecraft was under no illusions as to the literary status of the pulp magazines; he knew that they were meant to serve a generally ill-educated public, and the fact that he refused to mention any of this material in "Supernatural Horror in Literature" is one of many telltale signs of the low esteem in which he regarded this literary underworld. While Lovecraft never compromised his own literary standards to cater to popular formula, it becomes somewhat pitiable that he continued to hope against hope that he would encounter truly meritorious work in the pulps.

But the principal immediate result of the *Argosy* experience was, of course, his discovery of—or, rather, by—the world of amateur journalism. Edward F. Daas, then Official Editor of the United Amateur Press Association, noticed the poetic battle between Lovecraft and Russell and invited both to join the organisation. Both did so, Lovecraft officially enrolling on 6 April 1914. In a few years he would be transformed both as a writer and as a human being, eventually resuming the writing of that weird fiction which would ultimately bring him a small modicum of fame as a towering figure in this small realm. That we owe Lovecraft's later career even in part to the unreadable Fred Jackson and the illiterate F. V. Bennett must surely be one of the great ironies of literature.

Barbarism vs. Civilization: Robert E. Howard and H. P. Lovecraft in Their Correspondence

Robert E. Howard and H. P. Lovecraft, two of the towering figures of weird literature of their time, engaged in a six-year correspondence that currently constitutes more than 400,000 words—a treasure-trove of immense value to students and scholars of both writers. It is a shame that a variety of legal and logistical obstacles have so far prevented the full publication of this series of documents: we have seen large fragments of it in the last two volumes of Lovecraft's *Selected Letters* and in the two volumes of Howard's *Selected Letters*; but only a joint publication of their correspondence—as with the joint publication of the letters of Lovecraft and Clark Ashton Smith, which may also be imminent—can properly convey the rich texture of this variegated mass of letters, each so revelatory of their respective authors. For now, the best we can do is to convey some sense of the overall direction of the correspondence, focusing on the central intellectual questions that the two writers debated with such vigor.[1]

The very survival of the extant correspondence could be considered almost an accident. Lovecraft scrupulously preserved all of Howard's letters (the great majority of them typewritten), sending them down to Howard Payne University in Brownwood, Texas, following Howard's death. The fate of the Lovecraft side is less happy. Whether Howard himself preserved Lovecraft's letters entirely intact is not certain; in any event, after the death of both Howard and Lovecraft, Howard's father, Dr. I. M. Howard, allowed August Derleth to have the letters transcribed for ultimate publication in Lovecraft's *Selected Letters*. Derleth put the letters into the hands of his secretary, Alice Conger, having indicated which portions of the letters were to be transcribed. While Derleth did have substantial portions transcribed, he decided (as he

---

1. As the correspondence has now been published as *A Means to Freedom*, I will cite them only by date. The majority of Howard's letters are undated, and in some cases their exact dating is conjectural.

did with almost every other body of letters that came into his hands for this purpose) that some of the more ephemeral sections could be omitted. This would not be a problem if the original letters had not, through an apparent accident, been destroyed in the early 1940s. As a result, all we are left with, for Lovecraft's side of the correspondence, are the so-called Arkham House Transcripts—an amount totalling more than 150,000 words, but nonetheless not absolutely complete. Some entire letters appear to be missing—whether through Howard's own oversight, or through their loss before they reached Derleth, or through Derleth's decision not to transcribe them, cannot now be ascertained.

The rather peculiar initiation of the correspondence is well known. Lovecraft's "The Rats in the Walls" (first published in *Weird Tales*, March 1924) had been reprinted in *Weird Tales* in June 1930. When Howard read the story, he was struck by what he believed to be Lovecraft's advocacy of a minority view regarding the invasion of Britain by successive waves of Gaelic and Cymric peoples from mainland Europe, and wrote a letter to Farnsworth Wright, editor of *Weird Tales*, to this effect (see REH 1.48–49). Wright forwarded the letter to Lovecraft, who admitted sheepishly to Howard that he knew very little about the Gaelic or Cymric peoples and had merely borrowed some Gaelic phrases from Fiona Macleod's "The Sin-Eater" (1895) for his story. In this way, in the summer of 1930, an intense and voluminous correspondence, lasting till Howard's death, began—a correspondence of which a slight majority was written by Howard (although that may be in part a result, as just indicated, of the loss of some of Lovecraft's letters after Howard's death). The correspondence is unusual in being very largely philosophical, as each writer emphasizes—perhaps to excessive and repetitive length—his understanding of the nature of the universe and, more particularly, his preferences in regard to social and political matters. In the broadest terms, the fundamental divergence of views between the two writers can be encapsulated by Howard's preference for the barbarian life and Lovecraft's preference for civilization; but within this simple formulation lie masses of complexity and fine shades of meaning and emphasis that in some senses render these views not quite as antipodal as they may appear.

For much of the first year of their correspondence, Howard and Lovecraft were studiously respectful of each other: each expressed unbounded admiration for the other's writings, Howard declaring flamboyantly that "no writer, past or modern, has equalled you in the realm of bizarre fiction" ([c. 1 July 1930]), while Lovecraft praised the "suggestion of unholy antiquity" (20 July 1930) found in "The Moon of Skulls" (*Weird Tales*, June and July 1930). Howard also acknowledged his inferiority in book learning: in their early dis-

Barbarism vs. Civilization 75

cussion of prehistoric Britain, Howard admitted that "I am not scholar enough to present any logical argument" ([9 August 1930]), but this did not prevent him from quoting at substantial length a number of published books on the subject. Howard let himself in for another disillusionment when he innocently asked Lovecraft about the sources in folklore or myth of Cthulhu, Yog-Sothoth, and the like, especially in light of a letter to *Weird Tales* by N. J. O'Neail (published in the March 1930 issue) linking Cthulhu to Howard's Kathulos (in "Skull-Face" [*Weird Tales*, October, November, and December 1929]). Lovecraft wryly replied (14 August 1930) that the whole mythology was his own invention. Howard's reaction to this can be gauged by his letter to Tevis Clyde Smith ([c. September 1930]): "I got a letter from Lovecraft wherein he tells me, much to my chagrin, that Cthulhu, R'lyeh, Yuggoth, Yog Sothoth, and so on are figments of his own imagination" (REH 1.57).

To be frank, both writers were united in their racism: Lovecraft, in relating the history of Rhode Island and of New England, found occasion to note that the "foreign overrunning of America . . . [is] the most tragic event in the continent's history" (4 October 1930), while Howard, although engagingly relating the oral ghost stories he heard from the local Negroes ([c. September 1930]), could not help lamenting, "I'm afraid that in a few generations Texas will be over-run with mongrels." He goes on:

> On the Border there is a large Latin element, and on the coasts swarms of foreigners. The inevitable Jew infests the state in great numbers. You can hardly find a town of three thousand or more inhabitants that does not contain at least one Jew in business. And the Jew almost invariably has the country trade. It is a stock saying among rural Texans that if the Jew cannot sell his stuff at his price, he will sell it at yours. What they cannot seem to realize is that at whatever price he sells his shoddy junk, he is making a bigger profit than the legitimate merchant can make. No Aryan ever outwitted a Jew in business. . . . Houston, the largest city, has a vast alien population—Jews, Slavs, and Italians, the last drifting up from New Orleans. Dallas fairly swarms with Jews, in ever increasing numbers. ([c. January 1931])

This allowed Lovecraft to wax eloquent on his customary theme of the Semitization of New York City:

> Yes—New York is pretty well lost to the Aryan race, and the tragic and dramatic thing is the *speed* with which the change occurred. People hardly past middle age can still recall the pleasant, free and easy New York which really formed an American metropolis, and in which there was nothing more foreign than the wholesome, cheerful immigrants from Ireland and Germany. As late as 1900 this old New York was still the visible state of things on Manhattan Island—but then the packed East Side, which had been silently filling up

with Russian and Polish Jews since 1885 or 1890, began to disgorge its newly-prosperous foreign-born and first active generation. In 1905 certain troubles in Russia sent over countless hordes of cringing Jews; and by 1910 people began to notice the overwhelmingly Semitic tinge of the crowds on all the New York streets. (30 January 1931)

How exactly the correspondence veered to the matter of civilization vs. barbarism is not entirely clear, but it may have something to do with Howard's invention of the character of Conan, as he tells in a letter to Lovecraft of c. April 1931: "I've been working on a new character, providing him with a new epoch—the Hyborian Age, which men have forgotten, but which remains in classical names, and distorted myths. [Farnsworth] Wright rejected most of the series, but I did sell him one—'The Phoenix on the Sword' which deals with the adventures of King Conan the Cimmerian, in the kingdom of Aquilonia." This thread was not picked up immediately in the correspondence, but it eventually led Howard (who had already mentioned to Lovecraft [c. December 1930] his hatred of ancient Rome, especially the Romans in Britain) to confess that his interest in the ancient Greeks and Romans was quite limited:

> I can not understand their viewpoints. The Achaeans of the Heroic Age interest me, and to a lesser extent, the Romans of the early republic, when they were a struggling tribal-state, if they could be called that. But soon that interest dwindles. I attribute this, not to any real lack of interest those times contain, but to a defect in my own make-up. I am unable to rouse much interest in any highly civilized race, country or epoch, including this one. (9 August 1932)

This was a passage that—in spite of Howard's admission that his lack of interest was a result of "a defect in my own make-up"—caused Lovecraft to see red. After Howard's death, he would admit that "When I run up against a person with a strong anti-Roman bias—like the late Robert E. Howard, who championed the northern barbarians—I feel an almost personal affront" (SL 5.352). And so Lovecraft launched the first salvo of his defense of civilisation, in the course of a general defense of classical antiquity:

> To me Greece and Rome are prime realities because they had the same general problems and attitudes which the settled nations of modernity have. They had measurably conquered the salient natural phenomena around them, and had won sufficient material security to expand other parts of their mental and emotional endowment than those directly connected with self-defence and ego-assertion. Important brain areas—such as those connected with pure intellectual curiosity and with the finer nuances of rhythm and coördination—which had been necessarily underdeveloped in the peril-beset barbarian, be-

gan to expand and enrich life among the people who had reached a stage of relatively stable adjustment to nature and to the problem of group-defence. Where the barbarian had only a few simple motives and pleasures, and used only a small fraction of his heritage as a highly evolved primate, the civilised man had the infinitely vaster variety of stimuli and rewards which accrued from a more all-around development of his capacities. What he lost in the process was more than balanced by what he gained—so that not until his later decadence did he need to mourn any of the simple ruggednesses he had left behind. (16 August 1932)

All the tens of thousands of words of Lovecraft's subsequent debates with Howard on this issue amount to little more than elaborations and refinements of this basic utterance.

Lovecraft had also, perhaps unwittingly, made a passing remark that caused Howard to see red: "The ideology of the frontier could not work in a thickly settled community where everything depends upon the preservation of order." This remark had been made in the course of a discussion of police methods, and in a broader debate over the precise balance of personal liberty and government control—an issue to which I shall return later. Howard's response makes it abundantly clear that he considered his defense of barbarism part and parcel of his defense of the frontier, specifically the frontier of his own native Texas, from which he could legitimately consider himself scarcely a generation removed. But the precise nature of his initial defense (made in a letter that Lovecraft received around 22 September 1932) is of interest. Howard acknowledges that "if I should be suddenly confronted with the prospect of being transported back through the centuries into a former age, with the option of living where I wished, I would naturally select the most civilized country possible. That would be necessary, for I have always led a peaceful, sheltered life, and would be unable to cope with conditions of barbarism." (Lovecraft wryly remarked to another correspondent: "When [Howard] says his life is 'tame & uneventful', he is thinking only of Western standards. Actually, he sees a vast amount of violence" [*SL* 5.108].) But Howard went on to say, "if I were to be reborn in some earlier age and grow up knowing no other life or environment than that, I would choose to be born in a hut among the hills of western Ireland, the forests or Germany or the steppes of Southern Russia; to grow up hard and lean and wolfish, worshipping barbarian gods and living the hard barren life of a barbarian—which is, to the barbarian who has never tasted anything else—neither hard nor barren."

There would not seem, up to now, to be much room for debate, for Howard clearly appears to be expressing a mere *preference* rather than asserting some kind of quasi-objective superiority of barbarism over civilization. It was

Lovecraft, in his reply of 3 October 1932, who continued to harp on the issue. While admitting that "Both barbarism and civilisation have their advantages, and it is probable that some individuals naturally prefer one type to the other," he goes on to say: "I still think that the odds *may* be in favour of civilisation for those who utilise its advantages to the full." Later in the same letter Lovecraft accuses Howard of vaunting physical combat to such a degree that he cannot see the virtues of civilized life: "I certainly regard the intellect and aesthetic sense as the highest development of human personality, and believe that the goal of civilisation must necessarily be a state in which they can have the maximum opportunity for unhampered operation. At the same time I am not blind to the need of preserving a certain amount of the old physical stamina as a supplement to the newer qualities."

Howard's reply ([c. 2 November 1932]) is curious. He begins with an elaborate apology:

> I am afraid my last letter may have appeared rather churlish in spots, though rudeness was not my intention. The fact is, I wrote while in the grip of one of the black moods which occasionally—though fortunately rarely—descend upon me. With one of these moods riding me, I can see neither good nor hope in anything, and my main sensation is a blind, brooding rage directed at anything that may cross my path—a perfectly impersonal feeling, of course. At such times I am neither a fit companion nor a gentlemanly correspondent.

Now there was nothing in Howard's previous letter that could be interpreted as particularly "churlish"—certainly it was less so than several of the letters Howard would write in the next few years. Possibly Howard was frustrated by Lovecraft's apparent inability to understand the points he was trying to make ("When I get out of my depth—which is easy—the Devil himself couldn't get what I'm trying to say"), specifically on the all-important point that Howard was merely expressing a *preference* in regard to barbarism, physical activity over mental activity ("I would rather watch a football game than to see a scientist work out a really important problem in economics or mathematics"). In any case, Howard is emphatic that "when I voice a preference for anything I am not depreciating its opposite." And later in the same letter:

> I didn't say that barbarism was superior to civilization. For the world as a whole, civilization even in decaying form, is undoubtedly better for people as a whole. I have no idyllic view of barbarism—as near as I can learn it's a grim, bloody, ferocious and loveless condition. I have no patience with the depiction of the barbarian of any race as a stately, god-like child of Nature, endowed with strange wisdom and speaking in measured and sonorous phrases. Bah! my conception of a barbarian is very different. He had neither stability nor undue dignity. He was ferocious, vengeful, brutal and frequently squalid.

> He was haunted by dim and shadowy fears; he committed horrible crimes for strange monstrous reasons. As a race he hardly ever exhibited the steadfast courage often shown by civilized men. He was childish and terrible in his wrath, bloody and treacherous. . . . He had no mental freedom, as civilized man understands it, and very little personal freedom, being bound to his clan, his tribe, his chief.

Nevertheless, Howard concludes: "But I do say that if I had the choice of another existence, to be born into it and raised in it, knowing no other, I'd choose such an existence as I've just sought to depict. There's no question of the relative merits of barbarism and civilization here involved. It's just my own personal opinion and choice."

In his reply (7 November 1932) Lovecraft professes to understand Howard's attitude ("I can see your point of view completely, and do not believe that any real controversy is involved"), but then proceeds to argue as if Howard had really said something altogether different. (As early as August 1930, Howard had remarked to Tevis Clyde Smith on Lovecraft's method of debate: "He starts out by saying that most of my arguments seem logical enough and that he is about on the point of accepting my views—and then follows with about three or four closely written pages with which he rips practically all my theories to shreds" [REH 1.53].) Lovecraft himself puts forward his own views as merely a set of preferences ("To me, the few possible advantages of barbarism seem infinitely overshadowed by the overwhelming mass of hopeless lacks and disadvantages—so that I feel sure I would never have found enough to live for in primitive times, except perhaps as a history-chanting bard or mystery-making shaman"), and there he seems to leave the matter. Howard's reply ([December 1932]) picks up on the shaman comment:

> As for being a shaman or minstrel among barbarians—those are the very last things I should wish to be, were my lot cast among the uncivilized. It is evident that a shaman, however fantastic and barbarous his thoughts and methods, represents the nearest approach to civilized man, in his tribe and age. Therefore, he is able to glimpse, in a dim way, some of the vistas that lie above (I say "above" for the sake of argument; I am by no means sure that "progress" is necessarily a step upward.) and to feel the lack of intellectual attainment—oh, very, very dimly, without doubt.

That parenthetical comment may or may not conflict with Howard's previous attestation that he was not disparaging civilization when vaunting his own preference to barbarism, but Howard's continued emphasis on the physical over the mental ("We live, after all, in a physical world. Few of us are fortunate enough to be able to move in a mainly mental sphere. This is especially true of this part of the country") clearly set Lovecraft off, and in his reply (21 January 1933) he once again attempted to establish that there might indeed be a pseudo-objective standard or criterion whereby civilization could be considered "above" barbarism in an absolute sense:

> If anything is close to an axiom, it is that *superiority* in the organic field means *degree of evolutionary removal from* the unicellular stage. . . . the one real criterion of cosmic value is *degree of evolution*—advance from the gorilla, the Piltdown skull, the Neanderthaloid, the Australian blackfellow, or the nigger. *This advance of evolutionary degree, marking absolute superiority, is not in any way measured by physical strength, but is directly measured by the development of the intellect, the imagination, and the more complex and delicate emotions.* To me, at least, that argument seems unanswerable; and I cannot see how you can fail to concur in its essence. It does not mean that physical strength is contemptible or other than desirable, but is simply a reminder *to put first things first.*

Lovecraft is also keen to establish that, in regard to the relative happiness of barbarians over civilized people, the palm must be awarded to the latter:

> The happiness of primitively organised or undeveloped forms of life is to some extent—or in certain directions—more like the painlessness of oblivion, non-existence, or inorganic existence than like the active, varied, and poignant pleasure of a fully utilised consciousness, for even its most violent physical and crudely emotional forms are strongly localised in an extremely small part of the potential experience-field of the human species. The barbarian is really only a quarter or a sixteenth alive, since the most human and finely organised parts of his fabric are left inactive or dormant. For him the complex rhythms of energy-transformation which give consciousness its most intense vitality and pleasure-reactions do not exist.

Lovecraft even thinks he can quantify the relative happiness—or what he calls "the amount of pleasurable energy-conversion"—of various entities: "In the stick it will be 0; in the starfish it will be (let us say) 5; in the dog, 100; in the savage, 1000; and in the civilised man, 100,000." It is not clear on what basis Lovecraft has devised these figures, but it is evident that he is seeking an objective means of validating his preference for civilization over barbarism. He concludes by saying: "Only the sheerest academic quibbling can dispute the absolute and intrinsic improvement in the transition to civilisation."

Howard's reply ([6 March 1933]) begins by asserting that the physical-mental debate is "unnecessary," because "My position on the matter is much the same as yours, modified on my part only by a greater interest in physical things than you possess." Well, perhaps not exactly. He misinterprets Lovecraft's position as follows: "Simmered down, the real difference between our opinions is: you are interested wholly in the fruits of the mind, and I divide my interest between the fruits of the mind, and the exertions of the body." (Lovecraft had in fact stated that "no rational anti-physicalist objects to the continued athletic training of those whose actual occupation demands physical strength.") While Lovecraft had acknowledged that anti-physicalists did on occasion exhibit a certain contempt for physical strength because "under the existing social-economic order, only inferior individuals need to use physical strength in the struggle for survival," Howard replies that he is not about to endure the contempt of these anti-physicalists, because "I can not afford to neglect my physical side." Howard does not in fact address Lovecraft's regarding an entity's "degree of evolutionary removal from the unicellular stage," perhaps because he did not understand it or see its relevance to the discussion; but he then unloads a bombshell that Lovecraft would later seize upon:

> Leaving my own feelings and experiences aside, I see no reason why a fine athlete shouldn't feel a real pride in his athletic ability, when it brings him wealth, fame, and happiness that would not have been his had he depended on his mind. If Jack Dempsey's muscles pulled him up out of the gutter and the hobo-jungle into the ranks of the millionaires, while many a man infinitely his mental superior is still drudging away at a one-horse job, why shouldn't Jack be proud of his tigerish thews? I'd rather be an athlete with my pockets full of gold, than a university professor or a scientist with patches in the seat of my breeches.

How this constitutes a valid response to Lovecraft's argument is difficult to see. Even though Howard, later in the letter, declares that "What I'm trying to show is that the physical side of man—*admittedly inferior to the mental side*—is nevertheless a living vital factor in the development of society," Lovecraft was quite right in suspecting that Howard was really expressing a scorn for brainwork, especially since his example of Jack Dempsey emphasized the artificial criterion of money as the arbiter of value, something Lovecraft would vigorously reject.

In regard to the specific civilization-vs.-barbarism debate, Howard now declares that "if I could choose my age and place, there is no country and no time I would choose except the American frontier, between 1795 and 1895"—another indication of how intimately the notion of the frontier was fused with Howard's conception of barbarism, even though he would later admit that the people who colonized the frontier could in no precise sense be considered barbarians. He goes on to remark:

> Because I have read a few more books than my grandfathers read, and can scribble things on paper they couldn't, I am not such a conceited jackass as to fancy that my life is fuller and richer than theirs, who helped to fight a war, open a frontier and build up a new nation. Of all snobberies, the assumption

that intellectual endeavors, attainments and accomplishments are the only worth-while and important things in life, is the least justifiable.

But Lovecraft had never said that intellectual accomplishments were the "only" worthwhile things in life; only that they constituted a further degree of removal from the unicellular stage.

Lovecraft's reply (25-28 March 1933) begins by stating: "Your tendency to judge things merely in relation to the fulfilment of certain immediate material needs seemed to me (whether erroneously or not) to be blinding you emotionally (though perhaps not intellectually) to the actual relative values concerned in the problem at issue." This remark is clearly directed at Howard's comment on Jack Dempsey, as is a later and more exhaustive passage:

> You appeared to deny the supreme emotional value of intellectual and aesthetic experience for their own sakes—to regard as mythical or feigned the fact that for people of the highest type *the intrinsic acts of intellectual expansion or artistic creation are primary and satisfying ends in themselves,* forming the main and indispensable objects of life, and conducted without ulterior motives or hope of material gain. . . . Perhaps you did not specifically and consciously form this denial and repudiation, but you tended to show a certain ironic contempt in alluding to highly evolved experience—as in your recent letter, when you belittle rather bitterly the 'artists who smudge their canvas and scientists who pry into the secrets of the cosmos'; ignore the titanically increased opportunities for a full mental-aesthetic life which civilisation has brought; prefer gold-getting pugilists to idea-enjoying college professors; and (in asserting that you write for money alone) deny by implication the superlatively keen joy of literary creation—or any aesthetic craftsmanship for its own sake . . . a joy which for many forms the sole reason for remaining alive.

That remark about "artists who smudge their canvas" is worth examining: it actually occurred in Howard's letter in a very different context—that of the relative level of freedom possible in contemporary civilized society. Howard, asserting rather histrionically that the object of government today "is to emasculate all men, and make good little rabbits and guinea pigs out of them that will fit into the nooks designed for them," went on to say:

> Oh, no doubt we will have freedom of thought; a man sitting in a dungeon with his legs in iron stocks can think as he wishes. And no doubt our artists will be allowed to smudge their canvas and scribble their sheets just about as they desire. And our scientists will be allowed to pry into the secrets of the cosmos, no doubt. But what about the people who are neither artists, intellectuals, or scientists? They do exist, in large numbers.

Howard would later remark that "I was not aware that the expression 'smudge their canvas' reflected any particular bitterness" ([ca. May/June 1933]), and later in the same letter: "it seems to me that my unfortunate use of the word 'smudge' is still rankling a little bit." Whether this is the case or not, Lovecraft now resumed the civilization-vs.-barbarism debate by concluding that "My sole reason for debate is what seems to be an underlying assumption on your part that the barbaric state is *intrinsically superior*—in a serious sense—to civilisation"; but no such remark can be found in Howard's letters, and he is always careful to emphasize that he is merely expressing a preference. Whether there is an "underlying assumption" of intrinsic superiority is difficult to establish, since we have no way of ascertaining it—and Lovecraft had no way, either, aside from inferences from Howard's correspondence.

Howard, in his letter of c. May/June 1933, defended himself on various fronts. First, he denied that he was using financial success as a criterion of value: "I was merely trying to point out that a successful man need not be denied a real pride in his occupation just because it didn't happen to be of an intellectual nature." Howard goes on to say: "You criticize me for saying that I 'prefer a rich athlete to a poor professor'; as a matter of fact, I didn't say that, though perhaps I might have expressed myself more clearly. What I said was that *I would rather be the rich athlete*. This implies no belittling of the professor." I fear that this strikes me as both false (Howard is in fact expressing a preference for being a rich athlete than a poor professor) and disingenuous, since the remark about the professor's "patches in the seat of [his] breeches" certainly suggests a certain amount of contempt. Howard also denies that he is "anti-intellectual": "I have no hostility whatever toward either an intellectual or an artist." But "I refuse to place art on a pedestal above and beyond everything else; I refuse to believe that a million generations of human beings have lived, suffered, toiled and died in order that certain men may make marks on paper or canvas. In a word, I do not believe that artistic expression is the sole and only reason for evolution." Howard goes on to say: "The average artist is no more important in the scheme of things than is the average lawyer, physician, engineer, farmer or politician. A painting is of no more importance to a painter, or a story to an author, than a bridge is to the engineer, a well-pleaded case to the lawyer, or a fine crop to the farmer. It seems to me that artists as a whole are prone to exalt themselves and their work beyond all natural proportions."

To this, Lovecraft responded sharply in his letter of 24 July 1933:

> As for the status of art—by which I mean not only the process of creation but the whole development of personality which includes appreciation and general tasteful living—I don't know that I called it the 'only reason for evolu-

tion'; for indeed, evolution is a matter of chance which has no reason or object. Rather did I suggest that it is simply something which is *characteristic* of those types which are most evolved.

And later:

> No one has ever claimed that the artist is more important in the maintenance of some sort of civilisation than is the farmer, mechanic, engineer, or statesman.... It is not that we regard art as "sacred", but that we recognise the importance of something which naturally forms the chief life-interest of the most highly evolved types. Art certainly *is* more intrinsically removed from the unevolved protoplasmic stage of organic reaction than any other human manifestation except pure reason—hence our grouping of it as one of the "highest" things in life. By "highest" we do not mean "most important to survival", but simply "most advanced in intrinsic development."

Howard replied with a seemingly clever counter-argument—that the ability to appreciate both "high" and "low" aesthetic products is a sign of breadth of taste and outlook:

> It seems to me that a capacity for enjoying certain simple thing [sic], when combined with an ability to appreciate the "higher" things as well, is, if anything, the indication of a broader, rather than a narrower personality. If I can enjoy (for instance) both [Robert W.] Service and Baudelaire, I see no reason why I should feel inferior to the man who can enjoy only Baudelaire, any more than to the man who can enjoy only Service. You must admit the scope of enjoyment is broader, whatever is to be said about the aesthetic value.

It is that last remark that is the key; for there are clear limits to this kind of breadth of taste: if one enjoys both Baudelaire and, say, Nictzin Dyalhis, then this indicates not a commendable breadth but a deficiency in aesthetic sensibility, for *no* genuinely cultured person could derive aesthetic enjoyment out of the latter. Howard goes on to say, "It's really a matter of indifference to me whether or not my preferences, pursuits and desires are 'superior' according to some arbitrary standard"—but the standard is not "arbitrary," but based upon widely acknowledged aesthetic principles that have been recognized as sound for centuries. Howard predictably adds the typical anti-intellectual argument, "I know what I like, and what I want, and that's enough for me."

Lovecraft's response of 2 November 1933 emphasises these points, noting that there is a difference between genuine aesthetic appreciation and appreciation based on the arousal of "agreeable *associations* either consciously or subconsciously." He offers an example:

> It does not argue defective taste to be tickled by a jingle of Eddie Guest because it reminds us of something pleasing, although it does argue defective

taste to accept such junk as serious emotional expression. In the latter case, serious acceptance requires a defective receiving equipment because the material is so vapid, stale, ill-formed, and unrelated to anything in life or human feeling as intelligently understood, that it could not produce any response at all from a sensitive or well-developed receiving equipment.

Howard made another blunder: in arguing that "art is no more characteristically human than some other things" (an argument Lovecraft had never made), such as "treachery, and chicanery, and sex perversions," he claimed to adduce evidence from the animal world:

> . . . honesty and decency are not exclusively human characteristics. Most animals have them in larger abundance than man. It is just as impossible for an amoeba to crack the stock market and beggar thousands, plot and start a war in order to acquire valuable concessions, and having exhausted himself with debauchery, turn to perverse pleasures, as it is for him to paint a picture or write a book. . . . We call our enemies swine, dogs, skunks, etc. I never saw a dog, hog or pole-cat commit any of the crimes and vices that human beings perpetrate day after day.

Lovecraft replied that the very existence of such reprehensible traits as treachery and chicanery argued a superiority in human beings:

> Lower animals have the same natural greed and ferocity that man has; and if they get less through unscrupulous means, it is merely because they don't know enough. Man cheats more for two reasons—because he is more capable, and because some of his number erect standards higher than those of the other animals, to which the inferior specimens can't conform. If man as a whole did not strive to be better than the beasts, his narrower-visioned members wouldn't be (in some ways, if your allegation is true) worse than the beasts.

Howard did not give up on the point, however, writing in his next letter ([c. January 1934]):

> I have, it is true, noticed shadows of almost human depravity in animals—treachery, greed, cowardice, perversions—but I never saw an animal whose whole life was devoted to these things. And I never saw any bestial trait that was not possessed in greater volume by humanity. You say I say that animals are "superior" because "in my opinion" they are more "honest." I didn't say, or mean to say, that. I merely said that animals possess all the characteristics of courage, kindliness, and honesty that we are taught are the exclusive possessions of the human race. . . . I've spent all my life in the country and in small towns, among horses, cattle, hogs, dogs, cats and less domesticated beasts. And it is my judgment, borne upon me by experience and observation,

that the average animal is a cleanly, decent, respectable and altogether worthy citizen compared to the average man, when judged by moral standards.

Lovecraft responded (3 April 1934) with what he should have said previously—that the traits Howard is attributing to animals cannot be so attributed because animals in all likelihood are not self-conscious to the degree that they can recognize "honesty" or "treachery" as virtues or vices:

> What the bulk of organic creation does is simply to react to external stimuli in a fixed way—conditioned by the nature of each organism as determined by fortuitous evolution. There is no such thing as conscious choice of conduct. Each species is merely a machine which behaves in a certain way when certain buttons are pushed. Reflexes can be conditioned, but they are just as automatic for all that. Whether we like or dislike the typical reflexes of a certain species is wholly irrelevant. There is no more reason to call a lower animal (or a primitive man) "good" or "bad", "decent" or "evil" than there is to apply these terms to a volcano or wind or river or sandstorm.

By this time, the debate was becoming somewhat more acrimonious—at least on Howard's side. In his letter of January 1934 he felt that Lovecraft was accusing Howard of "refus[ing] to accept the basic standards of human development" because Howard was questioning the superiority of art or artists in human affairs. Howard countered by saying that many other human activities can indicate "superiority"; but in making this assertion Howard again put forward an implausible argument: "You have said that it is impossible for an inferior man to be a poet, a great novelist or a great painter. It is equally impossible for an inferior man to be a great physician, engineer, general, statesman, agriculturist or football coach." That last example of "greatness" (coming from one who had regaled Lovecraft with long accounts of some of the exciting college football games he had watched) was one Lovecraft could not pass up unrefuted, and his letter of 3 April makes pungent note of it:

> We call [certain] goals and pursuits "important" if they embody and provide for man's "higher" qualities (taste, intellectual curiosity, sense of order, intelligent civic and economic projects, art, drama, museums, literature, public works, etc. etc.), and "trivial" if they embody and provide only for the "lower" human qualities (physical sense-gratification, play of primitive instinct and immature, undeveloped emotion, etc.—as embodied in overemphasised sports, low-grade writing, acting, or iconography aimed at childish and undeveloped personalities, etc.) which do not involve man's greatest differentiation from other organisms in the direction of complexity. It may seem strange and unacceptable to you, at present, to have a distinction drawn between the human effort which seeks to measure the universe, or crystallise a phase of beauty, or evolve a more harmonious social order, and that which seeks to apply science

to the mutual slugging of two sullen giants—but that is something which must be left to time and to your instinctive *sense of proportion.*

Howard, in his reply of c. July 1934, professed amazement at the resurrection of the mental-vs.-physical argument; but it was Howard himself who had brought up the example of the football coach as an example of "greatness," and in that same letter he had also made an unwise comparison of the boxer Jim Corbett and Michelangelo: "That prize fighting is not to be compared with Angelo's [sic] artistic triumphs goes without saying. Nevertheless, Corbett can not be called an inferior man; certainly his accomplishments can not be compared with Angelo's. Nevertheless, Corbett was as supreme in his line as Angelo was in his." And yet, Howard now professes outrage at Lovecraft, and compounds the error by going on to assert that "it was not Corbett's physical development at all that caused my remark, but his mental equipment."

This letter of Howard's is particularly bitter and curt because he had taken umbrage at one particular passage in Lovecraft's April letter. Lovecraft had asserted that Howard's admiration for both barbarism and the frontier was essentially "moralistic" because

> You praise the frontier because it emphasises certain *moral qualities*—qualities of *character* like courage, resourcefulness, honesty, fairness, and so on—*at the same time ignoring its unfavourable effect on other phases of human development* . . . its absence of good educational facilities, etc. That would seem to argue *that you value moral qualities more than you value a general development of the personality.*

At this point Lovecraft seemed to get a bit carried away, producing a passage that was quite unfair to Howard and not a sound inference from his previous letters:

> You think a crude, narrow, ignorant man of few vistas and sensitivenesses, but of great physical strength, native keenness of judgment, acquisitive ability, courage, and honesty, represents just as perfect and worthy a development of the human raw material as does a man of balanced vision, trained sense of proportion, enlightened information, developed taste, and awakened sensitivenesses, possessing in addition many of the courageous and honourable qualities of the other type. . . . You would prefer that nothing be known of the world and universe beyond the savage's or barbarian's narrow ken; that no rhythmic eloquence ever fall from human lips, nor any painting, sculpture, music, and architecture ever flow from the human imagination . . . You would rather see three-fourths of man's personality—the ¾ involving those instincts highest in the scale of evolution—forever drugged to sleep and uselessness by ignorance, violence, and the material struggle.

And in conclusion Lovecraft made the breathtaking remark, "You sneer at human development—and as Dean Milman said (or rather, *quoted* from Paley) in his preface to Gibbon, 'Who can refute a sneer?'"

Howard was not about to take this lying down. In the first place, he misunderstood Lovecraft's "moralistic" comment by thinking that Lovecraft was accusing him of being a Puritan bluenose, when in fact Lovecraft was merely saying that Howard was overemphasizing the importance of morals in human affairs. While Howard did leave himself open to accusations of adhering to false values in vaunting Jim Corbett and a football coach as "great," he curtly enumerated the fundamentals of his views on these subjects:

1. I do not exalt physical strength above everything else.
2. I do not exalt ethics beyond the point that any normal, intelligent man does.
3. I do not repudiate, or fail to recognize the standards of basic development.

But Howard continues to insist that all these matters are mere personal preferences, and that Lovecraft is merely trying to change Howard's preferences so that they match his own. But Lovecraft was putting forward what he believed to be objective, if relative, standards to measure human development, and Howard never once addressed these standards.

Lovecraft tried to make this point in his reply of 27–28 July 1934:

> . . . I have tried to found my likes and dislikes on actual cosmic evidence and not on mere caprice. I know how hard it is to talk of external standards in dealing with human preferences, and would scarcely care to call my criteria infallible ones. On the other hand, I think the long biological, psychological, and philosophical explanations of these *proximate* or *pseudo-absolute* standards which I have made in former letters will convince you that they are not superficial, capriciously-adopted pieces of guesswork and prejudice. You may consider them *wrong*, but you can hardly consider them as *lightly or arbitrarily held*. . . . Thus when I say that civilisation is superior to barbarism, I am doing more than uttering a personal preference for civilised as distinguished from barbaric life. I am maintaining that civilisation utilises vast reservoirs of human capacity which barbarism leaves undeveloped; and that the effect of this utilisation is to make mankind an infinitely higher and more important being, as measured in distance from the condition of primitive slime, than he would otherwise be.

But Lovecraft went on to add a potentially (and, in the event, actually) inflammatory utterance:

> I believe that there are *certain real and specific reasons* for considering civilisation as different from barbarism in a direction intrinsically favourable to man's degree of importance, enjoyment, symmetry, and completeness in the cosmic flux; a direction to which we may logically apply the term "upward" (as

based on the only scale of progressive organisation in the cosmos), and which we cannot help endorsing if we are friends rather than enemies of mankind.

That last comment—even if, as Lovecraft would argue, not explicitly directed at Howard—sent Howard off the deep end. Clearly taking the remark personally, he exploded (in a letter of c. December 1934):

> Throughout our debate you have attributed to me the worst possible motives for my beliefs and tastes. Every time, when I have expressed an opinion that differed from yours, or even a personal taste, you have condemned it as sentimentalistic, romantic, a result of prejudice or distorted thinking; and denounced me as an enemy of development and enlightenment! Just as in this case, when you call me an enemy to humanity, and therefore imply that I am a villian [sic] of the deepest dye . . .

Now this itself is an overreaction to Lovecraft's "enemy of mankind" remark—and, in general, to Lovecraft's vigorous method of argumentation—but nevertheless it is undeniable that Lovecraft had opened the door for it. But once again Howard continues to insist that the debate is merely a matter of differing tastes ("there was never any real use in most of these arguments, anyway"), failing even to address the "pseudo-absolute" standards Lovecraft was putting forth. Howard also unjustly accused Lovecraft of vaunting his own New England region as the ideal to which the rest of the country (particularly Howard's Texas) failed to measure up—something that cannot be plausibly adduced from any of Lovecraft's remarks.

This phase of the debate now begins to peter out. Several of Lovecraft's responses of this period do not survive, so it is difficult to gauge the exact course of the discussion. In his letter of c. January–February 1935 Howard apologizes "if I have misunderstood any of your statements, or attitudes, or seemed to be doing you an injustice"; but since Howard continues to throw the "enemy of mankind" remark back in Lovecraft's teeth, it does not appear as if Lovecraft had withdrawn that remark just yet. Indeed, in an indication that Howard's resentment had not yet cooled, he accuses Lovecraft (in a letter of c. July 1935) of making a succession of charges against Howard as a person:

> Recalling off-hand the charges you have made against me, I remember that at various times you have accused me of being: Exalter-of-the-Physical-Above-the-Mental; Enemy of Humanity; Foe of Mankind; Apostle of Prejudice; Distorter of Fact; Repudiator of Evolutionary Standards; Over-Emphasizer of Ethics; Sympathizer of Criminals (that one broke all altitude records); Egotist; Poseur; Emotionalist; Defender of Ignorance; Sentimentalist; Romantist.

It need hardly be said that Lovecraft had not specifically directed many, or perhaps any, of these epithets at Howard; and it must also be said that in several regards Howard does lay himself open to these charges. He is outraged at the "Sympathizer of Criminals" accusation, but it was he who filled his letters with long, loving accounts of the bravery and courage of such outlaws as Billy the Kid and John Wesley Hardin. Lovecraft, in any case (in his letter of 7 August 1935), denied any "bitter resentment" at Howard's interpretation of his attitudes, and went on to say:

> As for what you appear to interpret as accusing or vituperative words on my part—let me repeat that the things I define adversely are *not persons but attitudes*. I may, for example, say that 'anyone who believes or wishes a certain thing' is an enemy of mankind or defender of ignorance—but that does not prove that any specific person really believes or wishes that thing in the light of all its implications. If I think, from his own utterances, that anyone in particular believes or wishes such a thing, I may be mistaken. I may fail to comprehend, through lack of a system of reference-associations in common, just what it is that he does believe and wish. Therefore there is nothing personal in anything I may say about a certain sort of attitude or method.

Howard's reply ([5 December 1935]) noted: "As for the charge of 'enemy of humanity,' the distinction you draw between attitudes and individuals seems a bit fine to me. I see no difference between telling a man he is an enemy of humanity and telling him that his attitude constitutes an enmity to humanity." Lovecraft's reply to this is not extant, but in his reply ([11 February 1936]) Howard observed dryly:

> I'm glad you've decided that I'm not an "enemy of humanity" after all. You say you use the term only to designate such people who "would voluntarily destroy the kind of life prevailing in Scandinavia or Britain or pre-war Germany in favour of the kind of life prevailing in Borneo or ancient Gaul or the Djuka country." Well, that must let everybody out for I can't imagine any sane person having such an ambition as this.

But to this Lovecraft responded (in a letter of 7 May 1936—the last letter he wrote to Howard):

> As for the term "enemy of humanity" as I used it—I think there is always present in society a small minority to whom that term can be applied in the given sense. While not all of this minority would care to lower the prevailing life-level to the wholly savage state, it is undeniable that they would like to see it pulled down to an intolerable degree of mediocrity. This actual hostility to the best human achievements is found in many proletarian groups and peasantries, and was markedly manifest in the earlier stage of both French and Russian revolutions.

The debate over personal freedom, specifically in an industrialized society, is an interesting offshoot of the whole debate regarding barbarism (or the frontier) and civilization, as Howard—who, in today's political jargon, would be regarded as a libertarian—was lamenting what he believed to be the decreasing amount of liberty in modern society, while Lovecraft—who was moving toward his distinctive final position of "fascistic socialism," whereby economic wealth would be equitably distributed to the many but political power (specifically the right to vote) be restricted to the few—argued that the necessity for law and order in heavily populated areas necessitated some minimal restrictions of freedom from earlier eras. As in the other debates, much of this dispute was based upon mutual misunderstanding and a failure to clarify the exact terms and parameters of the discussion.

Howard raised the issue first by casually remarking: "Personal liberty, it would seem, is to be a thing of the past." This occurs in his letter of [2 March 1932], in the course of a discussion of the current international scene and the possibility of tyranny in the United States: "It seems we must choose between a strong soviet government, and a strong dictatorship on the fascist style." Lovecraft did not pick up on this immediately—in spite of his unfortunate devotion to the word "fascism" as a characterization of his political philosophy—and Howard himself returned to the issue in his letter of [9 August 1932], speaking of impending tyranny in America both because of the violent suppression of the "bonus army"—the impoverished World War I veterans who had come from all parts of the country to Washington, D.C., and demanded the early payment of a bonus that was not to be paid to them for a decade or more—and because of what he regarded as "the detestable police practise of grilling prisoners." This theme of police brutality would become a dominant one in Howard's letters. In his reply of 16 August, Lovecraft put in some words on the other side, remarking that sometimes a certain harshness by the police is necessary to extract information out of "known members of the toughest criminal class." His letter of 7 November 1932 outlines the essentials of his "fascistic socialism," which includes such features as "the government's control of industry in a manner designed to spread work and reward it adequately, and to eliminate the profit motive as much as possible in favour of the demand-supplying motive," as well as "adequate public education both for industry and for the increased leisure of a mechanised era." In regard to the current situation, Lovecraft is pungent: "Democracy—as distinguished from universal opportunity and good treatment—is today a fallacy and impossibility so great that any serious attempt to apply it cannot be considered as other than a mockery and a jest."

Howard, in his reply ([December 1932]), actually expressed agreement with Lovecraft in regard to the limitation of the suffrage, and did not see it as conflicting with his professed yearning for freedom: "Individual liberty doesn't necessarily entail blind dabbling in governmental affairs." Howard did express skepticism as to whether the tidy political scheme Lovecraft had outlined could ever be put into effect, or, even if it were put into effect, whether it would remain stable and not descend into actual tyranny. He concluded:

> I do not expect a permanent state of slavery, but I do look for a period of more or less length, in which class and individual liberty will be practically unknown—oh, it won't be called slavery or serfdom. They'll have another name for it—Communism, or Fascism, or Nationalism, or some other -ism; but under the surface it will be the same old tyranny, modified, no doubt, to fit modern conditions.

It seems that Howard is not expressing some sound opinion on modern political conditions but rather an emotional reaction to the necessary restrictions of contemporary social existence. In any case, Lovecraft's reply of 21 January 1933 rejected the notion of an imminent tyranny: "I can't agree that anything resembling wholesale slavery is likely to result from the present confusion, since (as I said before) such a course would demand a greater concentration of obedient man-power than the controlling elements are ever likely to command again during the life of this civilisation." Lovecraft went on to remark that "Untrammelled individual freedom of action is nothing sacred or necessarily inviolate," but added: "To my mind, the irreducible minimum of personal independence worth fighting for till the last is *freedom of thought, opinion, research and art*. These are the things which really constitute human personality in its finest sense, and without them all the boasted physical freedom of the savage means nothing. Grant them, and slavery cannot exist."

Howard, in his reply of [6 March 1933], somewhat recklessly remarked, "Slavery? If three-quarters of the world isn't enslaved now I'm much mistaken," and went on to say: "I don't know as I said it was anybody's fault that there's no such thing as individual freedom any more. Unless I'm much mistaken I said it is a dream which is outworn. . . . I realize that such a state is impossible in a highly developed civilization; which is one thing I have against such civilizations." Exactly what Howard's ideal of freedom actually constituted is by no means clear. It was, let us recall, in this letter that he made the remark that "a man sitting in a dungeon with his legs in iron stocks can think as he wishes," and he also noted somewhat hysterically that the purpose of modern government "is to emasculate all men, and make good little rabbits and guinea pigs out of them that will fit into the nooks designed for them, and stay there contentedly nibbling their fodder until they die of inanition"—a remark whose precise application to American or European society is difficult to specify.

Lovecraft's response, in his letter of 25-28 March 1933, was frank:

> Just *what is* the wild and untrammeled "freedom" that our modern radicals are so vociferously clamouring for? What is it that they *want* to do that they *can't* do? I am curious to know, for they never seem to convey a clear idea. I don't see many honest and well-disposed people 'sitting in dungeons with their legs in iron stocks', nor do I see in the varied and active life of the modern average man anything resembling emasculation or reduction to the guinea-pig or rabbit stage. Just what do our "free souls" *want* to do? Ride bicycles on the sidewalks, disregard traffic signals and collide with other people's cars, play the radio at 3 a.m., shoot and carve people for fun, or what?

Howard's response (in his letter of [23 April 1933]) was perhaps not what Lovecraft was expecting:

> Well, in Cross Plains I can ride a bicycle on the sidewalk; there are no traffic signals; I can—and do—play the radio at all hours of the day and night, and I'd like to see anybody try to stop me; I have never yet shot or carved anybody for fun, but so far I have never been arrested for emptying my pistol into the air or using trash cans for targets in moments of alcoholic exuberance, and if we step outside the corporation lines, a friend and I can pummel each other unmolested by police interference. I don't suppose I would be allowed to pitch a tent, as you suggest, in the middle of the main street, but so far I have never experienced any overpowering desire to pitch such a tent.

It does not appear that Howard has given sufficient thought as to whether such actions—representing "liberty" for him—might in fact constitute a diminution or infringement of "liberty" to others, specifically the liberty to be left alone and not be unnecessarily bothered by others. More seriously, Howard does acknowledge that his ideal of freedom is impossible, and also that it is intimately tied to his thirst for frontier life:

> What I want is impossible, as I've told you before; I want, in a word, the frontier—which is compassed in the phrase, new land, open land, free land—land rich and unbroken and virgin, swarming with game and laden with fresh forests and sweet cold streams, where a man could live by the sweat of his hands unharried by taxes, crowds, noise, unemployment, bank-failures, gang-extortions, laws, and all the other wearisome things of civilization. Failing in that, I want as much personal freedom as is possible under this system, and if I can't have at least as much as I have now, I don't want to live at all.

Lovecraft's reply (24 July 1933) argued that "It was impossible for an industrialised nation to return to the agrarian-handicraft stage typified by the frontier and its transient conditions" (something Howard had not at all suggested), and went on to say, more sensibly, "nor is it logical to assume that frontier conditions were necessarily superior, as a whole, to those of a more settled order. Advantages have vanished, but other compensating advantages have appeared in their place—so that the net result is at least highly debatable."

At this point the discussion shifted to current political and economic conditions, and Howard (in his letter of c. September 1933) could not resist poking a finger in the eye of modern civilization by pointing out the catastrophic effects of the Depression: "You can't dismiss twelve and a half million men and women without work and on the point of starvation as theories. It would be well for the capitalists, perhaps, if they could be so dismissed. As for the 'alleged horrors' of civilization—if you would inquire into the condition of some of these people, and if you had ever seen what modern machinery can do to the human frame, you'd realize that all the horrors are not 'alleged.'" Lovecraft had a pungent response (2 November 1933), in which he again put forth the virtues of his socialistic scheme:

> The present year, just before the beginning of the new administration's remedial programme, marks the low point of the workman's fortunes in America. The tendencies crushing him under a "free" or laissez-faire economic system were steadily growing, yet the "free" system of Hoover individualism was unchecked. Now, under the "slavery" of a governmentally regulated economy, there will be a steady but slow trend toward relief. . . . "Freedom" means concentrated power for the strong and servitude and starvation for the weak. *Government*—which he calls "slavery"—is *the only possible avenue of rescue he has.*

It was at this point, as noted earlier, that Howard, believing Lovecraft to have accused him of "hating human development," became quite hostile and even a bit irrational, stating ([c. July 1934]): "If we were living under your ideal intellectual-ruled government, you could doubtless have me burned at the stake as a heretic. But since we haven't reached that enviable stage of civilization, it looks like you'll just have to classify me as another of the imperfections and crudities allowed to exist under a democratic form of government, and let it go at that." There was no justification for Howard to make this kind of snide comment, and Lovecraft responded vehemently but tactfully (27–28 July 1934):

> You say you do not hate human development, and yet you sneer at my ideal of a government restricted to men who are properly trained for the job and who know what they are doing! Moreover, you say that if my ideal of government were in force, I would—or could—have you burned at the stake because of your tastes and interests. Now that is *precisely the opposite* of anything which my kind of government would ever do, want to do, or permit to be done! The *absolute first* requisite of any mature or genuine civilisation is *complete intellectual and artistic freedom*; so that no restriction whatever would be placed upon any sort of individual thought or tastes.

Lovecraft, however, did not help his cause by adding lamely, "Do not judge the sort of fascism I advocate by any form now existing." What Lovecraft was really advocating was not fascism in any meaningful sense of the term, but democracy—only a democracy circumscribed by limitation of the suffrage.

Howard replied forcefully ([c. December 1934]): "I do not condemn the reforms you say would be possible under Fascism. I simply do not believe they would exist under a Fascist government. Of course you can draw glowing pictures of a Fascist Utopia. But you can not prove that Fascism is anything but a sordid, retrogressive despotism, which crushes the individual liberty and strangles the intellectual life of every country it inflicts with its slimy presence." Lovecraft's next several responses are missing, so it is difficult to gauge the course of the debate. The crux of the matter, of course, is Lovecraft's putting forth an idealized scheme that sounds good on paper, and Howard noting keenly that the actual instances of oligarchical government then in existence are very far from the tidy formulations of Lovecraft's political theory.

In the end, what can we say about the overall progression of the Lovecraft-Howard correspondence? In large measure, it appears that on nearly every issue there was considerable misunderstanding on both sides, as each writer struggled to convey to the other the precise shades of meaning in the issues in question. Howard, in his letter of [December 1932], admitted that temperamental differences between the two often caused difficulties ("Your impartial viewpoint is admirable. For myself, I must admit that I am motivated more often by emotion and sentiment than by cold logic"), and toward the end of their correspondence Howard made a keen analysis of their differing psychologies and upbringings:

> My life has been almost antipodal, in its associations, to yours. I've had little acquaintance with scholars, artists and literary people, whereas these types obviously have formed the bulk of your companions. Not being familiar with these types, it's easy for me to misunderstand their ideas and opinions. I'm also but little fitted to deal with abstract ideas which do not, apparently, have any connection with everyday reality as I know it. I've never had much time to devote to theories and philosophies.... On the other hand it seems obvious from your own arguments that you've had little if any first-hand contact with the rough sides and the raw edges of existence; if you had, you couldn't possibly have some of the ideas you have, and so many of my views and statements wouldn't seem so inexplicable and outrageous to you. It is inevitable that we should constantly misunderstand each other. ([5 December 1935])

Both writers were also aware that their differing methods of argumentation—Lovecraft's at times excessively involved rationalizations and use of highly abstract philosophical conceptions that Howard had difficulty applying to any reality within his sphere of knowledge, and Howard's at times blunt and clumsy debating style that frequently resulted in a lack of clarity as to his true ideas and feelings (this in spite of the fact that, as Rusty Burke has told me, actual rough drafts of Howard's letters to Lovecraft have been unearthed, indicating his painstaking care in holding up his end of the debate)—resulted in considerable misconstrual of even the essence of the discussion, let alone its finer points. In the last two or three years, as we have seen, Howard also exhibited a considerable hostility and resentment (precisely as many of his recent devotees do) at what he fancied to be Lovecraft's insulting treatment of him. Some Howard fans, perhaps adopting the inferiority complex Howard himself occasionally did when confronting a man of substantially greater education, have asserted somewhat truculently that Howard definitively "won" the various debates in which he engaged with Lovecraft—as if their correspondence was some kind of sporting event. But at this point there is no need to act as some kind of referee in determining who "won" or "lost" their multifaceted discussion. Both writers scored some key rhetorical points, and both suffered rhetorical defeats. But the real value of their correspondence—as they frequently acknowledged both to each other and to other associates—was the broadening of outlook that both experienced as a result of the clash of two such opposing viewpoints on central questions of life, society, freedom, civilization, and moral values.

Works Cited

Howard, Robert E. *Selected Letters 1923–1936*. Edited by Glenn Lord et al. West Warwick, RI: Necronomicon Press, 1989–91. [Abbreviated in the text as REH 1 and 2.]

H. P. Lovecraft and Robert E. Howard. *A Means to Freedom: The Letters of H. P. Lovecraft and Robert E. Howard.* Edited by S. T. Joshi, David E. Schultz, and Rusty Burke. New York: Hippocampus Press, 2010. 2 vols.

II. Philosophical Studies

The Political and Economic Thought of H. P. Lovecraft

The task of exploring and explaining H. P. Lovecraft's ideas on politics and economics is a vast one; for not only are these ideas merely a part of his whole philosophical outlook (related more to his aesthetic views than, as with Aristotle, his ethical views), but we have as yet little evidence to examine their finer points. The last two volumes of Lovecraft's *Selected Letters* reveal (perhaps to excess) many of Lovecraft's basic political and economic beliefs; and certain of his essays, published and unpublished, shed light on the development of his political philosophy as he lived through and assessed the turbulent events of the 1920s and 1930s. Nonetheless, this paper can claim only to lay the foundations for more penetrating studies of Lovecraft's political and economic thought.

Not only, as Robert Bloch has said, was Lovecraft "very much alive in the Twentieth Century of Picasso, Proust, Joyce, Spengler, Einstein, and Adolf Hitler" (174), but he was in many ways a remarkably astute observer of the political developments of his time. Lovecraft's tongue-in-cheek stance as an eighteenth-century gentleman, his identification with Periclean Athens, Augustan Rome, and the England of Elizabeth or of Dr. Johnson have resulted in the mistaken belief that he was "a recluse . . . living outside this century in a distant past" (Penzoldt 165). While it may be true that in his adolescence Lovecraft paid more attention to literature than to politics, it cannot be denied that the problems of government and the distribution of wealth became primary concerns toward the end of his life.

Lovecraft's earliest political utterances—expressed in letters and essays dating from the 1910s—reveal a dogmatic and cocksure attitude that might indicate their derivation, not from impartial observation, but from literary sources and untested prejudices. Before his entrance into amateur journalism, his beliefs were shaped largely by his extensive readings and by his family (whence many of his racialist views clearly stemmed); and his early opinions on race relations and the ideal form of government in many ways reflect those of his social class. Lovecraft stands up for the Ku Klux Klan, "that noble but much maligned band of Southerners" ("In a Major Key" [1915], CE 1.57); he berates American pacifism during World War I ("The Renaissance of Manhood" [1915], CE 5.15–16); he vaunts the "Teutonic" race, which is "masterful, temperate, and just" ("The Crime of the Century" [1915], CE 5.14); he advocates "Pan-Saxonism, or the domination by the English and kindred races over the lesser divisions of mankind" ("Editorial" [*Conservative*, July 1915], CE 1.51).

But while many of Lovecraft's early political views were wholly dropped or transformed through the years—indeed, his political thought underwent more changes than any other facet of his philosophy—there was one belief that in essence stood firm from the beginning to the end of his life: his advocacy of oligarchy. Even this stance, however, underwent important modifications. In his early years Lovecraft championed a ruthless aristocracy (to which, of course, he would belong) at the expense of all other elements of the population: "What does the condition of the rabble matter? All we need to do is to keep it as quiet as we can. . . . The blood of a million men is well shed in producing one glorious legend which thrills posterity . . . and it is not at all important *why* it was shed. A coat of arms won in a crusade is worth a thousand slavering compliments bandied about amongst a rabble" (SL 1.208). In the late 1920s this view had softened somewhat and became more rationalised; and he noted the difference between his position and that of the reformer by saying: "He is a democrat at all times, and because he *wants* to be. I am one only occasionally, and when I *have* to be" (SL 2.290). In the 1930s Lovecraft justified his opposition to democracy by pointing to the incredibly complex nature of the political decisions facing modern government. As he noted in his significant essay, "Some Repetitions on the Times" (1933), unpublished during his lifetime:

> No bungling democratic government could even begin to accomplish the delicate adjustments which loom ahead. Laymen of slight education and low intelligence are wholly useless and potentially harmful as determiners of the national course, and even laymen of wide education and high intelligence can do no more than roughly (and often erroneously) judge the general executive calibre of certain administrators from watching their performances in a few fields which may happen to be familiar. No non-technician, be he artist, philosopher, or scientist, can even begin to judge the labyrinthine governmental problems with which these administrators must deal.
>
> Accordingly we must expect any adequate government to be of the sort now generally called "fascistic"—forming, as it were, an oligarchy of intelligence and education. (CE 5.93)

Thus we see that Lovecraft advocated some form of oligarchy throughout his life. The reasons for this stance seem, interestingly enough, closely related to his aesthetic views. For Lovecraft, the essence of a civilisation is the quality and quantity of its artistic products. "All that I care about is *the civilisation*—the state of development and organisation which is capable of gratifying the complex mental-emotional-aesthetic needs of highly evolved and acutely sensitive men" (SL 2.290). He well realised the political havoc of the disunited Greek city-states in the fifth century B.C., but valued that era because of its unparalleled literary and artistic achievements. So, too, the products of an autocratic Rome or a politically chaotic Georgian England. Lovecraft valued any political system that would ensure the preservation of culture and civilisation. For much of his life he felt that the only such system was aristocracy, though he in time admitted that socialism could achieve similar ends.

Lovecraft's oligarchical stance, then, is clearly dissociated from the militaristic fascism of a Hitler or a Mussolini; and is instead, as he wrote, an "oligarchy of intelligence." But how to evade the problem of corruption that seems to be inherent in any oligarchy? How to escape Lord Acton's dictum that "Power tends to corrupt; absolute power corrupts absolutely"? The problem fazed Aristotle, who in the *Politics* favoured monarchy as the best ideal government, but nonetheless felt that democracy would in practise be the most workable political form given the inherent imperfections of mankind. Lovecraft, however, did not give in so easily, and felt that the combination of the "oligarchy of intelligence" with limited voting would ensure a better government than that which democracy could provide. He writes in "Some Repetitions on the Times":

> Office-holding must be limited to men of high technical training, and the franchise which elects them must be granted only to those able to pass rigorous educational examinations (emphasising civic and economic subjects) and scientific intelligence tests. Elective offices ought to be very few—perhaps no more than a single dictator—in order to ensure harmony and speed in the execution of necessary measures. That would make such a system perfectly fair and representative would be, of course, the equal availability of franchise-earning education to all—an effective reality in view of the leisure of the future. Corruption, naturally, could not be entirely abolished; but there would undoubtedly be far less of it in a government of the educated and the intelligent than in the haphazard governments of today. (CE 5.93-94)

One of the most interesting aspects of Lovecraft's thought is the clear dichotomy between his political and economic views; such that it makes much sense to use the almost paradoxical term "fascistic socialism" (as he himself did to denote the governmental organisation of the Great Race in "The Shadow out of Time") to describe this facet of his philosophy. Whereas, as we have seen, Lovecraft advocates the limiting of *political power* to the hands of a few, he as forcefully advised the spread of *economic wealth* among the many.

Lovecraft's growing disillusion with laissez-faire capitalism and his eventual adoption of socialism in light of the Great Depression is one of the greatest mental reversals that he ever effected.

It would be facile to say that this change stemmed solely—or even largely—from Lovecraft's own declining financial situation over the decades: the vehemence and rationality with which he sets forth his views preclude the possibility that his urging the distribution of wealth was merely self-serving. Moreover, he never adopted socialism to the full; advising instead that wealth not be spread in strict equality (i.e., communism) but only insofar as the individual contributes—whether physically or intellectually—to society. How far he was from Marxist political thought can be seen from his statement in "Some Repetitions on the Times" that "the existing equilibrium must not be disrupted by a violent overthrow of all the safeguards of property in moderate quantities" (CE 5.86). As with his political reforms, Lovecraft's suggested economic modifications were designed largely for the benefit of the civilisation as a whole; and he realised that no civilisation can thrive or remain stable if millions of its members are permanently unemployed.

The basis for Lovecraft's abandonment of capitalism for socialism was his realisation of the ineradicable establishment of mechanisation and technology in modern society.

> I realise that the wholesale application of machinery to industry has totally destroyed the old relationships between individuals and the total amount of work to be done—so that laissez-faire capitalism has actually come to the end of its rope. There is absolutely no way in which, under the old order, more than a small fraction of the idle population can ever (even amidst the greatest commercial prosperity) be employed again—since with labour-saving machinery all the possible work of the world (including the supplying of new demands such as the blind reactionaries rave about) can be performed by a relatively few persons. (SL 5.38)

Given such a situation, what were Lovecraft's solutions for rampant unemployment? At the base was the total abandonement of the profit motive from the economy. Next would come a "bald assertion of government control over large accumulations of resources . . . the state coordination and operation of the wider fundamental industries on a basis of service rather than profit." This would enable the hours and conditions of labour to be artificially regulated with a view to distributing work among the whole population, no matter how little is left by machinery to be done, or how little profit could be obtained from the employment of many persons at a really living wage for only a few hours per week" ("Some Repetitions on the Times,"

CE 5.92). In addition, "a really substantial unemployment insurance" and "liberal old-age pensions" would be necessary" (CE 5.92).

It is interesting to note that, although Lovecraft showed admirable foresight in feeling the need for many of the benefits now in effect through Social Security, his basic wish to see the artificial division of labour has not as yet been realised. Lovecraft saw three basic options in curing the problem of unemployment: "feeding this residue charitably, starving it into a civilisation-ending revolt, or restoring it to self-respecting effectiveness by artificially spreading work" (CE 5.86). While Lovecraft felt that the "third is the obvious choice," America has instead chosen to follow the first in its welfare system. But Lovecraft's knowledge of history suggested the disadvantages of this system, for he saw that it would soon descend to a mere dole as practised in imperial Rome. As in a number of other points, Lovecraft here seems again to have been vindicated by the future.

Such an economic reform as Lovecraft proposed would naturally cause significant alterations in social organisation; the major effect being the radical increase of leisure for all classes. This circumstance could be turned to the good by increasing the level of education, thus perhaps raising the general level of culture.

> On the cultural side the existing tradition need not be menaced. Education, however, will require amplification in order to meet the needs of a radically increased leisure among all classes of society. It is probable that the number of persons possessing a sound general culture will be greatly increased, with correspondingly good results to the civilisation. On the other hand, it would be foolish to assume that the more mentally sluggish types will ever lose their present cultural inferiority. Curricula will naturally be shaped to fit existing conditions; and in view of the complex nature of government and industry, civics and economics will receive enhanced attention. (CE 5.93)

Lovecraft was, in fact, concerned with preserving as much as possible in the social structure, modifying only those elements of the political and economic machinery which would no longer meet the needs of a mechanised society: "What is to be sought is not the preservation of a parcel of commercial methods and economic ideals, but a rational apportionment of the resources and a continuation of our hereditary way of life as regards art, ethics, intellectual perspective, and the niceties of personal existence" (CE 5.86). His loathing of Russian bolshevism, then, can easily be understood: in its economic reforms it overthrew "the whole background of tradition which made life endurable for persons of a higher degree of imagination and richer store of cultivation" (CE 5.90).

For all that Lovecraft so forcefully advocated his political and economic theories in letters and essays, one of his most interesting political statements comes in a fictional work—"The Shadow out of Time." Here—as, less extensively, in the earlier *At the Mountains of Madness*—Lovecraft spends much space in depicting his version of a social utopia, and incorporates in it many of his ideas on social organisation:

> The Great Race seemed to form a single loosely knit nation or league, with major institutions in common, though there were four definite divisions. The political and economic system of each unit was a sort of fascistic socialism, with major resources rationally distributed, and power delegated to a small governing board elected by the votes of all able to pass certain educational and psychological tests. Family organisation was not overstressed, though ties among persons of common descent were recognised, and the young were generally reared by their parents. . . . The sciences were carried to an unbelievable height of development, and art was a vital part of life. . . . (*DH* 399)

The final phrase is particularly to be noted: advocating reform only where needed, Lovecraft urged continuity in social and cultural traditions. For it is only through continuity, Lovecraft felt, that a real civilisation can take root and thus make life worth living for the sensitive and cultivated individual.

This cursory examination can only claim to display the skeleton of Lovecraft's ideas on government. As with his metaphysical, ethical, and aesthetic views, his political and economic stances have yet to be probed in detail. And yet, the writing of Lovecraft's intellectual biography is of the greatest moment; for the recluse of Providence was as much a thinker as a dreamer.

Works Cited

Bloch, Robert. "Out of the Ivory Tower." In *The Shuttered Room and Other Pieces* by H. P. Lovecraft and Divers Hands. Sauk City, WI: Arkham House, 1959. 171–77.

Penzoldt, Peter. *The Supernatural in Fiction*. London: Peter Nevill, 1952.

"Reality" and Knowledge: Some Notes on Lovecraft's Aesthetic

One of the more misunderstood aspects of Lovecraft's theory of aesthetics—misunderstood because, perhaps, Lovecraft himself uttered it in a peculiar way—is his concept of "reality" as expressed through his fiction. One of his favourite remarks was that he wrote weird fiction so as to create the image of defying natural law. Taken literally, this idea is quite contradictory and impossible: how is it possible, we might ask, that natural law can be "defied"? Any event that occurs in reality—or that, in fiction, is postulated as occurring in reality, as is the case with the majority of Lovecraft's tales—must perforce be obeying some natural law. There can, in effect, logically be no such thing as a "supernatural" occurrence, since its very occurrence implies its adherence to the laws of nature and entity. Are we to conclude that Lovecraft naively failed to realise this, and that his fiction, aesthetically and philosophically, is an excursion into futility?

Care must be taken in interpreting Lovecraft's remarks. His most forceful statement of his aesthetic of horror is found in "Notes on Writing Weird Fiction," where he states:

> I choose weird stories because they suit my inclination best—one of my strongest and most persistent wishes being to achieve, momentarily, the *illusion* [my italics] of some strange suspension or violation of the galling limitations of time, space, and natural law which for ever imprison us and frustrate our curiosity about the infinite cosmic spaces beyond the radius of our sight and analysis. (CE 2.175-76)

The final section of this credo is the most important. Here we see that Lovecraft understood the notion that natural law is inviolable and that it is simply the limitations of the human mind that prevent us from conceiving "reality" in its ultimate state. When he speaks of the "galling limitations of time, space, and natural law," he is really referring to the galling limitations of our mental and sensory apparatus. Lovecraft knew that time and space "at bottom possess no distinct and definite existence" ("Hypnos" [D 166]—he had read his Einstein well—but were themselves "illusions" engendered by a human mind incapable of conceiving reality other than spatially and sequentially. What Lovecraft, then, sought to do in his fiction was to hint of these other realms beyond "reality" as we know it, and thereby to achieve that sense of liberation from the "galling limitations" of the ordinary reality that he failed to find "interesting and satisfying" (SL 3.140).

Note that Lovecraft wished to achieve only the "illusion" of defying natural law: he was certainly no mystic, and did not believe in the "reality" of the bizarre realms he depicted. His appreciation of them was aesthetic rather than intellectual.

> My big kick comes from *taking reality just as it is*—accepting all the limitations of the most orthodox science—and then permitting my symbolising faculty to build outward from the existing facts; rearing a structure of *indefinite promise and possibility* whose topless towers are in no cosmos or dimension penetrable by the contradicting-power of the tyrannous and inexorable intellect. But the whole secret of the kick is *that I know damn well it isn't so*." (SL 3.140)

The whole Lovecraftian universe presents "images forming *supplements* rather than *contradictions* of the visible & mensurable universe" (SL 3.295-96). Lovecraft's materialistic stance could not allow him to conceive of realms that overtly contradicted reality as known to science: instead, he chose to work in what E. F. Benson called "the strange uncharted places that lie on the confines and borders of science" (Benson 289), borders that the "tyrannous and inexorable intellect" does not yet have the power to refute. When Lovecraft defined "the crux of a weird tale [as] something which *could not possibly happen*," he meant something that could not be explained by present-day science. "If any unexpected advance of physics, chemistry, or biology were to indicate the *possibility* of any phenomena related by the weird tale, that particular set of phenomena would cease to be *weird* in the ultimate sense" (SL 3.434).

"From Beyond" (1920) contains one of the earliest concrete expressions of this whole idea. Here the means for perceiving this "supra-reality" (as I term it) is a mechanical device invented by Crawford Tillinghast. The story is more interesting because it states, through the character Tillinghast, Lovecraft's views on reality and the feebleness of the human mind perhaps more clearly than anywhere in his other fiction or letters:

> "What do we know," he had said, "of the world and the universe about us? Our means of receiving impressions are absurdly few, and our notions of surrounding objects infinitely narrow. We see things only as we are constructed to see them, and can gain no idea of their absolute nature. With five feeble senses we pretend to comprehend the boundlessly complex cosmos, yet other beings with a wider, stronger, or different range of senses might not only see

very differently the things we see, but might see and study whole worlds of matter, energy, and life which lie at hand yet can never be detected with the senses we have." (*D* 91)

Another story that reiterates this idea is "Hypnos" (1922), but here the mechanism used to perceive realms beyond reality is drugs, which launch the two characters into "dreams" or, more properly, visions. Lovecraft's use of the word "dream" may be somewhat paradoxical unless we collate fragments from other tales: in "Beyond the Wall of Sleep" it is postulated that certain "dreams" are not the usual "nocturnal visions [that] are perhaps no more than faint and fantastic reflections of our waking experiences" but are in effect "possible minute glimpses into a sphere of mental existence" (*D* 25) not usually exhibited to human beings. Dreams, then, are of two sorts, and it is this second sort—this perception of supra-reality—in which the characters in "Hypnos" engage. It is significant that Lovecraft frequently equates the terms "dream" and "vision" (cf. "Dagon": "I do not know why my dreams were so wild that night; . . . Such visions as I had experienced were too much for me to endure again" [*D* 16])—the latter of which would perhaps better describe these glimpses of supra-reality. "Hypnos," too, enunciates this same conception:

> . . . our studies . . . were of that vaster and more appalling universe of dim entity and consciousness which lies deeper than matter, time, and space [i.e., as we normally conceive them], and whose existence we suspect only in certain forms of sleep—those rare dreams beyond dreams which come never to common men, and but once or twice in the lifetime of imaginative men. The cosmos of our waking knowledge, born from such an universe as a bubble is born from the pipe of a jester, touches it only as such a bubble may touch its sardonic source when sucked back by the jester's whim. (*D* 165)

We need not catalogue the other tales that express this concept; in effect, all Lovecraft's fiction does. The means, however, of perceiving this "reality" beyond reality are quite varied. "Dreams" or visions are often used, as in "Beyond the Wall of Sleep," "The Dreams in the Witch House," and several others (as well as the poem "The Poe-et's Nightmare"). Sometimes the accidental presence of a character in a certain geographical area results in his perception of "reality," or an embodiment of it—i.e., an entity or event not explainable by present scientific knowledge. Tales of this type are "Dagon," "The Call of Cthulhu," "The Whisperer in Darkness," *At the Mountains of Madness*, "The Shadow out of Time," and many others. In effect, Lovecraft's entire myth-cycle of fantastic entities could be interpreted merely as the vast revelation of that level or plane of reality that normal human beings cannot perceive but which certain individuals, usually by chance, stumble upon.

In effecting this "convincing illusion of the thwarting, suspension, or disturbance of . . . basic natural forces" (*SL* 3.436), it was important to Lovecraft that the characters experiencing visions of supra-reality could not explain them away by recourse to hallucination or (ordinary) dream. Although Lovecraft sought to depict only the "illusion" of a defiance of natural law (since an actual defiance is, as noted, logically impossible), that illusion had to be convincing if it were to give him the aesthetic and imaginative thrill he sought: he required that the illusion be so realistic, so based upon reality as we know it, that it could neither blatantly defy known laws of matter and entity nor be dispensed with as the phantasms of a disordered mind. Thus when, in "The Dreams in the Witch House," Gilman finds in his room the "exotic spiky figure which in his monstrous dream he had broken off the fantastic balustrade" (*MM* 279), he becomes increasingly unable to pass off his visions of hyperspace as mere dreams. Indeed, the title of the story reflects Gilman's frantic wish to deny the reality of his cosmic voyages—voyages that he finds at once fascinating and appalling. But such a wish now becomes difficult as he is faced with this material, objective proof of these voyages. In "The Shadow out of Time," the narrator's witnessing of the manuscript that he must have written millions of years ago forms the proof that his psychic displacement by a member of the Great Race was not a dream, as he would have liked to believe, but a reality. Lovecraft conveniently allows the narrator to lose this manuscript when he returns to his excavation party, but it is made all too clear that the manuscript actually existed, and was not a product of the narrator's imagination. So, too, when Wilmarth, in "The Whisperer in Darkness," sees the face and hands of Henry Wentworth Akeley. In other tales this is made even clearer: Arthur Jermyn sees the hideous contents of a box from Africa; the narrator of "The Shadow over Innsmouth" notes the changing of his features into the Innsmouth look; the narrator of "The Lurking Fear" sees the horde of deformed entities chasing one another; and so on throughout Lovecraft's fiction. Always does he assert the brutal, objective reality of these sights of supra-reality: although in some instances no concrete evidence is available as proof, it is precisely because the narrators cannot pass off their adventures as dreams or hallucinations that their minds are shattered.

Related to this idea of perceiving supra-reality, or fragments of it, is the role of knowledge. It is knowledge that usually permits the characters to break through "normal consciousness and reality" ("Hypnos" [*D* 165]) to perceive this other reality. This applies even in some of the tales where "dreams" are used: in "Beyond the Wall of Sleep," it is the central character's mechanical device—a "cosmic 'radio'" (*D* 32)—that allows him to glimpse a different reality through Joe Slater's brain; in "The Dreams in the Witch House," it is Gilman's formidable knowledge of "Non-Euclidean calculus and quantum physics" (*MM* 263)—and, perhaps, his fortuitous occupancy of the queerly angled room in the Witch House—that permits him to jaunt through hyperspace.

Science, then, is one of the major keys to the revelation of reality. This readily harmonises with Lovecraft's strongly positivistic and empirical outlook, forcefully expressed through his letters.

Yet some of Lovecraft's remarks seem to indicate a loathing and hatred of this very science that is leading man to visions beyond his five senses. Do we not read in "Facts concerning the Late Arthur Jermyn and His Family" (1920) that "Science, already oppressive with its shocking revelations, will perhaps be the ultimate exterminator of our human species" (*D* 73), or in "The Call of Cthulhu" (1926) that although "The sciences . . . have hitherto harmed us little; . . . some day the piecing together of dissociated knowledge will open up . . . terrifying vistas of reality" (*DH* 125)? Moreover, do not many of his characters who pursue this knowledge end disastrously, either in death or madness? Does this not reveal a fear of knowledge and reality?[1]

Such a view can be gleaned only through a careless reading of Lovecraft's work. Surely his letters reveal that he could not have hated knowledge—else, we wonder, why did he so arduously pursue it throughout his life?—nor dreaded "reality." Lovecraft was possessed of an "acute, persistent, unquenchable craving TO KNOW"; this meant an "overpowering desire to know whether I am asleep or awake—whether the environment and laws which affect me are external and permanent, or the transitory products of my own brain." Moreover, "If there be not some virtue in plain TRUTH; then our fair dreams, delusions, and follies are as much to be esteemed as our sober waking hours and the comforts they bring. If TRUTH amounts to nothing, then we must regard the phantasmata of our slumbers just as seriously as the events of our daily lives" (*SL* 1.61-63). Yet do we not here encounter another contradiction? Did not Lovecraft say in "Beyond the Wall of Sleep" that "Sometimes I believe that this less material life [revealed through dreams] is our truer life, and that our vain presence on the terraqueous globe is itself the secondary or merely virtual phenomenon" (*D* 26)? But here he is alluding to that less material and normal life which those apocalyptic visions of supra-reality reveal to us, not our normal dreams, which "are no more than faint and fantastic reflections of our waking experiences"; and it is only logical to believe that supra-reality is "truer" than the illusory reality that we normally perceive through our senses.

Clearly, then, Lovecraft did not hate either knowledge or reality. One way of interpreting the themes in his stories is to believe that "Lovecraft is not deploring knowledge, but rather, *man's inability to cope with it*" (Mosig 105). This

---

1. Such a view has actually been adopted by some critics: Colin Wilson believes that HPL "rejected 'reality'" (Wilson 2), while Maurice Lévy feels that HPL "hated reality" (Lévy 25). Barton L. St Armand maintains that HPL thought it "dangerous to know too much" (St Armand 14).

certainly explains the events in certain tales and poems, particularly "Facts Concerning the Late Arthur Jermyn and His Family," "The Poe-et's Nightmare," "The Call of Cthulhu," and others. But an even stronger statement is that Lovecraft, while certainly not deploring knowledge as such, is deploring either the *misuse* of knowledge or the *effects*—often cataclysmic—that knowledge can have.

Observe that in such tales as "From Beyond" and "Hypnos," it is not knowledge itself but the ends to which that knowledge was to have been directed that caused the doom of the central characters. Both Crawford Tillinghast and the unnamed character in "Hypnos" who leads the narrator in their peregrinations through time and space (it is immaterial for our purposes whether he actually existed or was merely a figment of the narrator's imagination) intend to use the knowledge that they have acquired for pernicious ends: Tillinghast shouts, in a burst of pure hubris, "I have harnessed the shades that stride from world to world to sow death and madness. . . . Space belongs to me, do you hear?" (*D* 96). The central character in "Hypnos" "had designs which involved the rulership of the visible universe and more; designs whereby the earth and the stars would move at his command, and the destinies of all living things be his" (*D* 166). Rather than questing for knowledge simply for their own enlightenment, these characters are aiming for goals that are ludicrously and impiously vast; and—perhaps because Lovecraft, believing man so inconsequential in the realms of space and time, felt that the idea of a human being ruling all entity was so grotesquely ridiculous that anyone's thinking such a thing was only indulging in vainglory—the result is not their success, but their fitting doom.

The ancient Greek idea of hubris—"overweening pride"—was a strong one in Lovecraft. But while the Greeks applied it to a man's belief that he was the equal or superior of the gods (who would then castigate him for such a notion), Lovecraft seemed to apply it to a human being's notion that he could subvert or control natural law—and who, in many cases, came very close to doing it. Lovecraft seemed to take a rich satisfaction in condemning such figures in his fiction to utter annihilation.

One of the finest examples of this is *The Case of Charles Dexter Ward*. Some commentators have believed that Ward himself is the quasi-villain of this novel—for does he not aspire to unholy knowledge?—and that Willett is the "hero." But this is a fatal misreading of the tale. Ward is certainly the "tragic hero," but the true villain is of course Joseph Curwen, who has not only used his diabolical knowledge to perpetuate himself far beyond the normal lifespan of a human being, but who aspires for goals that could affect "all civilisation, all natural law, perhaps even the fate of the solar system and the universe" (MM 181-82). Ward, on the other hand, is never deemed "evil"—at least, not when he is still himself, before he is supplanted by Curwen—precisely because his searches into the past were done "for the sake of knowledge" (MM 182). This comment is Ward's sole—and, for Lovecraft, sufficient—justification for all the actions he has undertaken in resurrecting Curwen and relearning his unholy secrets of the resurrection of the dead. Ward, like Lovecraft, was simply attempting to quench his own thirst for knowledge, and Lovecraft never condemns him for doing so; and if he has "brought to light a monstrous abnormality" (MM 182), then it was not really through his own doing but through the evil influence of Curwen. Ward certainly perishes, but he ends almost happily, buried in his family plot at the North Burial Ground. It is Curwen, the villain, who dies hideously, and Lovecraft gains much satisfaction from it; Willett, in effect, is only the instrument of his death. It is to be observed, also, that the death of Curwen's associates, Orne and Hutchinson, is caused by the very things they called up from the dust of centuries; they thus suffer a doom similar to that of Herbert West in "Herbert West—Reanimator," who tried to subvert natural law by reanimating the dead.

The same incidents roughly occur in "The Dreams in the Witch House." Gilman is never blamed or castigated for venturing into hyperspace, since he is venturing there as a student and learner, with no ulterior aims. Gilman also perishes, and hideously enough, but rather than passing a moral judgment upon him, Lovecraft only remarks wryly, "Possibly Gilman ought not to have studied so hard" (MM 263). The real villains are Keziah Mason and Brown Jenkin, and they too suffer death—indeed, partly through Gilman's own actions. Gilman's death is perhaps a necessary effect of the destruction of two such cosmic villains.

An early tale that features the hubris theme in a more purely Greek fashion—i.e., as an offence to the gods—is "The Other Gods." Barzai, given the ironic soubriquet of "The Wise," was "a man deeply learned in the Seven Cryptical Books of Hsan, and familiar with the Pnakotic Manuscripts of distant and frozen Lomar"; but not satisfied with mere knowledge, Barzai, who "knew so much of the gods that . . . he was deemed half a god himself," determines to see the gods on the peak of Hatheg-Kla. He declares: "The wisdom of Barzai hath made him greater than earth's gods, and against his will their spells and barriers are as naught. . . ." But this outburst of hubris does not go unpunished by the gods, who "suffer no man to tell that he hath looked upon them": Barzai falls into the sky through "the *other* gods! The gods of the outer hells that guard the feeble gods of earth!" (D 127–32). The quaintly simple moral of this tale should not allow us to believe that Lovecraft was abandoning the cosmic and rationalistic approach of his other narratives: this tale, along with several of his other early fantasies, shows how pervasive was the influence of Lord Dunsany at this time. Lovecraft was captivated by Dunsany's artlessly simple and moralistic tales, which themselves show the strong influence of pagan mythology in their themes of divine retribution and human hubris; and Lovecraft sought to capture this intentionally and ostensibly naive manner of story-telling, reminiscent of folklore, in many of his early tales, notably "The Cats of Ulthar," "The Quest of Iranon," "The Tree" (which of all Lovecraft's tales is the most strongly Grecian in theme and flavour), and others. It is not to be wondered that, as Lovecraft's rationalistic outlook grew, the Dunsanian influenced waned, and that his theme of hubris began to be manifested in a less classically Grecian manner.

Closely related to this notion of the misuse of knowledge by hubristic human beings is the idea that certain revelations of life, matter, and entity as they "really" are could result in disaster, either for human civilisation or for the cosmos at large. Thus in *At the Mountains of Madness* the narrator strives to prevent the exploration of the Antarctic because any further study—particularly one involving "a thoroughness far beyond anything our outfit attempted" (MM 35)—would surely result, not only in mental perturbation (as with Danforth) at the realisation of the existence of such an entity as a shoggoth, but in the possible loosing of this entity (and however many others may still be lurking) upon the world, with the subsequent destruction of mankind. Lovecraft makes it clear that what is involved here is not merely the threat of madness through revelation—not merely "the inability to cope" with knowledge—but the fate of the world:

> It is absolutely necessary, for the peace and safety of mankind, that some of earth's dark, dead corners and unplumbed depths be let alone; lest sleeping abnormalities wake to resurgent life, and blasphemously surviving nightmares squirm and splash out of their black lairs to newer and wider conquests. (MM 105)

This sentiment is expressed, though not as strongly, in "The Shadow out of Time." Here the narrator is urging "a final abandonment of all attempts at unearthing those fragments of unknown, primordial masonry which my expedition set out to investigate" because if further discoveries are made,

> then man must be prepared to accept notions of the cosmos, and of his own place in the seething vortex of time, whose merest mention is paralysing. He must, too, be placed on guard against a specific, lurking peril which, though it will never engulf the whole race, may impose monstrous and unguessable horrors upon certain venturesome members of it. (*DH* 368)

Here again is the notion that we may be unable to cope with the knowledge of our own ludicrously insignificant position in the cosmos and that this knowledge—or rather the actions that may be implemented based upon it—could lead to destruction, if only of "certain venturesome" individuals.

Yet there are undoubtedly other tales where the inability to cope with knowledge—a comment not on the evil of knowledge but on the feebleness of humanity's psychological state—seems to be the main theme. Arthur Jermyn certainly kills himself because of what the knowledge he gleaned from his African explorations implied; and in "The Call of Cthulhu" the narrator discourages the "piecing together of dissociated knowledge" such as he did because it would result only in our going "mad from the revelation or flee[ing] from the deadly light into the peace and safety of a new dark age" (*DH* 125). Here mental, not physical, destruction might result from knowledge. In either case it would lead to the destruction of civilisation as we know it. But unlike *At the Mountains of Madness*, it seems that here the knowledge—or even the acting upon the knowledge—that Cthulhu exists would not directly endanger the physical well-being of mankind. Cthulhu cannot rise, as might a shoggoth, through any direct actions of human beings: he rose in 1925 only because of a freak earthquake that momentarily brought R'lyeh to the surface, but he and his minions will be freed from their underwater prison only when the "stars and the earth might once more be ready for Them" (*DH* 140), and there is no telling how many years or millennia in the future that may be. So, too, in "The Colour out of Space": to be sure, "something terrible" (*DH* 81) still remains after all the events of the tale; and that something will presumably grow and spread regardless of the wishes or knowledge of mankind. In such instances, Lovecraft seems to be saying, where men can have no effect on the suppression or releasing of these cosmic forces, it is best not to know about them; not because the knowledge is in itself an evil, but because with this knowledge, "even the skies of spring and the flowers of summer must ever afterward be poison" ("The Call of Cthulhu" [*DH* 154]). For our own peace of mind, it is better to preserve the illusion of our safety than to face the existence of cosmic forces that may destroy mankind and the universe and against which man can have no deterrent effect in any case.

We can note that this concept of the dire effects of knowledge is manifested in the more "amoral" of Lovecraft's tales, where there is no real "villain" but only forces and entities working in their own interest. It is only logical that the hubris theme could not apply here, since there would be no character through whom it could be expressed. Certainly we cannot regard Cthulhu as the "villain" of "The Call of Cthulhu" who is questing for power beyond his "station": Cthulhu simply exists and is only "evil" in relation to mankind. The hubris theme seems to have been applied only to human beings who tried to exalt themselves to some level of cosmic rulership. It certainly cannot be applied to any characters in the tales of Lovecraft's pseudomythology: not to the titanic extra-terrestrial entities such as Yog-Sothoth or Nyarlathotep, who *already* rule the cosmos; not to the other intergalactic races, most of whom (such as the fungi from Yuggoth in "The Whisperer in Darkness," the Old Ones in *At the Mountains of Madness,* and the Great Race in "The Shadow out of Time") are themselves questing scientifically and disinterestedly for knowledge; not even to the human characters who piece together the facts of the case, since they too are working in a scientific spirit. The hubris theme seems to have been generally an early one in Lovecraft—despite its occurrence in "The Dreams in the Witch House" (1932) and perhaps in "The Thing on the Doorstep" (1933), in the figure of Asenath/Ephraim Waite—when he was still strongly under the influence of the heavy classical reading of his youth. Moreover, the hubris theme, with its connotations of morality even in Lovecraft's modified and rationalistic form, may have seemed to him out of place in his "cosmic" narratives, since he readily recognised the aimlessness and amorality of a blindly impersonal cosmos.

It is clear, then, that Lovecraft the positivistic materialist envisaged realms of reality beyond that revealed by our mental and sensory data; and although he did not believe in the literal reality of these realms—did not believe in the literal existence of a Cthulhu—he nonetheless felt them symbolically true, i.e., felt that such realms might be true if only our senses were keener or our knowledge of the universe greater. But if this supra-reality is in his work almost always horrifying—although on one occasion it is deemed "picturesque" ("The Dreams in the Witch House" [MM 285])—then it only underscores Lovecraft's belief in the inconsequentiality of mankind, belittled as it is by cosmic forces that could easily crush it; forces not only beyond humanity's comprehension, but even its imagination.

Works Cited

Benson, E. F. "Mrs. Amworth." In *The Collected Ghost Stories of E. F. Benson.* New York: Carroll & Graf, 1992.

Lévy, Maurice. *Lovecraft: A Study in the Fantastic.* Trans. S. T. Joshi. Detroit: Wayne State University Press, 1988.

Mosig, Dirk W. "H. P. Lovecraft: Myth-Maker." 1976. In S. T. Joshi, ed., *H. P. Lovecraft: Four Decades of Criticism.* Athens: Ohio University Press, 1980. 104–12.

St Armand, Barton L. "Facts in the Case of H. P. Lovecraft." *Rhode Island History* 31, No. 2 (February 1972): 3–19.

Wilson, Colin. *The Strength to Dream: Literature and the Imagination.* Boston: Houghton Mifflin, 1962.

In Defence of Dagon and Lovecraft's Philosophy

The Transatlantic Circulator may still form one of the minor mysteries in the study of H. P. Lovecraft, no less from a biographical than from a bibliographical standpoint. While the affair of the Transatlantic Circulator may not be exactly pivotal in Lovecraft's life and thought, it did represent one of the earliest occasions in which he defined his literary theory and championed his philosophy of mechanistic materialism over idealism or religiosity or uncritical mysticism.

The Transatlantic Circulator was a loose organisation of amateur journalists in England and the United States who exchanged stories and poems in manuscript and criticised them. How long the organisation was in existence before Lovecraft's entrance into it in July 1920 is unknown, but it is certainly not correct, as L. Sprague de Camp has said, that Lovecraft himself "organized . . . the Transatlantic Circulator" (de Camp 115). Indeed, there is nothing to suggest either this or that the organisation collapsed after Lovecraft's exit from it in September 1921, for new members were entering it at precisely the time Lovecraft was withdrawing.

Also in doubt is the matter of who introduced Lovecraft to the Circulator. The choice would perhaps fall on John Ravenor Bullen, a major member of the organisation. Bullen is the only one of the known members of the Circulator with whom Lovecraft continued an acquaintance in later life; but did he know Bullen as early as 1920? There is no especial reason to doubt it. Lovecraft published a poem of Bullen's in the July 1923 issue of the *Conservative*, but this issue appears to have been prepared much earlier; and in 1927 Lovecraft edited and wrote the preface to Bullen's posthumous collection of poems, *White Fire*.

These matters are, however, relatively unimportant; the crux of the affair is Lovecraft's own activities in the Circulator. Being at the time both a critic and a creative writer of poetry and fiction, Lovecraft found the organisation very congenial. In this group, as (more successfully) with his other correspondence cycles, the Kleicomolo and the Gallomo, and later with his literary associates to whom he almost invariably sent manuscripts of his tales for criticism before submitting them to a publisher, he could indulge in literature as a form of "self-expression" without any thought of a preconceived audience. In Lovecraft's mind, the aesthetic enjoyment and satisfaction of literary creation itself—the act of capturing in an artistic manner images, moods, and attitudes that are clamouring to be captured—is the sole reward for that literary creation. This product need reach only the eyes of a few discerning friends and critics; whether it reaches a wider audience is immaterial.

The very fact that Lovecraft felt compelled to write at least four essays defending his literary philosophy (one of them, the first, is non-extant) shows that some members of the Circulator were perhaps not as discerning as Lovecraft would have liked. This is, however, not to say that they were either incompetent or immature literary critics; in some of their remarks we find astute and even prophetic comments on Lovecraft's work. A Dr John Munday recorded: "I suspect that [Lovecraft's] letters are more interesting than his stories"—a view held by at least a few current scholars. In saying that Lovecraft "makes one *think*" and that "Mr Lovecraft does not write for lazy readers," Elsye Tash Sater was a vague and perhaps unintentional precursor of that school of critics—of which T. O. Mabbott is one of the earliest notable examples—who regarded Lovecraft's works as expressions of a distinctive philosophy rather than as fiction intended merely to horrify. John Ravenor Bullen, perhaps the keenest of the Circulator's critics, recognised Lovecraft's "art for art's sake" attitude, and mentions him in the same breath as Wells and Maeterlinck.[1] The conclusion, then, cannot be drawn that the critical abilities of the Circulator in general were inadequate, or that the members failed (again in general) to satisfy Lovecraft's desire for friendly yet perspicacious criticism of his work. The fact that he granted the logic of several remarks on his pieces, and that he even revised slightly one work—"Psychopompos"—on the basis of a suggestion made in the Circulator, shows that Lovecraft did enjoy the intellectual stimulus provided by the Circulator. Only illness and overwork forced him to remove himself from the organisation in September 1921.

It was, however, those particular comments by some members—comments that Lovecraft considered subjective, irrelevant, or simply a different viewpoint from his own—that spurred the three essays now referred to as *In Defence of Dagon*. Important in this regard is a comment of John Munday's on "Dagon": "Do you remember Kipling's little poem with the refrain 'But is it

---

1. "In 'The Island of Dr. Moreau' H. G. Wells makes animals into men. In 'Dagon' H. P. Lovecraft makes men into fish and vice versa. In a recent paper Maeterlinck reveals that every animal, fish, and insect since creation is bound up in man to-day...." All comments by members of the Transatlantic Circulator survive in ms. at JHL.

art'? So would I courteously ask: 'Is it wholesome' of Mr Lovecraft's story." Here we see the impetus for the writing of "The Defence Reopens!" Munday later says, "You are . . . giving us food for thought. But, unless I am very greatly mistaken, your 'The White Ship' will be succeeded by cleverer, and (pardon me) healthier, writings." To this Lovecraft brandished Oscar Wilde's dictum that "no artist is ever morbid." One of Bullen's observations also prompted a response by Lovecraft: ". . . the reader, search and probe as he may, is unable to discover any trace of humour in [the stories]. The essence of a man's whole work (noticeable in these contributions) generally presents itself more or less in the form of a view of the universe. Can a view of the universe which does not take humour into consideration be complete or correct?" And, of course, A. H. Brown's remark that Lovecraft's work should more fully reflect "the thoughts and actions of ordinary people," thereby allowing them "to appeal to a larger class," again caused Lovecraft to unearth the major tenets of his literary aesthetic.

What these comments by the Circulator really allowed Lovecraft to do was, for the first time, to defend his view of weird fiction as a significant art form. In so doing he anticipated many of the remarks he would make in the introduction to "Supernatural Horror in Literature" (1925-27), although by that time Lovecraft's "art for art's sake" stance—inspired by his reading of the critical theory of Poe, Wilde, and the Decadents—had been merged into a broader aesthetic emphasising a need for sincerity and disinterested self-expression. By dividing literature, somewhat unorthodoxly, into three categories—romantic, realistic, and imaginative—he stresses the importance of the last by declaring that it draws upon the best features of both the other two: like romanticism, imaginative fiction bases its appeal on emotions (the emotions of fear, wonder, and terror); from realism it derives the important principle of truth—not truth to fact, as in realism, but truth to human feeling. As a result, Lovecraft comes up with the somewhat startling deduction that "The imaginative writer devotes himself to art in its most essential sense."

In defending himself, and his writing, from charges of "unwholesomeness" and immorality (charges still made today against weird fiction), Lovecraft states that the weird, the fantastic, and even the horrible are as deserving of artistic treatment as the wholesome and the ordinary. No realm of human existence can be denied to the artist; everything depends upon the treatment, not the subject matter. Lovecraft cites Wilde's pretty paradox that

> a healthy work of art is one the choice of whose subject is conditioned by the temperament of the artist, and comes directly out of it. . . . An unhealthy work of art, on the other hand, is a work . . . whose subject is deliberately chosen, not because the artist has any pleasure in it, but because he thinks that the public

will pay him for it. In fact, the popular novel that the public calls healthy is always a thoroughly unhealthy production; and what the public calls an unhealthy novel is always a beautiful and healthy work of art.

In this way Lovecraft neatly justifies his unusual subject-matter while simultaneously condemning the popular best-seller as a product of insincere hackwork. And yet, because Lovecraft realises that weird fiction is necessarily a cultivated taste, he is compelled to note repeatedly that he writes only for the "sensitive"—the select few whose imaginations are sufficiently liberated from the minutiae of daily life to appreciate images, moods, and incidents that do not exist in the world as we know and experience it. As a result, Lovecraft does not want to write for or about "ordinary people"—not only because, as he declares, he has no interest in them, but because they in turn have no particular interest in his imaginative work.

Lovecraft's defence of weird fiction as the literature of pure imagination and as the preserve of a select few is a compelling one, and we can see how well it justifies the work of such of his contemporaries and successors as Lord Dunsany, E. R. Eddison, Arthur Machen, Clark Ashton Smith, Ramsey Campbell, T. E. D. Klein, and Thomas Ligotti. The bestsellerdom of Stephen King, Clive Barker, and Anne Rice, on the other hand, seem motivated by exactly that sort of "unhealthiness" that Wilde detected in the popular novel, and there can hardly be a doubt as to which group of writers will survive as exponents of genuine literature and which will be banished to the oblivion of superficial, if lucrative, hackdom.

Although Lovecraft vindicates his own theories at length in these essays, he is well aware that the situation is not one of right and wrong but, fundamentally, of differing taste and outlook. Lovecraft summed up the matter in a note he wrote on a Circulator member's comment: ". . . Since all my 'literary' emanations are more or less grotesque and arabesque . . . it occurred to me that [they] might be rather boresome . . . [to] an audience predominantly pro-realistic."

It is not the case that Lovecraft's work was uniformly unpopular with the members of the Circulator; to some his stories were indeed powerful. Virtually all at least realised that Lovecraft was "a writer . . . undeniably possessed of fine powers of imagination and a really exceptional ability to say things in a striking way" (as John Munday commented in regard to "Dagon"), and Elsye Tash Sator even understood vaguely the cosmic quality that is the notable feature of Lovecraft's work when she hypothesised on the reasons for the final madness of the narrator of "Dagon": "Is it the immensity of space that overwhelms [him], or [his] feeling of powerlessness? Or is it loneliness in its intensest form that shatters the brain cells?" In a way she is right, although the crux of the tale lies in the narrator's (and the reader's) awareness of the "terrible and acknowledged antiquity of the earth and man's tenuous sinecure thereon," as Matthew H. Onderdonk termed it.

John Ravenor Bullen recognised the allegorical nature of "The White Ship" when he noted that it was a "powerful prose-poem in which the allegorist informs us somewhat sorrowfully that he was once an idealist but is now a materialist—that he once dwelt happily in the land of Sona-Nyl but foolishly forsook it and pushed on to explore forbidden territory—only to find the Cathuria of his hopes a hollow hell." The interpretation seems, however, somewhat unlikely, since—even judging solely from the passages in these essays—there is no indication that Lovecraft either was ever idealistic or ever regretted his materialistic stance.

Turning to the Circulator's opinion of Lovecraft's poetry, we find one comment by the poet Bullen on "Old Christmas" that is startlingly perceptive and may stand as one of the finer general comments passed on Lovecraft's verse:

> May I point out that poets of each period have forged their lines in the temper and accent of their age, whereas Mr Lovecraft purposefully "plates over" his poetical works with "the impenetrable rococo" of his predecessors' days, thereby running great risks. But it may be that his discerning eyes perceive that many modern methods are mongrel and ephemeral. His devotion to Queen Anne style may make his compositions seem artificial, rhetorical descriptions to contemporary critics, but the ever-growing charm of eloquence (to which assonance, alliteration, onomatopoeic sound and rhythm, and tone colour contribute their entrancing effect) displayed in the poem under analysis, proclaims Mr Lovecraft a genuine poet, and "Old Christmas" an example of poetical architecture well-equipped to stand the test of time.

This may be a somewhat charitable assessment of Lovecraft's poetry in general and of "Old Christmas" in particular, but it touches upon some important issues. Lovecraft indeed considered "modern methods" in poetry "mongrel and ephemeral" (see his comments on Whitman and T. S. Eliot), and did indeed choose to follow the Augustan poets of eighteenth-century England in form and substance. Much later, in the essay "Heritage or Modernism: Common Sense in Art Forms" (1935), Lovecraft attempted a justification for artistic archaism:

> When a given age has no new *natural* impulse toward change, is it not better to continue building on the established forms than to concoct grotesque and meaningless novelties out of thin academic theory?
>
> Indeed, under certain conditions is not a policy of frank and virile antiquarianism—a healthy, vigorous revival of old forms still justified by their relation to life—infinitely sounder than a feverish mania for the destruction of

familiar things and the laboured, freakish, uninspired search for strange shapes which nobody wants and which really mean nothing? (CE 5.124)

This is sound enough in theory, but it cannot actually be used as a justification for Lovecraft's archaistic poetry (it should be pointed out that the above remarks were intended to apply not to poetry but to architecture); for no one could possibly maintain that eighteenth-century verse—at least the sort of quaint, mechanical eighteenth-century verse written by Lovecraft—was one of the "old forms still justified by their relation to life." Indeed, it was exactly because his poems were merely playful—and, to be honest, fundamentally insincere—excursions into antiquarianism that they fail as aesthetic products. Lovecraft ultimately realised this, and not only repudiated much of his earlier verse but, in *Fungi from Yuggoth* (1929-30), finally began using the language of his own day to convey his message.

Lovecraft's philosophical remarks in the *In Defence of Dagon* essays must also concern us, insofar as they occupy a large body of the text. It is unfortunate that no remarks of the Mr Wickenden whom Lovecraft so took to task survive; but the context allows us to assume that the matter must have been the familiar idealism vs. materialism debate in which Lovecraft and some of his other correspondents—Maurice W. Moe, James F. Morton, Rheinhart Kleiner—engaged. Just as his literary remarks represent the first significant enunciation of his theory of the weird, so do Lovecraft's philosophical remarks put forth—more vigorously and pointedly than even such essays as "Idealism and Materialism: A Reflection" (1919)—the secular, positivist world view that would, with some modifications, remain his dominant outlook for the whole of his life.

Several important features emerge in Lovecraft's comments which allow us to gauge exactly how far he had evolved certain facets of his metaphysics and ethics. By 1921 he had not only absorbed what were for him the most important branches of ancient thought—particularly Leucippus' determinism, the atomic theory of Leucippus and Democritus (probably through the *De Rerum Natura* of Lucretius), and (also in part through Lucretius) the ethical philosophy of Epicurus—but also such modern thinkers as Nietzsche, Thomas Henry Huxley, Ernst Haeckel (*The Riddle of the Universe*), and Hugh Elliot (*Modern Science and Materialism*). He had not yet, however, embraced Einstein or other advanced astrophysicists such as Planck, de Sitter, and Heisenberg, and therefore had yet to harmonise his old-style mechanistic materialism with the advances of modern science, as he would do in a later letter (see *SL* 2.266f.).

But Wickenden's repeated criticism of Lovecraft's use of the word "know"—how did Lovecraft "know" that there is no life after death?—forced him to shed belief in the absolute certainty of scientific discovery and to base all his arguments—on the existence of God or the soul; on survival after death; on the place of humanity in the universe—on *probability*. This belief in probability—i.e., a belief as to the *"is or isn'tness"* of things (SL 3.307) as derived from the most up-to-date findings of science—would serve as the foundation for Lovecraft's metaphysics for the rest of his life.

In ethics Lovecraft had already accepted the teachings of Epicurus that *pleasure*—interpreted widely as that which fosters well-being—as the aim of terrestrial existence. Like Epicurus, Lovecraft saw pleasure as the natural goal of all organisms, and later made pleasure the foundation for his aesthetic thought as well:

> False or insincere amusement is the sort of activity which does not meet the real psychological demands of the human glandular-nervous system, but merely affects to do so. Real amusement is the sort which is based on a knowledge of real needs, and which therefore hits the spot. *This latter kind of amusement is what art is.* (SL 3.21)

Darwinian and Huxleyan evolution plays a considerable role in Lovecraft's debate with Wickenden, and he uses it as his trump-card in refuting Wickenden's notion of the human soul: if human beings have a soul and animals do not, exactly where along the course of our evolution from apes to human beings did we acquire this mysterious element? In battling the theist Wickenden, Lovecraft also relies upon anthropological work for a natural account of the origin of religious belief in primitive man. Lovecraft had by this time probably absorbed such seminal works as Edward Burnett Tylor's *Primitive Culture* (1871), John Fiske's *Myths and Myth-Makers* (1872), and James George Frazer's *The Golden Bough* (1890), which to his mind explained in a wholly satisfactory way the inevitable religiosity instilled in the human race by ignorance of the true workings of natural phenomena, thereby giving rise to notions of deity, soul, and immortality. Lovecraft maintained that "This matter of the explanation of 'spiritual' feelings is really the most important of all materialistic arguments; since the explanations are not only overwhelmingly forcible, but so adequate as to shew that man could not possibly have developed without acquiring just such false impressions." There is, indeed, every reason to believe that Lovecraft is correct on this point.

Works Cited

de Camp, L. Sprague. *Lovecraft: A Biography*. Garden City, NY: Doubleday, 1975.

Onderdonk, Matthew H. "The Lord of R'lyeh." 1945. *Lovecraft Studies* No. 7 (Fall 1982): 8–17.

Lovecraft's Alien Civilisations: A Political Interpretation

In "The Political and Economic Thought of H. P. Lovecraft" I attempted to outline the major tenets of Lovecraft's political and economic thought, particularly as they evolved toward the end of his life, when, with the onset of the Depression, his attention became directed more and more to the problems of employment, social organisation, and particularly the place of aesthetics in modern society. But these views are not only reflected in his letters and in such essays as "Some Repetitions on the Times" (1933), but also in his later fiction. Fritz Leiber was among the earliest to hint that Lovecraft's later tales—notably *At the Mountains of Madness* (1931) and "The Shadow out of Time" (1934-35)—contain much discussion of the political, social, and cultural aspects of his alien civilisations (see Leiber, "Through Hyperspace"); but it is now clear that in several of Lovecraft's late narratives—not only the two mentioned but other such tales as "The Mound" (1929-30),[1] "The Whisperer in Darkness" (1930), "The Shadow over Innsmouth" (1931), and "In the Walls of Eryx" (1936)[2]—these alien civilisations either represent a sort of Lovecraftian utopia or are predictions of the possible future of mankind. The six extra-terrestrial races involved—the Great Race, the Old Ones, the mound denizens,[3] the fungi from Yuggoth, the Innsmouth folk, and the Venusians—are, in varying degrees, embodiments of Lovecraft's political and economic views; but while some are utopias, others are very much dystopias.

It is interesting to note, however, that all the alien civilisations involved

---

1. It need not concern us that the tale was "revised" (or, rather, ghostwritten) for Zealia Bishop, since it is obvious that HPL not only wrote but conceived the entire tale. See my article "Who Wrote 'The Mound'?" (p. 343).

2. Here the amount of work that can definitely be ascribed to HPL (as opposed to his collaborator, Kenneth Sterling) is less certain; but the descriptions of the natives of Venus seem to be HPL's. Nevertheless, caution must be exercised.

3. They too are curiously called the "Old Ones"; I shall, however, not use this designation for the mound dwellers but shall restrict it to the alien race in *At the Mountains of Madness*.

are in many ways superior to human beings—or, at least, to human beings in their present state. Lovecraft declares flatly that the Great Race (which probably represents his quintessential utopia, since it is called "the greatest race of all," having "learned all things that ever were known or ever would be known on earth" [DH 385]) had an intelligence "enormously greater than man's" (DH 393). Similarly, the "scientific and mechanical knowledge" of the Old Ones in At the Mountains of Madness "far surpassed man's today" (MM 62) (the final word is to be noted), while the "brain capacity [of the fungi from Yuggoth] exceeds that of any other surviving life-form" (DH 240). (This appears to be hyperbole, since the Great Race and the Old Ones—despite the fact that the latter were defeated in warfare by the fungi at the dawn of our planet's history [see MM 68]—seem clearly superior to the fungi in pure intelligence; but as this remark is found in a letter to Wilmarth written by one of the fungi themselves, one may legitimately suspect that it is an instance of self-congratulatory egotism.) The mound denizens can also boast superiority in intelligence to human beings: they have gained the power of dematerialisation, converse purely by telepathy, and have also conquered old age.

This last quality is an interesting one; for while the incredible longevity of the Great Race and the Old Ones seems to be a product of their anatomical structures, the mound denizens have triumphed over old age apparently through sheer strength of mind. In a less intellectual way, the Innsmouth folk have become immortal by returning to the sea, the original habitat—so Lovecraft has Zadok Allen declare[4]—of all terrestrial life. The longevity of the fungi from Yuggoth is not stated, and is thus probably not notable.

Lovecraft conveys the great intelligence of his alien races in other ways. Several of them possess more (or keener) senses than human beings: the Great Race "had but two of the senses which we recognise—sight and hearing . . . [but] of other and incomprehensible senses . . . they possessed many" (DH 398); the protagonists of At the Mountains of Madness have difficulty in understanding some of the bas-reliefs that they see, since "certain touches here and there gave vague hints of latent symbols and stimuli which another mental and emotional background, and a fuller or different sensory equipment, might have made of profound and poignant significance to us" (MM 57); while even the Venusians seem to have a "special sense" (D 293) for the crystals which they worship.

The ability for space-travel is noted for all the races save the Innsmouth folk and the Venusians. Both the Old Ones and the fungi from Yuggoth are

---

4. "Seems that . . . everything alive come aout o' the water onct": "The Shadow over Innsmouth" (DH 331).

said to have flown through the aether on their "vast membranous" (*MM* 61) wings. This idea has been ridiculed by Richard L. Tierney; and perhaps Lovecraft himself saw the improbability of the device, for he declares that the Great Race flew through space and time by projecting their minds forward (or, more rarely, backward) through time with "suitable mechanical aid" (*DH* 386) (presumably the curious mechanism of "rods, wheels, and mirrors" [*DH* 374] seen in Peaslee's home just before the end of his "amnesia"). In "The Mound" it is said that the people of K'n-yan "had come from a distant part of space where physical conditions are much like those of the earth" (*HM* 131); this idea is still harder to swallow, particularly in view of Lovecraft's condemnation of the use of anthropomorphic alien races in such essays as "Some Notes on Interplanetary Fiction." Lovecraft adds the qualification, "All this ... was legend now; and one could not say how much truth was in it" (*HM* 131); but, we wonder, if the origin of the mound denizens were not extra-terrestrial, how could they have had such notions of extra-terrestriality to begin with? Suffice it to say that, with the exception of "The Shadow out of Time," Lovecraft's conceptions of space travel were somewhat primitive.

Three of Lovecraft's alien civilisations possess the power of hypnosis and telepathy. The mound denizens not only converse telepathically but control their slaves by "streams of thought" (*HM* 119). The Old Ones maintain a similar control over their slaves, the shoggoths. In "The Whisperer in Darkness" the "undoubted telepathic and hypnotic powers of the hill creatures and their agents" (*DH* 231) is noted.

Scientific research is high among several of Lovecraft's alien races. The prodigious scientific intelligence required to build the "mechanical aid" that permits mind-exchange certainly argues a high development of physics, electronics, astronomy, and perhaps psychology on the part of the Great Race. As for the Old Ones, not only does Lovecraft say (as noted above) that their "scientific and mechanical knowledge" greatly exceeded that of human beings, but remarks that the information revealed in their maps and diagrams is "uncannily close to the latest findings of mathematics and astrophysics" (*MM* 60). The pseudo-Akeley in "The Whisperer in Darkness" tells Wilmarth: "You can't imagine the degree to which those beings [i.e., the fungi from Yuggoth] have carried science" (*DH* 253). Among the mound denizens "scientific curiosity ... was keen," and "science had been profound and accurate, and all-embracing save in the one direction of astronomy" (*HM* 132, 135).

The Venusians seem to have excelled in only a single branch of science (or art)—that of architecture. The narrator of "In the Walls of Eryx" categorically states: "They haven't any skill except building" (*D* 293). Indeed, we cannot place the Venusians too high on the intellectual scale; for if we believe (as the narrator comes to do) that they had constructed their invisible labyrinth solely to entrap human beings greedy for their crystals, we can only wonder at the stupendous waste of energy and effort. Lovecraft's other civilisations are, however, also notable builders: Zamacona is stupefied at the sight of the "monstrous, gigantic, and omnipotent city of Tsath" (HM 143), while the two protagonists of At the Mountains of Madness experience still greater amazement at the site of the Old Ones' immemorial megalopolis. Peaslee admires the imposing and Cyclopean architecture of the Great Race's city, remarking that "the principle of the arch was known as fully and used as extensively as by the Romans" (DH 379). On Yuggoth the fungi have built "great houses and temples"; although the "mysterious Cyclopean bridges . . . [were] built by some elder race extinct and forgotten before the beings came to Yuggoth from the ultimate voids" (DH 254). Even the Innsmouth denizens (clearly at the bottom of the scale among Lovecraft's alien civilisations) have a distinctive architecture, but only in their underwater homes: who can forget the conclusion of the tale, when the narrator longs to behold "Cyclopean and many-columned Y'hanthlei" (DH 367)?

History is a major pursuit among the alien races in Lovecraft, particularly the Great Race, in whose "vast libraries were volumes of texts and pictures holding the whole of earth's annals—histories and descriptions of every species that had ever been or that ever would be, with full records of their arts, their achievements, their languages, and their psychologies" (DH 386). Lovecraft emphasises the "abnormal historic-mindedness" (MM 57) of the Old Ones, adding somewhat dryly that the continental drift theory of Taylor, Wegener, and Joly received "striking support from [the] uncanny source" (MM 66) of the Old Ones' maps. History was certainly a high priority among the mound denizens, although it was "more and more neglected" (HM 136) at the time of Zamacona's visit. Even the fungi from Yuggoth have some interest in history or ethnography, since "they like to take away men of learning once in a while, to keep informed of the state of things in the human world" (DH 218). One senses, however, that this curiosity is not so much academic as practical and even strategical.

Finally, medicine has been carried to a high level by many of the aliens. Here the fungi from Yuggoth seem to be paramount, since "surgery is an incredibly expert and every-day thing among them" (DH 240). In other tales this medical capacity is only implied: certainly the mound denizens must be skilled in surgery to create their bizarrely composite reanimated slaves, while the Old Ones, if not skilled in medicine, are at least curious about the human and canine anatomies (cf. MM 37, 86). No particular mention is made of the Great Race's medical capacities.

In social organisation Lovecraft's alien civilisations are in some respects strikingly similar and in others notably divergent. In the final analysis the Great Race clearly emerges as the most enlightened and "model" race in Lovecraft, with the Old Ones some distance back and the mound denizens well behind. The social structure of the fungi, the Venusians, and the Innsmouth folk is scarcely described, but we can assume that all these societies—despite the intelligence of the fungi—represent Lovecraftian dystopias in greater or lesser degrees. Lovecraft's attitude toward the social and political structure of his alien races will be studied in greater detail later.

It is a fact of no small interest that all three of Lovecraft's comparatively utopian societies have done away with sex in the normal human fashion. This is understandable in the cases of the Great Race and the Old Ones, since both these races are totally non-human in biology and could thus hardly propagate like humans. Both reproduce by spores; consequently there is little place for family life in the two civilisations. Normal family life has also been done away with among the mound denizens (cf. *HM* 344).[5] In the early period of the mound denizens' history, the "ruling type" had practised "selective breeding" (*HM* 134) to gain supremacy; and long before Zamacona's visit "births had ceased," since people "could easily become young again when they felt like it" (*HM* 132). Indeed, the "naturally inferior members of the ruling race" (*HM* 134) became slaves so that the ruling type remained uncorrupted. Similarly, the Great Race disposed of its "defective individuals . . . as soon as their defects were noticed" (*DH* 399), while the Old Ones did away with any "bothersome forms" (*MM* 65) which they happened to create. A particularly surprising detail is that the inferior stock of the mound denizens not only became slaves but actually contributed to the meat supply (*HM* 139).

That Lovecraft was essentially reflecting his own social views when writing such passages is obvious from the manifestly sympathetic tone in which they are written. While, certainly, Lovecraft would surely not have wished to make a feast of such of his characters as Joe Slater in "Beyond the Wall of Sleep," it is clear that the idea of racial purity and the elimination of "bad blood" remained central to his thought even at the end of his life (as the correspondence to J. Vernon Shea indicates), and is all of a piece with his comparative admiration of Hitler. Both the Old Ones and the mound denizens make extensive use of slaves; and while slavery has no place in the socialistic order

---

5. The resemblance in this detail to Plato's utopia in the *Republic* need not be stressed, since HPL, having no great respect for Plato, probably derived his ideas independently of him—largely through keen observation of the political and social developments of his own time.

embraced by Lovecraft in his later years, he was nonetheless sympathetic to slavery: in "Medusa's Coil" he wrote that "to hear [negro slaves upon a southern plantation] singing and laughing and playing the banjo at night was to know the fullest charm of a civilisation and social order now sadly extinct" (HM 169). It is true that both the Old Ones and the mound denizens went into a decline, and that the former were actually extirpated by the slaves of their own creation; but the causes of their decline (to be examined in greater detail later) were not restricted to their being a slave-owning society, hence we can infer no moral condemnation of slavery by Lovecraft in these cases.

In more minor particulars of social organisation, we may note that the Great Race does without sleep altogether (DH 398) and no longer hunts for its food, it being wholly "vegetable and synthetic" (DH 397). In these details—which allow the beings to engage the more extensively in intellection—the Great Race again asserts its superiority to the other alien civilisations in Lovecraft. Even the Old Ones continue to hunt and practise herding (MM 65), while the same holds true for the mound denizens. Both the Old Ones and the Innsmouth folk are fishermen. Little is said on the eating habits of the Venusians or the fungi (although the pseudo-Akeley's refusal to share a dinner with Wilmarth at the conclusion of "The Whisperer in Darkness" may imply that the fungi cannot eat human food); but they presumably require some sort of sustenance, probably gained from the land through rudimentary agriculture.

It is in the political structure of some of Lovecraft's alien civilisations that we trace the clearest reflections of his own political views. The Great Race in particular seems to represent the governmental utopia toward which Lovecraft wished mankind to strive:

> The Great Race seemed to form a single, loosely knit nation or league, with major institutions in common, though there were four definite divisions. The political and economic system of each unit was a sort of fascistic socialism, with major resources rationally distributed, and power delegated to a small governing board elected by the vote of all able to pass certain educational and psychological tests. (DH 399)

I have elsewhere pointed out the startling similarities of these remarks to Lovecraft's views as crystallised in "Some Repetitions on the Times." In that essay Lovecraft clearly advocates the limiting of franchise to those "able to pass rigorous educational examinations (emphasising civic and economic subjects) and scientific intelligence tests" (CE 5.93), the limiting of power to a small "oligarchy of intelligence," the wider distribution of wealth (including government control "over large accumulations of resources"), and other such measures.

The two stories, "The Mound" and *At the Mountains of Madness*, provide interesting insights into the gradual development of Lovecraft's political and economic thought. "The Mound" (1929–30), the first tale where political remarks (and even satire) are inserted, shows that Lovecraft had not yet evolved the views codified in "Some Repetitions on the Times." The mound denizens' government "was a kind of communistic or semi-anarchical state; habit rather than law determining the daily order of things" (*HM* 135). This is most surprising, since Lovecraft was never sympathetic to communism, much less anarchism; writing in 1931: "I think no conceivable system of communism could bring civilised people any possible recompense for the damage its establishment would inevitably involve" (*SL* 3.377). But it appears that the mound denizens had drifted into communism through "paralysing ennui" (*HM* 135) rather than through the violent revolution predicted by Marx and realised in the Russia of 1917. Indeed, the mound society is hardly communistic, but rather aristocratic; hence Lovecraft's frequent mentions of the "ruling race" or the "ruling type." It is precisely the aristocratic temperament—whose noblest features were, as Lovecraft wrote, "good manners, taste, intelligence, responsibility, and a certain sense of honour" (*SL* 4.423)—that makes possible a government ruled by "habit rather than law." "The Mound," then, indicates that Lovecraft had yet to abandon the vestigial predilection for aristocracy gained through his early readings and upbringing, and had not yet fully adopted socialism. His aristocratic or elitist views never in fact left him; for even the socialistic Great Race has four "definite" classes. But Lovecraft easily reconciled aristocracy with socialism, since to the end of his life he believed that progress in intellectual and aesthetic life—in effect, the distinctive features of civilisation—were determined by a very small segment of the population.[6] But Lovecraft's "oligarchy of intelligence" (which might better have been called an oligarchy of specialists) does not necessarily consist of these intellectual leaders; for in "Some Repetitions on the Times" he writes: "No non-technician, be he artist, philosopher, or scientist, can even begin to judge the labyrinthine governmental problems with which . . . administrators must deal" (*CE* 5.93).

The political system of the Old Ones in *At the Mountains of Madness* is quite different from that of the mound denizens. Lovecraft flatly declares that their "government was evidently complex and probably socialistic"; adding, however, that "no certainties in this regard could be deduced from the sculptures we saw" (*MM* 65). Lovecraft's comparative lack of detail on the governmental structure of the Old Ones may be explained not only through the

---

6. Here he is an agreement with, among others, Bertrand Russell; see his essay "Western Civilization" in *In Praise of Idleness and Other Essays* (1935).

exigencies of plot—since, as he wrote, it would be exceedingly difficult to ascertain an entire social system merely from bas-reliefs, however extensive and detailed—and not only through his imperfect adoption of socialism, but through a lack of conviction as to the necessity for social reform in his own time. "Some Repetitions on the Times," however—written in the bleakest days of the Depression, just before the inauguration of Roosevelt—burns with a sense of urgency for reform lest we "starve and goad the people into an uprising," which "is likely to mean bolshevism in the end . . . a thing worth going to any length to escape" (CE 5.89–90). This sense of urgency not only colours his letters from the period but also accounts for the notably detailed presentation of the Great Race's political and social structure in "The Shadow out of Time."

It is noteworthy that two of Lovecraft's three highly evolved races—the Old Ones and the mound denizens—had passed through a stage of mechanised culture but had discarded it because they found it unsatisfying (MM 62, HM 343). This is in strict accordance with Lovecraft's loathing of the rampant mechanisation which was altering the whole structure of his society: "The future civilisation of mechanical standardisation of life and thought is a monstrous and artificial thing which can never find embodiment either in art or in religion" (SL 2.104–5). What, then, are we to make of the fact that the Great Race still maintains its mechanised society? "Industry, highly mechanised, demanded but little time from each citizen; and the abundant leisure was filled with intellectual and aesthetic activities of various sorts" (DH 399). Here again we must look to "Some Repetitions on the Times": Lovecraft had there suggested a rational distribution of work to solve unemployment; hence, given the "radically increased leisure among all classes of society . . . education . . . will require amplification. . . . It is probable that the number of persons possessing a sound general culture will be greatly increased, with corresponding good results to the civilisation" (CE 5.93).

The development of Lovecraft's views now becomes clear: when he wrote "The Mound" and At the Mountains of Madness, he still felt it possible to reverse the tide of mechanisation and return to the rural-based aristocracy of the past;[7] but with the writing of "Some Repetitions on the Times" and "The Shadow out of Time," we see that Lovecraft has accepted the inevitability of a mechanised future—though by no means sympathising with it—and feels that proper

---

7. "Granted the machine-victim has leisure. What is he going to do with it? What memories and experiences has he to form a background to give significance to anything he can do? What can he see or do that will mean anything to him? If he takes an aeroplane trip to the country, what will such a glimpse mean to one whose natural connexion to the rural landscape is hopelessly shattered?" (SL 2.308).

education and the reorganisation of society (particularly the abolishment of democracy and capitalism) could perhaps provide a meaningful and aesthetically satisfying existence. Lovecraft had ceased to want a *restoration* of the past, but now looks to *reform* for the future.

Lovecraft notes that "crime was surprisingly scant" among the Great Race, "and was dealt with through highly efficient policing" (*DH* 400). Indeed, the Great Race seems to be the only one of Lovecraft's alien races to have a police force: none is mentioned in *At the Mountains of Madness*, while the lack of one among the mound denizens is implied by the fact that Zamacona was given ten slaves to "protect him from thieves and sadists and religious orgiasts on the public highways" (*HM* 146). The government of the mound people must have been anarchical, indeed!

All the alien civilisations—with the exception, perhaps, of the Innsmouth folk[8]—seem to deal in warfare on a lesser or greater level; and the Great Race, the Old Ones, and the fungi from Yuggoth all battled one another in massive wars long before the emergence of humanity. All the races, however, conduct their wars in a roughly similar fashion—through the use of a vast army. The use of such a large force is interesting, for it implies the failure on the part of the races to develop weapons that—as with modern nuclear weapons—would render the use of large bodies of men needless. True, the Great Race has "camera-like weapons which produced tremendous electrical effects," but it also has an "enormous army" (*DH* 400). The mound denizens had sent a "suitably armed and equipped exploring party . . . to Yoth" (*HM* 141), while the fungi from Yuggoth "could easily conquer earth, but have not tried so far because they have not needed to. They would rather leave things as they are to save bother" (*DH* 218); and their battles with Akeley imply that they fight largely through the strength of numbers than through any powerful devices. It is true that the Old Ones "used curious weapons of molecular disturbance" (*MM* 67) against both the shoggoths and their extra-terrestrial rivals; but these seem to have availed them little, since the Old Ones were defeated not only by the Cthulhu spawn and the fungi from Yuggoth but ultimately by the shoggoths themselves. Lovecraft thus apparently failed to predict the revolutionary effect upon warfare which such weapons as the atomic bomb (the physical effects of which were so precisely if accidentally predicted in "The Colour out of Space") would have, for in "Some Repetitions on the Times"

---

8. There are, however, a few hints of the Innsmouth folk's warlike tendencies: their alliance with the shoggoths (see below) may imply that they use those entities for militaristic purposes; while the Innsmouth folk pursue the narrator in a "limitless stream" (*DH* 360), though apparently lacking any real coordination or organisation.

he continues to emphasise the need for "an army and navy of great strength," possibly involving "universal training" (CE 5.93). Of course, even today nuclear weapons seem to be used largely as a strategic tool, and the need for conventional weapons and a large standing army has by no means diminished.

All the alien races—the Venusians apparently excepted—practise trade or commerce in one form or another. The Innsmouth folk subsist on "fishing and lobstering. Everybody trades mostly either here [i.e., Newburyport] or in Arkham or Ipswich" (DH 306), and they also sell their "queer foreign kind of jewellery . . . on the sly" (DH 309). The fungi appear to do no trading with human beings, but have come to earth "to get metals from mines that go deep under the hills" (DH 218). The mound denizens once traded extensively with the surface civilisations, but "traffic with the lands of sun and starlight abruptly ceased" (HM 131) when the mound people gained a sudden prejudice of the men of the outer earth. Among the Old Ones "there was extensive commerce, both local and between different cities; certain small, flat counters, five-pointed and inscribed, serving as money" (MM 65). Trade among the Great Race is curiously not mentioned by Lovecraft, although it must have existed; perhaps it was conducted along the same lines as that of the Old Ones.

Aesthetic activity is high among each of Lovecraft's alien civilisations, although the fungi can only boast of their Cyclopean architecture upon Yuggoth. The Innsmouth folk produce a fascinating type of jewellery that "clearly belonged to some settled technique of infinite maturity and perfection," but which ultimately inspires dread in the narrator because it was "overflowing with the ultimate quintessence of unknown and inhuman evil" (DH 312). As for the invisible labyrinth on Venus, the narrator of "In the Walls of Eryx" is so impressed with its construction that he refuses to believe that the Venusians could have built it: "There must have been another race aeons ago, of which this is perhaps the last relique" (D 301). The art of the Old Ones "was mature, accomplished, and aesthetically evolved to the highest degree of civilised mastery. . . . In delicacy of execution no sculpture I have ever seen could approach it" (MM 56). As for the Great Race, "art was a vital part of [their] life" (DH 399).

The mound denizens are among the most interesting in this regard, for their whole lives are conducted in a quest for "pleasure-seeking" (HM 135)—the traditional perversion of Epicureanism.[9] Indeed, even their intellectual activities—science, history, and philosophy—seem to be carried out rather in the pursuit of amusement than of knowledge:

---

9. "Remember that the goal of the great Epicurus was not an earthly *hedone* (Hedonism), or pleasure, but a lofty *ataraxia*, or freedom from cares and trivial thoughts" (SL 1.87).

> Science had been profound and accurate. . . . Of late, however, it was falling into decay, as people found it increasingly useless to tax their minds by recalling its maddening infinitude of details and ramifications. It was thought more sensible to abandon the deepest speculations and to confine philosophy to conventional forms. . . . History was more and more neglected . . . [but] it was still an *interesting* [my italics] subject. . . . In general, though, the modern tendency was to feel rather than think; so that men were now more highly esteemed for inventing new diversions than for preserving old facts or pushing back the frontier of cosmic mystery. (HM 135–36)

Which view comes closest to Lovecraft's own—the quest for pleasure or the quest for knowledge? There is no denying that, on occasion, Lovecraft confessed himself more given toward the former than the latter:

> The truth is, that I am really most emphatically non-intellectual, if not positively anti-intellectual. I abhor mathematics, take no interest in feats of mental sprightliness, have no especial quickness of apprehension, and am certainly not at all distinguisht for holding in my head the many simultaneous threads of a complex matter. What liking I have for logick and analysis is purely an aesthetick one—a wish to *arrange* and *classify* things in patterns whose configuration shall possess, in the realm of ideas, that decorative *beauty of form* possesst by tangible objects of art and nature in the realm of matter. (SL 2.52)

I have already discussed, in a previous essay ("'Reality' and Knowledge"), Lovecraft's devotion to knowledge; the statement above—made, perhaps, when he was still under the influence of the Decadent philosophy of his earlier years, and betraying disingenuousness with its use of pretentious archaisms—can perhaps be contrasted with one made only a few years later:

> The process of delving into the black abyss is to me the keenest form of fascination, and it is my conviction that this process demands the exercise of those parts of the human organism which represent the latest and most complex degrees of evolution. I burn, I admire, I respect . . . and what I crave, admire, and respect is the pure and abstract abyss-plunging which enthralled Anaxagoras, Anaximines, and Anaximander. Dry, utilitarian mechanism? John L. Sullivan's ass! Don't make an old man hee-haw! I want the straight dope on the clear *is or isn't* proposition as far as it can be pushed, and a weeding out of all silly, unmotivated, and gratuitous guess-work and lie-faking in the unknown gulph beyond the present radius of the *is or isn't* searchlight. (SL 3.299)

It is clear that Lovecraft valued intellection for his own sake; and the inference we must draw from the relevant passages of "The Shadow out of Time," *At the Mountains of Madness*, and "The Mound" is that, in his mind, the Great Race and the Old Ones are significantly higher on the cultural scale for practising *both* intellection and aesthetics than the mound denizens, who practise a type of intellection *because* of their aesthetic tastes.

The conclusion is confirmed when we note that the normal activities of the mound denizens do not consist in intellectual activity but in "games, intoxication, torture of slaves, day-dreaming, gastronomic and emotional orgies, religious exercises, exotic experiments, artistic and philosophical discussions, and the like" (HM 135). The student of Lovecraft will readily acknowledge that few of these activities found sympathy with him. Indeed, the "torture of slaves" immediately brings to mind the gladiator displays that formed part of the *panem et circenses* of the later Romans: "[There were] many amphitheatres where curious sports and sensations were provided for the weary people of K'n-yan" (HM 145).

In the end Lovecraft condemns the mound denizens' lifestyle—and in the process declares his ultimate rejection of the Decadent philosophy:

> He [Zamacona] felt that the people of Tsath were a lost and dangerous race—more dangerous to themselves than they knew—and that their growing frenzy of monotony-warfare and novelty-quest was leading them rapidly toward a precipice of disintegration and horror. . . . As time progressed, he noticed an increasing tendency of the people to resort to dematerialisation as an amusement; so that the apartments and amphitheatres of Tsath became a veritable witches' sabbath of transmutations, age-adjustments, death-experiments, and projections. With the growth of boredom and restlessness, he saw, cruelty and subtlety and revolt were growing apace. There was more and more cosmic abnormality, more and more curious sadism, more and more ignorance and superstition, and more and more desire to escape out of physical life into a half-spectral state of electronic dispersion. (HM 147–48)

The significance of this decadence—as well as the less complete decline of the Great Race and the Old Ones—shall be examined later.

The final aspect of social life upon which Lovecraft dwells in his tales of extra-terrestrial races is religion. Lovecraft's views on religion are well known, and it is interesting to note that only the Great Race seems almost wholly free of religious tendencies. It is true that their "dead were incinerated with dignified ceremonies" (DH 399), but no religious connotation need be drawn from this fact. The closest that the Great Race comes to any sense of religion is a quasi-superstitious dread or "fear of the basalt ruins and trap-doors," since it was "the one subject lying altogether under a taboo among the Great Race" (DH 400). Even this fear is understandable, however, since the trap-doors concealed "elder beings" whose "successful irruption" would "one day . . . send millions of keen minds [of the Great Race] across the chasm of time to strange bodies in the safer future" (DH 402).

The Old Ones have not banished religion from their sphere of existence—a curiosity considering their supreme intellectual achievements. Not only do they regard the Antarctic as a "sacred spot" (MM 70), but their city has "great temples" (MM 74) and, "in the decadent days," they "made strange prayers" to the vast mountains to the west representing the "fabled nightmare Plateau of Leng" (MM 70). The Venusians, of course, seem irrationally to worship their crystals, not realising that they are a source of energy: "They have no use for the crystals except to pray to" (D 293).

The three other alien races—the mound denizens, the fungi from Yuggoth, and the Innsmouth folk—are all related in their religious practices, since they worship either Cthulhu ("Tulu" in "The Mound") or Tsathoggua or Nyarlathotep. Indeed, a strange linkage between the Innsmouth folk and the shoggoths is implied in "The Shadow over Innsmouth" (cf. DH 340, 367), and may confirm William Fulwiler's view that "The Shadow over Innsmouth" is a partial sequel to *At the Mountains of Madness*. Moreover, this connexion with the shoggoths—a species toward which Lovecraft has no sympathy whatever—further condemns the Innsmouth folk as representatives of a Lovecraftian dystopia. The religious practices of the three races are, indeed, quite odious in their superstitiousness, mysticism, and barbarity; and it is clear that Lovecraft is passing a negative judgment upon the races, as they show themselves to be similar to the "degraded and ignorant" worshippers in Louisiana described in "The Call of Cthulhu" (DH 139).

The religion of the mound denizens is of particular interest, and is in fact the key to understanding the decadence of the race. Lovecraft initially describes their religion before the decline set in: "Religion was a leading interest in Tsath, though very few actually believed in the supernatural. What was desired was the aesthetic and emotional exaltation bred by the mystical moods and sensuous rites which attended the colourful ancestral faith" (HM 136). This aesthetic religiosity was, indeed, approved after a fashion by Lovecraft, and he spoke of the Roman Catholic church in a similarly sympathetic vein:

> It seems to me—an atheist of Protestant ancestry—that Catholicism is really an admirable faith for those artists whose tastes are wholly Gothic and mystical without any mixture of the classic or the intellectual. It is the inheritory of ancient and beautiful rhythms of thought, cadence, and gesture which thousands of years of human feeling have woven symbolically and expressively around the various significant points of mortal experience; and as such it cannot help having a profound and genuine artistic importance and satisfyingness. It is the oldest continuously surviving poem of life that the races of Western Europe possess, and as such has an authority which no other one system of symbolic expression can claim. It seems to me that if one is to have an-

ything so extra-rational as religion of any sort the Catholic and Episcopal systems are the only two sects with enough roots and anchors in the past to make them worthy of the affiliation of the artist. (SL 2.104)[10]

But the mound religion does not remain in this enlightened and artistic spirit for long: "The more Zamacona studied these things the more apprehensive about the future he became.... Rationalism degenerated more and more into fanatical and orgiastic superstition, centreing in a lavish adoration of the magnetic Tulu-metal" (HM 149). As with the Romans of the late Empire (whose Stoic philosophy is curiously reflected in the mound denizens[11]), the mound people's increasing religiosity is a testimony to their decay; and they thus fully deserve the condemnation that Lovecraft the atheistic rationalist dealt them.

Lovecraft's attitude toward his own alien civilisations is not always clear, since we obviously cannot impute to Lovecraft all the remarks made by his narrators. "The Mound" is a case in point: initially we note a tone of sarcasm directed toward Zamacona for his lack of perspective and pious horror at the mound civilisation:

> Zamacona found difficulty in describing conditions so unlike anything he had previously known; and the text of his manuscript proved unusually puzzling at this point.... He himself never participated in any of the rites save those which he mistook for perversions of his own faith; nor did he ever lose an opportunity to convert the people to that faith of the Cross which the Spaniards hoped to make universal. (HM 135–36)

But as the narrative proceeds, more and more sympathy is accorded to Zamacona; and Lovecraft, after describing the decadent (or, rather, Decadent) lifestyle of the mound denizens, agrees with Zamacona's attitudes and identifies with him. In "The Whisperer in Darkness" the reverse is the case: Akeley is obviously Lovecraft's mouthpiece, and the reader's sympathy for

---

10. One wonders whether HPL gained this view from George Santayana, who acknowledged a belief in Roman Catholicism for somewhat analogous reasons. HPL had, indeed, encountered Santayana at this time (see SL 2.226). It may also be possible that in the above passage, written to August Derleth, HPL was attempting to deal gingerly with Derleth's own religious beliefs.

11. "Temples to Great Tulu, a spirit of universal harmony, anciently symbolised as the octopus-headed god who had brought all men down from the stars, were the most richly decorated objects in K'n-yan" (HM 136). The similarity to the Stoic philosophy—which also emphasised the brotherhood of all human beings, and which HPL probably encountered in the work of the younger Seneca—is striking.

him continues to grow as the fungi engage in increasingly vicious battles with him; but the final letter from "Akeley"—and particularly Wilmarth's meeting of the pseudo-Akeley—reverses the situation. "Akeley's" defence of the fungi—"All that the Outer Ones wish of man is peace and non-molestation and an increasing intellectual rapport" (*DH* 239)—only confirms our opinion of their loathsomeness; for to physical horror is added a sinister deceitfulness which makes all "Akeley's" words have a double meaning and which causes us to be repelled by them just as we are by the decadent mound denizens, the Innsmouth folk, and the Venusians. Hence only the Great Race and the Old Ones appear as "model" civilisations in Lovecraft's mind.

But not one of Lovecraft's alien races fails to inspire horror within the human characters in the story—hence, to a certain degree, in Lovecraft. The Great Race and the Old Ones, however benign and enlightened, are nonetheless a source of terror in the tales in which they appear. The fact that Peaslee "waked half of Arkham with [his] screaming" when, in his "dreams," he found himself in the "monstrous form" (*DH* 394) of his extra-terrestrial captor is a sufficient indication of the terror which the Great Race's *outré* appearance inspires in him; while the equally bizarre outlines of the Old Ones, with their "stench" and "noisome dark-green ichor," cause the narrator at one point to declare them not merely horrible but "blasphemous" (*MM* 95). We need quote no passages to convey the loathsomeness of the Innsmouth folk, the fungi from Yuggoth, and the Venusians: the narrators' distaste is evident on every page. Only the mound denizens—so uncannily like human beings for all their extra-terrestrial origin—seem to have inspired no horror in the narrator; instead, their ugliness is entirely moral.

How do we account for the horror that even the two "model" races inspire in Lovecraft's characters? Several factors must here be considered. Note, firstly, Wilmarth's comment in "The Whisperer in Darkness": "Close contact with the utterly bizarre is often more terrifying than inspiring" (*DH* 249). To this we may add Lovecraft's celebrated explanation of his predilection for fantasy: "I *know* that my most poignant emotional experiences are those which concern the lure of unplumbed space, the *terror* [my italics] of the encroaching void" (*SL* 3.197). All Lovecraft's alien races are, in greater or lesser degree, embodiments of the "encroaching void," and as such are a source of terror.

In a certain way, moreover, Lovecraft adhered to the dictum that "man is the measure of all things," that the human scale is the standard of measure upon this world; hence his remark in "The Shadow out of Time" that "it is not wholesome to watch monstrous objects doing what we had known only human beings to do" (*DH* 392). The belief connects with Lovecraft's political and racial views, and made him write to J. Vernon Shea:

The *primary* reason [for racial segregation] is simply a sensible wish to keep *every* settled culture (Nordic or not) true *to itself* for the sake of human values involved. No one wishes to force Nordicism on the non-Nordic—indeed, a real friend of civilisation wishes merely to make the Germans *more German*, the French *more French*, the Spaniards *more Spanish*, and so on. (SL 4.253)

While such a statement hardly indicates (as some have believed) that Lovecraft "feared" or even "hated" other races and cultures, it nevertheless helps us to understand that his narrators' terror at the sight of aliens stems from the latter's sheer difference from human beings—what the pseudo-Akeley called "man's eternal tendency to hate and fear and shrink away from the *utterly different*" (DH 238).

Furthermore, the Great Race is an added source of terror because it has robbed the narrator of his own body—although for no nefarious purpose—and thus forces the narrator to feel that "loss of identity" than which, as is written in "Through the Gates of the Silver Key," "no death, no doom, no anguish can arouse [greater] despair.... To be aware ... that one no longer has a *self* ... is the nameless summit of agony and dread" (MM 438).[12]

But in mitigation we can note that the horror inspired by the Great Race and the Old Ones lessens gradually as the respective narratives advance—to the point that Lovecraft can make his celebrated declaration that the Old Ones were "scientists to the last.... Whatever they had been, they were men!" (MM 96). Indeed, in both tales we notice that the horror is slowly transferred from the extra-terrestrial races to the even more *outré* beings—the Blind Beings and the shoggoths, respectively—who are their enemies; as Fritz Leiber said, "The author shows us horrors and then pulls back the curtain a little farther, letting us glimpse the horrors of which even the horrors are afraid!" (Leiber, "Copernicus" 462). No such mitigation occurs in respect to the four other entities concerned—the Innsmouth folk, the Venusians, the fungi, and the mound denizens. Instead, the horror they inspire grows at every moment; culminating in "The Whisperer in Darkness" with the pseudo-Akeley and in "The Shadow over Innsmouth" with the metamorphosis of the narrator himself into a monster.

* * *

---

12. This passage was originally written by HPL's collaborator E. Hoffmann Price (see his original sequel to "The Silver Key," entitled "The Lord of Illusion"; *Crypt of Cthulhu* No. 10 [1982]: 47–56). But the sentiment was frequently expressed by HPL elsewhere; indeed, the fact that this was one of the few passages by Price which HPL retained in "Through the Gates of the Silver Key" indicates his approval of the sentiment.

We must now give attention to Lovecraft's ideas on the decadence of civilisations. In four of the six tales under consideration—"The Shadow out of Time," *At the Mountains of Madness*, "The Mound," and "The Shadow over Innsmouth"—the alien races undergo a greater or lesser decline. It is now well known that Lovecraft quickly adopted the theory of the successive rise and fall of world civilisations as propounded by Oswald Spengler in *The Decline of the West*, the first volume of which he read around 1927 (see *SL* 2.103). The idea of decadence is so strong in Lovecraft that it has led some commentators to believe that he actually took a "pleasure uncertain even in himself over [the] collapse of [Western civilisation] and the rages of excess that the calamity would unloose" (Buhle 204). Barton L. St Armand (11) quotes the following letter as proof of Lovecraft's "fascination with decadence":

> There may be some—such as the 19th century decadents in France—who can derive a sort of pleasurable tragic exaltation from the picture of themselves as the crew of a sinking ship—a ship which is sinking, no matter how many other ships may later put to sea from other ports. To be a Psamettichus in a dying Egypt, a Lucian in a fading Hellenistic world, a Boëthius or a Venantius Fortunatus in a doomed Rome—there is quite a kick in the idea for those who like that kind of thing. (*SL* 3.41)

That such a passage reveals a "fascination with decadence" is clear; but that it implies a "pleasure" at the prospect is a more debatable matter. Indeed, the passage quoted above leads one to believe that Lovecraft would *not* have been one of those who might enjoy the experience of witnessing civilisation's collapse. In balance to the above we can quote his remark that "no civilisation has lasted for ever, and perhaps our own is perishing of natural old age. If so, the end cannot well be deferred" (*CE* 5.61)—a remark that reveals an historical awareness of the impermanence of any civilisation, from the greatest to the worst.

It is precisely this awareness that explains the decadence of the two "model" civilisations in Lovecraft. The Great Race, indeed, has scarcely declined at all; and Lovecraft's only remark to that effect is that its art had "at the period of [Peaslee's] dreams . . . passed its crest and meridian" (*DH* 399). The vast intelligence of the Great Race will prevent it from a wholesale decadence such as that of the mound denizens; and the species will simply transfer itself into the bodies of other beings as soon as its present habitat becomes too dangerous. This comparative absence of decadence on the part of the Great Race not only underscores Lovecraft's relative distaste for the decline of civilisation—a distaste that helps us to understand his remarks on racial purity—but again establishes the Great Race as the supreme example of a Lovecraftian utopia.

The Old Ones have declined rather more significantly: not only do they have difficulty in controlling their synthetic slaves, but "with the march of time . . . the art of creating new life from inorganic matter had been lost" (MM 67); they are no longer able to "sally forth into the planetary ether" (MM 68), and, like the Great Race, their art has become "decadent," although even "these latest carvings had a truly epic quality" (MM 75); they have even gained some of the irrational superstitiousness of the later mound denizens. The conclusion to be drawn is that the decadence of the Great Race—slight as it was—and of the Old Ones was due largely to inevitable historical forces.

It is quite otherwise for the mound denizens and the Innsmouth folk: their decadence is manifestly caused by a moral and social collapse. The mound civilisation declined because it reacted "with mixed apathy and hysteria against the standardised and time-tabled life of stultifying regularity which machinery had brought it during its middle period" (*HM* 149). As with the Great Race and the Old Ones, "art and intellect . . . had become listless and decadent" (*HM* 135). As for the Innsmouth folk, their decadence is, interestingly, due to the unnatural inbreeding instigated by Obed Marsh—we need not be reminded that the Great Race, the Old Ones, and even the mound denizens do without the normal forms of sexuality. But rather than engaging in superficial Freudianism, we may note instead that the Innsmouth folk's decline—labelled a "biological degeneration" (*DH* 314)—not only is similar to the decline of the Martense family in "The Lurking Fear" and the Catskill denizens in "Beyond the Wall of Sleep,"[13] but again indicates Lovecraft's desire for racial purity. Throughout the novelette we can detect parallels between the Innsmouth folk and the "foreigners" with whom Lovecraft was so concerned: the ticket agent remarks significantly that the fear of the Innsmouth folk by the surrounding populace is largely a matter of "race prejudice," and draws an important parallel with the Innsmouth folk: "You've probably heard about the Salem man that came home with a Chinese wife, or maybe you know there's still a bunch of Fiji Islanders somewhere around Cape Cod" (*DH* 307). He also makes note of the "foreign talk" (*DH* 309) heard in the Gilman House. The narrator once speculates, "Just what foreign blood was in him [Joe Sargent] I could not even guess" (*DH* 314), and goes on to say that the "people . . . had certain peculiarities of face and motions which I instinctively disliked" (*DH* 317), and, finally, that there is an "alien strain" (*DH* 325) in the Innsmouth folk.

---

13. It is significant that both the Catskill folk and the Innsmouth residents are given the label "'white trash'"; see "The Shadow over Innsmouth" (*DH* 309) and "Beyond the Wall of Sleep" (*D* 26).

What is more interesting about the Innsmouth folk is that their decline is not merely a "strange and insidious disease-phenomenon" (*DH* 321), but a sort of reversion to type. As Zadok Allen says: "Seems that human folks has got a kind o' relation to sech water-beasts—that everything alive came aout o' the water onct, an' only needs a little change to back agin" (*DH* 331). Hence the Innsmouth folk are returning gradually to the state which Walter de la Poer reached instantly at the conclusion of "The Rats in the Walls." On a political level we can relate this decline to Lovecraft's belief that miscegenation can lead to the collapse of civilisation: "It is easy to see the ultimate result of the wholesale pollution of highly evolved blood by definitely inferior strains. It happened in ancient Egypt—and made a race of supine fellaheen out of what was once a noble stock" (*SL* 4.230).

It is clear from the above analyses that, in the depiction of his alien civilisations—notably the Great Race, the Old Ones, the mound denizens, and the Innsmouth folk—Lovecraft was either making predictions on the fate of modern society or was creating enlightened cultures toward the realisation of which human beings ought to strive. A unified examination of each of these four civilisations will the more clearly reveal Lovecraft's intentions.

By all accounts the Great Race deserves its appellation as "the greatest race of all" (*DH* 385). They are unreservedly at the top of Lovecraft's pantheon of bizarre entities. The reasons for their supremacy are equally clear: they are not merely intelligent but are filled with a thirst for knowledge that is far greater than that of any other civilisation or race, and that is so vigorous that it impels them to make hazardous trips through time and space in order to learn about civilisations "from every corner of the solar system" (*DH* 395). Their political system—fascistic socialism with all its ramifications—is precisely the one Lovecraft declared to be the only workable system in a mechanised age. Art "was a vital part of life" (*DH* 399), crime and warfare were scant. Their only failings were a slight decline of artistic excellence at the time of Peaslee's visit and their fear—well founded, indeed—of the Blind Beings. They are the Lovecraftian utopia par excellence.

The Old Ones are not very far behind; for they too have a keen thirst for knowledge—especially science and history—and have a keen sense of aesthetics, perhaps greater than that of the Great Race. Their political system seems roughly akin to that of the Great Race, although Lovecraft does not describe it in any great detail. They passed through a stage of mechanisation, but ultimately rejected it as aesthetically unsatisfying; and now no longer use their knowledge, as Lovecraft sarcastically remarked of modern science, to "serve useful ends in a civically acceptable fashion" (*SL* 3.298). They have, however, declined more than the Great Race: their power to create new forms of life is gone, they cannot fly through space, they have become more superstitious, and their art has declined. Nevertheless, "they were men!"

"The Mound," the first of Lovecraft's major tales to include a significant amount of political and social speculation, is the more interesting because in it he draws obvious parallels between the development of the mound denizens and the development of modern human society. At first their civilisation seems as nearly utopian as that of the Great Race or the Old Ones: they have conquered old age, have the power of dematerialisation, use religion merely as an aesthetic ornament, practise selective breeding to ensure the vigour of the "ruling type," and—like the Old Ones—have abandoned a life of mechanisation. But this utopia very quickly turns to a dystopia. Lovecraft makes us realise the similarity of the mound denizens to modern American and European civilisation, then presents a bleak picture of the development of that civilisation:

> The nation [had] gone through a period of idealistic industrial democracy which gave equal opportunities to all, and thus, by raising the naturally intelligent to power, drained the masses of all their brains and stamina. . . . Physical comfort was ensured by an urban mechanisation of standardised and easily maintained pattern. . . . Literature was all highly individual and analytical. . . . The modern tendency was to feel rather than to think. . . . (HM 134-36)

The cause of their decline was obviously mechanisation—and, perhaps more importantly, their inability to overcome it as had the Old Ones:

> The dominance of machinery had at one time broken up the growth of normal aesthetics, introducing a lifelessly geometrical tradition fatal to sound expression. This had soon been outgrown, but had left its mark upon all pictorial and decorative attempts; so that except for conventionalised religious designs, there was little depth or feeling in any later work. Archaistic reproductions of earlier work had been found much preferable for general enjoyment. (HM 135)

The similarity of these remarks to those on modern art and architecture as found in "Heritage or Modernism: Common Sense in Art Forms" (1935) is clear:

> They [the modernists] launch new decorative designs of cones and cubes and triangles and segments—wheels and belts, smokestacks and stream-lined sausage moulders—problems in Euclid and nightmares from alcoholic orgies—and tell us that these things are the only authentic symbols of the age in which we live. (CE 5.123)

Lovecraft makes it obvious that it was precisely the mound civilisation's reaction "against the standardised and time-tabled life of stultifying regularity which machinery had brought it during its middle period" (*HM* 149) that caused its decline; adding significantly that in "bygone eras . . . K'n-yan had held ideas much like those of the classic and renaissance outer world, and had possessed a natural character and art full of what Europeans regard as dignity, kindness, and nobility" (*HM* 149).

These identical sentiments are found in Lovecraft's letters: remarking that "nothing good can be said of that cancerous machine-culture" (*SL* 2.304), he speculates bitterly on the fate of the masses in such an age:

> We shall hear of all sorts of futile reforms and reformers—standardised culture-outlines, synthetic sports and spectacles, professional play-leaders and study-guides, and kindred examples of machine-made uplift and brotherly spirit. And it will amount to just about as much as most reforms do! Meanwhile the tension of boredom and unsatisfied imagination will increase—breaking out with increasing frequency in crimes of morbid perversity and explosive violence. (*SL* 2.309)

Enough has been said on the rather different dystopia predicted in "The Shadow over Innsmouth"—a dystopia caused not by mechanisation but by unhealthy inbreeding. Maurice Lévy rightly remarked that the Innsmouth denizens could be seen as a "testimonial to the failure of America's politics of racial assimilation, a deliberate rejection of the notion of the 'melting pot,' which forms so integral a part of the American dream" (Lévy 61). That they so correspond with Lovecraft's views of "foreigners" is at least suggestive.

The political and social systems of the two other alien races here considered—the fungi from Yuggoth and the Venusians—is little described, and we can draw few conclusions from them. The former seem rather more highly evolved than the latter, who—despite their ingenuity in building the invisible maze—seem to have risen hardly above a primitive level. Rather than being reflections of the future development of Western man, they are pure embodiments of the "terror of the encroaching void" that Lovecraft sensed so keenly. They seem not quite as loathsome as the Innsmouth folk, but cannot claim even the few virtues of the mound denizens.

In conclusion, we can single out three traits which distinguish Lovecraft's higher alien civilisations—pure intelligence, sound political organisation, and aesthetic sensibility—and which in turn represent the goals for which Lovecraft wished modern society to aim. That these utopian concerns entered his fiction precisely at the time of the Depression—for "The Mound" was begun in late 1929—is of no small interest; and the extensive political, economic, and social speculation that fills not only his letters but his later fiction reveals the widening scope of his intellectual horizons. No longer concerned solely with Augustan England or Imperial Rome or colonial New England, Lovecraft consolidated his extensive historical and philosophical knowledge with keen observations of his own time; and, in "The Shadow out of Time," depicted a utopian society that—in brutal contrast with modern America—was as enlightened and aesthetically developed as the great cultures of Greece and Rome to which Lovecraft was ever allied and which he ever held up as great and model civilisations.

Works Cited

Buhle, Paul. "Dystopia as Utopia: Howard Phillips Lovecraft and the Unknown Content of American Horror Literature." 1976. In S. T. Joshi, ed. *H. P. Lovecraft: Four Decades of Criticism*. Athens: Ohio University Press, 1980. 196–210.

Joshi, S. T. *H. P. Lovecraft: The Decline of the West*. Mercer Island, WA: Starmont House, 1990. Rpt. Berkeley Heights, NJ: Wildside Press, [2001].

Leiber, Fritz. "A Literary Copernicus." 1949. In Peter Cannon, ed. *Lovecraft Remembered*. Sauk City, WI: Arkham House, 1998. 455–66.

———. "Through Hyperspace with Brown Jenkin: Lovecraft's Contribution to Speculative Fiction." 1966. In Peter Cannon, ed. *Lovecraft Remembered*. Sauk City, WI: Arkham House, 1998. 472–83.

Lévy, Maurice. *Lovecraft: A Study in the Fantastic*. Trans. S. T. Joshi. Detroit: Wayne State University Press, 1988.

St Armand, Barton Levi. *H. P. Lovecraft: New England Decadent*. Albuquerque: Silver Scarab Press, 1979.

Tierney, Richard L. Letter to the editor. *Nyctalops* 1, No. 5 (October 1971): 51.

Lovecraft and a World in Transition

For too long has H. P. Lovecraft been regarded solely within the narrow context of horror fiction. His philosophy, when it has been considered at all, has been either ignorantly scorned or judged by the standards of our own time and *Zeitgeist*. But Lovecraft was very much more than the greatest supernaturalist of the twentieth century; he was a man both of and above his time, one who adopted many of the conventional shibboleths of his day but also, through his strength of mind and character, transcended them and evolved a philosophy unlike that of any thinker before or since.

One historian (Barraclough 10f.) has singled out the very year of Lovecraft's birth, 1890, as the great watershed of modern history; it is precisely from this date that many see a new age of history begin, as different from the Renaissance, Reformation, and Enlightenment that preceded it as those ages are different from the ancient and medieval worlds they succeeded. Lovecraft and those of his generation were caught in this period of dizzying change—change that saw, in the next sixty years, two world wars, the overthrow of hereditary regimes in Russia and China, the emergence of mass democracy, and a profound disruption and alteration in intellectual and cultural history. Thirty years after the death of Tennyson (1892) T. S. Eliot published *The Waste Land*; fifty years after the Second Reform Bill in England (1867) the Russian Revolution occurred. However much Lovecraft tried to picture himself as an "outsider . . . a stranger in this century" (*DH* 52), the fact is that he was not an outsider but—almost in spite of himself—an acute commentator on his times. His fiction, moreover, reflects the changes undergone both in his own thought and in the temper of his times, so that his latest tales reveal a preoccupation with science, politics, economics, and culture which in his earlier, archaistic work he consciously eschewed.

Lovecraft was born in the presidency of Benjamin Harrison; Victoria would still reign for more than a decade in England. His response to the political and social issues of the 1890s and 1900s remain unknown: we do not know what he thought—if anything—of the Populists or the Progressives (when Theodore Roosevelt died in 1919 Lovecraft wrote an elegy on him, but his praise of Roosevelt as a strong leader is platitudinous), of the female suffrage movement, of the curtailing of the power of the House of Lords (1911), and other important developments. Lovecraft's attention was instead fixed on matters close to home. His views were initially shaped, almost passively, by familial and societal influence and by his early reading. When he remarked how he nostalgically read James Thomson's *The Seasons* in Quinsnicket Park (*SL* 1.90), he may not have been aware that this harmless indulgence in antiquarianism was also a reflection of that longing for the rural landscape which is still a part of the American myth, and which the Populists—a movement of the American farming class against the urban moneyed interests—used as the symbol for their campaign. The rapid urbanisation of America was something of which Lovecraft was virtually an eyewitness, as he saw his own birthplace, then on the outskirts of the town and bordering the rural countryside, gradually swallowed up by the encroaching suburbs of Providence.

Lovecraft's first real political consciousness is evinced in the matters of racial purity and the influx of foreigners to his native land. These views have become notorious, and much abuse has been heaped upon him for his alleged "racism." But the route to take in defending Lovecraft is not to deny the importance of these views—for it is clear, as we shall shortly see, that they entered his fiction from an early date—but to ascertain their origin and purpose. Lovecraft's opinions have been aired widely by hostile critics, but it has not been noticed how commonplace they were to the majority of educated people at the turn of the century. Moreover, the intent of Lovecraft's racialist views changed over the course of his life, so that in the 1930s he could tentatively embrace Hitler but not for the same reasons that he had trumpeted "Aryan supremacy" twenty years before.

His earliest writing is not free from the racialist strain. In "De Triumpho Naturae" (1905) the young Lovecraft could speak of "The savage black, the ape-resembling beast" (*AT* 33); in "Providence in 2000 A.D." (1912) he could satirically envision a future in which the "true" American would be singled out as a rarity amidst hordes of immigrants; in "New-England Fallen" (1913) he could write:

> The village rings with ribald foreign cries;
> Around the wine-shops loaf with bleary eyes
> A vicious crew, that mock the name of "man,"
> Yet dare to call themselves "American." (*AT* 388)

The prose-poem "The Street" (1920) is a transparent allegory on the future ethnicisation of urban America; "The Horror at Red Hook" and "He," written in the depths of his despair in New York, create a phantasmagoria of horror around the evil-looking foreigners in Brooklyn; and the culmination is "The Shadow over Innsmouth" (1931), where Lovecraft's horror of miscegenation and racial interbreeding is transmuted into a tale of cosmic abnormality where sea-creatures mate with humans to produce an appalling blight over an entire New England community.

Where did these ideas originate? Clearly they were inbred in him initially by his family: when the Lovecrafts were living at 454 Angell Street they had four black servants, whom Lovecraft later remembered fondly; moreover, New England long remained the most politically and socially conservative area of the nation, and the upper-class Bostonian's notions of aristocracy could easily lead to segregationalism. But just as clearly Lovecraft early began investigating the matter himself: "De Triumpho Naturae" is dedicated to William Benjamin Smith, author of *The Color Line: A Brief in Behalf of the Unborn* (1905). Some of his early essays on the matter are clearly influenced by T. H. Huxley, Spencer, and other Social Darwinists. But to Americans the issue of racial purity was at this time no longer an abstract one: the unprecedented influx of immigrants at the turn of the century—by 1910, 13,345,000 foreign-born persons were settled in the U.S. (Hofstadter 177)—was a source of great concern to "old Americans," especially since the immigrants came this time not from Ireland, Germany, and Scandinavia but from Eastern Europe, Asia, and Latin America. The key to Lovecraft's racialism—and, indeed, to the whole of his political and social thought—is not biology (save in the case of the African American, who was, as Lovecraft and many leading scientists of the day believed, demonstrably inferior biologically to the "Aryan") but the concept of *culture*.

Lovecraft derived greatest pleasure from "symbolic identification with the landscape and tradition-stream to which I belong" (*SL* 2.288). Lovecraft was a great *conservative* (hence the aptness of the title of the journal he edited as a young man), even when he adopted socialism at the end of his life. His great desire—a desire exacerbated by the accelerated rate of change in the age in which he lived—was to preserve as much of the past as possible, in the name of culture. It is easy to say that this position was a mere rationalisation of his early influences—his upbringing in a town filled with reminiscences of colonial days; his learning Latin and the rudiments of Greek at a time when these accomplishments were already becoming uncommon among the educated classes; his reading eighteenth-century books in the dusty attic of his birthplace; his early sense of dislocation from his own age—but, if so, the rationalisation was a singularly persuasive and intellectually challenging one.

Of course, his early views on blacks, Jews, and foreigners are very naive and dogmatic, and are largely the products of bookishness, sequestration, and simply an ignorance of the world. It is easy (and perhaps justifiable) to laugh when Lovecraft speaks of the "pan-Teutonic ideal" (*SL* 1.54); it is less comforting to hear him supporting the Ku Klux Klan. And his early Anglophilia (initially inspired purely by literature and the trappings of royalty and aristocracy so tempting to certain uncritical Americans) led him to condemn the Sinn Fein and Irish Home Rule movements and, as late as 1921, to make the astonishing statement that "the early 'English oppression' [of Ireland] . . . was never as severe as is popularly stated" ("Lucubrations Lovecraftian," *CE* 1.279). But his views on race and culture steadily grew more thoughtful with the years, so that toward the end of his life he could justify segregation in the name of cultural autonomy: "A real friend of civilisation wishes merely to make the Germans *more German*, the French *more French*, the Spaniards *more Spanish*, and so on" (*SL* 4.253). Perhaps this is merely a cover for segregation, but it is not an intrinsically vicious or ignorant stance.

Many have pointed to the paradox of, on the one hand, Lovecraft's theoretical anti-Semitism and, on the other hand, his marrying a Ukrainian Jew, Sonia Greene, and his friendship with the poet Samuel Loveman; but there is no inconsistency, and the answer is not to found in the view (espoused by his wife) that Lovecraft "hated humanity in the abstract" (Davis, *Private Life* 3) but singled out individuals for approval. Rather, his hatred for the Jews of New York, the Italians and Portuguese of Providence, rested precisely on the ground that, in his view, they refused to adopt the dominant Anglo-American culture of the nation and remained unassimilated, steadfastly guarding their own heritage, language, and traditions. It is because Loveman (an erudite scholar whose poetry revealed a sort of languorous, *fin-de-siècle* classicism that Lovecraft appreciated) and Sonia Greene had become Americans (or, more to Lovecraft's liking, Nietzsche's "good Europeans") that Lovecraft found their race little or no barrier.

In his preferences for political organisation Lovecraft again made it clear that the preservation of a rich and thriving culture was all that concerned him:

> All I care about is *the civilisation*—the state of development and organisation which is capable of gratifying the complex mental-emotional-aesthetic needs of highly evolved and acutely sensitive men. Any indignation I may feel in the whole matter is not for the woes of the downtrodden, but for the threat of social unrest to the traditional institutions of the civilisation. The reformer cares only for the masses, but may make concessions to the civilisation. I care only for the civilisation, but may make concessions to the masses. (*SL* 2.290)

Initially Lovecraft felt that a frank hereditary aristocracy was the only political system to ensure a high level of civilisation; but as the prosperous twenties gave way to the Depression of the thirties, he began to realise that a restoration of the sort of aristocracy of privilege, cultivation, and civic-mindedness advocated (and represented) by Henry Adams was highly unlikely, in the days of labor unions, political bosses, and crass plutocrats of business who had not sufficient refinement to be the leaders of any civilisation Lovecraft cared about. The solution for Lovecraft was socialism.

This is not nearly as much an about-face as it is sometimes conceived; for both aristocracy and Lovecraft's brand of "fascistic socialism" would eliminate what were for him the two great threats to culture—capitalism (because it brought to the fore the false values of money, speed, and calculativeness) and democracy (because it inculcated the illusion of justice and illegitimately extended the principle of equality from the legal to the social and intellectual realm):

> What I used to respect was not really aristocracy, but a set of personal qualities which aristocracy then developed better than any other system . . . a set of qualities, however, whose merit lay only in a psychology of non-calculative, non-competitive disinterestedness, truthfulness, courage, and generosity fostered by good education, minimum economic stress, and assumed position, AND JUST AS ACHIEVABLE THROUGH SOCIALISM AS THROUGH ARISTOCRACY. (SL 5.321)

The "fascistic" element in Lovecraft's system (he had in fact welcomed Mussolini's rise to power in 1922) would really be what he called an "aristocracy of intelligence": the vote would be restricted to those who could pass certain intellectual and psychological tests, and the actual government run not by "geniuses"—for there is no guarantee that an Einstein would make a good head of state—but specialists in political science and economics. While real political power would be restricted to the few, economic wealth would be spread to many, through government control of important utilities, social security, old-age pensions, and fewer working hours so that all who were capable of working could have an opportunity to work. The increased leisure time accruing from such a programme would be spent in increased educational and cultural activity, so that more people than ever before could enjoy the fruits of civilisation.

It all sounds very utopian; did Lovecraft actually think it could come about? Or was it the case that he—like the many others, from T. S. Eliot to Arnold Toynbee, who were strongly influenced by Oswald Spengler's monumental *Decline of the West*—felt that he was on a sinking ship, that the coming decades and centuries would bring only an ultimate collapse of civilisation and a return to barbarism? This view was certainly dominant in Lovecraft's thinking in the 1920s, and he arrived at it years before he read Spengler in 1926; in 1921 he had already written: "No civilisation has lasted for ever, and perhaps our own is perishing of natural old age. If so, the end cannot well be deferred" ("The Defence Remains Open!," CE 5.61). The major culprit, which evilly united with capitalism and democracy, that "catchword and illusion of inferior classes, visionaries, and dying civilizations" (SL 1.207), was (and here too he anticipated Spengler and many others) mechanisation:

But nothing good can be said of that cancerous machine-culture itself. It is not a true civilisation, and has nothing in it to satisfy a mature and fully-developed human mind. It is attuned to the mentality and imagination of the galley-slave and the moron, and crushes relentlessly with disapproval, ridicule, and economic annihilation, any sign of actually independent thought and civilised feeling which chances to rise above its sodden level. It is a treadmill, squirrel-trap culture—drugged and frenzied with the hasheesh of industrial servitude and material luxury. It is wholly a material body-culture, and its symbol is the tiled bathroom and steam radiator rather than the Doric portico and the temple of philosophy. Its denizens do not live or know how to live. (SL 2.304)

But again, by the 1930s Lovecraft finally admitted that the technological age was here to stay; and his socialism, with its plan for fewer working hours for all, took account of the fact that mechanisation had made it possible for a few to do as much work as it had taken many to do before. This whole shift in attitude can, interestingly enough, be traced quite precisely in some of his later stories: in "The Mound" (1929–30), *At the Mountains of Madness* (1931), and "The Shadow out of Time" (1934–35) he depicts various alien races and describes their political and social structure with some exactitude. I have elsewhere described this progression of thought—from an initial attempt to turn back the clock and return to the rural-based aristocracy of the eighteenth century to a frank (if resigned) acceptance of the radical changes affecting modern society and the hammering out of a political system that might ensure both the comfort and sustenance of all and a sufficiently high grade of culture for those able to appreciate it. It was not a system Lovecraft lived to see, for World War II—which he had in a nebulous way predicted as early as 1917 (SL 1.53)—changed the course of history once again and made his solution farther from realisation than ever, by temporarily bolstering precisely those forces of democracy and capitalism which Lovecraft felt were the harbingers of barbarism.

The progress of Lovecraft's literary work not merely is strikingly uniform—for there is no question but that his later work is systematically superior to his earlier—but reveals again a gradual, often ambiguous, attempt to bring his work up to date. Lovecraft's archaism has been vastly exaggerated: there is a difference between archaism of style (such as we find in that curious tongue-in-cheek story "A Reminiscence of Dr. Samuel Johnson" [1917]) and erudition of complexity of style (such as we find in most of his stories). Nevertheless, when we first see Lovecraft the writer he is a dyed-in-the-wool classicist: his first extant poem is a retelling of the *Odyssey*, "The Poem of Ulysses" (1897); the manuscripts of his very early horror stories employ the "long s," although otherwise they are not notably archaistic; his poems from 1911—the date of his revival of literary studies after a brief hiatus—well into the 1920s are competent but frequently lifeless imitations of his favourite poets, Dryden, Pope, Johnson, Gray, Poe; while the first story of his "mature" period, "The Tomb" (1917), is a faithful echo of Poe and contains a hilarious drinking song similar to (and in some ways a parody of) the poems included in Poe's "Ligeia" and "The Fall of the House of Usher." There is nothing in this story to indicate that it was written during World War I: it could as easily have been written in the Civil War, or the Seven Years War. "Dagon" (1917), on the other hand, is peculiarly modern in its use of modern science—in this case biology and anthropology (a glancing reference to the Piltdown man)—and its relative absence of archaism.

But from this point into the 1920s Lovecraft's fiction retreats into imitations of Poe ("Memory," "The Transition of Juan Romero," "The Outsider," "The Music of Erich Zann") or Lovecraft's new idol Lord Dunsany, whom he discovered in 1919 ("The White Ship," "The Doom That Came to Sarnath," "The Cats of Ulthar," "The Quest or Iranon," "The Other Gods"). The Dunsany influence reinstated to his fiction the archaic cast which it seemed—with such a "modern" tale as "The Statement of Randolph Carter" (1919)—on the threshold of shaking off. "The Rats in the Walls" (1923) is so quintessentially Poesque—it is Lovecraft's "Fall of the House of Usher," just as "The Shunned House" (1924) is Lovecraft's *House of Seven Gables*—that a passing reference to "the death of the President [i.e., Harding]" (*DH* 40) in 1923 comes as a jarring note.

It is as if Lovecraft required two brutal years in New York to bring him into modern world; for then his fiction not merely takes a radical turn for the better but the archaism of manner is shed like an old skin. "The Call of Cthulhu" (1926) is for the most part written in a cold, spare style like that of a scientific report; only toward the end, with the actual appearance of the hoary entity Cthulhu, does Lovecraft allow his prose (very calculatingly) to wax poetic: "There is a sense of spectral whirling through liquid gulfs of infinity, of dizzying rides through reeling universes on a comet's tail, and of hysterical plunges from the pit to the moon and from the moon back again to the pit, all livened by a cachinnating chorus of the distorted, hilarious elder gods and the green, bat-winged mocking imps of Tartarus" (*DH* 153–54). Lovecraft then wrote his two short novels in quick succession—*The Dream-Quest of Unknown Kadath*, where he has deliberately cultivated a playful Dunsanian archaism almost as a vast in-joke; and *The Case of Charles Dexter Ward*, whose modernism of tone is emphasised by the remarkably faithful reproduction of seventeenth-century prose in the purported documents of Joseph Curwen and his cohorts—followed by "The Colour out of Space" (1927), a sustained prose-poem that requires no archaism for its effects. From this point Lovecraft's characteristic work is modern and scientific—"The Whisperer in Darkness" (1930), At the Mountains of Madness (1931), "The Shadow over Innsmouth" (1931), "The Shadow out of Time" (1934-35)—to such a degree that several of these works have been seen (quite rightly) as forerunners of mainstream science fiction; At the Mountains of Madness and "The Shadow out of Time" even appeared in Astounding Stories in 1936.

Augmenting the realism and contemporaneity of Lovecraft's tales was his increasing use of topographical accuracy, particularly of the New England countryside he knew so well. While "The Tomb" is nominally set in New England, it is really in a sort of never-never land owing its background more to Poe than to Providence. It is only with "The Festival" (1923)—with its spectral re-creation of "Kingsport," a lightly fictionalised version of Marblehead, Massachusetts, that living museum of colonial New England which Lovecraft stumbled upon ecstatically in December 1922—that the element of realism enters the tales. From now on he tamed his Anglophilia and no longer used the conventional English settings he had employed in "The Hound" (1922) and "The Rats in the Walls" (1923). "The Shunned House" panoramically recreates the entire history of New England as centred on a single dubious old home in Providence; "He," "The Horror at Red Hook," and "Cool Air" make the clangour and heterogeneity of New York—which Lovecraft had by now learned at first hand—come alive; his trips into western Massachusetts are transmogrified into "The Dunwich Horror" (1928); his fondness for the hoary woods of Vermont is given a sinister turn in "The Whisperer in Darkness" (1930); in "The Shadow over Innsmouth" we can almost taste and smell the stench of fishy decay in a Massachusetts backwater. It is in these late stories that Lovecraft can claim to be the true descendant of Hawthorne, and his New England can take its place next to Machen's Wales, Hardy's Wessex, and Faulkner's South as one of the great fictional topographies in literature.

Lovecraft's poetry ultimately shewed a similar modernism. From 1922 to 1928 almost no poetry flowed from his pen: clearly his creative energies had shifted to fiction. Even some of this poetry reveals an incipient shaking off of eighteenth-century models: "My Favourite Character" and "A Year Off" (both 1925) have something of the flavour of Locker-Lampson and the *vers de société* of the later nineteenth century, and could well have been influenced by Lovecraft's friend Rheinhart Kleiner, a forgotten master of this light form. But then—suddenly—we come upon the sonnet "Recapture" (November 1929; later incorporated into *Fungi from Yuggoth*), which is so unlike anything Lovecraft had written before that both W. T. Scott and Edmund Wilson were led to suspect (groundlessly, as it happens) that in it, as well as in the other sonnets of *Fungi from Yuggoth* (1929-30), Lovecraft was influenced by the contemporary poet Edwin Arlington Robinson. But if we study Lovecraft's aesthetic thought of this time, we learn that the change was perhaps not so sudden. By 1928 he is already railing against the use of the archaisms, inversions, and "poetic language" which had cluttered his earlier verse. He had begun to realise that living poetry cannot wear the garments of a prior day and saw that his own previous poetry had merely been a vast psychological game he had played with himself—an attempt to retreat into the eighteenth century as feeble and pathetic as his longing for a periwig and knee-breeches. When he sent a batch of this old poetry to a correspondent he appended a very revelatory disclaimer:

> You will see evidences of all my various metrical stages—pure eighteenth century, pseudo-Poe-etry, and halting attempts at emancipation which didn't get very far from the standard models. Nowadays I write no verse except when forced to it by demands for elegies, birthday lines, and so on, which I cannot civilly refuse. . . . In all these verses you will note with ironic amusement that I freely use all the archaisms, inversions, and poeticisms against which I so constantly warn others! This is because I do not try at all to be a poet in any serious sense. My verse is simply antiquarianism and nothing more. And to other bards I give the time-honored advice—"Do as I say, not as I do!" (*Letters to Elizabeth Toldridge* 41)

This was only eight months before "Recapture"; and when he sent that sonnet to the same correspondent he added: "Speaking of my stuff—I enclose another recent specimen illustrative of my efforts to practice what I preach regarding direct and unaffected diction—a sort of irregular semi-sonnet, based on an actual dream" (*Letters to Elizabeth Toldridge* 116).

What had triggered this radical shift? There must have been a number of factors. Principally it was simply his realisation that the twentieth century was not a nightmare from which one could simply wake up and walk away but an age whose uniqueness demanded expression in art and literature; secondly, Lovecraft may have been struck by the brilliant poetry of his friend Clark Ashton Smith, who might have shown Lovecraft how to harmonise a selective use of archaism with a generally modern and vigorous approach; most directly, there was Lovecraft's work on a poetic handbook, *Doorways to Poetry*, for his friend Maurice W. Moe, and his reading of Donald Wandrei's *Sonnets of the Midnight Hours* (1927), probably the direct model for Lovecraft's *Fungi*. In any case, that sonnet series, while by no means radical, can take its place with the work of other conservative poets of the day—Rupert Brooke, Ralph Hodgson, Robert Hillyer, John Masefield, Walter de la Mare, and others.

Lovecraft had finally come out of the eighteenth century; but this did not mean that he either betrayed his earlier classical models or adopted modernist theories in any freakish way. In his literary theory he remained true, to the end of his career, to the utterance he had made toward the beginning of it: "the literary genius of Greece and Rome, developed under peculiarly favourable circumstances, may fairly be said to have completed the art and science of expression. Unhurried and profound, the classical author achieved a standard of simplicity, moderation, and elegance of taste, which all succeeding time has been powerless to excel or even to equal" ("The Case for Classicism" [1919], CE 2.37). Lovecraft's hostility to the poetry of T. S. Eliot, Amy Lowell, and e. e. cummings is well known; he confessed that he "had nearly fallen asleep over the tame backstairs gossip of Anderson's *Winesburg, Ohio*" (letter to Edwin Baird, c. early November 1923; MW 508), and yet this novel indirectly inspired a domestic drama of a very different order, "Facts concerning the Late Arthur Jermyn and His Family" (1920); he was distinctly cool toward the other realists of his day, Dreiser, Sinclair Lewis, Ben Hecht (the only virtue of his *Erik Dorn* was that "it contained a hatred for mankind which itself forms an unique and refreshing element in literature" [SL 1.283]); and he admitted that he never even made the effort to read *Ulysses*,

> because such extracts as I have seen convince me that it would hardly be worth the time and energy. Without doubt it forms an important landmark in the history of prose expression, but so far as I can see it is of theoretical significance rather than actual aesthetic value. It represents the intensive development—the concentration or exaggeration—of a literary principle which will greatly affect future writing, but which defeats its own ends of normally-proportioned portrayal when isolated and intensified to this extreme degree. (SL 4.14)

And yet, this somewhat backhanded compliment to Joyce is a clue to one of the most important and misunderstood features of Lovecraft's literary theory. The traditional image of Lovecraft—the one we think of when we see Virgil Finlay's exquisite portrait of him as a periwigged gentleman—as the eighteenth-century fossil completely ignorant of and hostile to the twentieth century ignores the fact that Lovecraft's real scorn (and here he is actually in comparative agreement with many modernists of his day) was reserved not for literary modernism—as early as 1924 he could refer to *Ulysses* and Cabell's *Jurgen* as "significant contributions to contemporary art" ("The Omnipresent Philistine," CE 2.77)—but for the age that directly preceded it, Victorianism, that "desert of illusions, pomposities, and hypocrisies" (SL 3.50). It was Lovecraft's nemesis T. S. Eliot who was influential in resurrecting the reputations of the Augustan poets (especially Dryden) in the twentieth century. And yet Lovecraft felt that his generation's backlash against Victorianism had led some of its members too far into radicalism—whether it be in prose (Joyce, Gertrude Stein), poetry (the Imagists, Eliot, cummings), art (the Cubists, the Dadaists), or architecture (the extreme functionalists). Lovecraft's reaction was ultimately more restrained: no one vilified Victorian hollowness more vociferously than he, but his solution was simply to skip the whole nineteenth century (at least after the early Romantics—Keats was the last great poet he recognised before Swinburne and Yeats; and of course there were Poe and the Decadents) and bring back the saner, more honest values of the eighteenth century. Lovecraft could quite rightly defend Augustan prose precisely because it was more natural and direct than either the floridity of Carlyle or the "machine-gun fire" of Hemingway:

> I refuse to be taken in by the god-dam bunk of this aera just as totally as I refused to fall for the pompous, polite bull of Victorianism—and one of the chief fallacies of the present is that smoothness, even when involving no sacrifice of directness, is a defect. The best prose is vigorous, direct, unadorn'd, and closely related (as is the best verse) to the language of actual discourse; but it has its natural rhythms and smoothness just as good oral speech has. There has never been any prose as good as that of the early eighteenth century, and anyone who thinks he can improve upon Swift, Steele and Addison is a blockhead. (SL 4.32–33)

But if Lovecraft's purity of diction brings the Augustans to mind, several other features show that he was tentatively led to break—or at least bend—the boundaries of the classicism he cherished. We are hardly in Dr. Johnson's century when we see and hear the narrator of "The Rats in the Walls" gibbering madly in archaic English, Celtic, debased Latin, and finally primitive apecries; *The Dream-Quest of Unknown Kadath* and "The Dreams in the Witch House" occasionally bring to mind certain conceptions of the most advanced Surrealists; and Lovecraft knew when to abandon formal prose and descend into a telling colloquialism (as when Lake, in *At the Mountains of Madness*, glimpses the tallest mountains in the world in Antarctica and laconically declares: "Everest out of the running" [MM 14]) or the barbarous dialect of the backwoods New England farmer. Who cannot fail to be moved by the poignant dying words of Nahum Gardner as he succumbs to the "colour out of space?"—". . . the colour . . . it burns . . . cold an' wet, but it burns . . . it beats down your mind an' then gits ye . . . burns ye up . . .ye know summ'at's comin', but 'tain't no use . . . sucks the life out . . ." (DH 71–72).

It is true that Lovecraft used dialogue infrequently (most of his dialogue actually resolves itself into monologue); there may be only random (and perhaps parodic) attempts to employ stream-of-consciousness; but his stated goal in weird fiction—"No weird story can truly produce terror unless it is devised with all the care and verisimilitude of an actual *hoax*" (SL 3.193)—meant that he was compelled at least to modify the classical ideal of "moderation" in ways of which Addison might not approve but which result in a realism—both topographical and psychological—whose power is rivalled by few.

Lovecraft is frequently not given credit for simply being master of, rather than slave to, his style. The Dunsanianism of his early tales was quite consciously adopted, and became openly parodic in *The Dream-Quest of Unknown Kadath*; he could write a Dunsanian tale ("Celephaïs"), a Poe-esque tale ("The Picture in the House"), and a "modern" tale of World War I ("The Temple") in a single year; and the fact that such an anticipation of his late scientific narratives as "Beyond the Wall of Sleep" (1919) preceded the height of his Dunsanian and Poe-esque periods should tell us that Lovecraft could write in the manner he wished when he wished.

What have we learned of Lovecraft at the end of this investigation? Principally, we have learned that he was a unique writer and a unique thinker. This platitude would be more interesting and closer to the truth if we said instead that he *became* a unique writer and thinker. His early writing—up to at least 1925—was heavily dominated by the literary influence of Poe, Machen, Dunsany, Blackwood, Hawthorne, and others in fiction, and Dryden, Gray, and Poe in poetry; but from then on he showed that he had assimilated these influences and added to them his distinctive "cosmic" philosophy to produce that unclassifiable amalgam we call a Lovecraft story. In his thought he was dominated initially by the influence of his time (in his racial and political views) and by that of the philosophers he had early absorbed, from Democritus to Ernst Haeckel; in later life, although he continued to read and be affected by the work of Spengler, Russell, Santayana, J. G. Frazer, and modern astrophysicists, his fertile mind was able to digest these influences and produce again one of the more original philosophies of our time. It was a hard struggle for Lovecraft to leave the ancient world and the eighteenth century behind—or, rather, to learn how these could be made viable in the twentieth century—but he ultimately forced himself to come to terms with modernity, whether in the form of T. S. Eliot or of Max Planck. His thought was evolving as dynamically as his work; his early ignorance of his social milieu had given way to a keen interest in the state of civilisation.

We may chide him for his praise of Hitler, for his remarks on blacks and Jews, for his generally bleak vision of the world and of humanity's place in it; but we can approach even these views with greater understanding if we study how he came to hold them. It is unlikely that Lovecraft will ever be considered solely for his philosophical thought, interesting and worthy of further explication as it is; rather, his greatness lies in expressing so distinctive a philosophy so brilliantly in fiction. The time is past when we can think of Lovecraft merely as a clever wordsmith or calculating spine-tingler; the intellectual backbone of his tales is now too evident to miss. Much work remains to be done in the analysis of his work and thought; and there are now not many who will refuse to admit that such a thing is long overdue.

Works Cited

Barraclough, Geoffrey. *An Introduction to Contemporary History.* Harmondsworth, UK: Penguin, 1967.

Davis, Sonia H. *The Private Life of H. P. Lovecraft.* Ed. S. T. Joshi. West Warwick, RI: Necronomicon Press, 1985.

Hofstadter, Richard. *The Age of Reform.* New York: Vintage, 1955.

Lovecraft, H. P. *Letters to Elizabeth Toldridge and Anne Tillery Renshaw.* Ed. David E. Schultz and S. T. Joshi. New York: Hippocampus Press, 2014.

Lovecraft and the "Big Issue"

In a recent article Wheeler Winston Dixon wrote: "Lovecraft is a minor writer, but a major talent in his narrowly defined area. This does not diminish his considerable talents, but placed in context with his contemporaries—Hemingway, Fitzgerald, Stein, or even Lewis—Lovecraft is clearly the smaller voice. Yet that voice is original and unique." It should be emphasised that this article was on the whole sympathetic to Lovecraft; and yet, when Dixon concludes axiomatically that Lovecraft was not a "major writer," he seems to be making certain standard and unquestioned assumptions about what constitutes great or serious literature. These assumptions, commonly made by many readers and critics, appear to be as follows:

1) "Major" literature must deal with the complexities of the human personality and human relationships, generally in a realistic setting;

2) "Major" literature must have broader philosophical or social or political implications (hence, one supposes, Dixon's citing of F. Scott Fitzgerald and Sinclair Lewis, whose work lays bare the cultural climate of the 1920s);

3) Horror fiction (or, as I prefer to call it, weird fiction) can never be "major" literature save perhaps—as in the case of Poe—when such writing focuses upon human personality.

I maintain, however, that Lovecraft was one of the first to rebel against the dominance of what might be called the *humanocentric* bias in literature. What Lovecraft was saying is simply this: Are human beings really *important* enough to devote one's attention to? If literature is really supposed to deal with "big issues," can the day-to-day activities of human beings—or even the whole history of the human race—be thought of as a "big issue"? To these queries Lovecraft responded with a resounding no.

"I could not write about 'ordinary people' because I am not in the least interested in them," Lovecraft wrote in 1921. "Man's relations to man do not captivate my fancy. It is man's relations to the cosmos—to the unknown—which alone arouses in me the spark of creative imagination. The humanocentric pose is impossible to me, for I cannot acquire the primitive myopia which magnifies the earth and ignores the background."

It is from this point of view that Lovecraft evolved his cosmic philosophy, and made it the centrepiece of his fiction. It is a truism that there are no especially memorable characters in Lovecraft; but by the rules of his own philosophy, there couldn't be. In 1934 he wrote: "Individuals are all momentary trifles bound from a common nothingness toward another common nothingness." I think we have to recognise what an enormous break with the prevailing literary tradition Lovecraft is making here. Could such writers as Dickens or Thackeray or Trollope—or Henry James or James Joyce or Virginia Woolf—have ever concluded that "individuals are all momentary trifles" or that (as he wrote in "The Silver Key") "the blind cosmos grinds aimlessly on from nothing to something and from something back to nothing again, neither heeding nor knowing the wishes or existence of the minds that flicker for a second now and then in the darkness"? For the warmth of human passion, Lovecraft has substituted the chill of the outer void. It is notable that, in grudging praise of his great contemporary William Faulkner, he criticises Faulkner's "philosophy assigning too much significance to the human personality and emotions." All this argues that Lovecraft came to his non-humanocentric vision quite consciously, and did so because the facts of science seemed to him to require it. Human beings *really are* insignificant in cosmic terms; should there not be a literature that reflects that fact?

The means Lovecraft chose to depict his vision of the universe was what might be termed the misanthropic tale of horror. As early as 1923 Lovecraft wrote: "Only a cynic can create horror—for behind every masterpiece of the sort must reside a driving daemonic force that despises the human race and its illusions, and longs to pull them to pieces and mock them" (MW 509). Lovecraft later toned this down, referring to himself not as a misanthrope or a pessimist but an "indifferentist" who didn't think that the cosmos "gives a damn one way or the other about the especial wants and ultimate welfare of mosquitoes, rats, lice, dogs, men, horses, pterodactyls, trees, fungi, dodos, or other forms of biological energy" (SL 3.39). Now Lovecraft's misanthropy was not the active hatred of a Jonathan Swift or an Ambrose Bierce; and of course this misanthropy did not emerge in personal behaviour (his unfailing courtesy, kindness, and generosity is remarked upon by all his friends). But perhaps bland indifference to human concerns was in the end an even purer form of misanthropy.

How do these attitudes emerge in his fiction? When we see Cthulhu rising from the waters ("A mountain walked or stumbled"), we suddenly find that human beings occupy the same relation to such a creature as ants do to us. If such titanic beings exist, how can we possibly believe in our own importance? We do not even have the virtue of having evolved to our present state of existence. Lovecraft is endlessly fond of postulating an ignominious origin of our species: in *At the Mountains of Madness* the Old Ones—huge barrel-shaped entities from the depths of space who colonised our planet aeons ago—appear to have created all earth life (including human beings) "as jest or mistake." In "The Shadow over Innsmouth" it is suggested that we are ultimately related to the loathsome fish-frogs that populate the sinister New England backwater of Innsmouth.

Lovecraft never passes up an opportunity to diminish human achievements. In "The Shadow out of Time" there is a hint that all the great geniuses of human history were really the result of a process of mind-exchange with a "Great Race" incalculably superior to us in intellect. The final impression we come away with from Lovecraft's stories is a brutal and humbling one. We are *not* the masters of the earth; we are *not* made in God's image, because there are no "gods" but only extraterrestrial aliens; the human race is destined to complete extinction in a few thousand or million years. A second ago in cosmic time we did not exist; a second hence the universe shall have forgotten that we did exist.

This is not a comforting vision, but it is the vision Lovecraft felt was the inevitable outcome of his philosophy. Even if we do not share the vision, we must still admit that Lovecraft had the artistry to portray it vividly and chillingly. In so doing he showed that weird fiction at least has the potential of rising to the level of great art, even if that art completely repudiates the "humanocentric pose." And no one can deny that Lovecraft dealt with "big issues," indeed the "biggest" issue of all: What are we doing in the universe?

Works Cited

Dixon, Wheeler Winston. "H. P. Lovecraft: A Critical Reevaluation." *West Virginia University Philological Papers* 34 (1988): 102-9.

H. P. Lovecraft: The Fiction of Materialism

> Now all my tales are based on the fundamental premise that common human laws and interests and emotions have no validity or significance in the vast cosmos-at-large. To me there is nothing but puerility in a tale in which the human form—and the local human passions and conditions and standards—are depicted as native to other worlds or other universes. To achieve the essence of real externality, whether of time or space or dimension, one must forget that such things as organic life, good and evil, love and hate, and all such local attributes of a negligible and temporary race called mankind, have any existence at all. Only the human scenes and characters must have human qualities. *These must be handled with unsparing realism, (not catch-penny romanticism) but when we cross the line to the boundless and hideous unknown—the shadow-haunted Outside—we must remember to leave our humanity and terrestrialism at the threshold.* (SL 2.150)

This landmark statement, made in a letter by H. P. Lovecraft upon the resubmittal of his seminal tale, "The Call of Cthulhu," to *Weird Tales* in 1927 (the story had been rejected a few months earlier), can stand as one of the central documents of Lovecraft's aesthetic of the weird, and it also justifies a philosophical approach to his work as a whole. Lovecraft is remarkable in having articulated a highly complex, detailed, and carefully considered world view that structured his entire work. This world view, which underwent significant modifications in various particulars over the course of his life, is embodied not so much in his relatively few and insignificant philosophical essays as in tens of thousands of letters, published and unpublished, in which he tirelessly debated points of philosophy and conduct with colleagues of both like and dissimilar temperament. It will repay us, therefore, to consider briefly the fundamentals of Lovecraft's philosophical thought before we attempt to see how that thought provides the underpinning for his weird fiction.[1]

---

1. In this article I have intentionally avoided any discussion of HPL's political philosophy, not only because it is extremely complex—it underwent more radical changes over the course of his life than any other aspect of his thought—but because it is not intimately related to his metaphysics and ethics, which are what I wish to focus on here. A political analysis, in particular dealing with the racialist element in HPL's fiction, would

I. Materialism

Lovecraft's early readings in the *Arabian Nights*, Grimm's fairy tales, and the tales of Poe (all of which he encountered before the age of eight) impelled a lifelong love of the strange and the bizarre; but almost coincident with this absorption of the weird were two other influences of equal importance: the discovery of classical antiquity—literature, philosophy, and art—and fascination with the sciences, particularly chemistry and astronomy. Lovecraft speaks of the significance of these two interests in a charming essay, "A Confession of Unfaith" (1922):

> The most poignant sensations of my existence are those of 1896, when I discovered the Hellenic world, and of 1902, when I discovered the myriad suns and worlds of infinite space. Sometimes I think the latter event the greater, for the grandeur of that growing conception of the universe still excites a thrill hardly to be duplicated.... By my thirteenth birthday I was thoroughly impressed with man's impermanence and insignificance, and by my seventeenth, ... I had formed in all essential particulars my present pessimistic cosmic views. (CE 5.147)

I shall return to that final sentence presently; what is important to emphasise here is how early Lovecraft's "cosmic" point of view—an awareness of the vast size of the known universe and a consequent appreciation of the relative insignificance of all human life when measured on the scale of cosmic infinity—was imbued in him.

In some ways Lovecraft's classical and scientific interests worked in tandem, for among his classical readings was the philosophy of materialism as embodied in Leucippus and Democritus and its ethical corollary in the philosophy of Epicurus. If nothing else, ancient materialism and modern science—the nebular hypothesis of Laplace; Dalton's analysis of the atom; the evolutionary theory of Darwin and Huxley; the anthropological work of Edward Burnett Tylor (*Primitive Culture*, 1871), John Fiske (*Myths and Myth-Makers*, 1872), and Sir James George Frazer (*The Golden Bough*, 1890) —allowed Lovecraft to slough off whatever remnants of religious belief his early upbringing may have instilled in him. In "A Confession of Unfaith" he speaks wryly of his pestiferous questioning of a Sunday school teacher and his eventual removal from the class: "No doubt I was regarded as a corrupter of the simple faith of the other 'infants'" (CE 5.145). Much later in life Lovecraft codified his religious views:

---

be very welcome. For some guidance, see my chapter on HPL in *The Weird Tale* (Austin: University of Texas Press, 1990), 214-28, and my lengthier philosophical study, *H. P. Lovecraft: The Decline of the West* (Mercer Island, WA: Starmont House, 1990; rpt. Berkeley Heights, NJ: Wildside Press, 2001).

> I certainly can't see any sensible position to assume aside from that of *complete scepticism tempered by a leaning toward that which existing evidence makes most probable*. All I say is that I think it is *damned unlikely* that anything like a central cosmic will, a spirit world, or an eternal survival of personality exist. They are the most preposterous and unjustified of all the guesses which can be made about the universe, and I am not enough of a hair-splitter to pretend that I don't regard them as arrant and negligible moonshine. In theory I am an *agnostic*, but pending the appearance of rational evidence I must be classed, practically and provisionally, as an *atheist*. The chances of theism's truth being to my mind so microscopically small, I would be a pedant and a hypocrite to call myself anything else. (SL 4.57)

Lovecraft defended his atheism in a spirited series of articles in 1921 (now titled *In Defence of Dagon*), whose scintillating rhetoric and logical force must be read to be appreciated.

Around this time Lovecraft began solidifying his entire metaphysics, reading such works as Ernst Haeckel's *The Riddle of the Universe* (1899) and Hugh Elliot's *Modern Science and Materialism* (1919). Elliot enunciates three main principles of materialism, all of which Lovecraft accepted:

> 1. The uniformity of law.
> 2. The denial of teleology.
> 3. The denial of any form of existence other than those envisaged by physics and chemistry, that is to say, other existences that have some kind of palpable material characteristics and qualities. (Elliot 138–41)

The uniformity of law means that the sequence of cause and effect is constant throughout the universe, from the smallest sub-atomic particle to the largest quasar or nebula. This principle is important to Lovecraft's aesthetic of the weird because the sense of imaginative liberation he sought depends upon it:

> I choose weird stories because they suit my inclinations best—one of my strongest and most persistent wishes being to achieve, momentarily, the illusion of some strange suspension or violation of the galling limitations of time, space, and natural law which for ever imprison us and frustrate our curiosity about the infinite cosmic spaces beyond the radius of our sight and analysis. ("Notes on Writing Weird Fiction" [CE 2.175–76])

It is important not to be led astray here: Lovecraft is not somehow renouncing his materialism—his belief in the uniformity of law—by seeking an imaginative escape from it; indeed, it is precisely *because* he believes that "time, space, and natural law" *are* uniform, and that the human mind cannot defeat or confound them, that an imaginative escape is sought. Lovecraft emphasises this point in a letter:

> The real *raison d'être* of [weird] art is to give one a temporary illusion of emancipation from the galling and intolerable tyranny of time, space, change, and natural law. If we can give ourselves even for rather a brief moment the illusory sense that some law of the ruthless cosmos has been—or could be—invalidated or defeated, we acquire a certain flush of triumphant emancipation comparable in its comforting power to the opiate dreams of religion. Indeed, religion itself is merely a pompous formalisation of fantastic art. Its disadvantage is that it demands an *intellectual* belief in the impossible, whereas fantastic art does not. (SL 4.417-18)

The contrast with religion is to be noted. If Lovecraft actually believed in the defiance of natural law—if, for example, he actually believed in the literal reality of his entity Cthulhu (as, regrettably, some occultist enthusiasts appear to do)—he would simply feel like a fool, since he knew that Cthulhu does not and cannot exist in the real world; it is, instead, a metaphor for that defiance of natural law which Lovecraft required as an aesthetic escape.

The point about teleology—the belief that either the human race or the cosmos as a whole is progressing toward some goal, usually under the direction of some deity—need not be discussed in detail: Lovecraft wholeheartedly rejected this notion, once accusing an adversary of misusing the theory of evolution to bolster a teleological view of the universe:

> He sees a process of evolution in operation at one particular cosmic moment in one particular point in space; and at once assumes gratuitously that *all the cosmos* is evolving steadily *in one direction* toward a fixed goal. . . . So when it is shewn that life on our world will (relatively) soon be extinct through the cooling of the sun; that space is full of such worlds which have died; that human life and the solar system itself are the merest *novelties* in an eternal cosmos; and that all indications point to a gradual breaking down of both matter and energy which will eventually nullify the results of evolution in any particular corner of space; when these things are shewn Mr. Wickenden recoils, and . . . cries out that it's all nonsense—it just *can't* be so!! (CE 5.51-52)

In Lovecraft's fiction we shall see this denial of teleology appear in some rather dismal predictions as to the humiliating petering-out of the human race and the eventual entropic decline of the universe as a whole. As early as 1915 he painted a vivid portrait of such a universe in an astronomy column:

> A vast, sepulchral universe of unbroken midnight gloom and perpetual arctic frigidity, through which will roll dark, cold suns with their hordes of dead, frozen planets, on which will lie the dust of those unhappy mortals who will have perished as their dominant stars faded from their skies. Such is the depressing picture of a future too remote for calculation. ("Clusters and Nebulae: Part II," *Asheville Gazette-News*, 6 April 1915; CE 3.311)

For Lovecraft, both philosophically and aesthetically, the most important aspect of materialism was the denial of "any form of existence other than those envisaged by physics and chemistry." Specifically, this refers to the existence of an immaterial soul, and Lovecraft has great fun demolishing theistic views of the immaterial and immortal soul:

> How may we . . . assume in one wild guess the existence of a whole world of entity, distinct from any provable substance, giving no evidence of itself, and independent of the known laws of matter? If it was hard to conceive of life as the product of lifeless matter, is it indeed easier to conceive of the existence of an airy nothing which can have no source at all, but which is claimed without proof or probability to hover around certain substances for certain periods, and subsequently to retain the personality of the substance around which it last hovers? (CE 5.55–56)

But for Lovecraft the whole notion is broader, and he wishes to deny the existence of *any* substance or entity not encompassed by current science. This point gains importance when, as we shall see presently, he is compelled to defend his materialism against the potentially threatening discoveries of modern astrophysics.

II. The Ethics of Materialism

Some of the ethical ramifications of Lovecraft's materialism are worth investigating here, as they shall have some bearing on our analysis of his fiction. I now wish to return to that curious phrase in "A Confession of Unfaith," wherein Lovecraft states that his awareness of the vastness of the cosmos and the insignificance of human beings led to his "pessimistic cosmic views." The fact is that there are several fallacies in his thinking at this point. Dale J. Nelson has recently remarked astutely: "Sometimes Lovecraft makes a category error: given the perhaps infinitely greater physical dimensions of the universe than those of mankind and the earth (quantitative), mankind and the earth are insignificant (qualitative)" (4n). Even if mankind's insignificance is accepted as a valid inference from the vastness of the universe, why should this lead to pessimism or misanthropy, as it seems to have done in the early Lovecraft? In fact, Lovecraft was at this time strongly under the influence of Schopenhauer, whose *Studies in Pessimism* he quotes frequently and with clear approval in his essay, "Nietzscheism and Realism" (1922).[2] Even later in life, when he had become more of an "indifferentist" and less of a pessimist, he was still adhering to certain of Schopenhauer's beliefs:

---

2. Actually, this is a series of letter excerpts to his future wife, Sonia H. Greene.

Ol' Art Schopenhauer had the straight goods—however you look at it, there's so goddam much *more* pain than pleasure in any average human life, that it's a losing game unless a guy can pep it up with pure moonshine—either the literal 95-proof pink-snake-evoker, or the churchly hootch of belief in immortality and a benign old gentleman with long whiskers . . . and a cosmick purpose . . . or else the Dunsanian conjuration of an illusion of *fantastick and indefinite possibility* as shadow'd forth in certain aesthetic interpretations of selected objective phenomena, time-sequences, and cosmical and dimensional speculations. (SL 3.139–40)

This is all very neat, and again shows the *unity* of Lovecraft's thought: given that life has so much more pain than pleasure, the option for someone like Lovecraft, who does not drink and cannot accept the opiate of religion, is to write weird fiction. This sort of cynical cosmicism made for an interesting aesthetic argument, as he wrote to Edwin Baird in 1923: "Only a cynic can create horror—for behind every masterpiece of the sort must reside a driving daemonic force that despises the human race and its illusions, and longs to pull them to pieces and mock them" (MW 509). Although Lovecraft toned this down later, he never wholly repudiated it, and we shall see instances in his fiction where this sort of misanthropy exhibits itself very powerfully. I have no wish, incidentally, to condemn Lovecraft for any misanthropic tendencies he may have had, since there is every reason to believe that the misanthropy of such writers as Swift, Bierce, Lovecraft, and Shirley Jackson has much philosophical justification. If nothing else, Lovecraft could express his misanthropy very piquantly: "Honestly, my hatred of the human animal mounts by leaps and bounds the more I see of the miserable vermin" (SL 1.211).

But, as I said, Lovecraft came to amend this view. A lifelong believer in Epicurean *ataraxia* ("freedom from cares and trivial thoughts" [SL 1.87]), he came to realise that misanthropy may be both a limiting and a philosophically invalid position if taken too far:

> Anti-humanism, in its extreme phases, becomes exceedingly ridiculous; since it assumes as many values of purely arbitrary unreality as does pro-humanism. Both attitudes are essentially silly and unscientific, since mankind is merely one type of matter among many, and no more to be loved and respected, or hated and repudiated, than any other type of matter. (SL 2.165)

This leads the way to Lovecraft's mature ethical stance:

> Contrary to what you may assume, I am *not a pessimist* but an *indifferentist*—that is, I don't make the mistake of thinking that the resultant of the natural forces surrounding and governing organic life will have any connexion with the wishes or tastes of any part of that organic life-process. Pessimists are just as illogical as optimists; insomuch as both envisage the aims of mankind as unified, and as

having a direct relationship (either of frustration or of fulfilment) to the inevitable flow of terrestrial motivation and events. That is—both schools retain in a vestigial way the primitive concept of a conscious teleology—of a cosmos which gives a damn one way or the other about the especial wants and ultimate welfare of mosquitoes, rats, lice, dogs, men, horses, pterodactyls, trees, fungi, dodos, or other forms of biological energy. (SL 3.39)

This is a brilliant encapsulation of Lovecraft's entire metaphysical and ethical philosophy: cosmicism makes both pessimism and optimism irrelevant because human beings are simply too *insignificant* to be worth bothering about.

I do not wish to suggest that Lovecraft wholly scorned all human concerns in his ethical thought; indeed, his later views—once he had sloughed off the extreme Schopenhauerianism and Nietzscheism of his early period—are in every sense broad-minded (except in the one issue of race), humane, and civilised. His urgent pleas for social and economic reform in the wake of the depression of the 1930s testifies to his anxiety for the fate of Western culture; and his evolved ethical stance, while still placing humanity on a very humble plane in cosmic entity, brings the humanism of Bertrand Russell to mind:

> Now since man means nothing in the cosmos, it is plain that his only logical goal (a goal whose sole reference is to *himself*) is simply the achievement of a reasonable equilibrium which shall enhance his likelihood of experiencing the sort of reactions he wishes, and which shall help along his natural impulse to increase his differentiation from unorganised force and matter. This goal can be reached only through teaching individual men how best to keep out of each other's way, and how best to reconcile the various conflicting instincts which a haphazard cosmic drift has placed within the breast of the same person. Here, then, is a practical and imperative system of ethics, resting upon the firmest possible foundation and being essentially that taught by Epicurus and Lucretius. (SL 5.241)

III. The Defence of Materialism

The year 1923 was a critical one for Lovecraft—not so much because it marked his entry into *Weird Tales*, the magazine that published the bulk of his mature fiction, but because it was then that he was no longer able to shield himself from the effects of certain advances in astrophysics, so that he was forced to modify his materialism significantly. First on the scene, as far as his awareness is concerned, was Einstein's relativity theory, one of the first blows against the somewhat cocksure materialism of Hugh Elliot and other late nineteenth-century thinkers. Lovecraft must have known something about relativity before 1923: Elliot himself mentions it with some perplexity in *Modern Science and Materialism* (38), and there is a very curious allusion to Einstein in the story

"Hypnos" (1922) ("One man with Oriental eyes has said that all time and space are relative, and men have laughed" [D 165]); but observations made during a solar eclipse in 1923 appeared to confirm the relativity beyond reasonable doubt. Lovecraft's response is perhaps typical of that of many intellectuals of the time:

> My cynicism and scepticism are increasing, and from an entirely new cause—the Einstein theory. The latest eclipse observations seem to place this system among the facts which cannot be dismissed, and assumedly it removes the last hold which reality or the universe can have on the independent mind. All is chance, accident, and ephemeral illusion—a fly may be greater than Arcturus, and Durfee Hill may surpass Mount Everest—assuming them to be removed from the present planet and differently environed in the continuum of space-time. There are no values in all infinity—the least idea that there are is the supreme mockery of all. All the cosmos is a jest, and one thing is as true as another. I believe everything and nothing—for all is chaos, always has been, and always will be. (SL 1.231)

Particularly interesting (and fallacious) is the ethical corollary Lovecraft draws from Einstein ("There are no values in all infinity . . ."). In a few years, however, he had snapped out of this nihilistic attitude and harmonised Einstein into a philosophy that was still broadly materialistic, but modified in certain important respects. Throughout all this Lovecraft is keen on preserving at least two of the fundamental tenets of materialism as enunciated by Hugh Elliot: the denial of teleology and the denial of spirit. As for the first:

> The actual cosmos of pattern'd energy, including what we know as matter, is of a contour and nature absolutely impossible of realisation by the human brain; and the more we learn of it the more we perceive this circumstance. All we can say of it, is that it contains no visible central principle so like the physical brains of terrestrial mammals that we may reasonably attribute to it the purely terrestrial and biological phenomenon call'd *conscious purpose*; and that we form, even allowing for the most radical conceptions of the relativist, so insignificant and temporary a part of it (whether all space be infinite or curved, and transgalactic distances constant or variable, we know that within the bounds of our stellar system no relativistic circumstance can banish the approximate dimensions we recognise. The relative place of our solar system among the stars is as much a proximate reality as the relative positions of Providence, N.Y., and Chicago) that all notions of special relationships and names and destinies expressed in human conduct must necessarily be vestigial myths. (SL 2.261)

It can be seen here that Lovecraft's denial of teleology is tied to his belief in the cosmic insignificance of the human race: if the cosmos were in fact evolving in some definite direction under the guidance of a deity, then there might be cause for thinking that a "special relationship" exists between human beings and that deity, something Lovecraft emphatically denies. As for the second point:

> The truth is, that the discovery of matter's identity with energy—and of its consequent lack of vital intrinsic difference from empty space—is *an absolute coup de grace to the primitive and irresponsible myth of "spirit". For matter, it appears, really is exactly what "spirit" was always supposed to be.* Thus it is proved *that wandering energy always has a detectable form*—that if it doesn't take the form of waves or electron-streams, *it becomes matter itself;* and that the absence of matter or any other detectable energy-form indicates *not the presence of spirit, but the absence of anything whatever.* (SL 2.266-67)

This is really rather clever, and it may even be reasonably similar to the modified materialism adopted by Lovecraft's later philosophical mentors, Bertrand Russell and George Santayana.

Lovecraft had a little more difficulty with quantum theory, which was hailed initially (as it occasionally still is) as spelling the downfall of determinism and even of the basic laws of cause and effect. Lovecraft does not discuss it at all frequently, and he never seems to have understood it fully:

> What most physicists take the quantum theory, at present, to mean, is *not that any cosmic uncertainty exists* as to which of several courses a given reaction will take; but that in certain instances *no conceivable channel of information shall ever tell human beings which courses will be taken,* or by what exact course a certain observed result came about. (SL 3.228)

Lovecraft wants to render the "uncertainty" of quantum theory epistemological, not ontological: he wants to believe that it is our inability to predict the behaviour of sub-atomic particles that results in uncertainty. This is in fact incorrect, as Bertrand Russell has pointed out ("There are reasons for believing that th[e] absence of complete determinism is not due to any incompleteness in the theory, but is a genuine characteristic of small-scale occurrences"); but Russell himself went on to say that "Phenomena involving large numbers of atoms remain deterministic" (Russell 23-24), something Lovecraft would have noted with relief. In terms of any ethical consequences—specifically as regards free will—Lovecraft would also have taken heart in J. L. Mackie's statement:

> . . . the crucial but so far unanswered question is whether there are processes by which random sub-atomic occurrences trigger larger scale neural processes and so introduce some randomness into them. There could be a forceful case for indeterminism about actions along these lines. But what it would give us instead of causal regularity is literally randomness, and this is not the kind of contra-causal freedom for which the moralists who dislike determinism are looking. (220)

In the end Lovecraft managed to take relativity, quantum theory, and even Heisenberg's indeterminacy principle in stride, maintaining the core of his materialist thought at a time when many others were lapsing into confused mysticism or wholesale scepticism. Recall that as late as 1933 he is still referring to "the galling limitations of time, space, and natural law" —by which he means the galling limitations of our consciousness to surpass or confound the laws of entity, laws that present such an obstacle to the imagination precisely because they are seen to be inflexible.

IV. The Fiction of Materialism

The relevance of Lovecraft's metaphysical and ethical thought to his fiction may not be immediately obvious to the casual reader, for his tales simply seem filled with outlandish monsters with unpronounceable names. And yet, the manifesto of 1927 quoted at the beginning of this essay suggests that his entire fictional work is an outgrowth of his philosophy, and that work can be seen to undergo significant changes of conception and purpose as his philosophy itself evolved in the 1920s and 1930s. Moreover, it was because Lovecraft was a materialist that he effected one of the boldest changes in the entire course of modern weird fiction, shifting the locus of horror from the terrestrial to the cosmic. It is this that led Fritz Leiber to call Lovecraft a "literary Copernicus."

Let us first notice that there is in Lovecraft's work a near-complete absence of the standard monsters of horror fiction—the ghost, the vampire, the werewolf. A ghost, with its suggestions of duality and spiritualism, would have been completely incomprehensible for Lovecraft—it is something to which he could not even extend aesthetic belief, let alone intellectual credence. The only vampire we find in Lovecraft may perhaps be the peculiar entity in "The Shunned House" (1924), and that story is worth examining for some highly provocative statements that already exhibit his coming to terms with advanced astrophysics. The critical passage is as follows:

> We were not . . . in any sense childishly superstitious, but scientific study and reflection had taught us that the known universe of three dimensions embraces the merest fraction of the whole cosmos of substance and energy. . . . To say that we actually believed in vampires or werewolves would be a carelessly inclusive statement. Rather must it be said that we were not prepared to deny the possibility of certain unfamiliar and unclassified modifications of vital force and attenuated matter; existing very infrequently in three-dimensional space because of its more intimate connexion with other spatial units, yet close enough to the boundary of our own to furnish us occasional manifestations which we, for lack of a proper vantage-point, may never hope to understand. . . .
>
> Such a thing was surely not a physical or biochemical impossibility in the light of a newer science which includes the theories of relativity and intra-atomic action. (MM 251–52)

Indeed, it is the very *materiality* of his monsters that is the trump card for the assertion of a unity between Lovecraft's philosophy and his fiction. The nature of their materiality is, to be sure, peculiar: Cthulhu, in "The Call of Cthulhu" (1926), is capable of reintegrating parts of itself that have been separated, and the fungi from Yuggoth in "The Whisperer in Darkness" (1930) may be able to travel faster than the speed of light (something Lovecraft knew to be impossible given the relativity theory). But there is nothing in his tales that stretches the limits of materialism beyond recognition. Indeed, the "vampire" in "The Shunned House" is completely dispatched by the use of hydrochloric acid, not by a cross and stake. Of course, in order for Lovecraft to receive the imaginative liberation he sought from weird fiction, his entities or phenomena *did* have to defy "natural law" in some fashion; if they didn't, the tale would not be *weird* but merely mundane. As Lovecraft stated in a discussion of Faulkner's tale of necrophilia, "A Rose for Emily":

> Manifestly, this is a dark and horrible thing which *could* happen, whereas the crux of a *weird* tale is something which *could not possibly happen*. If any unexpected advance of physics, chemistry, or biology were to indicate the *possibility* of any phenomena related by the weird tale, that particular set of phenomena would cease to be *weird* in the ultimate sense because it would become surrounded by a different set of emotions. It would no longer represent imaginative liberation, because it would no longer indicate a suspension or violation of the natural laws against whose universal dominance our fancies rebel. (SL 3.434)

This is why, from his earliest to his latest fiction, Lovecraft observed the laws of materialism except in one particular direction where a "violation" seems to occur, as in Cthulhu's reintegration of himself. This became a conscious principle in his later years:

> The time has come when the normal revolt against time, space, and matter must assume a form not overtly incompatible with what is known of reality—when it must be gratified by images forming *supplements* rather than *contradictions* of the visible and mensurable universe. And what, if not a form of *nonsupernatural cosmic art*, is to pacify this sense of revolt—as well as gratify the cognate sense of curiosity? (SL 3.295-96)

Lovecraft employed such "supplements" by creating entities that emerge from the depths of cosmic space (where natural laws may be very different from those governing our planet) or by setting his tales in geographically remote areas, where disproof is difficult. The very first tale of Lovecraft's mature period, "Dagon" (1917), is of the latter sort. The strange fishlike entity encountered by the narrator after the anomalous upheaval of a land mass in the middle of the Pacific clearly anticipates the emergence of Cthulhu from the depths of his sunken city R'lyeh in "The Call of Cthulhu"; but the palpable materialism of the creature is stressed at every turn. Later tales are set in the wilds of rural Massachusetts ("The Colour out of Space" [1927], "The Dunwich Horror" [1928]) or Vermont ("The Whisperer in Darkness"), in the Antarctic (*At the Mountains of Madness*), or in the Australian desert ("The Shadow out of Time" [1934–35]). But with exploration continuing unabated during Lovecraft's maturity (he speaks ominously of what the "Starkweather-Moore Expedition" [MM 5] may unearth in the Antarctic, and the whole of *At the Mountains of Madness* is a warning against such unwholesome curiosity), the hitherto unknown corners of this planet were slowly disappearing; so that Lovecraft had no option but to transfer the origin of his entities to the boundless depths of space. In so doing, he perhaps accidentally but very powerfully effected a union between the horror tale and the emerging genre of science fiction.

Cosmicism is certainly the hallmark of Lovecraft's fiction, but this feature manifests itself in many different ways in tales both early and late. Recall his statement of 1923 that "only a cynic can create horror"; this sort of cynicism, shading at times into actual misanthropy, may be the source of a celebrated utterance of 1921, when Lovecraft defended himself against charges that he did not write about "ordinary people" in his stories:

> I could not write about "ordinary people" because I am not in the least interested in them. Man's relations to man do not captivate my fancy. It is man's relation to the cosmos—to the unknown—which alone arouses in me the spark of creative imagination. The humanocentric pose is impossible to me, for I cannot acquire the primitive myopia which magnifies the earth and ignores the background. (CE 5.53)

This is a position that, with some modifications, remained fixed throughout his literary career, and in itself it constitutes a defence against the accusations of many critics that Lovecraft is incapable of drawing "real" characters. In the first place, he had no interest in such people ("Individuals are all momentary trifles bound from a common nothingness toward another common nothingness" [SL 5.19]); in the second place, characters who become too "real" or distinctive will actually militate against the perception of the vastness of the cosmos that was his aim. All Lovecraft seeks from his characters is that they be *representative*: that they allow the reader to see events through their eyes, so as to create a genuine and powerful sensation of the "violation of natural law." We cannot be concerned about their individual fates, for in the later stories it is the fate of the entire human race, the entire planet, or even the entire cosmos that is in question. It is also critical for Lovecraft's narrators to be, on the whole, intelligent and rational men (and they are all men): if these people can be convinced that something bizarre has happened, then how can the reader refrain from being convinced? It is for this reason that the narrator of "The Call of Cthulhu" notes toward the end of the tale: "My attitude was still one of absolute materialism, *as I wish it still were*" (DH 144). Here again one should not assume that it is Lovecraft who is renouncing his materialism: rather, the fact that the narrator cannot encompass Cthulhu within his materialistic scheme must mean that some awful suspension of what we know of the laws of nature has taken place.

Some of Lovecraft's misanthropy remained to the end of his life, and it emerges pungently in some of his tales. He is endlessly fond of postulating an ignominious origin of the human race: in *At the Mountains of Madness* the Old Ones—huge barrel-shaped entities from the depths of space who colonized our planet eons ago—appear to have created all earth life (including human beings) "as jest or mistake" (MM 22). When the narrators explore the millennia-abandoned city of the Old Ones in the Antarctic, they find bas-reliefs supplying a detailed history of the alien race on this planet; at one point they remark: "It interested us to see in some of the very last and most decadent sculptures a shambling primitive mammal, used sometimes for food and sometimes as an amusing buffoon by the land dwellers, whose vaguely simian and human foreshadowings were unmistakable" (MM 65). This is probably one of the most fiercely cynical and misanthropic utterances ever made: the degradation of humanity can go no further. In "The Shadow over Innsmouth" (1931) it is suggested that we are ultimately related to the loathsome fish-frogs that populate that sinister New England backwater; as Zadok Allen tells the narrator: "'Seems that human folks has got a kind o' relation to sech water-beasts—that everything alive came aout o' the water onct, an' only needs a little change to go back agin'" (DH 331). Here again the guiding principle is the utter decimation of human self-importance by the attribution of a grotesque or contemptible origin of our species.

Lovecraft rarely passes up an opportunity to diminish human achievements. In many tales it is suggested that all the accomplishments of human civilisation are as nothing when gauged against the incalculably greater works of the alien civilisations that have occupied—and will in the future, after humanity's demise, occupy—the planet. In "The Shadow out of Time" there is a hint that all the great geniuses of human history were really the result of a process of mind-exchange with a "Great Race" inconceivably superior to us in intellect. When the narrator of this tale stumbles upon the archives of the Great Race, where repose the histories of all the varied entities throughout the universe, the narrator's account lies in the "lowest or vertebrate level" (DH 396). Here not only humanity but nearly all earthly life is seen to occupy a derisively inferior status in the realm of cosmic entity.

Those of Lovecraft's alien races who still inhabit the dark corners of our

H. P. Lovecraft: The Fiction of Materialism 173

planet are not cowering in fear of humanity; indeed, they are allowing *us* to dwell on this planet by *their* sufferance. Of the fungi from Yuggoth in "The Whisperer in Darkness" it is said: "They could easily conquer the earth, but have not tried to so far because they have not needed to. They would rather leave things as they are to save bother" (*DH* 218). It is not even worth their while to destroy us. The hybrid entities of "The Shadow over Innsmouth" feel superiority to human beings: "They seemed sullenly banded together in some sort of fellowship and understanding—despising the world as if they had access to other and preferable spheres of entity" (*DH* 321). And Zadok Allen lets us know of their power: "'They cud wipe aout the hull brood o' humans ef they was willin' to bother'" (*DH* 331).

Even when Lovecraft modified his misanthropy into "indifferentism," a certain anti-humanist bias remained: his canonical statement of 1927 still refers to "a negligible and temporary race called mankind." We can finally address that statement and its manifold implications. On the surface, Lovecraft is simply noting that alien entities, if they are said to have emerged from the cosmic void, should not have human attributes. This seems to us unexceptionable, but we must recall that Lovecraft was battling against a tidal wave of naive science fiction of the "space opera" type that was achieving widespread publication in the pulp magazines. As he remarked in "Some Notes on Interplanetary Fiction" (1935): "The human-like aspect, psychology, and proper names commonly attributed to other-planetarians by the bulk of cheap authors is at once hilarious and pathetic" (*CE* 2.181). The absurdity of naming an entity "Cthulhu" vanishes when placed in this perspective; it is a name that, as Lovecraft frequented noted in letters, "was invented by beings whose vocal organs were not like man's . . . *hence could never be uttered perfectly by human throats*" (*SL* 5.10–11). Why should such an extraterrestrial entity have a humanoid name? Such names as Yog-Sothoth, Azathoth, and Nyarlathotep are less exotic, and their roots in Arabic, Egyptian, and other languages has been traced; but this does not mean that these entities are Arabic or Egyptian, but rather that their names were set down in this approximate fashion by ancient Arabic and Egyptian scholars such as Abdul Alhazred, author of the *Necronomicon*. Lovecraft takes extraordinary care in nomenclature, a care he learnt from his mentor Lord Dunsany.

But what Lovecraft is really claiming in his statement of 1927 is a sort of moral independence of his alien entities from any sort of human psychology or motivation. They cannot—or at least need not be—motivated by "good and evil, love and hate, and all such local attributes" of the human race. This is why it is stated, in reference to the entity in "The Shunned House": "It might be actively hostile, or it might be dictated merely by blind motives of self-preservation" (*MM* 252). It is, however, not a contradiction for Lovecraft's character to add: "In any case such a monster must of necessity be in our scheme of things an anomaly and an intruder, whose extirpation forms a primary duty with every man not an enemy to the world's life, health, and sanity" (MM 252). This is the human perspective on the matter: of course, in "our scheme of things," we must destroy this entity, lest it destroy us; but nothing is said about the moral superiority or inferiority of the entity in relation to human beings.

Similarly, what is it that Cthulhu actually wants when it emerges from the waves? To be sure, his human followers foresee an overthrow of mankind upon Cthulhu's release:

> . . . then mankind would have become as the Great Old Ones; free and wild and beyond good and evil, with laws and morals thrown aside and all men shouting and killing and revelling in joy. Then the liberated Old Ones would teach them new ways to shout and kill and revel and enjoy themselves, and all the earth would flame with a holocaust of ecstasy and freedom. (DH 141)

But can these emotions be attributed to Cthulhu? This is doubtful, even though the narrator, paraphrasing the account of an encounter with Cthulhu by a hapless Norwegian sailor, states: "After vigintillions of years great Cthulhu was loose again, and ravening for delight" (DH 152). But there is no reason to believe that either the narrator or the sailor is correct in attributing such motives to Cthulhu. Indeed, it should be remarked that all the cult-followers of the alien entities in Lovecraft's fiction appear to be on the whole misguided as to the nature and purpose of the creatures they worship. In particular, they assume that such creatures are gods, when by and large they appear to be simply extraterrestrials who have come into contact with the earth and its denizens by accident. An entity like Azathoth, "that last amorphous blight of nethermost confusion which blasphemes and bubbles at the centre of all infinity" (MM 308), seems nothing more than a symbol for the unknowability of a boundless cosmos.

Lovecraft's most successful portrayal of an amoral entity—or, rather, an entity whose motivations human beings are wholly at a loss to fathom—is in his masterpiece of subtlety and atmosphere, "The Colour out of Space" (1927). This landmark tale of a creature—or perhaps a group of creatures—that comes to the earth when a meteorite lands in the property of a rustic Massachusetts farmer and slowly corrupts everything it encounters, is horrifying precisely because the entity exhibits none of the traits attributable to any sentient being on this planet or perhaps in the known universe. Consider the poignant dying utterance of Nahum Gardner, the farmer whose land and family is inexorably destroyed by this alien force:

> "'. . . the colour . . . it burns . . . cold an' wet, but it burns . . . it lived in the well . . . I seen it . . . a kind o' smoke . . . suckin' the life out of everything . . . it must

a' come in that stone . . . pizened the whole place . . . dun't know what it wants . . . it beats down your mind an' then gits ye . . . burns ye up . . . can't git away . . . draws ye . . . ye know summ'at's comin', but 'tain't no use . . . it come from some place whar things ain't as they is here . . .'" (*DH* 71–72)

In the midst of frank admissions of the incomprehensibility of the entity's motives ("'dun't know what it wants'"), its paradoxical nature ("'cold an' wet, but it burns'"), and an awareness of its utterly non-mundane origin ("'it come from some place whar things ain't as they is here'"), Gardner can still not help pitiably anthropomorphising the creature, as does a character later on: "'it come from beyond, whar things ain't like they be here . . . now it's goin' home . . .'" (*DH* 77). The expression of these sentiments in the crude patois of rustics only augments the horror and the tragedy.

Alien entities in Lovecraft's later tales, curiously, seem more motivated by comprehensible—and reprehensible—human motives than these. There can hardly be a doubt that the monster in "The Dunwich Horror" is impelled by blind rage against the human race, and when Professor Henry Armitage dispatches the creature by implausibly muttering some sort or counter-incantation, he delivers a naive and bombastic moral lecture:

> "It was—well, it was mostly a kind of force that doesn't belong in our part of space; a kind of force that acts and grows and shapes itself by other laws than those of our sort of Nature. We have no business calling in such things from outside, and only very wicked people and very wicked cults ever try to." (*DH* 197)

The purport of this passage is perhaps subject to debate. I would very much like to see it, as Donald R. Burleson has, as a parody, but I have my doubts about the matter. Armitage is very similar in function to Dr. Willett of *The Case of Charles Dexter Ward* (1927), who utters a similar sort of moral catechism to Joseph Curwen. Curwen, who has devoted his life to the resurrection of the dead in order to drain whatever knowledge their "essential salts" may contain, remarks in defence of his actions: "'There is no evil to any in what I do, so long as I do it rightly'" (*MM* 181), an amusing appeal to moral relativism; but we are clearly meant to side with Willett on the matter, who notes harshly: "'Curwen, a man can't tamper with Nature beyond certain limits, and every horror you have woven will rise up to wipe you out'" (*MM* 233). This attribution of pure evil to Curwen may be plausible, in that Curwen is indeed a human being even if he has by sorcery far exceeded his rightful tenure on this planet; but the similar attribution to the "very wicked people and very wicked cults" who "called in" the Dunwich horror strains credulity. "The Dunwich Horror" is, indeed, in spite of its evident popularity with readers, one of Lovecraft's great failures in its clumsy moral didacticism and ludicrous use of white magic versus black magic; it is exactly the sort of pulpish tripe Lovecraft so despised in the pages of *Weird Tales*.

"The Whisperer in Darkness" is similarly troubled by a peculiar ambivalence in the portrayal of its alien entities. These creatures, the fungi from Yuggoth, have clearly come from the depths of space—indeed, Yuggoth (Pluto) is not even their place of origin but only their "main *immediate* abode" (*DH* 240). And yet, they seem strangely motivated by such conventional moral failings as violence and treachery. They engage in a furious—and somewhat comical—battle, involving guns and dogs, with Henry Wentworth Akeley, an isolated Vermont rustic who resists their attempts to remove his brain from his body and take it with them on vast cosmic voyagings. Then at one point Albert Wilmarth, who has been trying to assist Akeley through correspondence, receives a letter from Akeley stating that the hostilities are over and that he has become reconciled to his erstwhile foes.

> All that the Outer Ones wish of man is peace and non-molestation and an increasing intellectual rapport. This latter is absolutely necessary now that our inventions and devices are expanding our knowledge and motions, and making it more and more impossible for the Outer Ones' necessary outposts to exist *secretly* on this planet. The alien beings desire to know mankind more fully and to have a few of mankind's philosophic and scientific leaders know more about them. With such an exchange of knowledge all perils will pass, and a satisfactory *modus vivendi* be established. The very idea of any attempt to *enslave* or *degrade* mankind is ridiculous. (*DH* 239)

On the face of it this idea sounds perfectly rational; but, since this letter is not in fact written by Akeley but forged by one of the aliens, it is in reality a sort of slick attempt to pull the wool over Wilmarth's eyes to prevent him from disseminating information about the entities. The aliens, even though "their brain-capacity exceeds that of any other surviving life-form" (*DH* 240), do not even seem very adept at forgery, as earlier they had sent a telegram to Wilmarth but misspelled Akeley's name (*DH* 232). "The Whisperer in Darkness" is still one of Lovecraft's great tales, full of a densely textured atmosphere derived from realistic but poetic descriptions of the dark woods of Vermont; but he does not appear to have been entirely clear on the motivations of his alien entities.

But with *At the Mountains of Madness* and "The Shadow out of Time" all such problems have passed. In both instances the extraterrestrial entities are *initially* presented as horrifying—although only from a human perspective, and only because of their extreme *difference* in appearance from human beings—but gradually they become, as it were, the "heroes" of the tale as opposed to entities still more alien than they. Who can forget that paean to the Old Ones delivered by the narrator after he has seen what a rich, flourishing civilisation they once had on the Antarctic, and understood that their prime motivation was a pure and disinterested pursuit of knowledge?

> Scientists to the last—what had they done that we would not have done in their place? God, what intelligence and persistence! What a facing of the incredible, just as those carven kinsmen and forbears had faced things only a little less incredible! Radiates, vegetables, monstrosities, star-spawn—whatever they had been, they were men! (MM 96)

It certainly does not appear as if "men" are a "negligible and temporary race" here. In "The Shadow out of Time" the pattern is completed. The Great Race "had learned all things that ever were known or ever would be known on the earth" (*DH* 385); they are the supreme entities in the universe. It is true that, early in the tale, the narrator is filled with horror and loathing as he sees them in his dreams: "Their actions, though harmless, horrified me even more than their appearance—for it is not wholesome to watch monstrous objects doing what one had known only human beings to do" (*DH* 392). But this fear dissipates once the narrator learns that the Great Race does the things that only human beings are supposed to do—reading, writing, speaking, learning—far better than we.

Lovecraft's belittling of the human race might be called the negative side of his cosmicism; on the positive side he is capable of suggesting the vast gulfs of space and time as powerfully as any writer in the history of literature. Again *At the Mountains of Madness* and "The Shadow out of Time" are the two masterworks here, and the fact that both appeared in *Astounding Stories* shows what an exquisite union of horror and science fiction Lovecraft has accomplished in these lengthy tales. Indeed, length is one of their important features; for Lovecraft was among the first to realise the value of the novelette or short novel form for the expression of complex weird scenarios. Incredibly, his first draft of "The Shadow out of Time" was a mere sixteen pages (*SL* 5.71), and he rightly discarded this version in lieu of one approximately four times as long. What this length allows a writer like Lovecraft—who, let us recall, does not rely upon character but atmosphere to sustain a tale—is to develop the plot with enormous richness but without destroying that unity of effect which he, like Poe, felt essential to the short story. In both tales we have extensive discourses on the biology, history, and even politics of his alien species, as well as a compact history of the entire cosmos, beginning millions of years before humanity's emergence on this planet and continuing long after the human race shall have ceased to exist. Indeed, at one point the narrator of "The Shadow out of Time" writes harriedly: "What was hinted . . . of the fate of mankind produced such an effect on me that I will not set it down here"

(*DH* 396). This single sentence casts such a cloud of doom upon the future of humanity that all our achievements seem trivial and futile.

V. Style

In conclusion I wish to address an issue that is not directly connected to the philosophy of Lovecraft's fiction, but one that has evidently led many critics to condemn his work out of hand. Edmund Wilson was among the first to dismiss Lovecraft's stories as "bad taste and bad art" (47), largely because of his style. This criticism has, with little variation, been made on many occasions, and Jacques Barzun has referred to the "frequently portentous but unintelligible H. P. Lovecraft" (xxvi), a remark that unwittingly testifies to nothing more than Barzun's inability to understand Lovecraft.

There is no denying that Lovecraft evolved a very idiosyncratic style to express his horrific conceptions—a style that is a union of the stateliness of the eighteenth century ("I suppose I picked up my peculiar style from Addison, Steele, Johnson, and Gibbon" [*SL* 1.11]), the atmospheric floridity of Poe and Wilde (the latter a much ignored but very significant influence on Lovecraft's style as well as on his entire aesthetic theory), and the precision of nineteenth- and twentieth-century philosophic writing. But what is forgotten in all this is, firstly, that Lovecraft's style actually *works*—it is as appropriate to his subject-matter as any style can be—and, secondly, that his style *evolved* over the course of his life, so that it progressively became less archaic and less florid. Let us examine both these points in greater detail.

Lovecraft is frequently not given credit for being master, not slave, of his style. As Steven J. Mariconda has pointed out in two brilliant papers on Lovecraft's style,[3] such a coldly reportorial story as "Beyond the Wall of Sleep" (1919) actually preceded by three years the wildly—and intentionally—overwritten tale "The Hound" (1922), the latter so obviously a self-parody that it is remarkable how few critics have picked up on the fact. It is nevertheless true that in his writing up to 1926 Lovecraft did not always seem entirely in control, and his early work suffers not so much from shoddiness of style but the immaturity of his own temperament, brought on by reclusiveness, bookishness, and a general ignorance of the world. Such tales as "The Tomb" (1917) and "The Outsider" (1921) could indeed have been written by Poe—not only because of their archaic diction, but because they show almost no awareness that the twentieth century actually exists.

But, as in so many other ways, "The Call of Cthulhu" (1926) changes all

---

3. Now collected in Mariconda's *H. P. Lovecraft: Art, Artifact, and Reality* (New York: Hippocampus Press, 2013).

H. P. Lovecraft: The Fiction of Materialism

this. The opening paragraph must be quoted not only for its restraint but for its subtle modulation of prose rhythm and its powerful manipulation of symbol and metaphor:

> The most merciful thing in the world, I think, is the inability of the human mind to correlate all its contents. We live on a placid island of ignorance in the midst of black seas of infinity, and it was not meant that we should voyage far. The sciences, each straining in its own direction, have hitherto harmed us little; but some day the piecing together of dissociated knowledge will open up such terrifying vistas of reality, and of our frightful position therein, that we shall either go mad from the revelation or flee from the deadly light into the peace and safety of a new dark age. (*DH* 125)

Several factors united in giving Lovecraft a new lease on his life and his work around this time. First, there was his ecstatic return to his native Providence, Rhode Island, in the spring of 1926 after two hellish years spent in New York, where he saw his brief marriage collapse and found himself unable to secure regular work. Perhaps more important, in late 1925 he had been asked by his friend W. Paul Cook to write a treatise on the horror tale for Cook's amateur magazine, *The Recluse*; Lovecraft immediately plunged into work, and the result is the masterful essay "Supernatural Horror in Literature" (1927). The virtues of this treatise speak for themselves: its unfailingly pithy and sympathetic analyses of the weird work of Poe, Hawthorne, Bierce, Machen, Dunsany, Blackwood, M. R. James, and a host of other writers; its important statements on the nature and function of the weird tale; and its clear delineation of the historical progression of this branch of literature. But the reading of all these weird classics gave a forceful impetus to Lovecraft's own work—not in the manner of transparent imitation, as he had done in the early 1920s in a group of generally undistinguished tales modelled after Lord Dunsany, but in terms of a finely honed awareness of the metaphysical and psychological bases for the weird tale and of its most skilful and artistic examples.

From "The Call of Cthulhu" onward, Lovecraft becomes an increasingly assured stylist, aside from curious lapses such as "The Dunwich Horror," "The Dreams in the Witch House" (1932), and "The Thing on the Doorstep" (1933), the latter two being among his most disappointing late stories. By this time, moreover, Lovecraft had evolved a clear theory of weird writing:

> In writing a weird story I always try very carefully to achieve the right mood and atmosphere, and place the emphasis where it belongs. One cannot, except in immature pulp charlatan-fiction, present an account of impossible, improbable, or inconceivable phenomena as a commonplace narrative of objective acts and conventional emotions. Inconceivable events and conditions have a special handicap to overcome, and this can be accomplished only through the mainte-

nance of a careful realism in every phase of the story *except* that touching on the one given marvel. This marvel must be treated very impressively and deliberately—with a careful emotional "build-up"—else it will seem flat and unconvincing. Being the principal thing in the story, its mere existence should overshadow the characters and events. ("Notes on Writing Weird Fiction" [CE 2.177])

It may seem surprising that Lovecraft is promoting "realism," but in fact realism—realism of landscape, realism in scientific detail, realism in terms of human emotions toward the bizarre—is the foundation for his fiction. But among his great gifts was an extremely sure sense of narrative pacing, and it is this that leads to a passage toward the end of "The Call of Cthulhu" that may appear overwritten but which in fact has been prepared for by thirty pages of "careful emotional 'build-up'":

> The Thing cannot be described—there is no language for such abysms of shrieking and immemorial lunacy, such eldritch contradictions of all matter, force, and cosmic order. A mountain walked or stumbled. God! What wonder that across the earth a great architect went mad, and poor Wilcox raved with fever in that telepathic instant? The Thing of the idols, the green, sticky spawn of the stars, had awaked to claim his own. The stars were right again, and what an age-old cult had failed to do by design, a band of innocent sailors had done by accident. After vigintillions of years great Cthulhu was loose again, and ravening for delight. (DH 152)

One is at liberty to dislike things like this, but one cannot in fairness condemn them without an awareness of Lovecraft's purpose and of the context in which they are placed.

The study of H. P. Lovecraft—his life, his work, and his thought—has of late been burgeoning; but it has largely taken place away from the academic arena. The best work on Lovecraft continues to be written by independent scholars or enthusiasts, most of whom have emerged from the realm of science fiction and fantasy fandom. Work of this sort has its limitations—many such scholars do not appear as thoroughly versed in critical method as one would like—but for the time being Lovecraft's fate rests in their hands.[4]

One of the great difficulties in understanding Lovecraft is the sheer quantity of ancillary material that has built up around him—letters, essays, poetry, mem-

---

4. Some of this material is at last becoming available to an academic audience; see Donald R. Burleson's *Lovecraft: Disturbing the Universe* (Lexington: University Press of Kentucky, 1990) and *An Epicure in the Terrible: A Centennial Anthology of Essays in Honor of H. P. Lovecraft*, ed. David E. Schultz and S. T. Joshi (Rutherford, NJ: Fairleigh Dickinson University Press, 1991; rpt. New York: Hippocampus Press, 2011).

oirs and criticism from as early as 1915 to the present day—much of which has been published in relatively obscure sources and by specialty publishers largely outside the academic community. Even if we acknowledge that Lovecraft's fiction is, in the short term, the primary basis for his reputation (I think, however, that a case could be made for his letters as his greatest achievement), much valuable insight can be gained from access to this ancillary material, in particular his letters. It is largely the ignorance of his letters, and the complex intellect they reveal, that has led to many academics' hasty dismissal of Lovecraft as a pulp hack. Even a casual reading of the letters will show that Lovecraft had a carefully evolved philosophy, a scorn of the pulp magazines in which he was forced to publish, and a very clear idea of his motives in writing weird fiction. Lovecraft is, indeed, one of the most articulate spokesmen for the weird tale as a distinctive art form, and few have written more poignantly on the subject than he:

> The imaginative writer devotes himself to art in its most essential sense. . . . He is a painter of moods and mind-pictures—a capturer and amplifier of elusive dreams and fancies—a voyager into those unheard-of lands which are glimpsed through the veil of actuality but rarely, and only by the most sensitive. . . . Pleasure to me is wonder—the unexplored, the unexpected, the thing that is hidden and the changeless thing that lurks behind superficial mutability. To trace the remote in the immediate; the eternal in the ephemeral; the past in the present; the infinite in the finite; these are to me the springs of delight and beauty. (CE 5.47)

Works Cited

Barzun, Jacques. "Introduction." In *The Penguin Encyclopedia of Horror and the Supernatural*, ed. Jack Sullivan. New York: Viking Penguin, 1986. xix–xxviii.

Burleson, Donald R. "The Mythic Hero Archetype in 'The Dunwich Horror.'" *Lovecraft Studies* No. 4 (Spring 1981): 1–9.

Elliot, Hugh. *Modern Science and Materialism*. London: Longman, 1919.

Leiber, Fritz. "A Literary Copernicus." 1949. In *H. P. Lovecraft: Four Decades of Criticism*, ed. S. T. Joshi. Athens: Ohio University Press, 1980. 50–62.

Mackie, J. L. *Ethics*. Harmondsworth, UK: Penguin, 1977.

Nelson, Dale J. "Lovecraft and the Burkean Sublime." *Lovecraft Studies* No. 24 (Spring 1991): 2–5.

Russell, Bertrand. *Human Knowledge: Its Scope and Limits*. New York: Simon & Schuster, 1948.

Wilson, Edmund. "Tales of the Marvellous and the Ridiculous." 1945. In *H. P. Lovecraft: Four Decades of Criticism*, ed. S. T. Joshi. Athens: Ohio University Press, 1980. 45–49.

Lovecraft and Religion

How does it happen that a man like H. P. Lovecraft—almost entirely unknown in his time except as the author of seemingly lurid and flamboyant tales of "cosmic" horror, and who contributed almost nothing to the public discussion of the central questions of religion, politics, and society—has become, more than a half-century after his death, a kind of patron saint of atheism? The conundrum might be explained in part by considering his remarkable posthumous reputation, a reputation that has seen not only the publication of his relatively small corpus of fiction in the most prestigious of venues (capped, in 2005, by the Library of America's edition of his *Tales*) but also the issuance of his essays, poetry, and especially his thousands of letters; for it is these letters, clearly not designed for publication and written to friends and colleagues who were themselves little-known, that show him to have been one of the keenest minds of his generation, one who fashioned a comprehensive worldview that saw no place for God in the fabric of the universe and that appealed largely to science as the arbiter of truth, but nonetheless left room for the imaginative stimulus of art. And yet, to explain Lovecraft's eminence, both as a writer and as a thinker, we may also have to look to the nearly mythic figure he has become as the gaunt, lantern-jawed creator of a plethora of "gods" in his stories but who nonetheless heaped scorn on the central religious tenets of the existence of a deity, the immortality of the soul, and the cosmic significance of humankind.

Lovecraft's early life and upbringing laid the foundations for both his impressive intellect and his supernatural fiction. Born on August 20, 1890, in Providence, Rhode Island, to a Baptist mother (Sarah Susan Phillips Lovecraft) and an Anglican father (Winfield Scott Lovecraft), Lovecraft early developed a keen taste for what he would call "the supremely rational 18th century" (SL 3.146)—the century of David Hume, Edward Gibbon, and the *philosophes*. In his early childhood years, of course, it was not philosophy but literature—especially poetry—that fascinated him; and his enthusiasm for the elegant translations of Greek and Latin poetry by such poets as John Dryden and Alexander Pope led him back to classical antiquity itself. One of his earliest surviving writings is an 88-line verse paraphrase of the *Odyssey*, dating to 1897. In the piquant essay "A Confession of Unfaith" (1922) Lovecraft admits that his absorption of classical myth and literature had much to do with his later atheism. In that same essay, however, he dates his first sceptical utterances to a Sunday school class he attended at the age of five. This would appear to conflict with a 1920 letter in which he dates his Sunday school clashes to a somewhat later period:

> How well I recall my tilts with Sunday-School teachers during my last period of compulsory attendance! I was 12 years old, and the despair of the institution. None of the answers of my pious preceptors would satisfy me, and my demands that they cease taking things for granted quite upset them. Close reasoning was something new in their little world of Semitic mythology. At last I saw that they were hopelessly bound to unfounded dogmata and traditions, and thenceforth ceased to treat them seriously. Sunday-School became to me simply a place wherein to have a little harmless fun spoofing the pious mossbacks. My mother observed this, and no longer sought to enforce my attendance. (SL 1.110–11)

Perhaps there is no strict contradiction: Lovecraft's memories, in "A Confession of Unfaith," of attending the "infant class" of the Sunday school at the First Baptist Church in Providence seem authentic, but one suspects he may be exaggerating the degree to which he was able to "tilt" with his teachers at the tender age of five.

Lovecraft's imagination, meanwhile, had been stimulated by his early readings of Grimm's fairy tales (age four), the *Arabian Nights* (age five), and Coleridge's *The Rime of the Ancient Mariner*, in the edition illustrated by Gustave Doré (age six). These and other influences awakened his love of the fantastic, and he was writing short horror tales as early as the age of six. These specimens are very crude, but they laid the groundwork for his later "cosmic" narratives. Equally important, however, was Lovecraft's precocious absorption of science—first chemistry, at the age of eight, and then astronomy, at the age of eleven. Lovecraft speaks truly in "A Confession of Unfaith" that these studies definitively transformed him from agnosticism to full-fledged atheism. The "myriad suns and worlds of infinite space" (CE 5.147) seemed to reduce all earth life to vanishing insignificance, and Lovecraft admits that he actually entered a period of cosmic pessimism. "The futility of all existence began to impress and oppress me" (CE 5.147).

Lovecraft's devotion to the eighteenth century should not deceive us into thinking that he was much influenced by—or, to be frank, even very familiar with—the writings of the leading secular thinkers of that century. Although he charmingly affected eighteenth-century diction in his letters, there is little reason to assume that he was intimately conversant with the writings of (to quote more fully the letter cited earlier) "La Mettrie, Diderot, Helvetius, Hume, and dozens of others . . . in the supremely rational 18th century" (SL 3.146). Even

Voltaire, the most forceful opponent of religious obscurantism and intolerance in the eighteenth century, was probably not one of Lovecraft's favourite reads, although no doubt he would have enjoyed Voltaire's unrestrained flair in attacking the "infamy" of the church.

Lovecraft's atheism was based, as was that of so many others in the early part of the twentieth century, upon a remarkable convergence of scientific advance in the course of the nineteenth century that systematically destroyed many previously unassailable pillars of religious thought. Both the "hard" sciences—astrophysics, chemistry, biology—and the social sciences, such as history and (especially) anthropology, each pursuing their own courses of research, presented naturalistic explanations for phenomena previously thought to be the work of a deity; and anthropological advances were, in a way, the capstone of this process, for it accounted with unfailing accuracy and plausibility for the origin of religious belief. Such works as Edward Burnett Tylor's *Primitive Culture* (1871) and Sir James George Frazer's *The Golden Bough* (1890-1915) added an immense quantity of fieldwork to the highly theoretical accounts found in David Hume's *The Natural History of Religion* (1757) and other works. (Lovecraft himself may not have read Tylor's dense work, but he unquestionably read John Fiske's popularisation of contemporary anthropology, *Myths and Myth-Makers* [1872].)

Of course, Lovecraft was well-versed in the hard sciences as well, and his absorption of Darwinian evolution—as well as of the work of Darwin's two most prominent disciples and advocates, Thomas Henry Huxley and Ernst Haeckel—laid strong foundations for his criticism of religion. His refutation of the immortality of the soul rested largely on Darwinian principles; for, as he cleverly notes, "One must ask . . . just how the evolving organism began to acquire 'spirit' after it crossed the boundary betwixt advanced ape and primitive human" (CE 5.64). His understanding of chemistry and biology led him to speculate (correctly) that life would one day be generated in the laboratory (as was in fact done in the 1950s), thereby confounding the religious conception that life and consciousness could only have been bestowed by a god.

Astrophysics presented the greatest difficulties for Lovecraft, chiefly because his essentially layman's training prevented him from understanding some of the more abstruse theories propounded in the early twentieth century. Lovecraft early announced himself as a "mechanistic materialist"—one who believed the universe was a "mechanism" (i.e., governed by fixed deterministic laws) and was composed wholly of matter (i.e., that "soul" or "spirit" does not and cannot exist). In an early letter he presents a keen understanding of the implications of determinism, distinguishing it from the fallacy of fatalism:

Determinism—what you call Destiny—rules inexorably; though not exactly in the personal way you seem to fancy. We have no specific destiny against which we can fight—for the fighting would be as much a part of the destiny as the final end. The real fact is simply that every event in the cosmos is caused by the action of antecedent and circumjacent forces, so that whatever we do is unconsciously the inevitable product of Nature rather than of our own volition. If an act corresponds with our wish, it is Nature that made the wish, and ensured its fulfilment. When we see an apparent chain of circumstances leading toward some striking denouement, we say it is "Fate". That is not true in the sense meant, for all of those circumstances might have been deceptive, so that a hidden and unexpected cause would have turned matters to an utterly opposite conclusion. The chain of appearances are [sic] as much a part of fate as the result, whichever the latter may be. (SL 1.132)

Mechanistic materialism was, of course, challenged on two fronts—by Einstein's theory of relativity (which saw matter and energy as interchangeable) and by Max Planck's quantum theory (which was thought by many to have destroyed causality in its ultimate sense). Lovecraft's initial response to Einstein was little short of traumatic. In 1923, when certain solar observations rendered the theory all but irrefutable, Lovecraft reacted as follows:

My cynicism and scepticism are increasing, and from an entirely new cause—the Einstein theory. The latest eclipse observations seem to place this system among the facts which cannot be dismissed, and assumedly it removes the last hold which reality or the universe can have on the independent mind. All is chance, accident, and ephemeral illusion—a fly may be greater than Arcturus, and Durfee Hill may surpass Mount Everest—assuming them to be removed from the present planet and differently environed in the continuum of space-time. There are no values in all infinity—the least idea that there are is the supreme mockery of all. All the cosmos is a jest, and fit to be treated only as a jest, and one thing is as true as another. I believe everything and nothing—for all is chaos, always has been, and always will be. (SL 1.231)

There is no need to examine the multiple fallacies of this statement, especially Lovecraft's rash assumption of moral nihilism. What is remarkable is that, only six years after writing the above, he came to terms with relativity and saw it, not as a threat to materialism (and, hence, to his ongoing attack on religious conceptions of "soul" or "spirit"), but as an ally. His 1929 letter, reprinted here, warns a correspondent not to be tricked by the "Einstein-twisters"—of whom there were many both among scientists and littérateurs, who were using Einstein to bolster previously outmoded views regarding both God and the soul. Lovecraft concludes:

> Matter, we learn, is a definite phenomenon instituted by certain modifications of energy; *but does this circumstance make it less distinctive in itself or permit us to imagine the presence of another kind of modified energy in places where no sign or result of energy can be discovered?* It is to laugh! The truth is, that the discovery of matter's identity with energy—and of its consequent lack of vital intrinsic difference from empty space—is *an absolute coup de grace to the primitive and irresponsible myth of "spirit". For matter, it appears, really is exactly what "spirit" was always supposed to be. Thus it is proved that wandering energy always has a detectable form*—that if it doesn't take the form of waves or electron-streams, *it becomes matter itself;* and that the absence of matter or any other detectable energy-form indicates *not the presence of spirit, but the absence of anything whatever.* (SL 2.266-67)

Whether an astrophysicist would accept this conclusion or not, it is a clever resolution of the difficulty.

Quantum theory gave Lovecraft more difficulty. He maintained in a 1930 letter: "What most physicists take the quantum theory, at present, to mean, is *not that any cosmic uncertainty exists* as to which of several courses a given reaction will take; but that in certain instances *no conceivable channel of information can ever tell human beings which course will be taken*, or by what exact course a certain observed result came about" (*SL* 3.228). Lovecraft wants to believe that the "uncertainty" of quantum theory is not ontological but epistemological. This conclusion is apparently false, for the "uncertainty" really does persist—on a subatomic level. But there is no question that macro-atomic phenomena remain largely materialistic and deterministic, so that Lovecraft's materialism—the word, as he recognised, being used in a purely historical sense—remains largely intact.

Lovecraft was merciless in his skewering of muddle-headed thinkers who were using relativity, quantum theory, and other scientific advances to lobby for the resurrection of religious theories that had already been conclusively shown to be false. He speaks of a

> ... new mysticism or neo-metaphysics bred of the advertised uncertainties of recent science—Einstein, the quantum theory, and the resolution of matter into force. Although these new turns of science don't really mean a thing in relation to the myth of cosmic consciousness and teleology, a new brood of despairing and horrified moderns is seizing on the doubt of all positive knowledge which they imply; and is deducing therefrom that, since nothing is true, therefore anything can be true ... whence one may invent or revive any sort of mythology that fancy or nostalgia or desperation may dictate, and defy anyone to prove that it isn't emotionally true—whatever that means. This sickly, decadent neo-mysticism—a protest not only against machine materialism but against pure science with its destruction of the mystery and dignity of

human emotion and experience—will be the dominant creed of middle twentieth century aesthetes, as the [T. S.] Eliot and [Aldous] Huxley penumbra well prognosticate. (SL 3.53)

It may be worth noting that Lovecraft did not appear to be much interested in, or very aware of, another important advance that severely called into question the inerrancy of the Bible—the school of biblical criticism called the "higher criticism," emerging in Germany in the late eighteenth century and popularised by many important books such as Ernest Renan's *Life of Jesus* (1864). This school systematically studied the origins and sources of the Bible, establishing conclusively that it was written over a long period of time—spanning perhaps as much as a millennium—and finally assembled in a manner that can only be called haphazard. The work of the "higher criticism" dethroned the conception of the Bible as a work dictated or inspired by God, especially when other commentators pointed out that it contained not a few traces of barbarism that could not possibly be suitable for contemporary society, such as the death penalty for witches (Exodus 22:18), homosexuals (Leviticus 20:13), and sabbath-breakers (Exodus 31:15), the ownership of wives by the husbands (Exodus 20:10), and so forth.

Lovecraft, as I say, did not pay much attention to this work, probably because he couldn't credit how any sane person could believe that the Bible was the product of some kind of stenographic dictation from God. His own (northern) Baptist tradition emphasised the Bible as a guide to moral conduct, and even here Lovecraft saw reason to be sceptical: "Half of what Buddha or Christus or Mahomet said is either simply idiocy or downright destructiveness, as applied to the western world of the twentieth century; whilst virtually all of the emotional-imaginative background of assumptions from which they spoke, is now proved to be sheer childish primitiveness" (SL 3.47–48). Lovecraft was familiar with the Bible as a literary document, and he was highly taken with the style of the Anglo-Irish writer Lord Dunsany, who (although he himself was also an atheist) consciously used the King James Bible as the basis of his fantastic prose; but beyond that, Lovecraft exhibited little interest in the Bible as a religious text.

Lovecraft, in the final analysis, appealed to *probability* as the ultimate basis for his atheism; and, interestingly, he used probability as a means of distinguishing his atheism from agnosticism. In his mind, the probability of the truth of theism was so vanishingly small that he felt it irresponsible to think of himself as a mere agnostic:

> All I say is that I think it is *damned unlikely* that anything like a central cosmic will, a spirit world, or an eternal survival of personality exist. They are the most preposterous and unjustified of all the guesses which can be made about

the universe, and I am not enough of a hair-splitter to pretend that I don't regard them as arrant and negligible moonshine. In theory I am an *agnostic*, but pending the appearance of radical evidence I must be classed, practically and provisionally, as an *atheist*. (SL 4.57)

One of the most provocative questions pertaining to Lovecraft and religion is the seeming paradox of a vigorously atheistic writer producing stories filled to the brim with "gods" and their worshippers. His so-called Cthulhu Mythos (a term invented by his disciple, August Derleth), a mythology that dominates the stories of the last decade of his life, seems to envision a universe populated by all-powerful gods who can crush the human race—or at least certain venturesome individuals—at will. How can this be squared with the materialistic atheist of his letters? The matter is considerably complex, but some hints can be provided here.

Some commentators have believed that Lovecraft's "evil" gods—Cthulhu, Yog-Sothoth, Nyarlathotep, Azathoth, Shub-Niggurath, and so forth—are themselves representative of the evils of religious belief, since they embody the viciousness that many of the actual gods invented by human beings, not excluding the Christian god, appear to display. I am not entirely convinced of this notion, largely because Lovecraft's "gods" are not "evil" in any meaningful sense. They are inimical to human beings only because they render our position on this earth highly tenuous and fragile, but they are as much "beyond good and evil" (as Lovecraft actually states in "The Call of Cthulhu") as we ourselves would be from an ant's perspective. Lovecraft's "gods" are, in large part, symbols for the inscrutability of the cosmos: scientific materialist that he was, he knew that the universe held an infinite reservoir of mystery, and even scientific advance could do little to minimize it; as he wrote in a late letter, "the more we learn about the cosmos, the more bewildering does it appear" (SL 4.324).

And, in the end, Lovecraft's "gods" aren't really gods at all. It is true that, in "The Call of Cthulhu" and "The Dunwich Horror," various cults are stated as worshipping Cthulhu and Yog-Sothoth; indeed, in the former story one of these worshippers gives a history of the eon-old cult:

Then . . . those first men formed the cult around small idols which the Great Ones shewed them; idols brought in dim aeras from dark stars. That cult would never die till the stars came right again, and the secret priests would take great Cthulhu from His tomb to revive His subjects and resume His rule of earth. The time would be easy to know, for then mankind would have become as the Great Old Ones; free and wild and beyond good and evil, with laws and morals thrown aside and all men shouting and killing and revelling in joy. Then the liberated Old Ones would teach them new ways to shout and kill and revel and enjoy themselves, and all the earth would flame with a holocaust of ecstasy and freedom. (DH 140-41)

The overriding question is: Are we to take this statement at face value? It is true that a virtual library of "forbidden" books invented by Lovecraft and his colleagues—ranging from the *Necronomicon* of the mad Arab, Abdul Alhazred, to the *Unaussprechlichen Kulten* of von Juntz—appear to speak in like terms of the old gods; but what one gradually discovers, as Lovecraft's work progresses, is that these cultists are as pathetically deluded about the nature of the "gods" they worship as most human beings are in their devotion to Yahweh or Allah. The critical passage comes in the short novel *At the Mountains of Madness* (1931), where an immense stone city evidently built by extraterrestrials, coming from the depths of space, is discovered by explorers penetrating a previously unknown corner of Antarctica:

> The things rearing and dwelling in this frightful masonry in the age of dinosaurs were not indeed dinosaurs, but far worse. Mere dinosaurs were new and almost brainless objects—but the builders of the city were wise and old, and had left certain traces in rocks even then laid down well-nigh a thousand million years . . . rocks laid down before the true life of earth had advanced beyond plastic groups of cells . . . rocks laid down before the true life of earth had existed at all. They were the makers and enslavers of that life, and above all doubt the originals of the fiendish elder myths which things like the Pnakotic Manuscripts and the *Necronomicon* affrightedly hint about. (MM 59)

So now the stories about the "gods" as found in the *Necronomicon* have been reduced to "myths"! The "gods" are merely space aliens. This appears to have been Lovecraft's conception right from the beginning, for even in "The Call of Cthulhu," which launched the Cthulhu Mythos, Cthulhu and his "spawn" are merely extraterrestrials who come from some infinitely far galaxy to the earth, where they are unwittingly trapped in the underwater city of R'lyeh beneath the Pacific. Cthulhu and R'lyeh rise up in that story, but not because the "stars are right" or because of any actions taken by his human cult, but merely by accident—an earthquake—and they sink back under the waves by a similar accident.

Lovecraft's signature element in his fiction is its "cosmic" quality—its suggestion of the infinite gulfs of space and time, and the resulting inconsequence of humanity within these gulfs. It is an element that Lovecraft may well have conveyed more powerfully and poignantly than any writer in literature, and it constitutes one of the chief justifications of the canonical status he has attained today. But it should be made clear that that cosmic vision is strictly dependent on Lovecraft's metaphysical—and, specifically, his atheistic—viewpoint. For in Lovecraft's universe, humanity is indeed alone in the cosmos; and whereas the object of most religions is, in John Milton's words, to "justify the ways of God to men," Lovecraft's "anti-mythology," as it has been appropriately called (see Schultz 222), establishes that human beings can appeal to no higher power when faced with threats to our fleeting sinecure on this earth. A moment ago, in cosmic terms, we did not exist; a moment hence, the universe shall have forgotten that we did exist.

It is, in truth, a bleak vision, but the prose-poetry with which Lovecraft infuses it in his stories lends it a strange and exhilarating beauty. In scarcely less powerful a fashion, the liveliness, vigour, and at times satirical flair of his discussions of religion and atheism in his letters and essays exhibit a mind wrestling with the central questions of existence and hammering out a cogent, forward-looking philosophy shorn of outmoded religious belief and courageously prepared to face a universe in which humanity is indeed alone and friendless. Comforting as Lovecraft knew the myths of religion may be, he was determined to contemplate the universe with the blinkers removed from his eyes and mind.

Works Cited

Schultz, David E. "From Microcosm to Macrocosm: The Growth of Lovecraft's Cosmic Vision." In David E. Schultz and S. T. Joshi, ed. *An Epicure in the Terrible: A Centennial Anthology of Essays in Honor of H. P. Lovecraft.* 1991. New York: Hippocampus Press, 2011. 208-29.

Time, Space, and Natural Law:
Science and Pseudo-Science in Lovecraft

I. A Tripartite Nature

In 1920 H. P. Lovecraft made the following analysis of his own temperament:

> I should describe mine own nature as tripartite, my interests consisting of three parallel and dissociated groups—(a) Love of the strange and the fantastic. (b) Love of the abstract truth and of scientific logick. (c) Love of the ancient and the permanent. Sundry combinations of these three strains will probably account for all my odd tastes and eccentricities. (SL 1.110)

This is a remarkably perspicacious and prescient remark, and it is exactly those "sundry combinations" that not only clarify many of the "eccentricities" of his personality (his simultaneous adoration of the past—ranging from ancient Rome to the colonial remains of his native Providence, Rhode Island—and his enthusiasm for the most recent findings in the sciences, from Einstein's theory of relativity to the exploration of the Antarctic) but also help to illuminate the most distinctive features of his literary work. In a literary career that spanned less than two decades and comprised no more than sixty works of fiction (all of them short stories with the exception of three short novels and several novellas), Lovecraft performed a critical function in the development of supernatural fiction; Fritz Leiber, a late colleague and perhaps his most distinguished disciple, put it best when he wrote that Lovecraft "shifted the focus of supernatural dread from man and his little world and his gods, to the stars and the black and unplumbed gulfs of intergalactic space" (Leiber, "Literary Copernicus" 455). In effect, Leiber is maintaining that Lovecraft fashioned a unique hybrid, mingling those elements of the traditional supernatural tale that still remained scientifically and aesthetically viable with the emerging genre of science fiction, at whose birth Lovecraft could be said to have been a bemused eyewitness.

In order to effect this union, Lovecraft required not only a thorough grounding in the history of supernatural literature (a history he himself ably charted in his monograph, "Supernatural Horror in Literature" [1927]) but an awareness of the many sciences—physics, biology, chemistry, astronomy, geology, palaeontology—that could conceivably be drawn upon for the new kind of horror tale he was writing. To be sure, Lovecraft did not set out with such a goal in mind; rather, that "tripartite" nature he noted in 1920 led inexorably to this result, so that by around 1930 Lovecraft was quite aware that he himself was fashioning something new in the realm of fantastic literature.

All three aspects of Lovecraft's tripartite nature were remarkably early in manifesting themselves. His enthusiasm for such works as Grimm's fairy tales, Coleridge's *Rime of the Ancient Mariner,* and the tales of Poe—all absorbed by the age of eight—instilled in him a lifelong love of the "strange and the fantastic." His birth in an ancient colonial town, with tangible landmarks dating back two centuries, and his early absorption of the myths of classical Greece and Rome (initially through Bulfinch's *Age of Fable* and later through translations of classical texts and then first-hand knowledge of those texts after he learned Latin), did much to foster his taste for the "ancient and the permanent." But where did his taste for "abstract truth and . . . scientifick logic" originate? It is, of course, impossible to specify with precision, but Lovecraft himself provides an engaging account of one of his earliest encounters with science:

> The science of chemistry . . . first captivated me in the Year of Our Lord 1898—in a rather peculiar way. With the insatiable curiosity of early childhood, I used to spend hours poring over the pictures in the back of Webster's *Unabridged Dictionary*—absorbing a miscellaneous variety of ideas. After familiarising myself with antiquities, mediaeval dress and armour, birds, animals, reptiles, fishes, flags of all nations, heraldry, etc., etc., I lit upon the section devoted to "Philosophical and Scientific Instruments". I was veritably hypnotised with it. Chemical apparatus especially attracted me, and I resolved (before knowing a thing about the science!) to have a laboratory. . . . By 1901 or thereabouts I had a fair knowledge of the principles of chemistry and the details of the inorganic part—about the equivalent of a high-school course, and not including analysis of any kind. Then my fickle fancy turned away to the intensive study of geography, geology, anthropology, and above all *astronomy* . . . (SL 1.74)

There are a number of interesting features in this account, to which I shall return shortly. But first, let us now read of his discovery of astronomy in 1902, which Lovecraft himself admitted did more to shape his entire worldview than any other single event:

> I began to study astronomy in 1902—age 12. My interest came through two sources—discovery of an old book of my grandmother's in the attic, and a previous interest in physical geography. Within a year I was thinking of virtually nothing but astronomy, yet my keenest interest did not lie outside the solar system. I think I really ignored the abysses of space in my interest in the habit-

ability of the various planets of the solar system. My observations (for I purchased a telescope early in 1903) were confined mostly to the moon and the planet Venus. You will ask, why the latter, since its markings are doubtful even in the largest instruments? I answer—this very MYSTERY was what attracted me. (SL 1.69)

Several things now become clear, chiefly the fact that Lovecraft was already combining his "love of the strange and the fantastic" with his burgeoning interest in science: it was exactly because the world revealed by science was, potentially, a world of mystery and even terror that he became enraptured with the sciences. Science was, certainly, a way of penetrating those mysteries, but there would always be further mysteries to be explored, and perhaps many that could never be fully explicated. Lovecraft speaks of writing many stories at this time—not only horror tales in the old-time Gothic mode but tales inspired by Jules Verne and by W. Frank Russell's histrionic tale of Antarctic adventure, *The Frozen Pirate* (1887). Many of these tales, if they survived, would certainly be considered proto-science fiction, dim antecedents of such later works as *At the Mountains of Madness* and "The Shadow out of Time."

At this point it is hardly necessary to examine in detail the prodigious amount of scientific writing in which Lovecraft engaged between 1899 and 1908. This material, still largely unpublished, includes such things as two long-running papers, *The Scientific Gazette* (which began as a *daily* on March 4, 1899, later lapsing into a weekly and maintained at least until 1905 or 1906; its focus was chiefly on chemistry) and *The Rhode Island Journal of Astronomy* (begun on August 2, 1903 as a weekly and continued until at least 1907), numerous small booklets on special subjects (e.g., *A Good Anaesthetic*), and even such things as (apparently daily) weather forecasts, a result of Lovecraft's new-found interest in meteorology. Lovecraft had, of course, abundant leisure to engage in this literary work, since he attended grade school only in the years 1898-99 and 1902-03 and high school from 1904-05 and 1906-08, leaving abruptly without a diploma. His first appearances in print were astronomy columns written for local papers—the *Pawtuxet Valley Gleaner* (1906) and the Providence *Tribune* (1906-08). Fiction and poetry were also being written during this period, but Lovecraft later admits that he destroyed all but two stories written between 1903 and 1908: "The Beast in the Cave" (1905) and "The Alchemist" (1908).

The importance of all this scientific work for the course of his fiction writing would become apparent only after the passage of a decade or more; but Lovecraft was aware of a more immediate result—the formation of a scientific world-view. He prefaces the above account of his discovery of astronomy with the words: "To trace, then, my philosophical views." And in the seminal essay "A Confession of Unfaith" (1922) he states unequivocally:

> The most poignant sensations of my existence are those of 1896, when I discovered the Hellenic world, and of 1902, when I discovered the myriad suns and worlds of infinite space. Sometimes I think the latter event the greater, for the grandeur of that growing conception of the universe still excites a thrill hardly to be duplicated. . . . By my thirteenth birthday I was thoroughly impressed with man's impermanence and insignificance, and by my seventeenth, about which time I did some particularly detailed writing on the subject, I had formed in all essential particulars my present pessimistic cosmic views. (CE 5.147)

That last sentence is critical, although Lovecraft would shed the "pessimism" that he found in the cosmic viewpoint. As the title of this essay makes clear, Lovecraft used both the discovery of pre-Christian literature and the discovery of science as supports for the religious skepticism that he maintains developed as early as the age of five. In later years he was not shy in declaring himself an atheist (see SL 4.57), and he was endlessly fond of twitting pious associates such as Maurice W. Moe, who plaintively asked Lovecraft what he had against religion, to which he replied that his chief objection was that "the Judaeo-Christian mythology is NOT TRUE" (SL 1.60).

Lovecraft came to maturity at a time when the findings of nineteenth-century science—notably Darwin's theory of evolution, which was seen by many as destroying the last remaining intellectual support for the notion of an omnipotent deity in its implicit refutation of the "argument from design"—were being synthesized by a wide range of philosophers and scientists who, following Thomas Henry Huxley and Friedrich Nietzsche, were becoming increasingly bold in advancing purely secular theories both of cosmic origins and human motivations. Lovecraft came upon both Huxley and Nietzsche before 1920, and later absorbed Freud, Bertrand Russell, and many other secularists; but his chief bulwark remained astronomy, and in 1917 he made the pungent declaration:

> A mere knowledge of the approximate dimensions of the visible universe is enough to destroy forever the notion of a personal godhead whose whole care is expended upon puny mankind, and whose only genuine and original Messiah was dispatched to save the insignificant vermin, or men, who inhabit this one relatively microscopic globe. Not that science positively refutes religion—it merely makes religion seem so monstrously improbable that a large majority of men can no longer believe in it. (SL 1.44)

Lovecraft may be guilty of a category error here, for there is no intrinsic reason why the size of the universe (a matter of *quantity*) should necessarily imply the insignificance of humanity (a matter of *quality*); but it becomes clear that he is relying on the argument from probability, since there now seems no particular reason why a god should have singled out this tiny corner of the unbounded universe for his special interest and concern. Elsewhere in this same letter Lovecraft flatly declares that "life, animal and vegetable, including human life, is a mode of motion which ceases absolutely upon the death of the body containing it," and appeals to several sciences for further support for this destruction of the myth of the "soul":

> . . . sooner or later the relation betwixt organic and inorganic life will be discovered. It will be clearly demonstrated how carbon, hydrogen, oxygen, nitrogen, and other elements combine to form substances possessing vital energy. Probably the chemist or biologist will be able to create in his laboratory some very primitive sort of animal or vegetable organism. This will be the death knell of superstition and theology alike . . . (SL 1.44)

In this as elsewhere, Lovecraft exaggerates the ability of the average person to absorb scientific information and also the influence of even generally diffused scientific knowledge in the religious and moral spheres; but it is evident that the advance of science had the effect of destroying forever any belief Lovecraft himself may have had in the human soul, in the existence of a deity, and in the role of that deity in guiding human affairs. Lovecraft could well be said to have been one of the most secular temperaments in modern literature and thought.

II. Cannibals and Aliens

It is not my place here to trace the manifold ramifications of science upon Lovecraft's philosophical thought.[1] More to the purpose is the role of science in Lovecraft's own literary work, particularly his fiction. It will become manifest that science provides the intellectual backbone of nearly all his short stories; but at the same time Lovecraft seems to suggest that that science will itself will ultimately be a source of horror and destruction. Did he not write, in the early story "Facts concerning the Late Arthur Jermyn and His Family" (1920), that "Science, already oppressive with its shocking revelations, will perhaps be the ultimate exterminator of our human species" (D 73)? Is this mere hyperbolic rhetoric, or an indication of Lovecraft's conflicted attitudes toward a science that was relentlessly tearing away the remaining shreds of

---

1. See my treatise *H. P. Lovecraft: The Decline of the West* (Mercer Island, WA: Starmont House; rpt. Berkeley Heights, NJ: Wildside Press, 2001), a study of HPL's philosophical thought.

mystery in the cosmos? And consider the more subtle expression of the same idea in the celebrated opening paragraph of "The Call of Cthulhu" (1926): "The sciences, each straining in its own direction, have hitherto harmed us little; but some day the piecing together of dissociated knowledge will open up such terrifying vistas of reality, and of our frightful position therein, that we shall either go mad from the revelation or flee from the deadly light into the peace and safety of a new dark age" (*DH* 125). The elucidation and contextualization of these passages may require considerable analysis, but in the course of it we may come to gain a better sense of what science actually meant to Lovecraft.

Some of Lovecraft's reliance on science is of an amusingly trivial sort. In the minor tale "The Transition of Juan Romero" (1919) he speaks in passing of a "gibbous moon," and then writes a self-important footnote: "Here is a lesson in scientific accuracy for fiction writers. I have just looked up the moon's phases for October, 1894, to find when a gibbous moon was visible at 2 a.m., and have changed the dates to fit!!" (*D* 340). Expressing early admiration for the work of Edgar Rice Burroughs, Lovecraft was nonetheless irritated at the scientific errors in both the Tarzan and the Mars stories (see *MW* 497); and he was tireless in correcting his colleagues' scientific errors, even going so far as to buy planispheres for Frank Belknap Long and Donald Wandrei "so that those young rascals won't get the constellations wrong in their future stories, as they have done in the past!"[2] All this is very entertaining, and at a minimum it shows the emphasis Lovecraft placed on rigid scientific accuracy. This kind of "realism" became a central tenet of his entire theory of weird fiction, as he explained in "Notes on Writing Weird Fiction": "Inconceivable events and conditions have a special handicap to overcome, and this can be accomplished only through the maintenance of a careful realism in every phase of the story *except* that touching on the one given marvel" (*CE* 2.177).

Science of a marginally more significant sort appears in "The Beast in the Cave"—in this case, biology, or, more specifically, the theory of evolution. This story could be said to have initiated a wide range of Lovecraft tales that feature a potential reversal along the evolutionary ladder. Here the narrator, lost in the labyrinthine depths of Mammoth Cave, feels threatened by some entity who appears to be pursuing him; upon his first sight of the creature—after a guide comes to rescue him and shines a flashlight upon the dying figure—he identifies it as "an anthropoid ape of large proportions" (*D* 327); of course, the creature turns out to be a man who had been lost in the cave for

---

2. HPL to August Derleth, 16 January 1936 (*ES* 724).

months or years. The reasons why the narrator thought the entity to be nonhuman are of interest: unable to see him, but only hearing his footsteps, the narrator becomes convinced that "these footfalls were *not like those of any mortal man*" because "*at times,* when I listened carefully, I seemed to trace the falls of *four* instead of *two* feet" (D 324; Lovecraft's emphasis). In other words, the man, in his "fallen" state, had renounced the prototypical badge of humanity—an upright gait—for the savagery of the animal.

This story immediately brings "Arthur Jermyn" to mind; for just as the narrator of "The Beast in the Cave" is struck by "the all-pervading and almost unearthly *whiteness* so characteristic of the whole anatomy" (D 327) of the hapless man, so in "Arthur Jermyn" we appear to be dealing with a "mummified white ape of some unknown species, less hairy than any recorded variety, and infinitely nearer mankind—quite shockingly so" (D 82). This is, indeed, the ape that Sir Wade Jermyn had mated with in the eighteenth century, leading to the "subtly odd and repellent cast" (D 78) of the entire Jermyn line from that point onward. But it is not only this that leads Arthur Jermyn, a sensitive poet and last of the Jermyns, to set himself ablaze on a moor one night: rather, it is his realization that the peculiarities of his own heredity are, to a lesser degree, implicit in the entire human race: by subtle clues Lovecraft makes it clear that all humanity is derived from the "prehistoric white Congolese civilisation" (D 74) of which that white ape was a descendant. For someone of Lovecraft's well-known racialist inclinations (for which see Section IV), this would be the acme of horror; but more broadly, Lovecraft is emphasizing human "insignificance" by postulating—as he would repeatedly do in many different ways in later stories—a degrading or ignominious origin of our species.

For Lovecraft, devolution can occur in several ways: unwholesome inbreeding, psychological trauma, cannibalism, and miscegenation (interbreeding with alien species). Psychological trauma could conceivably be the reason for the degeneration of the man in "The Beast in the Cave," forced as he is to adopt animalistic behavior as a means of self-preservation (presumably he eats, without the benefit of cooking, any stray animals that cross his path). A similar trauma appears to cause the spectacular descent upon the evolutionary scale of the otherwise refined narrator of "The Rats in the Walls" (1923). Science would appear to be a critical component in this story, as at one point the narrator, Delapore, brings in a band of scientists to assist in elucidating the apparently supernatural phenomena by which his restored home, Exham Priory, is plagued: the "five eminent authorities" (DH 39) include "Sir William Brinton, whose excavations in the Troad excited most of the world in their day" (DH 40); the suggestion is that most of the five are archaeologists or anthropologists, although oddly enough one of them, Thornton, proves to be a "psychic investigator" (*DH* 41). And yet, the source of the horror in this story remains a bit unclear. It appears that Delapore comes upon evidence that his family, and by extension all the previous occupants of Exham Priory going back to prehistory, had practiced cannibalism, sadism, and other monstrous acts, and is so horrified that he immediately devolves from a modern, civilized man to a cannibalistic monster: after uttering wild cries in increasing ancient languages (archaic English, Anglo-Saxon, Latin, Gaelic, and what in a letter he terms "pithecanthropoid" [*SL* 1.258]) he is found "crouching in the blackness over the plump, half-eaten body of Capt. Norrys" (*DH* 45). In reality, the science in "The Rats in the Walls" is only a kind of gloss or patina that seeks to lend a vague sort of plausibility to a story that is otherwise fully in the old Gothic mode: it is, in fact, Lovecraft's "Fall of the House of Usher."

Much the same can be said for "The Picture in the House" (1920), where unnatural longevity—if not actual devolution—is attributed to cannibalism. The large old man with "abnormally ruddy" (*DH* 120) cheeks has not merely maintained his robust physique by devouring humans ("His height could not have been less than six feet, and despite a general air of age and poverty he was stout and powerful in proportion" [*DH* 120]); it is that he has extended the span of his life far beyond the normal, for it becomes evident that he was actually born in the eighteenth century. Once again, the scientific rationale for the story is relatively slight: the old man himself, in his crude patois, appeals to Biblical precedent when he remarks, "They say meat makes blood an' flesh, an' gives ye new life, so I wondered ef 'twudn't make a man live longer an' longer ef 'twas *more the same*" (*DH* 123), a manifest reference to "For the blood is the life" (Deut. 12:23). But the story is worth contrasting with another one written a few months earlier, "The Terrible Old Man" (1920): here no rationale at all is provided for the anomalous longevity of the old sea captain of the title; if anything, there is a suggestion that sorcery of some kind is involved, if those "many peculiar bottles, in each [of which] a small piece of lead suspended pendulum-wise from a string" (*DH* 273) are any indication: they appear to contain the souls of the old man's former crew. Can the magic that has confined the souls of his shipmates also have helped to give him unnatural life?

Things do not get much better, from a scientific perspective, in "The Lurking Fear" (1922), a potboiler written to order for what Lovecraft later called a "vile rag" (*SL* 4.170) named *Home Brew*. Here one can assume that some sort of inbreeding caused the degeneration of the Martense family, who dwelt in a once-sumptuous mansion in the Catskill mountain region of New York State. The narrator, seeking to learn the source of the repeated attacks upon the outlying regions—attacks that had occurred randomly for more than a century—in the end learns that it is not a single entity that is responsible for the mayhem but an entire colony of "deformed hairy devils or apes" (*D* 198) that have dug endless tunnels all through Tempest Mountain, where the mansion stands. In a cataclysmic vision the narrator finally sees one of them clearly: "The object was nauseous; a filthy whitish gorilla thing with sharp yellow fangs and matted fur. It was the ultimate product of mammalian degeneration; the frightful outcome of isolated spawning, multiplication, and cannibal nutrition above and below the ground; the embodiment of all the snarling chaos and grinning fear that lurk behind life" (*D* 199). That final, hysterical phrase makes it clear that what Lovecraft was seeking in this story was not a plausible scientific rationale but merely a lurid shudder, made all the more flamboyant by the fevered prose with which the entire tale is written.

If any scientific element predominates in the first decade (1917–26) of Lovecraft's mature fiction-writing career, it is the notion of alien races—races that, either emerging from the depths of space or nurtured in the secret corners of the earth, menace humanity from below and make our own dominance of the planet tenuous indeed. One of his earliest stories, "Dagon" (1917), involves a narrator who, having escaped from a German prison-ship and drifting in the open sea in a rowboat, awakens to find that an entire land mass has emerged from the depths of the sea. The bas-reliefs the narrator finds on a monolith depict some anomalous entities: "I think that these things were supposed to depict men—at least, a certain sort of men; though the creatures were shewn disporting like fishes in the waters of some marine grotto" (*D* 18). But the story ends shortly thereafter, and not much is made of this. What Lovecraft is hinting in this story is that there are not merely isolated non-human—or not fully human—entities lurking in hidden places, but entire civilizations of which we know nothing. "The Temple" (1920) conveys this idea somewhat more effectively. The commander of a disabled German submarine that is sinking to the bottom of the Atlantic comes upon evidence of an entire city on the sea-bottom; what is more, the art that the commander sees adorning an immense temple in this city "imparts the impression of terrible antiquity, as though it were the remotest rather than the immediate ancestor of Greek art" (*D* 67). In other words, Lovecraft is saying that Greek art—one of the greatest sources of aesthetic pride of which we as human beings can boast—is, in the end, a degraded echo of a much more refined art produced by an alien species. In "The Nameless City" (1921) an archaeologist encounters clear evidence that a forgotten city in Arabia was built by "monstrosities" (*D* 104) who, as he learns cataclysmically at the end of the story, are still existing. Lovecraft, however, does not seem to have thought through the physiology of these creatures particularly carefully:

> They were of the reptile kind, with body lines suggesting sometimes the crocodile, sometimes the seal, but more often nothing of which either the naturalist or the palaeontologist ever heard of. In size they approximated a small man, and their fore legs bore delicate and evidently flexible feet curiously like human hands and fingers. But strangest of all were their heads, which presented a contour violating all known biological principles. To nothing can such things be well compared—in one flash I thought of comparisons as varied as the cat, the bulldog, the mythic Satyr, and the human being. Not Jove himself had so colossal and protuberant a forehead, yet the horns and the noselessness and the alligator-like jaw placed the things outside all established categories. (D 104)

All this is very piquant; but, if these creatures were the products of terrestrial evolution, how could they have gained such anomalously hybrid features? Analogous entities are found in "The Festival" (1923): "They were not altogether crows, nor moles, nor buzzards, nor ants, nor vampire bats, nor decomposed human beings; but something I cannot and must not recall" (D 215). That last comment is particularly unhelpful, and one would never know that, as Lovecraft would admit years later (see SL 4.297), this broodingly atmospheric story—which chiefly seeks to evoke the antique atmosphere of Marblehead, Massachusetts—was even in part inspired by Margaret A. Murray's controversial anthropological treatise, *The Witch-Cult in Western Europe* (1921), which advocated the theory (now regarded as highly unlikely) that the medieval witch-cult was the product of a pre-Aryan race of stunted human beings who retreated into caves and other secret places but managed to carry on their nefarious practices. Lovecraft, who had just encountered the Welsh writer Arthur Machen, whose horror fiction embodies an approximately similar conception in its use of the legends of the "little people," found the apparent scientific confirmation of the idea fatally enticing, and he repeated it as proven fact to the end of his life.

It is evident that, although science peeps out here and there in many early Lovecraft tales, it is largely used as a makeshift to enhance the *aesthetic* plausibility of the scenarios, which remain overwhelmingly supernatural in their overall thrust. The best that can be said for these stories is that they make a *gesture* toward scientific plausibility, as Lovecraft is coming to recognize that the standard ghost, goblin, witch, werewolf, or vampire is no longer convincing to a sophisticated readership that has learned too much about biology, chemistry, and physics, and that has also shed the naive religious belief that formed at least a part of the pseudo-intellectual support for these entities.

All this makes us stop short in amazement when we encounter "The Shunned House" (1924). On the surface, this appears to be nothing more than an artfully told haunted house tale set in Lovecraft's native Providence. The narrator and his uncle strive to ascertain why so many deaths—and certain other anomalies—have occurred in a house in the oldest district of the city; a house that, as a matter of fact, "was never regarded by the solid part of the community as in any real sense 'haunted'" but merely "'unlucky'" (MM 237). But as the narrator explores the history of the house and its occupants and seems forced to the conclusion that some vampiric entity is sucking the life out of anyone who lives there too long, we suddenly come upon this remarkable passage:

> We were not, as I have said, in any sense childishly superstitious, but scientific study and reflection had taught us that the known universe of three dimensions embraces the merest fraction of the whole cosmos of substance and energy. In this case an overwhelming preponderance of evidence from numerous authentic sources pointed to the tenacious existence of certain forces of great power and, so far as the human point of view is concerned, exceptional malignancy. To say that we actually believed in vampires or werewolves would be a carelessly inclusive statement. Rather must it be said that we were not prepared to deny the possibility of certain unfamiliar and unclassified modifications of vital force and attenuated matter; existing very infrequently in three-dimensional space because of its more intimate connexion with other spatial units, yet close enough to the boundary of our own to furnish us occasional manifestations which we, for lack of a proper vantage-point, may never hope to understand....
>
> Such a thing was surely not a physical or biochemical impossibility in the light of a newer science which includes the theories of relativity and intra-atomic action. One might easily imagine an alien nucleus of substance or energy, formless or otherwise, kept alive by imperceptible or immaterial subtractions from the life-force or bodily tissues and fluids of other and more palpably living things into which it penetrates and with whose fabric it sometimes completely merges itself. (MM 251-52)

A treatise could be written on this passage. That first sentence brings to mind the earlier tale "From Beyond" (1920), a florid and confused tale whose only interest lies in its embodiment (as I have demonstrated elsewhere [see Joshi, "The Sources for 'From Beyond'"]) of certain principles found in Hugh Elliot's *Modern Science and Materialism* (1919), a major source for Lovecraft's views on science and philosophy. In essence, "From Beyond" is a kind of horrific instantiation of the common fact that all material entities are in fact largely composed of the empty space between atoms and molecules. The histrionic scientist in that story, Crawford Tillinghast, declares pompously: "What do we know ... of the world and the universe about us? Our means of receiving impressions are absurdly few, and our notions of surrounding objects infinitely narrow" (*D* 91). Tillinghast has invented a machine that can "*break down the barriers*" (*D* 91; Lovecraft's emphasis) that prevent our seeing what the universe is "really" like; accordingly, the narrator sees a succession of hideous entities "brushing past me and occasionally *walking or drifting through my supposedly solid body*" (*D* 95; Lovecraft's emphasis).

Far more interesting in "The Shunned House" is the reference to "relativity and intra-atomic action." The remarkable thing about this is that, just a year previously, Lovecraft felt that his entire world-view was in tatters because recent eclipse observations had confirmed the truth of the Einstein theory:

> My cynicism and scepticism are increasing, and from an entirely new cause—the Einstein theory.... All is chance, accident and ephemeral illusion—a fly may be greater than Arcturus, and Durfee Hill may surpass Mount Everest—assuming them to be removed from the present planet and differently environed in the continuum of space-time. There are no values in all infinity—the least idea that there are is the supreme mockery of all. (*SL* 1.231)

Lovecraft snapped out of this naive response to Einstein fairly quickly, although many other intellectuals saw in relativity the downfall of much of the nineteenth century's cocksure materialism. Lovecraft rebuked such careless thinkers in a late letter:

> Although these new turns of science don't really mean a thing in relation to the myth of cosmic consciousness and teleology, a new brood of despairing and horrified moderns is seizing on the doubt of all positive knowledge which they imply; and is deducing therefrom that, *since nothing is true*, therefore *anything can be true* . . . whence one may invent or revive any sort of mythology that fancy or nostalgia or desperation may dictate, and defy anyone to prove that it isn't "emotionally" true—whatever that means. This sickly, decadent neomysticism—a protest not only against machine materialism but against pure science with its destruction of the mystery and dignity of human emotion and experience—will be the dominant creed of middle twentieth century aesthetes . . . (*SL* 3.53)

What Lovecraft is saying, in essence, is that Einstein's devising of the precise formula for the transformation of matter into energy does not make the archaic notion of "spirit" (i.e., "soul") any more plausible than before; indeed, as he says in another letter:

> For matter, it appears, really is exactly what "spirit" was always supposed to be. Thus it is proved *that wandering energy always has a detectable form*—that if it doesn't take the form of waves or electron-streams, *it becomes matter itself*; and that the

absence of matter or any other detectable energy-form indicates *not the presence of spirit, but the absence of anything whatever.* (SL 2.266–67)

This is all very clever, and pretty much on the mark. Lovecraft had a bit more difficulty with quantum theory, and the one passage I have found in his correspondence where he discusses it (SL 3.228) reveals a fundamental misunderstanding of it: Lovecraft wants to maintain that the "uncertainty" in regard to the action of sub-atomic particles is an *epistemological*, not an *ontological*, uncertainty; that is, it is only our human inability to predict the movement of sub-atomic particles that causes the uncertainty, and that the uncertainty is not inherent in nature. This conclusion is erroneous, but Lovecraft can be pardoned for not fully grasping this highly complex theory—which many thinkers seized upon as spelling the downfall of all causality, a conclusion that is itself highly likely to be erroneous, and is certainly erroneous where atomic or molecular action is concerned.

What we have in "The Shunned House," then, is, for the first time in Lovecraft's literary career, a coherently conceived scientific rationale that reinterprets the standard myth of the vampire and recasts it into something much more complex—and, as it happens, much more mysterious and horrifying. The appeal to advanced science is also an appeal to the scientific method—the method of keeping an open mind in regard to phenomena that may appear bizarre or even contrary to nature, but which may in the end be incorporated into an expanded conception of the universe that is still predominantly materialistic. And whereas the conventional vampire could be dealt with by such hackneyed means as a crucifix or exposure to the light of day, the vampiric entity in "The Shunned House" is a far more redoubtable creature; and it requires nothing less material than "six carboys of sulphuric acid" (MM 260) which, when poured upon the entity, elicits a "hideous roar" (MM 261) heard throughout the city.

III. The Brain in the Canister

The rest of Lovecraft's fiction shows a constant if unsystematic attempt to embody scientific principles as an intellectual substratum, even if some of them radically exceed the bounds of the known laws of nature. Moreover, it is in the stories of his last decade of writing that we finally come upon an extensive use of those sciences—especially chemistry, geology, and astronomy—that Lovecraft professed to have been his first loves, and which, taken as a whole, fostered the sense of "cosmicism" that is his defining characteristic as a fiction writer. Even though cosmicism was stated as an aesthetic principle at least as early as 1921 ("Man's relations to man do not captivate my fancy. It is man's relation to the cosmos—to the unknown—which alone arouses in me the spark of creative imagination" [CE 5.53]), it is embodied in relatively few tales prior to 1926. "Dagon," "Beyond the Wall of Sleep" (1919), and "The Temple" only hint at cosmicism; perhaps Lovecraft's most interesting treatment is found in the prose poem "Nyarlathotep" (1920), which powerfully suggests the decline of human civilization as a corollary to the collapse of the entire fabric of the universe.

All that changes with "The Call of Cthulhu" (1926). This story is important not so much for its introduction of the so-called Cthulhu Mythos (a term never coined by Lovecraft), but rather for its coherent and plausible use of the theme that would come to dominate his subsequent tales: alien races dwelling on the underside of the known world. And because these alien races are now postulated as having emerged from the depths of space, they evade the dilemma (found in various ways in "Dagon," "The Temple," and "The Nameless City") of incorporating these entities within the scope of terrestrial evolution.

The stories of this type—"The Colour out of Space" (1927), "The Dunwich Horror" (1928), "The Whisperer in Darkness" (1930), At the Mountains of Madness (1931), "The Shadow out of Time" (1934-35)—are all of such length and complexity as to preclude detailed analysis; but some hints as to their distinctive features can be made here. In a sense it could be said that Lovecraft is choosing the easy way out by hypothesizing an extraterrestrial origin for his various alien species, thereby obviating the need to harmonize them within the known laws of terrestrial biology and physics; but the mass of circumstantial detail Lovecraft provides shows how much thought he took in fashioning his creatures, and in rendering them simultaneously plausible and outré. He is careful not to make them *too* bizarre, *too* defiant of the known laws of nature; for he knows (as he states in his discussion of the ramifications of the Einstein theory) that the universe within the scope of our knowledge

> *isn't big enough* to let relativity get in its major effects—*hence we can rely on the never-failing laws of earth to give absolutely reliable results in the nearer heavens*. . . . If we can study the relation of a race of ants to a coral atoll or a volcanic islet which has risen and will sink again—and nobody dares deny that we can—then it will be *equally possible* for us, if we have suitable instruments and methods, to study the relation of man and the earth to the solar system and the nearer stars. The result will, when obtained, be just as conclusive as that of a study in terrestrial zoölogy or geology. (SL 2.265; Lovecraft's emphasis)

Accordingly, the only physical anomaly revealed by the baleful entity Cthulhu is his (its?) ability to recombine disparate parts of himself after they have been scattered. Old Castro, who "remembered bits of hideous legend" about Cthulhu and his "spawn," states that they "were not composed altogether of flesh and blood. They had shape . . . but that shape was not made of matter. When the stars were right, They could plunge from world to world through the sky; but when the stars were wrong, They could not live. But although They no longer lived, They would never really die" (*DH* 140). All this is expressed in a deliberately mystical fashion, for Castro is a naive and ignorant worshipper of Cthulhu and his minions; but underneath this language one can see Lovecraft *stretching*—but not *breaking*—the laws of nature to accommodate the existence of an alien species just outside the bounds of the known. That Cthulhu is made up of a substance not quite material as we recognize it; that there is some obscure connection between him and the stars of the outer cosmos; that his manner of existence is somewhere between "life" and "death" as we are accustomed to understand them—all this is hinted, and no more than hinted, in Castro's maunderings.

"The Colour out of Space" is perhaps Lovecraft's greatest triumph in the depiction of an extraterrestrial entity. The creature (or creatures?) that came in the meteorite that landed in a central Massachusetts farm cannot be analyzed by chemical means: the substance of the meteorite itself, when collected by scientists from Miskatonic University, "had faded wholly away when they put it in a glass beaker" (*DH* 58) and, when another specimen was gathered, it failed to respond to numerous tests—water, hydrochloric acid, nitric acid, carbon disulphide, and several others (*DH* 58). Lovecraft's chemical experiments, conducted from the age of eight onwards, certainly stood him in good stead here. But more significantly, it is the *psychology* of the nebulous entities that is least amenable to human analysis; whereas an obviously malevolent motive is at one point attributed to Cthulhu ("After vigintillions of years great Cthulhu was loose again, and ravening for delight" [*DH* 152]), the entities in the meteorite are utterly inscrutable as to their goals or purpose. Lovecraft effectively conveys both their physical and their moral incomprehensibility in the simple words of the dying farmer Nahum Gardner: ". . . the colour . . . cold an' wet, but it burns . . . dun't know what it wants . . . it beats down your mind an' then gits ye . . . it come from some place whar things ain't as they is here . . ." (*DH* 71-72).

From this perspective, "The Dunwich Horror" and even "The Whisperer in Darkness"—the latter a masterful evocation of the terror to be found in the remote backwoods of Vermont—represent a regression; for the entities in these tales are all too obviously intent on harming human beings and perhaps even in dominating them. "The Dunwich Horror," indeed, is in many ways a reprise of the short novel *The Case of Charles Dexter Ward* (1927), which in its use of alchemy and witchcraft can be said to be the pinnacle of Lovecraft's work in the old-time Gothic mode; it is, in effect, his *House of the Seven Gables* in its tracing of a curse that spans the generations. "The Dunwich Horror" is remarkably similar in many details. The cosmic entity Yog-Sothoth has mated with a backwoods farm girl, Lavinia Whateley, and spawned twin monsters—one of them, Wilbur Whateley, approximately human, and the other, his twin, quite otherwise. Although Wilbur reveals some interesting physiological traits when his dead body is analyzed, the science here is merely a sop to plausibility in a tale that otherwise is entirely dependent on the supernatural and on sorcery (three professors from Miskatonic University destroy the twin by the use of incantations). More to be censured is the obvious good-vs.-evil scenario that Lovecraft sets up between the valiant Professor Armitage and the Whateley clan; at one point he speaks wildly and bombastically of a "plan for the extirpation of the entire human race and all animal and vegetable life from the earth by some terrible elder race of beings from another dimension" (DH 185), and then emits a self-important lecture at the end: "We have no business calling in such things from outside, and only very wicked people and very wicked cults ever try to" (DH 197).

In "The Whisperer in Darkness" Lovecraft seems to dance nervously around the issue of what the fungi from Yuggoth are actually after. Once again, a lone farmer, Henry W. Akeley, is besieged by extraterrestrials—they come from Yuggoth (Pluto), although Lovecraft is careful to specify that "Yuggoth . . . is only the stepping-stone" and that "the main body of the beings inhabits strangely organised abysses wholly beyond the utmost reach of any human imagination" (DH 240). This is no doubt why they cannot be photographed by ordinary cameras. But the critical issue of motive emerges when a correspondent of Akeley's, Albert N. Wilmarth, comes up to Vermont for a visit at Akeley's urging, finding that Akeley has unexpectedly taken ill and can hardly speak except in a whisper, and is otherwise wrapped from head to foot in blankets. Akeley tells him of the remarkable abilities of the aliens ("The Outer Beings are perhaps the most marvellous organic things in or beyond all space and time—members of a cosmos-wide race of which all other life-forms are merely degenerate variants" [DH 239]), and especially of their surgical skill—they can extract a human brain, encase it in a canister, and take it on cosmos-wide voyagings where it can perceive all the wonders of the universe, "with elaborate instruments capable of duplicating the three vital faculties of sight, hearing, and speech" (DH 257). At one point Wilmarth finds such a prospect intoxicatingly exciting: "To shake off the maddening and wearying limitations of time and space and natural law—to be linked with the vast *outside*—to come close to the nighted and abysmal secrets of the infinite and the ultimate—surely such a thing was worth the risk of one's life, soul, and sanity!" (DH 243). But in the end he draws back in fear and flees the place—perhaps because he has come to realize that the letter inviting him up to Vermont was written not by Akeley but by the aliens themselves, and that the whispering figure he saw in the dimly lit room of the farmhouse was one of the aliens in disguise. Hence, the statement in the letter—"The alien beings desire to know mankind more fully, and to have a few of mankind's philosophic and scientific leaders know more about them. . . . The very idea of any attempt to *enslave* or *degrade* mankind is ridiculous" (DH 239)—would seem to carry the very opposite connotation.

The contradictions in Lovecraft's depiction of alien races seem to have been resolved in his two great science fiction stories, At the Mountains of Madness and "The Shadow out of Time." In these tales there is not only an enormously elaborate anatomical description of the alien species, but a careful working out of their psychology, morality, and even politics. Both works were, fittingly, published in the science fiction pulp magazine *Astounding Stories*. One passage in the former tale is of surpassing interest. As the protagonists decipher the bas-reliefs of the ancient Antarctic city of the barrel-shaped Old Ones, they discover that these semi-vegetable, semi-animal creatures had had encounters with both the "Cthulhu spawn" and the fungi from Yuggoth (here termed the "Mi-Go" because of their apparent resemblance to the "Mi-Go, or Abominable Snow-Men"):

> It was curious to note from the pictured battles that both the Cthulhu spawn and the Mi-Go seem to have been composed of matter more widely different from that which we know than was the substance of the Old Ones. They were able to undergo transformations and reintegrations impossible for their adversaries, and seem therefore to have originally come from even remoter gulfs of cosmic space. The Old Ones, but for their abnormal toughness and peculiar vital properties, were strictly material, and must have had their absolute origin within the known space-time continuum. (MM 68)

This is exactly the distinction Lovecraft was emphasizing in his letter discussing the ramifications of the Einstein theory.

At the Mountains of Madness is significant because it appears to be the first tale written by Lovecraft after he had formulated a momentous new theory of weird fiction—one that took far more cognizance of the advance of science than any theory he had previously articulated. The canonical utterance occurs in a letter to Frank Belknap Long dating to February 27, 1931, only three days after he had begun writing his Antarctic novel:

> The time has come when the normal revolt against time, space, & matter must assume a form not overtly incompatible with what is known of reality—when it must be gratified by images forming *supplements* rather than *contradictions* of the visible & mensurable universe. And what, if not a form of *non-*

supernatural cosmic art, is to pacify this sense of revolt—as well as gratify the cognate sense of curiosity? (*SL* 3.296-97)

The context of this utterance is worth examining. Lovecraft, fresh from a reading of Joseph Wood Krutch's *The Modern Temper* (1929), had agreed emphatically with Krutch's belief that (as he expressed it) "some former art attitudes—like sentimental romance, loud heroics, ethical didacticism, &c.— are so patently hollow as to be visibly absurd & non-usable from the start" (*SL* 3.293). The advance of knowledge—and this includes not only our understanding of the universe but our understanding of our own psychologies—had destroyed many of the intellectual foundations that had supported previous "art attitudes," and there was a danger that weird fiction itself—especially fiction that still relied on outdated concepts like the ghost or the vampire—would cease to be of any relevance to the knowledgeable and sophisticated reader. The only recourse, as Lovecraft saw it, was the notion of *supplementing* rather than *defying* known natural law—a principle he had perhaps unconsciously observed since "The Call of Cthulhu," but one that now became conscious. *At the Mountains of Madness* is one of his most vigorous expressions of this new aesthetic: nothing in the story—even the final emergence of the loathsome shoggoth, a fifteen-foot protoplasmic entity that the Old Ones had created as a beast of burden, but which had ultimately overthrown its masters—stretches the bounds of credulity to the breaking point, as, say, the mating of Yog-Sothoth with a human being in "The Dunwich Horror" does. The enormous care that Lovecraft took in establishing the scientific basis for the entire scenario—employing the sciences of geology, palaeontology, biology, and physics in particular—and the slow, gradual accumulation of convincing detail make this novel a triumph of scientific realism. And of course, one cannot fail to quote Lovecraft's celebrated praise of the Old Ones, as the protagonists come to express the highest admiration for their courage and perseverence in traversing the cosmos, colonizing the earth, and establishing a rich and flourishing civilization: "Scientists to the last—what had they done that we would not have done in their place? God, what intelligence and persistence! What a facing of the incredible . . . Radiates, vegetables, monstrosities, star-spawn— whatever they had been, they were men!" (*MM* 96).

"The Shadow out of Time," while featuring many of the same elements of scientific verisimilitude, also represents the culmination of a theme that we can detect throughout Lovecraft's work—the theme of mind- or personality-exchange. In this novella an alien species termed the Great Race has "conquered the secret of time" (*SOT* 48) by its ability to send its minds forward (and, more rarely, backward) in time, displace the mind of some member of another species, and inhabit that mind for shorter or longer periods, learning everything about that species and its historical period; in the meantime, the captive mind is thrust into the body of its captor, and writes the history of its own time for the immense archives of the Great Race. Eventually, a reversal is effected, and the two minds occupy their own bodies once again. Lovecraft, while initially portraying the idea as existentially terrifying, later suggests that the prospect is not at all to be despised:

> When the captive mind's amazement and resentment had worn off, and when (assuming that it came from a body vastly different from the Great Race's) it had lost its horror at its unfamiliar temporary form, it was permitted to study its new environment and experience a wonder and wisdom approximating that of its displacer. With suitable precautions, and in exchange for suitable services, it was allowed to rove all over the habitable world in titan airships or on the huge boat-like atomic-engined vehicles which traversed the great roads, and to delve freely into the libraries containing the records of the planet's past and future. This reconciled many captive minds to their lot; since none were other than keen, and to such minds the unveiling of hidden mysteries earth—closed chapters of inconceivable pasts and dizzying vortices of future time which include the years ahead of their own natural ages—forms always, despite the abysmal horrors often unveiled, the supreme experience of life. (SOT 49)

The scenario of this story is a vast expansion and subtilization of the scenario found in the early tale "Beyond the Wall of Sleep," where the notion was handled in a sadly bungled manner. There, a cosmic entity had been trapped in the body of a backwoods farmer named Joe Slater, and only manages to escape its human prison upon Slater's death. But Lovecraft has not thought through *why* or *by what means* this entity had ended up in the body of this uncouth individual, and the story collapses of its own absurdity.

What is more interesting is that Lovecraft has employed the notion of mind-exchange as a means of obviating both the scientific and the philosophical difficulties involved in the traditional idea of psychic possession, especially in the highly conventionalized form of possession by a demon or by the Devil himself. Lovecraft the atheist could of course never utilize the trope in that form, but earlier tales do make use of it in a relatively standard manner. *The Case of Charles Dexter Ward* is frequently thought to involve psychic possession, but, if it occurs at all, it does so in a manner somewhat more covert than many commentators believe. It is not that the seventeenth-century alchemist Joseph Curwen literally possesses the soul or mind of his twentieth-century descendant, Charles Dexter Ward; rather, it is that Ward, after stumbling upon his relation to Curwen, manages to revive him *bodily* (by the gathering of his "essential Saltes" and the use of suitable incantations), whereupon Curwen kills Ward (whose double he proves to be) and tries to pass himself off as Ward. But psychic possession from a different angle may come into play, as it is suggested that the very interest that Ward initially takes in his relation to Curwen was a result of the latter's exercise of mental powers beyond the grave.

This scenario is roughly duplicated in the late story "The Thing on the Doorstep" (1933), which is an anomaly in its reversion to a traditional Gothic mode in the midst of Lovecraft's period of scientific realism. Here a college student named Asenath Waite seems to have an anomalous power of hypnosis: "By gazing peculiarly at a fellow-student she would often give the latter a distinct feeling of *exchanged personality*—as if the subject were placed momentarily in the magician's body and able to stare half across the room at her real body, whose eyes blazed and protruded with an alien expression" (*DH* 281). Sure enough, she does exactly that with the man she marries, the weak-willed Edward Derby; and her power also extends beyond the grave, for she manages to switch minds with Derby even after he has killed her; in turn, Derby's mind is flung back into her decaying corpse.

All this is delectably ghoulish, but the handling is crude and obvious, and "The Thing on the Doorstep" is one of the most disappointing of Lovecraft's later tales. And yet, it becomes clear that he has duplicated its basic scenario in "The Shadow out of Time," although introducing the notion of *mind-exchange over time* and, of course, rendering the entire conception far more plausible and compelling. There is, however, one philosophical issue that Lovecraft does no more than skirt in all these tales of mind-exchange: exactly what is being exchanged? In the early story "Herbert West—Reanimator" (1921–22), a flamboyant and possibly self-parodic account of a mad scientist's repeated attempts to reanimate the dead, the narrator states that Herbert West believed "with Haeckel that all life is a chemical and physical process, and that the so-called 'soul' is a myth" (*D* 134). The reference is to Ernst Haeckel (1834–1919), the German biologist and naturalist whose vigorous support of the theory of evolution is embodied in several works, notably *Die Welträthsel* (1899; translated into English in 1900 as *The Riddle of the Universe*), a book that markedly influenced Lovecraft when he read it around 1920. If, with Haeckel, Lovecraft had dispensed with the notion of an immaterial "soul," how then could he envision a (presumably material) mind cast out of its own body and thrust into that of another? He never really addresses the issue in the tales in question, and perhaps we are to believe that he retained this conception, even in such a purely science-fictional tale as "The Shadow out of Time," as the one supernatural "safety-valve" in a work that otherwise rigorously observes every known scientific principle.

IV. Shuddering Physical Repugnance

The one major late story I have not studied so far is "The Shadow over Innsmouth" (1931). This can readily be seen to be the culmination of Lovecraft's recurrent theme of miscegenation—the denizens of the Massachusetts coastal city of Innsmouth have become physically and mentally corrupted through interbreeding with a hideous race of fish-frogs, the Deep Ones, who appear to have underwater colonies throughout the world—but this supremely masterful evocation of urban decay is perhaps worth studying from a very different context: the context of Lovecraft's racism.

It is scarcely to be denied that H. P. Lovecraft was a racist for the whole of his life. Initially deriving his views from familial influence and from his upbringing in an old Yankee town that was, in the opinion of the once-dominant Anglo-Saxons, already being overrun by such "foreigners" as Italians, Poles, and Portuguese, Lovecraft became a systematic racist who maintained resolutely that African Americans were biological inferior to Caucasians, that Jews represented an "alien" force in American culture, and that the "the one supreme race is the Teuton" (SL 1.18). Perhaps from the influence of younger colleagues who objected to his doctrinaire views, Lovecraft grudgingly came to abandon the notion of *biological* superiority or inferiority (except where African Americans were concerned) and posited an extreme notion of *cultural disharmony*, maintaining that even a tiny admixture of a foreign culture produced incompatibilities that could potentially lead to the downfall of civilization. The formulation he evolved late in life—"a real friend of civilisation wishes merely to make the Germans *more German*, the French *more French*, the Spaniards *more Spanish*, & so on" (SL 4.253)—sounds superficially laudable, but it is based upon this notion of the radical incompatibility of even the smallest presence of "foreign" blood or culture in a predominantly homogeneous society.

The tracing of the intellectual origin of these views is a vexed issue. Certainly, the unprecedented influx of immigrants into the United States from 1890 to 1920 inspired not only the severe immigration restriction laws of 1917, 1921, and 1924, but also an unprecedented wave of pseudo-scientific defenses of racism in the teens and twenties. How much of this literature Lovecraft read is a difficult question. One of his earliest surviving poems is the embarrassing "De Triumpho Naturae: The Triumph of Nature over Northern Ignorance" (1905), a vicious attack on African Americans ("The savage black, the ape-resembling beast, / Hath held too long his Saturnalian feast" [AT 33]), is dedicated to one William Benjamin Smith, author of the racist treatise *The Color Line* (1905), which Lovecraft clearly read and relished. The early essay "The Crime of the Century" (1915) appeals to Thomas Henry

Huxley for its division of mankind into separate racial groups, and no doubt Lovecraft may have picked up some hints from Friedrich Nietzsche, whom he read around 1919. Neither Huxley nor Nietzsche can be termed racists in any simple or obvious sense, although it is possible to read some of their writings in that way. Whether Lovecraft ever read Madison Grant's best-selling treatise *The Passing of the Great Race* (1916) is difficult to ascertain; I myself doubt it, in spite of the odd coincidence of Lovecraft's using the term "Great Race" twenty years later in "The Shadow out of Time." I similarly find no evidence that Lovecraft read another popular work, Lothrop Stoddard's *The Rising Tide of Color Against White World-Supremacy* (1920), although no doubt he would have sympathized with its message.

The plain fact is that Lovecraft believed he had scientific support for his racial views. In arguing with his old friend James F. Morton, who had written a brief tract called *The Curse of Race Prejudice* (1906), Lovecraft pontificates: "The black *is* vastly inferior. There can be no question of this among contemporary and unsentimental biologists—eminent Europeans for whom the prejudice-problem does not exist" (SL 3.253). Lovecraft, always eager to pick up information second-hand from reviews, newspapers, and magazine articles, does not cite any of these "eminent Europeans," but he was correct in believing that a fair number of scientists were still harboring racist beliefs well into the 1920s. It required generations of pioneering work by the anthropologist Franz Boas (1857–1942) and his students to persuade even biologists and anthropologists to discard racist presuppositions, and, as we are all aware, it has taken even longer for racialism to become intellectually and morally discreditable to the general public.

The incursion of racist presuppositions in Lovecraft's fiction is in large part covert, but it becomes visible once we realize the extent to which he ascribed to such views. Many of the tales of miscegenation now take on racial overtones: the mating of a distinguished, even aristocratic, Caucasian clan with apes in "Arthur Jermyn"; the unwholesome inbreeding that leads to degeneration in "The Lurking Fear"; even the mating of a white woman (however backward and degraded) with a "god" in "The Dunwich Horror," with the monstrosities that result. A more purely racialist story is "The Horror at Red Hook" (1925), written in the depths of Lovecraft's despair during his two miserable years (1924–26) in New York. This is nothing but a hostile snarl at the "foreigners" infesting the city that, in his view, had been established by Anglo-Saxons for the use of Anglo-Saxons; one of the worst parts of the city, the Red Hook district of Brooklyn, had now become "a maze of hybrid squalor" whose "population is a hopeless tangle and enigma; Syrian, Spanish, Italian, and negro elements impinging upon one another, and fragments of

Scandinavian and American belts lying not far distant" (D 247). Lurid, pulpish, and confused, "The Horror at Red Hook" possesses only biographical importance as a sign that Lovecraft was near the end of his psychological tether in a city he had come to despise—a city in which, ironically, he felt himself to be an "unassimilated alien" (SL 2.176).

With "The Shadow over Innsmouth" we are in very different territory. The existence of racialist elements does not detract from the aesthetic supremacy of this tale, which in its skillful mingling of external horror (the horror of an alien species impinging upon our civilization) and internal horror (the narrator, after struggling so valiantly to escape the aliens' clutches, finds that he is, by heredity, himself related to them) may stand at the very pinnacle of Lovecraft's artistic achievement. And yet, the racism certainly enters into the tale. The narrator is first repelled by the physical anomalies of the Innsmouth people; of the bus driver who takes him into the city from Arkham, he writes:

> He had a narrow head, bulging, watery blue eyes that seemed never to wink, a flat nose, a receding forehead and chin, and singularly undeveloped ears. His long, thick lip and coarse-pored, greyish cheeks seemed almost beardess except for some sparse yellow hairs that straggled and curled in irregular patches; and in places the surface seemed queerly irregular, as if peeling from some cutaneous disease. His hands were large and heavily veined, and had a very unusual greyish-blue tinge. (DH 314)

How can we not think of the "Arab with a hatefully negroid mouth" (D 258) found in "The Horror at Red Hook," or, even more pertinently, Lovecraft's admission in reference to Jews that "On our side there is a shuddering physical repugnance to most Semitic types"[3]—a clear reference to what Lovecraft took to be the anomalies of the Jewish physiognomy.

When the narrator of "The Shadow over Innsmouth" is compelled to spend a night in the seedy Gilman Hotel, further details unnerve him. Outside the hotel he is unnerved to hear that the passengers from a bus "shambled to the sidewalk and exchanged some faint guttural words with a loafer in a language I could have sworn was not English" (DH 341); the point is repeated once he flees the hotel and is being pursued by the Innsmouth denizens: "a large crowd of doubtful shapes was pouring [out of the Gilman House]—lanterns bobbing in the darkness, and horrible croaking voices exchanging low cries in what was certainly not English" (DH 350). It is probable that the presence of "foreigners" in conservative New England backwaters of this type was still uncommon in Lovecraft's day, but the emphasis he puts on the matter—as

---

3. HPL to Lillian D. Clark, 11 January 1926 (ms., JHL).

if the use of a foreign language is indicative of some kind of cosmic abnormality—is extraordinary. Lovecraft does not say that the language used by the inhabitants was not "human"—something that would indeed be productive of acute horror; rather, it was not "English."

It should, incidentally, be pointed out that Lovecraft's desire for homogeneity of culture is not intrinsically objectionable, just as the current tendency toward multiculturalism is not intrinsically virtuous. Lovecraft realized that there were virtues and drawbacks to both these forms of social organization, and he simply preferred the former. Where he is to be censured is (a) his refusal to take cognizance of the advances in anthropology and other sciences that had destroyed the racialist presuppositions on which he relied throughout his life, and (b) his assumption—on no compelling evidence—that even the tiniest admixture of "foreigners" would produce cultural chaos. As a social critic Lovecraft made many keen points, and his screeds on the baleful dominance of machinery, on the need to abandon *laissez-faire* capitalism for moderate socialism, and on the benefits of broadened education to yield an intelligent electorate and to foster civilized values have much to recommend them; but in his racial theories Lovecraft comes up short both as an intellect and as a compassionate human being. It is the one black mark against his otherwise admirable character.

Epilogue: The Big Kick

This essay hardly exhausts the use of science in Lovecraft's fiction. I have not even touched upon "The Dreams in the Witch House" (1932), which elegantly reinterprets ancient witchcraft legendry by means of higher mathematics, as a seventeenth-century witch develops the ability to enter into hyperspace (the fourth dimension); but Fritz Leiber's comprehensive discussion of this tale (see Leiber, "Through Hyperspace") leaves little for later commentators to say.

What I wish to do is to return, at last, to a query I raised earlier. How can Lovecraft, the supreme scientific rationalist, still find himself able to say (albeit in fiction, not in essays or letters) that science "will perhaps be the ultimate exterminator of our human species," or that its findings might initiate a "new dark age"? Does this not indicate a hostility to science starkly at odds with his general philosophy?

Two points can be made in extenuation of Lovecraft's remarks. In the first place, it is possible that what Lovecraft is suggesting is not that science, as such, is dangerous, but that its results can produce *psychological* trauma in sensitive temperaments. Lovecraft does in fact seem to have had an unusually low opinion of humanity's ability to deal with unpleasant truths; as early as 1918 he wrote: "In many cases the truth may cause suicidal or nearly suicidal depression" (SL 1.65). The stories exemplify this sentiment over and over again, preeminently "The Call of Cthulhu." Here we learn that Cthulhu's underwater city, R'lyeh, emerged by accident as a result of an earthquake, but—presumably because the "stars were not right"—it sank shortly thereafter, taking Cthulhu back down to the depths of the sea. As a result, the earth is presumably spared any reemergence of the loathsome entity for the foreseeable future; and yet the narrator, having now become aware of the mere existence of such an appalling contradiction to known laws of entity, writes plangently: "I have looked upon all that the universe has to hold of horror, and even the skies of spring and the flowers of summer must ever afterward be poison to me" (DH 154).

From another perspective, Lovecraft's "attack" on science can be seen as part and parcel of his aesthetic (as opposed to his metaphysical) enterprise. In other words, Lovecraft used weird fiction to create "the *illusion* of some strange suspension or violation of the galling limitations of time, space, and natural law" (CE 2.176); but he knew that such a gesture was not to be confused with an actual acceptance of the *reality* of a suspension of natural law. Convinced, to his own satisfaction (in spite of the findings of Einstein, Planck, and others), of the invariability of natural laws, Lovecraft nonetheless enjoyed giving himself the *frisson* of contemplating—at least for the duration of a story—the *possibility* that natural laws had been suspended or subverted. To suggest that science did not have *all* the answers to the universe was critical to his ability to preserve the sense of wonder and awe that he believed all weird writers must retain. To adapt his own terminology, the suggestion of the limitations of science was not a *contradiction* of his materialist philosophy, but a *supplement* to it. In 1930 he wrote:

> I get no kick at all from *postulating what isn't so*, as religionists and idealists do. That leaves me cold . . . My big kick comes from *taking reality just as it is*—accepting all the limitations of the most orthodox science—and then permitting my symbolising faculty to *build outward* from the existing facts; rearing a structure of *indefinite promise and possibility* whose topless towers are in no cosmos or dimension penetrable by the contradicting-power of the tyrannous and inexorable intellect. But the whole secret of the kick is *that I know damn well it isn't so.* (SL 3.140)

The point about religion is of interest, for Lovecraft believed it was exactly the error of religionists to take *literally* what could only have a *symbolic* reality: "religion itself is merely a pompous formalisation of fantastic art. Its disadvantage is that it demands an *intellectual* belief in the impossible, whereas fantastic art does not" (SL 4.417-18).

Lovecraft the scientific rationalist, then, produced a literature in which the boundaries of rationalism and science are pushed to their limits; but he could only get the "kick" he wanted by adhering to the most rigid and up-to-date findings of that science, which to him was the arbiter of all truth. And yet, science was in no way a hindrance to the functioning of the imagination; indeed, quite the reverse: "The more we learn of the cosmos, the more bewildering does it appear" (SL 4.324).

Works Cited

Leiber, Fritz. "A Literary Copernicus." 1949. In Peter Cannon, ed. *Lovecraft Remembered*. Sauk City, WI: Arkham House, 1998. 455–66.

———. "Through Hyperspace with Brown Jenkin: Lovecraft's Contribution to Speculative Fiction." 1966. In Peter Cannon, ed. *Lovecraft Remembered*. Sauk City, WI: Arkham House, 1998. 472–83.

Lovecraft, H. P. *The Shadow out of Time*. Edited by S. T. Joshi and David E. Schultz. New York: Hippocampus Press, 2001. [Abbreviated in the text as SOT.]

III. Thematic and Textual Studies

Autobiography in Lovecraft

On a certain level we can all accept Maurice Lévy's dictum that "in most of Lovecraft's tales, the main character—whether his name be Charles Dexter Ward, Edward Derby, Olney, Malone, or simply 'I'—*is* the author" (Lévy 118). This fact, Lévy contends, allows us to assume that Lovecraft is vicariously attempting to bestow the horror in his tales upon himself. While there are many points of validity in this interpretation, one flaw emerges in the obvious fact that Lovecraft's characters are autobiographical in radically differing degrees. There are some tales where the character or characters are only superficially autobiographical; where they are given various external characteristics that are not central to the tale as a whole. On the other hand, other tales gain some of their poignancy and significance precisely through the central character's sharing important attitudes with his author. An exploration of the relative degrees of autobiography present in Lovecraft's fiction may help us the better to understand his oft-misunderstood theory of characterisation.

In many of Lovecraft's tales one or the other of the characters is given a trait shared by Lovecraft himself. The narrator of "The Shadow over Innsmouth" is essentially a colourless character—since the main emphasis of the tale is not on what he *is* but on what he will *become*—but has certain idiosyncrasies that were Lovecraft's own. He embarks upon a tour of New England for "sightseeing, antiquarian, and genealogical" (*DH* 305) purposes; so, too, did Lovecraft visit many antiquarian (Marblehead, Portsmouth, Salem) and ancestral (Foster and Greene, R.I.) sites in his life. When the narrator, forced to stay in Innsmouth for the night, dines in a restaurant, he declares: "A bowl of vegetable soup with crackers was enough for me" (*DH* 342). Clearly he is reflecting Lovecraft's own parsimonious diet. (He is, indeed, one of the few characters in Lovecraft's fiction who partakes of any food at all. Another is Albert Wilmarth in "The Whisperer in Darkness," whose eating of a meal is similarly crucial to the development of the plot.) A still obscurer reference is the narrator's description of the Order of Dagon Hall with the "black and gold sign on the pediment" (*DH* 318). From a letter we learn that "I never liked any other colour combination so well as *black-and-gold* . . . perhaps because that was the scheme in the front hall of my birthplace, 454 Angell

Street" (*SL* 2.165). Whether the mention of "black and gold" is even a conscious reference to his favourite colours can certainly be doubted; it only underscores the relatively insignificant nature of the autobiographical elements in the tale. The narrator is not even important save as a conveyer of data, as the victim of the pursuit by the entities of Innsmouth, and as the subject of the final twist where he himself becomes one with the monsters. The narrative clearly centres upon the horrors at Innsmouth—the result of an unholy inbreeding—and the narrator is merely the vehicle for the exposition of this theme.

Elsewhere the autobiographical element is equally trivial. In one amusing passage in "Herbert West—Reanimator" the narrator tells that West "secretly sneered at my occasional martial enthusiasms and censures of supine neutrality" (*D* 142). Here we see Lovecraft ridiculing the militaristic attitudes he expressed during World War I, exhibited in such essays as "The League," "The Renaissance of Manhood," and "At the Root," and in such poems as "The Peace Advocate." The cause of temperance, which initially found Lovecraft a staunch supporter ("A Remarkable Document," "Liquor and Its Friends," "Temperance Song"), is similarly undermined hilariously in the celebrated drinking song (the manuscript of which bears the title "Gaudeamus" = "Let us delight") in "The Tomb." But neither of these two autobiographical touches is at all central to the two stories in question.

In other tales certain autobiographical elements hold somewhat more importance to the theme of the tale, but cannot be considered significant enough to warrant the conclusion that the tale hinges upon these elements. In "The Tomb" the central character certainly shares Lovecraft's antiquarianism, but this antiquarianism is born only of his unusual fascination with death. To be sure, the narrator is "temperamentally unfitted for the formal studies and social recreations of my acquaintances" (*D* 9), as Lovecraft perhaps was, and spent "my youth and adolescence in ancient and little-known books, and in roaming the fields and groves of the regions near my ancestral home," as Lovecraft certainly did; but the narrator ultimately resembles not Lovecraft but some of Poe's characters, whom Lovecraft described aptly as "melancholy, intellectual, highly sensitive, capricious, introspective, isolated, and sometimes slightly mad" (*D* 379). The whole tale is saturated with Poesque elements—the narrator's remark that he is a "dreamer and visionary" echoes phrases found in Poe's tales, as in "Berenice" where the narrator declares that his "line has been called a race of visionaries"—to the point that Lovecraft's character never achieves true vitality.

The antiquarianism so significant to Lovecraft's personality is utilised with still greater strength and with much less affectation in *The Case of Charles Dexter Ward*. The autobiographical details in the novel—the external elements of Ward's character, the careful descriptions of Providence sites—are almost too numerous to mention: especially striking is Ward's return home to Providence from his three-year trip to Europe, which so parallels Lovecraft's own return to his native city from two years in New York; and the fact that Lovecraft transcribed into the novel, almost verbatim, certain passages from his letters describing Providence[1] clearly shows that he incorporated many details of his personal existence into the tale. But in the final analysis these details remain only details. Ward's antiquarianism is only a device to introduce the machinations of the real central character, Joseph Curwen; Ward becomes only the hapless victim whose death is in the end avenged by Dr Willett. Only in random passages do we sense that Lovecraft is drawing authentic parallels with incidents in his own life and with ideas central to his thought.

Two other ambivalent cases are "Cool Air" and "The Outsider." That the former was, at least in part, inspired by Lovecraft's inability to stand the cold seems undeniable; but from this nucleus he has created a plot which ties in with an important theme in his work: the Faustian theme of questing for knowledge that will conquer death (manifested in wholly different ways in *The Case of Charles Dexter Ward*, "The Thing on the Doorstep," and "Herbert West—Reanimator"). The autobiographical inspiration is entirely dwarfed by this theme, and cannot be said to be of importance to the tale proper; just as this same element has even less importance in *At the Mountains of Madness*, although here again it could have partly served as inspiration. As for "The Outsider," it is certainly tempting to look upon the central character as embodying Lovecraft's view of himself; and an attractive autobiographical interpretation may be derived from the possibility (suggested by Dirk W. Mosig) that the tale was written not long after the death of Lovecraft's mother in May 1921. Unfortunately, no concrete evidence to corroborate this theory has emerged.[2] But the central character's unhappy childhood does not at all find

---

1. Compare particularly a passage from the letter to the *Providence Sunday Journal* of 5 October 1926 (SL 2.75) with the description of South Water Street in Chap. 1, Sec. 2 of *The Case of Charles Dexter Ward* (MM 108).

2. The tale must have been written after the writing of "The Quest of Iranon" (28 February 1921; cf. A.Ms., JHL) and before that of "The Other Gods" (14 August 1921; cf. A.Ms., JHL). HPL never hints at the date of writing in any letters seen by me. There may even be slight evidence that the tale was written *before* the death of his mother. On 23 April 1921 he wrote to Rheinhart Kleiner (SL 1.128): "I am picking up a new style lately—running to pathos as well as horror. The best thing I have yet done is 'The Quest of Iranon'." Now a "new style" cannot consist of merely one tale; and the only other tale written in this period that can claim both pathos and horror is "The Outsider." It could then have been written between 28 February and 23 April 1921. The fact that HPL

an echo in Lovecraft, who always looked back with fondness to his childhood, unusual though it may have been; so that he once declared: "Adulthood is hell" (SL 1.106). The narrator's discovery of his own monstrous appearance does seem to relate to the fact that Lovecraft's mother deemed him "ugly" and "hideous"; there seems no denying that he had a severe inferiority complex about his facial appearance, most poignantly embodied in what he once said to his future wife: "How can any woman love a face like mine?" (Davis, *Private Life* 12). Nevertheless, "The Outsider," like "The Tomb," is so clearly derivative of Poe (as Lovecraft himself admitted[3]) that it may not be possible to draw many authentic parallels with Lovecraft's own life and character. The first four paragraphs of the tale—which seem to contain many autobiographical elements—are almost a paraphrase of the opening paragraphs of "Berenice."

In "The Shadow out of Time" occurs an autobiographical element that, though intriguing, is merely incidental to the tale. Nathaniel Peaslee suffered his "amnesia" from 14 May 1908 to 27 September 1913 (*DH* 370, 374); can we not parallel this with Lovecraft's own hermitry during this time? In 1908 his "health completely gave way" (SL 1.40-41), and he did not recover until late 1913, when he began to engage in his celebrated epistolary battles in the *Argosy* and subsequently joined amateur journalism. This coincidence of dates is, as mentioned, not at all central to the tale's theme, but may be seen as an interesting "in-joke" on Lovecraft's part—a joke which none but he and his closest associates could understand.[4]

In many early stories, however (and in some later ones as well), the central characters are imbued with attitudes so central to Lovecraft's thought that these tales read virtually like fictionalised essays. The celebrated and bitter opening of "He," recording Lovecraft's increasing hatred of New York—with its "squalor and alienage, and the noxious elephantiasis of climbing, spreading stone . . . and the throngs of people that seethed through the flume-like streets" (*D* 231)—certainly comes from Lovecraft's heart, and the narrator's

---

does not mention it in the letter to Kleiner may simply imply that he did not believe it to be as good a tale as "The Quest of Iranon." In any case, it is certainly possible that the stress caused by his mother's hospitalisation may have inspired the tale, as it inspired the bitter poem "Despair," even though her death (as a result of a gall bladder operation) was quite unexpected. For this autobiographical interpretation see Dirk W. Mosig, "The Four Faces of 'The Outsider,'" *Nyctalops* 2, No. 2 (July 1974): 3-10. Mosig, incidentally, ultimately rejects the autobiographical interpretation.

3. "It represents my literal though unconscious imitation of Poe at its very height" (SL 3.379).

4. I owe this observation to Donald R. Burleson.

fleeing this garish reality for the night and the past certainly reflects his disgust for the metropolis' uncouth modernity. Especially poignant is the narrator's concluding remark that he has now "gone home to the pure New England lanes up which fragrant sea-winds sweep at evening" (*D* 239), when in fact Lovecraft would not return to Providence until nine months after the writing of "He": there can hardly be a clearer expression of a wish-fulfilment fantasy than this. "The Horror at Red Hook," written only a week before "He" in early August 1925, also reflects Lovecraft's loathing of New York, but this time not directly through the central character, Thomas Malone, whose mysticism ("Daily life had for him come to be a phantasmagoria of macabre shadow-studies; now glittering and leering with concealed rottenness as in Beardsley's best manner, now hinting terrors behind the commonest shapes and objects as in the subtler and less obvious work of Gustave Doré" [*D* 242]) Lovecraft certainly did not share. Indeed, although Malone "had the Celt's far vision of weird and hidden things" (*D* 241), Lovecraft makes the following remark in a late letter: "Oddly—for one whose Devonian and Welsh and Cornish lines imply a good proportion of Celtic blood—my weird imagination is not at all Celtic. I not only lack but dislike the Celt's whimsical angle toward the unreal world" (*OFF* 347). One wonders, in fact, whether the character of Malone might not have been based upon the Welshman Arthur Machen, whose work Lovecraft had discovered in 1923. The engulfing of the poetic Malone in the filth and decadence of Brooklyn might be Lovecraft's fictional parallel to Machen's hard years in London (as recorded in his autobiographies) and to the similar experiences of Machen's autobiographical character Lucian Taylor in *The Hill of Dreams*.

In "The Horror at Red Hook" the autobiographical element is manifested only through the setting, for which Lovecraft has drawn upon his own travels and residences. Of this same type are many of the tales set either in Providence ("The Shunned House," "The Call of Cthulhu," *The Case of Charles Dexter Ward*, "The Haunter of the Dark") or in New England ("The Picture in the House," "The Festival," "In the Vault," "Pickman's Model," "The Dunwich Horror," "The Whisperer in Darkness"). It is well known that Lovecraft based "Pickman's Model" upon an actual site in Boston, while of "The Festival" he wrote: "It formed a sincere attempt to capture the feeling that Marblehead gave me when I saw it for the first time—at sunset under the snow, Dec. 17, 1922" (*SL* 4.275). In the present study, however, I shall restrict myself to the analysis of the autobiographical element in Lovecraft's fiction as manifested by his characters.

In "Celephaïs" the central character bears important traits found in Lovecraft himself. Not only is King Kuranes "the last of his family," with "his money and lands gone," but "he did not care for the ways of people about him, but preferred to dream and write of his dreams." Moreover, Kuranes "was not modern, and did not think like others who wrote. Whilst they strove to strip from life its embroidered robes of myth, and to shew in naked ugliness the foul thing that is reality, Kuranes sought it in fancy and illusion, and found it on his very doorstep, amid the nebulous memories of childhood tales and dreams" (D 60). Not only is this a faithful recording of Lovecraft's attitudes (at this stage of his life, at any rate), but it is also the nucleus for Randolph Carter's great quest for his "sunset city," told in *The Dream-Quest of Unknown Kadath* and "The Silver Key." Moreover, it is precisely the personality of King Kuranes that engenders the events recorded in "Celephaïs"; so that it can truly be said that the autobiographical element is pivotal to the tale.

"The Thing on the Doorstep" is the tale where Lovecraft perhaps mined the greatest amount of material from his own life. With some oddities which we must consider later, the character of Edward Derby certainly emerges as that of Lovecraft himself:

> Perhaps his private education and coddled seclusion had something to do with his premature flowering. As an only child, he had organic weaknesses which startled his doting parents and caused them to keep him closely chained to their side. He was never allowed out without his nurse, and seldom had a chance to play unconstrainedly with other children. All this doubtless fostered a strange, secretive inner life in the boy, with imagination as his one avenue of freedom. (DH 277)[5]

Later on it is written: "Edward's mother died when he was thirty-four, and for months he was incapacitated by some odd psychological malady." Lovecraft's mother died when he was thirty-one; he too was psychologically disturbed for a long period following. "Afterward he seemed to feel a sort of grotesque exhilaration, as if of partial escape from some unseen bondage. He began to mingle in the more 'advanced' college set despite his middle age" (DH 279). This last detail may perhaps be paralleled with Lovecraft's frequent trips to New York after his mother's death (his first trip to the metropolis was in April 1922) and his friendship with such sophisticates as Frank Belknap Long, Samuel Loveman, Alfred Galpin, and even—sporadically—Hart Crane. In the character of Asenath Waite we may trace the over-possessive and domineering nature that made up the personalities of both his wife Sonia and his mother. In all this Lovecraft reveals an acute ability at self-psychoanalysis; and his noting of significant connexions between Derby's affection for his

---

5. Steven J. Mariconda has suggested to me that even this passage may not be strictly autobiographical, but could be an allusion to Frank Belknap Long.

mother and for Asenath (hence Lovecraft's mother and Sonia) anticipates the views of many recent critics. Although, as mentioned previously, the theme of the tale involves the unholy prolongation of life through superhuman means, the philosophical message that marriage is not a healthy institution—at least for such a one as Lovecraft or Derby—is clear. It is expressed in a different context in "The Horror at Red Hook."

There remains one group of tales whose autobiographical elements have yet to be examined. These are the so-called Randolph Carter stories. While it may be a truism to say that Carter is Lovecraft, it seems to have gone unnoticed that the personality of Carter differs in every one of the four (or five) tales involving him. The most that can be said is that Carter embodies various aspects of Lovecraft's character in each of the tales. The least significant tale, from the autobiographical context, is "The Statement of Randolph Carter." Since this tale is simply the transcription of a dream, the characters are not at all important; instead, Lovecraft was attempting to capture the images of horror presented by his dream. Carter is given some of Lovecraft's external characteristics—most particularly "frail nerves" (MM 286)—only as a plot device and because Lovecraft himself filled the role of Carter in his dream, just as Samuel Loveman filled that of Harley Warren. The autobiographical element is certainly not significant to the tale.[6]

In "The Unnamable" (often inexplicably ignored as one of the Randolph Carter tales) the precisely opposite circumstance holds true. Here no physical characteristics of either character are described, but only their respective attitudes as they debate the merit of the weird tale. The story is actually a significant enough statement of Lovecraft's aesthetic principles, though often the language is couched in a Biercian cynicism and satire which slightly lessen the seriousness of the message through exaggeration. Carter, here the author of weird fiction, is certainly Lovecraft; but who is Joel Manton?[7] It must clearly be Maurice W. Moe. Manton is "principal of the East High School" (D 196); Moe taught English at West Division High School in Milwaukee. Manton believes that "We know things . . . only through our five senses or our religious

---

6. Similarly, in "The Hound," the character St John is modelled upon Rheinhart Kleiner (whom HPL often referred to as a descendant of Henry St John, Viscount Bolingbroke), but his personality—which is hardly described—is wholly unimportant to the tale, as it seems more intent on displaying Poesque rhetoric than on making any serious parallels with HPL's life or with that of his associate.

7. The name might perhaps have been derived from Bierce, the character of whose "The Middle Toe of the Right Foot" is named Manton; see "Supernatural Horror in Literature" (D 386). There is also a Manton Street in Providence.

intuitions" (*D* 196); Lovecraft frequently engaged in arguments with Moe over religion, once declaring nastily: "Perhaps it is better to be near-sighted and orthodox like Mo[e], trusting all to a Divine Providence, R. I." (*SL* 1.57). "The Unnamable" is not so much a story as a fictionalised essay; and thus resembles such of Poe's works as "The Imp of the Perverse" or "The Premature Burial." It is true, however, that the tale does not fit as well into what has come to be the "Randolph Carter cycle" (never so termed by Lovecraft) as the other four tales involving him; it merely presents certain of his aesthetic attitudes that are more fully developed in the three succeeding tales.

The chronology of the next Randolph Carter tales is somewhat confused, since it appears that "The Silver Key" was written before the writing (or, at any rate, before the completion) of *The Dream-Quest of Unknown Kadath*, although the former records events occurring to Carter subsequent to those in the latter. This can only indicate that Lovecraft certainly had a clear idea of the denouement of the *Dream-Quest*, although August Derleth curiously wrote that he seemed to have "had no very clear plan" for the novel (x). Certainly, Carter's quest for his "sunset city" and his discovery of it in the memories of his childhood find significant echoes in Lovecraft's thought, although it can hardly be imagined that very many of the episodic, odysseylike incidents throughout the novel (often told with an unwonted tongue-in-cheek humour) have any autobiographical significance. The more concise and serious (and bitterly cynical) "Silver Key" returns to the central theme of "Celephaïs" and the *Dream-Quest*, but there are of course many details of Carter's life that certainly find no echo in Lovecraft's own: Lovecraft never attempted to find solace in religion (even if to be repelled by it), nor to "taste ... modern freedoms" (*MM* 388) (unless we see in this a dim allusion to his period of decadent sophistication in the 1920s); instead, Carter's sampling of these various aspects of life are obvious symbols meant to show "how shallow, fickle, and meaningless all human aspirations are" (*MM* 387). "The Silver Key" is still less of a story than "The Unnamable," and is as close to a philosophical allegory as anything in Lovecraft.

Carter completes his metamorphosis from trivial character ("The Statement of Randolph Carter") to mouthpiece for Lovecraft's ideas ("The Unnamable") to pure symbol (*The Dream-Quest of Unknown Kadath*, "The Silver Key") in "Through the Gates of the Silver Key." Being an artificial collaborative effort forced upon Lovecraft by E. Hoffmann Price, the tale is somewhat lacking in unity and is clumsy in structure, although containing some of the most superbly cosmic writing in all Lovecraft's fiction. Here Carter wavers between a mere device for the conveyance of the central philosophical message and a strikingly animated figure, showing more vigour than almost any other

Lovecraft character save perhaps Thomas Malone, the central character of "The Shadow over Innsmouth," and Carter himself in the *Dream-Quest*. In neither of these guises does Carter reveal either a similarity to Lovecraft or to his persona as sketched in other of the Randolph Carter tales. Thus, as we have seen, the statement that "Carter is Lovecraft" must be severely qualified; applicable to the first four Randolph Carter tales in significantly different ways, and evidently applicable to the last tale not at all.

At this point we must consider some curiosities in Lovecraft's descriptions of some of the characters whom we have discussed above. Let us return first to "The Thing on the Doorstep." If we have satisfactorily determined that Edward Derby is Lovecraft, what then are we to make of this remark: "He [Derby] was the most phenomenal child scholar I have known" (*DH* 277)? Would Lovecraft have been so arrogant as to have written such a thing about himself? It hardly seems likely. Yet his early letters reveal a great admiration for the precocity of his associate Alfred Galpin. "He is intellectually *exactly like me* save in degree. In degree he is immensely my superior," Lovecraft wrote in 1921 (*SL* 1.128); and in 1923 he called Galpin "the most brilliant, accurate, steel-cold intellect I have ever encountered" (*SL* 1.256). Galpin was Lovecraft's junior by eleven years, just as Derby is eight years younger than Daniel Upton, the narrator of "The Thing on the Doorstep." Moreover, Galpin was in his youth somewhat susceptible to female charms: Lovecraft's pastoral poems involving the character "Damon" (i.e., Galpin) all tell of Damon's ensnarement at the hands of various beauteous nymphs (see Galpin 165). The play *Alfredo* (whose central character is obviously Galpin) also concerns this theme, which ties in with Derby's later involvement with Asenath Waite.

Yet this identification of Galpin with certain of Derby's traits raises some further curiosities: Galpin certainly never wrote "verse of a sombre, fantastic, almost morbid cast" (*DH* 277), nor did he publish a volume of verse, *Azathoth and Other Horrors*, at the age of eighteen. But did not Clark Ashton Smith, Lovecraft's associate since 1922, create a stir by the publication of *The Star-Treader and Other Poems* in 1912, when he was nineteen? Moreover, it is mentioned that Derby "was a close correspondent of the notorious Baudelairean poet Justin Geoffrey, who . . . died in a madhouse in 1926" (*DH* 277). Now Smith was a close associate of George Sterling, who, curiously, died by suicide in 1926. The figure of Justin Geoffrey was, however, the creation of Robert E. Howard, in "The Black Stone" (1931); and the date of his death as given by Lovecraft does seem to tally with that supplied by Howard (who mentions that Geoffrey died five years previously), so it appears to be a fortuitous coincidence that Geoffrey and Sterling died in the same year. Derby, in any event, seems to have been an interesting amalgam of Lovecraft, Galpin, and Smith, and perhaps also Samuel Loveman or Frank Belknap Long, whose extreme sensitivity and shyness is shared by Derby. While Derby's basic personality can be said to be Lovecraft's, he also owns some traits and surface details of Lovecraft's associates.

Turning now to "The Silver Key," we find some equally curious descriptions of Randolph Carter:

> Then he began once more the writing of books, which he had left off when dreams first failed him. But here, too, was there no satisfaction or fulfilment; for the touch of earth was upon his mind, and he could not think of lovely things as he had done of yore. Ironic humour dragged down all the twilight minarets he reared, and the earthy fear of improbability blasted all the delicate and amazing flowers in his faery gardens. The convention of assumed pity spilt mawkishness on his characters, while the myth of an important reality and significant human events and emotions debased all his high fantasy into thin-veiled allegory and cheap social satire. His new novels were successful as his old ones had never been; and because he knew how empty they must be to please an empty herd, he burned them and ceased his writing. They were very graceful novels, in which he urbanely laughed at the dreams he lightly sketched; but he saw that their sophistication had sapped all their life away. (MM 389–90)

This certainly does not sound like a description of Lovecraft's own work, since he always claimed that he wrote only for "self-expression" in spite of whatever unconscious corrupting influences were gained through incessant writing for the pulp market. Lovecraft certainly used "ironic humour" very infrequently in his fiction: it appears only in "The Silver Key" itself, "The Strange High House in the Mist" (with similar Juvenalian bitterness), and in a few other tales. But if the description does not apply to Lovecraft, to whom could it apply if it is not meant as only an element in the tale? Note this comment on the work of Lord Dunsany written in 1936:

> Of course Dunsany is uneven, and his later work . . . cannot be compared to his early productions. As he gained in age and sophistication, he lost in freshness and simplicity. He was ashamed to be uncritically naive, and began to step aside from his tales and visibly smile at them even as they unfolded. Instead of remaining what the true fantaisiste must be—a child in a child's world of dream—he became anxious to shew that he was really an adult good-naturedly pretending to be a child in a child's world. (SL 5.353–54)

Dunsany then appears as a very fitting model for this aspect of Carter's personality; indeed, the choice is the more apt since Dunsany's work inspired imitations by Lovecraft, of which *The Dream-Quest of Unknown Kadath* and "The Silver Key" may be said to form the final examples. Here again we encounter in Carter an amalgam of Lovecraft and a figure—Dunsany—who played an important part in his philosophical and literary development.

Another interesting example of autobiography occurs in "The Whisperer in Darkness." Researches by Donald R. Burleson indicate that the character of Henry Akeley was based in part upon Lovecraft's Vermont associate Vrest Orton, although there was a real Vermont rustic named Bert G. Akley whom Lovecraft met in his travels of 1928, and whose character figures indirectly in the portrayal of Akeley; indeed, the whole setting of the tale seems to be a compendium of impressions received in Vermont—in travels with Orton and visits with the poet Arthur Goodenough—during his trips there in 1927 and 1928. (Descriptive passages from the essay "Vermont: A First Impression" [1927] were incorporated directly into the tale, although the element of weirdness in the landscape was heightened.) But Akeley also bears some resemblances to Lovecraft. Aside from delving into scholarship that borders upon the weird, Akeley is as firmly tied to his native soil as Lovecraft was: "It is not easy to give up the place you were born in, and where your family has lived for six generations," Akeley writes to Wilmarth; and again: "[I] suppose I'll be ready for moving in a week or two, though it nearly kills me to think of it" (*DH* 218, 234). Indeed, it is precisely Akeley's reluctance to depart that causes his doom—although this should not allow us to assume that Lovecraft ever regretted his "sense of place"; rather, it is this facet of Akeley's character that explains why he did not flee the horrors long before, and we are meant to regard it as an entirely understandable motivation. Nevertheless, Akeley's personality is not wholly central to the tale (the major emphasis is upon the setting and the machinations of the fungi from Yuggoth—the "phenomena" that Lovecraft recognised as the true "heroes" for a fantastic tale), hence the autobiographical element—such as it is—is of less importance.

One final case does not concern an amalgamation of several real figures in the personality of a fictional character, but a relation between a fictional character and a real figure that has hitherto passed unnoticed. In "The Shadow over Innsmouth" we are presented the following description of Barnabas ("Old Man") Marsh, whose grandfather's dealings in the South Seas caused the decadence of Innsmouth's race stock: "He had once been a great dandy, and people said he still wore the frock-coated finery of the Edwardian age, curiously adapted to certain deformities" (*DH* 323). Compare Lovecraft's judgment upon Oscar Wilde as written in a letter to August Derleth:

> As a man, however, Wilde admits of absolutely no defence. His character, notwithstanding a daintiness of manners which imposed an exterior shell of decorative decency and decorum, was as thoroughly rotten & contemptible as it is possible for a human character to be. . . . So thorough was his absence of that

> form of taste which we call a moral sense, that his derelictions comprised not only the greater & grosser offences, but all those petty dishonesties, shiftinesses, pusillanimities, & affected contemptibilities which mark the mere "cad" or "bounder" as well as the actual "villain." It is an ironic circumstance that he who succeeded for a time in being the Prince of Dandies, was never in any basic sense what one likes to call a gentleman. . . . It is hard to feel much charity or affection toward the bloated, dissipated, & diseased old high-liver who virtually rotted to pieces & exploded in "Valdemar" fashion on that grey winter day of 1900. (ES 1.64)

Of particular note is the use of the word "dandy." Certainly Lovecraft condemns both Old Man Marsh and Oscar Wilde for their unorthodox sexual practices, although of course the nature of those practices was radically different in the two cases.

Thus we emerge with the conclusion that Lovecraft's characters—when they are not absolutely colourless—tend to share some traits not only with their creator but with figures whom that creator encountered either in life or in literature. Let it be noted, however, that in the overwhelming bulk of cases the autobiographical element (as regards the personalities of the fictional characters) is not central to the tales' theme, and in some cases is not even present. We are hard put to find any significant Lovecraftian echoes in the figures who people such tales as *At the Mountains of Madness*, "The Shadow out of Time," "The Colour out of Space," "The Dunwich Horror," "The Call of Cthulhu," and many other important tales, as well as most of the "Dunsanian fantasies." The characters in most of these tales are not significant save as devices for the unfolding of the plot; and in those stories where the characters do hold some intrinsic importance, Lovecraft gives them a semblance of realism by basing them upon his own attitudes or those of his associates. As he wrote to E. Hoffmann Price:

> All of us are more or less complex, so that our personalities have more than one side. If we are reasonably clever we can make as many different characters out of ourselves as there are sides to our personalities—taking in each case the isolated essence and filling out the rest of the character with fictitious material as different as possible from anything either in our own lives or in any other characters we may have manufactured from other sides of ourselves. . . . Another mode of deriving varied characters is that of simple and accurate observation. Often we may be neither fertile in imagining alien motives and manners nor apt in personifying different sides of ourselves; yet may be able to record varied characters through our clear perception and faithful memory of the way other people whom we have actually known act and seem to think and feel. When we are of this type it is obligatory for us to possess a wide ac-

quaintance among a great variety of people of all classes, in order that we may have an ample reservoir on which to draw. We are then able to populate a story not only with a character drawn from ourselves (although that will naturally be the strongest and most vivid one, since we can never know anybody else as well as we know ourselves), but with other characters drawn from those whom we have studied. (SL 4.117-18)

But it is obvious that characterisation was not important to Lovecraft because it would not serve his fictional goal: the depiction of the vastness of the cosmos and the inconsequence of humanity within it. With such a principle as the basis for his work it would be positively detrimental to have characters who obtrude from the tale by their distinctiveness:

Individuals and their fortunes within natural law move me very little. They are all momentary trifles bound from a common nothingness toward another common nothingness. Only the cosmic framework itself—or such individuals as symbolise principles (or defiances of principles) of the cosmic framework—can gain a deep grip on my imagination and set it to work creating. In other words, the only "heroes" I can write about are *phenomena*. (SL 5.19)

Characterisation, then, was decidedly a secondary matter to Lovecraft; and his only care was to make his characters sufficiently realistic as not to be noticeably unconvincing. And the obvious mine for the traits of his characters was himself, "since we can never know anybody else as well as we know ourselves."

Works Cited

Davis, Sonia H. *The Private Life of H. P. Lovecraft.* Edited by S. T. Joshi. West Warwick, RI: Necronomicon Press, 1985.

Derleth, August. "H. P. Lovecraft's Novels." In Lovecraft's *At the Mountains of Madness and Other Novels.* Sauk City, WI: Arkham House, 1964. ix-xi.

Galpin, Alfred. "Memories of a Friendship." 1959. In Peter Cannon, ed. *Lovecraft Remembered.* Sauk City, WI: Arkham House, 1998. 164-72.

Lovecraft's Other Planets

We all know that Lovecraft invented many species of extra-terrestrial denizens who become involved not merely in the distant past but the present and future of the earth; and his imaginativeness in creating and so precisely describing such species as the Old Ones (in *At the Mountains of Madness*), the fungi from Yuggoth (in "The Whisperer in Darkness"), and the Great Race (in "The Shadow out of Time") would alone suffice to give him a place as a forerunner in interplanetary or science fiction. What is not so well known, however, is that in his later fiction Lovecraft was also fond either of populating the planets of this solar system with peculiar entities or of inventing entirely new planets either in this system or in the dim corners of the cosmos. It will be our purpose to examine these planets in this paper.

The study of Lovecraft's "other" planets, however, cannot be separated from the analysis of his use of space travel, time travel, and the actual astronomical findings known in his day. It may be of interest to note that Lovecraft intentionally puts aside or even flagrantly contradicts what was then known about the stars and planets in an effort to augment the awesomeness of his conceptions.

That Lovecraft, however, did not make these violations of astronomical truth (or probability) in an unthinking way can, of course, easily be proven by observation of his lifelong love and study of astronomy. Who can forget his statement that "The most poignant sensations of my existence are those . . . of 1902, when I discovered the myriad suns and worlds of infinite space" (*SL* 1.302)? From the start, then, Lovecraft's intellectual study of the heavens was conjoined with an emotional or aesthetic thrill at the vastness of the cosmos; and we need look no further than this in understanding the origin of his unique "cosmic" point of view which minimised mankind to an infinitesimal inkblot in the vast gulfs of the cosmos: "Our philosophy is all childishly subjective—we imagine that the welfare of our race is the paramount consideration, when as a matter of fact the very existence of the race may be an obstacle to the predestined course of the aggregated universes of infinity!" (*SL* 1.24).[1]

---

1. There is a certain amount of hyperbole here, of course: in a deterministic system

I. Lovecraft's Use of the Existing Solar System

In a number of early astronomical articles Lovecraft alludes to the possibility of life on other planets in our solar system. Mars is particularly singled out in this regard, and in "The Truth about Mars" (1917) Lovecraft portentously declares: "It is . . . not impossible that LIVING BEINGS OF SOME SORT MAY DWELL UPON THE SURFACE OF MARS" (CE 3.320). The moon, Lovecraft feels, is "not wholly dead" ("Is There Life on the Moon?" [1906], CE 3.27), although probably it contains only low vegetation; and the possibility of the inhabitability of Venus ("Mysteries of the Heavens IV: The Inferior Planets" [1915], CE 3.284) and the satellites of Jupiter ("Mysteries of the Heavens VIII: The Outer Planets" [1915], CE 3.295) is also noted. It is somewhat interesting, then, that Lovecraft in his fiction places no imaginary creatures on Mars, but does populate Mercury, Venus, and Jupiter's satellites (of which only eight were known in his day); note the significant passage in "The Shadow out of Time" (1934–35):

> There was a mind from the planet we know as Venus, which would live incalculable epochs to come, and one from an outer moon of Jupiter six million years in the past. . . . The Great Race . . . would again migrate [to] . . . the bodies of the bulbous vegetable entities of Mercury. (*DH* 395)

Later we are told that the Great Race's enemies, the Blind Beings, had "come through space from immeasurably distant universes [one supposes Lovecraft means galaxies] and had dominated the earth and three other solar planets about 600 million years ago" (*DH* 400); perhaps one of these was Yuggoth, since, as we know from "The Whisperer in Darkness" (1930), the buildings on Yuggoth, having no windows, would be admirably suited to these sightless denizens! So early as "Beyond the Wall of Sleep" (1919), however, we find interesting references: "'You and I have . . . dwelt in the bodies of the insect-philosophers that crawl proudly over the fourth moon of Jupiter'" (*D* 34). The mention of insects is interesting, since we know that in "The Shadow out of Time" a "mighty beetle civilisation" (*DH* 396) would supersede man on this planet. Here Lovecraft was working on the soundest findings of science, and in a marginal note to R. H. Barlow's "'Till A' the Seas'" (1935) he writes: "Actually, insects and other life-forms will undoubtedly outlast man and his fellow-mammals" (quoted in *HM* [1970 ed.] 103).

We also know, of course, of Lovecraft's extensive use of Venus as a setting for the collaboration "In the Walls of Eryx" (1936), although the idea for using

---

nothing can be an "obstacle" to anything else except in relative terms, since its very existence as an obstacle would be a part of the broader plan of destiny. See *SL* 1.132.

Venus was arrived at by his collaborator, Kenneth Sterling. Here Lovecraft again adhered to current astronomical knowledge, and postulates earthmen wandering all over the planet, sometimes without protective headgear: the discovery that the surface of the planet was much too hot and gaseous to allow such a thing was only made several decades after Lovecraft's death.

This extensive use of the planets of the solar system is of great interest because, much later in life, Lovecraft realised the extreme improbability of highly developed life existing on any of the planets: "In our solar system, no planet but the earth is likely to possess complexly evolved organisms at the present moment" (SL 5.154)—a remark made only a month after the completion of "The Shadow out of Time." We must examine later the implications and intent of this wilful contradiction of scientific probability in Lovecraft's tales.

II. Lovecraft's Invented Planets

Lovecraft was manifestly fond of inventing planets and inhabited solar systems, but a number of these he merely cited tantalisingly without giving any indication of their physical nature. Hence in "Star-Winds" (*Fungi from Yuggoth* XIV) we read of "what scents / And tints of flowers fill Nithon's continents." Nithon is nowhere else mentioned in Lovecraft; the name, however, has a Greek ring (although there is no root *nith-* in classical Greek), and may be related to the verb *nēthō*, to spin.

Another pseudo-Greek coinage is Kythanil, "the double planet that once revolved around Arcturus" (MM 443–44), mentioned in "Through the Gates of the Silver Key" (1932–33). *Kyth-* is a good Greek stem, and is most commonly known in the name *Kythereia* (Lat. Cytherea), eponym of Aphrodite (Venus). Also in "Through the Gates of the Silver Key" we hear of Shonhi, Mthura, and Kath (MM 444, 447), but are told little of these worlds. All we know, moreover, of Yith is that it is an "obscure, trans-galactic world" (*DH* 401) where dwelt the minds of the Great Race before they occupied the bodies of the cone-shaped beings on earth. Little more about Yith can be learned from Lovecraft's revision of Duane W. Rimel's sonnet-cycle "Dreams of Yith" (1934). Similarly, Shaggai is mentioned in "The Haunter of the Dark" (1935), and is apparently "more distant" (*DH* 114) than Yuggoth, hence may be the tenth planet of our solar system. This honour, however, might have to go to Kynarth, which is mentioned once in "Through the Gates of the Silver Key": "He [Randolph Carter] saw Kynarth and Yuggoth on the rim, [and] passed close to Neptune" (MM 451). Now since Carter (in the form of Zkauba) is returning to the earth from the gulfs of space, he would be passing successively the remotest planets of the system; hence Kynarth seems to be placed as tenth. There is also a curious allusion in "The Shadow out of Time" to "a half-plastic denizen of the hollow interior of an unknown trans-Neptunian planet" (*DH* 418).

The two most interesting worlds invented by Lovecraft are clearly Yuggoth and Yaddith. The concept of Yuggoth is one of the most interesting in all Lovecraft, and its genesis can be traced to so early a date as 1906. The idea of a ninth planet in the solar system had long intrigued astronomers since the discovery of Neptune in 1846. Neptune itself was discovered, as Lovecraft knew, when scientists observed irregularities in the orbit of Uranus (discovered 1781) which hinted at the existence of another planet exercising some sort of gravitational attraction (see "Mysteries of the Heavens VIII, Part II: The Outer Planets" [1915], *CE* 3.297); and similar irregularities in Neptune's orbit ultimately led to Pluto's discovery in 1930. One of Lovecraft's earliest published letters—his famous missive to the *Scientific American* (published in the issue for 25 August 1906)—discusses the idea, and must be quoted in full:

TRANS-NEPTUNIAN PLANETS

To the Editor of the *Scientific American*:

In these days of large telescopes and modern astronomical methods, it seems strange that no vigorous efforts are being made to discover planets beyond the orbit of Neptune, which is now considered the outermost limit of the solar system.

It has been noticed that seven comets have their aphelia at a point that would correspond to the orbit of a planet revolving around the sun at a distance of about 100 astronomical units (9,300,000,000 miles).[2]

Now several have suggested that such a planet exists, and has captured the comets by attraction. This is possible, as Jupiter and others also mark the aphelia of many celestial wanderers. The writer has noticed that a great many comets cluster around a point 50 units out, where a large body might revolve.

If the great mathematicians of the day should try to compute orbits from these aphelia, it is doubtful if they could succeed; but if all the observatories that possess celestial cameras should band together and minutely photograph the ecliptic, as is done in asteroid hunting, the bodies might be revealed on their plates. Even if no discoveries were made, the accurate star photographs would almost be worth the time and trouble.

H. P. LOVECRAFT

Providence, R.I., July 16, 1906.

---

2. Either there is an error in the text, or HPL's calculations are far off, for Pluto's distance from the sun is now calculated at 3,680,000,000 miles.

In 1915 Lovecraft again mentions the idea, but curiously remarks that, while trans-Neptunian planets "in all probability exist, . . . that we shall ever discover them is not likely" ("Mysteries of the Heavens VIII, Part II"; *CE* 3.298). Evidently he had little faith in the advances of modern science.

It is often forgotten that the name Yuggoth is first cited not in "The Whisperer in Darkness" (1930), but in the sonnet series *Fungi from Yuggoth* (1929–30). It is not clear, however, whether Yuggoth is at this time established as the solar system's ninth planet: in "Recognition" (*Fungi from Yuggoth* IV) occurs the first mention of Yuggoth in Lovecraft, but it is merely described as "past the starry voids"—the implication seems to be that it is entirely outside the solar system and even the known cosmos; and the mention of Yuggoth in "Star-Winds" ("This is the hour when moonstruck poets know / What fungi sprout in Yuggoth") is still more inconclusive.

It is, of course, in "The Whisperer in Darkness" where we are given the first important and substantial information on Yuggoth. The first citation here is in Akeley's recording of a gathering of the aliens in the woods near his home: ". . . to That whereof Yuggoth is the youngest child, rolling alone in black aether at the rim" (*DH* 226)—presumably we are to supply ". . . of the solar system." Finally, in the forged letter by "Akeley" to Wilmarth we are at last told that Yuggoth is "a still undiscovered and almost lightless planet at the very edge of our solar system—beyond Neptune, and the ninth in distance from the sun" (*DH* 240); the mention of "still undiscovered" is particularly subtle, since, although Lovecraft knew of the very recent discovery of Pluto in early 1930, in the context of the story (taking place in 1927–28) the planet's existence could not be confirmed. Indeed, "Akeley" goes on to mention that Yuggoth/Pluto "will soon be the scene of a strange focussing of thought upon our world" (*DH* 240)—a remark that Wilmarth later recalls when noting anxiously:

> Those wild hills are surely the outpost of a frightful cosmic race—as I doubt all the less since reading that a new ninth planet has been glimpsed beyond Neptune, just as those influences had said it would be glimpsed. Astronomers, with a hideous appropriateness they little suspect, have named this thing "Pluto" [the Greek god of the underworld]. I feel, beyond question, that it is nothing less than nighted Yuggoth—and I shiver when I try to figure out the real reason *why* its monstrous denizens wish it to be known in this way at this especial time. (*DH* 264–65)

The pseudo-Akeley goes into some detail about the nature of Yuggoth (*DH* 254), and his remarks are sufficiently well known not to require citation. In other tales, however, Lovecraft elaborates upon the idea of Yuggoth and its denizens. The first tale in which he does so is, curiously, the revision "Out of the Aeons," ghostwritten for Hazel Heald in 1932. Here we learn that, on an ancient (earthly) continent equated with Mu, a "gigantic fortress of Cyclopean stone" was reared by "the alien spawn of the dark planet Yuggoth, which had colonised the earth before the birth of terrestrial life" (*HM* 272). This spawn is not to be equated with the fungi from Yuggoth who harass Akeley, but rather with an older (and perhaps native) race that, as we know from "The Whisperer in Darkness," built "mysterious Cyclopean bridges" on Yuggoth (*DH* 254); the pseudo-Akeley goes on to remark that these were built "by some elder race extinct and forgotten before the beings [i.e. the fungi] came to Yuggoth from the ultimate voids" (*DH* 254)—Yuggoth was, after all, merely a "stepping-stone" (*DH* 240) for the fungi. Moreover, while the fungi came to earth to seek a metal not found on their planet (see *DH* 218), the builders of the fortress on Mu themselves had a metal—named *lagh*—that is "found in no mine of earth" (*HM* 274).

A further elaboration on the Yuggoth-idea occurs in "The Haunter of the Dark" (1935), where we are told that the Shining Trapezohedron "was fashioned on dark Yuggoth" (*DH* 106). This is interesting, since it appears to confirm a connexion of Nyarlathotep to Yuggoth hinted in "The Whisperer in Darkness"—recall that the fungi appear to worship the Dark God: "To Nyarlathotep, Mighty Messenger, must all things be told" (*DH* 226). The concept of Yuggoth, then, gains increasing depth and detail in the course of Lovecraft's later writing, and it is clear that the idea fascinated him.

Yaddith is not so well worked out. It is first cited in "Alienation" (*Fungi from Yuggoth* XXXII)—"He had seen Yaddith, yet retained his mind"—but nothing is made of it until "Through the Gates of the Silver Key"; the entire latter part of the tale takes place on Yaddith (and this was entirely Lovecraft's idea, not that of his collaborator E. Hoffmann Price), as Carter (whose personality is trapped in the body of Zkauba the Wizard) strives to return to the earth from Yaddith. The planet is manifestly very far from the earth, since Carter realises that he will have to traverse "aeons of light-years" (*MM* 448) to return to his home planet. That he was ultimately successful in effecting his return we all know not merely from the ending of "Through the Gates of the Silver Key" but from "Out of the Aeons," where reference is made to "a dark, turbaned, and bushily bearded man with a laboured, unnatural voice, curiously expressionless face, clumsy hands covered with absurd white mittens, who . . . called himself Swami Chandraputra" (*HM* 270); this figure visited the Cabot Museum in Boston in 1931—apparently before he made his appearance at the New Orleans meeting described in "Through the Gates of the Silver Key," which appears to take place "four years" (*MM* 421) after Carter disappeared in October 1928.

Yaddith is also glancingly cited in "Out of the Aeons," since the great volcano housing the god Ghatanothoa is named "Mount Yaddith-Gho" (*HM* 272), although the planet itself never seems to come into play. Robert Blake mentions Yaddith in an oath: "Yaddith grant it will keep up!" (*DH* 114), as does Alonzo Typer: "And may the Lords of Yaddith succour me" (*HM* 319).

III. Space Travel and Time Travel

Related to the idea of strange planets and galaxies is the notion of the various species travelling both in space and in time to reach the earth. The creatures, indeed, effect this space- and time-travel with singular alacrity, and it must be noted that it is here that Lovecraft makes the greatest strain upon our credulity by postulating means for travelling in space and time which are exceedingly improbable even in light of the scientific knowledge of his day.

Space-travel enters into a number of the later tales, and takes remarkably similar forms. In both "The Whisperer in Darkness" and *At the Mountains of Madness* the creatures have flown through space by wings: the fungi are endowed with "ether-resisting wings" that allow the race "to traverse the heatless and airless interstellar void in full corporeal form" (*DH* 240), while the Old Ones "traverse the interstellar ether on their vast membraneous wings" (*MM* 57). On the face of it this concept appears slightly ridiculous, and Richard L. Tierney has not been slow to criticise Lovecraft on the point. What is more, we learn that the fungi have threatened to take Akeley "beyond the last curved rim of space" (*DH* 239). This idea is even more fantastic, given the vastness of the cosmos: Lovecraft in an early astronomical article ("Mysteries of the Heavens X: The Stars" [1915], *CE* 3.304) noted that one star had been sighted that was 578,000 light-years away; to surpass this point would take aeons, even if the fungi could proceed at or greater than the speed of light (as is hinted—perhaps to account for this very point—by the pseudo-Akeley: "'Do you know that Einstein is wrong, and that certain objects and forces *can* move with a velocity greater than that of light?'"—*DH* 253). Whether the fungi's anomalous molecular structure (recall that they could not be photographed with an ordinary camera) allowed them to attain such a speed is not made clear, but even so the mention of wings is incongruous.

In passing let us clear up a matter about Lovecraft's citation of the "interstellar ether." The ether (what Leiber [144] called a "fringe-fashionable science concept" in Lovecraft's day) was a postulation of pre-Einsteinian physics and was thought to be a sort of undetectable substance permeating all space and transmitting waves of light and energy. Its postulation derived from the old Aristotelian notion—accepted through the nineteenth century—against the possibility of *actio in distans*: nothing—not even light—could proceed through a vacuum. The idea was not nearly as old-fashioned in Lovecraft's day as Tierney (who severely criticises Lovecraft for it) suggests; it was accepted axiomatically by Ernst Haeckel in *The Riddle of the Universe* (Eng. tr. 1900), and in 1929 Sir James Jeans wrote:

> The ether has dropped out of science, not because scientists as a whole have formed a reasoned judgment that no such thing exists, but because they find they can describe all the phenomena of nature quite perfectly without it. It merely cumbers the picture, so they leave it out. If at some future time they find they need it, they will put it back again. (318)

Similarly, Lovecraft in 1936 reports hearing a lecture where the results of the Michaelson-Morley experiment (which, as we now know, did away with the ether) were being questioned, so that a "luminiferous ether" could still—"contrary to Einstein"—be hypothesised (*SL* 5.254). There is, then, no need to censure Lovecraft's use of the ether in even his latest fiction.

Another idea rather less defensible is broached in "The Mound" (1929-30). Here we are told that the underground denizens of K'n-yan "had come from a distant part of space where physical conditions are much like those of the earth" (*HM* 131). This idea is, it must be admitted, frankly puerile, and Lovecraft knew it: in 1935 he told Emil Petaja that "it is inconceivable that any of the higher organic species we know can be duplicated or even closely resembled on any other planet" (*SL* 5.152-53) given the very specific environmental conditions which produced man on this globe. One wonders why Lovecraft even bothered to imagine the K'n-yan denizens as having an extraterrestrial origin, since in terms of the plot they could just as well have been early inhabitants of the earth who descended to their underground habitat aeons ago.

One interesting conception related to space-travel is alluded to in "The Call of Cthulhu" (1926), where it is mentioned that Cthulhu would emerge "when the stars were ready" or "when the stars had come around again to the right position in the cycle of eternity" (*DH* 139-40). This seems to hint of astrology, where the linkage of the planets and stars is brought into play as predicting man's destiny; but the whole concept is really given a much broader cosmic scope, and Lovecraft seems to be postulating not merely a conjunction of heavenly bodies as seen from the earth (where such conjunctions are merely the result of our point of perspective) but a conjunction in absolute terms. Lovecraft's scorn of astrology (as revealed in his merciless parodying of the hapless astrologer J. F. Hartmann in 1914) was such as not to allow him to use it in any conventional way in his own fiction.

Time travel is handled with vast ingenuity in one tale—"The Shadow out of Time"—and in a rather inept fashion in another—"Through the Gates of the Silver Key." The brilliance of using mind-exchange as the vehicle of time-travel is in completely obviating the problem of how one can travel in time and not thereby disrupt the events of the past (or future). Lovecraft, of course, as a determinist was particularly aware of the interconnectedness of all events:

> If a man stubs his toe in a certain place on a certain day, it is because of an infinity of antecedent elements—hereditary factors, etc.—which have caused him to be in the given place when he is; which have caused the obstacle to exist where it does; and which have caused the man to react to the obstacle as he does. If the man had had another great-great-great-grandfather, or if a certain glacier had not been at a certain stage of plasticity when encountering a mountain 200 miles to the north 25,000 years ago, or if the man's great-great-grandmother in a wholly different line of heredity, then unknown to any other of his lines, had not died when she did instead of a year later, etc., etc.; this particular incident, involving as it does a particular conjunction of elements, could not possibly occur. (Letters to Nils Frome, 8 February 1937; *Uncollected Letters* 41)

Moreover, in the unfinished novel *The Dark Tower* C. S. Lewis observed that conventional time-travel is "absolutely impossible" because

> "Time-travelling clearly means going into the future or the past. Now where will the particles that compose your body be five hundred years hence? They'll be all over the place—some in the earth, some in plants and animals, and some in the bodies of your descendants, if you have any. Thus, to go to the year 3000 A.D. means going to a time at which your body doesn't exist; and that means, according to one hypothesis becoming nothing, and, according to the other, becoming a dis- embodied spirit." (17-18)

But in "The Shadow out of Time" Lovecraft was able to have his cake and eat it, too, for it is not the body that travels but merely the mind or consciousness; in this way Lovecraft's narrator was able to experience the horrifying sight of a scroll he must have written millions of years ago (and this was, after all, the central image that Lovecraft had conceived years before writing the story: see *SL* 3.217) without the paradoxes that this might otherwise entail.

The matter is not nearly so well handled in "Through the Gates of the Silver Key," and Lovecraft does not seem to be concerned with the fact that, if Randolph Carter actually went back in time from the age of fifty-four in 1928 (MM 422) to the age of nine in 1883 (MM 423), then he would, as it were, be trapped in an unending cycle: when he reached age fifty-four, he would simply double back again to the age of nine, and so on ad infinitum; in the process, of course, all time would be involved in this anomalous loop. Lovecraft was surely aware of this (which is why he probably would never have written a sequel to

"The Silver Key" on his own initiative, since the concept—allowable in so poetic and even allegorical a fantasy as "The Silver Key"—would be untenable in any tale where the idea would be assumed to be even nominally plausible), and in fact tries to get around it by noting that Carter, from the age of nine onwards, had strange abilities to see the future, but that "he had never spoken of anything to happen after 1928" (MM 424). But in no way could Carter then get out of this cycle and become Zkauba the Wizard and then return to earth in 1932 as Swami Chandraputra! In a marginal note to Price's original draft of the sequel to "The Silver Key" Lovecraft has written—at the point where begins the explanation that there is in fact only one archetypal "Carter" at all periods of time—that "There are paradoxes in this conception, but let it stand." Apparently he did let it stand, much to the detriment of the logic of the tale.

What, then, are we to make of Lovecraft's use of planets and his populating them with such a multifarious array of peculiar entities? It is first somewhat amusing that all these entities seem to have made their way to the earth, even from the dimmest corners of space; Edmund Wilson already poked fun at this idea when he remarked that in Lovecraft "a race of outlandish gods and grotesque prehistoric peoples . . . are always playing tricks with time and space and breaking through into the contemporary world, usually somewhere in Massachusetts" (47). It is also quite remarkable that so many species inhabit our own solar system, since—in spite of Lovecraft's early claims that a number of planets in the solar system may be inhabited—he later realised that the phenomenon of highly developed life was surely an extreme rarity in the entire cosmos: in 1935 he remarked that "I think [Arthur] Eddington has ventured the guess that . . . the cosmos may possess about *six* worlds with highly developed life at any one time" (SL 5.154). But in fact the creation of all these species—along with the extensive use of time- and space-travel—was merely in accord with Lovecraft's avowed purposes in writing weird fiction. It was because he felt a "galling sense of intolerable restraint" (SL 3.295) at the mind's inability to probe the deeper corners of the cosmos that he pictured in his imagination a world enlivened by the most bizarre—yet scientifically plausible—species. This sense of the probability of his creations was important to Lovecraft, since he rarely found satisfaction in overt defiances of scientific truth; and though some of his concepts strain credulity, most of them are indeed plausible and allow the extension of the imagination that Lovecraft sought: "The time has come when the normal revolt against time, space, and matter must assume a form not overtly incompatible with what is known of reality—when it must be gratified by images forming *supplements* rather than *contradictions* of the visible and mensurable universe" (SL 3.295-96).

Works Cited

Jeans, Sir James. *The Universe Around Us.* New York: Macmillan, 1929.

Leiber, Fritz. "Through Hyperspace with Brown Jenkin: Lovecraft's Contribution to Speculative Fiction." 1966. In Peter Cannon, ed. *Lovecraft Remembered.* Sauk City, WI: Arkham House, 1998. 472–83.

Lewis, C. S. *The Dark Tower and Other Stories.* New York: Harcourt Brace Jovanovich, 1977.

Lovecraft, H. P. *Uncollected Letters.* Edited by S. T. Joshi. West Warwick, RI: Necronomicon Press, 1986.

Tierney, Richard L. Letter to the Editor. *Nyctalops* 1, No. 5 (October 1971): 51.

Wilson, Edmund. "Tales of the Marvellous and the Ridiculous." 1945. In S. T. Joshi, ed. *H. P. Lovecraft: Four Decades of Criticism.* Athens: Ohio University Press, 1980. 46–49.

Textual Problems in Lovecraft: A Preliminary Survey

It is now known to the majority of Lovecraft scholars that the printed texts of Lovecraft's work—particularly the editions of his fiction published by Arkham House, from which all other editions derive[1]—are notoriously corrupt and misprinted; some texts bearing over 1000 errors, including the omission of whole passages. The reasons for this state of affairs are manifold, and stem both from Lovecraft's idiosyncratic use of English and from the oftentimes curious transmission of his texts. The fact that Lovecraft did not, as with Bierce, live to supervise an edition of his work, and the fact that his posthumous editors August Derleth and Donald Wandrei were not authorities in textual scholarship and (in Derleth's case) were oftentimes very careless in the preparation of their editions,[2] has resulted in a textual chaos

---

1. The Arkham House editions of HPL's fiction date from *The Outsider and Others* (1939) to *The Horror in the Museum and Other Revisions* (1970). The earlier Arkham House editions were the source for the early British editions from Gollancz, while the later Gollancz editions derive from (and in some cases are facsimile reprints of) the later Arkham House editions beginning with *The Dunwich Horror and Others* (1963), itself largely a facsimile reprint of the *Best Supernatural Stories of H. P. Lovecraft* (1945). The Ballantine editions derive from the newer Arkham House editions (the two paper editions originally published by Lancer Books and later by Zebra and Jove derive from the earlier Arkham House editions, hence are somewhat securer textually), while the Panther editions stem from Gollancz. The earlier foreign editions (especially the French), as noted by Derleth in "H. P. Lovecraft: The Making of a Literary Reputation, 1937–1971" (19), were largely triggered by the earlier Gollancz editions.

2. The question of how competently R. H. Barlow would have edited HPL's work had he been given a chance is an interesting one, but in all probability he would have done even worse than Derleth: Barlow could not read HPL's hand as well as Derleth could (as the manifold errors in his edition of the *Commonplace Book* [Futile Press, 1938] indicate), although he was more respectful of HPL's work and less interested in presenting it in an "orthodox" format excluding HPL's many idiosyncrasies of orthography, grammar, and the like. Barlow's main importance to HPL textual studies is simply in the assiduity with which he collected and preserved HPL's original manuscripts so that textual reparation could, however belatedly, be made.

from which only a whole new edition—founded on the extensive number of manuscripts of Lovecraft's fiction still preserved, thanks largely to the diligence of R. H. Barlow—can rescue Lovecraft's work. Such an edition is now being undertaken by the author, but for the time being a preliminary examination of the nature of the textual problems in Lovecraft's work may not be out of order. For the sake of simplicity only Lovecraft's prose shall be dealt with in this article, as his poetry involves wholly different textual problems of a rather less complex nature.

The reasons for the plethora of errors in the published texts of Lovecraft's work stem, as has been noted, both from his own style and from vagaries in the textual history of individual works. Let us consider the former.

Lovecraft, nurtured upon the old books in his grandfather's library, gained from youth an archaic, complex style of writing which never wholly left him, in spite of his later attempts to exorcise the most extreme of the archaisms. (The actual archaism of Lovecraft's mature style has perhaps been exaggerated by critics, and certain of his spelling preferences—e.g., *shew*,[3] *phantasy*, *connexion*,[4] *whilst*, etc.—were common not only in his day but afterwards.) Lovecraft, however, never abandoned his usage of British spellings, in spite of the fact that most magazines in which he appeared did not allow them in their "style sheets."

The most common of Lovecraft's British spellings are these:

-*our* for -*or*: *honour*, *colour*, etc.

    At times Lovecraft would use the improper *glamourous*, but he knew that *honorary* and *vaporise* are the proper forms. (See *SL* 3.101.)

-*ise* for -*ize*: *rationalise*, *recognise*, etc.

    Curiously, *Weird Tales* would sometimes alter *surprise* (so both in British and American orthography) to the unintentionally Elizabethan *surprize*!

-*xion* for -*ction*: *connexion*.

    Lovecraft never uses the form *reflexion* (*complexion* is so both in England and America).

-*ae* or -*oe* for -*e*: *palaeontologist*, *daemon*, *mediaeval*, *foetor*, etc.

    Primaeval occurs intermittently, but *primeval* is more common. *Aera* for *era* is rare in the fiction (less so in the letters).

-*re* for -*er*: *centre* (hence *centring*, *centred*), *lustre*, *mitre*, etc.

---

3. Regularly used by Evelyn Waugh (d. 1966); see the Chapman & Hall editions of his novels.

4. Still employed by many British writers.

-ce for -se: *defence* (but *defensive*), *licence* (not consistent in Lovecraft), *pretence*, etc.

Lovecraft always used the American *practice*, although *Weird Tales* paradoxically changed this to *practise*.

-ll for -l: *travelling*, *jewellery* (for jewelry), etc.

Individual words: *programme*, *shew* (for *show*—only as verb; not wholly consistent in Lovecraft), *plough*, *despatch* (for *dispatch*), et al.

Certain non-British spellings used regularly by Lovecraft are *practice* (for *practise* [verb only]), *judgment* (although *judgement* is not exclusively British), *inquiry* (for *enquiry*),[5] *reflection*. *Eery* occurs more often than *eerie*. Lovecraft did not employ the British mode of abbreviating personal titles (e.g., Mr for Mr.) or of telling time (*3.10* for *3:10*).[6]

Lovecraft employed certain archaisms of syntax and spelling that have not always been preserved in his printed texts. In particular we may speak of his use of punctuation. Note the comma in the construction "He affirms (or knows or says), that" found regularly in eighteenth-century prose (see Dobrée); the use of two commas in the enumeration of three items (*apples, pears, and bananas*)—even now not wholly out of fashion; *an* (not *a*) before some words beginning with an *h* or a consonantal vowel (in *At the Mountains of Madness* alone we find *an Euclid, an hypothesis, an hundred*, and the formerly common *such an one*); the use of a semicolon before a present participle ("The Dunwich Horror": "they rode around Dunwich; questioning the natives . . .") or before an adversative clause ("The Whisperer in Darkness": "But while . . . the creatures would appear to have harmed only those trespassing on their privacy; there were later accounts . . .") or before a clause beginning with *for* ("The Festival": "The nethermost caverns . . . are not for the fathoming of eyes that see; for their marvels are strange and terrific"); the use of a semicolon for a colon (*The Case of Charles Dexter Ward*: "The new withdrawals were all modern items; histories, scientific treatises, [etc.]"); and numerous other forms. Lovecraft hyphenated many words and compounds in which hyphenation has now been abandoned. All cases were the suffix *-like* is used are hyphenated in Lovecraft (save very common words such as *warlike* or *godlike*); hyphens are used for the prefixes *pre-, trans-, post-, half-, ultra-, extra-, sub-, semi-* (save only *semicircle*), some words with *non-*, and some verbs with *re-*. Other hyphenated words in Lovecraft are *breath-taking, far-away, first-hand, burying-ground*,

---

5. *Enquiry* occurs very rarely in HPL: see, e.g., letter to W. F. Anger, 14 August 1934 (ms., Univ. of Minnesota).

6. The only exceptions are the astronomy articles for the *Pawtuxet Valley Gleaner* (1906) and the juvenile fiction.

copy-book, and words with the compound *-place* (e.g., *meeting-place*). The diaeresis is used in such words as *coördinate, coöperate, reënter,* and the like (an earlier form in Lovecraft is *co-operate* [cf. *The United Co-operative*, edited by Lovecraft] or *coòperate*).

Lovecraft had a tendency not to italicise certain foreign words that he felt were sufficiently incorporated into English; hence the non-italicisation of *fantaisiste, en masse, facade* (without the cedille), *outré, cul de sac,* and others. Latin is usually italicised (see *ex nihilo nihil fit* from "The Whisperer in Darkness").

There are a number of other idiosyncratic or archaic syntactical arrangements employed by Lovecraft that have caused difficulties for his editors; moreover, there are indications that certain of these idiosyncrasies changed toward the end of his career, so that we can speak definitely of a "late" orthographical or syntactical style in Lovecraft. One feature alone is the replacement of a semicolon by a dash; note "The Dreams in the Witch House": "The other three were what sent him unconscious—for they were living entities. . . ."

Another point of difficulty in Lovecraft's texts is his handwriting. The illegibility of his handwriting has perhaps been exaggerated by some (certainly Clark Ashton Smith's is much worse), and after a certain interval his hand becomes actually fairly effortless to read; albeit his handwriting became smaller and smaller toward the end of his life. This initial difficulty in reading Lovecraft's hand, compounded with the fact that he often allowed associates to prepare typescripts of his work through his own disinclination to type, have resulted in some curious misreadings.[7]

Both *The Dream-Quest of Unknown Kadath* and *The Case of Charles Dexter Ward* remained in manuscript until after Lovecraft's death. August Derleth and Donald Wandrei have spoken of their difficulty in preparing the latter for publication: "Lovecraft's handwriting was not easy to read under the best of circumstances; he had his own peculiarities of spelling, often used Latin and Greek phrases [but there is no Greek in *Ward*], and often used coined words of his own. These made the problem of deciphering his complex puzzle-pages even more difficult" (letter to *Weird Tales*, May 1941; in Joshi, *Weird Writer* 99). The results are often amusing. The Arkham House text of the novel bears such readings as "wholly" for "vitally," "sad" for "and," "contacts" for "contents," "wrested" for "arrested," "here" for "well," "ruins" for "rims," and others. Neither Derleth nor Wandrei seemed to know Latin (this is certainly borne out in some wild misreadings in the *Selected Letters*—e.g., the

---

7. I have pointed out many misreadings made by Tom Collins (due to his inability to read HPL's handwriting) in his edition of HPL's poetry, *A Winter Wish* (1977); see "A Textual Commentary on *A Winter Wish*," *Miskatonic* 6, No. 2 (May 1978): [11–21].

butchery of Virgil at *SL* 3.313 [= *Aeneid* 6.847–55]), although Wandrei knew Greek; and both editors' lack of knowledge of archaic English caused them to be unaware of such things as the archaic doubling of the lower-case *f* to indicate a capital *f* (e.g. *ffortunes,* not *Fortunes*); hence in the Arkham House text such words are—in the letters between Curwen and his cohorts—repeatedly spelled with one *f,* save when the word happens to be at the beginning of a sentence (where the capital *f* is improperly used). Other errors are the failures to capitalise nouns. Indeed, Derleth, as if in some sort of frenzy, has added archaisms in these letters where they do not belong (e.g., *calle* for *call*).

Problems in the *Dream-Quest* stem partly from Lovecraft's coining of place-names: hence "Inquanok" is actually "Inganok" (the editors misread the *g* as a *q,* then inserted a *u* after it; believing that not even a fictitious name could lack the *u* after *q,* in spite of such Middle Eastern place-names as *Qatar*); and all the species names (gug, zoog, shantak, etc.) ought to be in lower case. Other comical misreadings are "air out" for "an ant," "beings" for "priests," "goodly" for "grisly," "putrid" for "foetid," and others.

A final matter concerns the deliberate tampering of Lovecraft's texts by his editors. This is a comparatively rare phenomenon, and the reasons for it are usually obvious. When R. H. Barlow published "Cats and Dogs" (retitled "Something about Cats" by Derleth) in *Leaves* (1937), he removed certain of Lovecraft's attacks upon democracy and his praises of fascism and aristocracy; hence "aristocratic" becomes "unshackled," "even the fascist sentiment" becomes "any hand," and—in a similar light—"negroes" becomes "tradesmen." The date of original publication must always be kept in mind. Similarly, when Derleth printed "Observations on Several Parts of America" (not "North America") in *Marginalia* (1944), he altered "oily Jews" to "foreigners."

A more culpable instance of tampering occurs in Lovecraft's revisions of Zealia Bishop's "The Mound" and "Medusa's Coil." Both these stories lay in manuscript (or, rather, in typescripts prepared by Frank Belknap Long, then Bishop's agent) after Lovecraft's death; and Derleth, in an effort to sell them to a pulp market, decided to alter and abridge both texts. (As it was, "The Mound" was published in a still more abridged form in *Weird Tales,* although fortunately no subsequent edition followed this text.) His changes in "The Mound" amount to excisions of about 500 words, and countless changes in spelling and punctuation (some resulting in incoherence; hence in a sentence reading "And if any room for doubt remained, that room was abolished . . .," Derleth changed the second "room" to "crypt," destroying the idiom and producing nonsense).[8] "Medusa's Coil" fared still worse under Derleth's pen-

---

8. "Crypt" appears in the *Beyond the Wall of Sleep* (1943) text; in the *Horror in the Museum* (1970) text the word "doubt" is substituted for "crypt," a makeshift change that

cil, and whole sections have been removed and abridged. These texts were only restored to their unadulterated state in 1989.

In the majority of Lovecraft's texts (particularly the fiction), textual errors have crept in not so much through the bungling of any particular editor, as in the fossilisation of errors through repeated publications. Hence to account for all textual errors in a work, we must ascertain the details of the transmission of the text, beginning with the autograph manuscript and proceeding to the latest edition. In such a procedure we often need not examine all publications of a work; very often the text is transmitted through a relatively small number of publications, rendering other publications textually irrelevant. Hence, since the Arkham House editions usually derive from the first *Weird Tales* appearance of a story, the second or third *Weird Tales* appearance of that story is textually irrelevant. (This is not the case with "Under the Pyramids" [commonly known as "Imprisoned with the Pharaohs"], where the Arkham House text derived from the second *Weird Tales* text, textually much inferior to the first.)

After examining all relevant publications and extant manuscripts of a work, we can, in most cases, readily determine the order and process of transmission. In some instances we must hypothesise the existence of manuscripts not now extant to account for all textual deviations; and, in cases where no manuscript of a work survives, more weight must be given to those publications that seem closer to the source (i.e., the original manuscript) than to those that are secondary (i.e., derive from other publications). For "The Beast in the Cave," there survive the autograph manuscript, a typescript (prepared by Barlow), and published versions in the *Vagrant* (June 1919) and the Arkham House editions beginning with *Marginalia*. (The appearance in the *Acolyte* of Fall 1943 is textually irrelevant.) Since the *Vagrant* appearance reveals a text revised from the original manuscript, a now non-extant typescript (presumably by Lovecraft) must be postulated, so that the *stemma* or textual genealogy of the tale would be as follows (bracketed text represents the hypothetical T.Ms.):

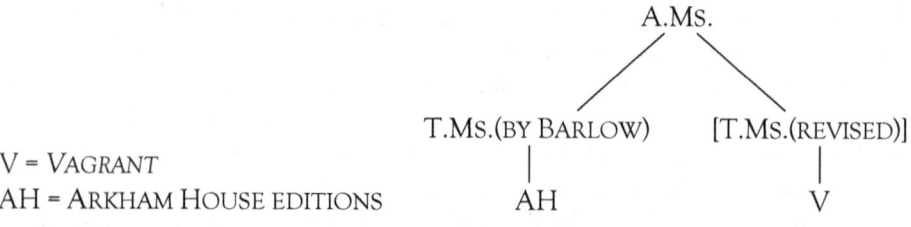

at least preserves the sense.

We have noticed that many of Lovecraft's manuscripts—particularly his long later works—were typed by other hands, whose ability to read Lovecraft's hand varied widely. Hence August Derleth typed "The Dreams in the Witch House" (surprisingly accurately); Donald Wandrei (the best of Lovecraft's amanuenses) typed (or probably retyped) many of Lovecraft's earlier stories, e.g., "The Quest of Iranon" (see *SL* 2.211), "The Other Gods," etc.; R. H. Barlow typed a great many of Lovecraft's texts, including the T.Ms. (non-extant) of "The Shadow out of Time" (see below) and the partial T.Mss. of *The Case of Charles Dexter Ward* and *The Dream-Quest of Unknown Kadath* (the latter followed by Arkham House until it ceased; the former ought to have been followed by Arkham House, since Lovecraft had written some revisions on the T.Ms.); E. Hoffmann Price prepared a T.Ms. of "The Picture in the House" (very poor) for use in an anthology he was planning (see *SL* 4.112f.); Lovecraft writes that "a delinquent [revision] client" (*SL* 4.310) typed "The Thing on the Doorstep" (the T.Ms. is very bad, confusing Lovecraft's chapter divisions of the tale; unfortunately it has been followed in all publications), but I have not ascertained who this is (perhaps Hazel Heald).

If a story has emerged relatively unscathed textually at this level, it must begin its ventures into print; here is where the majority of textual errors arise. Lovecraft had to be content to appear in the lowest and humblest of places—amateur journals, pulp magazines, "fan" journals, cheap anthologies, and the like. The result is not pleasant to behold. Surprisingly, some of his soundest publications are found in the amateur journals, in spite of the unprepossessing appearance of many of them. Thus the appearance of "The White Ship" in the *United Amateur* (November 1919; typeset by W. Paul Cook) is word-for-word perfect with the surviving T.Ms. (by Lovecraft); although in an A.Ms. fair copy prepared by Lovecraft at a later time,[9] he has made some apparent revisions that must be incorporated in any text claiming to be definitive.

Unfortunately, the value of many of these amateur journal appearances is lessened by the fact that Lovecraft often revised many of his earlier tales for subsequent publications; hence a double tradition arises which makes the establishment of the text sometimes difficult, especially when a reliable manuscript for the tale is not extant. The *stemma* for "The Picture in the House" is as follows (texts in brackets indicate non-extant manuscripts):

---

9. Prepared in 1934 for Alvin Earl Perry; published in facsimile in *Whispers* (July 1974).

N = *NATIONAL AMATEUR*
("JULY 1919")
W = *WEIRD TALES* (JAN. 1924)
AH = ARKHAM HOUSE EDITIONS

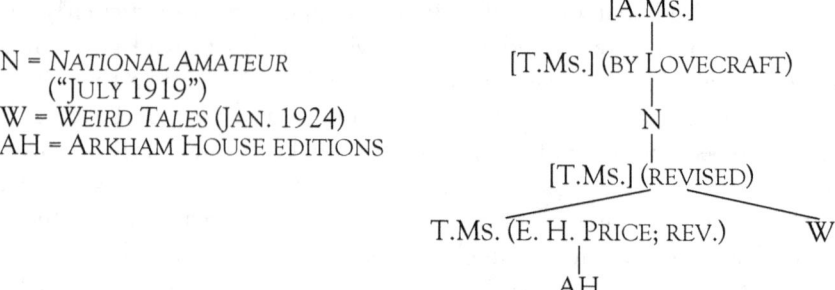

This text was apparently revised twice; first for the *Weird Tales* appearance, then for the appearance in Price's anthology (which, of course, never appeared). Many other stories were similarly revised after initial publication.

When we turn to appearances in the pulp magazines, we find not only certain standard alterations that were made in Lovecraft's texts—Americanisation of his British spellings, simplification of his punctuation, etc.—but also some bizarre alterations or errors hard to account for. Thus in the appearance of "The Call of Cthulhu" in *Weird Tales* (followed by Arkham House), the long newspaper article from the *Sydney Bulletin* hinting of Johansen's encounter with Cthulhu, which in Lovecraft's text consists of four long paragraphs, has been broken up into thirteen paragraphs; apparently Farnsworth Wright, editor of *Weird Tales*, felt that these short paragraphs were more in keeping with journalistic style. *Weird Tales* almost always spelled out Lovecraft's abbreviated forms "Mr.," "Prof.," "St." (street), "Dr.," and the like. Lovecraft notes some bewildering printer's errors in "The Dreams in the Witch House": "love" for "lore," and "human element" for "known element." He is correct when he remarks that such errors cause the author (and not his editors) to become "laid open to the suspicion of rambling feebleness and semi-illiteracy" (*SL* 4.213). Lovecraft had, indeed, when submitting his first manuscripts to *Weird Tales* in 1923, laid down the dictum that "If the tale cannot be printed as written, down to the very last semicolon and comma, it must gratefully accept rejection" (Joshi-Michaud, "Eyrie" 15);[10] but the injunction was never followed. *Weird Tales* actually made few typographical errors (here it bested the amateur journals); most of the textual changes were quite deliberate. The textual problems encountered in the science-fiction journals in which Lovecraft appeared—*Amazing Stories, Astounding Stories*—must be considered later.

The "fan" magazines—the *Fantasy Fan, Fantasy Magazine, Fanciful Tales,* the *Phantagraph,* etc.—were the poorest of all in the presentation of texts: Lovecraft remarks that the appearance of "The Nameless City" in *Fanciful Tales* had "59

---

10. "Accept rejection" is as exquisite an oxymoron as anything in HPL.

bad misprints . . . surely something of a record!" (*SL* 5.368). The *Fantasy Fan* perpetrated the horrible misreading "seven cryptical books of earth" for "seven cryptical books of Hsan" in "The Other Gods," leading L. Sprague de Camp to believe that the latter title (used in the *Dream-Quest*) was a deliberate change by Lovecraft to make the title sound "more impressive" (167).

Unfortunately, when Derleth and Wandrei came to prepare their Arkham House editions, they ordinarily picked the very worst printed texts to follow—indeed, they seemed to have an uncanny knack for so doing. The reason for this circumstance is simply that they usually used the printed text most readily available to them; this generally happened to be the latest appearance, wherein the greatest number of errors had encrusted. Hence the *stemma* for "The Doom That Came to Sarnath" is as follows:

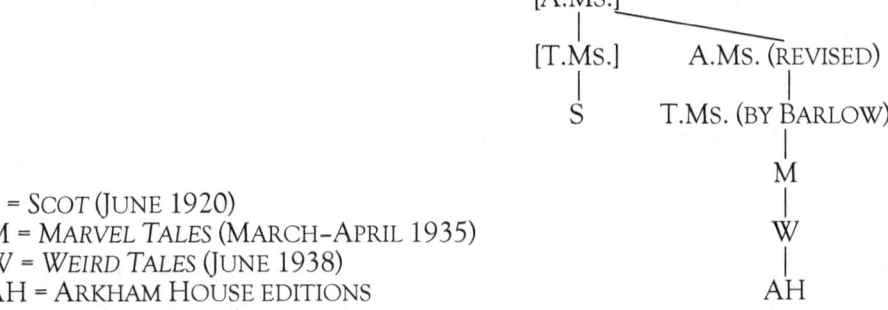

S = *Scot* (June 1920)
M = *Marvel Tales* (March–April 1935)
W = *Weird Tales* (June 1938)
AH = Arkham House editions

This is one of the tales revised after its initial appearance; the T.Ms. by Barlow introduced a number of errors, and each publication added new errors. Moreover, the later Arkham House edition—*Dagon and Other Macabre Tales* (1965)—introduced many errors from its own predecessor, *Beyond the Wall of Sleep* (1943). The story as now printed is a textual nightmare.

Arkham House did in certain instances follow Lovecraft's typescripts where they existed; but, save in the prose poem "What the Moon Brings," avoided following the A.Ms. if any published appearance at all, however poor, survived. The following are some of the more important stories followed from the T.Ms. (hence relatively accurate): "The Dunwich Horror," "The Whisperer in Darkness," "He," "The Horror at Red Hook," "Pickman's Model," "The Silver Key," and some others.

Arkham House often failed to realise that some published versions of a tale were better than others. Lovecraft rarely remarked upon the relative textual accuracy of the published versions of his work (save, as in the cases of "The Nameless City" and *At the Mountains of Madness*, where the appearances were extremely bad), so that Derleth and Wandrei had no way of distinguishing textually poor from textually sound printed texts—a distinction that only actual collation with manuscripts could elicit. Thus Arkham House followed the poor *Weird Tales* appearance of "The Call of Cthulhu," not realising that the appearance in Harré's *Beware After Dark!* (1929) had followed the T.Ms., hence was notably superior to the *Weird Tales* text. As noted earlier, the first *Weird Tales* appearance of "Under the Pyramids" is much superior to the second *Weird Tales* appearance, but Arkham House followed the latter.

Vagaries in the transmission between various Arkham House editions themselves exist. For *The Outsider and Others* Derleth and Wandrei followed Derleth's T.Ms. for "The Dreams in the Witch House," but in the appearance in *At the Mountains of Madness and Other Novels* (1964) Derleth used the poor *Weird Tales* text; one is at a loss to understand why he did not follow his own earlier text rather than return to another one which had much less authority. In the 1964 reprint of "The Statement of Randolph Carter" from *The Outsider and Others,* part of a paragraph is curiously omitted;[11] part of the second paragraph has been dropped in the 1964 reprint of "The Silver Key," completely reversing the meaning of the passage. T. G. L. Cockcroft has at various times pointed out certain lines dropped from one Arkham House edition to another: two celebrated instances occur in the text of "The Dunwich Horror" in *The Dunwich Horror and Others* (1963), although one exists in the first paragraph of the 1963 edition of "The Whisperer in Darkness," hitherto unknown.

The task of restoring the texts of Lovecraft's fiction is in essence simple, thanks to the survival of manuscripts for nearly all his original tales and even some of his revisions. Some of these manuscripts are, of course, typescripts not by Lovecraft, but they have a certain value in any case. (Lovecraft was not notably careful in correcting blunders made by his typists, and rarely if ever made any word-by-word collation between his A.Ms. and the T.Ms.) Important tales for which no manuscripts exist are: "The Alchemist," "The Tomb," "Polaris," "The Temple," "The Street," "The Moon-Bog," "The Outsider," "The Music of Erich Zann," "Hypnos," "The Rats in the Walls," "The Unnamable," and "The Shunned House." Even here we have some published versions that are quite reliable: Cook's pamphlet of *The Shunned House* and his *Vagrant* text of "The Tomb"; Galpin's text of "Polaris" in the *Philosopher* (although the tale was subsequently revised); and others. In the *Weird Tales* text of "The Rats in the Walls," however, there may have been some tampering with the paragraphing of the tale, as there was in the second *Weird Tales* appearance of "Under the Pyramids." In the one instance of "From Beyond," we have a manuscript that is not the final or revised text: in its appearance in the *Fantasy Fan* the text bears some divergences from the A.Ms. (the T.Ms. is non-extant) that are manifestly revisions by Lovecraft (e.g.,

---

11. As pointed out by R. Alain Everts in his edition of the tale (Strange Co., 1976).

the addition of phrases), but other divergences may be printing errors. The manuscript of "The Haunter of the Dark" was given to Donald A. Wollheim, and it appears that this manuscript was lost or misplaced; at any rate, it has not turned up among Wollheim's effects following his death in 1990. We are therefore reliant on a possibly inaccurate *Weird Tales* text.

Aside from countless minor problems involved in establishing a definitive text of Lovecraft's work, one problem stands out foremost—the text of *At the Mountains of Madness*. This was one of the two tales published in *Astounding Stories*, and its textual history is so bizarre that enormous difficulty may be had in establishing the text.

The tale was conceived in late 1930. Clark Ashton Smith wrote to Lovecraft in mid-December 1930: "I think your idea for an Antarctic story would be excellent, in spite of 'Pym' and subsequent tales" (*Letters to H. P. Lovecraft* 23). The A.Ms. records that the actual writing took place from 24 February to 22 March 1931. Lovecraft then himself prepared the 115-page T.Ms., finishing it (as he notes on the last page) on 1 May 1931. The tale of its submission to *Weird Tales* and its rejection there (causing Lovecraft an enormous psychological setback that "did more than anything else to end my effective fictional career" [*SL* 5.224]) is well known. It lay in manuscript for five years, until (through the agency of Julius Schwartz) it was accepted by *Astounding Stories* and published as a three-part serial in the February, March, and April 1936 issues.

In the interim, however, had occurred Admiral Byrd's expedition to the Antarctic (1933–35); and among its results was the confirmation that an hypothesis made by Lovecraft in his novel (that the Antarctic continent was actually two continents divided by a frozen sea) was incorrect. Lovecraft was apparently concerned with correcting this error (which is alluded to three times in his novel); but he must have made the correction on the carbon copy of the novel (assuming that one were made), for no such revisions are found either on the existing T.Ms. or the A.Ms., although the revisions (clearly the work of Lovecraft) appear in the printed text. This carbon copy must have been sent to *Astounding* for publication; it has, I have discovered, now been destroyed.[12]

When the tale was actually published, however, hundreds if not thousands of deliberate alterations and deletions appear to have been made in the text by editor F. Orlin Tremaine (whom Lovecraft once called a "god-damned dung of a hyaena" [*OFF* 335]). Apparently Tremaine considered Lovecraft's text too difficult for easy comprehension by his readers, so that he felt com-

---

12. In a recent talk with Kirby McCauley, who discussed this matter with Stanley Schmidt, current editor of *Analog* (formerly *Astounding*), I learned that the old files of *Astounding* were destroyed c. 1960.

pelled to simplify Lovecraft's English and extensively alter his paragraphing. Lovecraft was forced laboriously to pencil in corrections in his own copies of *Astounding*; but unfortunately, he seems to have corrected only a fraction of the errors, since even after his corrected text there remain hundreds of divergences between the *Astounding* text and the original T.Ms.

The problem becomes: How much did Lovecraft revise the text of his tale when submitting it to *Astounding*? Did he revise not merely his scientific hypothesis, but other portions (particularly the punctuation of the tale, which accounts for most of the divergences between *Astounding* and the T.Ms.) as well? The point is a delicate one, although I tend to doubt that Lovecraft revised his text much: the punctuational forms found in the *Astounding* text seem less typical of Lovecraft's normal punctuational style (although it is unfortunately exactly at this time when his style shifted to the "late" punctuational style noted earlier), and we know (see below) that *Astounding* altered the punctuation of "The Shadow out of Time." In his copies of *Astounding* (still extant in the John Hay Library) Lovecraft has failed to correct certain obvious errors (e.g., the Americanisation of his British spellings), a thing accountable only by oversight or by his unconcern about these lesser errors. Lovecraft has in almost every case corrected the misparagraphing of the tale in *Astounding*—a point of considerable importance in our examination of the text of "The Shadow out of Time"—as well as most of the actual omissions of passages.

Two passages, however, omitted in the first part of the serial were not pencilled in by Lovecraft; and the question again arises as to whether he deleted the two passages in his revised T.Ms. or whether he had failed to notice their omission in the printed text. The latter is—in spite of the relative bulk of the omitted passages—not improbable, since Lovecraft did not appear to realise the extreme corruption of the printed text until he examined the third part of the serial, where by far the most omissions occurred. Moreover, the second of the two omitted sections seems so important to the smooth transition of the passage that its absence is difficult to endure.[13] I claim, therefore, that both passages are authentic and must be restored.

---

13. The second passage (here indicated by diagonal brackets) would occur on p. 36 of the 1964 Arkham House edition: "The whole general formation, it must be made clear, seemed abominably suggestive of the starfish-head of the archaean entities; and we agreed that the suggestion must have worked potently upon the sensitised minds of Lake's overwrought party. <Our own first sight of the actual buried entities formed a horrible moment, and sent the imaginations of Pabodie and myself back to some of the shocking primal myths we had read and heard. We all agreed that the mere sight and continued presence of the things must have cooperated with the oppressive polar solitude and daemon mountain wind in driving Lake's party mad.> ¶ For madness—

There are, however, additional complications at this stage. Lovecraft wrote (*OFF* 336) that he corrected the *Astounding* text from his A.Ms., not having the T.Ms. at hand. Now in preparing his T.Ms. Lovecraft had made certain revisions—usually phraseological—as is normal when any writer prepares a typescript of his own work. Unfortunately, in the five years between the preparation of the T.Ms. and the publication of the tale, Lovecraft seems to have forgotten some of these revisions when correcting the *Astounding* text with his A.Ms.; hence the following oddity:

At the beginning of Chapter IV there occurs the phrase "mountains of madness" in the A.Ms.; this was changed to "frightful mountain wall" in the T.Ms., presumably because the phrase "mountains of madness" had just appeared in the last paragraph of Chapter III. In *Astounding Stories* the text reads "awful mountain wall"; this appears to be a deliberate alteration (probably by Tremaine or his copy editor rather than by Lovecraft) from the T.Ms.; but Lovecraft has corrected his copy of *Astounding* here to read "mountains of madness" again, and the Arkham House editions follow this reading. Lovecraft seems to have forgotten his revision of the phrase in the T.Ms., and has restored what is actually an incorrect reading in terms of what appear to be his final wishes for the wording of the passage. Hence a proper text of the tale should here read "frightful mountain wall"; this reading, at least, has some manuscript authority, and the possibility that Lovecraft changed "frightful" to "awful" in the T.Ms. sent to *Astounding* is too dim and uncertain for reliance (Lovecraft, in any case, normally used "awful" as an archaic synonym for "awesome"). Similar problems occur elsewhere in the text. It thus appears that the existing T.Ms. must be followed in nearly all instances where a deliberate revision has not taken place, and that Lovecraft's "corrected" copies of *Astounding* must not be allowed to carry great weight save as corroboration.

Unfortunately, Derleth and Wandrei, when preparing the first Arkham House edition of the tale—*The Outsider and Others* (1939)—based their text on Lovecraft's copies of *Astounding*.[14] They apparently knew that Lovecraft had revised his text after preparing the T.Ms. and that the *Astounding* version was not at all reliable; hence they felt that Lovecraft's corrected copies of *Astounding* would provide as secure a text as could easily be obtained. That the 1964 Arkham House edition (very little different from the 1939 edition) still con-

---

centreing in Gedney as the only possible surviving agent—was the explanation spontaneously adopted by everybody so far as spoken utterance was concerned. . . ." The word *for* beginning the new paragraph must obviously refer to a previous mention of madness—a mention we find precisely in the omitted section.

14. See August Derleth to R. H. Barlow, 21 March [1937] (ms., JHL).

tains some 1500 errors need not strictly be attributed to Derleth and Wandrei; for only an enormously laborious collation of all existing manuscripts and publications of the novel can produce a text that has even a modest claim to authority. In the end there shall always remain doubt as to what Lovecraft's final wishes for the novel were, and which of the uncorrected divergences between *Astounding* and the existing T.Ms. are the result of deliberate revision by Lovecraft and which the result of editorial alteration.[15]

Still greater uncertainty previously surrounded the text of the other story published by *Astounding*, "The Shadow out of Time"—but the difficulties have now been resolved by the fortuitous recovery of the A.Ms. in 1994. Nevertheless, the textual problems in the text are still worth exploring. Instead of being faced with a plethora of texts as with *At the Mountains of Madness*, we here have too few. Before the discovery of the A.Ms., we were only left with the published version (Lovecraft's annotated copy of the issue) and the Arkham House texts that must derive from it.

There was, however, one additional clue. Years ago I discovered a fragment of a manuscript of the tale in the John Hay Library, where it was badly miscatalogued. This fragment is in pen, is labelled at the top as p. 58, and at the bottom bears the note: "Copied Aug. 15, 1935." I hypothesised that this is a copy of the pencil draft made by Lovecraft (who on August 15 was still in Florida) for Barlow, perhaps because Barlow was unable to read this portion of the pencil draft. Comparison between this manuscript fragment and the published text reveals that on two occasions *Astounding* has divided Lovecraft's original paragraphs into two or more paragraphs, precisely as was done for *At the Mountains of Madness*. Consultation of the complete A.Ms. establishes conclusively that the paragraphing of the whole novelette is wrong. Amazingly, Lovecraft continually remarked that the tale was more or less soundly printed in *Astounding*. He wrote on one occasion: "It [the tale] was made rather worse by the careless printing—the crazy 'style sheet' of A. S., with its irresponsible overcapitalisation (*Moon, Moonlight,* &c.!) & overpunctuation (redundant commas by the bushel), & occasional outright misprints. This story wasn't intentionally mangled."[16] True enough, Lovecraft's copy of *Astounding* bears some slight corrections, but nowhere does he correct the paragraphing of the tale as he did laboriously and carefully with the printed text of *At the Mountains of Madness*.

---

15. It is, therefore, somewhat ironic that the 2005 Modern Library edition of *At the Mountains of Madness*, reprinting the text I established in 1985, is called "The Definitive Text." There can be no definitive text of this novel unless by some miracle the T.Ms. submitted to *Astounding* were to turn up.

16. HPL to Duane W. Rimel, 20 June 1936 (ms., JHL).

It is puzzling that Lovecraft forgot or overlooked the paragraphing of his own story only a year after its writing. Surely he cannot have approved of some of the paragraphing in the *Astounding* appearance; in one instance the following brief sentence—"Flowers were small, colourless, and unrecognisable, blooming in geometrical beds and at large among the greenery"—is made a separate paragraph, and this in spite of the fact that the whole passage is a discussion of the "omnipresent gardens" seen by the narrator in his "dreams." Such small paragraphs are absolutely non-existent in Lovecraft's fiction, save in dramatic instances: note the final paragraph of "The Whisperer in Darkness," the third to last paragraph of "The Dunwich Horror," and the like. Moreover, the fact that similar paragraph divisions were made in the *Astounding* text of *At the Mountains of Madness* and in the passage of "The Shadow out of Time" as revealed in the one-page manuscript forces us to dismiss outright Lovecraft's statements as to the textual security of the tale.

These are only some of the most complex problems faced in restoring the texts of Lovecraft's fiction. The restoration of his essays and poetry is made much the simpler due to their existence in relatively sound amateur journal appearances or in manuscript. In these cases there has been almost no transmission of the text, and in many instances we have only one ultimate source with which to deal.

All aspects of scholarship are affected by textual study; and it is certain that the analysis of Lovecraft's work will rise substantially in quality once we are aware of what he actually wrote.[17]

Works Cited

de Camp, L. Sprague. *Lovecraft: A Biography*. Garden City, NY: Doubleday, 1975.

Dobrée, Bonamy. "Note on the Text." In *The Mysteries of Udolpho* by Ann Radcliffe. Oxford: Oxford University Press, 1966. xvii.

Derleth, August. "H. P. Lovecraft: The Making of a Literary Reputation, 1937–1971." *Books at Brown* 25 (1977): 13–25.

Joshi, S. T., ed. *A Weird Writer in Our Midst: Early Criticism of H. P. Lovecraft*. New York: Hippocampus Press, 2010.

Joshi, S. T., and Marc A. Michaud, ed. *H. P. Lovecraft in "The Eyrie."* West Warwick, RI: Necronomicon Press, 1979.

Smith, Clark Ashton. *Letters to H. P. Lovecraft*. Edited by Steve Behrends. West Warwick, RI: Necronomicon Press, 1987.

---

17. I am grateful to Edward S. Lauterbach for suggestions on the revision of this paper.

The Structure of Lovecraft's Longer Narratives

As early as 1952 Peter Penzoldt, in *The Supernatural in Fiction*, remarked that Lovecraft's tales are "nearly always perfect in structure" (69); but neither Penzoldt himself nor subsequent scholars have actually made a detailed examination of this structural perfection. Lovecraft is, indeed, a master almost unrivalled in the writing of novelettes, novellas, and short novels; and his best tales are almost without exception his longer narratives. It may, then, be well to give closer attention to the structural devices employed by Lovecraft in his longer works.

We can, I think, distinguish four structural patterns in Lovecraft's novelettes, although a given tale may happen to employ, in differing degrees, two or even three of the patterns. The four patterns can be enumerated as 1) strict chronology (i.e., where the incidents of a tale are narrated without a break in chronological sequence); 2) flashback; 3) double or multiple climax; and 4) narrative within narrative. Let us examine these four methods in greater detail.

The tales that are narrated without any interruption or rearrangement of chronological time are usually the simplest in structure; and are, in a sense, mere outgrowths of the short story. It may, then, be significant that Lovecraft's first true novelette (excluding the two serials "Herbert West— Reanimator" and "The Lurking Fear"), "The Rats in the Walls" (1923), employs this structure; indeed, the tale is hardly much longer than a short story itself. The opening of the tale has become celebrated: "On July 16, 1923, I moved into Exham Priory after the last workman had finished his labours" (*DH* 25). The tale can actually be regarded as a huge flashback, since in the last paragraph we are finally told of the present state of the narrator: "Now they have blown up Exham Priory, taken my Nigger-Man away from me, and shut me into this barred room at Hanwell" (*DH* 45). Indeed, there is a certain deception in the narration of this tale (as with several others of the flashback type in Lovecraft), since the narrator, although fully aware of the horrific events he is telling, nevertheless expounds his tale quite rationally at the beginning, as if he is unaware of what is to be. (One supposes that Lovecraft might have justified this device by implying that the narrator, as he begins relating the increasingly horrible events of the tale, gradually loses his self-control and descends to the gibbering of the penultimate paragraph.) This tale cannot strictly qualify as a flashback as I propose to define it, since we are not aware that it is a flashback until the end of the narrative; moreover, although the tale involves a brief exposition of the history of Exham Priory and of the narrator's ancestry (hence perhaps belonging to the class of narrative within narrative), the narrator clearly and emphatically brings us back to present time by concluding his digression with the words: "As I have said, I moved in on July 16, 1923" (*DH* 32).

More purely adhering to strict chronology is, surprisingly, Lovecraft's first novel, *The Dream-Quest of Unknown Kadath* (1926-27)—surprisingly because a strictly chronological framework is difficult to manage in a very long work without the danger of tedium. Lovecraft, however, clearly intended such a structure for his work, since he could thus achieve that sense of wonder and amazement at the successive encounters with odd beings and events which is typical of works embodying the "Odyssey theme"—a theme we find in Lovecraft's earlier tale "The White Ship" (1919). (The *Odyssey*, of course, is of immensely intricate construction in its plot structure alone, to say nothing of subtle thematic parallels. See Whitman, ch. 12.)[1] Lovecraft declared, indeed, that "This tale is one of picaresque adventure—a quest for the gods through varied and incredible scenes and perils—and is written continuously like *Vathek* without any subdivision into chapters" (*SL* 2.94); a passage that recalls Lovecraft's description of his inchoate novel *Azathoth* ("The weird *Vathek*-like novel *Azathoth*" [*SL* 1.185]), which appears to have been similarly designed in a strict chronological framework, as the opening lines reveal: "When age fell upon the world, and wonder went out of the minds of men; . . . there was a man who travelled out of life on a quest into the spaces whither the world's dreams had fled" (*D* 357). That *Azathoth* is thus an adumbration or precursor to the *Dream-Quest* (whose "moral" seems to have been based on the earlier "Celephaïs" [1920]) is very likely.

The flashbacks or narratives within narratives in the *Dream-Quest* are all very brief and usually involve allusions to previous works by Lovecraft whose incidents he is attempting to tie into the thread of his novel. Thus we find hints of such tales as "The White Ship," "Celephaïs," "Pickman's Model," "The Other Gods," and the like, but the time spent in recounting the plots of these tales is scant, as can be seen in the summary of "The White Ship":

---

1. It is interesting to note that HPL, in his juvenile retelling of the *Odyssey* ("The Poem of Ulysses," 1897), simplifies the structure of the epic vastly and narrates the plot strictly chronologically, to the point of omitting entirely the Adventures of Telemachus of Books I-IV.

> He [Carter] saw slip past him the glorious lands and cities of which a fellow-dreamer of earth—a lighthouse-keeper in ancient Kingsport—had often discoursed in the old days, and recognised the templed terraces of Zak, abode of forgotten dreams; the spires of infamous Thalarion, that daemon-city of a thousand wonders where the eidolon Lathi reigns; the charnel gardens of Xura, land of pleasures unattained, and the twin headlands of crystal, meeting above in a resplendent arch, which guard the harbour of Sona-Nyl, blessed land of fancy. (MM 317)

The description of the "Basalt Pillars of the West, beyond which simple folk say splendid Cathuria lies," takes only another paragraph. The whole point of the novel, then, is the almost kaleidoscopic display of bizarre scenes one upon the other, and to the accomplishment of this design the simple narrative structure of strict chronology is clearly the best suited. That Lovecraft employed this simple technique deliberately and not through any incompetency in structural design can be seen in *The Case of Charles Dexter Ward*, one of the most structurally complex of Lovecraft's works, written directly after the *Dream-Quest*.

"The Dreams in the Witch House" (1932) presents a deceptively simple pattern; for although ostensibly a strictly chronological narrative (proceeding from the moment Gilman enters the Witch House to his eventual death), the tale actually becomes a quasi-"narrative within a narrative" (i.e., Gilman's "dreams" of hyperspace), although in both "narratives" Gilman is the central figure. The tale is thus somewhat akin to "The Shadow out of Time," where the narrator similarly "dreams" of himself in a wholly different environment; but here the two "narratives"—Gilman's "real-life" existence in Arkham and his dream-journeys—are so intricately knit together and alternate so rapidly back and forth (unlike "The Shadow out of Time," which, because of the extended description of the narrator's experiences as a member of the Great Race, qualifies as a true narrative within a narrative) that the tale becomes—fascinatingly and brilliantly—a structural anomaly.[2] Ultimately the two "narratives" cannot be separated, in spite of the fact that Gilman himself tries to make a distinction between his "real" and his "dream" existence—a distinction difficult to maintain when certain concrete particulars from the "dream" world (e.g., the spiky image from the dream-balustrade) obtrude upon his "real" world. The employment of these two simultaneous narratives was the only means by which Lovecraft could imply that Gilman was actually living on two

---

2. This is not to imply that the tale is necessarily one of HPL's best: indeed, in certain of its philosophical bases, uses of language, and plot elements it is distinctly inferior to many of his longer tales.

planes of reality—i.e., three-dimensional space and hyperspace—at the same time. This is only one of several examples where the philosophical bases of a tale has actually inspired or necessitated a specific narrative technique.

The second narrative structure—the flashback—has been used by Lovecraft in varying degrees in many tales, long and short. Indeed, this is perhaps the most common type of structure employed by Lovecraft. On a minor level we find it in many short tales; note the opening of "Dagon" (1917): "I am writing this under an appreciable mental strain, since by tonight I shall be no more" (*D* 14). Or "The Tomb" (1917): "In relating the circumstances which have led to my confinement within this refuge for the demented, I am aware that my present position will create a natural doubt of the authenticity of my narrative" (*D* 3). Often the flashback method opens with a grand and almost philosophical series of reflections impelled by the events through which the narrator has passed; note "Beyond the Wall of Sleep" (1919): "I have frequently wondered if the majority of mankind ever pause to reflect upon the occasionally titanic significance of dreams" (*D* 25). Or "Under the Pyramids" (1924): "Mystery attracts mystery" (*D* 217). Or the very famous opening of "The Call of Cthulhu" (1926): "The most merciful thing in the world, I think, is the inability of the human mind to correlate all its contents" (*DH* 125).

At its simplest, the flashback technique becomes little more than the strict chronological technique with a brief introduction where the narrator reflects upon his experiences; note that in "The Tomb" the narrative proceeds directly after a paragraph where the narrator speculates that "there is no sharp distinction betwixt the real and the unreal" (*D* 3). Almost all Lovecraft's shorter tales are of this very simple type.

In other cases, however, the flashback becomes a rather more significant device; and in the longer tales we are given a proportionately longer introduction to the tale proper—an introduction full of reflections about the incidents about to be, told from the standpoint of the chronological end of the events. The first adumbration of this device we find in "The Horror at Red Hook" (1925), where the whole first chapter is given over to a description and analysis of Thomas Malone's curious "lapse of behaviour" (*D* 244) in the village of Pascoag, where he loses control of himself after seeing some tall buildings. In this opening chapter—which in the chronology of the tale occurs some time after the events narrated in the bulk of the story—Lovecraft can arouse our curiosity first by the seeming psychological absurdity of the event, and then by hints of the causes for Malone's lapse—"There had been a collapse of several old brick buildings [in New York] during a raid in which he had shared, and something about the wholesale loss of life, both of prisoners and of his companions, had peculiarly appalled him" (*D* 245). Here again, as with all the tales of the flashback type, we encounter a certain deception in the narration; for the omniscient third-person narrator of the tale obviously knows the real reason for Malone's collapse, but fails to record it at this time.

In "The Colour out of Space" (1927) and "The Dunwich Horror" (1928) the flashback technique is slightly altered. We are, at the tales' beginning, presented with an essentially "timeless" description of the unhealthy environment of the respective regions: "When a traveller in north central Massachusetts takes the wrong fork at the junction of the Aylesbury pike beyond Dean's Corners he comes upon a lonely and curious country" (*DH* 155-56). In both tales reference is made—almost in passing—to the horrific events about to be described (in "The Dunwich Horror": "In our sensible age—since the Dunwich horror of 1928 was hushed up by those who had the town's and the world's welfare at heart—people shun it without knowing exactly why" [*DH* 157]), but this flashback is not central to the description. Indeed, in "The Dunwich Horror" reference is made not merely to the "Dunwich horror of 1928" but to the Salem witch trials and to Rev. Hoadley's sermon of 1747. The difference between the flashback openings here and that of "The Horror at Red Hook" is that in the former tales the description is general, timeless, and does not involve any of the central characters of the tale proper. "The Whisperer in Darkness" (1930), with its very brief flashback opening, is thus more similar to "The Horror at Red Hook" or even to Lovecraft's shorter tales.

"Through the Gates of the Silver Key" (1932-33) presents a combination of the flashback and the narrative within a narrative; the opening scene (in the New Orleans home of de Marigny) is not set chronologically after *all* the incidents of the tale, but only some of them (i.e., those describing Carter's odd adventures through space and time); the opening is in fact somewhat clumsy, as it must (like the successive episodes of "Herbert West—Reanimator") initially describe the events of "The Silver Key" of which the story is a sequel. The New Orleans setting thus recurs after the "Swami Chandraputra" narrates Carter's adventures. (It is interesting to note that Price's original version of the sequel similarly opens with a two-paragraph recounting of the events of "The Silver Key," although without any New Orleans scene.) It is difficult to see how this structural clumsiness—perhaps inherent in sequels—could have been avoided, and it is thus not difficult to understand Lovecraft's displeasure at completing this forced collaboration.

As for the double or multiple climax, we naturally find it initially in the two serial tales "Herbert West—Reanimator" (1921-22) and "The Lurking Fear" (1922); Lovecraft, indeed, remarking of the former that "To write to order, and to drag one figure through a series of artificial episodes, involves the violation of all that spontaneity and singleness of impression which should characterise short story work" (SL 1.158). There are several important points in this statement: first, it reveals that Lovecraft was at this time (1921) still exclusively concerned with writing short stories that had "singleness of impression" (we are reminded of his later remark of Poe's "maintenance of a single mood and achievement of a single impression in a tale": "Supernatural Horror in Literature" [D 396]); and secondly, we learn that he was not certain as to the aesthetic value of multiple climaxes in a single tale—particularly when the respective climaxes were of equal importance or power. Indeed, although Lovecraft was, for "The Lurking Fear," forced to tack on a climax at the end of each of the four sections, it is significant that here the final climax is much more potent than the three subsidiary ones; the tale in effect reveals his growing mastery of structure in the employment of several subsidiary climaxes but only one major climax at the conclusion, thus preserving—after a fashion—the "singleness of impression" he desired. "The Lurking Fear" is notably lacking in the redundant synopses of previous episodes which makes "Herbert West—Reanimator" so tedious, and it maintains a unity far more than its predecessor. Significantly, Lovecraft's first true novelette—"The Rats in the Walls"—was written less than a year after the writing of "The Lurking Fear."

"The Call of Cthulhu" (1926) is built somewhat on the same pattern (although this is more probably one of a narrative—or, rather, two narratives—within a narrative), but there is only one real climax: the actual encountering of Cthulhu by Johansen's ship. The end of the first chapter—that impressive listing of bizarre happenings all over the world as culled from Prof. Angell's "press cuttings" (DH 132)—is not a climax in the strictest sense, for it merely causes a certain perturbation and wonderment in the reader, who is at a loss to account for so many odd occurrences at a single time. The conclusion of the second chapter provides still less of a climax, since the function of the chapter is to provide the clue for the strange incidents of Chapter I and to supply information on the Old Ones. Only with the actual sight of Cthulhu do we encounter a true climax; and even here Lovecraft is striving to escape from any sensationalism or floridity: we find no italicised last sentence, but after the narrator's calm conclusion of Johansen's experience ("That was all" [DH 153]), he continues for four paragraphs with some general remarks that serve to conclude the tale tranquilly. For in fact the true climax of the tale is not the emergence of Cthulhu (who in any case vanishes after a few moments), but the *implication* of the narrative—the implication that hideous, vastly powerful entities lurk just behind our consciousness. This is the point of the narrator's offhand remark "Cthulhu still lives, I suppose," and his much more harried thought that "Loathsomeness awaits and dreams in the deep, and decay spreads over the tottering cities of men. A time will come—but I must not and cannot think!" (*DH* 154). Although in a certain sense employing the multiple climax technique, Lovecraft has here escaped the need of making any overt climax at all.

The double climax is authentically employed in "The Dunwich Horror," a tale whose structure—like that of "The Shadow over Innsmouth" (1931)—has frequently been misunderstood. Drake Douglas, commenting on Lovecraft's detailed description of the death of Wilbur Whateley, wrote: "One wonders why, in this particular instance, Lovecraft decided to go to so much trouble to provide an exact description which, in truth, is not very satisfying. A rather vaguely defined horror is often more terrifying than the one which is clearly outlined for us" (268). The last sentence is, of course, a truism of weird literature; but Douglas finds the description here unsatisfying precisely because he seems to conceive it as the major climax, when in fact it is only a subsidiary climax and the first real indication of the "non-human side of [Whateley's] ancestry" (*DH* 174). Lovecraft was perfectly aware of the importance of mere suggestion as opposed to overt description in a tale; of Blackwood's "The Willows" he remarked that "the lack of *anything concrete* is the *great asset* of the story" (*SL* 3.429). Indeed, Lovecraft may have employed such a detailed, almost clinical description of Whateley's death precisely as an indication of the greater horror of his brother. The fact that this first climax occurs precisely halfway through the narrative may confirm this view.

The situation is the same with "The Shadow over Innsmouth" (1931). Far from believing L. Sprague de Camp's remarkable statement of "Lovecraft's blunder of putting the climax [i.e., the narrator's pursuit by the Innsmouth denizens] in the middle" (354), we must understand that this subsidiary climax is only a preparation for the enormously greater climax of the narrator's gradual awareness that he has gained "the Innsmouth look." Here we note Lovecraft's preference for climaxes of a deceptively quiet or mental nature, in contrast to those of an "action" or physical sort.

Two tales with double climaxes somewhat similar to those of "The Dunwich Horror" are *At the Mountains of Madness* (1931) and "The Shadow out of Time" (1934–35). In the broadest terms, the first "climax" in both tales (although it is really not presented as such) is the encounter with the first genus of extra-terrestrial beings—i.e., the Old Ones and the Great Race. These beings are both initially portrayed as horrifying from a human perspective; but in the course of the narrative we actually come to gain a certain sympathy with them, and the real horror (the "second" climax) emerges with the appearance of the shoggoth and the Blind Beings. Fritz Leiber brilliantly characterised this pattern by speaking (in reference to *At the Mountains of Madness*) of the "transition whereby the feared entities [i.e. the Old Ones] become the fearing; the author shows us horrors and then pulls back the curtain a little farther, letting us glimpse the horrors of which even the horrors are afraid!" (462). Precisely as in "The Dunwich Horror" with the description of Wilbur Whateley, the first "horrors" (Old Ones and Great Race) are described in some detail, whereas the second or real horrors are merely adumbrated; indeed, the Blind Beings never make an actual appearance in "The Shadow out of Time," while in *At the Mountains of Madness* the climax—the witnessing of the shoggoth—is prepared by an elaborate series of sub-climaxes: the narrators first stumble across the material from Lake's camp transported by the Old Ones, then the three sledges and the body of Gedney, then the gigantic albino penguins (actually a deliberate anticlimax), then the decapitated bodies of the Old Ones, and then finally the shoggoth itself. The real climaxes to both stories are prepared with almost excessive care and detail: in *At the Mountains of Madness* the narrators' "glance backward" (MM 99) is described in five excruciatingly long paragraphs (a remarkable example of the "freezing" of time), while in "The Shadow out of Time" the narrator's descent into the primal ruins fills nearly a third of the narrative, and the narrator's hesitation actually to tell the horrible truth (that he saw the record he himself had written millions of years ago) is emphasised by the thrice-repeated anaphoric utterance "Had I . . .?" toward the close of the tale. Indeed, the very fact that the Old Ones and Great Race are described in such a calm and rational manner, whereas the real horrors are narrated feverishly and almost poetically, ought to inform us of Lovecraft's true climactic intentions.

The revision "Medusa's Coil" also contains several climaxes (the deaths of Marsh and Denis, the emergence of Marceline's hair from its grave after the narrator shoots the picture, the discovery that the mansion had actually burned down five or six years before the narrator's visit, and finally the discovery that Marceline had been a negress), but there are actually too many of them, and they do not fit together into a coherent whole. Indeed, the revelation of the mansion's razing five years before the narrator's arrival seems particularly gratuitous, and is difficult to explain even by supernatural means. Clearly Lovecraft did not take much trouble in working out the plot for this tale—or perhaps this part of the plot was the nucleus by Zealia Bishop upon which he based the rest of the story.

In the case of the narrative within a narrative technique, we may subdivide it into two types: the indirect narrative (i.e., where the narrator himself has not pieced together the subsidiary narrative) and its converse, the direct narrative. The former is a cruder form and sometimes entails structural difficulties, while the latter creates a much more unified effect. In no instance, however, ought to employment of the narrative within a narrative device be considered in itself a structural defect. We are, of course, reminded of Lovecraft's criticism of *Melmoth the Wanderer,* where the subsidiary narrative of John and Monçada "takes up the bulk of Maturin's four-volume book; this disproportion being considered one of the chief technical faults of the composition" (*D* 382). Lovecraft avoided this structural flaw even in his worst-constructed tales by sufficiently integrating the subsidiary narrative with the principal one. Thus in "Medusa's Coil," the bulk of the work is given over to de Russy's tale of his son, Marceline, and the portrait by Marsh; but this narrative is followed by actions based upon it leading to the (presumably) major climax—the destruction of the mansion. There is, nonetheless, a certain awkwardness in the whole procedure, and this tale is clearly the crudest example of Lovecraft's use of the narrative within a narrative. Rarely does he allow a subsidiary character actually to tell the subordinate narrative (another example, causing equal structural clumsiness, is "Through the Gates of the Silver Key"); we are usually presented with the main narrator's discovery of a document that presents the subsidiary narrative (as in "The Mound"), and rarely is this document quoted directly; rather it undergoes constant interpretation by the narrator (the best example is *At the Mountains of Madness,* where the narrator constantly comments upon the bas-reliefs being examined) and as a result the narrator is constantly kept before our eyes. Lovecraft's failure to adopt this subtler device in "Medusa's Coil" (one presumes that the narrator could have found some document in the house—a diary, perhaps—that could have told him the gist of de Russy's narrative) again indicates his lack of concern in the refinement of this tale.

"Medusa's Coil" nonetheless indicates an important trait inherent in Lovecraft's use of the indirect narrative within a narrative: in the subsidiary narrative one character gradually emerges with a personality of his own, and the reader comes to identify with him. This happens in a trilogy of stories—"The Horror at Red Hook," "The Whisperer in Darkness," and "The Thing on the Doorstep"—whose subsidiary narratives are so intricately woven into the central narrative that we can hardly speak of two narratives at all. In "The Horror at Red Hook," the central narrative ostensibly concerns Malone's attempts to purge Red Hook of its sinister horrors; but through Malone's eyes and through his gradual accumulation of data another narrative emerges—the tale of Robert Suydam, who is initially portrayed as unpleasant and vaguely horrific but who ultimately becomes a subordinate "hero" by nullifying the black magic being performed at the underground waterfront. It cannot, of course, be said that the two narratives are distinct; in fact, they are intimately connected. But the process of expounding the Suydam narrative is indirect—i.e., through Malone—hence can be considered subordinate.

Similarly, in "The Whisperer in Darkness" Akeley emerges as a separate character—in spite of the fact that Wilmarth is the narrator and ostensibly the central figure—but here again the means is indirect: it is accomplished wholly through the correspondence between Akeley and Wilmarth. In "The Thing on the Doorstep" the narrator is not the central character at all, but it is he who tells the story of Edward Derby and Asenath Waite—for reasons obviously essential to the plot (although it might have been fascinating had Lovecraft attempted to narrate the tale from Derby's point of view;[3] Derby's intermittent possession by Asenath might have been conveyed by the employment of a radically different style—note Wilmarth's detecting the psychological difference between Akeley's letters and the final letter from the aliens ["Word-choice, spelling—all were subtly different" (*DH* 242)]—while Derby's emergence from the grave in the rotting corpse of Asenath might have brought forth a scene similar to the conclusion of "The Outsider").

All these tales and other of Lovecraft's longer stories reveal the care with which he debated on the best narrative point of view and structure to employ for a given tale. The use of correspondence to expound Akeley's involvement with the Winged Ones keeps these horrific events at a proper narrative "distance," similar perhaps to the use of the messenger to narrate the climax of Greek tragedies (one thinks especially of the *Medea* of Euripides, where the Messenger tells the grisly tale of the deaths of Glauke and her father Kreon).[4]

This creation of a narrative "distance" is most emphatically displayed in "The Call of Cthulhu," the last of the indirect narrative-within-a-narrative tales to be studied here. This tale is remarkable in having not merely one but as many as three narratives within the basic narrative. An outline might more clearly depict the structure:

I. Narrative of Francis Wayland Thurston
   A. Narrative of Prof. Angell's discussions with Henry Wilcox
   B. Narrative of Prof. Angell's account of the account of Inspector Legrasse.
      1. Inspector Legrasse's cross-examination of Castro (information about Old Ones)
   C. Narrator's discovery of newspaper article telling of Johansen's ship
   D. Narrator's discovery and recital of Johansen's manuscript

---

3. This was suggested to me by Donald R. Burleson.

4. See Kitto, *Greek Tragedy*: "The horrible death of Glauce and Creon is described exhaustively in the terrible style of which Euripides was such a master. It is sheer Grand Guignol. We have yet seen nothing like it in Greek Tragedy" (199).

In this elaborate structure we may note several things: first, the number of characters or elements required to tell the entire narrative (Thurston, Angell, Wilcox, Legrasse, Castro, the newspaper article, Johansen); and secondly, the fact that the most sensational parts of the narrative—the explanation of the Old Ones by Castro and the encounter with Cthulhu—are told in an extremely circumspect way; indeed, the Castro narrative is *three* times removed from the central one: Thurston–Angell–Legrasse–Castro. This can be depicted by the following chart of the narrative voices:

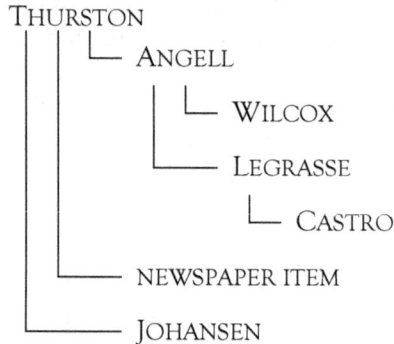

This structure, however, never becomes clumsy, since we always keep the principal narrator in view, as he continually interprets the evidence and brings himself forward; at one point he actually interviews Wilcox again after reading his uncle's papers, charmingly concluding: "I took leave of him amicably, and wish him all the success his talent promises" (*DH* 144).

"The Call of Cthulhu" provides a transition to what I have called the direct narrative within a narrative, for in that tale the narrator himself has pieced together some of the information representing the subsidiary narratives (i.e., his discovery of the newspaper item and the Johansen narrative). It is this device—one much more conducive to unity, in spite of the much greater length of the subsidiary narratives that we generally find in this group—that Lovecraft has employed in some of his most impressive tales; namely, "The Shunned House," *The Case of Charles Dexter Ward*, "The Mound," *At the Mountains of Madness*, "The Shadow out of Time," and "The Haunter of the Dark."

For the direct narrative within a narrative the earliest example on an extended scale seems to be "The Lurking Fear" (1922), where the narrator, in order to understand why "Fear had lurked on Tempest Mountain for more than a century" (*D* 180), must do much research into the history of the Martense family. Indeed, the narrator remarks with a certain poignancy that "History . . . was all I had after everything else ended in mocking Satanism" (*D* 190)—a remark that makes us realise that all the narratives within narratives in this group involve a reaching backward through time, a technique frequent in Lovecraft even in tales technically outside this specific group (e.g., "The Rats in the Walls," "Facts concerning the Late Arthur Jermyn and His Family," even so early a tale as "The Alchemist"). In any case, the whole historical research in the tale is performed by the narrator; and through his direct exposition of his findings the tale gains an unity lacking in such a tale as "Medusa's Coil." The exigencies of the serial form of "The Lurking Fear" forced Lovecraft to confine the subsidiary narrative of the Martenses to a single chapter (the third); in later tales he greatly expands the narrative, to the point that (e.g., in "The Mound") it occupies more than half the length of the whole tale.

In "The Shunned House" (1924) the technique of employing a subsidiary narrative is subtilised; for not only is the history of the shunned house not told all at one time—the narrator's discovery of the "French element" (MM 248) (i.e., the tale of Etienne Roulet) being delayed after the preliminary exposition of the house's history—but the narrator is constantly kept in our view: Chapter II begins: "Not till my adult years did my uncle set before me the notes and data which he had collected concerning the shunned house"; Chapter III opens: "It may well be imagined how powerfully I was affected by the annals of the Harrises"; and finally the narrator begins his own researches, carrying forward his uncle's work.

This same device is found in *The Case of Charles Dexter Ward* (1927), upon whose rich complexity we can here only touch. The subsidiary narrative—the tale of Joseph Curwen's doings in the seventeenth and eighteenth centuries—is ostensibly limited to Part II ("An Antecedent and a Horror"), and throughout this section we find Ward intruding as the information is being presented: "Charles Ward told his father, when they discussed Curwen one winter morning . . ."; "The collection of Durfee-Arnold letters, discovered by Charles Ward . . ."; "Parts of [a letter], copied and preserved in the private archives of the family where Charles Ward found it . . ."; "Charles Ward, however, discovered another vague sidelight in some Fenner correspondence" (MM 120, 126, 138, 143); and the like. But this intrusion of a twentieth-century character into an eighteenth-century world then reverses, as the hoary Curwen, as it were, bursts out of his narrative and comes more and more to dominate Ward. In Part III, we find Ward still accumulating data, coming across more letters written in the crabbed archaism of the seventeenth century; and throughout the rest of the novel, which is supposed to be set in the contemporary age, we constantly encounter intrusions of archaism: Curwen's diary, letters written to Curwen/Ward so late as 1928 (letters contrasting harshly with Ward's own epistle to Willett of March 8, 1928), and finally Curwen's complete replacement of Ward, conveyed—as in "The Whisperer in Darkness" and "The Thing on the Doorstep"—through a telltale stylistic difference; this time a difference of speech, as Curwen reveals his age with such terms as "bigness," "phthisical," and the like (MM 186-87). (Lovecraft's omnivorous reading of eighteenth-century literature held him in good stead here.) As in "The Call of Cthulhu," the use of many types of documents—letters, diaries, newspaper articles, even the scrap of eighth-century Latin minuscule—serves to "distance" the narrative and subtilise it; indeed, we must pay enormously close attention to ascertain exactly when Curwen finally kills Ward and supplants him permanently (hence the constant debates by the alienists as to the precise commencement of Ward's "madness" [i.e., replacement], which help not only to clarify the structure of the novel but to provide clues as to when we are to understand that the final transition has occurred). As in many of Lovecraft's tales, the "subsidiary" historical narratives comes ultimately to dominate the rest of the narrative; a technique which can be interpreted philosophically as indicating Lovecraft's belief in the deathlessness of the past and its power over the present.

"The Mound" (1929-30) is not so sound structurally as some of Lovecraft's original narratives, for here the narrative of Zamacona—an actual parchment found by the narrator, and presented in a paraphrase—occupies the whole of Chapters III to VI, and this great length forces us almost to lose track of the central, contemporary narrative: indeed, when, at the opening of Chapter VII, we read "When I looked up from my half-stupefied reading and note-making" (*HM* 155), we have almost forgotten that the narrative is in the first person. Nonetheless, the tale is indicative of Lovecraft's interest in increasingly alien civilisations: the tale, though apparently reporting a fifteenth-century Spaniard's narrative, actually tells an incalculably older tale—the settlement and civilisation of the underground race that came from the stars; the tale thus becomes a triple narrative within a narrative within a narrative (modern times—Zamacona—mound civilisation), and reaches farther back in time than any of Lovecraft's previous historical interludes.

This temporally distant sub-narrative is employed in two of Lovecraft's most brilliant tales, *At the Mountains of Madness* and "The Shadow out of Time." In both tales the means for expounding the alternate civilisations here presented (Old Ones and Great Race) is no mere manuscript, but, in the first case, the bas-reliefs of the Old Ones' city, and in the second case, the narrator's "dreams" of his experiences in the Great Race's city. In *At the Mountains of Madness* we again note the enormously subtle device of using *style* or *aesthetics* to tell an historical narrative; a technique carried still farther here, when the narrators encounter—well after the exposition of the basic historical segment in Chapters VII and VIII—the "new and degenerate work [that] was coarse, bold, and wholly lacking in delicacy of detail" (MM 92); the work, of course, of the shoggoths. The historical segment does not, as in "The Mound," dominate the novel: instead, enormously elaborate descriptions of the voyage to the Antarctic, Lake's sub-expedition, and the protagonists' exploration of the Old Ones' dead city preface the subsidiary tale, so that we never lose track of the central story line. In "The Shadow out of Time" similar restraint is used: we learn the whole history and civilisation of the Great Race gradually and sporadically through the successive dreams of the narrator; and we have seen how the last third of the tale is wholly occupied with the narrator's maniacal trip through the ruined city.

Some general remarks about Lovecraft's varied structural patterns can now be made. In regard to the strictly chronological or flashback technique, we have noted how the majority of his shorter tales and some of his longer works fall into this pattern; indeed, the pattern is almost mandatory for stories narrated in the first person (and it is to be noted that the majority of Lovecraft's tales that are not narrated in the first person—e.g., "The Dreams in the Witch House"—still centre so much around one character that the distinction becomes nominal). We must actually commend Lovecraft for his ability to incorporate the narrative within a narrative technique into a first-person account—successfully in *At the Mountains of Madness* and "The Shadow out of Time" and perhaps less so in "The Mound." The double or multiple climax can be handled either in first- or third-person narrative (e.g., "The Shadow over Innsmouth" and "The Dunwich Horror").

We have already cited Lovecraft's criticism of Maturin's *Melmoth* in its use of the narrative within a narrative; and we may well ask how he managed generally to escape such a flaw in construction when he used the device. The answer appears to lie in the fact that in nearly all cases the narrator or central character (e.g., Ward) either tells the facts of the case himself (and has usually assembled or collected them) or paraphrases the account of someone else (e.g., "The Call of Cthulhu," "The Mound"). Moreover, the "subsidiary" narrative in all cases is so fundamental to the plot of the story that it in effect cannot be considered subsidiary at all; indeed, it may well be that the narrative that frames it is the really subsidiary narrative. In "The Mound," for example, the central plot of the narrative is the fate of Zamacona in the underground world; the actual narrator has merely unearthed the data and, at the end, comes upon a definite confirmation[5] of Zamacona's fate. Similarly, in "The Call of Cthulhu" the actual narrator has acted merely as an industrious detective in unearthing the facts about the Cthulhu cult and of Johan-

---

5. See Fritz Leiber's explanation of this concept in "A Literary Copernicus" (461).

sen's encounter with the being. In several instances, however, the "subsidiary" historical narrative reaches out of the plot and has an effect upon the future: in "The Shunned House" and *The Case of Charles Dexter Ward*, the horror is averted and the tales end "happily"; in others—e.g., "The Haunter of the Dark"—the reverse is the case.

That Lovecraft himself was fully aware of the importance of structure in fiction can be fully observed in some of his essays, notably "Notes on Writing Weird Fiction," where he recommends the preparation of two synopses for a tale, one explaining the events in order of chronological occurrence, and the second in order of narration in the story. That these two synopses could be widely different (indeed, the degree of their difference may point to the structural complexity of a given tale) can be seen if we attempt to form two synopses of "The Call of Cthulhu":

1. Order of Occurrence	2. Order of Narration
History of arrival of Old Ones	Death of Prof. Angell—narrator begins examination of papers
American Archaeological Society meeting of 1908	American Archaeological Society meeting—Castro's narrative of Old Ones
Dreams of Henry Wilcox (1925)	
Johansen's encounter with Cthulhu (1925)	Johansen's encounter with Cthulhu (after narrator discovers newspaper item and locates Johansen's narrative)
Death of Prof. Angell (late 1926)	
Narrator begins examination of Prof. Angell's papers—discovers truth	

An even more intricate design can be formed for, e.g., *The Case of Charles Dexter Ward* or for "The Shadow out of Time," where Leiber has pointed out that the use of the "terminal climax" necessitates an elaborately convoluted structure (461f.).

We may tread on shaky ground when we attempt to find any *literary influences* for the structural complexity of Lovecraft's longer tales. Narrative structure does not lend itself to influence as do images or phraseology or themes, since each tale normally requires a structure peculiar to it because of the exigencies of the plot and the author's philosophical goal; and in Lovecraft's case we can find several early tales which prefigure the profound complexity of his later tales—in "The Nameless City" (1921) we find a device for narrating the history of alien civilisations repeated in much elaborated form in *At the Mountains of Madness*; in "Beyond the Wall of Sleep" (1919) "dreams" are used to convey fragments of an alternate reality, as was done much more extensively in "The Dreams in the Witch House" and "The Shadow out of Time." We may in any case hazard some speculations on particular authors or works that may have suggested structural patterns. Lovecraft probably derived little from the Gothic novelists, while Poe's short tales fall almost wholly into the strictly chronological or modest flashback type. Some of Ambrose Bierce's longer narratives—notably "The Death of Halpin Frayser" and "The Damned Thing" —have what Maurice Lévy called an "architectural framework" (15) that may have impressed Lovecraft.

I think, however, that Lovecraft learned most about narrative structure from two fantaisistes whose output consists largely of novelettes or novels — Arthur Machen and especially M. R. James. Of "The Great God Pan" Lovecraft wrote: "But the charm is in the telling. No one could begin to describe the cumulative suspense and ultimate horror with which every paragraph abounds without following fully the precise order in which Mr. Machen unfolds his gradual hints and revelations" (*D* 423)—a remark that tells us how faithfully Lovecraft studied Machen's construction. Indeed, we may suppose that the structure of "The Call of Cthulhu"—the gradual piecing together of widely disparate data of equally disparate form (a bas-relief, newspaper cuttings, the results of an archaeological meeting, documents and narratives by various individuals) may have been triggered by the similar amassing of evidence found in Machen's "Novel of the Black Seal." M. R. James, however, was the great master of structure—something Lovecraft confirms by his almost disproportionately long plot description of "Count Magnus" in "Supernatural Horror in Literature." Here Lovecraft has done nothing but tell the story *in order of chronological occurrence,* since the James tale is so intricately convoluted in its construction that such a thing is necessary in order to explain the story at all. One may wonder whether even Lovecraft carried structural complexity to this level. But we must remember that the tracing of an influence in narrative structure is an exceedingly tenuous and tentative business; and at best Machen, James, and others only provided analogies that Lovecraft used in his own unique way.

We may, then, agree with Peter Penzoldt as to the structural perfection of most of Lovecraft's narratives; always—save perhaps in revisions or ghost-written tales where he may have been less concerned about the excellence, structural or otherwise, of a tale—do we note his extreme care about such elements as the arrangement and order of incidents, the selection of a narrative voice, the incorporation of subsidiary or coordinate narratives or of multiple climaxes, and countless other subtler techniques. We have attempted here only the broadest of structural analyses; and a study of each of his longer tales could in truth fill the space of this essay. In the end we must agree with Lovecraft when he wrote that *"the synopsis is the real heart of the story"* (CE 2.171); and it is unfortunate that we have the notes and synopses for so few of his finished tales. Lovecraft's prose style, his use of images, the philosophical depth of his tales, all have been commended by critics; and it is time that readers and scholars alike found an almost architectural beauty in the structure of his narratives.

Works Cited

De Camp, L. Sprague. *Lovecraft: A Biography*. Garden City, NY: Doubleday, 1975.

Douglas, Drake. *Horror!* New York: Macmillan, 1966.

Kitto, H. D. F. *Greek Tragedy*. London: Methuen, 1954.

Leiber, Fritz. "A Literary Copernicus." 1949. In Peter Cannon, ed. *Lovecraft Remembered*. Sauk City, WI: Arkham House, 1998. 455–66.

Lévy, Maurice. *Lovecraft: A Study in the Fantastic*. Trans. S. T. Joshi. Detroit: Wayne State University Press, 1988.

Penzoldt, Peter. *The Supernatural in Fiction*. 1952. Extracts in S. T. Joshi, ed. *H. P. Lovecraft: Four Decades of Criticism*. Athens: Ohio University Press, 1980. 63–77.

Whitman, Cedric. *Homer and the Heroic Tradition*. Cambridge, MA: Harvard University Press, 1958.

The Dream World and the Real World in Lovecraft

I am perhaps not the only one who has been puzzled at the singular fashion in which sites, characters, and even gods from Lovecraft's "dream world" find their way into those of his tales that are presented as taking place in the "real" world. Why, for example, does Abdul Alhazred, in the passage from the *Necronomicon* cited in "The Dunwich Horror," refer to "Kadath in the cold waste" (*DH* 170) when the very title of *The Dream-Quest of Unknown Kadath* reveals that Kadath is in the world of dream? Why does Dr Willett mention the sign of Koth (MM 214) in *The Case of Charles Dexter Ward*—when Koth was a place where Randolph Carter had one of his most harrowing dream-experiences? How did Richard Upton Pickman go from the very real world of Boston's North End in "Pickman's Model" to meet Randolph Carter in the land of Deeper Slumber? Was Lovecraft merely amusing himself with playful interrelations that he knew to be impossible? Did he not realise the apparent paradoxes of such an intermingling? Or did he have a coherent system for effecting such an interpenetration of dream and reality? My own conclusion is that, while a certain method can be traced in this apparent madness, Lovecraft did in fact fail to detect some contradictions when—especially in *The Dream-Quest of Unknown Kadath*—he made attempts to show that the realms of dream and reality are not entirely distinct. That a certain element of playfulness entered into the matter seems also inescapable.

It is, in the first place, important to establish which of Lovecraft's tales occur in a dream-setting. The number is far fewer than many seem to have assumed. It can be demonstrated that only three (perhaps four) tales are conclusively set in a dream world; of these, two—when taken in conjunction with other tales—turn out not to be actual dream-narratives at all. It seems a common assumption that Lovecraft's Dunsanian tales all take place in a dream world, in spite of the fact that in at least one instance—"The Tree"—we are dealing with a very real if historical world (i.e., ancient Greece). There is in fact no justification, in the great majority of his Dunsanian tales, for the inference that they are set in a dream world. It may be true that the use of such imagined place-names as Ulthar, Nir, Lomar, Sona-Nyl, and the like—and the absence of overt references to places in the real world—seem to imply a "never-never land" existing only in the author's imagination; but the actual narratives of many of these tales are not postulated explicitly as being in a dream world, and testimony from other tales proves conclusively that many are not so situated. Dunsany himself rarely admitted openly that his narratives took place in a dream world: we find, for example, a mention of "Europeans" in "Bethmoora" (Dunsany 54, 56); and in "Poltarnees, Beholder of Ocean" we are told that "the name of the river is Oriathon, but men call it Ocean [here meaning the Greek concept of a single body of water surrounding all the land masses of the earth]" (Dunsany 6). It is true that in "Idle Days on the Yann" the narrator tells his ship-captain that "I came from Ireland, which is of Europe, whereat the captain and all the sailors laughed, for they said, 'There are no such places in all the land of dreams'" (Dunsany 60), but such a specific indication that a tale is set in a dream world is as rare in Dunsany as it is in Lovecraft.

"Polaris" (1918) appears manifestly to be in a dream setting, for the narrator remarks: "After the beams came clouds, and then I slept" (*D* 19); there follows his description of his adventures in Olathoë, in the land of Lomar. Indeed, it appears superficially that the narrator has so confused the worlds of dream and reality that he believes his "real-life" existence to be the dream: "My head, heavy and reeling, drooped to my breast, and when next I looked up it was in a dream, with the Pole Star grinning at me through a window from over the horrible swaying trees of a dream swamp. And I am still dreaming" (*D* 23). But we know, of course, that the narrator has somehow managed to tap a source of ancestral memory and actually go back to a prehistoric age; this is suggested by the poem in the tale (especially the lines ". . . till the spheres, / Six and twenty thousand years, / Have revolv'd" [*D* 23], which effectively places the fall of Lomar at c. 24,000 B.C.E.) and by the implication that the Esquimaux are the descendants of the "squat, hellish yellow" (*D* 22) Inutos who overwhelm Lomar. All later mentions of Lomar in Lovecraft's fiction (even in the *Dream-Quest*) confirm the impression that Lomar is postulated by Lovecraft as existing in the real world; note At the Mountains of Madness: "The ultimate blow, of course, was the coming of the great cold [i.e., the Ice Age] which . . . put an end to the fabled lands of Lomar and Hyperborea" (*MM* 73).[1] Note, too, that it is in "Polaris" where occurs the first citation of

---

1. The term "fabled" need not imply that Lomar is "fabulous" (i.e., existing only in fable), but merely that it is extremely old. An earlier passage in At the Mountains of Madness makes this clear: "Here sprawled a palaeogean megalopolis compared with which the fabled Atlantis and Olathoë in the land of Lomar are recent things of today—not even of yesterday" (*MM* 47).

the Pnakotic Manuscripts (*D* 22), which are again universally regarded as being in the real world; even in the otherwise ambiguous *Dream-Quest* it is noted that "those inconceivably old Pnakotic Manuscripts [were] made by waking men in forgotten boreal kingdoms" (MM 310). All this confirms that "Polaris" describes a "forgotten" civilisation in the real world before the birth of history. Indeed, in "Through the Gates of the Silver Key" it is implied that Lomar may in fact be the first true human civilisation (as opposed to those, such as Ib, whose inhabitants seem not to be fully human): "For this shape [i.e., 'Umr at-Tawil] was nothing less than that which all the world had feared since Lomar rose out of the sea" (MM 432).

It seems difficult to deny that "The White Ship" (1919) is a dream-journey; but it is odd that no explicit mention of such a thing occurs in the tale. The story was, of course, manifestly inspired by Dunsany's "Idle Days on the Yann," which takes place in a dream world; and the narrator of "The White Ship," as that in "Idle Days on the Yann," seems at least initially to be in the real world, although even this cannot be conclusively proven: "I am Basil Elton, keeper of the North Point light that my father and grandfather kept before me" (*D* 36).[2] When the White Ship comes Elton makes a supernatural ascent upon it ("I walked out over the waters to the White Ship on a bridge of moonbeams" [*D* 37]); but recall that Denys Barry seems to do roughly the same thing at the end of "The Moon-Bog," which is clearly set in the real world of Ireland. But the question of whether the events in "The White Ship" take place in the real or dream world becomes academic; for not only is the tale a virtual allegory, but none of the sites or characters mentioned in it recur anywhere in Lovecraft's fiction save in the ambiguous *Dream-Quest*.

In "The Doom That Came to Sarnath" (1919) we are explicitly told that the "grey stone city of Ib" stood "when the world was young" (*D* 43), and that Sarnath itself existed "ten thousand years ago" (*D* 43). Manifestly, then, the land of Mnar is in a prehistoric world, and not in a dream world; and in "The Nameless City" (1921) we are told that Sarnath was inhabited by early human beings while Ib was pre-human: ". . . I thought of Sarnath the Doomed, that

---

2. In the *Dream-Quest* allusion is made to the story, and Elton is now described as a "fellow-dreamer of earth—a lighthouse-keeper in ancient Kingsport" (MM 317). The evidence here is singularly ambiguous (does "fellow-dreamer" imply that Elton dreamed his journey on the White Ship or merely that he was given to dreaming?), but at least we know that Elton started from "earth." His location in Kingsport is merely an "in-joke," one supposes: Kingsport was not created until "The Terrible Old Man" (1920); and even so, Kingsport (along with HPL's other "mythical" towns, Arkham, Dunwich, and Innsmouth) is not postulated as being in a dream world but in the "actual" world of New England.

stood in the land of Mnar when mankind was young, and of Ib, that was carven of grey stone before mankind existed" (D 100). In *At the Mountains of Madness* we learn that the great megalopolis of the Old Ones ranks "with such whispered pre-human blasphemies as . . . Ib in the land of Mnar" (MM 47). There may even be a veiled reference to Ib in "The Moon-Bog," where mention is made to tales "of an imagined city of stone deep down below the swampy surface" (D 119). Note that this tale seems to contain an allusion to "The Tree" ("that monotonous piping . . . made me think of some dance of fauns on distant Maenalus" [D 121]), so that such a reference to Ib is not impossible. All references, then, confirm that Mnar was actually a prehistoric land in the real world. If this is the case, then the other sites mentioned in the tale are no less real: "There were [in Sarnath] many palaces, the least of which were mightier than any in Thraa or Ilarnek or Kadatheron" (D 45).

We must briefly withhold judgment as to whether Lovecraft's next Dunsanian tale, "The Cats of Ulthar" (1920), is in the real or the dream world; let us note again that no explicit remark places the story in the land of dream. For the solution of the problem we must turn to "The Other Gods" (1921), where we learn that Barzai the Wise was "familiar with the Pnakotic Manuscripts of distant and frozen Lomar" (D 128). Barzai, it turns out, is from Ulthar (D 128), and the clear implication is that this tale too takes place in a prehistoric civilisation. Indeed, if—as seems indisputable—the Pnakotic Manuscripts were written in the "real" world, then not merely must Ulthar, Nir, Hatheg, and other towns mentioned in the tale be real, but so too must "Kadath in the cold waste" (D 127) and Mt. Hatheg-Kla, upon which the "gods of earth" (D 127) used to dance. Note this remark: "Now it is told in the mouldy Pnakotic Manuscripts that Sansu found naught but wordless ice and rock when he did climb Hatheg-Kla *in the youth of the world*" (D 131; my emphasis). It is to be noted that Atal, who was a mere "innkeeper's son" (D 58) in "The Cats of Ulthar," has now become a "young priest" (D 128) in "The Other Gods." In *The Dream-Quest of Unknown Kadath* he is "fully three centuries old" (MM 311).

"The Quest of Iranon" (1921) also makes reference to Lomar and to the sites mentioned in "The Doom That Came to Sarnath": "I [Iranon] have been to Thraa, Ilarnek, and Kadatheron on the winding river Ai, and have dwelt long in Olathoë in the land of Lomar" (D 114). As a result, the sites in "The Quest of Iranon"—Teloth, the river Zuro, etc.—must also be in the prehistoric world; although Iranon's city of Aira exists only in his imagination, since the name of Aira came only "from the lips of a playmate, a beggar's boy given to strange dreams" (D 117). Here the whole crux of the tale depends on the poignant distinction between a prosy real world (Teloth, Oonai, etc.) and the magical dream world imagined by Iranon. And recall the final sentence of he story, commenting on Iranon's death: "That night something of youth and beauty died in the *elder* world" (*D* 117; my emphasis).

"Celephaïs" (1920) resembles "Polaris" in that a sort of dream is employed in penetrating other worlds or other planes of reality; and since the tale so closely foreshadows the problematical *Dream-Quest* in theme, it is of the utmost importance to ascertain the precise nature of the realm of Celephaïs. It is true that, as in "The Quest of Iranon," the point of the tale consists in the dichotomy between the real world of London with its "indifferent millions" (*D* 83) and the imagined world of Celephaïs. The very opening of the tale tells us that Kuranes (and this was, after all, his dream name) saw Celephaïs "in a dream" (*D* 83); and that "when truth and experience failed to reveal [beauty], he sought it in fancy and illusion" (*D* 82-83)—but what does that "fancy and illusion" consist of? Nothing but the "nebulous memories of childhood tales and dreams" (*D* 84)—in other words, memories of the real world. The problematical nature of Celephaïs' existence is underscored by Kuranes' final (and permanent) journey there, for he initially starts the journey by a literal descent into time:

> . . . they . . . all rode majestically through the downs of Surrey and onward toward the region where Kuranes and his ancestors were born. It was very strange, but as the riders went on they seemed to gallop back through Time; for whenever they passed through a village in the twilight they saw only such houses and villagers as Chaucer or men before him might have seen . . . (*D* 88)

What seems to have happened is that Kuranes has somehow gone back in time to the town of his ancestors; Celephaïs is merely a name invented by Kuranes in his childhood fancies, but stands for some real locale (presumably in Surrey). It may be, indeed, that, like the narrator of "Polaris," Kuranes is prey to ancestral memory, and that his "dreams" are merely a means of escaping into a world that is very real, but which is merely set in the historical past. The fantastic or "dreamlike" details of Celephaïs may be merely the products of Kuranes' boyhood imagination.

It may well be that the fragment "Azathoth" (1922)—the last of Lovecraft's quasi-Dunsanian tales before the *Dream-Quest*—is the only tale in which an actual dream-journey is involved. Here the narrator is said specifically to have "travelled out of life on a quest into the spaces whither the world's dreams had fled" (*D* 357). Hence the character seems authentically to have fled the "real" world; but where precisely is the region "whither the world's dreams had fled"? The answer to this question may perhaps be found in the *Dream-Quest*, since Randolph Carter seems to have undertaken a journey very akin to that of the narrator of "Azathoth."

We have seen, then, that virtually all the characters and sites in Lovecraft's Dunsanian tales can conclusively be set not in the world of dream but in a prehistoric (or, as in the case of "Celephaïs," an historical) land where a series of civilisations—Ib, Sarnath, Ulthar, Lomar, and the rest—have risen and fallen. There is striking uniformity in this conception, and—at least in the tales written before 1926—we have no justification for making any clear distinction between the Dunsanian tales and the real-world tales; there is nothing paradoxical about the intermixture of these worlds, since they can all be incorporated into a history of the planet that, though (obviously) imagined by Lovecraft, is postulated to be as "real" as the imagined cities of Dunwich, Arkham, Kingsport, and Innsmouth. Indeed, when in *At the Mountains of Madness* Lovecraft mentions a parade of lost civilisations—Atlantis, Lemuria, Commoriom, Uzuldaroum, Lomar, Valusia, R'lyeh, Ib, the Nameless City (MM 47)—he is, because they are cited in a definitely "real-world" tale, implicitly acknowledging their actual existence on this planet (for fictional purposes, it need hardly be added). It is, in fact, only with *The Dream-Quest of Unknown Kadath* and (to a lesser degree) "The Silver Key" that confusion enters into the picture.

We have already seen that Kadath, first mentioned in "The Other Gods" (D 127, 132), has been placed in the real world. This conception persists throughout the whole of Lovecraft's work except the *Dream-Quest* itself. Alhazred's mention of it—"Kadath in the cold waste hath known Them [the Old Ones], but what man knows Kadath?" (DH 170)—would not be paradoxical at all if, in the *Dream-Quest* (and only there), Kadath were not placed emphatically in the dream world. Even if we discount the title of the novel (and it was only the last of half a dozen titles devised by Lovecraft for the work, nearly all emphasising the dreamlike aspect of the narrative),[3] there is too much textual evidence in the novel to leave any doubt as to the dream-world status of Kadath. Carter, after being denied the sight of his sunset city, "prayed . . . to the hidden *gods of dream* that brood capricious above the clouds on unknown Kadath" (MM 307). Then, after Carter descends the "seventy steps" in "light slumber" (MM 307), he is told by the priests Nasht and Kaman-Thah that "not only had no man ever been to Kadath, but no man had ever suspected in what part of space it might lie" (MM 307–8). The mention of "space" here is slightly odd, apparently implying that Kadath occupies some space in the "real" world, but this implication is immediately dispelled by the subsequent remark—"whether in the *dreamlands* around our own world,

---

3. The others are recorded on the verso of p. 1 of the A.Ms. (JHL): *The Dream-Quest of Randolph Carter; A Pilgrim in Dreamland; A Dreamland Quest/Pilgrimage; The Seeking of Dreamland's Gods; Past the Gate of Deeper Slumber; In the Gulfs of Dream; A Seeker in Gulfs of Dream; The Quest of the Gods on Kadath.*

or in those surrounding some unguessed companion of Fomalhaut or Aldebaran" (MM 308). This is itself a little paradoxical, for if Kadath holds only the gods of earth (as stated in "The Other Gods"), then there would presumably be no reason why the gods (hence Kadath) would be anywhere but on or around our planet. This confusion is cleared up by Atal the priest, who tells Carter that the gods "are indeed only earth's gods, ruling feebly our own dreamland and having no power of habitation elsewhere" (MM 311-12). It therefore seems conclusive that Kadath is—in the *Dream-Quest*—in the dream world.

But if Carter has to descend the "seven hundred steps to the Gate of Deeper Slumber" (MM 308) to find Kadath, then all his journeys described in the novel must take place in the dream world. This means that nearly all the sites invented in Lovecraft's earlier Dunsanian tales are suddenly transported from the real (if prehistoric) world to the world of dream. Only Lomar seems to preserve its real-world status, since we learn that the Pnakotic Manuscripts had been "made by waking men in forgotten boreal kingdoms . . . when the hairy cannibal Gnophkehs overcame many-templed Olathoë and slew all the heroes of the land of Lomar" (MM 310). But these very Pnakotic Manuscripts have now been "borne into the land of dream" (MM 310). This copy of the Pnakotic Manuscripts has been taken to Ulthar (MM 310), which means that it must now be in the land of dream. All the other sites which Carter visits—the land of the zoogs (who "know many obscure secrets of the dream world and a few of the waking world" [MM 308]), Dylath-Leen, Mt. Ngranek, Celephaïs, Inganok, and presumably Leng itself—must equally be in the dream world. The case of Leng is singularly bizarre. It was first cited in "Celephaïs," although nothing conclusive about its existence in the real or dream world can be drawn from that mention; but in "The Hound" (1922) we are clearly told that Leng is in "Central Asia" (D 174). It is true that its location here is dependent upon the testimony of Alhazred's *Necronomicon*, and Lovecraft takes the opportunity in *At the Mountains of Madness* of transferring it to the Antarctic (MM 103); but nevertheless Leng is always postulated as existing in the real world. Here again the *Dream-Quest* flies in the face of all the testimony found in Lovecraft's other tales.

I maintain that Lovecraft never carefully thought out the *Dream-Quest*, for there are certain internal inconsistencies in the novel that are puzzling in the extreme. First, we learn from Atal that "at least twice in the world's history the Other Gods set their seal upon earth's primal granite; once in antediluvian times, as guessed from a drawing in . . . the Pnakotic Manuscripts . . ., and once on Hatheg-Kla when Barzai the Wise tried to see earth's gods dancing by moonlight" (MM 312). We have seen that the Pnakotic Manuscripts, even in the *Dream-Quest*, are postulated as being written by people of the "waking" world (MM 310); therefore the mention of the first instance of the gods' setting their seal must also have taken place in the real world, and specifically in the ancient (perhaps prehistoric) world.[4] The incident with Barzai, if the *Dream-Quest* is here being consistent with "The Other Gods," must also have taken place in the real world; but of course this is contradicted by other parts of the novel, where Ulthar and Hatheg-Kla are set in the dream world. Similarly, it is remarked that "Ninety aeons ago, before even the gods had danced upon its [Ngranek's] pointed peak . . ." (MM 330), which tallies with a comment in "The Strange High House in the Mist": "the host grew timid when he spoke of the dim first age of chaos before the gods or even the Elder Ones [= the Great Ones of the *Dream-Quest*] were born, and when *the other gods* [Lovecraft's italics] came to dance on the peak of Hatheg-Kla in the stony desert near Ulthar" (D 282). As in all other tales, Hatheg-Kla (of which Ngranek is the name given to it by the gods—cf. "The Other Gods" [D 127]) is now set in the real world, along with the various gods who dwell or once dwelt upon it; but how can this be reconciled with the "gods of dream" (MM 307) whom Carter seeks in the dream world in the *Dream-Quest*? Finally, there is a stupendous internal contradiction when, after Carter escapes from the "almost-humans" who transport him to the moon to deliver him to Nyarlathotep, it is remarked that "on an unhallowed summit of the moon-mountains still vainly waited the crawling chaos Nyarlathotep" (MM 307). But how can Kadath (hence Leng), where Nyarlathotep must be waiting, be on the moon? As we know, the onyx castle is transferred back to the earth's dreamland at the conclusion of the *Dream-Quest*.

If we try to examine how precisely the dream world in the *Dream-Quest* is related to the real world, we will either discover more paradoxes and contradictions or be unable to integrate the relation into that found in other of Lovecraft's Dunsanian tales. There seem four ways in which we may conceive the dream world: 1) it is Carter's own dream world; 2) it is (literally) under the earth; 3) it is a prehistoric world (as in all the other Dunsanian tales) but Carter, by dreaming, has found a way to enter into it; 4) it is a "general" or "universal" dream world superimposed upon the real world. Let us examine each of these possibilities further.

The first hypothesis is ruled out almost automatically by Atal's remark that Carter's sunset city "probably . . . belonged to his [Carter's] especial dream world and not to the general land of vision that many know" (MM 312). Note, moreover, that the dream world continues to exist after Carter (at the end of

---

4. It is unlikely that by "antediluvian" HPL specifically means "before the Flood"; the adjective in HPL means nothing more than "ancient."

the *Dream-Quest*) has woken up: "So . . . Randolph Carter leaped shoutingly awake within his Boston room. . . . And vast infinities away, past the Gate of Deeper Slumber and the enchanted wood . . . [etc.]" (MM 406). It appears, therefore, that the dream world in which Carter travels is a sort of "universal" dream world and not his own; and it is probably to this that the fragment "Azathoth" refers when it is said that the character there went on a "quest into the spaces whither the world's dreams had fled" (D 357). These dreams "that men have lost" (D 358) must similarly form a general body of dream accessible to all human beings (or, at least, to those who are powerful dreamers like Carter).

The case of Kuranes in the *Dream-Quest* is both enlightening and confusing in this regard. Although in "Celaphaïs" it was said that "it was he [Kuranes] who had created Ooth-Nargai in his dreams" (D 88), Ooth-Nargai and Celephaïs now appear to have become part of the general world of dream, while Kuranes now longs for the waking world and his boyhood memories of England. But "he could not go back to these things in the waking world because his body was dead; but he had done the next best thing and dreamed a small tract of such countryside in the region east of the city [sc. Celephaïs]" (MM 354). Kuranes has therefore created his own private world of dream in the land of dream. But why is Carter's similar private "sunset city" not in the (general) land of dream as well? Presumably (although this is never stated or even implied by Lovecraft) it is because Carter is not dead in the real world, so that all he has to do (and does do at the end of the novel) is to wake up and recapture his boyhood memories. But it is peculiar that Kuranes seems not to have any great control over his own dream world: "there hobbled to meet him [Carter] no robed and anointed lackey but a small stubby old man in a smock who spoke as best he could in the quaint tones of far Cornwall" (MM 355). If Kuranes, clearly an experienced dreamer, has created his own dream world, why can he not make the old man speak actually and perfectly in the tones of far Cornwall? And Kuranes furthermore was "seeking ever to teach them [the inhabitants of a "little Cornish fishing village" that Kuranes had dreamed] the dear remembered accents of old Cornwall fishers" (MM 354). But why do the people not know these accents already if they are merely creations of Kuranes? Here again Lovecraft has created, certainly, a poignant episode and one that clearly foreshadows Carter's discovery at the end of the novel, but he has not thought through the details of the concept very well. But whatever the situation with Kuranes, it is at least clear that there is both a general dream world and separate dream worlds that can be created by individual dreamers.

There are many indications that the general dream world into which

Carter enters is in some fashion under the earth.[5] We have already noted that Carter initially descends the seventy steps to the cavern of flame (MM 307) and then the 700 steps to the Gate of Deeper Slumber (MM 308). Indeed, as Maurice Lévy wryly remarked, "We could almost say that Carter moves more often vertically, in height or in depth, than horizontally" (Lévy 103). We know that the Enchanted Wood housing the zoogs "at two places touches the land of men" (MM 308), which implies that it is geographically very close to the surface of the real world; and recall Carter's apprehension that in the land of the ghouls "he was probably nearer the waking world than at any other time . . ." (MM 338)—this too seems to imply a vertical arrangement whereby the land of the ghouls is on the underside of the world. We may even draw support for this from "Pickman's Model," since we learn there that the ghouls have made a vast series of underground tunnels under Boston. That these tunnels are not, however, very far underground can be inferred from the fact that Pickman can presumably call upon and photograph the ghouls in his "cellar studio" (*DH* 25) by lifting "the circular brick curb of what was evidently a great well in the earthen floor" (*DH* 21). It is even remarked in the *Dream-Quest* that "these ghouls of the waking world would do no business in the graveyards of upper dreamland" (MM 338). It would be cumbrous to attempt to distinguish the various layers of Lovecraft's dream world (note, for example, that Sarkomand is "the valley *below* Leng" [MM 339]), but one remark may be significant. When the night-gaunts snatch Carter as he is ascending Mt. Ngranek, he suspects that they are taking him to the "primal mists of the earth's core" (MM 335); but Lovecraft's looseness of terminology—there is throughout the novel a confusion as to whether "earth" means the real world or the dream world—does not allow us to ascertain whether the literal earth's core is meant.

Nevertheless, the evidence seems overwhelming that the dream world is literally situated below the earth. But this theory encounters apparently insuperable obstacles. If Carter is actually under the earth, how can he see in the sky such galaxies and constellations as the Milky Way (MM 334), Charles' Wain, and the Little Bear (MM 357)? How can there be a sky at all? Most paradoxically, how can the black galley suddenly leap into space and go to the

---

5. This was realised by Wetzel, who compared the dream world to the Hades of Greek myth, since Kuranes has died in the real world to descend into the dream world (see Wetzel 84–85). The comparison to Hades is interesting, but Kuranes is the only one in the dream world of whom we know who is dead in the real world. There is no sign that Richard Upton Pickman died on earth, for the narrator of "Pickman's Model" merely remarks: "He's gone—back into the fabulous darkness he loved to haunt" (*DH* 24-25).

(apparently real) moon? How can the cats make similar leaps to and from the moon? Finally—and this seems to be a major obstacle to this theory and the next—if the "dream world" in the *Dream-Quest* is only a loose way of referring to a portion of the real world, what are we to make of the fact that the leader of the cats on the moon recognised Carter "as the sworn friend of his kind on earth and in the land of dream" (MM 324)? What is the distinction being drawn here? and did Lovecraft not realise that nearly all his other Dunsanian tales seem to take place in the real world? But here we are faced with yet another internal inconsistency: if Ulthar has now been placed in the dream world in this novel, how are we to understand the remark that "it was fortunate that the moon was not up, so that all the cats were *on earth*" (MM 346)? How can this be? Are not the cats in the dream world? or does "earth" merely refer to the dream world? If this is so, the distinction between "earth" and the "land of dream" noted above can have no meaning. Clearly Lovecraft is guilty of either extreme inconsistency or extreme looseness and vagueness of language.

When we turn to the third hypothesis—that the dream world is actually in the prehistoric past, as with nearly all the other "Dunsanian" tales, and that dream is simply a means of reaching this realm—we are in no better situation; for the theory seems not only inherently inappropriate to the *Dream-Quest* but may be tacitly contradicted by it at various points. First, we note that the law forbidding the killing of cats in Ulthar is now regarded as "ancient and significant" (MM 311); one cannot be sure what scope to give to the term "ancient," but just previous to this we are told that the stone bridge across the river Skai was built "thirteen-hundred years before [sc. Carter's arrival there]" (MM 311); presumably the law is much more ancient than this. Parts of the Pnakotic Manuscripts are now regarded as "too ancient to be read" (MM 312)—although it must be noted that they were termed "mouldy" in "The Other Gods" (D 131)—and Sarkomand's ruins are said to have "bleached for a million years before the first true human saw the light" (MM 371), which at least hints that we are far from the prehistoric age. In sum, although there is nothing explicitly forbidding the belief that the dream world is merely the prehistoric past, there is nothing in the novel to suggest such a view. In any case, the repeated hints that we are either literally or figuratively under the earth could not be incorporated into this scheme. We seem manifestly to be in a world not temporally distant from our own; moreover, the artist Pickman does not seem to have penetrated into the dream world by dreaming (as with Carter), but literally through one of the openings between the real world of the surface and the dream world below.

We are then left only with the theory that the dream world is somehow superimposed upon the real world, but how this is done is never explained (save in the curious remark about "dreamlands *around* our own world" [MM 308], which seems to imply some sort of outer membrane or atmosphere). Moreover, this would force us to ignore the very frequent hints that the dream world is underground ("the inner world has strange laws" [MM 337]). I can only conclude that Lovecraft never clearly thought out the relations between the real world and the dream world in this novel, and—in wilfully ignoring the fact that his previous "Dunsanian" stories had clearly been set in the prehistoric past of the real world—subsumed all his previous Dunsanian sites into the dream world in order to make Carter's discovery of the real-world nature of his "sunset city" the more poignant. One could live with the mere failure of the *Dream-Quest* to tally with Lovecraft's other "Dunsanian" tales, for Lovecraft was not obliged to be uniformly systematic from one story to the next; but we may well express a certain irritation in not being able to ascertain even an internally consistent dream world within the confines of the *Dream-Quest* itself.

It remains to explore some later tales where Lovecraft seems consciously to have modified his previous conceptions of his "Dunsanian" sites and characters. Of the mention of the sign of Koth in *The Case of Charles Dexter Ward* ("It was the sign of Koth, that dreamers see fixed above the archway of a certain black tower standing alone in twilight—and Willett did not like what his friend Randolph Carter had said of its powers" [MM 214]) we need take little notice: this seems a completely frivolous and joking reference that, in any case, has no bearing on the outcome of the novel. More important is Alhazred's remark that "Kadath in the cold waste has known Them [i.e., the Old Ones]" (*DH* 170). But who are the Old Ones? or rather, how can Kadath have known them? If the Ones Ones are to be identified with any gods in the *Dream-Quest*, it must be with the Other Gods, for the Great Ones are merely the "mild gods of earth" (MM 399), hardly to be equated with the titanic entities depicted by Alhazred. This harmonises both with the *Dream-Quest*—since Nyarlathotep is there called "the soul and messenger" (MM 308) of the Other Gods, a designation commonly applied to him in other tales—and with "Through the Gates of the Silver Key," where the Old Ones or Other Gods have not merely been given yet another name but have returned to their dreamlike state: "He [Carter] wondered at the vast conceit of those who babbled of the *malignant* Ancient Ones, as if They could pause from their everlasting dreams to wreak a wrath on mankind" (MM 433). It appears that both Nyarlathotep and the Old Ones/Other Gods/Ancient Ones have the power of dwelling simultaneously in the dream world and the real world, although it is inevitably never explained how this is possible.

At the Mountains of Madness (1931) both clarifies and casts further confusion upon the whole picture. We have seen that the novel confirms the real-

The Dream World and the Real World in Lovecraft 287

world existence of Lomar and Ib by incorporating them into Lovecraft's history of life on this planet; and we have also seen that Kadath has been transferred from Central Asia to the Antarctic (although this shift was anticipated in "The Mound" [1929-30], where we are told that the underground denizens of K'n-yan "had had some remarkable civilisations, especially one at the South Pole near the mountain Kadath" [HM 131]). But note Lovecraft's terminology when he makes the shift in At the Mountains of Madness: "For this far violet line could be nothing else than the terrible mountains of the forbidden land ... the unknown *archetype* of that dreaded Kadath in the Cold Waste beyond abhorrent Leng whereof *primal legends* hint evasively" (MM 103). Kadath has now become merely a "legend," hence presumably has no concrete existence at all. Leng is similarly transformed: "Mythologists have placed Leng in Central Asia" (MM 20); "... I thought again of the eldritch primal *myths* ... of the daemoniac plateau of Leng" (MM 45). What seems to be going on in this novel is a general "demythologising" (see Price) of the myth-cycle evidenced by the fact that the very real barrel-shaped entities are themselves "the originals of the fiendish elder myths which things like the Pnakotic Manuscripts and the *Necronomicon* affrightedly hint about. They were the great 'Old Ones' that had filtered down from the stars ..." (MM 59). Hence not merely Kadath and Leng, of which Alhazred had spoken, but the Old Ones themselves whom he had deemed divine, are all myths and legends—or rather, there were very real causes or "archetypes" that gave rise to these myths. How we are to reconcile this with the fact that, in "Through the Gates of the Silver Key" (1932-33), the Old Ones or Ancient Ones seem to have regained their ethereal divinity is anyone's guess. But Kadath at any rate has evolved from a real site in the prehistoric past ("The Other Gods") to a dream site (*The Dream-Quest of Unknown Kadath*) to a mere myth whose real model is the range of unexplored mountains in the Antarctic. Indeed, Lovecraft in At the Mountains of Madness may be trying to imply that all his previous tales about Kadath, Ulthar, Lomar, and the rest are merely fragments of this body of legend.

The results of this investigation are, inevitably, tentative and confused. In nearly all the tales before the *Dream-Quest*, the characters and sites of Lovecraft's "Dunsanian" tales seem to be emphatically placed in a prehistoric setting; the *Dream-Quest* causes great confusion to this schema, placing most of the sites in the dream world but doing so in a paradoxical and self-inconsistent fashion; finally, in later tales Lovecraft develops or changes his conceptions at will, and finally transforms them into myth or legend in the manner of a J. G. Frazer or Margaret Murray. All this is, doubtless, somewhat strange for a writer who is otherwise remarkably self-consistent; but this investigation—aside from indicating that *The Dream-Quest of Unknown Kadath* cannot be used indiscriminately as a source for many aspects of the Lovecraft Mythos unless its internal inconsistencies be resolved—shows the singular fertility of Lovecraft's mind, not content to let the smallest details of his various invented characters, gods, and civilisations go unaltered in the course of his fictional career. I suspect, however, that Lovecraft would have been comparatively unconcerned at the non-synchronisation of all aspects of his fictional geography, for he knew that

> the final criterion of authenticity [in a weird tale] is not the dovetailing of a plot but the creation of a given sensation. . . . The one test of the really weird is simply this—whether or not there be excited in the reader a profound sense of dread, and of contact with unknown spheres and powers; a subtle attitude of awed listening, as if for the beating of black wings or the scratching of outside shapes and entities on the known universe's utmost rim. ("Supernatural Horror in Literature" [D 368-69])

There can hardly be any question that, judged from these standards, Lovecraft's tales succeed as few others ever have.

Works Cited

Dunsany, Lord. *A Dreamer's Tales.* 1910. Rpt. Boston: John W. Luce, [1917].

Lévy, Maurice. *Lovecraft: A Study in the Fantastic.* Trans. S. T. Joshi. Detroit: Wayne State University Press, 1988.

Price, Robert M. "Demythologizing Cthulhu." *Lovecraft Studies* No. 8 (Spring 1984): 3-9, 24.

Wetzel, George T. "The Cthulhu Mythos: A Study." 1972. In S. T. Joshi, ed., *H. P. Lovecraft: Four Decades of Criticism.* Athens: Ohio University Press, 1980.

Topical References in Lovecraft

The myth that H. P. Lovecraft was completely detached from the political, social, literary, and philosophical movements of his day is one whose death has been anomalously slow, despite the volumes of comment on the contemporary scene found not merely in his letters but also in his essays from so early as "The Crime of the Century" (1915). Lovecraft is in a way partially to blame for this state of affairs, since he was fond of portraying himself (more often than not with tongue in cheek) as an eighteenth-century gentleman with allegiance to the traditions of Republican Rome, and could also write such a line as "I know always that I am an outsider; a stranger in this century and among those who are still men" ("The Outsider" [DH 52]). And while there can be no question of Lovecraft's sincere adherence to the standards of the past, there can equally be no doubt, as Robert Bloch wrote, "but that H. P. Lovecraft was very much alive in the Twentieth Century of Picasso, Proust, Joyce, Spengler, Einstein, and Adolf Hitler" (Bloch [1959] 174).

Bloch himself, however, felt that Lovecraft's fiction was almost wholly—and quite consciously—devoid of reference to the political and social upheavals of the time. "Lovecraft ignores the post WWI Jazz Age in its entirety: Coolidge, Hoover, FDR, Lindbergh, Babe Ruth, Al Capone, Valentino, Mencken, and the prototypes of Babbitt have no existence in H. P. L.'s realm. It is difficult to believe that Howard Phillips Lovecraft was a literary contemporary of Ernest Hemingway" (Bloch [1972] 159). This remark itself is not correct in its details, and I maintain that it may not even be entirely true in the general sense in which Bloch meant it. The fact is that there are many topical references in Lovecraft's fiction, and these references—sometimes glancing, sometimes more or less central to the tale—are echoes of lengthier and more detailed remarks on modern literature, politics, and society as found in his letters and essays.

It is, of course, true that Lovecraft's tales frequently seem so remote from the time in which they were written that certain topical references become almost jarring in their abruptness. "The Rats in the Walls" (1923) is a classic example; and although we are at the outset told that the tale takes place in 1923 ("On July 16, 1923, I moved into Exham Priory after the last workman had finished his labours" [DH 26]), we tend to forget the date as the tale becomes involved in the ancient past of the mansion, reaching back even beyond the Roman foundations. Then, as if out of nowhere, we are given this allusion: "As we all took the train for Anchester I felt myself poised on the brink of frightful revelations, a sensation symbolised by the air of mourning among the many Americans at the unexpected death of the President on the other side of the world" (*DH* 40). This of course refers to Warren G. Harding, who died on 2 August 1923—a date that harmonises perfectly with the chronology of the tale, and which makes me wonder whether the story was actually being written during this event. Lovecraft did indeed take notice of Harding's death, remarking rather cynically: "Harding was a handsome bimbo—I'm sure sorry he had the good luck to get clear of this beastly planet" (*SL* 1.253). Another odd and unexpected allusion occurs in "Out of the Aeons" (1933), where it is noted that the curious mummy on display in the Cabot Museum "formed—for imaginative people—a close rival to the depression as chief topic of 1931 and 1932" (*HM* 271). This is the only direct reference to the Great Depression I have found in all Lovecraft's fiction—a circumstance the more unusual in that his later letters are filled with discussions on possible means for the alleviation of unemployment and for general economic recovery.

Many other references to the political scene are not so irrelevant to a tale. World War I receives much mention in the fiction, and one of the most poignant references is at the end of "Dagon" (1917), where the narrator reflects: "I dream of a day when they [the things of the deep sea] may rise above the billows to drag down in their reeking talons the remnants of a puny, war-exhausted mankind" (*D* 19). The remark is vaguely echoed in the final paragraph of "The Call of Cthulhu" (1926), although here the reference is made broader and cannot actually be deemed topical: "Loathsomeness waits and dreams in the deep, and decay spreads over the tottering cities of men" (*DH* 154). It may be going too far to read into these references an indication of Lovecraft's adherence to the Spenglerian notion of a "decline of the west" (although he did ascribe generally to Spengler's notions on this subject), and even the reference at the opening of "The Call of Cthulhu" ("the peace and safety of a new dark age" [*DH* 125]) cannot be adduced in favour of the idea, since there Lovecraft postulates (for fictional purposes, obviously) that the "piecing together of dissociated knowledge" will bring about the dark age, while in his letters he notes (as Spengler himself did) that mechanisation will perhaps be the ultimate cause of the collapse of Western civilisation. Still, the references in "Dagon"—observe that the very premise of the tale is that a man has escaped from a "German sea-raider" when "the great war was . . . at its beginning, and the ocean forces of the Hun[1] had not completely sunk to their later degradation" (*D* 14)—are to be noted. "Dagon" is, as we know, only the second tale of Lovecraft's mature fictional career; and its realism of setting and employment of a major "current event" place it in an entirely different category from the intentionally archaic and Poesque "The Tomb."

Most of the other mentions of World War I are brief and insignificant, but in three stories the references are a little more vital to the tale's import. "The Temple" (1920) purports to be the document of a commander of a German submarine, and tries ironically to present the war from his point of view; but the satire against the German is so clumsily handled that the tale never amounts either to a penetrating social and political commentary or to a successful weird tale. In "Herbert West—Reanimator" (1921-22) one of the six episodes is set in Flanders in early 1915, since, like the narrator of "The Loved Dead," Herbert West and his companion were "one of many Americans to precede the government itself into the gigantic struggle" (*D* 153). This of course was true, although I have not been able to discover any figures on how many Americans actually entered the war before the United States' declaration of war in April 1917.[2] We have a dim connexion with Lovecraft's continual criticisms of American pacifism in the early stages of the war (see especially the essay "The Renaissance of Manhood" [1915]), although later in the story we find that West "secretly sneered at my occasional martial enthusiasms and censures of supine neutrality" (*D* 154–"craven pacifism" in "The Renaissance of Manhood"), which may indicate that by 1921 Lovecraft was finding his earlier words on the subject somewhat embarrassing. Finally, in "The Mound" (1929-30) we find that interest in the mound has been rekindled by "the daredeviltry of some of the youths back from service in France" (*HM* 103). It is precisely two of these "prematurely hardened young veterans"—the Clay brothers—who meet horrible fates on the mound. Here, then, is certainly a moderately significant social commentary used for horrific purposes.

Prohibition enters two stories, and in at least one is important for the development of the plot. In *The Case of Charles Dexter Ward* we learn of an anomalous event in conjunction with bootlegging: "In a lonely spot near Hope Valley had occurred one of the frequent sordid waylayings of trucks by 'hi-jackers' in quest of liquor shipments, but this time the robbers had been

---

1. In the first appearance of the tale (*Vagrant*, November 1919) the text read "Kaiser."

2. Edwin W. Morse, one contemporary writer, speaks of "hundreds of young Americans" going abroad before America's declaration of war. See *The Vanguard of American Volunteers: In the Fighting Lines and Humanitarian Service, August, 1914–April, 1917* (New York: Scribners, 1918), 4.

destined to receive the greater shock" (MM 180). What they find are coffins being delivered to Ward. In "The Shadow over Innsmouth" (1931) a significant moment occurs when the narrator entices Zadok Allen with a bottle of bootleg whiskey. Lovecraft's comment is illuminating: "A quart bottle of whiskey was easily, though not cheaply, obtained in the rear of a dingy variety-store just off the Square in Eliot Street" (DH 327). This single sentence vividly conveys the furtiveness, expense, and sordidness of purchasing alcohol during those fourteen long years when it was illegal. Lovecraft's attitude on the subject is well-known: having begun as an emphatic supporter of Prohibition (see such essays as "More *Chain-Lightning*" [1915] and "A Remarkable Document" [1917]), he later realised that Prohibition was simply too clumsy a means to cure the problem, although he continued to regard the consumption of alcohol a disgusting practice and maintained a strict teetotalism to the end of his life.

Certain other references apply more particularly to the New England region in which Lovecraft lived and travelled. In *The Case of Charles Dexter Ward* he makes reference to such things as the "vast new Christian Science dome" (MM 115) on Prospect Street in Providence, built between 1906 and 1913; and the mention of the State House earlier in the text (MM 113) could conceivably provide a *terminus post quem* for the story (if we needed one), since it was completed only in 1901. In "Pickman's Model" (1926) there are telling references to the Boston subways and the horrors that may be lurking there; indeed, the subways seemed to affect Lovecraft powerfully, and one of his most brilliant horrific strokes was in *At the Mountains of Madness*, when Danforth begins a crazy series of utterances after seeing the shoggoth: "'South Station Under—Washington Under—Park Street Under—Kendall—Central—Harvard . . .' The poor fellow was chanting the familiar stations of the Boston-Cambridge tunnel that burrowed through our peaceful native soil thousands of miles away in New England" (MM 100). One can still travel this exact subway route today, and Lovecraft must have ridden the line countless times. Indeed, it can be argued that the very notion of the shoggoth was inspired by the subway, since the shoggoth's "nearest comprehensible analogue is a vast, onrushing subway train as one sees it from a station platform—the great black front looming colossally out of infinite subterranean distance, constellated with strangely coloured lights and filling the prodigious burrow as a piston fills a cylinder" (MM 101). Here, then, is certainly one example of a modern—even prosaic—device inspiring Lovecraft's imagination!

In "The Colour out of Space" (1927) we find mentions of the "new reservoir" (DH 54) that is being designed for western Massachusetts. This is of course the Quabbin Reservoir, plans for which were undertaken by a special commission of the Massachusetts legislature in 1926, and work on which was begun as early as the fall of 1926, continuing sporadically for the next twenty years (see Clark, passim). Again, it is possible that Lovecraft's hearing of this impending project began his imagination working. And then there is the very familiar reference to the Vermont floods of November 1927 which provides the starting point for the events in "The Whisperer in Darkness" (1930). Lovecraft had visited Vermont earlier that year, and must have kept close watch of the floods as he read about them in the newspaper. Finally, that anomalous reference in "The Shadow over Innsmouth" (1931)—"'Maybe you know there's still a bunch of Fiji Islanders somewhere around Cape Cod'" (*DH* 307)—has a real source, as Lovecraft wrote to his aunt in 1930 that "The drive to Onset was uneventful—though it was interesting to have [Frank] Belknap [Long] point out a colony of *Fiji-Islanders* near Onset."[3] I do not know what has happened to this colony, but presumably it has since become mingled with the surrounding population.

Some topical references are not so much central to a tale as rather amusing indications that we are in fact in the early decades of the twentieth century. In "Facts concerning the Late Arthur Jermyn and His Family" (1920) occur several charming references. Recall that Sir Alfred Jermyn, father of Arthur Jermyn, who "at thirty-six had deserted his wife and child to travel with an itinerant American circus" (*D* 77), suffered so hideous an end that the "members of 'The Greatest Show on Earth' do not like to speak" (*D* 77) of it. This glancing allusion to the Barnum and Bailey circus is the more revealing in that Lovecraft clearly intends the reader to understand the reference without his having to mention the circus by name. Later in the story we are told that the "once mighty N'bangus were now the submissive servants of King Albert's government" (*D* 80), an obvious reference to the annexation of the Congo by Belgium in 1908; Albert himself became king in 1909 and ruled until his death in 1934. This obviously accounts for the Belgian agent, M. Verhaeren, who sends the strange "white ape" to Jermyn. In *The Case of Charles Dexter Ward* there is one particularly succulent reference, where at the end of the novel Curwen (pretending to be Ward) "could recall how the creaking of Epenetus Olney's new signboard . . . was exactly like the first few notes of the new jazz piece all the radios in Pawtuxet were playing" (*MM* 188). Here again the very point of the modern reference is not merely to place the novel in the contest of the 1920s, but to indicate in a particularly vivid way the unnatural longevity of the wizard Curwen: the implication is that only a person who has actually lived in the eighteenth and the twentieth centuries could make such a comparison.

---

3. HPL to Mrs. F. C. Clark, 15–16 August 1930 (ms., JHL).

Some indications of the modernity (or, rather, contemporaneity) of Lovecraft's fiction can be derived from his reference to previous epochs. Hence there are frequent references to the Victorian age in the tales, and these occur in such a fashion as to suggest that that age is hopelessly outmoded and antiquated. Lovecraft here actually shares the outlook of his time in his rejection of nineteenth-century standards, although he claimed to do so simply so as to return to (what he felt were) the truer and more rationally based attitudes of the eighteenth century. This stance was, however, a little disingenuous, since part of the initiative for Lovecraft's condemnation of nineteenth-century values was his adoption of very advanced philosophical views from Nietzsche, Haeckel, T. H. Huxley, Spengler, Russell, and Santayana. Hence part of Lovecraft's scorn of the "pathetic Puritanism" (*D* 140) of Dr. Allan Halsey in "Herbert West—Reanimator" is in its acceptance of "sins like ... anti-Darwinism [and] anti-Nietzscheism." The Darwin controversy is, of course, still with us, amazing as it may seem; and it may be well to note that Nietzsche died only in 1900. The very remoteness of the Victorian age is hinted more directly in "The Silver Key" (1926), where Randolph Carter decides to refurbish his home "as it was in his early boyhood—purple panes, Victorian furniture, and all" (*MM* 413). And note the description of Old Man Marsh in "The Shadow over Innsmouth," who "still [my italics] wore the frock-coated finery of the Edwardian era" (*DH* 323). This emphatically places the tale in at least the late 1920s, since the reign of Edward VII spanned the years 1901 to 1910.

I have elsewhere briefly discussed some elements of social satire found in Lovecraft's later tales, especially "The Mound," *At the Mountains of Madness*, and "The Shadow out of Time."[4] Some earlier examples of it may, however, be noted. We can hardly fail to note the acidity of his allusion to the "notably fat and especially offensive millionaire brewer" (*D* 89) who has taken over Trevor Towers after the death of Kuranes in "Celephaïs"; this, certainly, is an instance where Lovecraft reveals his adherence to the aristocratic standards of a previous epoch. A similar sort of satire, more topical this time, is found in "The Moon-Bog" (1920), where it is said of Denys Barry: "For all his love of Ireland, America had not left him untouched, and he hated the beautiful wasted space [i.e., the bog] where peat might be cut and land opened up" (*D* 119)—a reference that accidentally relates the story to the theme of Lord Dunsany's later novel, *The Curse of the Wise Woman* (1933). Here again it is precisely this "modern" stance of Barry's that leads directly to his doom.

Lovecraft's references to modern literature, art, and the general aesthetic

---

4. See my "Humour and Satire in Lovecraft" and "Lovecraft's Alien Civilisations: A Political Interpretation."

movements of his time are surprisingly scant in the fiction, although they are of course voluminously recorded in his letters and essays. One odd mention occurs as early as "The Crawling Chaos" (1920/21): "My mind wandered back to an ancient and classical story of tigers which I had read; I strove to recall the author but had difficulty. Then in the midst of my fear I remembered that the tale was by Rudyard Kipling; nor did the grotesqueness of deeming him an ancient author occur to me" (*HM* 13). All this is a bit clumsy, but we may at least note that the very point of the reference is that Kipling is a contemporary author (he would not die until 1936). The attack on free verse in "Poetry and the Gods" (1920) is somewhat more amusing, and Lovecraft's remarks tally with those found in his essays and letters: "It was only a bit of *vers libre*, that pitiful compromise of the poet who overleaps prose yet falls short of the divine melody of numbers" (*D* 350).

References to the "Yellow Nineties" are tolerably frequent in Lovecraft, but are ambivalent in import: Lovecraft was probably repelled by the general excesses of the period, but had fondness for individual writers such as Machen, Wilde, Huysmans, Chambers, and others. Hence the decadence of the two protagonists of "The Hound" (1922) is typified by the remark that "Baudelaire and Huysmans were soon exhausted of thrills" and that "the enigmas of the symbolists and the ecstasies of the pre-Raphaelites all were ours in their time" (*D* 171). Huysmans is mentioned to no especial purpose in "The Rats in the Walls" (*DH* 42), but some significant mentions occur in "Medusa's Coil" (1930). Here the phrase "yellow nineties" is actually used (*HM* 170), and the painter Frank Marsh is said to be a "disciple of Lafcadio Hearn and Gaugin and Van Gogh" (*HM* 170). The mention of Hearn is a little odd, but at least serves to give a *terminus ante quem* to the events of the tale, since Hearn died in 1904. A later reference is still more significant, when Marsh is said to be "like a Durtal or a des Esseintes at the most jaded point of his curious orbit" (*HM*, 278). These are the central characters of Huysmans' *Là-Bas* (1891) and *À Rebours* (1884), respectively. Again the very allusiveness of the reference implies their familiarity in Lovecraft's day, at least among the circle of *littérateurs*. The various mentions of Sidney Sime and Clark Ashton Smith fall more into the class of "in-jokes" than actual topical references.

Lovecraft's disapproval of the general radical trend of modern literature—particularly its abandonment of traditional form and its excessive dwelling on the day-to-day realities of mundane life—comes out frequently in both early and late fiction. "Celephaïs" (1920) provides perhaps the first example, and pungent remarks are made about modern writers who "strove to strip from life its embroidered robes of myth, and to shew in naked ugliness the foul thing that is reality" (*D* 83). The theme is refined in "Azathoth" (1922), where we find that "learning stripped earth of her mantle of beauty, and poets sang no more save of twisted phantoms seen with bleared and inward-looking eyes" (*D* 357). This is actually not an inaccurate description of the obscurity and subjectivity of modern poetry, although the remark was made just before Lovecraft read the most celebrated and revolutionary of modern poems, *The Waste Land* of T. S. Eliot. Lovecraft seems to have read this almost immediately upon first American publication (*Dial*, November 1922), and jumped upon it in an editorial in the *Conservative* of March 1923. The parody "Waste Paper" probably dates to about this time, although its appearance in "the newspaper" (*SL* 4.159)—presumably the *Providence Journal* or the *Providence Evening Bulletin*—has yet to be located. In any case, the most celebrated reference to Eliot in all Lovecraft is the mention at the end of *The Case of Charles Dexter Ward* where Willett, in the basement of Ward's bungalow, tries to calm himself by muttering the Lord's Prayer, "eventually trailing off into a mnemonic hodge-podge like the modernistic *Waste Land* of Mr. T. S. Eliot" (*MM* 209). The very use of the word "Mr." implies a reference to a living contemporary.

But Lovecraft's hostility to the sort of literary realism epitomised by Ben Hecht's teeth-gnashing *Erik Dorn* or the novels of Sinclair Lewis emerges more pungently in "The Silver Key," where Carter "did not dissent when they told him that the animal pain of a stuck pig or dyspeptic ploughman in real life is a greater thing than the peerless beauty of Narath" (*MM* 409)—a position that, if stripped of its vicious satire, is certainly a legitimate one (recall the triumphant first sentence of the preface to Wilde's *Picture of Dorian Gray*: "The artist is the creator of beautiful things"), although certainly out of tune with its time. Later a more general condemnation of the "Bohemian" or "Greenwich Village" sect is made, in a passage both virulent and noble:

> But when he [Carter] came to study those who had thrown off the old myths, he found them even more ugly than those who had not. They did not know that beauty lies in harmony, and that loveliness of life has no standard amidst an aimless cosmos save only its harmony with the dreams and the feelings which have gone before and blindly moulded our little spheres out of the rest of chaos. They did not see that good and evil and beauty and ugliness are only ornamental fruits of perspective, whose sole value lies in their linkage to what chance made our fathers think and feel, and whose finer details are different for every race and culture. Instead, they either denied these things altogether or transferred them to the crude, vague instincts which they shared with the beasts and peasants; so that their lives were dragged malodorously out in pain, ugliness, and disproportion, yet filled with a ludicrous pride at having escaped from something no more unsound than that which still held them. They had traded the false gods of fear and blind piety for those of licence and anarchy. (*MM* 410)

Nearly every sentence here has an analogue in Lovecraft's correspondence. Lovecraft could even parody more directly the literary fashions of his day; "Waste Paper" is certainly a brilliant example, but it can be wondered whether Lovecraft was trying to have fun at the expense of the "stream-of-consciousness" school in "Hypnos" (1922) when he wrote at one point: "Clocks—time—space—infinity . . ." (D 169).

The glancing allusion to the art of the pulp magazines in "Pickman's Model" (1926) may be worth noting ("Any magazine-cover hack can splash paint around wildly and call it a nightmare or a Witches' Sabbath or a portrait of the devil" [DH 13]). Note the significant difference in "The Colour out of Space": "It was too much like a landscape of Salvator Rosa; too much like some forbidden woodcut in a tale of terror" (DH 54), where "tale of terror" refers to the Gothic novels of the late eighteenth and early nineteenth centuries. Here a modern allusion would have been inappropriate, since this introductory passage depicts timelessly a hoary land where horrors have been lurking for hundreds of years. Then, of course, there is that curious mention in "The Unnamable" (1923), where a magazine containing one of Randolph Carter's stories was taken "off the stands at the complaints of silly milksops" (D 202). We immediately think of the similar temporary banning of *Weird Tales* when it published C. M. Eddy's "The Loved Dead"; but since that tale did not appear until the issue for May–June–July 1924, we must either believe that the parallel is coincidental or that Lovecraft revised the tale before its appearance in *Weird Tales* for July 1925 to include the reference.

It is, however, in the realms of science and philosophy that Lovecraft's tales gain their greatest sense of topicality; for, as his letters amply testify, Lovecraft kept closely abreast of the latest findings in astronomy, astrophysics, anthropology, and many other of the sciences, and was also very well read in contemporary philosophy. Bloch himself came to this conclusion when he wrote that the fundamental link between Poe and Lovecraft was "their mutual interest in science," and that this interest "softens the charge that the two writers were totally unaware of the actual world and unrealistic in their treatment of their times" (Bloch [1972] 159). Bloch made no attempt to treat this topicality in detail, but we shall try to provide at least a few hints here.

As with the political and literary references, some of Lovecraft's allusions to current science and philosophy are merely by the way, but in their very allusiveness serve to root the works in their time. Hence the two references to the Piltdown man in Lovecraft ("The Tomb" [D 18] and "The Rats in the Walls" [DH 42]) force us to date the events of these tales to after 1912, when it was first brought to public attention. Lovecraft, of course, had no way of knowing that it was a hoax, since nearly all leading anthropologists accepted the finding as genuine, if anomalous and difficult to place within the framework of primitive man's history. Only in 1949 did widespread scepticism emerge, and in 1953 the hoax was finally uncovered. Another brief archaeological note in "The Rats in the Walls" may be of interest, where it is remarked that Sir William Brinton's "excavations in the Troad excited most of the world in their day" (*DH* 40). The very nature of the reference places these excavations well before 1923, the date of the tale's events, and Brinton's work must surely have occurred after Schliemann's spectacular discovery of the site of Troy in 1867. Schliemann's last work at Troy dates to 1890, and from then until the early 1930s little of consequence was done, although the discovery received wide publicity through books by Schliemann and others; hence Brinton's excavations could plausibly be placed in the first decade of the twentieth century.

Some other anthropological references are of interest as well. Fritz Leiber recognised that the "authors Akeley lists [in "The Whisperer in Darkness"] to prove his competency in those fields are a nice selection" (Leiber 476); the list includes E. B. Tylor, Sir John Lubbock, Sir J. G. Frazer, Jean Louis Armand de Quatrefages de Breau, Margaret Murray, Henry Fairfield Osborn, Sir Arthur Keith, Pierre Marcellin Boule, and G. Elliott Smith (*DH* 216). All these are rough contemporaries of Lovecraft, although several did their best work in the last two decades of the nineteenth century. Tylor, incidentally, aside from writing the seminal *Primitive Culture* (1871), which may have given Lovecraft much of his information on anthropology, primitive man, and the origin of religion, also wrote the article on "Magic" in the 9th edition of the *Encyclopaedia Britannica*, which Lovecraft pillaged for "The Horror at Red Hook" (1925). Lovecraft read Margaret Murray's *Witch-Cult in Western Europe* (1921) a few years after it came out—apparently in 1924, since he wrote to Clark Ashton Smith in October 1925: "Meanwhile let me urge you, as I did over a year ago, to read *The Witch-Cult in Western Europe*. . . . It ought to be full of inspiration for you" (*SL* 2.28). That it was full of inspiration for Lovecraft is abundantly clear, since it receives first mention in "The Horror at Red Hook" (*D* 249). It is then cited in "The Call of Cthulhu" (1926), but let us recall that that tale was conceived more than a year previously: in October 1926 Lovecraft notes that "I've written two new tales, one of which is the sunken-land thing I described in advance last year" (*SL* 2.77). In his diary for 1925, under the dates of August 12-13 (only a day after the writing of "He" and about two weeks after writing "The Horror at Red Hook") Lovecraft notes: "Write out story plot—'The Call of Cthulhu'" (*CE* 5.165). Indeed, the tale is set generally in March-April 1925, so perhaps Lovecraft had sketched out a timetable of events in the story plot and maintained it when he wrote the tale—he seems to have done something similar in "The Whisperer in Darkness" (1930), most of which is set in late 1927 and 1928.

Mentions of modern occultist works can perhaps be noted here. The mention of Charles Fort in "The Descendant" (D 361) does not help much to date that fragment. Fort had written two of his major books by this time, *The Book of the Damned* (1919) and *New Lands* (1923); Lovecraft, however, did not read the latter until late 1927, when he notes that he "didn't find it as interesting as *The Book of the Damned*" (SL 2.174); I have not been able to determine when Lovecraft read that volume. The mention of "Ignatius Donnelly's chimerical account of Atlantis" (D 361) in the same fragment is of even less help, since Donnelly's *Atlantis: The Antediluvian World* was published so early as 1882. In "Out of the Aeons" (1933) we have mentions of Colonel Churchward and Lewis Spence (HM 269). Churchward's books on the lost continent Mu all date to the 1920s and 1930s;[5] Lovecraft confessed, however, that "I've never seen [Churchward's] books, but have read fairly indicative reviews of them."[6] These reviews must at least have told Lovecraft of the ancient Naacal language that Churchward claimed to have discovered, since Naacal is mentioned extensively in "Through the Gates of the Silver Key" and "Out of the Aeons." As for Spence, Lovecraft owned his *Encyclopedia of Occultism* (1920) and may have been familiar with such other of his books as *Atlantis in America* (1925) and *The Problem of Lemuria* (1932). No doubt Lovecraft, if he read any of these books at all, would have done so only because of their possible imaginative stimulus: he says of Fort that he "scraped up all sorts of press anecdotes of a certain type—which in turn were typical misstatements, misinterpretations, exaggerations, and distortions of actually observed things, or else hallucinations or fabrications" (SL 5.172–73).

References to modern psychology enter into only a few tales, but in a telling manner. It is interesting to note that both "Beyond the Wall of Sleep" (1919) and "From Beyond" (1920) were revised after initial publication to incorporate some rather snide references to Freud. In the former tale, as Wetzel long ago pointed out, the cynical insertion "—Freud to the contrary with his puerile symbolism—" (D 25) was added subsequent to the tale's appearance in *Pine Cones* (October 1919). Wetzel did not realise that a similar addition was made in "From Beyond": in the original manuscript the sentence "I laugh at the shallow endocrinologist, fellow-dupe and fellow-parvenu of the Freudian" (D 93) is missing and must have been added at some point preceding the tale's first appearance in the *Fantasy Fan* (June 1934). Can we date these insertions? They may well have occurred quite early, for in June 1921 Lovecraft

---

5. Cf. *The Lost Continent of Mu* (1926); *The Children of Mu* (1931); *The Sacred Symbols of Mu* (1933); *Cosmic Forces of Mu* (1934).

6. HPL to E. Hoffmann Price, 15 February 1933 (ms., JHL).

announces: "Dr. Sigmund Freud of Vienna, whose system of psycho-analysis I have begun to investigate, will probably prove the end of idealistic thought" (*SL* 1.134). Lovecraft was unfortunately mistaken in his prediction (just as he was wrong when he noted that "a mere knowledge of the approximate dimensions of the visible universe is enough to destroy forever the notion of a personal godhead" [*SL* 1.44], even though this knowledge seems to have had such an effect upon him), and no contradiction need be assumed between the tolerably favourable mentions of Freud in the letters and the rather sarcastic ones in the two tales in question: Lovecraft is merely criticising Freud's single-minded attribution of all human impulses to the libido (a position that most modern Freudians have themselves abandoned), since, as he remarked, "I am inclined to accept the modifications of Adler, who in placing the ego above the eros makes a scientific return to the position which Nietzsche assumed for wholly philosophical reasons" (*SL* 1.136). The glancing reference to the "big three" of early twentieth-century psychology in "The Trap" (1931)—"Even the most prosaic scientists affirm, with Freud, Jung, and Adler, that the subconscious mind is most open to external impression in sleep" (*HM* 384)—can be noted in brief.

It is, actually, somewhat curious that pure philosophers do not receive much notice in the fiction. We have observed the passing reference to "anti-Nietzscheism" in "Herbert West—Reanimator"; and in the same story Lovecraft notes that West believed "with Haeckel that all life is a chemical and physical process, and that the so-called 'soul' is a myth" (*D* 134). Ernst Haeckel (1834–1919) was probably the greatest of the biologist-philosophers of the late nineteenth and early twentieth centuries, and the great apostle for materialistic monism in his time (although Santayana could note, as early as 1923, that "In natural philosophy I am a decided materialist—apparently the only one living";[7] certainly Santayana would have amended his statement if he had read Lovecraft's trenchant essay, "Idealism and Materialism: A Reflection"!) and Lovecraft was greatly influenced by Haeckel's seminal volume, *The Riddle of the Universe* (1899; English translation 1900), which he seems to have read in late 1919 or 1920 (*SL* 1.87, 141). But of other philosophers we find no mention.

Einstein, however, runs through Lovecraft's fiction like an elusive thread, although here, of course, we are treading the borderline between astrophysics and metaphysics (as, indeed, physics since Einstein has tended increasingly to do). The first—and very allusive—citation occurs so early as "Hypnos" (1922), where it is remarked that "one man with Oriental eyes has said that all time and space are relative, and men have laughed" (*D* 165); this mention is actually anomalously early, for only in May 1923 does Lovecraft announce: "My

---

7. Santayana, "Preface" to *Scepticism and Animal Faith* (1923). HPL later read this volume.

cynicism and scepticism are increasing, and from an entirely new cause—the Einstein theory.... All is chance, accident, and ephemeral illusion—a fly may be greater than Arcturus, and Durfee Hill may surpass Mount Everest—assuming them to be removed from the present planet and differently environed in the continuum of space-time" (SL 1.231). Indeed, Lovecraft's remark here that "All the cosmos is a jest" is peculiarly reminiscent of what he had written a year before in "Hypnos": "The cosmos of our waking knowledge, born from such an universe as a bubble is born from the pipe of a jester, touches it only as such a bubble may touch its sardonic source when sucked back by the jester's whim" (D 165).

Lovecraft first cites Einstein in a letter to the Gallomo that probably dates to April 1920 (see *Letters to Alfred Galpin* 75-79). He then took note of the eclipse observations in May 1923 (reported on the front page of the *New York Times*) that, in the minds of most physicists, definitively confirmed the truth of the theory. Another sentence from "Hypnos"—"But even that man with Oriental eyes has done no more than suspect"—suggests that Lovecraft (along with most members of the intelligentsia) felt that the theory of relativity was, in 1922, still a theory, lacking empirical proof. In any event, Lovecraft's immediate reaction to Einstein is typical of that of many intellectuals, especially those lacking technical training in physics; indeed, it is precisely this sort of misunderstanding and false application of the theory of relativity that led many philosophers to reject the positivism of the later nineteenth century and to usher in a new age of idealism and mysticism. Lovecraft, of course, snapped out of his naive perceptions of the Einstein theory quite early, and by 1929 was telling Frank Belknap Long: "If any mystic thinks that matter has lost its known properties because it's been found made of invisible energy, just let him read Einstein and try to apply his new conception by butting his head into a stone wall" (SL 2.267)—which is amusingly reminiscent of Dr. Johnson's refutation of Berkeley. Lovecraft knew, however, that in the "nearer heavens" the "given area *isn't big enough* to let relativity get in its major effects"—hence he wisely warned Long: "Don't let the Einstein-twisters catch you here!" (SL 2.265). All this reveals an admirable grasp of the Einstein theory and its integration into a positivist and even materialist scheme, at least partially similar to that produced by Russell and Santayana.

In any case, Einstein reappears in vivid fashion in "The Whisperer in Darkness" (1930), where the pseudo-Akeley boldly announces: "'Do you know that Einstein is wrong, and that certain objects and forces *can* move with a velocity greater than that of light?'" (DH 253). One wonders whether this remark was inspired by Frank Belknap Long's "The Hounds of Tindalos," where the protagonist notes: "What do we know of time, really? Einstein believes that it is relative, that it can be interpreted in terms of space, of *curved* space. But why must we stop there?" And compare pseudo-Akeley's statement—"With the proper aid I expect to go backward and forward in time" (*DH* 253)—with the remark of Long's character: "With . . . the aid of my mathematical knowledge I believe that I can *go back through time*" (Long 94-95). Lovecraft almost certainly read "The Hounds of Tindalos" in manuscript, and even if he did not he could have read it in its appearance in *Weird Tales* (March 1929) in time to use it in his own tale.

But the two most interesting citations of the Einstein theory—as well as other advances in modern physics—occur in "The Shunned House" (1924) and "The Dreams in the Witch House" (1932). The former is particularly interesting in that it reinterprets the traditional vampire legend in terms of modern physics. Note these passages:

> To say that we actually believed in vampires or werewolves would be a carelessly inclusive statement. Rather must it be said that we were not prepared to deny the possibility of certain unfamiliar and unclassified modifications of vital force and attenuated matter; existing very infrequently in three-dimensional space because of its more intimate connexion with other spatial units, yet close enough to the boundary of our own to furnish us occasional manifestations which we, for lack of a proper vantage-point, may never hope to understand. . . .
>
> Such a thing was surely not a physical or biochemical impossibility in the light of a newer science which includes the theories of relativity and intra-atomic action. One might easily imagine an alien nucleus of substance or energy, formless or otherwise, kept alive by imperceptible or immaterial subtractions from the life-force or bodily tissue and fluids of other and more palpably living things into which it penetrates and with whose fabric it sometimes completely merges itself. (MM 251-52)

The overt mention of relativity is to be observed, and the mention of "intra-atomic action" presumably alludes to the quantum theory. What Lovecraft actually made of the quantum theory is not easy to deduce from the letters, where neither the theory itself nor Max Planck is mentioned at all frequently. Like the Einstein theory, Planck's findings were hailed by idealists as spelling the downfall of determinism and a *carte blanche* for all sorts of previously outmoded notions about the universe and humanity's relation to it. Lovecraft knew better, and by the time he assimilated the quantum theory he felt that it posed no real threat to determinism. "What most physicists take the quantum theory, at present, to mean, is *not that any cosmic uncertainty exists* as to which of several courses a given reaction will take; but that in certain instances *no conceivable channel of information can ever tell human beings which course will be taken"* (*SL* 3.228). Lovecraft thus seems to regard the "uncertainty" revealed by the quantum theory as epistemological and not ontological—i.e., it is simply our inability to predict the movement of sub-atomic particles that produces the "uncertainty," but the uncertainty does not inhere in Nature. This conclusion (although also adopted by Einstein, who made the celebrated remark that "God does not play dice with the universe") does not appear to be correct, since, in the words of Russell:

> In quantum theory, individual atomic occurrences are not determined by the equations; these suffice only to show that the possibilities form a discrete series, and that there are rules of determining how often each possibility will be realized in a large number of cases. There are reasons for believing that this absence of complete determinism is not due to any incompleteness in the theory, but is a genuine characteristic of small-scale occurrences. The regularity which is found in macroscopic phenomena is a statistical regularity. Phenomena involving large numbers of atoms remain deterministic, but what an individual atom may do in given circumstances is uncertain, not only because our knowledge is limited but because there are no physical laws giving a determinate result. (23–24)

Nevertheless, determinism as a philosophical position is by no means undermined, since "the crucial but so far unanswered question is whether there are processes by which random sub-atomic occurrences trigger larger scale neural processes and so introduce some randomness into them" (Mackie 220). Hence Lovecraft's belief that "the future, though wholly determinate, is . . . essentially unknown" (*SL* 3.31)—where again the distinction is made between ontological determinism and human epistemological uncertainty—is still viable, although the case for determinism now tends to be based rather on psychological than metaphysical foundations.

The point of all these reflections is that Lovecraft could use the findings of modern physics to produce an "updated" or "modernised" version of such standard supernatural themes as the vampire in "The Shunned House." A similar transformation occurs in "The Dreams in the Witch House," where witchcraft and time travel are reinterpreted through Einstein. At the very beginning of the tale is a mention of "quantum physics" (MM 263)—nowadays called quantum mechanics—and shortly after we are given a hint as to the possible sources of Keziah Mason's powers: "some circumstance had more or less suddenly given a mediocre old woman of the seventeenth century an insight into mathematical depths perhaps beyond the utmost modern delvings of Planck, Heisenberg, Einstein, and de Sitter" (MM 264).

The mention of Einstein and Planck is not unusual, but the other two call for some notice. Willem de Sitter (1872–1934) was chiefly known for having been instrumental in introducing the theory of relativity into the English-speaking world in a series of articles published during 1916-17, and he worked extensively on the relation of relativity to cosmology; in so doing he evolved a view of the universe sufficiently different from Einstein's as to earn it the nickname of the "De Sitter Universe." Lovecraft heard a lecture by him on 9 November 1931 (SL 3.437), which probably accounts for the mention of him in "The Dreams in the Witch House," written in February 1932. The mention of Werner Karl Heisenberg (1901-1976) is even more interesting; for, basing his work on the quantum theory, he produced in 1927 the celebrated Indeterminacy Principle, whereby "natural laws" previously thought to be fixed were reduced to mere statistical averages. It might be thought that Lovecraft would be highly inspired by this theory, since his whole aesthetic of weird fiction centred on the depiction of "the illusion of some strange suspension or violation of the galling limitations of time, space, and natural law" (CE 2.176); but in fact the reverse would be the case, since Lovecraft's "suspension or violation" of the laws of Nature could be aesthetically effective only if those laws were assumed to be immutable and eternal. In any case, I am not certain how well Lovecraft ever explored the Indeterminacy Principle, although it is certainly rather curious that Heisenberg was awarded the Nobel Prize for Physics in the very year (1932) Lovecraft wrote "The Dreams in the Witch House."

The discussions of time travel and hyperspace travel later in the tale have already been examined by Fritz Leiber, and we need remark on only a few particulars. Compare, for example, the bold statement "Time could not exist in certain belts of space" (MM 285) and the subsequent logical development of the idea with the earlier, nebulous, and poetic expression of the same idea in "The White Ship": "In the land of Sona-Nyl there is neither time nor space, neither suffering nor death; and there I dwelt for many aeons" (D 39). Granted that the intent of the two tales is wholly dissimilar, and that in the earlier tale a scientific exposition would be entirely inappropriate, it may still be observed how the discoveries of modern physics—and Lovecraft's early and intelligent absorption of them—have led to a tightening of the intellectual and philosophical foundations of his later tales, and even perhaps to an expansion in imaginative scope, since, as Lovecraft knew, "the more we learn about the cosmos, the more bewildering does it appear" (SL 4.324).

As we move to the realm of pure astronomy, we may examine the one great example of Lovecraft's topicality: the mention of the discovery of Pluto in "The Whisperer in Darkness." Although the core of the tale was inspired by Lovecraft's trips to Vermont in 1927 and 1928, it may be of interest to note that the actual writing of the tale was begun on 24 February 1930. The discovery of Pluto was made by C. W. Tombaugh at the Lowell Observatory on 23 January 1930, but the earliest announcement of the discovery that I can find is the front page of the *New York Times* for 14 March 1930; it was announced in various scientific journals shortly thereafter. It cannot, therefore, precisely be said that the discovery impelled the actual commencement of a tale whose genesis had occurred several years earlier, but it is still clear that Lovecraft was eager to incorporate this great discovery into his story. It may also be of some interest to note that the search for a trans-Neptunian planet was instigated as early as 1915 by Percival Lowell (with whose work Lovecraft was quite familiar) in a manner not wholly dissimilar to that advised by Lovecraft himself in his letter to the *Scientific American* of July 1906.

The last example of Lovecraft's scientific topicality to be considered here is his mention of the continental drift theory in *At the Mountains of Madness*. I have elsewhere noted that one example of Lovecraft's attempts to keep this tale "up to date" was the elimination of some references to an incorrect theory that the Antarctic continent was actually two land masses separated by a frozen strait between the Weddell and Ross Seas;[8] this elimination must have been made just prior to the submission of the tale to *Astounding Stories* in late 1935 (SL 5.209-10). I had, however, previously thought that these changes were triggered by information derived from Admiral Byrd's expedition to the Antarctic (1933-35); it now appears that the widely held theory of the frozen strait was effectively refuted by a plane flight from the Weddell to the Ross Sea made by Lincoln Ellsworth and Herbert Hollick-Kenyon in late 1934 and early 1935 (see Chapman 240). Whatever the situation, it is clear that Lovecraft was intent on eliminating any obsolete scientific references in the novel—perhaps he did so in March 1935, when he told Emil Petaja that "Before long I'll try to dig it [the novel] up and shoot it along" (SL 5.120).

But it is fortunate that Lovecraft did not alter the two references to the continental drift theory, which he actually notes had been "lately advanced by Taylor, Wegener, and Joly" (MM 66). For the fact is that the continental drift theory was very controversial throughout the 1920s and 1930s, and the majority of scientists tended to reject it; only after World War II did it gain widespread acceptance (although in a slightly altered form from that expounded by its originators). Lovecraft was here remarkably advanced and prophetic in embracing the theory.[9] Even the order in which Lovecraft mentions the three proponents of the theory is chronologically correct. Frank Bursley Taylor (1860-1938) published a paper on the theory in 1910 but did not himself expand upon it. The major advocate and elaborator of the theory

---

8. See "Textual Problems in Lovecraft."

9. I am grateful to John Shaw for first alerting me to this circumstance.

was Alfred Lothar Wegener (1880–1930), who himself announced the theory in 1912 and went on to write a volume on the subject translated as *The Origin of Continents and Oceans* (1924). Wegener's work was adopted by John Joly (1857–1933), who published his *Surface History of the Earth* in 1925; but Joly does not seem to have advanced the theory much farther than Wegener. I do not believe that Lovecraft actually read either Wegener's or Joly's book, but he was certainly conversant with the major principles of the theory and uses it in a brilliant and clever fashion in his novel, remarking wryly that the theory "receives striking support from [the] uncanny source" (MM 69) of the Old Ones' bas-reliefs in their millennia-abandoned megalopolis.

Lovecraft, then, was not merely very much alive in the era of Hitler, T. S. Eliot, and Einstein (as his letters clearly prove), but he was not above making overt references to contemporary political, social, literary, and scientific movements in his fiction. It is true that these references rarely occupy a large or central place in his tales, and we have nothing akin to the minute descriptions of life in seventeenth- and eighteenth-century Providence forming the sub-narrative about Curwen in *The Case of Charles Dexter Ward*; but it is clear that Lovecraft assumes knowledge of the culture in which he was writing and makes few attempts to depict a consciously archaic environment or to write in an archaic idiom. Indeed, the belief that Lovecraft's work is "antiquated" either in theme or in style has been greatly exaggerated by critics. The very allusiveness of many of the references—note the mention of "the President" and not "President Harding" in "The Rats in the Walls"—signifies a shared body of information that Lovecraft expected of his reader. Even if Lovecraft intended his fiction to be, as with Thucydides, a "possession for all time," there can be no doubt but that it is firmly rooted in the culture of the inter-war years in America and Europe which Lovecraft observed so perceptively in his life and letters.

Works Cited

Bloch, Robert. "Out of the Ivory Tower." In Lovecraft's *The Shuttered Room and Other Pieces*. Sauk City, WI: Arkham House, 1959. 178–90.

———. "Poe and Lovecraft." 1972. Rpt. in S. T. Joshi, ed. *H. P. Lovecraft: Four Decades of Criticism*. Athens: Ohio University Press, 1980. 168–70.

Chapman, Walker. *The Loneliest Continent: The Story of Antarctic Discovery*. Greenwich, CT: New York Graphic Society, 1964.

Clark, Walter E. *Quabbin Reservoir*. New York: Hobson Book Press, 1946.

Leiber, Fritz. "Through Hyperspace with Brown Jenkin: Lovecraft's Contribution to Speculative Fiction." 1966. Rpt. in Peter Cannon, ed. *Lovecraft Remembered*. Sauk City, WI: Arkham House, 1998. 472–83.

Long, Frank Belknap. "The Hounds of Tindalos." In *The Hounds of Tindalos*. New York: Jove/HBJ, 1978.

Lovecraft, H. P. *Letters to Alfred Galpin*. Edited by S. T. Joshi and David E. Schultz. New York: Hippocampus Press, 2003.

Mackie, J. L. *Ethics: Inventing Right and Wrong*. Harmondsworth: Penguin, 1977.

Russell, Bertrand. *Human Knowledge: Its Scope and Limits*. New York: Simon & Schuster, 1948.

Humour and Satire in Lovecraft

The publication of Lovecraft's letters ought to have eradicated the long-held belief that Lovecraft was wholly lacking in humour. While it is true that humour, satire, and irony generally take bitter, Juvenalian forms in his work, his letters reveal an appreciation and expression of many types of humour: from punning to playful lapses into Georgian archaism to imitations of African American, Jewish, and foreign dialect to the most ferocious cynicism directed toward religion, modern civilisation and literature, and other of Lovecraft's bêtes noires. Indeed, the impression of his humourlessness arose only through a disregard for all his work save his fiction; for essays and poems alike display a penchant for satire, polemic, and repartee.

And yet, those very letters and essays seem to indicate a distaste for the use of humour and satire, notably in weird fiction. "I don't care for humour as an ingredient of the weird tale—in fact, I think it is a definitely diluting element," wrote Lovecraft in 1932 (*SL* 4.83). In "Some Notes on Interplanetary Fiction" we find that "Social and political satire are always undesirable [in science fiction] since such intellectual and ulterior objects detract from the story's power as a crystallisation of a mood" (*CE* 2.181); this in spite of the fact that, as I have tried to show elsewhere,[1] such satire enters extensively into much of his later fiction. Poe's "blundering ventures in stilted and laboured pseudo-humour" (*D* 396) clearly did not meet with Lovecraft's favour. In many other remarks we find a similar belief that humour and fantasy do not mix well.

It is very easy, however, to discover many traces of humour, irony, and satire in even the most serious of Lovecraft's tales. I shall not here be concerned greatly with those marginal tales where the element of humour is consciously paramount—"A Reminiscence of Dr. Samuel Johnson" (1917), "Ibid" (1928), "The Battle That Ended the Century" (1934), "Collapsing Cosmoses" (1935), and "Sweet Ermengarde"[2]—but shall restrict my attention to those "weird tales"

---

1. See "The Political and Economic Thought of H. P. Lovecraft" and "Lovecraft's Alien Civilisations: A Political Interpretation."

2. The precise date of this last work has not been satisfactorily determined; but, from the handwriting of the A.Ms. (JHL, Brown University), it seems a comparatively early

that, in spite of Lovecraft's remarks, contain varying types and degrees of humour. The sources for this element of humour shall then be considered.

Humour seems to take three distinct forms in Lovecraft's fiction, although they are frequently combined in a given tale. These three types can be classified as puns, "in-jokes," and bitter, mirthless satire and cynicism. The first two are prevalent in many of his later tales, while the third is found rather less frequently but enters early as well as later tales.

The number of verbal puns in Lovecraft's tales can scarcely be enumerated, but I seem to find them more prevalent in those tales which he did not write for immediate publication, whether in *Weird Tales* or elsewhere. *The Case of Charles Dexter Ward* is particularly rich both in puns and in-jokes, as is *The Dream-Quest of Unknown Kadath*; and this fact may confirm the impression that the two novels were written almost wholly without any immediate market in mind, as some of his earlier tales—e.g., "The Horror at Red Hook"—seems to have been. Indeed, Lovecraft dismissed the latter novel merely as "useful practice for later and more authentic attempts in the novel form" (SL 2.95), and disavowed both when he came to make a chronology of his fiction in 1937 (Conover 225).

The puns in *The Case of Charles Dexter Ward* come, surprisingly, more toward the end of the novel, where the climax is approaching, than toward the beginning. Note Lovecraft's remark that Dr. Willett, despite the horror of his first trip through the basement of Ward's (i.e., Curwen's) bungalow, was determined to "leave no stone unturned in his search for the hideous facts behind Charles Ward's bizarre madness" (MM 210), a play on Willett's earlier discovery of the things that lay beneath the stone trap-doors in the basement. It may surprise us that this pun—which must surely be intentional—comes at one of the high points of the novel, where the danger of humour might deflate the entire atmosphere. But few readers would probably catch the pun on first reading, since the atmosphere has by then made us oblivious to such subtle and dry humour. Another type of pun that runs through the whole of *The Case of Charles Dexter Ward* is Lovecraft's reference to Ward/Curwen as a "youth"; this pun in fact relates to the central plot of the novel, where the youthful Ward comes increasingly under the control of the preternaturally aged Curwen. A similar example of humour or satire integral to the tale is found in the opening paragraph, where it is noted that the person who escaped "from a private hospital for the insane near Providence, Rhode Island . . . *bore the name* of Charles Dexter Ward" (MM 107), since the name was all that he bore.[3]

---

story, probably c. 1919-25.

3. This detail was pointed out to me by Donald R. Burleson.

In-jokes—jokes which could be understood only by Lovecraft and his close associates—also abound in *The Case of Charles Dexter Ward*. Hazard Weeden, for example, lives at 598 Angell Street, Lovecraft's home from 1904 to 1924, while Willett lives in the very residence where Lovecraft wrote the novel, 10 Barnes Street.

Other examples of humour in *The Case of Charles Dexter Ward* that do not specifically fall into the categories of puns or in-jokes are the fact that Willett visited Ward/Curwen for the last time on Friday the 13th of April, 1928 (MM 231), and the fact that Ward/Curwen and his cohorts were trying to procure the "essential Saltes" of a certain "B. F." in Philadelphia (MM 197)—a somewhat undignified allusion to the venerable Benjamin Franklin.

In *The Dream-Quest of Unknown Kadath* the humour is not displayed in specific puns but in the general tone; and this fact certainly underscores the personal and autobiographical nature of the tale. Who cannot smile, for example, at this dryly humorous description of the ghouls:

> The ghouls were in general respectful, even if one did attempt to pinch him [Carter] while several others eyed his leanness speculatively. Through patient glibbering he made inquiries regarding his vanished friend [R. U. Pickman], and found he had become a ghoul of some prominence in abysses nearer the waking world. A greenish elderly ghoul offered to conduct him to Pickman's present habitation, so despite a natural loathing he followed the creature into a capacious burrow and crawled after him for hours in the blackness of rank mould.... There, on a tombstone of 1768 stolen from the Granary Burying Ground in Boston, sat the ghoul which was once the artist Richard Upton Pickman. It was naked and rubbery, and had acquired so much of the ghoulish physiognomy that its human origin was already obscure. But it still remembered a little English, and was able to converse with Carter in grunts and monosyllables, helped out now and then by the glibbering of ghouls. (MM 338)

The description of King Kuranes, who has attempted to recreate the "little Cornish village" that was his during his childhood, is less bitter than most satirical passages in Lovecraft, and there is an element of pathos when Carter is greeted by a "small stubbly old man in a smock who spoke as best he could in the quaint tones of far Cornwall" (MM 355). Kuranes has managed to preserve his illusion (although he knows it to be an illusion); and it is thus no surprise that when Iranon, in "The Quest of Iranon," finds that his illusion is shattered, the satire and irony become extremely bitter. "The Quest of Iranon" is, indeed, one of the most poignantly bitter tales in all Lovecraft, and embodies an *irony of situation* that is one of the ways in which Lovecraft subtly employs his more cynical vein of satire.

The humorous passages of *The Dream-Quest of Unknown Kadath* are too numerous for citation, and the whole novel (save the ending) is full of a witty grotesqueness quite uncommon in Lovecraft. Indeed, it is not unlikely that the bizarre incident where the galley jumps off of the earth and goes to the far side of the moon is taken from a similar passage in the Greek satirist Lucian's *True History*. In-joke here takes the form of Lovecraft's constant references to his earlier "Dunsanian" stories; we here encounter such figures as Kuranes ("Celephaïs"), the cats of Ulthar, Atal the priest ("The Other Gods"), and the like; "The White Ship" is alluded to in such names as Xura and Sona-Nyl; and even "The Temple"—not generally considered a "Dunsanian" tale—may perhaps be echoed in one passage describing a sea-voyage by Carter.[4]

Two stories contain elements that fall somewhere between puns and in-jokes: "Herbert West—Reanimator" (1921-22) and "The Hound" (1922). In effect, both stories can be read as parodies—chiefly parodies of themselves, or more generally of the kind of flamboyant, over-the-top kind of horror fiction that was already causing the early pulp magazines to fall into literary disrepute. Lovecraft makes no secret of the onus of writing "Herbert West," a task that reduced him to the level of a Grub Street hack:

> To write to order, to drag one figure through a series of artificial episodes, involves the violation of all that spontaneity and singleness of impression which should characterise short story work. It reduces the unhappy author from art to the commonplace level of mechanical and unimaginative hackwork. Nevertheless, when one needs the money one is not scrupulous—so I have accepted the job! (SL 1.158)

In order to amuse himself, it appears that Lovecraft wrote the successive episodes of the story in an increasingly lurid and bombastic manner. It is possible, indeed, that "Herbert West—Reanimator" did not *begin* as a parody, but *became* one as time went on and Lovecraft began to realise the absurdity of writing a "serious" weird tale on a subject so hackneyed and stale as the reanimation of the dead.

"The Hound" has been roundly abused for being overwritten; but it has somehow managed to escape most critics' attention that the story is an obvious self-parody. This becomes increasingly evident from many obvious literary allusions in the tale, and also from such grotesque utterances as "Bizarre manifestations were now too frequent to count" (*D* 176). And yet, the story is un-

---

4. See MM 326. This allusion to "The Temple" has been disputed by William Fulwiler (pers. comm.) because "The Temple" is manifestly set in the "real" or "waking" world. I am not convinced, however, that this distinction is a meaningful (or, at least, consistent) one in HPL; see my article "The Dream World and the Real World in Lovecraft."

deniably successful as an experiment in flamboyance and excess, so long as one keeps in mind that Lovecraft was aiming for such an effect and was doing so at least partially with tongue in cheek.

There are numerous in-jokes in the tale. While the narrator's friend St John is clearly meant to be Rheinhart Kleiner (whom Lovecraft customarily referred to as Randolph St John, as if he were a relative of the sophisticated British writer Henry St John, Viscount Bolingbroke), the connexion rests only in the name, as his character is not described in any detail. One wonders whether the museum of tomb-loot collected by the two protagonists is a playful reference to Samuel Loveman's impressive collection of *objets d'art* (not taken from tombs, one must hasten to add): Lovecraft first saw this collection in September 1922 and was much impressed by it.

Some of Lovecraft's revisions have a great many puns, and may represent his attempt to escape the drudgery of revision and ghost-writing by subtle humour. "The Mound" is particularly rich in this regard. It is mentioned that in 1891 "a young man named Heaton" had "resolved to get to the bottom of the mystery" (*HM* 100) of the mound—a common type of pun where an idiom is humorously used in a literal sense. Later, after the narrator has discovered the manuscript of Panfilo de Zamacona, the Spaniard is referred to as "the vanished writer" (*HM* 113); again a literal usage of a metaphor, since we learn at the end of the tale that Zamacona suffered "dematerialisation." Openly satirical passages occur later, where Zamacona is ridiculed for his narrow Christian outlook and his "desire to convert the [mound] people to that Faith of the Cross which the Spaniards hoped to make universal" (*HM* 136). More amusement is provoked by Lovecraft's statement that Zamacona was given slaves by the mound people to "protect him from thieves and sadists and religious orgiasts on the public highways" (*HM* 146). The humour of this passage is redoubled by Lovecraft's bland assumption that such anarchy ought to be no surprise in a race so wholly devoted to aesthetic appreciation.

The in-jokes in the collaboration "In the Walls of Eryx" (1936) have long been known; and we may note the number of unkind references to Forrest J Ackerman (the "wriggling akmans," the "efjay weeds"), indicating Lovecraft's continued irritation with Ackerman after their conflict in "The Boiling Point" letter column in the *Fantasy Fan* of 1933–34. The "sificlighs" (Science Fiction League) also make no reputable appearance, and the "farnoth-flies" (a reference to Farnsworth Wright) are depicted as devouring the dead body of Frederick N. Dwight "of Koenig's [= H. C. Koenig, associate of Lovecraft's] division" (*D* 320). This tale differs from Lovecraft's other satires on the science fiction tale, "The Battle That Ended the Century" and "Collapsing Cosmoses," in that the basic aim of the tale is serious; and readers not familiar with the specific literary controversies in which Lovecraft was engaged could understand few of these in-jokes.

"The Haunter of the Dark" (1935) is similar in this regard. We know that the tale was designed as a reply to Robert Bloch's "The Shambler from the Stars," where the central character—intended to be Lovecraft—is annihilated. Prompted by a suggestion by a reader of *Weird Tales* (*Uncollected Letters* 36), Lovecraft wrote his tale with Bloch ("Robert Blake") as the central character. But the comparatively obvious in-jokes—Blake, the author of weird fiction, lives in a home modelled upon Lovecraft's own residence at 66 College Street—give way quickly, and the majority of the narrative is quite serious. Humour and in-jokes are thus never made the core of the story, as they are in "The Battle That Ended the Century" (whose initial inspiration was R. H. Barlow's), although the tale's superficial genesis certainly has comic overtones.

In many other of Lovecraft's serious narratives do we find puns insinuated at random moments. Toward the close of *At the Mountains of Madness*, at the very moment when the climax is being reached, Lovecraft notes that Danforth's impressions about the "wind-pipings . . . around the lofty mountain caves. . . *chimed*" with the narrator's (MM 97). In "The Shadow out of Time" it is noted that the archaeologist Mackenzie seemed to have stumbled "upon the remains of an unknown civilisation [i.e., that of the Great Race] older than any *dreamed* of before" (*DH* 405), a sly allusion to Peaslee's dreams about the Great Race. One of Nahum Gardner's sons, in "The Colour out of Space," is said to have been "going to pieces for days" (*DH* 68), another use of a colloquial idiom made to serve literally. This reminds us of Lovecraft's description of Charles Dexter Ward, who is said to have been "thoroughly master of himself" (MM 160) all the way up to the time when Curwen finally supplanted him.

In "The Dreams in the Witch House" it is stated that "Dombrowski must attend to the poisoning of those rats in the walls" (MM 283)—an allusion, of course, to Lovecraft's own tale written a decade before. Although this particular example fits more into the category of in-joke (for those not knowledgeable of his previous work would not understand the reference), we may note Lovecraft's fondness for citing the actual title of a tale within the text. A more amusing example is found in *The Case of Charles Dexter Ward*, since Lovecraft was not sure whether to title the novel *The Case of Charles Dexter Ward* or *The Madness out of Time* (*SL* 2.100). He neatly solved the problem by naming both near the end: "The madness out of time had subsided, and the case of Charles Dexter Ward was closed" (MM 234).

The third type of humour in Lovecraft must now be considered. Here we are concerned with that bitter, cynical, Juvenalian satire which is directed toward two somewhat related matters, both central to his whole philosophical thought—the belief in the utter triviality of existence in a vast and purposeless universe, and a condemnation of the bland ignorance of common people, particularly those who have little appreciation of art. The first can be said to infuse the whole of Lovecraft's fictional work—since he himself stated that "all my tales are based on the fundamental premise that common human laws and interests and emotions have no validity or significance in the vast cosmos-at-large" (SL 2.150)—but more specifically we find it in certainly openly satirical passages where the monstrous futility of all life is stated or implied. The most obvious example of this cynicism is "The Silver Key," which is less a tale than, as Fritz Leiber long ago noted (488), a clear utterance of Lovecraft's philosophical stance. A passage near the opening contains some of the bitterest words in all Lovecraft:

> Wise men told him his simple fancies were inane and childish, and he believed it because he could see that they might easily be so. What he failed to recall was that the deeds of reality are just as inane and childish, and even more absurd because their actors persist in fancying them full of meaning and purpose as the blind cosmos grinds on aimlessly from nothing to something and from something to nothing again, neither heeding nor knowing the wishes or existence of the minds that flicker for a second now and then in the darkness. (MM 409)

Equally blunt is a statement written by Lovecraft at the end of R. H. Barlow's "'Till A' the Seas'":

> And now at last the earth is dead. The final, pitiful survivor had perished. All the teeming billions; the slow aeons; the empires and civilisations of mankind were summed up in this poor twisted form—and how titanically meaningless it all had been! Now indeed had come an end and climax to all the efforts of humanity—how monstrous and incredible a climax in the eyes of those poor complacent fools of the prosperous days! Not ever again would the planet know the thunderous trampling of human millions—or even the crawling of lizards and the buzz of insects, for they, too, had gone. Now was come the reign of sapless branches and endless fields of tough grasses. Earth, like its cold, imperturbable moon, was given over to silence and blackness for ever. (HM 428)

The idea is stated more subtly in *At the Mountains of Madness*. It is first noted that the Old Ones may have "created all earth-life as jest or mistake" (MM 22), and later the narrators see on the bas-reliefs "a shambling primitive mammal, used sometimes for food and sometimes as an amusing buffoon by the land dwellers, whose vaguely simian and human foreshadowings were unmistakable" (MM 65). This is probably one of the most cynical and misanthropic utterances ever made; the degradation of humanity can go no further. But even this is not the end; for at the last it is remarked even of the Old Ones that "Nature had played a hellish jest on them" (MM 95-96). Human beings are thus merely the dupes of dupes, and no life-form can escape the grinning phantom of Nature. We are reminded of Lovecraft's response to a query as to why he did not include more open humour in his tales:

> Humour itself is but a superficial view of that which is in truth both tragic and terrible—the contrast between human pretence and cosmic mechanical reality. Humour is but the faint terrestrial echo of the hideous laughter of the blind mad gods that squat leeringly and sardonically in caverns beyond the Milky Way. It is a hollow thing, sweet on the outside, but filled with the pathos of fruitless aspiration. . . . But I cannot help seeing beyond the tinsel of humour, and recognizing the pitiful basis of jest—the world is indeed comic, but the joke is on mankind. (CE 5.54)

We see here a connexion between this satire on the meaninglessness of existence and that directed toward the folly of mankind. The latter is also noted in *At the Mountains of Madness*, where it is written: "It would be tragic if any were to be allured to that realm of death [i.e., the Antarctic] by the very warning meant to discourage them" (MM 58). Lovecraft might have written that it would be *ironic* if such a thing occurred; and that he saw the frequent connexion between irony and tragedy (we think of Scalinger's deeming the satires of Juvenal as *satirae tragicae*) is seen by a letter in the *Providence Sunday Journal* in defence of "Brick Row": "To lose such a generous, vivid fragment of the poetry of history at this late date, and for no valid reason, would be a tragedy peculiarly ironic" (MW 512). More openly we see Lovecraft's condemnation of the unimaginativeness of the herd in "The Strange High House in the Mist," describing Olney's life after his meeting with the Terrible Old Man:

> And ever since that hour, through dull dragging years of greyness and weariness, the philosopher has laboured and eaten and slept and done uncomplaining the suitable deeds of a citizen. Not any more does he long for the magic of farther hills, or sigh for secrets that peer like green reefs from a bottomless sea. The sameness of his days no longer gives him sorrow, and well-disciplined thoughts have grown enough for his imagination. His good wife waxes stouter and his children older and prosier and more useful, and he never fails to smile correctly with pride when the occasion calls for it. In his glance there is not any restless light, and if he ever listens for solemn bells or elfin horns it is only at night when old dreams are wandering. He has never seen Kingsport again, for his family disliked the funny old houses, and complained that the drains were impossibly bad. They have a trim bungalow now

at Briston Highlands, where no tall crags tower, and the neighbors are urban and modern. (D 284)

The idea that the only criterion of value for human achievement is intellectual or aesthetic achievement runs like a leitmotif in Lovecraft's fiction and is in fact the core of the plot in "Beyond the Wall of Sleep," wherein an extraterrestrial entity remarks upon Joe Slater after his death:

> "He is better dead, for he was unfit to bear the active intellect of cosmic entity. His gross body could not undergo the needed adjustments between ethereal life and planet life. He was too much of an animal, too little a man; yet it is through his deficiency that you have come to discover me, for the cosmic and planet souls rightly should never meet. He has been my torment and diurnal prison for forty-two of your terrestrial years . . ." (D 34)

In "The Call of Cthulhu," too, we find that only certain intellects are affected by strange dreams inspired by Cthulhu:

> Average people in society and business—New England's traditional "salt of the earth"—gave an almost completely negative result, though scattered cases of uneasy but formless nocturnal impressions appear here and there, always between March 23d and April 2nd.—the period of young Wilcox's delirium. Scientific men were little more affected, though four cases of vague description suggest fugitive glimpses of strange landscapes, and in one case there is mentioned a dread of something abnormal.
>
> It was from the artists and poets that the pertinent answers came, and I know that panic would have broken loose had they been able to compare notes. (DH 131)

This somewhat bizarre elitism is also present in "The Shadow out of Time," where only certain human beings are selected for exchange with the Great Race:

> Another thing that worried me during my investigation was the somewhat greater frequency of cases where a brief, elusive glimpse of the typical nightmares was afforded to cases not visited by well-defined amnesia. These persons were largely of mediocre mind or less—some so primitive that they could scarcely be thought of as vehicle for abnormal scholarship and preternatural mental acquisitions. For a second they would be fired with alien force—then a backward lapse, and a thin, swift-fading memory of unhuman horrors. . . . Had something been groping blindly[5] through time from some unsuspected

---

5. "Blindly," of course, is not intended to be taken literally, since it is very obvious that the Great Race's gropings are anything but blind; rather, the word is to be understood in a quasi-passive sense similar to a common usage of the Latin *caecum* (lit. "blind," but also "unseen," "hidden"); cf. Lucretius 1.407-9.

abyss in Nature? Were these faint cases monstrous, sinister experiments of a kind and authorship utterly beyond sane belief? (*DH* 378)

Satire is also directed frequently toward those characters in Lovecraft's tales who flatly refuse to believe in the possibility of supernatural (or, rather, supernormal) occurrences. In "The Colour out of Space" the sceptical professors from Miskatonic University are called "wise men" and "sages" in a tone whose irony and sarcasm are hardly veiled. In "The Unnamable" a ferocious satire is waged against Joel Manton, whose literal-mindedness, religiosity, and aesthetic insensitivity are ridiculed:

> We know things, he said, only through our five senses or our religious intuitions; wherefore it is quite impossible to refer to any object or spectacle which cannot be clearly depicted by the solid definitions of fact or the correct doctrines of theology— preferably those of the Congregationalists, with whatever modifications tradition and Sir Arthur Conan Doyle may supply. . . . It was his view that only our normal, objective experiences possess any aesthetic significance, and that it is the province of the artist not so much to rouse strong emotion by action, ecstasy, and astonishment, as to maintain a placid interest and appreciation by accurate, detailed, transcripts of every-day affairs. (*D* 200-201)

In four of Lovecraft's major tales we find that the supernatural occurrences are ridiculed by the press. In "The Dunwich Horror" there was, "tucked away obscurely in a corner of the *Arkham Advertiser* . . . a facetious little item from the Associated Press, telling what a record-breaking monster the bootleg whiskey of Dunwich had raised up" (*DH* 186-87), while in "The Colour out of Space" "the editor of the *Gazette* [wrote] a humorous article . . . in which the dark fears of rustics were held up to polite ridicule" (*DH* 63). In "The Whisperer in Darkness" it is Wilmarth himself who, in the *Arkham Advertiser*, *Rutland Herald*, and *Brattleboro Reformer* scoffs at the wild suggestions of certain writers on the nature of the curious bodies floating down the rivers from the mountains. Blake, in "The Haunter of the Dark," is thrown "into a veritable fever of horror" by some "half-humorous items about the Federal Hill restlessness" (*DH* 107) in the *Providence Journal*. In all these cases Lovecraft is employing a type of dramatic irony; far from wishing to convey that the fantastic events in his tales are delusions, he means to imply that they have not only occurred but that those who, in their stolid and complacent rationalism, ridicule the idea of supra-rational (Onderdonk's "super-normal") events are the more foolish for their unimaginativeness. Indeed, the entire opening of "The Haunter of the Dark" is a case in point: it is precisely the third-person narrator's peremptory dismissal of "less rational [i.e., supra-rational] and commonplace theories" (*DH* 93) on Robert Blake's death that makes us the more certain that his death was not as commonplace as "cautious investigators" believe.

In sum we can say that it is precisely unimaginativeness—metaphysical and aesthetic—that, according to Lovecraft, allows most human beings to be unaware of their abysmal inconsequence in terms of space, time, and infinity, and which makes them suitable for the oftentimes brutal satire which we find not infrequently in his tales.

Now that we have briefly examined the various types of humour and satire in Lovecraft's serious "weird tales," we can now attempt to resolve the apparent contradictions between his declaration that humour was a weakening element in fantasy fiction and the occurrence of humour in his own work. The contradiction is merely apparent in a number of ways. First we must conclude that, despite all the examples cited above, humour and satire in the final analysis hold a quite small place in his serious work; they appear randomly, and are almost never the centre of the plot. This applies much more to puns and in-jokes than to satire, but even satire seems never to have inspired the very theme of a tale—with the possible exceptions of "Beyond the Wall of Sleep," "The Unnamable," "The Silver Key," and "The Strange High House in the Mist." In all these tales the satire is directed toward the ignorance, unimaginativeness, and commonplaceness of human beings lost in an aimless cosmos; and all manifest this idea in different ways.

"The Terrible Old Man" also has a satiric base, but its aim is quite different. Here is involved a cynical (and somewhat simplistic) display of the age-old axiom that "Crime does not pay," along with a satire not merely on the infiltration of foreigners into New England but on the social exclusivity of New England society itself: a satirical tone can hardly be missed in such a line as "Angelo Ricci and Joe Czanek and Manual Silva were not of Kingsport blood; they were of that new and heterogeneous alien stock which lies *outside the charmed circle of New-England life*" (DH 273; my emphasis). The satire here is double-edged, and L. Sprague de Camp has wholly misread the tale in deeming it "one of those hostile snarls at 'aliens' which . . . formed a *leitmotif* of Lovecraft's fiction" (148). It is no more a hostile snarl than is Lovecraft's playful comment that he wished to drink the hot blood of a Celt in his hollowed-out skull. Moreover, Lovecraft's own culture is not excluded from the satire; a satire that, indeed, is expressed with infinitely greater bitterness in the opening of "The Picture in the House." "The Terrible Old Man" is in fact a *jeu d'esprit*, similar both in tone and theme to "The Cats of Ulthar." Both tales would find better company beside "A Reminiscence of Dr. Samuel Johnson" than beside "The Dunwich Horror."

Granting, then, that humour and satire are comparatively rare and quite subordinate in Lovecraft's fiction, what are we to make of his remark that humour "as an ingredient of the weird tale . . . is a definitely diluting element"? It is clear that the type of humour to which Lovecraft refers is certainly not the "sardonic comedy and graveyard humour" ("Supernatural Horror in Literature," *D* 406) that he obviously enjoyed in Ambrose Bierce, but the humour where the author is merely laughing genially at his horrors rather than taking them seriously—the type of humour encountered in Wilde's "The Canterville Ghost." One gets the impression that Lovecraft regarded such humour as disrespectful of the dignity of the weird tale—an unseemly kind of mockery. He himself certainly used humour; but his humour is neither genial nor that of the grave—it is that of the abyss.

Finally, what is the purpose of Lovecraft's humour and satire? The motives are clearly different in connexion with the respective forms of humour being employed. Puns obviously indicate his fascination with language, while in-jokes seem to confirm his uncommercial and "amateur" concept of writing: Lovecraft never consciously intended his tales to appeal to a wide audience, and in employing in-jokes he was wilfully restricting still further the number of those who could fully understand his tales (insofar, of course, as it is possible for the most fully informed reader fully to understand the work of an author). In many cases the in-jokes could be comprehended only by his very closest associates, and in not a few cases it is likely that they could he comprehended only by Lovecraft himself.

With satire the case is somewhat different: the satire found in his tales clearly connects with his cynicism and his pessimism about the intellectual and aesthetic development of common people; and in many tales the satire is so prevalent and obvious that we must infer Lovecraft's conscious desire to convey these ideas and attitudes along with the "images" and "moods" so essential to his aesthetic theory. We know that, in his involvement with amateur journalism, Lovecraft was often taken to task for the severity of his views anent mankind in essays and poems alike; and certain sharper critics even noticed the pessimism in his early "Dunsanian" tales. John Ravenor Bullen, member of the Transatlantic Circulator, remarked of "The White Ship" that it was a "powerful prose-poem in which the allegorist informs us somewhat sorrowfully that he was once an idealist but is now a materialist" (*In Defence of Dagon* 5). And while the validity of Bullen's view can certainly be questioned, there is no denying that Lovecraft often wrote certain stories with an openly philosophical and satirical intent so as more emphatically to convey his worldview than might be possible in essays or poetry. Indeed, the very fact that Farnsworth Wright was so unwilling to print "The Silver Key," being forced to do so only because Lovecraft refused to send him other tales unless it found publication (SL 2.253), would alone prove its openly philosophical and manifestly non-commercial purpose.

The matter of whence Lovecraft was led to instil satire and humour in his fiction is not quite clear. Rheinhart Kleiner correctly remarked that in his satirical verse Lovecraft followed "familiar lines, particularly those laid down by Butler, Swift, and Pope" (402), but it is hard to see how the satirical element in these poets was transferred into his fiction. Lovecraft seemed either unaware or unappreciative of the satiric element in the fiction of his own time: he seemed not to care for Aldous Huxley, and not to have read Evelyn Waugh (whose first novel appeared in 1928) or Nathanael West. Ben Hecht's *Erik Dorn*, whose ferocious satire on the meaningless of existence is as bitter as anything in Lovecraft, met only with Lovecraft's scorn and distaste;[6] nor did he care for Hecht's two fantasy novels, *Fantazius Mallare* and *The Kingdom of Evil*, both of which contain teeth-gnashing satire on the plebianism of the herd (see especially the dedication to *Fantazius Mallare,* a torrent of uncontrolled invective in every way worthy of Juvenal).[7] Ambrose Bierce's cynicism and "graveyard humour" seem to have influenced him singularly little, save perhaps in "The Unnamable" and "In the Vault."[8] While it is evident that the particular ferocity of Lovecraft's satire owes something to that of Juvenal, Swift, Johnson, Voltaire, and others, we must look elsewhere for his whole conception of the joke that is existence.

The answer may be found in certain philosophers who shaped Lovecraft's worldview during his youth. Scientists—Darwin, Huxley Haeckel, and others—had laid the substructure for his materialist stance, and his early absorption of Schopenhauer and Nietzsche probably did as much as anything to imbue him with a bent for the mockery of mankind. Lovecraft could hardly have failed to notice the satire, sarcasm, and cynicism that occasionally enters the work of such other philosophers (whom he encountered in the later 1920s) as George Santayana, Bertrand Russell, and Joseph Wood Krutch. It may well have been his absorption of such philosophers that made him expand his satire from the mere mockery of manners employed by the poets of Augustan Rome and Au-

---

6. Cf., however his remark that "The *Erik Dorn* of Ben Hecht I did peruse because it contained a hatred for mankind which itself forms an unique and refreshing element in literature" (SL 1.284).

7. See HPL to R. H. Barlow, [25 March 1935], expressing his disapproval of the obscenity of *Fantazius Mallare* (OFF 227).

8. See Clark Ashton Smith to HPL, [11 March 1930]: "'In the Vault' . . . has the realistic grimness of Bierce" (ms., JHL).

gustan England to the more pervasive satire on the "tragedy, 'Man'" and the cosmic jest which the universe has played on life.

We have hardly covered the whole range of Lovecraft's humour and satire: his poetry abounds in it; his essays—particularly such polemics as "Lucubrations Lovecraftian" and "The Omnipresent Philistine," as well as many of his essays in the *Conservative* contain it in plenty; and his letters are rarely lacking in parody, sarcasm, and wit. A humourless Lovecraft has proven to be as much a myth as a humourless Poe; but in his tales the satire is so often of a particularly mirthless character that we the more frequently wince than laugh.

Works Cited

Conover, Willis, and H. P. Lovecraft. *Lovecraft at Last*. Arlington, VA: Carrollton-Clark, 1975.

de Camp, L Sprague. *Lovecraft: A Biography*. Garden City, NY: Doubleday, 1975.

Kleiner, Rheinhart. "A Note on Howard P. Lovecraft's Verse." 1919. In Peter Cannon, ed. *Lovecraft Remembered*. Sauk City, WI: Arkham House, 1998. 401–2.

Leiber, Fritz. "A Literary Copernicus." 1949. In Peter Cannon, ed. *Lovecraft Remembered*. Sauk City, WI: Arkham House, 1998. 455–66.

Lovecraft, H. P. *In Defence of Dagon*. Ed. S. T. Joshi. West Warwick, RI: Necronomicon Press, 1985.

———. *Uncollected Letters*. Ed. S. T. Joshi. West Warwick, RI: Necronomicon, Press, 1986.

A Guide to the Lovecraft Fiction Manuscripts at the John Hay Library

After the publication of my essay "Textual Problems in Lovecraft" (*Lovecraft Studies*, Spring 1982), and my three-volume corrected edition of Lovecraft's collected fiction (Arkham House, 1984–86), several critics have called for further information on the manuscript sources of Lovecraft's tales. I provide such information here. The following article will allow the reader to understand how and why I made certain decisions regarding the texts of Lovecraft's fiction. This essay was written before the emergence of my editions; accordingly, when I refer to "Arkham House editions," I allude to those editions prior to my own.

This listing is divided into two parts: a) works by Lovecraft alone; b) revisions and collaborations. Considerable attention has been given to the transmission of the texts from the autograph manuscript (A.Ms.) to the typewritten manuscript (T.Ms.) through important publications of the story to the present day. In many cases it has been revealed that the texts have suffered considerable damage in the course of forty to sixty years of transmission. The revisions and collaborations usually require an explanation of the very process of composition, since this usually has much to do with the textual history of the work. While manuscripts exist for almost all Lovecraft's original works, the manuscripts for his revisions and collaborations are comparatively few.

Some abbreviations have been used to denote important appearances of Lovecraft's work. They are as follows:

AH 1939   *The Outsider and Others* (Arkham House, 1939)
AH 1943   *Beyond the Wall of Sleep* (Arkham House, 1943)
AH 1944   *Marginalia* (Arkham House, 1944)
AH 1963   *The Dunwich Horror and Others* (Arkham House, 1963)
AH 1964   *At the Mountains of Madness and Other Novels* (Arkham House, 1964)
AH 1965   *Dagon and Other Macabre Tales* (Arkham House, 1965)
AH 1970   *The Horror in the Museum and Other Revisions* (Arkham House, 1970)

All the above editions of Lovecraft's tales were prepared by August Derleth.

A. Works by Lovecraft Alone

1. *At the Mountains of Madness.* a) A.Ms., 80 pp.; b) T.Ms., [1] + 115 pp.

The A.Ms. is Lovecraft's original draft, written in pen, extensively revised and interlined, and slightly revised at a later date in pencil. The last page records the dates of writing: "Begun Feby. 24, 1931. / Finish'd March 22, 1931." The T.Ms. was prepared by Lovecraft and was "Finished May 1, 1931" (see p. 115; how typical of Lovecraft to note the completion of what must have been an arduous series of sessions at the typewriter!). The title page of the T.Ms. bears a handwritten "Schedule of Circulation" (persons to whom the ms. was to be sent before publication): August Derleth to Donald Wandrei to Clark Ashton Smith to Bernard Austin Dwyer to Lovecraft.

Textually this work is the most curious of all Lovecraft's tales. Lovecraft revised the tale in the process of preparing the T.Ms.; but the text of the tale as ultimately printed (*Astounding Stories*, Feb.-Mar.-Apr. 1936; AH 1939, 1964) diverges radically from the T.Ms. Some of these divergences seem to stem from revisions made later by Lovecraft: the text contains several passages where the hypothesis is made that the Antarctic continent might originally have been two land masses separated by a frozen sea; this hypotheses was proven false by various expeditions to the Antarctic in 1933-35, hence Lovecraft must have revised the passages. These passages (see, e.g., AH 1964, p. 8) are revised in all printed appearances, but not in the T.Ms. or A.Ms.; Lovecraft must have made a carbon copy of the T.Ms., made the revisions there, and had this text sent (through Julius Schwartz) to *Astounding Stories*. The *Astounding* text, however, contains many other divergences from the T.Ms., and most of these are probably editorial alterations by *Astounding* and not revisions by Lovecraft. In some cases, however, it is difficult to decide whether the divergences are by Lovecraft or by *Astounding*. The Arkham House texts follow not the *Astounding* text nor the T.Ms., but Lovecraft's annotated copies of *Astounding* (now in the John Hay Library), where he has pencilled in many (but by no means all) the deletions and alterations made by *Astounding*. The Arkham House texts thus still contain some 1500 divergences from the text as Lovecraft probably intended it.

2. "Azathoth." A.Ms., 2 pp.

A fragment of a never-completed novel (see *SL* 1.185). The ms. is Lovecraft's original draft in pen, bearing some revisions and interlineations.

3. "Beyond the Wall of Sleep." T.Ms., 12 pp.

The T.Ms. was prepared by Lovecraft, but incorporates some revisions made after the tale's first appearance (*Pine Cones*, October 1919). Since the next publication (*Fantasy Fan*, October 1934) followed the T.Ms., it must have been prepared between 1919 and 1934; and since the verso of one sheet contains a letter to Lovecraft dated July 1925, the T.Ms. was probably prepared about this time. *Weird Tales* (March 1938) followed the *Fantasy Fan* appearance (which made numerous errors in the text), and the Arkham House editions followed the *Weird Tales* text.

4. ["The Book."] A.Ms., 3 pp.

The title, as well as the date of writing ("1934?"), were supplied by R. H. Barlow and are written on the ms. The draft is somewhat revised and interlined, suggesting an actual tale rather than merely the record of a dream. The date of writing is uncertain, but the script is the very small, close hand of Lovecraft's later years, hence 1933 or 1934 may be a probable conjecture (see my article "On 'The Book,'" where the dating of late 1933 is hypothesised). The last paragraph has been written at a somewhat later time in pencil.

All appearances derive from Barlow's edition in *Leaves* (1938), which followed the ms. accurately enough.

5. "The Call of Cthulhu." T.Ms., [1] + 32 pp.

The T.Ms. was prepared by Lovecraft. The first appearance (*Weird Tales*, February 1928) followed the T.Ms., but made its usual editorial alterations; this text was followed in the Arkham House editions. When the tale was to be anthologised in Harré's *Beware After Dark!* (1929), Lovecraft sent the T.Ms. (or a copy of it) to Harré, hence the text there is quite superior to the texts deriving from *Weird Tales*, although the Harré text is by no means wholly faithful to the T.Ms.

6. *The Case of Charles Dexter Ward.* a) A.Ms., [1] + 147 + [10] pp. b) T.Ms., 23 pp. (incomplete).

The A.Ms. is written on the back of correspondence to Lovecraft and other odd pieces of paper widely differing in size and shape. It contains extensive revisions, deletions, and interlineations, more toward the beginning than toward the end. The last page of the A.Ms. records the date of completion: March 1, 1927. (Contrast this with the date of November 1927 given by L. Sprague de Camp or 1927–28 given by Derleth.) The T.Ms. was prepared by R. H. Barlow and is partially corrected by Lovecraft.

The first printed appearance (excluding the abridged version in *Weird Tales*, May–July 1941) was in AH 1943; it did not follow the T.Ms., but worked wholly from the A.Ms. No sign of the T.Ms. prepared by Donald Wandrei (see Derleth and Wandrei, letter to the editor, *Weird Tales*, May 1941) has come to light; perhaps Lovecraft destroyed it (as Wandrei suggests in the letter). The Arkham House edition (especially AH 1964) contains many errors, largely because of Derleth's inability to read Lovecraft's handwriting. The T.Ms. also contains some revisions by Lovecraft that have obviously not been followed in the Arkham House editions.

7. "Celephaïs." T.Ms., 7 pp.

The T.Ms. was not prepared by Lovecraft (but bears the diaeresis that has not been followed in any printed versions) and may have been prepared by Donald Wandrei: the typewriter face does not appear to be Barlow's, and the text is apparently quite accurate—a fact not common to T.Mss. prepared by Barlow.

The first appearance (*Marvel Tales*, May 1934) followed the T.Ms., making several errors. This text was followed by the Arkham House editions, where a few more errors were made.

8. "Cool Air." T.Ms., 10 pp.

The T.Ms. was prepared by Lovecraft. The first appearance (*Tales of Magic and Mystery*, March 1928) followed the T.Ms., but made some curious editorial alterations of phrases. This text has been followed in all subsequent appearances.

9. "Dagon." T.Ms., 3 pp.

The T.Ms. was prepared by Lovecraft and is one of the five single-spaced mss. sent to *Weird Tales* in 1923 (it is numbered "4" at the top in pencil). No copy of the double-spaced T.Ms. that Lovecraft must have sent subsequently to *Weird Tales* has been found. The existing T.Ms. must date after the first appearance (*Vagrant*, November 1919), as it incorporates some slight revisions made after that appearance. *Weird Tales* (October 1923) followed the theoretical double-spaced T.Ms. (presumably identical to the existing T.Ms.), making a number of apparently deliberate alterations. Later *Weird Tales* appearances (January 1936, November 1951) made some abridgements and alterations in the text, but these are not relevant to the textual history of the tale. The Arkham House editions follow the T.Ms.

10. ["The Descendant."] A.Ms., 3 pp.

The title for this fragment was bestowed by R. H. Barlow, who wrote it on the ms. and used it in its first appearance (*Leaves*, 1938). The A.Ms. contains comparatively few revisions and interlineations and is, as Derleth hypothesised, probably the transcript of a dream.

The AH 1965 edition does not indicate that the brief first paragraph of the tale was deleted by Lovecraft in the A.Ms. See now my essay "On 'The Descendant'" for the view that this paragraph may not even belong to the fragment.

11. "The Doom That Came to Sarnath." a) A.Ms., [1] + 9 pp.; b) T.Ms., 9 pp.

The A.Ms. is not the original draft, as it bears no revisions and interlineations whatever; moreover, it incorporates some revisions made after the first appearance (*Scot*, June 1920), hence must date after that appearance. Perhaps Lovecraft recopied the text from the *Scot* appearance (a comparatively accurate one), making revisions along the way. The A.Ms. is still in a youthful hand, however, and probably does not date beyond 1925. The T.Ms. was probably prepared by Barlow, since it is rather inaccurate and bears some autograph marks that seem to be in his hand.

The second appearance (*Marvel Tales*, March–April 1935) followed the T.Ms.; the *Weird Tales* appearance (June 1938) followed the *Marvel Tales* text; AH 1943 followed the *Weird Tales* text; AH 1965 followed the AH 1943 text. Each appearance repeated the errors of the preceding text and made new ones, so that the latest text departs radically from the A.Ms.

12. *The Dream-Quest of Unknown Kadath.* a) A.Ms., 110 pp. b) T.Ms., [1] + 68 pp. (incomplete).

The A.Ms. is not as extensively revised and interlined as that of *The Case of Charles Dexter Ward*, indicating that less polishing was done on what Lovecraft regarded as "practice in carrying plot threads for a considerable distance" (*SL* 2.99). It is written entirely on the back of correspondence to Lovecraft. Lovecraft debated upon the title of the novel (see verso of p. 1), but finally settled on the one as we know it. The T.Ms. was prepared by Barlow and contains almost no corrections by Lovecraft: even some words that Barlow could not decipher from the A.Ms. (e.g., "immanent" in paragraph 2) were not supplied by Lovecraft. He did, however, alter some names on the T.Ms. (e.g., "Thok" for "Throk"; cf. "To a Dreamer," l. 13). In the first appearance (AH 1943) the editors followed the T.Ms. until it left off, then worked from the A.Ms. Their text is not bad (since August Derleth could read Lovecraft's hand somewhat better than Barlow), but there are still some ludicrous misreadings (e.g., "air out" for "an ant"—see AH 1964, p. 375). The Arkham House text contains some 400 errors.

13. "The Dreams in the Witch House." a) A.Ms., 34 + [1] pp. b) T.Ms., [1] + 35 pp.

The A.Ms. (which does not include a hyphen in "Witch House") is one of Lovecraft's few pencil drafts and is therefore somewhat difficult to read now. It contains extensive revisions, interlineations, and deletions. The last page records the date of completion: "Feby. 28, 1932." The T.Ms. was prepared (without Lovecraft's knowledge) by August Derleth (see *SL* 4.146), and, though making some severe errors, actually follows Lovecraft's text not inadequately.

Derleth sent the T.Ms. to *Weird Tales* (see *SL* 4.154), where it appeared—with the usual editorial alterations—in the issue for July 1933. The *Weird Tales* text made some celebrated blunders that Lovecraft pointed out when he read the galleys (see *SL* 4.213), but which were not corrected before publication. Lovecraft's copy of the issue (John Hay Library) contains only one correction in pencil ("known" for "human"). The first book appearance (AH 1939) wisely followed the T.Ms., hence its text is fairly sound; but the reprint (AH 1964) made the curious mistake of following the *Weird Tales* appearance, with the result that its text is very poor. One is at a loss to understand why Derleth did not use his own earlier text to prepare the later one.

14. "The Dunwich Horror." T.Ms., [1] + 48 pp.

The T.Ms. was prepared by Lovecraft, but bears curious marks made apparently by Barlow, where parts of the text have been bracketed off. These marks seem, however, to have had nothing to do with the transmission of the text. There is also a note by Barlow on the title page alerting Derleth to a typographical error between pp. 30 and 40 of the ms.; this error corresponds to a passage on p. 194, l. 4 of the AH 1963 text, where "out. 'It's . . ." was on the T.Ms. rendered as "out, 'It's . . ."

The textual history of the tale is simple. *Weird Tales* (April 1929) followed the T.Ms., making the usual alterations. AH 1939 also went back to the T.Ms., making few alterations; the AH 1963 text followed AH 1939. Few errors thus exist in the latest edition of the text.

15. "Facts concerning the Late Arthur Jermyn and His Family." T.Ms., 5 pp.

This is another of the T.Mss. prepared by Lovecraft and sent to *Weird Tales* in 1923 (numbered "5" at the top in pencil). It must date after the first appearance in the *Wolverine* (March–June 1921), since it incorporates revisions made after that appearance. The ms. (or a double-spaced version of it) was followed by *Weird Tales* when the tale appeared in the issue for April 1924. More than the usual amount of editorial alterations (primarily in paragraphing) were made, but fortunately all Arkham House editions derive from the T.Ms., hence are comparatively sound.

16. "The Festival." T.Ms., 10 pp.

The T.Ms. is not by Lovecraft and may be by Donald Wandrei (it seems comparatively accurate); moreover, it must date after the first appearance (*Weird Tales*, January 1925), since it incorporates revisions made after that appearance. It is not certain whether the second *Weird Tales* appearance (October 1933) followed the T.Ms. or the first *Weird Tales* printing: it does incorporate most of the revisions, but repeats many of the editorial alterations made in the first appearance. Probably Lovecraft merely sent to *Weird Tales* a list of the revisions in the tale. The Arkham House editions derive from the T.Ms., hence contain comparatively few divergences from it.

17. "From Beyond." A.Ms., 11 pp.

The A.Ms. is Lovecraft's original draft, written on the back of correspondence to him. The last page records the date of writing: "Novr. 16, 1920." No T.Ms. has come to light, but one must have prepared for the tale's first appearance (*Fantasy Fan*, June 1934). That appearance contains certain important divergences from the A.Ms. (particularly in paragraphing) that are probably not printing errors but revisions made in the hypothetical T.Ms. It appears, however, that Lovecraft may not have prepared the T.Ms. himself: although the *Fantasy Fan* appearance contains some phrases not in the A.Ms. (which might easily have been added on the T.Ms. by hand), there are other omissions and errors in the appearance that may be attributed more to its derivation from a faulty T.Ms. than from errors of its own. Moreover, the A.Ms. contains certain marks and annotations by Lovecraft (e.g., the fact that the central character's name is to be changed from "Henry Annesley" to "Crawford Tillinghast") that would be superfluous unless Lovecraft were making instructions for someone else preparing the T.Ms. Nevertheless, some of the divergences between the A.Ms. and the *Fantasy Fan* appearance are surely due to wilful revisions by Lovecraft. The Arkham House editions derive from the *Fantasy Fan* appearance, making some additional errors and correcting some obvious printing errors made there.

18. "He." T.Ms., 12 pp.

The T.Ms. was prepared by Lovecraft; the date of writing is written on the last page ("Aug. 11, 1925") but in Barlow's hand; the date is, nevertheless, corroborated by an entry in Lovecraft's Diary for 1925. The T.Ms. was sent to *Weird Tales*, where it appeared with the usual alterations in the issue for September 1926. The Arkham House editions derive, however, from the T.Ms., and thus are fairly accurate.

19. "Herbert West—Reanimator." T.Ms., 3 + 3 + 3 + 3 + 3 + 3 pp.

The T.Ms. is single-spaced and each of the six episodes is numbered separately; it is likely that Lovecraft sent each episode separately for the serialisation in *Home Brew* (February–July 1921). Arkham House seems to have followed the *Home Brew* appearance when reprinting the tale (AH 1943). The *Weird Tales* serialisation (March 1942–November 1943) is irrelevant to the textual history of the story, since all subsequent publications derive from AH 1943. AH 1965 leaves out some phrases from the text and makes many other errors.

20. "History of the Necronomicon." a) A.Ms., 2 pp. b) T.Ms., 2 + [1] pp. c) T.Ms., [1] + 3 pp.

The A.Ms. is written on the front and back of a letter to Lovecraft (see *Lovecraft at Last*, pp. 104–5); in the corner of the first page Lovecraft has given the ms. to Barlow ("the Curator of the Vaults of Yoh-Vombis") in exchange for preparing a T.Ms. of the work ([c]). The first T.Ms. ([b]) was prepared (apparently from the A.Ms.) by Wilson Shepherd and contains alterations and additions by him in pencil. Obviously he used this T.Ms. to prepare his pamphlet of 1938. Barlow's T.Ms. is not as inaccurate as Shepherd's but still contains some errors. All subsequent appearances derive from Shepherd's pamphlet.

21. "The Horror at Red Hook." T.Ms., 24 pp.

The T.Ms. (typed on the back of correspondence received by him) was prepared by Lovecraft; the A.Ms. is now in the New York Public Library. The last page of the T.Ms. records the date of writing ("August 1–2, 1925") in Barlow's hand, but it is confirmed by the aforementioned Diary of 1925 (see the description of "He").

The T.Ms. was sent to *Weird Tales*, where it appeared (January 1927) with the usual alterations. The Arkham House editions derive from the T.Ms., hence are quite accurate.

22. "The Hound." T.Ms., 5 pp.

This is another of the mss. sent to *Weird Tales* in 1923, although no number is written at the top. The T.Ms. contains some last-minute revisions by Lovecraft in pen (suggested by C. M. Eddy; see *SL* 1.292) which were incorporated in the first appearance—*Weird Tales*, February 1924. AH 1939 derives from the first *Weird Tales* printing and is as a result quite inaccurate, since *Weird Tales* made extensive alterations in the text (particularly in paragraphing). The second *Weird Tales* appearance (September 1929) follows the first, hence is textually irrelevant.

23. "In the Vault." T.Ms., [1] + 10 pp.

The T.Ms. was prepared by Lovecraft; it bears some revisions both in pencil and in pen by him, and apparently some marks made by Barlow and perhaps even August Derleth. Lovecraft sent the T.Ms. (before making the pencil revisions) for publication in the *Tryout* (November 1925); then, as Lovecraft was circulating the ms. to his associates, Derleth decided to type a new draft (see *SL* 4.25) and sent it to *Weird Tales*, where it was published in the issue for April 1932. Derleth apparently typed from the T.Ms. before it was revised in pencil, for the *Weird Tales* text does not include the revisions; moreover, aside from making errors, Derleth may have made wilful alterations in the text: the last line is italicised in *Weird Tales*, but is not italicised in the *Tryout* appearance; the line is underscored in pencil in the existing T.Ms., but in a pencil apparently different from that used by Lovecraft to make his revisions. Was this italicisation added by Derleth? Barlow's annotations include only elucidations of some of the revisions that Lovecraft had scribbled upon the T.Ms. The Arkham House editions derive from the *Weird Tales* appearance, hence are rather inaccurate, since *Weird Tales* made many alterations, aside from not incorporating the revisions that Lovecraft may have made after the *Weird Tales* appearance (or, at any rate, after Derleth prepared the new T.Ms.).

24. "The Lurking Fear." T.Ms., [1] + 12 + [1] pp.

Like "Herbert West—Reanimator," the T.Ms. (prepared by Lovecraft) is single-spaced, though numbered consecutively. Curiously, all important publications derive from the T.Ms.: the first appearance (*Home Brew*, January–April 1923), the *Weird Tales* appearance (June 1928), and the Arkham House editions (AH 1939, 1965). None can be said to be any better than the other: if anything, the *Home Brew* text (rpt. Necronomicon Press, 1977) is the least error-filled. The AH 1965 edition leaves out some lines from the earlier Arkham House editions.

25. "The Nameless City." T.Ms., [1] + 13 pp.

The T.Ms. was prepared by Lovecraft and is an early T.Ms., probably dating before 1925. It must, however, date after the first appearance (*Wolverine*, November 1921), since it incorporates revisions made after that appearance. The T.Ms. was sent to *Fanciful Tales*, appearing in the Fall 1936 issue; that publication made many errors in the text (see *SL* 5.368). Unfortunately, it was followed by AH 1939, and AH 1965 derives from AH 1939; hence the latest text bears many errors, largely in the omission of words and phrases.

26. "Of Evil Sorceries done in New-England of Daemons in no Humane Shape." A.Ms., 3 pp.

This is what Derleth included in the early pages of his "collaboration," *The Lurker at the Threshold* (1945). Derleth extensively altered (although also misread) the text to suit his plot. The A.Ms. is considerably revised and interlined, indicating a quite careful shaping of the archaic prose. The last page does not seem to connect with the first two, but is of the same general flavour; it largely bears a proposed title page for the volume, *Thaumaturgicall Prodigies in the New-English Canaan*, by the Rev. Ward Phillips, though also some fragments of prose.

27. "The Other Gods." a) A.Ms., 8 pp. b) T.Ms., 4 pp.

The A.Ms is Lovecraft's original draft, written on the back of correspondence to him; the first page records the date of writing: "Aug. 14, 1921." The T.Ms. was probably prepared by Donald Wandrei, since it is quite accurate; it is slightly corrected by Lovecraft. The *Fantasy Fan* followed the T.Ms. when it published the tale (November 1933), making comparatively few errors (though making the stupendous mistake of misreading "the seven cryptical books of Hsan" [A.Ms., T.Ms.] as "the seven cryptical books of earth"). The *Weird Tales* appearance (October 1938) derives from the *Fantasy Fan* text, repeating its errors and making the usual alterations. The Arkham House editions derive from the *Weird Tales* text. The *True Supernatural Stories* appearance (October 1934) has not been seen, but may not be textually relevant, since it is clear that all other appearances derive ultimately from the *Fantasy Fan* text. *True Supernatural Stories* may have followed the *Fantasy Fan*, and *Weird Tales* may have followed *True Supernatural Stories*; or the latter may have followed the T.Ms., in which case *Weird Tales* could not have derived from it. In either case the *True Supernatural Stories* appearance does not seem central to the transmission of the text.

28. "Pickman's Model." T.Ms., 15 pp.

The T.Ms. was prepared by Lovecraft, and it was sent to *Weird Tales*, appearing in the issue for October 1927. The T.Ms. bears an alteration in pencil, where the name "Marlborough Street" has been changed to "Newbury Street." The hand is not Lovecraft's, and may be Barlow's. The change, moreover, was made after the *Weird Tales* appearance, since the original reading is retained there. Whether this change was made on Lovecraft's or Barlow's initiative is unclear; although it is unlikely that Barlow would have made the change of his own accord. The Arkham House editions, deriving from the revised T.Ms., bear the reading of "Newbury" and make comparatively few errors in the text.

29. "The Picture in the House." T.Ms., 7 pp.

The T.Ms. was not prepared by Lovecraft and is in a wholly unfamiliar typeface. It must date both after the *National Amateur* (July 1919 [*sic*]) and the *Weird Tales* appearances, since it incorporates revisions made after both publications. It may possibly have been prepared by E. Hoffmann Price, who wished to reprint the tale in an anthology in the 1930s (see *SL* 4.112). Lovecraft may have prepared a T.Ms. from the *National Amateur* appearance and sent it to *Weird Tales*; this T.Ms. was apparently lost, and Lovecraft may have sent to Price the *National Amateur* text with the requisite revisions, so that Price could type the T.Ms. The T.Ms. is full of errors that Lovecraft did not correct, although there are still extensive corrections by him. The Arkham House editions derive from the T.Ms., hence contain all these errors plus others made by themselves. (The famous error in AH 1963–"Lopex" for "Lopez"–has been pointed out long ago.)

30. "The Quest of Iranon." a) A.Ms., 14 pp. b) T.Ms., 8 pp.

The A.Ms. is Lovecraft's original draft, though not containing a great many revisions; it is written on the back of correspondence to him, and the last page records the date of writing: "Feby. 28, 1921." The T.Ms. is by Donald Wandrei (see SL 2.211) and is quite accurate. It bears corrections by Lovecraft in pen. It was probably sent to Weird Tales by Derleth after Lovecraft's death, where it appeared in the issue for March 1939. The Arkham House editions derive from the T.Ms., hence are quite accurate.

31. "The Shadow out of Time." A.Ms., 65 pp.

The discovery of this ms.—Lovecraft gave it to R. H. Barlow, who took it with him to Mexico, then gave it to a female student, who retired to Hawaii, where it was found upon her death and then given to the John Hay Library— is a remarkable tale in itself. The text is written in a school composition book, possibly dating to Lovecraft's Hope Street High School days. It is full of crossouts, interlineations (some appearing vertically in the margins), and other indications that it is a heavily revised original draft. Barlow surreptitiously prepared an 88-page typescript when Lovecraft was in Florida in the summer of 1935, but he neglected to prepare the two carbons that Lovecraft habitually prepared. Lovecraft, in gratitude for Barlow's hard work, claimed that the text was transcribed accurately, but it is evident that there are any number of errors, including a critical omission near the beginning of the text dealing with the earlier life of the protagonist, Nathaniel Wingate Peaslee.

The typescript was submitted by Donald Wandrei to *Astounding*, where it was published in the June 1936 issue. Lovecraft inexplicably declares that the text was not tampered with in the same manner as was *At the Mountains of Madness*, but it is clear that the same kind of editorial alterations—changes in punctuation and especially the breaking up of Lovecraft's long paragraphs into shorter ones—have occurred here, although no actual cuts were made. The corrected text was only published in *The Shadow out of Time* (Hippocampus Press, 2001), subsequently reprinted in *The Dreams in the Witch House and Other Weird Stories* (Penguin, 2004) and the *Complete Fiction* (Barnes & Noble, 2008).

31. "The Shadow over Innsmouth." a) A.Ms., [2] + 68 + [25] pp. b) T.Ms., [1] + 72 + [2] pp.

The A.Ms. is a pencil draft that Lovecraft declared to be the fourth draft of the work (see SL 3.435-36). With the A.Ms. are two pages of notes, and other notes and additions are written on the backs of some of the pages of the text. Some pages of an earlier draft (published as "Discarded Draught: 'The Shadow over Innsmouth'") survive, since the revised draft was written on their versos; these include pp. 1-6, 17, and 21 of the earlier draft. A p. 15 is on the verso of one of the two pages of notes, but comparison reveals that it is a rough version of p. 15 of the final text. It may be, indeed, that part of this early draft was incorporated directly into the final draft, as some of the pages of the latter have been renumbered as if some parts of the text have been inserted here and there. The T.Ms. was in any case prepared by Lovecraft; both it and the A.Ms. record the date of completion on their respective last pages: "December 3, 1931." The T.Ms. (or a carbon of it) was apparently sent to William L. Crawford for the book he printed in late 1936 (not April 1936, as the copyright page declares; see *SL* 5.359), although Roy A. Squires—who discovered a partial carbon copy of a T.Ms. that was the actual printer's copy for the publication—feels that the T.Ms. and his carbon are not the same. The carbon copy has now been dispersed, as separate leaves were sold to collectors. It is extremely unlikely, however, that Lovecraft would have prepared a new T.Ms. or have had someone else prepare it for him. In any case, the Arkham House editions derive from Crawford's booklet—or perhaps Lovecraft's corrected copy of it (John Hay Library). Lovecraft actually distributed several copies which he corrected in pencil, and Derleth and Wandrei may have obtained one of these. As usual, Lovecraft corrected only some obvious typographical errors. The errata sheet lists only a fraction of the errors in the book appearance.

32. "The Shunned House." T.Ms., 25 pp.

Recently a single-spaced T.Ms. of this novelette has turned up in the John Hay Library; it is not by Lovecraft nor in any other recognisable typeface. Although it has not been examined in detail, it probably is not original but derives from W. Paul Cook's abortive pamphlet of 1928. The original A.Ms. was given to Samuel Loveman (see Lovecraft to R. H. Barlow, 12 July 1934; *OFF* 149); and although Lovecraft believed that Loveman had misplaced it, Loveman declared owning the text well after Lovecraft's death (see Samuel Loveman to Winfield Townley Scott, 19 April 1944; ms., JHL). The A.Ms. has now surfaced and is currently being offered for sale by the dealer L. W. Currey. No other ms. of the work has ever come to light. The Cook printing, however, is probably quite accurate; Cook was, in fact, the only one ever to print a Lovecraft story faultlessly: his printing of "The White Ship" (*United Amateur*, November 1919) follows the T.Ms. down to the last comma and semicolon.

33. "The Silver Key." T.Ms., 14 pp.

The T.Ms. was prepared by Lovecraft and was sent to *Weird Tales*, where it appeared (January 1929) with the usual editorial alterations. AH 1939 followed the T.Ms., hence its text is quite accurate; AH 1964 leaves out part of a sentence in the first paragraph that makes the whole passage sound contradictory, if not incoherent.

34. "The Statement of Randolph Carter." T.Ms., 4 pp.

This is another of Lovecraft's single-spaced T.Mss. sent to *Weird Tales* (not numbered at the top). An A.Ms. was discovered and published by R. Alain Everts (Madison, WI: The Strange Co., 1976); it is a clean copy of Lovecraft's original draft, but must date before the T.Ms., as the latter incorporates some revisions (which Everts believed to be errors in the printed texts). The T.Ms. was followed by Cook when he published the tale in the *Vagrant* (May 1920). *Weird Tales* also followed the T.Ms. (February 1925), and the Arkham House editions derive from the *Weird Tales* appearance. AH 1964 leaves out part of a paragraph (rightly pointed out by Everts), but it is included in AH 1939.

35. "The Strange High House in the Mist." A.Ms. and T.Ms., [1] + 10 pp.

The ms. is a strange compendium of the original autograph draft (pp. 1–7, 10) and a T.Ms. (pp. 8–9) extensively revised by Lovecraft in pen. The last page records the date of writing: "Novr. 9, 1926." The covering page of the ms. (written in a much later hand than the A.Ms. part of the text) declares that the story was to have been published in the second issue of the *Recluse*, and that the tale appeared in *Weird Tales* (October 1931). The ms. has been revised in pencil; some of these revisions must date after the *Weird Tales* appearance, since that publication prints those phrases in the text in their unrevised state. Arkham House editions derive from the *Weird Tales* text, hence do not incorporate these new revisions (of which there are comparatively few).

36. "Sweet Ermengarde; or, The Heart of a Country Girl." As by "Percy Simple." A.Ms., 10 pp.

The A.Ms. seems to be Lovecraft's original draft, but bears very few revisions: evidently he did not spend much time in polishing. The ms. is written on blank pages of stationery from the Edwin E. Phillips Refrigeration Co., Providence, R.I. There is no indication of the date of writing (nor does Lovecraft mention the farce in any correspondence seen by me), but the handwriting is comparatively youthful, so that it probably dates to 1925 or before. The first appearance (AH 1943) followed the text accurately enough.

37. "The Terrible Old Man." A.Ms., 4 pp.

The ms. is a fair copy (the original A.Ms. is now in the possession of Arthur Koki; see his M.A. thesis, "H. P. Lovecraft: An Introduction to His Life and Writings," Columbia University, 1962). The last page records the date of writing: "Jany. 28, 1920." The existing A.Ms. must date after the first appearance (*Tryout*, July 1921), since it incorporates a few revisions from that text. The *Weird Tales* text includes the revisions made in the A.Ms., but this may mean either that the A.Ms. was made before the *Weird Tales* appearance (in which case a T.Ms. would have been from the A.Ms.) or that the A.Ms. dates after the *Weird Tales* appearance and was copied from the hypothetical T.Ms. or from pages of *Weird Tales* themselves. There is little difference in either case, however, since the text of the A.Ms. is basically the same as that of *Weird Tales*.

38. "The Thing on the Doorstep." a) A.Ms., 37 pp. b) T.Ms., [2] + 28 pp.

The A.Ms. is Lovecraft's original draft, written in pencil; the last page records the date of writing: "Begun—Aug. 21, 1933 / Ended—Aug. 24, 1933." Lovecraft gave the A.Ms. to Duane Rimel (a presentation by Lovecraft in pen appears in the corner of the first page), but Rimel gave it to the John Hay Library in 1948. The T.Ms. (by an unknown hand: Lovecraft remarked that he had a "delinquent [revision] client [Hazel Heald?]" [*SL* 4.310] type the text) is none too accurate, changing Lovecraft's punctuation extensively, leaving out words and phrases, and confusing Lovecraft's chapter divisions of the story. The first covering page of the T.Ms. bears a "Circulation List" in pen by Lovecraft; the list of names here includes Clark Ashton Smith, Robert E. Howard, E. Hoffmann Price, August Derleth, Robert Bloch, J. Vernon Shea, Robert H. Barlow, F. Lee Baldwin, and Donald Wandrei (the last two are added with a typewriter).

The *Weird Tales* appearance (January 1937) followed the T.Ms.; the Arkham House editions also derive from the T.Ms., making still more errors.

39. "The Transition of Juan Romero." a) A.Ms., 10 pp. b) T.Ms., 9 pp. (2 copies).

The A.Ms. is a fair copy, though it is still in a youthful hand; this draft was probably recopied from the original draft before 1925. The last page bears the date of writing: "9/16/19." The T.Mss. (one a carbon of the other) were prepared by R. H. Barlow and are somewhat inaccurate, though not as much as the Arkham House editions that derive from it. The first publication was in AH 1944, and later editions (e.g., AH 1965) derive from it.

40. "The Tree." T.Ms., 3 pp.

The T.Ms. is single-spaced (though not one of those sent to *Weird Tales* in 1923) and was prepared by Lovecraft. It was followed by the *Tryout* when the tale was published there (October 1921). Lovecraft's copy of the issue (John Hay Library) bears many corrections of the text in pen (see *Writings in The Tryout*, 1977, where a facsimile of the corrected *Tryout* text is printed). It appears that the Arkham House editions derive from this corrected copy, since they in large measure repeat those mistakes made in the *Tryout* appearance that were not corrected by Lovecraft. Nonetheless, the Arkham House texts are comparatively sound. The *Weird Tales* appearance (August 1938) is not relevant to the tale's textual history.

41. "What the Moon Brings." A.Ms., 3 pp.

The A.Ms. is Lovecraft's original draft, written in pencil on the back of correspondence to him. The last page bears the date of writing: "June 5, 1922." The tale does not bear a great many revisions and interlineations, indicating that Lovecraft wrote the prose-poem quickly (though not necessarily carelessly). The first appearance (*National Amateur*, May 1923) derives from the A.Ms.

42. "The Whisperer in Darkness." a) A.Ms., 52 pp. b) T.Ms., [1] + 69 pp.

The A.Ms. is Lovecraft's original draft, written in pen and bearing some revision at a later time in pencil. It is written entirely on the back of correspondence to him. The last page records the date of writing: "Begun Providence, R.I. Feby. 24, 1930 / Provisionally finished Charleston, S.C., May 7, 1930 / Polishing completed Providence, R.I., Sept. 26, 1930." The T.Ms. was prepared by Lovecraft. It was sent to *Weird Tales*, where it appeared (August 1931) with the usual editorial changes. The Arkham House editions derive from the T.Ms., hence are—aside from a few curious errors—relatively accurate.

43. "The White Ship." T.Ms., 4 pp.

The T.Ms. is one of the single-spaced T.Mss. sent by Lovecraft to *Weird Tales* in 1923. Both the appearance there (March 1927) and the first appearance (*United Amateur*, November 1919) derive from the T.Ms.; the latter, as remarked earlier, is word-for-word perfect with the T.Ms. The Arkham House editions derive from the *Weird Tales* text, which is rather less well printed. Stuart D. Schiff came into possession of an A.Ms. that he published in facsimile in *Whispers*, July 1974. The A.Ms. is a fair copy made in the 1930s for one of Lovecraft's correspondents. Lovecraft must have followed the T.Ms. (or the *United Amateur* appearance) in copying out the tale; and, aside from a few apparent scribal errors and omissions, makes some evidently wilful revisions, though these are of a very minor sort.

B. Revisions and Collaborations

1. "Collapsing Cosmoses." A.Ms., 3 pp.

The work is a collaboration between Lovecraft and Barlow, where each author wrote every other paragraph or so. The work is apparently incomplete.

Its first appearance was in *Leaves* (1938), which clearly followed the A.Ms., making few errors. All subsequent printings have followed the *Leaves* text. In my edition of the text in *Uncollected Prose and Poetry II* (1980) I have indicated precisely which portions were written by each author.

2. "Composite Story." A.Ms., [3] + 9 pp.

This is Lovecraft's segment of the round-robin tale, "The Challenge from Beyond." The text consists of three pages of notes and illustrations (first published in *Lovecraft Studies* No. 9 [Fall 1984]: 72-73) and nine pages of text. Presumably Lovecraft prepared a T.Ms. and sent it to *Fantasy Magazine* for publication there (September 1935).

The *Fantasy Magazine* text does not follow the A.Ms. very well, deleting some words and phrases. Some of these deletions were corrected in a copy of *Fantasy Magazine* (John Hay Library). All subsequent appearances have followed the (uncorrected) *Fantasy Magazine* text.

3. "The Diary of Alonzo Typer." A.Ms., 20 pp.

The A.Ms. is written in a very late script with extremely small characters and many revisions and interlineations. The tale was ghostwritten for William Lumley; Lumley's version survives, and examination of it proves that Lovecraft wholly recast the story, retaining only a few phrases of the original. It is probable that Lovecraft had Lumley prepare the T.Ms. (even though he states that he would prepare it himself; see Lovecraft to R. H. Barlow, 21 October 1935; *OFF* 299), since the first appearance (*Weird Tales*, February 1938) makes many curious errors that cannot well be attributed to editorial emendation. All subsequent appearances derive from the *Weird Tales* text.

4. "In the Walls of Eryx." T.Ms., [2] + 45 pp.

The T.Ms. is one of two carbon copies made of the collaboration; the other carbon and the original T.Ms. (as well as the presumable A.Ms. by Lovecraft) are not to be found. The tale is credited to "Kenneth Sterling and H. P. Lovecraft"; and although it is clear that Lovecraft wrote most of it (though perhaps less so than in his other revisions and collaborations), it is probable that he himself recommended that the names be listed in this way. The T.Ms. is presumably by Sterling, since it is in a wholly unfamiliar typewriter face. The text appears to be fairly accurately copied from the theoretical A.Ms. It was sent to *Astounding Stories*, *Blue Book*, the *Argosy*, *Wonder Stories*, and possibly *Amazing Stories* (all these names, save the last, are crossed out on a covering page of the ms). Finally it was taken by *Weird Tales* for the October 1939 issue. The Arkham House editions derive from the T.Ms. and bear few divergences from it.

5. "Medusa's Coil." T.Ms., 48 pp.

The T.Ms. is presumably by Frank Belknap Long, working from a probable A.Ms. by Lovecraft. In some places Long does not appear to have been able to read Lovecraft's handwriting, and the text is garbled. Pp. 27-48 have been typed by another hand, probably R. H. Barlow; perhaps this copy was damaged or part of it was lost, and Barlow retyped it from a hypothetical carbon copy, as he seems to have done with "The Mound" (see below). Barlow has written on the top corner of the first page: "(Pencil additions & deletions by Derleth 1937)," referring to extensive changes in pencil on the ms. by August Derleth. These changes appear in all published versions of the story: *Weird Tales* (January 1939), AH 1944, *The Curse of Yig* (1953), and AH 1970. Both AH 1944 and AH 1970 followed *Weird Tales*, the former being slightly more accurate. I have not examined the *Curse of Yig* text, but it is irrelevant to the textual history of the tale, as AH 1970 does not derive from it.

6. "The Mound." a) T.Ms., 82 pp. b) T.Ms., [1] + 82 pp.

The somewhat complicated history of the tale's writing has been spelled out in my article "Who Wrote 'The Mound'?." where I conclude that the text was entirely ghostwritten by Lovecraft for Zealia Bishop. The T.Ms. was presumably typed by Frank Belknap Long from Lovecraft's theoretical A.Ms.; Long seems to have done a better job of transcription here than in "Medusa's Coil." T.Ms. (b) is a carbon of T.Ms. (a) and has a cover sheet with the title "The Mound / Zealia Brown Bishop Reed" in Zealia Bishop's handwriting plus a lengthy note by R. H. Barlow (reproduced in my article). Many pages of (b) have been retyped by Barlow, either because they were lost or because Long discarded pages when he abridged the story in an attempt to market it to the pulps. Long has added a few sentences to the ms. in pen at the top and bottom of various pages of T.Ms. (b) to provide links of continuity between the sections he omitted; these appear on pp. 15 (bottom), 17 (top), 19 (top), 21 (top), 25 (bottom), 27 (top), and 52 (top). Long accordingly renumbered the T.Ms. after he made the cuts so that it was 69 pp. All Long's handwritten additions have been deleted by Lovecraft and are now virtually impossible to read. Barlow has retyped pp. 1-4, 7-half of p. 13, 16, 18, 20, 26, 48-51, and 69. T.Ms. (b) also contains extensive alterations and deletions in pencil by August Derleth. This adulterated text was published (in abridged form) in *Weird Tales* for November 1940. The first complete appearance (AH 1943) derives from the altered T.Ms., while AH 1970 derives from AH 1943, though making many comical errors (e.g., "self-encrusted" for "salt-encrusted" and "Old Bones" for "Old Ones"). The text, as altered by Derleth, lacks about 250 words and contains many revisions in punctuation (some resulting in incoherency).

7. "Through the Gates of the Silver Key." a) A.Ms., 34 pp. b) T.Ms., [1] + 46 pp.

The A.Ms. is Lovecraft's original draft, written in pencil. The publication of Price's original sequel to "The Silver Key," titled by him "The Lord of Illusion" (*Crypt of Cthulhu* No. 10 [1982]: 46-56) allows us to see precisely how much of Price's draft Lovecraft retained; there is more of Price in "Through the Gates of the Silver Key" than Price's own statements would have led one to believe. The T.Ms. is by Price and bears many autograph notes by him commenting on portions of the text. Price's T.Ms. is quite inaccurate, omitting words, phrases, and sentences from the original draft. Another T.Ms., incorporating the revisions made by Lovecraft on the existing T.Ms. based on Price's comments, must have been made by Price and sent to *Weird Tales* (where it appeared in the issue for July 1934), and probably more errors were made in the process. The Arkham House editions derive from the *Weird Tales* appearance. This tale ranks among the most misprinted of Lovecraft's works; Price arbitrarily changed much of the text, including important quotations from the *Necronomicon*.

8. "'Till A' the Seas.'" T.Ms., 11 pp.

The T.Ms. was prepared by R. H. Barlow and contains extensive revisions in pen by Lovecraft; some corrections in pen are also by Barlow and were probably made prior to Lovecraft's revisions. Barlow has written on the top corner of the first page: "Second draft, with Lovecraft's corrections / final text." In the title "All" has been changed to "A'," but this change may have been made by Barlow. Lovecraft has introduced the major section division ("II.") on p. vi. On p. ix (actually p. x, as Barlow has misnumbered the ms.) Barlow has added the date of composition: "Dec. 8-9-10 34." Much of p. ix is in Barlow's handwriting; he has typed this up as p. x (actually xi), and Lovecraft has made extensive revisions. It is possible that this final page is what Barlow refers to as the "second draft," since the rest of the ms. seems to be a first draft on the typewriter, unless Barlow is referring to a hypothetical A.Ms. The first printing of the tale (*Californian*, Summer 1935) is not very sound, but is much better than AH 1970, where Derleth attempted to follow the T.Ms. (perhaps because he did not even know of the *Californian* appearance).

IV. Studies of Individual Works

Who Wrote "The Mound"?

In Zealia Brown Reed Bishop's oftentimes fantastic memoir, "H. P. Lovecraft: A Pupil's View," she declares expressly that Frank Belknap Long helped to revise a lengthy tale that Lovecraft ghostwrote for Bishop, "The Mound." Yet both Long and Lovecraft were and have been ceaselessly stating that Lovecraft, and Lovecraft alone, wrote the novelette. As recently as 1975, Long stated categorically: "I had nothing whatever to do with the writing of *The Mound*" (*Dreamer* xiii–xiv). Who actually authored this tale, a major Lovecraftian opus fully as long as "The Whisperer in Darkness"?

Evidence shows that, although Long did indeed have a hand in the process of revision (or ghostwriting) of "The Mound," he is nonetheless fundamentally correct when he states, "That brooding, somber, and magnificently atmospheric story is Lovecraftian from the first page to the last" (*Dreamer* xiv). However, behind this statement lies a wealth of detail that even yet is not completely unravelled. Indeed, the published versions of "The Mound" are certainly not Lovecraft's in every respect.

Bishop had given Lovecraft the task of revising or ghostwriting "The Mound" in late 1929. R. H. Barlow states that "*The Mound* was . . . written by Lovecraft . . . from a late synopsis [by Bishop], something like 'There is an Indian mound near here, which is haunted by a headless ghost. Sometimes it is a woman.'"[1] But Lovecraft found this plot-germ far too tame, and he began expanding it, incorporating into it many elements of his myth-cycle. He wrote to Elizabeth Toldridge: "Everything pertaining to the Mayan & Aztec civilisations is interesting, & I fancy I shall use the theme more than once. Indeed—my next revision job will give me a chance to practice, since it will require the introduction of this theme in such a way as to involve wholly original composition on my part" (*Letters to Elizabeth Toldridge* 114).

We next hear that the ghostwriting of "The Mound" is "proving to be rather an incubus, for the idea is spinning itself out into a veritable novelette" (*SL* 3.97–98). Evidently Lovecraft finished the entire tale in early 1930. It appears that he now handed on his autograph version of the tale to Long for

---

1. Note by Barlow on the title page of one of the T.Mss. of "The Mound" (JHL).

typing, and that Long actually prepared the typed version: the typewriter face of the typescript and carbon copy (still surviving in the John Hay Library) is identical to that of letters by Long for this period. Moreover, Long seems to have made certain transcriptional errors in the text due to his inability to read Lovecraft's handwriting; one word is rendered on the typescript as "atariousness," and I have still not been able to ascertain what Lovecraft's intention here was.[2] (Lovecraft's handwritten manuscript has of course perished.) After the typescript was finished in 82 pages, it was submitted—either by Long (who at this time was Bishop's major literary agent [see OFF 143]) or by Lovecraft—to Weird Tales, but editor Farnsworth Wright rejected it, presumably on account of its length; Long writes to Lovecraft (c. 19 March 1930): "It was incredibly asinine of him [Wright] to reject The Mound—and on such a flimsy pretext" (ms., JHL).

The decision was then evidently made (probably by Bishop, who desperately wished to sell this story and any other of "her" works) to revise or abridge the story so that it would be more saleable to a pulp market. Frank Belknap Long was entrusted with this task. All that Long did, however, was to abridge the text, and this is indicated by the fact that the pages of the surviving typescript (but not the carbon) are renumbered in pen, apparently by Long, In all, the text was shortened by about 20 pages. Long may perhaps have provided suitable transitional passages for the abridged version (although there are none such on either the typescript or the carbon), but this is the extent of his role in the tale. When Long completed this "revised version," he apparently made some attempts to sell it, but these efforts came to nothing.[3] Both the abridged and the unabridged versions of "The Mound" lay in manuscript (or, rather, typescript) for years.

When he visited Barlow in De Land, Florida, in the summer of 1934, Lovecraft evidently made mention of this lengthy ghostwriting effort; Barlow, with his eye ever toward publication (among his many book ventures were Lovecraft's *Fungi from Yuggoth* series; possibly the essays written to the Transatlantic Circulator in 1921 defending the story "Dagon"; another collection of poems by Lovecraft; and several other projects, all of which came to naught), expressed a desire to publish the tale, either in magazine form or as a separate

---

2. This word is simply omitted in the published versions of the tale and the sentence containing it amended accordingly.

3. Frank Belknap Long to S. T. Joshi, 17 May 1977. HPL himself seems to have doubted Long's efforts in this regard: "I assumed that Sonny Belknap . . . *had* done so [i.e., tried to market the story]; & am astonished to find that any stone was left unturned" (OFF 143).

chapbook. Lovecraft wrote to Bishop informing her of the plan, and she in turn wrote to Long and asked him to send the *original* version to Lovecraft and Barlow in Florida. Needless to say, Long did not think he had the full version, for although he had "preserved the sheets [he] omitted in making the revised version . . . . . they [later] sank from sight." Long rightfully complained to Lovecraft: "Did you actually imagine that I could store MS rejects for more than five years in perfect safety?"[4] Long did, however, send this abridged/revised version to Lovecraft.

As noted, the original typescript of "The Mound" was the one Long used in making the "revised version"; but the carbon was still with Bishop, although it was missing the first three pages.[5] Barlow (on Lovecraft's suggestion) asked Bishop to send him this copy, and she complied in mid-July 1934.[6] Barlow evidently decided that the original, unabridged version by Lovecraft should be the one published. In the meanwhile Long had managed to locate the pages that he had removed in his abridged version and sent them to Barlow. Barlow now possessed two complete typescripts of "The Mound," save that the carbon lacked the first three pages. He forthwith typed them himself.

In the unabridged text, Lovecraft had made slight revisions and corrections in pen; but the text was almost precisely the same as that written in 1929–30. Plans for publication were apparently carried on, but soon foundered and were abandoned. In early 1937, a month before Lovecraft's death, Barlow sent the original typescript back to Lovecraft (see OFF 391), keeping the carbon himself. After Lovecraft's death both copies were deposited in the John Hay Library.

Thus ends Frank Belknap Long's involvement in the affair; but the saga of "The Mound" is not yet over. A few years after Lovecraft's death, August Derleth acquired the typescript (probably borrowing it from the John Hay Library) and "touched [it] up . . . for sales purposes."[7] This involved radically altering Lovecraft's punctuation, deleting passages (a total of about 150 words), and rephrasing sentences. It was this adulterated version of "The Mound" that was published (in still more abridged form) in *Weird Tales* for November 1940 and (unabridged) in *Beyond the Wall of Sleep* (1943). The text was later reproduced in Bishop's *The Curse of Yig* (1953) and in Lovecraft's

---

4. Frank Belknap Long to HPL, [28 May 1934] (ms., JHL).

5. Bishop writes to HPL (26 May 1934): "Do you suppose Mr. Barlow would be interested in reading Medusa's Coil? I have it and a carbon copy of The Mound except for the first three pages" (ms., JHL).

6. See Zealia Bishop to R. H. Barlow, 11 July 1934 (ms., JHL).

7. R. H. Barlow, note on the title page of one of the T.Mss. of "The Mound" (JHL).

The Horror in the Museum and Other Revisions (1970). All published versions of "The Mound," prior to my revised edition of *The Horror in the Museum* (1989), while not being "by Lovecraft and Long," can certainly be regarded as "by Lovecraft and Derleth"; the adulterated text of the tale is certainly more a "collaboration" than are any of the sixteen so-called "posthumous collaborations" of Lovecraft and Derleth, from *The Lurker at the Threshold* (1945) to "The Watchers out of Time" (1971).

It is, then, not surprising that, amidst the bizarre circumstances surrounding the writing and attempted selling of "The Mound," all parties in question (save, of course, Lovecraft) should be confused as to the authorship of the tale. Barlow, indeed, wryly records an amusing comment on the affair by Lovecraft: "L[ovecraft] perceived that Belknap had written [on the typescript] By F. B. L. & Z. B. R.—'the two people who had nothing to do with it'—& thereupon suggested that I call it *The Mound, by R. H. Barlow!*"[8] One can well understand Lovecraft's irritation at being robbed of credit for this story, "in view of the labour I put into it back in dear old '29" (*OFF* 391)—and especially in view of the fact that its cosmic scope and brilliant social criticism of the underground mound civilisation can make it rank even with the best of his later narratives.

Works Cited

Bishop, Zealia Brown Reed. "H. P. Lovecraft: A Pupil's View." In *The Curse of Yig*. Sauk City, WI: Arkham House, 1953. 139-51.

Long, Frank Belknap. *Howard Phillips Lovecraft: Dreamer on the Nightside*. Sauk City, WI: Arkham House, 1975.

Lovecraft, H. P. *Letters to Elizabeth Toldridge and Anne Tillery Renshaw*. Ed. David E. Schultz and S. T. Joshi. New York: Hippocampus Press, 2014.

---

8. See n. 7.

On "The Book"

Lovecraft's fictional fragments have not received much attention from critics, and perhaps deservedly so; for by their very incompleteness they are aesthetically unsatisfying, the more so since we have no idea how he intended to finish them. The fragments can gain value only by the possible light they may shed upon the history and progression of his writing.

R. H. Barlow, who supplied the title to the untitled fragment "The Descendant," also devised the title for "The Book" (D 362–64) and dated it hesitantly to 1934. Brief as it is, it offers some insights into Lovecraft's techniques of fiction-writing which make it not entirely devoid of interest.

Let us first attempt to date the fragment as precisely as possible. Barlow's date of 1934 is probably not far off, for the manuscript is written in that tiny, spidery handwriting typical of Lovecraft's late works. We can, however, perhaps be a bit more exact. Note this passage from a letter of 2–5 November 1933:

> I am at a sort of standstill in writing—disgusted at much of my older work, & uncertain as to avenues of improvement. In recent weeks I have done a tremendous amount of experimenting in different styles and perspectives, but have destroyed *most* [my emphasis] of the results. (SL 4.297)

Perhaps "The Book" could be referred to here. We may also note that the dream of an evil clergyman that Lovecraft wrote into a brief tale (actually an excerpt from a letter to Bernard Dwyer) dates to October 1933.[1] This period seems to have been a time of great psychological stress for Lovecraft in terms of fiction-writing: he had suffered painful rejections (*At the Mountains of Madness*

---

1. See SL 4.289–90. Derleth's dating it to 1937 has no authority at all. Indeed, even the possibility that HPL wrote up the dream at a later time seems refuted by the following letter from Dwyer to Clark Ashton Smith (n.d., but soon after HPL's death): "I sent [Farnsworth] Wright [editor of *Weird Tales*] a short story of his [HPL's]—a dream—never published. . . . I copied it out of an *old* [my emphasis] letter to me. A very odd little story; I call it 'The Wicked Clergyman'" (ms., Clark Ashton Smith Coll., JHL).

by *Weird Tales*; collections of his work by Putnam's and Knopf), and appeared to have difficulty in recapturing the fluency in writing that had characterised his 1926-27 period (after his return from New York), when he produced *The Dream-Quest of Unknown Kadath* and *The Case of Charles Dexter Ward*, plus several shorter tales, in a period of about eleven months. Indeed, after writing "The Thing on the Doorstep" in August 1933, he would write no more original fiction save "The Shadow out of Time" (which itself went through three drafts [SL 5.346]) in November 1934-February 1935, and "The Haunter of the Dark" in November 1935.

"The Book" may then date to late 1933; but it is far more interesting not when considered by itself, but in connexion with one of Lovecraft's most celebrated works—the *Fungi from Yuggoth* sonnets, written in late 1929 and early 1930.

The relations between the *Fungi* and Lovecraft's prose fiction have perhaps not been fully realised. Some of the sonnets are echoes or—more interestingly—foreshadowings of themes and plots used in his fiction. "The Courtyard" (IX) perhaps contains vague references to the earlier story "He" (1925):

> As edging through the filth I saw the gate
> To the black courtyard where the man would be. (ll. 7-8)

"The Bells" (XIX) mentions the name "Innsmouth" (cited first in "Celephaïs" [1920], but set there in England), used later, of course, in "The Shadow over Innsmouth." "Night-Gaunts" (XX) of course employs the entities cited in the earlier *Dream-Quest* and stemming from Lovecraft's boyhood nightmares. "Nyarlathotep" (XXI) seems to be an exact retelling of the prose-poem of 1920, while "Azathoth" (XXII) may provide clues as to the theme of the unfinished novel of 1922. The "thing . . . [with] a silken mask" from "The Elder Pharos" (XXVII) had made a vivid appearance in the *Dream-Quest*, while "The Dweller" (XXXI) may be retelling the events of the very early "Statement of Randolph Carter" (1919). "Alienation" (XXXII) perhaps echoes the theme of "The Strange High House in the Mist" (1926). Such examples could be multiplied upon additional study.

Lovecraft made, indeed, a revealing remark soon after completing the *Fungi* sequence: "Some of the themes [expressed in the sonnets] are really more adapted to fiction—so that I shall probably make stories of them whenever I get that constantly deferred creative opportunity I am always waiting for" (SL 3.116-17). Is it possible that "The Book," written at a time when Lovecraft's creative urge may have been at a lull, was such an attempt to rewrite *Fungi from Yuggoth* into prose?

Only the first three of the *Fungi* sonnets are openly linked, although R. Boerem has attempted to find continuity in the whole sequence. Comparison between "The Book" and the first three sonnets reveals a striking similarity of theme, plot, and even language, such that we can hardly fail to conclude that the fragment bears a distinct relation to the sonnets.

The plot of both the prose tale and the poems is that of a man's discovery of a forbidden book (presumably, though not necessarily, the *Necronomicon*) and its effect upon him as he reads it. The setting of "The Book" tallies with that of the first sonnet "The Book" (I): in the former we read of a "dimly lighted place near the black, oily river where the mists always swirl." In the sonnet we read of "old alleys near the quays" (l. 2) and "queer curls of fog" (l. 4). The old bookshop is, in the fragment, "very old" (recall the "old alleys") and "[had] ceiling-high shelves full of rotting volumes." In the sonnet we find "the books, in piles like twisted trees, / Rotting from floor to roof" (ll. 6-7). In the fragment the narrator finds the book amidst "great formless heaps of books on the floor and in crude bins"; in the sonnet the narrator "from a cobwebbed heap / Took up the nearest tome and thumbed it through" (ll. 9-10).

At this point Lovecraft in the fragment makes a glancing reference to the third sonnet of the *Fungi* sequence, "The Key": "it was a key—a guide—to certain gateways and transitions...." Quickly, however, he appears to return to the first and second sonnets, and retells them in order. "I remember how the old man leered and tittered," says the narrator in the fragment. In the sonnet "The Book" we read

> Then, looking for some seller old in craft,
> I could find nothing but a voice that laughed. (ll. 13-14)

The narrator of the fragment then "hurried home through those narrow, winding, mist-choked waterfront streets." In "Pursuit" (II) the narrator is seen "Hurrying through the ancient harbour lanes / With often-turning head and nervous face" (ll. 3-4). In the fragment "I had a frightful impression of being stealthily followed by soft padding feet." At this point the verbal correspondence becomes almost exact, for in the sonnet "far behind me, unseen feet were padding" (l. 14). The narrator of the fragment speaks of "the centuried, tottering houses . . . with fishy, eye-like, diamond-paned windows that leered." In the sonnet "Dull, furtive windows in old tottering brick / Peered at me oddly as I hastened by" (ll. 5-6).

In the fragment Lovecraft now begins to describe the events as recorded in the third *Fungi* sonnet, "The Key." In the fragment the narrator "locked [himself] in the attic room. . . . Then came the first scratching and fumbling at the dormer window." Note the last line of the sonnet: "The attic window shook with a faint fumbling."

Here, in the last two paragraphs of the fragment, the correspondence with the *Fungi* becomes blurred, and may indicate Lovecraft's perplexity as to how to continue the tale, since the rest of the thirty-three sonnets of the *Fungi* are not, as previously noted, ostensibly linked, at least in terms of plot. Only a few parallels can be drawn. In the fragment the narrator confesses: "Nor could I ever after see the world as I had known it." We are reminded of "Alienation" (XXXII): "He waked that morning as an older man, / And nothing since has looked the same to him" (ll. 9-10). The narrator of the fragment continues: "Every once-familiar object loomed alien in the new perspective brought by my widened sight." In "Alienation" we read:

> Objects around float nebulous and dim—
> False, fleeting trifles of some vaster plan.
> His folk and friends are now an alien throng
> To which he struggles vainly to belong. (ll. 11-14)

Later, the narrator of "The Book" recalls: "I was swept by a black wind through gulfs of fathomless grey with the needle-like pinnacles of unknown mountains miles below me. After a while there was utter blackness, and then the light of myriad stars forming strange, alien constellations." This is vaguely reminiscent of "Azathoth" (XXII):

> Out of the mindless void the daemon bore me,
> Past the bright clusters of dimensioned space,
> Till neither time nor matter stretched before me,
> But only Chaos, without form or place. (ll. 1-4)

But the resemblance is vague, tenuous, and hardly exact, and the fragment soon ends. Whether Lovecraft simply tired of the attempt to rewrite the *Fungi* into prose (we may perhaps be thankful that he never fully did so) or whether he found it difficult to string all or even some of the sonnets together into a coherent story, we may never know. Boerem's thesis of a "continuity" in the *Fungi* sonnets is neither confirmed nor refuted by the above correspondences; for if we accept the theory that "The Book" is an attempt to write out the *Fungi* in prose, then we must equally accept the possibility that Lovecraft could have written all or some into a tale, or at least conceived the possibility of so doing.

As it is, the fundamental theme of both the fragment and the *Fungi* sonnets as a whole is that of time—a central concept in Lovecraft's writing. Throughout the fragment the narrator hints of the new conceptions of time gained from reading the book he has discovered: "At times I feel appalling vistas of years stretching behind me, while at other times it seems as if the present moment were an isolated point in a grey formless infinity.... That night

I passed the gateway to a vortex of twisted time and vision.... Mingled with the present scene was always a little of the past and a little of the future...." All this is expressed—if oftentimes with less a feeling of horror than of exhilaration or "adventurous expectancy"—in the sonnets:

> At last the key was mine to those vague visions
> Of sunset spires and twilight woods that brood
> Dim in the gulfs beyond this earth's precisions,
> Lurking as memories of infinitude. (III.9-12)

> The winter sunset . . .
> Opens great gates to some forgotten year. . . .
> It is a land where beauty's meaning flowers;
> Where every unplaced memory has a source;
> Where the great river Time begins its course
> Down the vast void in starlit streams of hours. (XIII.1, 2, 9-12)

> I do not know what land it is—or dare
> Ask when or why I was, or will be, there. (XXIII.13-14)

> In that strange light I feel I am not far
> From the fixt mass whose sides the ages are. (XXXVI.13-14)

"The Book," then, while not of great intrinsic interest, typifies Lovecraft's despair at his own ability to write fiction during his later years. Certainly his powers were not failing—rather, the reverse seems to be the case, if we take "The Shadow out of Time" into consideration. But Lovecraft felt increasingly that "I'm farther from doing what I want to do than I was 20 years ago" (*SL* 5.224); the result was a series of experiments dating as early as "The Shadow over Innsmouth,"[2] of which "The Book" may represent another example. In his later years Lovecraft confessed that his "right medium" might perhaps be "the cheapened and hackneyed term 'prose-poem'" (*SL* 5.230); and perhaps "The Book," its basis drawn from some of his best poetry, is a step in that direction.

Works Cited

Boerem, R. "The Continuity of the *Fungi from Yuggoth*." In S. T. Joshi, ed. *H. P. Lovecraft: Four Decades of Criticism*. Athens: Ohio University Press, 1980. 222-25.

---

2. Cf. *SL* 3.435: "I am using the new [story] idea as a basis for what might be called laboratory experimentation—writing it out in different manners, one after the other, in an effort to determine the mood & tempo best suited to the theme."

On "Polaris"

"Polaris" is rather interesting in that I wrote it in 1918, *before* I had ever read a word of Lord Dunsany's. Some find it hard to believe this, but I can give not only assurance but absolute proof that it is so. It is simply a case of similar types of vision facing the unknown, and harbouring similar stores of mythic and historical lore. Hence the parallelism in atmosphere, artificial nomenclature, treatment of the dream theme, etc. (SL 2.120)

This revealing passage, written in a letter of 1927, tells us many important things; in particular, the fact that not only Lovecraft himself but his colleagues were taken aback at the manner in which "Polaris" seemed to have anticipated Lovecraft's later "Dunsanian" imitations, beginning in late 1919 with "The White Ship." Modern scholars have not merely echoed Lovecraft's remarks about this remarkable instance of parallelism, but have used it to defend Lovecraft's "Dunsanian" tales from charges of derivativeness. Dirk W. Mosig unhesitatingly declared that "'Polaris' was written a whole year prior to his encounter with Lord Dunsany and his work, and clearly shows that Lovecraft's mind, at the time, was running in a parallel channel to Dunsany's. It is quite possible that, had Lovecraft never come across Lord Dunsany, he would still have written most of his 'Dunsanian' tales" (Mosig 186).

But both Lovecraft and his later critics seem to have been content with acknowledging this "proto-Dunsanianism" in "Polaris" and have not tried to ascertain whence it may have derived. An examination of the possible literary and philosophical sources of "Polaris" may help to place the tale in proper perspective and perhaps to render it a little less anomalous.

The fact is that both Lovecraft and Dunsany had one common and very powerful influence: Edgar Allan Poe. But whereas Lovecraft was primarily influenced by Poe's "pure" horror tales (he ranked "The Fall of the House of Usher" and "Ligeia" as Poe's two finest tales [see *D* 399]), Dunsany seems conversely to have been affected by some of Poe's more "poetic" narratives. In his autobiography, Dunsany makes no secret of the effect of Poe's stories and poems on his early imaginative development: "the haunted desolation and weird gloom of the misty mid-region of Weir remained for many years something that seemed to me more eerie than anything earth had" (Dunsany 32). Lovecraft himself conjectures that Poe's prose-poems (especially "Silence—A Fable" and "Shadow—A Parable"), which "employ[ed] that archaic and Orientalised style with jewelled phrase, quasi-Biblical repetition, and recurrent burthen," had left their mark upon such "later writers [as] Oscar Wilde and Lord Dunsany" (*D* 398). Can it be, then, that Poe's prose-poems were at least an indirect influence upon "Polaris"?

A very good case could be made for such an influence. Poe's prose-poems seem to have made a great impression upon Lovecraft in his early fiction. It has not been observed even by the defenders of Lovecraft's "Dunsanian" tales that "Memory"—which could well be classed as "proto-Dunsanian"—was written several months before Lovecraft's first encounter with the Irish fantaisiste.[1] Here too we have imaginary place-names (the "valley of Nis" [*MW* 31])[2] and a generally dreamlike and poetic atmosphere. But this tale almost certainly derives from Poe's "Silence—a Fable"; both tales contain a "Demon" as a character ("'Listen to me,' said the Demon" is the first sentence of Poe's tale; Lovecraft introduces us to a "Daemon of the Valley"), while the "Genie that haunts the moonbeams" in Lovecraft's tale may be paralleled by the mention of "Genii" in Poe's. Indeed, the very structure of the tale—a dialogue between two bizarre supernatural beings which takes on an unreal, almost allegorical air—may have found its source in such of Poe's tales as "The Conversation of Eiros and Charmion" and "The Colloquy of Monos and Una." Lovecraft's tale certainly contains that "quasi-Biblical repetition" which he observed in Poe's tales ("The Genie . . . spake to the Daemon of the Valley, saying, 'I am old, and forget much'"). Finally, in "The Picture in the House" (1920) Lovecraft borrowed a memorable phrase from the end of Poe's "Shadow—a Parable" ("I am SHADOW, and my dwelling is near to the Catacombs of Ptolemais"; "Searchers after horror haunt strange, far places. For them are the catacombs of Ptolemais" [*DH* 116]).

Poe's influence, then, was pervasive in Lovecraft's early tales, and "Polaris" may well fit into the pattern. It contains the same sort of Biblical style that is at the heart of both Poe's prose-poems and Dunsany's early work, and its inclusion of a ten-line poem ("Slumber, watcher, till the spheres . . .") is reminiscent of the poetic snatches in some of Poe's tales, notably "The

---

1. It was published in the June 1919 issue of the *United Co-operative*; HPL first read Dunsany in October 1919.

2. "The Valley Nis" is in fact an early title for Poe's poem "The Valley of Unrest," although HPL may have been unaware of the fact. Nis, in any event, is mentioned in the poem.

Haunted Palace" in "The Fall of the House of Usher" and "The Conqueror Worm" in "Ligeia." Lovecraft had already used the device in the hilarious drinking-song in "The Tomb" (1917) but never again employed it, although "The Nameless City" (1921) and "Under the Pyramids" (1924) contain some lines of poetry by other hands (in both cases Thomas Moore). A claim might even be made that Lovecraft's other original fictional work of 1918—the lost "dime-novel" "The Mystery of Murdon Grange"—owed something to Poe's detective tales, although in the absence of the actual text such a claim is tenuous.

The most unusual feature of "Polaris"—or, rather, the feature that links it most closely with the work of Dunsany—is the use of mythical names. Here too we may find in Poe the common source of this technique in Lovecraft and Dunsany. Many of the names invented by Lovecraft in "Polaris" are pseudo-Greek coinages—Olathoë, Sarkis (reminiscent of Sardis, the ancient capital of Lydia in Asia Minor), Noton, Kadiphonek, Alos, Zobna, Thapnen, and perhaps even the Gnophkehs. Poe, in fact, in "Shadow—a Parable" uses actual Greek names (Oinos, Corinnos, Zoilus, etc.), while the names in "The Colloquy of Monos and Una" are derived, respectively, from the Greek masculine and Latin feminine adjectives meaning "one." Lovecraft himself recognised that Dunsany's "amazing facility for devising musical, alluring, and wonder-making proper names . . . [derives from] classical and Oriental models" ("Lord Dunsany and His Work" [*CE* 2.58]), but he seems not to have made the connexion that Poe's Hellenic names may at least have helped to inspire his own and Dunsany's mythical coinages.

Finally, it must be noted that Lovecraft is in fact incorrect in believing that the "treatment of the dream theme" (*SL* 2.120) in "Polaris" finds a parallel in Dunsany. Few of Dunsany's tales are postulated as occurring in a dream; rather, they simply employ a mythical terrain and completely ignore its possible relations to the "real" world. Moreover, Dunsany seems not to have based many of his stories upon his own dreams: his most celebrated tale, "Idle Days on the Yann" (in *A Dreamer's Tales*), was written in anticipation (what Lovecraft might have called "adventurous expectancy") of a journey he was to take down the Nile. Indeed, Dunsany seems to have had few vivid dreams at all. We now know, however, that "Polaris" was founded upon a dream that Lovecraft had in May 1918:

> Several nights ago I had a strange dream of a strange city—a city of many palaces and gilded domes, lying in a hollow betwixt ranges of grey, horrible hills. There was not a soul in this vast region of stone-paved streets and marble walls and columns, and the numerous statues in the public places were of strange bearded men in robes the like whereof I have never seen before or since. I was, as I said, aware of this city visually. I was in it and around it. But

certainly I had no corporeal existence. I saw, it seemed, everything at once; without the limitations of direction. I did not move, but transferred my perception from point to point at will. I occupied no space and had no form. I was only a consciousness, a perceptive presence. I recall a lively curiosity at the scene, and a tormenting struggle to recall its identity; for I felt that I had once known it well, and that if I could remember, I should be carried back to a very remote period—many thousand years, when something vaguely horrible had happened. Once I was almost on the verge of realisation, and was frantic with fear at the prospect, though I did not know what it was that I should recall. But here I awaked—in a very cramped posture and with too much bedclothing for the steadily increasing temperature. I have related this in detail because it impressed me very vividly. (SL 1.62)

The context of these remarks is of the highest interest, as it seems to provide the philosophical motive for Lovecraft's subsequent writing of the tale. In this letter Lovecraft was discussing with Maurice W. Moe the "distinction between dream life and real life, between appearances and actualities" (SL 1.63). Moe, apparently influenced by the Pragmatism of William James, was trying to defend the usefulness of religious belief regardless of its metaphysical truth or falsity. James himself felt that there was no positive evidence either for or against religion, hence felt that the "will to believe"—a decision to believe one of two contrary propositions as true depending upon its usefulness—was applicable in this case. In spite of the severe logical fallacies behind this position,[3] it became very popular at the turn of the century and was used by orthodox religionists like Moe as a philosophical justification of belief. Lovecraft, however, cut the ground out from under this position by categorically asserting that "the Judaeo-Christian mythology is NOT TRUE" (SL 1.60). What Lovecraft, then, was trying to do in relating his dream to Moe was to show him the paradoxes that would follow if truth or falsity were not the first criterion for judging a phenomenon rather than its usefulness: "According to your pragmatism that dream was as real as my presence at this table, pen in hand! If the truth or falsity of our beliefs and impressions be immaterial, then I am, or was, actually and indisputably an unbodied spirit hovering over a very singular, very silent, and very ancient city somewhere between grey, dead hills. I thought I was at the time—so what else matters?" (SL 1.62-63). This remark is ironically echoed in the tale itself:

At first content to view the scene as an all-observant uncorporeal presence, I now desired to define my relation to it, and to speak my mind amongst the

---

3. See Bertrand Russell's devastating criticisms, "Pragmatism" and "William James' Conception of Truth," in his *Philosophical Essays* (1910).

grave men who conversed each day in the public squares. I said to myself, "This is no dream, for by what means can I prove the greater reality of that other life in the house of stone and brick south of the sinister swamp and the cemetery on the low hillock, where the Pole Star peers into my north window each night?" (D 21)

What conclusions can we now draw about "Polaris"? Its immediate origin was the dream of May 1918 (and it was probably written up shortly after this letter to Moe), and its philosophical source was the "distinction between dream life and real life" about which Moe and Lovecraft were arguing; its partial literary source was perhaps Poe's prose-poems, which made a great impression upon Lovecraft's early fiction; and its apparent resemblance to Dunsany's work may derive precisely from the possibility that Dunsany and Lovecraft shared a common influence in the work of Poe. We may then be justified in doubting whether Lovecraft would in fact have gone on to write his other "Dunsanian" tales had he never read Dunsany. It is a question, of course, that we can never answer and which it is probably idle to ask at all; for there can be no doubt of the importance of Dunsany's work in the development of Lovecraft's own fictional technique, as Lovecraft was fully aware: "As for [Dunsany's] influence on me—of course I had the same general cosmic attitude before, for that is why his discovery was such an event for me. But I couldn't even begin to formulate my attitude in artistic prose till I had him to follow as a model" (letter to Elizabeth Toldridge, 14 August 1929; *Letters to Elizabeth Toldridge* 95).

Works Cited

Dunsany, Lord. *Patches of Sunlight*. London: William Heinemann, 1938.

Lovecraft, H. P. *Letters to Elizabeth Toldridge and Anne Tillery Renshaw*. Ed. David E. Schultz and S. T. Joshi. New York: Hippocampus Press, 2014.

Mosig, Dirk W. "'The White Ship': A Psychological Odyssey." In S. T. Joshi, ed. *H. P. Lovecraft: Four Decades of Criticism*. Athens: Ohio University Press, 1980. 186–90.

On "The Tree on the Hill"

It is unquestionable that Lovecraft had a hand in the writing of Duane W. Rimel's "The Tree on the Hill" (1934; HM 400–409); the debate merely concerns the exact degree of his involvement. To me there seems little doubt that Lovecraft only very lightly touched up the first two portions of the tale, but entirely wrote the third and concluding portion. There are, however, some curiosities in all three sections that merit investigation.

At this time Rimel, though surely not more than twenty years old, had already proved himself a not incompetent imitator of Lovecraft, as the roughly contemporaneous "The Disinterment" proves—and it is very obvious that "The Tree on the Hill" is, at least in stylistic terms, an imitation of Lovecraft. Nothing in the first two sections of the tale would lead us to believe that we are here concerned with anything more than a pastiche of Lovecraft.

The very opening of the tale is an imitation of "The Colour out of Space," and not a bad one at that. One wonders whether the town used as the focal point of the adventures, Hampdon, reflects the original of Lovecraft's mythical Dunwich, which he declared to be a compendium of three towns in western Massachusetts, Wilbraham, Monson, and Hampden. But the other names—either of places or of characters—in the tale are entirely un-Lovecraftian, and the similarity of Hampdon to Hampden (assuming, as likely, that Rimel knew of the latter) may be coincidental. Lovecraft, of course, was scrupulous in selecting names according to the region of the country in which a tale was set; but we are not even informed precisely where "The Tree on the Hill" takes place—the mention of a Beacon Street in Hampdon might suggest New England, but the general landscape is more suggestive of Rimel's native West.

Two other names mentioned casually in the first two parts of the narrative are highly peculiar, and warrant the belief that Lovecraft made a few revisions and additions in these sections. Toward the close of the first section we are given this paragraph:

> Again the vast doorway yawned before me; and I was sucked within that black, writhing cloud. I seemed to be staring at space unlimited. I saw a void beyond my vocabulary to describe; a dark, bottomless gulf teeming with name-

less shapes and entities—things of madness and delirium, as tenuous as a mist from Shamballah.

I venture to state that the last sentence was added by Lovecraft; and the clue is the mention of Shamballah. This primal city was invented in *The Book of Dzyan*, and Lovecraft was informed of this pseudo-mythology by E. Hoffmann Price in early 1933. Lovecraft mentions to Clark Ashton Smith that *The Book of Dzyan* "is kept at the Holy City of Shamballah, and is regarded as the oldest book in the world—its language being 'Senzar' (ancestor of Sanscrit), which was brought to earth 18,000,000 years ago by the Lords of Venus" (*SL* 4.155). Now Lovecraft mentioned Shamballah in two works of fiction: "Through the Gates of the Silver Key" (1932-33) and "The Diary of Alonzo Typer" (1935). Rimel, however, could not have borrowed Shamballah from the former because Lovecraft's mention of it was removed by E. Hoffmann Price (with Lovecraft's agreement) long before the tale saw print in *Weird Tales* for July 1934. Rimel could thus never have known of Shamballah unless he had heard of it from Price (and I do not believe Price and Rimel were correspondents) or discovered it independently from *The Book of Dzyan*, which does not seem likely. The mention of Hermes Trismegistus later in the text might also hint at Lovecraftian intrusion (Lovecraft cites him in *The Case of Charles Dexter Ward*), but this figure is common enough in esoteric lore that Rimel could have arrived at it independently.

The other extremely peculiar mention occurs in the extract from the mythical *Chronicle of Nath* cited in the second part of the tale. It is unlikely that Lovecraft was the creator of the mythical tome, for he would then have to be author of the extract as well; and the whole citation seems so intimately connected with the course of the narrative that Lovecraftian authorship seems quite doubtful—the passage from the book is not, in any case, as evocative as corresponding passages from the *Necronomicon* and other of Lovecraft's fabricated tomes in his own work.[1] Even the mention of the "Year of the Black Goat" need not be attributed to Lovecraft: much has been made of the "Black Goat of the Woods" in "The Whisperer in Darkness" (1930; *Weird Tales*, August 1931), and Rimel could easily have picked it up himself.

What is, however, curious is this reference from the extract: "This none could do save through the Gem; wherefore did Ka-Nefer the High-Priest keep that gem sacred in the temple." Now to my knowledge Ka-Nefer is mentioned only once in Lovecraft—in an entry in the commonplace book; it is nearly im-

---

1. Rimel has in fact now confirmed that HPL was the inventor of the title *Chronicle of Nath* and of the extract in the story. See "A History of the Chronicle of Nath," *Etchings and Odysseys* No. 9 (1986): 80.

possible that Rimel could have coined this name independently of Lovecraft. The portion of this sentence following the semicolon is therefore very probably Lovecraft's, and perhaps replaces some less interesting phrase of Rimel's. Beyond this, however, we need not attribute any part of the extract, or very much of these first two sections generally, to Lovecraft. The extended use of dialogue in the second section immediately brands it as un-Lovecraftian. One passage toward the end of this section ("'You reason in terms of this tiny earth,' Theunis said. 'Surely you don't think that the world is a rule for measuring the universe'") voices a theme very dear to Lovecraft's "cosmic" philosophy, but it is expressed in a crude and childish way not commensurate with Lovecraft's mature utterances; in particular, the idea that "modern science is . . . proving that the mystics were not so far off the track" could not possibly have come from the positivist Lovecraft.

One peculiar feature of the tale is the "Gem" cited in the extract and elaborated upon by Theunis: "'It's more or less like a lens or prism, though one can't take photographs with it. Someone of peculiar sensitiveness might look through and sketch what he sees.'" In the third section Theunis warns the narrator: "Don't look through the box as it is—it would fix you as it's fixed me." Now this is suggestive of nothing else but the Shining Trapezohedron; but "The Haunter of the Dark" was written well over a year after the completion of "The Tree on the Hill." It is not, however, likely that this feature was added by Lovecraft; rather, it seems very possible that this detail in Rimel's story helped to inspire Lovecraft's later creation of the Shining Trapezohedron. The similarity is not, in any case, so marked as to suggest a single creative force behind both conceptions.

In the third section there are so many phraseological and thematic echoes of Lovecraft's other works that it is awkward to attempt to list them. Indeed, the distinction between Rimel and Lovecraft is embarrassingly obvious, even though Lovecraft is compelled by the plot to insert a small amount of dialogue (actually monologue, since only Theunis makes a recorded utterance—perhaps similar to the pseudo-Akeley's long monologue to Wilmarth toward the close of "The Whisperer in Darkness").

In the first paragraph of Part III occurs an interesting passage: "He [Theunis] spoke fragmentarily of 'refraction,' 'polarization,' and 'unknown angles of space and time. . . .'" This is strongly reminiscent of conclusion of *At the Mountains of Madness*, where it is noted that Danforth "has on rare occasions whispered disjointed and irresponsible things about 'the black pit', 'the carven rim', 'the proto-shoggoths'" (MM 105-6), etc. The mention of "unknown angles of space and time" might link the tale to several of Lovecraft's later works, especially "The Whisperer in Darkness" and "The Dreams in the Witch House." ("The Shadow out of Time" is also suggested, but this tale was written after "The Tree on the Hill.")

Of other relations between this third section and the rest of Lovecraft's work (which would require a detailed commentary to elucidate fully) I shall point out only one. At the end of the tale, after the narrator has seen the cataclysmic vision revealed by Theunis's sketch, he utters: "Since then I have never been quite the same. Even the fairest scenes have seemed to hold some vague, ambiguous hint of the nameless blasphemies which may underlie them and form their masquerading essence." This is a common motif in Lovecraft: one thinks of "The Call of Cthulhu" ("I have looked upon all that the universe has to hold of horror, and even the skies of spring and the flowers of summer must ever afterward be poison to me" [*DH* 154]), "The Strange High House in the Mist" ("And ever since that hour, through dull changing years of greyness and weariness, the philosopher has laboured and eaten and slept and done uncomplaining the suitable deeds of a citizen" [*D* 284]), and others. But the closest resemblance is with the fragment "The Book," which I have dated to late 1933 (see my article "On 'The Book'"): "Nor could I ever after see the world as I had known it. Mixed with the present scene was always a little of the past and a little of the future, and every once-familiar object loomed alien in the new perspective brought by my widened sight" (*D* 364).

In a letter to Rimel where he notes his revision of the tale, Lovecraft remarks that he found Rimel's original conclusion anticlimactic. One wonders what Rimel had originally written, and how much of what Lovecraft wrote was based upon this original portion. It seems likely that Lovecraft had adhered fairly closely in point of plot to Rimel's original: perhaps Rimel merely had Theunis tell the narrator what he did when he went with the Gem to the locale of the tree on the hill. Perhaps the concluding surprise ending—the tree revealed actually to be a gigantic hand—was also Lovecraft's.

In sum, we should classify this revision decidedly as one of those where Lovecraft worked from a pre-existing draft. I maintain that Lovecraft's revisions or additions in the first two sections are so insignificant as to be virtually nil, but that the third section is his from beginning to end—it is unlikely that he even retained much original prose from Rimel's original for this part of the tale. Since this third section is slightly less than a third of the tale, Lovecraft's total contribution can be no more than 30-40%.

The story itself is by no means to be despised and is much more than a literary curiosity. While the plot as outlined by Rimel is rather clumsy—it is too fortuitous a coincidence that the Year of the Goat falls in the precise year when the narrator sees the strange vision on the hill, and that the Gem is so easily unearthed from a museum—and the precise nature of the menace threatening the earth is never described, this tale is significantly better than several of Lovecraft's other revisions. Rimel himself was, even at this early date, a fictionist of some merit: his "Disinterment" is a notable Lovecraftian pastiche, and his later tale, "The Metal Chamber" (*Weird Tales*, March 1939), while having distinct connexions with "The Shadow out of Time" and "In the Walls of Eryx," is itself a fine tale. Rimel was actually one of Lovecraft's more promising young disciples, and it is unfortunate that he did not maintain his work in weird fiction.

Lovecraft and the *Regnum Congo*

The first object of my curiosity was a book of medium size lying upon the table and presenting such an antediluvian aspect that I marvelled at beholding it outside a museum or library. It was bound in leather with metal fittings, and was in an excellent state of preservation; being altogether an unusual sort of volume to encounter in an abode so lowly. When I opened it to the title page my wonder grew even greater, for it proved to be nothing less rare than Pigafetta's account of the Congo region, written in Latin from the notes of the sailor Lopez and printed at Frankfort in 1598. I had often heard of this work, with its curious illustrations by the brothers De Bry, hence for a moment forgot my uneasiness in my desire to turn the pages before me. (*DH* 119)

This celebrated passage from "The Picture in the House" (1920) has perhaps led many to marvel at Lovecraft's recondite knowledge of Renaissance science and literature. Further descriptions of Pigafetta's *Regnum Congo* later in the story would lead us to believe that Lovecraft had not only consulted the rare volume, but had actually read it in detail. Where, then, could he have gained access to the tome? A copy exists in the John Carter Brown Library of Brown University, and Lovecraft might have seen it there; but what could have led him even to suspect the existence of this volume? The answer is now not difficult to find; and it reveals, unfortunately, that Lovecraft did not in fact consult the actual volume and that, in relying on second-hand accounts of the book, he made embarrassing mistakes concerning it.

The source for Lovecraft's knowledge of Pigafetta is nothing less than Thomas Henry Huxley's collection of essays, *Man's Place in Nature and Other Anthropological Essays* (1894). Lovecraft certainly knew of and read this volume, since he cites from Huxley's essay "On the Methods and Results of Ethnology" in the early essay "The Crime of the Century" (1915). In that essay Lovecraft makes use of Huxley's coined term "Xanthochroi" in reference to the yellow-haired and pale-complexioned people whom Lovecraft identified with the Aryan race. But an earlier essay in Huxley's volume—"On the Natural History of the Man-like Apes" (1–75)—provided Lovecraft all his information on the *Regnum Congo*, and he has repeated some errors and omissions that Huxley made in his own essay. The essay deals with the history of scholarship on the simian species in the 200 years before Huxley's time, and in the very opening Huxley discusses the *Regnum Congo* in some detail: "I have not met with any notice of one of these *Man-like Apes* of earlier date than that contained in Pigafetta's 'Description of the kingdom of Congo,' drawn up from the notes of a Portuguese sailor, Eduardo Lopez, and published in 1598" (1–2). In a footnote Huxley gives the Latin title:

REGNUM CONGO: hoc est VERA DESCRIPTIO REGNI AFRICANI QUOD TAM AB INCOLIS QUAM LUSITANIS CONGUS APPELLATUR, per Philippum Pigafettam, olim ex Eduardo Lopez acroamatis lingua Italica excerpta, num Latio sermone donata ab August. Cassiod. Reinio. Iconibus et imaginibus rerum memorabilium quasi vivis, opera et industria Joan. Theodori et Joan. Israelis de Bry, fratrum exornata. Francofurti, MDXCVIII. (2 note)

(A translation of the above is as follows: REGNUM CONGO, i.e., a true description of the African kingdom which is called "Congo" both by its inhabitants and by Spaniards, previously rendered into Italian by Filippo Pigafetta from the verbal accounts of Eduardo Lopez, now translated into Latin by A. C. Reinius. Decorated with maps and virtually live illustrations of memorable phenomena by the toil and diligence of the brothers J. T. and J. I. De Bry. Frankfurt, 1598.)

Unfortunately, neither Huxley nor Lovecraft seemed to know that this is not the first printing of Pigafetta's account. Rather, it was first published in Italian (hence the *lingua Italica* above) in 1591. The title of this edition is as follows: *Relatione de reame di Congo et della cironvicine contrade, tratta dalli scritti & ragionamenti di Odoardo* [sic] *Lopez, Portoghese, per Filippo Pigafetta* (Roma: Appresso B. Grassi, 1591). What is more, there was a Dutch translation of this in 1596 (Amsterdam: Cornelis Claesz), an English translation in 1597 (London: John Wolfe), and a German translation in 1597 (Frankfurt am Mayn: Johan Saur). It was in this German edition that the De Bry plates first appeared, whence they were transferred to the Latin edition of the following year.[1] And the Latin translation is not the work of Pigafetta, as Lovecraft seems to have believed, but is by A. C. Reinius (*Latio sermone donata ab . . .*). In addition, the real name of

---

1. William Scott Home is therefore incorrect when he remarks that "it was very likely the 1598 Frankfurt edition in which the De Bry illustrations first appeared" (143). Indeed, Home ought to have known that this was not the case, since he reprints a plate (facing p. 134) that obviously derives from the German, and not Latin, edition, since all the accompanying text on the page is in German black-letter! It ought to be remarked that Home's essay is riddled with errors of detail and had best be used, if at all, with caution.

the "sailor Lopez" seems to have been Duarte Lopes.[2]

But what of Lovecraft's detailed descriptions of the plates by the brothers De Bry which he provides in the story? It happens that Huxley actually reprints (or, rather, has had redrawn) two plates from the *Regnum Congo*, including the important plate XII representing the butcher shop of the cannibal Anziques. Before discussing that plate, let us consider the other details in Lovecraft's account. His indication that the book "was bound in leather with metal fittings" is apparently derived from his imagination; and in any case such clasps need not have been affixed at the time of publication. (It may be worth noting that, although Lovecraft seems to imply that the book is rather large, it is in fact quite small; the Latin version is only 60 pages,[3] while a modern English translation[4] is 137 pages, and a modern French translation[5] is 147 pages.) Later in the story Lovecraft records some remarks by the preternaturally aged owner of the volume:

> "Queer haow picters kin set a body thinkin'. Take this un here near the front. Hev yew ever seed trees like thet, with big leaves a floppin' over an' daown? And them men—them can't be niggers—they dew beat all. Kinder like Injuns, I guess, even ef they be in Afriky. Some o' these here critters looks like monkeys, or half monkeys an' half men. (*DH* 122)

This is an exact description of a plate reproduced or redrawn in Huxley's volume. Huxley describes the plate as follows: "So much of the plate as contains these apes is faithfully copied in the woodcut (Fig. 1), and it will be observed that they are tail-less, long-armed, and large-eared; and about the size of Chimpanzees" (3).

Lovecraft's character then continues: "'. . . but I never heerd o' nothin' like this un.' Here he pointed to a fabulous creature of the artist, which one might describe as a sort of dragon with the head of an alligator" (*DH* 122). This too derives directly from Huxley, who writes: "It may be that these apes are as much figments of the imagination of the ingenious brothers [i.e., De

---

2. See the modern French translation of the *Regnum Congo* (*Description du Royaume de Congo et des Contrees Environnantes*) by Willy Bal (Louvain/Paris, 1965), whose introduction (esp. pp. xxif.) gives much information on early editions.

3. Cf. *Catalogue of Books Printed on the Continent of Europe 1501–1600 in Cambridge Libraries*, comp. H. M. Adams (Cambridge: Cambridge University Press, 1967), 2.79. I have not actually consulted the Latin edition.

4. *A Report of the Kingdom of Congo, and of the Surrounding Countries*, tr. Margarite Hutchinson (1881; rpt. New York: Negro Universities Press/Greenwood Press, 1969).

5. See note 2.

Bry] as the winged, two-legged, crocodile-headed dragon which adorns the same plate" (3). This dragon figure is not reproduced in Huxley's plate, and Lovecraft had to work merely from Huxley's verbal description.

Let us now return to Lovecraft's description of the twelfth De Bry plate:

> The engravings were indeed interesting, drawn wholly from imagination and careless descriptions, and represented negroes with white skins and Caucasian features; nor would I soon have closed the book had not an exceedingly trivial circumstance upset my tired nerves and revived my sensation of disquiet. What annoyed me was merely the persistent way in which the volume tended to fall open of itself at Plate XII, which represented in gruesome detail a butcher's shop of the cannibal Anziques. I experienced some shame at my susceptibility to so slight a thing, but the drawing nevertheless disturbed me, especially in connexion with some adjacent passages descriptive of Anzique gastronomy. (*DH* 119)

This entire description is drawn from an appendix to Huxley's essay (pp. 73–75), "African Cannibalism in the Sixteenth Century," where he recounts what Pigafetta says in chapter 5 of Book I of the *Regnum Congo*. It is here that the brothers De Bry's plate XII is reprinted—or, rather, redrawn as a woodcut by W. H. Wesley, who was presumably responsible for the redrawing of the earlier plate. Of the plate Huxley remarks: "The careful illustrators of Pigafetta have done their best to enable the reader to realize this account of the 'Anziques,' and the unexampled butcher's shop represented in Fig. 12 [i.e., of Huxley's book], is a facsimile of part of their Plate XII" (p. 75).

Lovecraft's aged character now describes the plate: "'That fellow bein' chopped up gives me a tickle every time I look at 'im—I hev ta keep lookin' at him—see whar the butcher cut off his feet? Thar's his head on thet bench, with one arm side of it, an' t' other arm's on the graound side o' the meat block'" (*DH* 122). All this again tallies with the illustration in Huxley's book. But comparison of this illustration with the actual De Bry plate from the German or Latin edition of the *Regnum Congo* (reprinted by W. S. Home in *The Dark Brotherhood*) brings to light some interesting facts. Wesley has chosen only to redraw the butcher shop at the far right of the original De Bry plate, and it seems to be he—and not the brothers De Bry—who has endowed the negroes "with white skins and Caucasian features"; the figures on the left side of the De Bry plate—left out by Wesley—are actually much more negroid in appearance.

The second-hand nature of Lovecraft's erudition in this case would be rather less culpable had he not himself accused Poe of doing similar things. In remarking on Poe's borrowing of the term "Afrasiab" in "The Premature Burial" Lovecraft notes: "[Poe] was a great boy for second-hand erudition"

(SL 4.162); while in "Supernatural Horror in Literature" he notes that among Poe's "defects and affectations" was his "pretence to profound and obscure scholarship" (D 396). I am not about to assert that most of Lovecraft's knowledge was second-hand—indeed, he had a far greater and more authentic grasp of classical literature and philosophy, modern science, and many other subjects than Poe, and he integrated this knowledge into a philosophy far more profound and coherent than Poe could ever have managed—but his second-hand borrowings and attempts to assert knowledge in subjects on which he was ignorant landed him on occasion in trouble; as witness his bumbling derivation of the Greek word *Necronomicon* (although later scholars such as George Wetzel, William Scott Home, E. F. Bleiler, and others, all blithely ignorant of Greek, have been no less incompetent at the task), or the embarrassing errors of detail he made when he tried to explain the Greek-Hebrew incantation he had cribbed from the *Encyclopaedia Britannica* for "The Horror at Red Hook." Other second-hand borrowings have come to light which, while not erroneous, perhaps ought to make us cautious of attributing all-encompassing knowledge to Lovecraft: the books on cryptography, for example, cited so impressively in "The Dunwich Horror" are all derived from the article on "Cryptography" (by John Eglinton Bailey) in the 9th edition of the *Britannica*.

But these borrowings are always minor and rarely affect the success of the story in which they appear; and Lovecraft's letters testify abundantly to the real knowledge he had acquired over a lifetime's scholarship in a large number of diverse fields. We all take short-cuts when it is convenient to do so, and there is no reason to believe that Lovecraft was exempt from the habit.

Works Cited

Home, William Scott. "The Lovecraft 'Books': Some Addenda and Corrigenda." In Lovecraft's *The Dark Brotherhood and Other Pieces*. Sauk City, WI: Arkham House, 1966. 134–52.

Huxley, Thomas Henry. *Man's Place in Nature and Other Anthropological Essays*. New York: D. Appleton & Co., 1894.

The Sources for "From Beyond"

It is unlikely that "From Beyond" (1920) will ever be regarded as one of Lovecraft's better tales; and such a judgment is perfectly justified, since in its slipshod style, melodramatic excess, and general triteness of plot, the tale compares ill even with some of his other early tales, such as "Dagon" (1917), "The Picture in the House" (1920), and "The Outsider" (1921). But, as with everything Lovecraft wrote, the tale's poor quality does not prevent it from displaying certain features of considerable interest. In the first place, the philosophical sources of the tale can now be traced with some certainty; secondly, the story seems itself to have provided sources for several later tales.

The philosophical interest of the tale is noteworthy, for it centres upon an issue of fundamental importance in all modern philosophical speculation since Descartes—the problem of knowledge. How do we know what we know? How can we be certain that the sense-impressions we receive are accurate reflections of external reality? Is there an external reality of which they are the reflections? This problem certainly occupied some of the ancient philosophers. Parmenides and Democritus questioned the truth-value of sense-perception, and Gorgias the sophist wrote a celebrated treatise, *On Not-Being* (c. 440 B.C.E.), wherein he maintained that 1) nothing exists; 2) even if anything existed, it would be incomprehensible; 3) even if it were comprehensible, it would be incommunicable—and his whole argument was based upon the unreliability of sense-perception (see Kerford, ch. 8). Finally, the ancient Sceptics similarly believed that nothing can be known (and some were as rigorously consistent as to doubt whether even this—that nothing can be known—can be known!), and waged extended polemics against their opponents (especially the Stoics and the Epicureans) who tried to assert both the possibility of knowledge and the reliability of sense-data. After Descartes instituted his system of "Cartesian doubt," the problem of knowledge became a focus—some would say a bane—of philosophical enquiry. Lovecraft reflects this problem in "From Beyond" by conceiving of a way to "break down the barriers" (*D* 91) that our five senses impose and which prevent our catching a glimpse of reality "as it really is."

Part of the philosophical foundation of the tale is indeed derived from Descartes, although in a parodic way. Crawford Tillinghast tells the unnamed narrator how it is that we may glimpse "vistas unknown to man": "'You have heard of the pineal gland? . . . That gland is the great sense-organ of organs—*I have found out*. It is like sight in the end, and transmits visual pictures to the brain'" (D 93). This is a joke at Descartes' expense: when Descartes, in the *Meditations on First Philosophy*, established the distinction (one of the most pernicious ideas in the history of philosophy, rivalled perhaps only by Plato's Forms or Kant's *a priori* knowledge) between a material body and an immaterial and immortal soul, he found himself in the awkward position of being unable to explain how two such fundamentally different entities could ever interact, as they clearly do in the human being; he then (in *The Passions of the Soul*) seized upon the pineal gland as the mediator between body and soul. Lovecraft was fully aware of this celebrated venture into fatuity (see "Some Causes of Self-Immolation" [MW 180]), and he is having a bit of fun with it in "From Beyond."

But a more immediate and pervasive influence for the genesis of the whole tale can be found—in the form of Hugh Elliot's *Modern Science and Materialism* (1919). Lovecraft first mentions this work in a letter of June 1921 (SL 1.134; see also SL 1.158), but it is almost certain that he had read it before November 1920, the date of writing of "From Beyond" (cf. SL 1.121). That he found this triumphant exposition of mechanistic materialism stimulating can be seen by a few entries in his commonplace book which I have hypothesised were inspired by the volume:

> 34 Moving away from earth more swiftly than light—past gradually unfolded—horrible revelation.
>
> 35 Special beings with special senses from remote universes. Advent of an external universe to view.
>
> 36 Disintegration of all matter to electrons and finally empty space assured, just as devolution of energy to radiant heat is known. Case of *acceleration*—man passes into space. (MW 89)

It can be shown that each of these entries has a correlation in various passages in Elliot's book that discuss the points in question. Entry 35 is particularly interesting for our purposes, since it is precisely such an "external universe" that is brought to view in "From Beyond."

A still more concrete case for Elliot's book as inspiration for "From Beyond" can be made by collation of actual passages from the two works. In Lovecraft's tale Tillinghast boldly dilates upon the fallibility of the senses in a striking passage:

> "What do we know," he had said, "of the world and the universe about us? Our means of receiving impressions are absurdly few, and our notions of surrounding objects infinitely narrow. We see things only as we are constructed to see them, and can gain no idea of their absolute nature. With five feeble

senses we pretend to comprehend the boundlessly complex cosmos, yet other beings with a wider, stronger, or different range of senses might not only see very differently the things we see, but might see and study whole worlds of matter, energy, and life which lie close at hand yet can never be detected with the senses we have." (D 91)

Note a very similar passage in the introduction to Elliot's book:

> Let us first ask why it is that all past efforts to solve ultimate riddles have failed, and why it is that they must continue to fail. It is, in the first place, due to the fact that all knowledge is based on sense-impressions, and cannot, therefore, go beyond what the senses can perceive. Men have five or six different senses only, and these are all founded on the one original sense of touch. Of these five or six senses, the three of most importance for the accumulation of knowledge are those of sight, hearing, and touch. By these senses we are able to detect three separate qualities of the external Universe. Now, supposing that we happened to have a thousand senses instead of five, it is clear that our conception of the Universe would be extremely different from what it now is. We cannot assume that the Universe has only five qualities because we have only five senses. We must assume, on the contrary, that the number of its qualities may be infinite, and that the more senses we had, the more we should discover about it. (Elliot 2–3)

Later in the tale the narrator is baffled by a "pale, outré colour or blend of colours which I could neither place nor describe"; Tillinghast replies: "'Do you know what that is? . . . *That is ultra-violet.*' He chuckled oddly at my surprise. 'You thought ultra-violet was invisible, and so it is—but you can see that and many other invisible things *now*'" (D 93). This has its exact correlate in Elliot:

> Not only are our senses few, but they are extremely limited in their range. The sense of sight can detect nothing but waves in aether; all sensations of light and colour are no more than aethereal waves striking upon the retina with varying strength and frequency. And even then, it is only special aethereal undulations that give rise to the sensation of sight. The majority cannot be perceived by the retina at all; it is only when the waves follow one another within certain limits of rapidity (between four hundred billion and seven hundred billion a second) that sight ensues. If the waves are below the lower limit of rapidity, they do not give rise to the sensation of light at all, though they may give rise to a sensation of heat. If they are more rapid than the higher limit (as in the case of ultra-violet rays) they are not discernible by any sense at all. (Elliot 3)

Finally, the narrator at one point experiences great alarm when he sees, as a result of Tillinghast's machine, "huge animate things brushing past me and occasionally *walking or drifting through my supposedly solid body*" (D 95). Lovecraft is here merely reflecting in a vivid way the simple physical fact that solid matter is largely empty space. Elliot writes of it at length:

> Let us now . . . see what matter would look like if magnified to, say, a thousand million diameters, so that the contents of a small thimble appeared to become the size of the earth. Even under this great magnification, the individual electrons would still be too small to be seen by the naked eye. Small aggregations of these invisible electrons, moving in invisible orbits round a centre, would be aggregated to form atoms, and these again to form molecules, appearing (if they could be seen) to occupy the same volume as a football. The first circumstance that strikes us is that nearly the whole structure of matter consists of the empty spaces between electrons. Matter, which appears to us so continuous in its structure, is really no more than empty space, in which at rare intervals here and there an inconceivably minute electron is travelling at high velocity upon its way. It ceases, therefore, to be remarkable that X-rays can penetrate matter and come out on the other side. How should the tiny electrons obstruct their passage? It ceases to be remarkable that an electron from radium can be shot clean through a plate of aluminium; for, from the electron's point of view, the aluminium plate is very little different from empty space. (Elliot 54)

Clearly, then, the immediate inspiration for "From Beyond" was Elliot's *Modern Science and Materialism* and the philosophical vistas it opened to Lovecraft's fertile and imaginative mind. But "From Beyond," however imperfect a product in itself, very clearly served as a springboard for certain of his later stories. It is as if Lovecraft, dissatisfied with the treatment of some themes in this early story, decided to give them fuller and better treatment elsewhere.

Firstly, the narrator of "From Beyond" remarks at the outset: "That Crawford Tillinghast should ever have studied science and philosophy was a mistake" (*D* 91). We are immediately reminded of "The Dreams in the Witch House," where it is said: "Perhaps Gilman ought not to have studied so hard. Non-Euclidean calculus and quantum physics are enough to stretch any brain" (*MM* 263). A later passage in "From Beyond" is also suggestive of Gilman's voyages into hyperspace: "I was now in a vortex of sound and motion, with confused pictures before my eyes. . . . After that the scene was almost wholly kaleidoscopic, and in the jumble of sights, sounds, and unidentified sense-impressions I felt that I was about to dissolve or in some way lose the solid form" (*D* 94–95).

We have already alluded to the "pale, outré colour or blend of colours" which the narrator of "From Beyond" sees—and we can hardly fail to recall "The Colour out of Space": "The colour . . . was almost impossible to describe; and it was only by analogy that they called it colour at all" (*DH* 59).

Finally, the central philosophical theme of "From Beyond"—the fallibility of the senses—is emphasised in several later stories. I have studied this concept elsewhere (see "'Reality' and Knowledge"), and the idea of what I have termed "supra-reality"—a reality beyond that revealed to us by the senses, or that which we experience in every-day life (what Onderdonk called the "supernormal")—is central to much of Lovecraft's fiction; finding expression particularly in "Hypnos" (1922), "The Unnamable" (1923), "The Colour out of Space" (1927), "The Dreams in the Witch House" (1932), "Through the Gates of the Silver Key" (1932-33), and others. Note also the following passage from "The Shunned House" (1924):

> To declare that we were not nervous on that rainy night of watching would be an exaggeration both gross and ridiculous. We were not, as I have said, in any sense childishly superstitious, but scientific study and reflection had taught us that the known universe of three dimensions embraces the merest fraction of the whole cosmos of substance and energy. . . . To say that we actually believed in vampires or werewolves would be a carelessly inclusive statement. Rather must it be said that we were not prepared to deny the possibility of certain unfamiliar and unclassified modifications of vital force and attenuated matter; existing very infrequently in three-dimensional space because of its more intimate connexion with other spatial units, yet close enough to the boundary of our own to furnish us occasional manifestations which we, for lack of a proper vantage-point, may never hope to understand. (MM 251-52)

The closeness of wording between this passage and parts of "From Beyond" suggests that the idea was one of recurrent fascination to Lovecraft—and it is an idea derived from his continuing researches into the findings of modern science and philosophy, especially such books as Elliot's *Modern Science and Materialism*, Ernst Haeckel's *The Riddle of the Universe*, and Bertrand Russell's *Our Knowledge of the External World*.

Hence "From Beyond" has in its clumsy way shown once again the unity and integration of Lovecraft's work and thought. Science and philosophy, far from being antagonistic to the creation of literature, were for Lovecraft direct stimuli for it; and his untiring delvings into the strange worlds revealed by astrophysicists, biologists, and philosophers proved to be a central—perhaps even a necessary—inspiration for some of the greatest weird tales of the twentieth century.

Works Cited

Elliott, Hugh. *Modern Science and Materialism*. London: Longmans, Green & Co., 1919.

Kerferd, G. B. *The Sophistic Movement*. Cambridge: Cambridge University Press, 1981.

On "The Descendant"

We know less about "The Descendant" than about any other single story or fragment by Lovecraft. The title was supplied by R. H. Barlow; the date of 1926 was supplied by August Derleth and is, apparently, entirely conjectural. Lovecraft never mentions the fragment in any correspondence I have seen. Whereas we can guess that "Azathoth" may be an early adumbration of *The Dream-Quest of Unknown Kadath*, and "The Book" in part a rewriting of *Fungi from Yuggoth*, we have no idea what "The Descendant" is about or where it is going. It is Lovecraft's most unsatisfying yet most tantalising piece.

It is unclear how Derleth arrived at the date of the work. My own belief is that it was written in early 1927. In April of that year Lovecraft reports "making a very careful study of *London* . . . in order to get back-ground for tales involving richer antiquities than America can furnish" (*ES* 1.83); and "The Descendant" is the only tale of this period set in London.

The very text of the fragment is confused. Editions previous to mine (*D* 358–62) printed an introductory paragraph or fragment: "Writing on what the doctor tells me is my deathbed, my most hideous fear is that the man is wrong. I suppose I shall seem to be buried next week, but . . ." When this was printed in *Marginalia*, Derleth added the note: "*(foregoing deleted).*" It was indeed crossed out on the ms., but Derleth did not explain that when Lovecraft began "The Descendant" proper ("In London there is a man who screams . . .") he turned the paper around, so that the "deleted" passage is now at the bottom of the first page of the ms., upside down. This—along with the apparently unrelated nature of the passage—leads me to believe that it does not belong with "The Descendant" at all; I have accordingly removed it from my text. The deleted passage is in the first person, while the fragment proper is in the third; and the "I" does not seem to represent either character of the fragment, Lord Northam or "young Williams." My inclination is to regard the deleted passage as yet another, separate fragment.

This still does not allow us to make much sense of "The Descendant" as it stands. Let us see what internal evidence provides in terms of dating and content. The mention of a "Nameless City" in the "desert of Araby" at the very end of the fragment clearly points to Lovecraft's own tale of 1921. The mentions of Charles Fort and Ignatius Donnelly seem promising, but not much can be made of them: we do not know when Lovecraft read Donnelly's *Atlantis: The Antediluvian World* (1882); as to Charles Fort, we learn that around September 1927 Lovecraft read *New Lands*, but "didn't find it as interesting as *The Book of the Damned*" (SL 2.174), which he must have read earlier.

More may be gleaned from the character of Lord Northam, the harried old man who has only one goal in life: "All he seeks from life is not to think." Some external features of his characterisation bring Arthur Machen and Lord Dunsany to mind, although in a superficial way. Northam lives at Gray's Inn, London; Machen lived for many years at 4 Verulam Buildings, Gray's Inn (this is what gives us the *terminus post quem* of 1923, since Lovecraft only encountered the work of Machen at this date). Northam is the "nineteenth Baron of a line whose beginnings went uncomfortably far back into the past"; Dunsany was the eighteenth Baron Dunsany in a line founded in the twelfth century.

Much of the fragment spins a peculiar tale about strange happenings in Roman Britain. Here the most interesting point is how many things Lovecraft gets wrong in his historical account. The biggest blunder is his mention of "the Third Augustan Legion then stationed at Lindum." Regrettably, Legio III Augusta was never stationed in England (it was almost always in Libya); rather, it was Legio II Augusta that was in England; and it was not, as far as I know, ever stationed in Lindum (Lincoln), but always in Isca Silurum (Caerleon-on-Usk), something Lovecraft should have known from reading Machen's *Hill of Dreams*. Lovecraft made the same mistake in "The Rats in the Walls" (1923), where he says that the legion camped at "Anchester." Here he has made three mistakes: 1) neither the second nor the third Augustan legion was ever stationed in Anchester because 2) the town never had a legionary fort, and 3) the town's name is Ancaster, not Anchester! (For the record, two other legions, IX Hispana and XX Valeria, were customarily stationed in England, at York and Chester, respectively. Other legions were transferred there as needed during revolts or to build Hadrian's Wall. Interestingly enough, IX Hispana seems to have vanished around 130 C.E., and to this day no satisfactory explanation of its disappearance has been made. Now there's a story idea for Lovecraft!) By 1933, however, when he read Arthur Weigall's *Wanderings in Roman Britain*, Lovecraft finally got the legions in Roman Britain straight (cf. SL 4.293).

Well, I think I have squeezed "The Descendant" dry; there does not seem anything more to be got out of it. If it was in fact written in 1926, it may have been written early in the year, when Lovecraft was still in New York: he frequently confessed to his inability to write fiction toward the end of his "New York exile." The Roman aspect is interesting in providing a link between

"The Rats in the Walls" and Lovecraft's great "Roman dream" of 1927; and the scene where young Williams buys the *Necronomicon* from a "gnarled old Levite" is uncannily similar to the scene in "The Book" (1933?) where the nameless narrator buys a nameless tome from an "old man [who] leered and tittered." We would like very much to know what Lovecraft was trying to do with "The Descendant"; it embodies central themes in his work—dubious heredity, ancient horror, a Faustian quest for forbidden knowledge—but never resolves them. It is one of Lovecraft's few false starts; and yet, we can learn something even from its unsatisfying paragraphs.

What Happens in "Arthur Jermyn"

I have always admired Lovecraft's "Facts Concerning the Late Arthur Jermyn and His Family" (1920; *D* 73–82) for its compactness and relatively sober narrative style, as opposed to the floridity (effective in its own way) of other such early tales as "The Doom That Came to Sarnath" (1919) or "Celephaïs" (1920). It has been considered a precursor to some of Lovecraft's greatest tales: its opening rumination on the potentially disastrous psychological effects of knowledge brings "The Call of Cthulhu" (1926) to mind, while its account of loathsome miscegenation foreshadows "The Shadow over Innsmouth" (1931). But "Arthur Jermyn" has been deprecated for a certain narrowness of focus: unlike the spectacular miscegenation affecting an entire clan or city (and potentially all civilisation) that we find in "The Lurking Fear" (1922) or "The Shadow over Innsmouth," we appear here to be concerned only with the corruption of a single family. As such, the tale has been seen as a bridge between those of Lovecraft's tales where horror envelops a single individual ("The Tomb," "Dagon") and those where all mankind is involved. If read carefully, however, "Arthur Jermyn" may show that this schema, while on the whole accurate, may be somewhat problematical.

Let us consider the celebrated opening utterance:

> Life is a hideous thing, and from the background behind what we know of it peer daemoniacal hints of truth which make it sometimes a thousandfold more hideous. Science, already oppressive with its shocking revelations, will perhaps be the ultimate exterminator of our human species—if separate species we be—for its reserve of unguessed horrors could never be borne by mortal brains if loosed upon the world. (*D* 73)

This passage is so well-known that critics have apparently not taken the trouble to note some anomalous details, especially if read with the whole of the tale in mind. In particular, what we have here is a *generalised* statement concerning the possibility that human beings may not be entirely "human" ("if separate species we be"); such a notion is not logically deducible from a *single* case of miscegenation, as we appear to have here. Was Lovecraft simply inept in feeling that all humanity (or at least some broad segment of humanity) is implicated in the corruption of the Jermyn line, or are there in fact broader conceptions at work here?

The crux of the tale is what Arthur Jermyn's great-great-great-grandfather, Sir Wade Jermyn, actually found in the depths of Africa. It is mentioned very early on that one of Sir Wade's "bizarre conjectures" was the existence of a "prehistoric *white* Congolese civilisation" (my emphasis). This detail seems to have passed almost entirely unnoticed by scholars: what would a white civilisation be doing in Africa? We get some description of it later on, as Sir Wade describes

> the gigantic walls and pillars of a forgotten city, crumbling and vine-grown, and . . . damp, silent, stone steps leading interminably down into the darkness of abysmal treasure-vaults and inconceivable catacombs . . . the living things that might haunt such a place [were] creatures half of the jungle and half of the impiously aged city—fabulous creatures which even a Pliny might describe with scepticism; things that might have sprung up after the great apes had overrun the dying city with the walls and the pillars, the vaults and the weird carvings. (D 74-75)

This passage is critical, for it tells us what this city was like prior to Sir Wade's expedition there. The real implication of the story, I believe, is that this city (erected by the "white Congolese civilisation") *is the true fount of all white civilisation*. For someone of Lovecraft's well-known racialist bent, such a thing would be a horror surpassing any isolated case of miscegenation. This story is, really speaking, a mirror-image of the later "Medusa's Coil" (1930), where the true horror—intended to exceed all the other supernatural manifestations throughout the story—is that Marceline, "though in deceitfully slight proportion, . . . was a negress" (HM 200). The white man really comes from Africa!

Let us be clear on one point, however. The "white ape" whom Sir Wade marries is not a member of the original white civilisation, but a product of the mingling of apes with the remaining members of this civilisation: note that the "living things" Sir Wade found were "creatures half of the jungle [i.e., apes] and half of the impiously aged city [i.e., the white civilisation]" (D 75). How else could the ape be "white"? The white ape is itself a result of miscegenation, and its ancestors must have migrated throughout the world to found all the known white races. By marrying this white ape, Sir Wade has, as it were, given his descendants an "extra dose" of the blood of this corrupt race, producing the physiognomic and temperamental anomalies of the Jermyn line. When the ape's mummified form is discovered by Arthur Jermyn's Belgian associate, M. Verhaeren, it is found to be "less hairy than any recorded variety [of ape], and infinitely nearer mankind—quite shockingly so" (D 82). Its existence not merely reveals the source of the Jermyns' peculiar appearance, but by extension confirms the truth of all the tales of the white civilisation told by Sir Wade.

The overall implication of "Arthur Jermyn" is that all white civilisation is derived from this primal race in Africa, a race that has corrupted itself by intermingling with apes. This is the only explanation for the narrator's opening statement, "If we knew what we are, we should do as Sir Arthur Jermyn did [i.e., commit suicide]" (D 73): we may not have a white ape in our immediate ancestry, but we are all the products of an ultimate miscegenation.

In *The Weird Tale* (1990) I first drew attention to the anomaly of the generalised opening of "Arthur Jermyn" and its seeming case of unique miscegenation; at that time I did not know the solution to the anomaly, and I wondered: "Does Lovecraft mean us to feel horror, by extension, at the truth of the Darwin theory? Surely even Lovecraft did not expect people to find evolution psychologically unbearable" (205). But in fact that is exactly what is happening. Lovecraft is suggesting that the distinction between apes and human beings is a highly tenuous one—not merely in the case of the Jermyns, but of us all. In the essay "At the Root" (1918) Lovecraft wrote: "We must recognise the essential underlying savagery in the animal called man . . . civilisation is but a slight coverlet beneath which the dominant beast sleeps lightly and ever ready to awake" (CE 5.29). This could serve as the motto for "Arthur Jermyn," where the opening conjecture "if separate species we be" is ultimately to be answered in the negative.

Works Cited

Joshi, S. T. *The Weird Tale.* Austin: University of Texas Press, 1990.

"The Tree" and Ancient History

"The Tree" (1920) is one of Lovecraft's least-regarded tales: since it was written in the midst of his initial "Dunsanian" period, it comes under general attack for being another of his wooden and lifeless imitations of Lord Dunsany; even so perceptive a critic as Donald R. Burleson dismisses the tale as "stylistically pleasing but otherwise little distinguished" (Burleson 70). And yet, "The Tree" stands out as being the only tale by Lovecraft set in the ancient world[1] (and in this fact alone it is to be distinguished from Dunsany, who rarely used historical settings for his early short stories); what is more, the tale reveals Lovecraft as a careful and profound student of ancient history, since the date when the tale's events take place can be almost exactly determined.

Lovecraft's fondness for classical civilisation needs no emphasis. His first extant poem, "The Poem of Ulysses" (second "edition," 8 November 1897), is a charming retelling of the *Odyssey* in 88 lines; and we know that he soon afterwards wrote similar verse retellings of other such epics as the *Iliad* and the *Aeneid* (both non-extant). Another non-extant juvenile work, *The Argonauts*, is presumably a retelling of the story of Jason and the Argonauts as related by Apollonius Rhodius in the *Argonautica* (mid-third century B.C.E.).

Lovecraft learnt Latin at a very early age—he may have begun at the age of eight. By the age of ten or so he produced a remarkable literal verse translation of the first 88 lines of Ovid's *Metamorphoses*; indeed, the existing manuscript of this work may be fragmentary, so that Lovecraft this time could well have translated much more of the text than we have. Lovecraft, however, never mastered Greek, although he studied it in high school. In a late letter he remarks that he "never got beyond the first six books of Xenophon" (*SL* 4.173), by which he probably refers to Xenophon's *Anabasis* (the "March Up Country"), although the *Hellenica* of Xenophon is in seven books. The *Anabasis* is still used today as a beginning Greek reader, as Xenophon employed a model Attic prose style.

---

1. Aside from his "Roman dream" of 1927, incorporated by Frank Belknap Long in *The Horror from the Hills* (1931).

When, however, Lovecraft had come to write "The Tree," he had comprehensively absorbed all branches of ancient culture—Greek philosophy (especially the Atomists and Epicurus, with such Latin thinkers as Lucretius and the Stoic Seneca), Greek and Roman history, ancient literature from Homer to Juvenal (there is little evidence that Lovecraft read much late Latin, i.e., beyond the third century C.E.), and even ancient art and archaeology. What is remarkable about this absorption is that Lovecraft had for the most part to rely on rather inadequate school manuals and handbooks. Of the books in Greek history found in his library after his death, only a few—Mahaffy's *Survey of Greek Civilization*, Sir William Smith's *History of Greece*—are today granted any scholarly value. Lovecraft, however, clearly supplemented these manuals with extensive reading from original sources (especially, in the realm of Greek history, from Thucydides, Herodotus, Xenophon, and Diodorus Siculus) and with reference to Smith's still useful *Classical Dictionary* and *Dictionary of Greek and Roman Antiquities*.

The internal dating of the events in "The Tree" is actually a relatively simple business for anyone versed in ancient history; for Lovecraft is careful to provide unambiguous references that allow an exact pinpointing of the historical period involved. The tale concerns a contest proposed by the "Tyrant of Syracuse" (*D* 51) between the two great sculptors, Kalos and Musides, to carve a statue of Tyche for the Tyrant's city. Although the two artists are reputed to be the closest of friends, we soon find that Kalos has suddenly taken ill and eventually dies; we are clearly meant to infer that Musides has in fact poisoned Kalos so that he will not be defeated in the contest.[2] But Kalos is weirdly avenged when a strange olive tree growing out of his tomb suddenly falls upon Musides' residence, destroying both him and his statue.

Every detail in this story fits perfectly. First, the artists' names: Kalos in Greek simply means "handsome" or "fair," while Musides is a regular Greek formation meaning "son of the Muse(s)"—both apt names for artists. Moreover, the epigraph of the tale—omitted in all publications save the first, in the *Tryout* for October 1921—reads "Fata viam invenient" ("The Fates will find a way"), derived from Virgil's *Aeneid* 3.395. The mention of Fate connects directly with the contest to build a statue of Tyche, for *tyche* is nothing more than the Greek word for "chance" or "fate." Indeed, the Greek philosopher

---

2. Burleson's remark that "The strong indication, of course, is that Musides has poisoned Kalos . . . but this cannot be proven from the text alone," and his subsequent belief that "we have in 'The Tree' one of HPL's most unreliable or dissembling narrators" is, I think, a bit perverse. Of course HPL never says directly that Musides poisoned Kalos; to do so would have completely destroyed the subtlety of the story.

Democritus (much admired by Lovecraft for his development of the Atomic theory) equated necessity (*ananke* in Greek) or fate with chance, explaining the latter as merely those workings of fate whose precise chains of causality are not perceived by human beings (see Guthrie 414f.). This seems to be the conception utilised in "The Tree": Musides was bound to perish because of his murder of Kalos, but to the human spectators his death seems to be an unexplained phenomenon of chance.

Turning to the specifically historical data, let us first consider which Tyrant of Syracuse may be in question. Syracuse, the most important Greek city in Sicily, was also one of the earliest overseas colonies of the Greeks: it was reputed to have been founded by the Corinthians in c. 734 B.C.E.[3] At this time, however, it was governed by an aristocratic group collectively called *gamoroi*; and it remained so governed for two and a half centuries. Syracuse then came under attack and was defeated by Hippocrates, the tyrant of neighbouring Gela (c. 495), but a certain Gelo espoused the cause of the *gamoroi* and became tyrant in c. 485. When Gelo died in 476, his brother Hiero succeeded to the tyranny; he ruled until his death in 467/6. It was at this time that Syracuse gained prominence as a cultural centre—many poets and philosophers (including the playwright Aeschylus) made trips there from mainland Greece.

After Hiero's death Syracuse became a democracy governed by an assembly and council, but Dionysius I re-established a tyranny in c. 406. He ruled until his death in 367, when his son Dionysius II took over, ruling in a turbulent period until 344, when he was finally overthrown and fled into exile.

Syracuse was thus under a tyranny for only two periods in its history—from 495 to 467/6 and from 406 to 344. The earlier period is, however, ruled out as the date of "The Tree," since we are told that "the Pallas of Musides surmounted a pillar in Athens, near the Parthenon." Now the Parthenon was begun only in 447, and completed in 432; hence Musides' statue can have been placed there only after these dates—perhaps a good deal after.

A date in the fourth century B.C.E. is suggested by the very fact that the Tyrant of Syracuse suggests the building of a statue of Tyche. As we have seen, the notion of Tyche is central to the philosophical interpretation of the tale. But the worship of Tyche as a goddess in Greece cannot be dated before the late fourth century; the first known cult was established in Thebes some time after

---

3. Most of the historical information presented here can be found in any comprehensive history of Greece; see in particular that by J. B. Bury and Russell Meiggs (4th ed. 1975); also various articles in the *Oxford Classical Dictionary*, 2nd ed., ed. N. G. L. Hammond and H. H. Scullard (Oxford: Oxford University Press, 1970).

371. Lovecraft would not have committed such an anachronism as postulating a cult in Greek society before such a cult was known to have existed; hence we are reduced to the period 371 to 344 for the dating of events in "The Tree."

But a final datum can be added. When Kalos is lying terminally ill, Musides is made to remark that he would build a tomb for Kalos "more lovely than the tomb of Mausolus"; but the tomb of Mausolus (satrap of Caria), or the Mausoleum, was constructed by his widow Artemisia only in 353. We must thus conclude that "The Tree" is set in the period 353–344, perhaps toward the very end of the reign of Dionysius II. It is interesting to note that the philosopher Plato visited Syracuse three times, in 387, 367, and 358; one wonders whether we are to imagine the two great artists and the philosopher (whom, be it noted, Lovecraft despised) hobnobbing either at the court of Dionysius II or in mainland Greece.

It may be asked why Lovecraft does not specifically name Dionysius II in the story. The answer is easily forthcoming: so specific a mention (as opposed to the very allusive nature of the other historical mentions) would mar the allegorical or symbolic nature of the tale. It is not the fact that the tale is set in the middle fourth century B.C.E. in Sicily that is of importance; rather, it is an age-old theme of human baseness and divine revenge which is at the heart of this story. Some time after finishing the tale, Lovecraft remarked pointedly: "It was the result of some rather cynical reflection on the possible real motives which may underlie even the most splendid-appearing acts of mankind. With this nucleus I developed a tale based on the Greek idea of divine justice and retribution (a very pretty though sadly mythical idea!), with the added Oriental notion of the soul of a man passing into something else" (SL 1.121).

Although in later years Lovecraft thought little of the story, on at least one occasion he took some pains to defend it. Lovecraft had sent the tale through the Transatlantic Circulator (the Anglo-American group of *littérateurs* who criticised one another's work in manuscript) in early 1921, and replied to some adverse criticisms of it:

> Regarding "The Tree"—Mr. Brown finds the climax insufficient, but I doubt if a tale of that type could possess a more obvious denouement. The climactic effect sought, is merely an emphasis—amounting to the first direct intimation—of the fact that there is something hidden behind the simple events of the tale; that the growing suspicion of Musides' crime and recognition of Kalos' posthumous vengeance is well founded. It is to proclaim what has hitherto been doubtful—to shew that the things of Nature see behind human hypocrisy and perceive the baseness at the heart of outward virtue. All the world deems Musides a model of fraternal piety and devotion although in truth he poisoned Kalos when he saw his laurels in peril. Did not the Tegeans

build to Musides a temple? But against all these illusions the trees whisper—the wise trees sacred to the gods—and reveal the truth to the midnight searcher as they chaunt knowingly over and over again *"Oida! Oida!"* [I know! I know!] This, then, is all the climax so nebulous a legend can possess. (CE 5.53–54)

This has not been an attempt to resurrect "The Tree" or to claim it as one of Lovecraft's masterpieces; rather, by pointing out the obvious care Lovecraft lavished both on the conception and the historicity of the tale, I hope I have demonstrated that even one of his minor tales can reveal beauties and subtleties not to be grasped by superficial reading. In 1921 Lovecraft made a celebrated utterance: "There are probably seven persons, in all, who really like my work; and they are enough. I should write even if I were the only patient reader, for my aim is merely self-expression" (CE 5.53). Truly, Lovecraft wrote for a discerning few; the few who could approach his own intelligence and sensitivity and appreciate the philosophical, stylistic, thematic, and historical profundities that lie beneath the surface of even his slightest products.

Works Cited

Burleson, Donald R. *H. P. Lovecraft: A Critical Study*. Westport, CT: Greenwood Press, 1983.

Guthrie, W. K. C. *A History of Greek Philosophy*. Volume 2. Cambridge: Cambridge University Press, 1965.

Joshi, S. T. *Lovecraft's Library: A Catalogue*. 3rd rev. ed. New York: Hippocampus Press, 2012.

Lovecraft and Dunsany's *Chronicles of Rodriguez*

The influence of Lord Dunsany upon the early work of H. P. Lovecraft is no secret; but only recently have efforts been made to trace this influence beyond the so-called "Dunsanian" fantasies of 1919-21. Robert M. Price has probed some Dunsanian resonances in such works as "The Music of Erich Zann" and "The Call of Cthulhu," but few other such attempts have been made. Part of the problem is that Lovecraft confessed that he did not care much for Dunsany's later work—i.e., work subsequent to his first collections of short stories, from *The Gods of Pegāna* (1905) to *Tales of Three Hemispheres* (1919)—so that it has not occurred to readers and critics to trace influences from this body of work upon Lovecraft's fiction of the 1920s and 1930s. Lovecraft confessed that *A Dreamer's Tales* (1910) affected him "as with an electric shock" (SL 2.328), but of even so fine a novel as *The Curse of the Wise Woman* (1933), he merely remarks tepidly that it has a "different sort of charm" (SL 5.353).

It may therefore come as a surprise that Dunsany's first novel, *The Chronicles of Rodriguez* (1922; published in the U.S. as *Don Rodriguez: Chronicles of Shadow Valley*) may contain, in a single chapter, the nucleus of two of Lovecraft's stories, "He" (1925) and "The Strange High House in the Mist" (1926).

Our first order of business in establishing such an influence is determining when Lovecraft actually read *The Chronicles of Rodriguez*. After his discovery of Dunsany in 1919, Lovecraft appears to have kept abreast of Dunsany's publications, reading them shortly after publication. The American edition of *Rodriguez* came out in October 1922, and in a letter of January 1923 Lovecraft remarks: "I hope that 'Don Rodriguez' represents a return to the earlier mood" (SL 1.203). An unpublished letter to Samuel Loveman states clearly: "I read . . . 'Don Rodriguez' last month, & advise you to do the same." This letter, from internal evidence, must date to 1923.[1] Lovecraft, therefore, clearly

---

1. The letter is dated only "29 April," but it is addressed from "Old 598"; and since HPL moved out of 598 Angell Street and moved to Brooklyn in March 1924, the letter must date to 1923. I am grateful to Mara Kirk Hart for providing the text of this

read the novel well before writing either "He" or "The Strange High House in the Mist."

The Chronicles of Rodriguez is, as Lovecraft notes, a picaresque novel about Don Rodriguez, the eldest son of a nobleman who is sent by his dying father to seek his fortune in the world. Rodriguez longs to distinguish himself in battle and win a castle for himself, and to this end he traverses the byways of Spain looking for "the wars"; along the way he picks up, as a Sancho Panza–like sidekick, a lowly but eager peasant named Morano.

The third chapter of the novel, "How He Came to the House of Wonder," relates how Rodriguez and Morano approach the house of a Professor of Magic, high up on a nearly inaccessible crag of a lofty mountain. Their climb is arduous:

> Nothing invited them there in the look of that house, but they were now in such a forbidding waste that shelter had to be found; they were all among edges of rock as black as the night and hard as the material of which Cosmos was formed, at first upon Chaos' brink. . . . Then they pushed on over rocks that seemed never trodden by man, so sharp were they and slanting, all piled together: it seemed the last waste, to which all shapeless rocks had been thrown. (R 66–67)

Finally they reach the house:

> In the wall that their hands had reached there was no door, so they felt along it till they came to the corner, and beyond the corner was the front wall of the house. In it was the front door. But so nearly did this door open upon the abyss that the bats that fled from their coming, from where they hunt above the door of oak, had little more to do than fall from their crannies, slanting ever so slightly, to find themselves safe from man in the velvet darkness, that lay between cliffs so lonely they were almost strangers to Echo. (R 67)

Few readers of Lovecraft can have failed to notice the resemblance to Thomas Olney's climb up the cliff in Kingsport to see the mysterious occupant of the lofty house described in "The Strange High House in the Mist." Speaking of Olney's attempt to "find a path to the inaccessible pinnacle" (D 280), Lovecraft goes on to remark:

> As he climbed slowly east, higher and higher above the estuary on his left and nearer and nearer the sea, he found the way growing in difficulty; till he won-

---

letter. It has now been published in *Letters to Samuel Loveman and Vincent Starrett*, ed. S. T. Joshi and David E. Schultz (West Warwick, RI: Necronomicon Press, 1994), 17.

dered how ever the dwellers in that disliked place managed to reach the world outside, and whether they came often to market in Arkham. (D 280)

Olney finally reaches the dwelling and finds that it—like the professor's house in *Rodriguez*—has a door that is flush with the abyss over which it is perched:

> When he climbed out of the chasm a morning mist was gathering, but he clearly saw the lofty and unhallowed cottage ahead; walls as grey as the rock, and high peak standing bold against the milky white of the seaward vapours. And he perceived that there was no door on this landward end, but only a couple of small lattice windows with dingy bull's-eye panes leaded in seventeenth-century fashion. All around him was cloud and chaos, and he could see nothing below but the whiteness of illimitable space. He was alone in the sky with this queer and very disturbing house; and when he sidled around to the front and saw that the wall stood flush with the cliff's edge, so that the single narrow door was not to be reached save from the empty aether, he felt a distinct terror that altitude could not wholly explain. (D 280-81)

While the occupant of the house, who imparts a strange lore to Olney, bears some resemblance to the Professor of Magic in Dunsany's novel, an even closer resemblance can be found, oddly, in the story "He." This tale of the squalor of present-day New York would seem the furthest imaginable from Dunsany's novel of picaresque adventure, in spite of the mention of Carcassonne early in the story (D 266), a possible allusion to a magnificently poetic story of that name in *A Dreamer's Tales*. And yet, the actual actions of the Professor bear comparison with the visions shown to the unnamed narrator by the anomalously aged central figure in "He." Rodriguez is asked by the Professor where his interests lie; the former promptly replies, "In war." The Professor then makes a startling claim:

> He had a window, he explained, through which Rodriguez should see clearly the ancient wars, while another window beside it looked on all wars of the future except those which were planned already or were coming soon to earth, and which were either invisible or seen dim as through mist. (R 72-73)

The sight of the ancient wars through the first magic window thrills Rodriguez and Morano; the latter, in his pious simplicity, even cheers on the Christians as they battle the infidel during the Crusades. But the other window reveals something very different:

> But in the other window through that deep, beautiful blue Rodriguez saw Man make a new ally, an ally who was only cruel and strong and had no purpose but killing, who had no pretences or pose, no mask and no manner, but was only the slave of Death and had no care but for his business. He saw it

grow bigger and stronger. Heart it had none, but he saw its cold steel core scheming methodical plans and dreaming always destruction. Before it faded men and their fields and their houses. Rodriguez saw the machine. (R 81–82)

In some of the most gripping pages in all Dunsany, Rodriguez sees the horrors of World War I, which Dunsany had witnessed at first hand in the battlefields of Flanders and of which he had written poignantly in *Tales of War* (1918) and *Unhappy Far-Off Things* (1919): "Rodriguez lifted his eyes and glanced from city to city, to Albert, Bapaume, and Arras, his gaze moved over a plain with its harvest of desolation lying forlorn and ungathered, lit by the flashing clouds and the moon and peering rockets. He turned from the window and wept" (R 83).

Who cannot recall the visions of past and future New York as revealed by the aged squire in "He"? Of course, the visions are not of war, but there is an exactly analogous contrast between the past, with its closeness to Nature ("It was Greenwich, the Greenwich that used to be, with here and there a roof or row of houses as we see it now, yet with lovely green lanes and fields and bits of grassy common" [D 273]) and the cataclysmically mechanised future:

> I saw the heavens verminous with strange flying things, and beneath them a hellish black city of giant stone terraces with impious pyramids flung savagely to the moon, and devil-lights burning from unnumbered windows. And swarming loathsomely on aërial galleries I saw the yellow, squint-eyed people of that city, robed horribly in orange and red, and dancing insanely to the pounding of fevered kettle-drums, the clatter of obscene crotala, and the maniacal moaning of muted horns whose ceaseless dirges rose and fell undulantly like the waves of an unhallowed ocean of bitumen. (D 273–74)

It is, of course, unlikely that Lovecraft derived this contrast directly from Dunsany: both writers were keenly concerned about the advent of the machine age and the resultant loss of our intimate connexion with the natural rhythms of the earth. This, indeed, is really the overriding theme in all Dunsany's work, even that early otherworldly fantasy which Lovecraft mistakenly believed to have been the product of pure imagination. Nevertheless, I think that Lovecraft's idea in "He" of contrasting the past and future through apocalyptic visions might well have been derived from this arresting tableau in Dunsany's *The Chronicles of Rodriguez*.

It is not to be assumed that this one chapter in Dunsany's novel was the sole inspiration for these two very different tales by Lovecraft; indeed, attempts have been made to find a real counterpart for the clifftop house in Marblehead (the basis for Kingsport) or the surrounding area. But it is still possible that Lovecraft's reading of *The Chronicles of Rodriguez* suggested to him a means of utilising these conceptions effectively. It is not surprising that he did not develop the ideas in "He" and "The Strange High House in the Mist" until several years after his reading of Dunsany's work: he continually remarked on his difficulty in writing fiction during his stay in New York (1924-26), and "He" was one of only five stories he wrote in this period. "The Strange High House in the Mist," of course, was one of the several stories and novels—from "The Call of Cthulhu" to "The Colour out of Space," and including *The Dream-Quest of Unknown Kadath* and *The Case of Charles Dexter Ward*—that Lovecraft wrote in the first year after his return to Providence in April 1926. "The Strange High House in the Mist" is, indeed, virtually his swan-song to the Dunsanian manner, and it would be fitting if the root conception of that story were derived from the work of the writer who had given Lovecraft's fiction such a tremendous impetus in 1919.

Works Cited

Dunsany, Lord. *Don Rodriguez: Chronicles of Shadow Valley*. New York: G. P. Putnam's Sons, 1922. [Abbreviated in the text as *R*.]

Price, Robert M. "Dunsanian Influence on Lovecraft Outside His 'Dunsanian' Tales." *Crypt of Cthulhu* No. 76 (Hallowmass 1990): 3-5.

Some Sources for "The Mound" and *At the Mountains of Madness*

"The Mound" was begun in December 1929 and completed in January 1930. It appears to have been written—or, rather, ghostwritten, as it was based upon the flimsiest of plot-germs supplied by Lovecraft's revision client Zealia Brown Reed—at one of several low points in Lovecraft's fiction-writing career: he had written no original work of fiction since "The Dunwich Horror" (completed in August 1928), and he would not write another original tale until he began "The Whisperer in Darkness" in February 1930. So "The Mound" appears to have provided some practice for renewed fictional composition, especially on the extended scale of a novelette or short novel. It is therefore not surprising that, in order to augment the flow of creativity, Lovecraft looked to other works of fiction for inspiration. He himself makes no secret that Clark Ashton Smith's "The Tale of Satampra Zeiros"—which he read in manuscript only in early December 1929 (SL 3.88)—was a key influence, as he immediately incorporated Smith's invented deity Tsathoggua into his tale; but another work of earlier vintage, found in his own library, may also have supplied suggestive hints.

A Strange Manuscript Found in a Copper Cylinder (1888) is a "lost race" novel by a Canadian popular novelist, James De Mille (1833–1880). Although apparently written in the 1860s, it was published only posthumously. Lovecraft, although owning the book, makes no mention of it in any letters I have seen; but I have little doubt that he read it prior to writing "The Mound." In this novel, the crewmen of a yacht sailing near the Canary Islands in the year 1850 come upon a copper cylinder floating in the ocean. This cylinder, when opened, contains a lengthy manuscript written on papyrus, telling the story of one Adam More, who in the year 1843 was shipwrecked in the South Pacific and managed to reach a land mass that he believes is Antarctica, although it is a land of lush and almost tropical vegetation. There he encounters a bizarre and previously unknown society of human beings, the Kosekin, whose moral and social customs are in many ways antipodal to those of the rest of the species: they hate life and are in love with death; they scorn wealth and yearn for poverty; they believe that unrequited love is the highest and most beautiful human emotion. The ending of the novel is somewhat unsatisfying; there is evidence that De Mille was uncertain how to conclude his novel, and that he worked on the ending for years, right up to the end of his life—a circumstance that probably accounts for its failure to be published in his lifetime.[1] More, who has fallen in love with a seemingly normal woman named Almah, who has been brought over from another island, becomes the Kosekin's god when he rebels at being a sacrificial victim and instead kills his captors.

The very title of A Strange Manuscript Found in a Copper Cylinder would appear to suggest an obvious influence on "The Mound," for of course that novelette concerns a modern-day archaeologist who, in investigating a mound in Oklahoma that appears to be haunted, finds in it a "heavy object of cylindrical shape—about a foot long and four inches in diameter" (HM 112), which contains the incredible narrative of Pánfilo de Zamacona in the underground civilisation of K'n-yan. More's cylinder is "about eighteen inches long and eight wide" (S 5). Lovecraft, of course, did not wish to have his cylinder composed of something so common as copper, so he asserts that it was "made of [some] heavy, lustrous unknown metal" (HM 112)—a metal found, presumably, only in the underground realm of K'n-yan. But like More's manuscript, Zamacona's account tells of a fantastic and previously unknown humanlike civilisation—Lovecraft adding somewhat implausibly that the people of K'n-yan had "come from a distant part of space where physical conditions are much like those of the earth" (HM 131). More struggles to learn the language of the Kosekin (which one of the crewmen on the yacht believes is related to Semitic), just as Zamacona takes months or years to master the utterly outré language of K'n-yan.

Where Lovecraft and De Mille part company is in the depiction of their respective "lost race" civilisations. De Mille's novel is evidently intended as an anti-utopia, but his satire is crude and unfocused: he never makes plausible the moral characteristics of the Kosekin, and it is not clear what message he is seeking to convey in his portrayal of this death-loving race. Lovecraft, by contrast, etches with considerable care and attention both the rise and fall of the mound civilisation, morally and intellectually, and manifestly wishes to suggest that their fate may well be our own if we do not renounce the corrupting influence of mechanisation. Whether De Mille's novel actually inspired Lovecraft in this depiction of an alien civilisation is not at all certain; but he appears to have used A Strange Manuscript as a suggestive framework for his own ruminations on the decline of the West.

---

1. See Malcolm G. Parks's critical edition of A Strange Manuscript Found in a Copper Cylinder (Ottawa: Carleton University Press, 1986) for an exhaustive account of the writing of the novel. This edition will be cited in the text, under the abbreviation S.

Some features of *A Strange Manuscript Found in a Copper Cylinder* may also have found their way into another of Lovecraft's major works, *At the Mountains of Madness* (1931). The crewmen who had discovered More's manuscript conduct frequent debates as to its authenticity, one member asserting that it is a pure hoax; but another remarks, in reference to More's belief that he had reached Antarctica: "'The observations of Ross and of More show us that there is a chain of mountains of immense height, which seem to encircle the pole'" (S 70). This sentence would surely have piqued Lovecraft's curiosity, although possibly he already knew of that immense chain of mountains from the reports of James Clark Ross himself (recall Lovecraft's juvenile treatise, *The Voyages of Capt. Ross, R.N.* [SL 4.67]). A little later this same character states:

> ". . . the idea that I have gathered from his [More's] manuscript is that of a vast sea like the Mediterranean, surrounded by impassable mountains; by great and fertile countries, peopled with an immense variety of animals, with a fauna and flora quite unlike those of the rest of the world; and, above all, with great nations possessing a rare and unique civilization, and belonging to a race altogether different from any of the known races of men." (S 70-71)

Possibly that final sentence triggered something in Lovecraft's mind: his civilisation, however, would not be merely humanoid in appearance, but entirely and frighteningly alien—the barrel-shaped Old Ones, who themselves give way to the even more outré creature known as the shoggoth.

And yet, another work found in Lovecraft's library—W. Clark Russell's *The Frozen Pirate* (1887)—appears to have been an even more central influence on *At the Mountains of Madness*. Lovecraft's short novel, of course, is the final and triumphant product of a lifetime's interest in the Antarctic; and yet, that interest may well have been initially triggered not by his admitted fascination with the history of Antarctic exploration, but by Russell's novel itself. Here we have no need to speculate as to whether Lovecraft read the work, for he writes of it: "I read it in extreme youth—when 8 or 9—& was utterly fascinated by it . . . writing several yarns of my own under its influence" (*Letters to Richard F. Searight* 34). Note that this reading—which, if Lovecraft's word is to be trusted, occurred in 1898 or 1899—apparently predates his interest in Antarctic exploration, which cannot be dated any earlier than 1900 (Joshi, *I Am Providence* 1.57-58).

W. Clark Russell (1844-1911) was, like the later William Hope Hodgson, an Englishman who used his own experiences as a sailor to become a hugely popular author of sea stories. Of the dozens of novels he wrote, only two—*The Frozen Pirate* and *The Death Ship* (1888), sometimes titled *The Flying Dutchman* in pirated American editions—are suggestive of the supernatural; and it is no accident that it is exactly these two novels that are found in Lovecraft's library. *The Frozen Pirate* is just the sort of work to have fascinated an imaginative youth interested in the weird and fantastic. In 1801 a shipwrecked sailor, Paul Rodney, stumbles upon an icebound pirate ship, the *Boca del Dragon*, near Antarctica and finds several of its crewmen apparently frozen to death. Rodney inadvertently resuscitates one of them, a French pirate named Jules Tassard, when he brings Tassard's body close to a fire in the ship's kitchen. He learns that Tassard has been frozen since 1754, although Tassard himself refuses to believe it. Shortly after his revival, Tassard suddenly ages half a century in a few hours, dying a hideously decrepit old man. The rest of the novel is a letdown as it merely concerns Rodney's efforts to free the ship from the ice and sail it back to England while protecting the ship's immense stolen booty from thieves or customs agents.

How can we not think of the discovery of the frozen Old Ones by Lake's sub-expedition, and the accidental revival of those entities when their bodies are warmed by the heat of the Antarctic summer sun? Lovecraft has taken the core of Russell's plot and, as it were, *cosmicised* it: he has vastly expanded its imaginative scope by depicting the revival, not merely of a rather scoundrelly human being, but of a group of fantastically bizarre extraterrestrials.

One further element in *The Frozen Pirate* may have inspired Lovecraft. As Rodney, in a lifeboat, is approaching the immense ice shelf within which the pirate ship is frozen, he sees a bizarre sight:

> . . . the sun, being low with westering, shone redly, and the range of ice stood in a kind of gold atmosphere which gave an extraordinary richness to the shadowings of its rocks and peaks, and a particular fullness of mellow whiteness to its lustrous parts, softening the dazzle into an airy tenderness of brightness, so that the whole mass shone out with the blandness visible in a glorious star. But its main beauty lay in those features which I knew it to be ice—I mean in a vast surprising variety of forms, such as steeples, towers, columns, pyramids, ruins as might be of temples, grotesque shapes as of mighty statues, left unfinished by the hands of Titans, domes as of cathedrals, castellated heights, fragments of ramparts, and the like. These features lay in groups, as if veritably the line of coast were dotted with gatherings of royal mansions and remains of imperial magnificence, all of white marble, yet with a glassy tincture as though the material owned something of a Parian quality. (44)

Does not Dyer, when approaching the Antarctic continent, see a similar sight? "On many occasions the curious atmospheric effects enchanted me vastly; these including a strikingly vivid mirage—the first I had ever seen—in which distant bergs became the battlements of unimaginable cosmic castles" (MM 6). Later Dyer realises that this "mirage" was nothing less than a strange reflection of the immense city of the Old Ones that he and Danforth come upon—a city featuring buildings that "tended to be conical, pyramidal, or terraced; though there were many perfect cylinders, perfect cubes, clusters of cubes, and other rectangular forms, and a peculiar sprinkling of angled edifices whose five-pointed ground plan roughly suggested modern fortifications" (MM 46).

The novels of De Mille and Russell are only two of the literary works that appear to have inspired *At the Mountains of Madness*. One can hardly ignore the influence of Poe's *Narrative of Arthur Gordon Pym*, mentioned several times in the novel. David E. Schultz's conjecture that a mediocre story by Katharine Metcalf Roof, "A Million Years After," may have been the immediate trigger for the writing of *At the Mountains of Madness* remains valid: Lovecraft seems to have been so annoyed that this hackneyed tale of the hatching of a dinosaur's egg was the cover story for the November 1930 issue of *Weird Tales* that he perhaps envisioned his own "dinosaur egg" story, although of a vastly broader scope and different focus. But it seems clear that *The Frozen Pirate* provided the kernels of some central plot features in Lovecraft's novel, and that *A Strange Manuscript* may have lingered in the back of his mind as well.

There is of course no need to censure Lovecraft for borrowing key components of his tales from previous works of fiction; for, like Handel, he almost always improved upon what he borrowed. The underground civilisation of K'n-yan is incalculably more cogently and dramatically presented than that of De Mille's Kosekin; the cosmic narrative of the Old Ones makes Russell's account of the frozen pirate seem absurdly unimaginative. Nevertheless, it does appear that Lovecraft at times needed the impetus of previous literary works to fashion his own weird masterpieces—as if, perhaps half-unconsciously, he saw in these predecessors the nucleus of themes, conceptions, and images that deserved better treatment.

Works Cited

Joshi, S. T. *I Am Providence: The Life and Times of H. P. Lovecraft.* New York: Hippocampus Press, 2010. 2 vols.

Lovecraft, H. P. *Letters to Richard F. Searight.* Edited by S. T. Joshi and David E. Schultz. West Warwick, RI: Necronomicon Press, 1992.

Russell, W. Clark. *The Frozen Pirate.* Chicago: M. A. Donahue & Co., n.d.

The Case of Charles Dexter Ward

I

The Case of Charles Dexter Ward was written at almost the exact midpoint of H. P. Lovecraft's relatively brief literary career. Composed in perhaps as little as five weeks in the early months of 1927, this 51,000-word short novel is a kind of Janus-figure in the Lovecraftian corpus—a work that simultaneously looks backward, both to the tales that Lovecraft wrote in the first decade of his career, beginning with "The Tomb" in the summer of 1917, and looks forward to the dynamic stories and novellas of 1927-36, including his tales of the so-called Cthulhu Mythos.

The longest of Lovecraft's fictional works, Charles Dexter Ward is also his most personal. Even those readers unfamiliar with the basic facts of Lovecraft's biography can scarcely doubt that the opening pages, describing Ward's birth and upbringing in the old colonial town of Providence, Rhode Island, are thinly veiled allusions to his own childhood. Providence, indeed, becomes a kind of character in its own right in Charles Dexter Ward. Lovecraft was well aware of the witchcraft panic that had tainted the early history of Massachusetts, but he was likewise aware that Rhode Island—founded as a haven for the religiously unorthodox by Roger Williams in 1636, and as a counterweight to the Puritan theocracy of its northern neighbor—was, as it were, providentially free of the religious neuroticism that led to the outbreak of the Salem witch trials of 1692. For fictional purposes, however, it was convenient for Lovecraft to allude in his novel to the unsavory history of Massachusetts; indeed, we will find that the Salem witchcraft may have played at least an indirect role in the inspiration and writing of the novel.

Lovecraft's career as a fiction writer—not counting his amusing juvenile writings of 1897-1902, or even such teenage works as "The Beast in the Cave" (1905) and "The Alchemist" (1908)—commenced in 1917, when he wrote "The Tomb" and "Dagon" in quick succession. These two works themselves reflect the past and the future in Lovecraft's writing: the former could be considered a virtual pastiche of Poe (whom Lovecraft early declared his "God of Fiction" [SL 1.20]), while the latter, with its reliance on science and its departure from conventional supernaturalism, could be said to look forward to such scientifically based narratives as "The Call of Cthulhu" (1926) and "The Shadow over Innsmouth" (1931), both of which, in their own ways, could be regarded as "Dagon" writ large. (For these and other "cosmic rewrites" of Lovecraft's early tales, see Schultz.) At this time, however, Lovecraft had little thought of becoming a professional fiction writer, or a professional writer of any kind. Having spent half a decade in hermitry following his abrupt withdrawal from high school (without a diploma) in 1908, he was rescued from a life of unproductive vegetation by the amateur journalism movement. He joined one of the two major amateur journalism organizations—the United Amateur Press Association (UAPA)—in 1914, and a few years later would join the other, the National Amateur Press Assocation (NAPA), although he remained loyal to the UAPA until its demise in 1926. It was through the amateur movement—a relatively modest cadre of individuals around the country and the world who produced their own papers and contributed written matter of various sorts to one another's journals—that Lovecraft, initially devoting himself extensively to the writing of poetry, essays, and editorials, gradually contemplated the prospect of making fiction his chief aesthetic outlet. W. Paul Cook, a leading figure in both the UAPA and the NAPA, was enthusiastic about Lovecraft's early stories and published them in his journal, the *Vagrant*. Lovecraft was aware that many members of the amateur associations were—like the general public—unresponsive to weird or supernatural literature, and, always sensitive to criticism, he was grateful for the commendations of his fiction by Cook and other close colleagues, including Rheinhart Kleiner, Maurice W. Moe, and Alfred Galpin.

"The Tomb" is set in New England, but in a never-never land that lacks specificity. As Lovecraft continued his fictional experiments over the next decade, he came to realize that his strong sense of place, and in particular his fervent devotion to his home state and region, would allow for a solid grounding in realism that could make the supernatural incursions he depicted even more potent and dramatically effective. Late in life Lovecraft embodied this principle as a central component of his theory of supernatural writing. Consider the following from "Notes on Writing Fiction" (1933):

> Inconceivable events and conditions have a special handicap to overcome, and this can be accomplished only through the maintenance of a careful realism in every phase of the story *except* that touching on the one given marvel. This marvel must be treated very impressively and deliberately—with a careful emotional "build-up"—else it will seem flat and unconvincing. Being the principal thing in the story, its mere existence should overshadow the characters and events. But the characters and events must be consistent and natural except where they touch the single marvel. (CE 2.177)

It took Lovecraft some time to realize the value of this principle. His rapturous devotion to the work of the Irish fantasist Lord Dunsany, which resulted in a dozen or so pastiches in 1919-21, could in one sense be considered a deviation from the quest for topographical and scientific realism that would come to dominate Lovecraft's later work; but in another sense, Lovecraft did learn from Dunsany the value of musical prose in generating an atmosphere of weirdness and fantasy. But Lovecraft, who at one point naively declared that "Dunsany *is myself*" (SL 1.234), would later come to a different conclusion:

> What I do *not* think I shall use much in future is the Dunsanian pseudo-poetic vein—not because I don't admire it, but because I don't think it is natural to me. The fact that I used it only sparingly before reading Dunsany, but immediately began to overwork it upon doing so, gives me a strong suspicion of its artificiality so far as I am concerned. That kind of thing takes a better poet than I. (SL 3.212)

(Curiously enough, Dunsany's own work would follow a path not wholly dissimilar to Lovecraft's: by the late 1920s and 1930s Dunsany came to infuse more and more of his work with his deep feeling for the topography, history, and culture of his native Ireland, producing such masterworks as *The Curse of the Wise Woman* [1933] and *The Story of Mona Sheehy* [1939].)

Such of Lovecraft's early tales as "The Terrible Old Man" (1920), "From Beyond" (1920), "The Picture in the House" (1920), "The Festival" (1923), and "The Shunned House" (1924) all embody, in widely varying ways, Lovecraft's evolving understanding of the historical richness of his native terrain. Although "From Beyond" is the first of his tales set in Providence, its evocation of the city is superficial at best; one finds more amusement than profundity in the narrator's remark that he drew "from my hip pocket the revolver I always carried after dark since the night I was held up in East Providence" (D 93). But the last three tales cited are a very different story. "The Picture in the House" not only introduces us to the most celebrated of Lovecraft's imaginary New England cities—the town of Arkham, later the home of Miskatonic University—but unveils an archaic New England dialect that Lovecraft would use in telling fashion in such tales as "The Dunwich Horror" (1928) and "The Shadow over Innsmouth." In later years Lovecraft rightly pointed to this tale as evocative of his understanding—the perhaps scornful understanding of an avowed atheist looking upon the religious vagaries of a credulous populace that took literally the biblical command, "Thou shalt not suffer a witch to live"—of the mental and social environment that led to the Salem panic:

> . . . it is the night-black Massachusetts legendry which packs the really macabre "kick". Here is material for a really profound study in group-neuroticism; for

certainly, no one can deny the existence of a profoundly morbid stream in the Puritan imagination. What you say of the dark Saxon-Scandinavian heritage as a possible source of the atavistic impulses brought out by emotional repression, isolation, climatic rigour, and the nearness of the vast unknown forest with its coppery savages, is of vast interest to me; insomuch as I have often both said and written exactly the same thing! Have you seen my old story "The Picture in the House"? If not, I must send you a copy. The introductory paragraph virtually sums up the idea you advance. (SL 3.174-75)

"The Festival" is Lovecraft's paean to the coastal town of Marblehead, Massachusetts, which he stumbled upon by accident on 17 December 1922, marveling at its near-perfect preservation of colonial antiquity. It is in this tale, perhaps, that the heavy burden of New England history for the first time truly manifests itself. In a 1930 letter Lovecraft poignantly expresses the overwhelming emotions he felt upon seeing the town:

In a flash all the past of New England—all the past of Old England—all the past of Anglo-Saxondom and the Western World—swept over me and identified me with the stupendous totality of all things in such a way as it never did before and never will again. That was the high-tide of my life. I was thirty-two then—and since that hour there has been merely a recession to senile tameness; merely a striving to recapture the wonders of revelation and intimation and cosmic identification which that sight brought. (SL 3.126-27)

As for "The Shunned House"—Lovecraft's most exhaustive treatment of Providence prior to *Charles Dexter Ward*—its very composition requires a more searching examination of Lovecraft's life at that critical juncture.

On March 3, 1924, Lovecraft, to the astonishment of nearly all his friends and family, married Sonia Haft Greene, a Russian Jewish immigrant who lived in Brooklyn and operated a successful millinery business in Manhattan. How did two such seemingly opposite personalities—Lovecraft shy, introspective, intellectual, devoted to his New England heritage and scornful of the many "foreigners" who had flooded into the country in the past generation; Sonia vibrant, dynamic, business-oriented, modern, perhaps overly emotional—decide to unite in matrimony? The tale perhaps begins with the unexpected death of Lovecraft's mother on 24 May 1921. Susie Lovecraft had herself been confined to Butler Hospital since 1919, having suffered a serious nervous breakdown brought on in part through financial worries—especially worries over her "useless" son, who seemed so intellectually brilliant but so clueless as to how to earn a living. Her death, however, was the result of a botched gall-bladder operation and did not seem to have any direct connection with her psychological condition. Lovecraft was momentarily stunned by the loss of this emotional fixture in his household; for a time he openly contemplated suicide. Lillian D. Clark and Annie E. P. Gamwell, the two aunts who had moved into 598 Angell Street—the house that Lovecraft and his mother had lived in since 1904—to take care of their nephew, evidently did not figure much in the equation, although in later years Lovecraft exhibited a great tenderness to both of them as the sole remaining members of the once-proud Phillips family. It was, however, on 4 July 1921 that Lovecraft, at a Boston gathering of the NAPA, met Sonia Greene for the first time. It would be a facile and clumsy psychoanalysis to assert that he was looking for some kind of mother substitute; Sonia, although seven years older than Lovecraft and now a widow, was herself the polar opposite of Lovecraft's reserved and emotionally disturbed mother, and he himself proclaimed at the outset that it was intellectual comity that initiated their mutual attraction. Sonia, for her part, made no secret of wanting more from Lovecraft than purely literary or philosophical discussion; she made frequent trips to Providence to visit him, and in April 1922 she boldly invited him to stay in her own Brooklyn apartment so that he could taste the myriad wonders of New York for the first time and meet the many friends and correspondents he had in the metropolis.

Lovecraft's decision to marry, and to move to New York, seemed at the time a sensible move, both personally and financially. Sonia was making a substantial income, relieving Lovecraft of the immediate necessity of becoming a breadwinner; and it seemed likely that, in spite of his previous inexperience, he would be able to find either staff work or freelance opportunities in New York publishing. But things went sour almost from the start for the hapless couple: Sonia unwisely gave up her job and attempted to start her own millinery business, which promptly failed; Lovecraft's clumsy efforts to secure work were met with uniform rejections; he had declined (probably wisely) an offer to take over the editorship of *Weird Tales* (the pulp magazine, founded in 1923, that would become the haven of most of his later work), as it would have required a move to Chicago; and, most significant of all, the emotional trauma he suffered in the midst of a teeming megalopolis where "foreigners" seemed to outnumber the native-born Americans Lovecraft was accustomed to seeing in the streets of Providence and Boston brought him to the depths of enraged despair. Why were these brash newcomers so financially successful when he, gifted with intellect and a proud lineage, was flirting with poverty? At the beginning of 1925, after only ten months of cohabitation, Sonia was forced to accept positions at various department stores in the Midwest, leaving Lovecraft alone to manage housekeeping by himself. Insult was added to injury when in May 1925, after he moved into a small one-room flat in the then seedy area of Brooklyn Heights, he was robbed of nearly all his clothing, forcing him to practice extreme economies until he could replenish his wardrobe. Even the many friends

Lovecraft had in the city—the members of the so-called Kalem Club (Kleiner, James F. Morton, Arthur Leeds, Samuel Loveman, and especially Frank Belknap Long), all of whose members' last names began with K, L, or M—were not enough to ward off a growing neuroticism and sense of victimization.

During this trying period, Lovecraft could only look with wistful longing at the Providence he had unwisely left. "The Shunned House," written at a time when the couple's finances were perilous and Sonia's own health problematical, constitutes a kind of mental deception—an attempt to envisage the long history of Lovecraft's native city as encapsulated in the successive occupants of a sinister house at 135 Benefit Street, in the heart of the colonial district. Lovecraft had already written a poem about the house ("The House," 1920), and may well have had actual familiarity with the structure: his elder aunt, Lillian D. Clark, is listed as a housekeeper in that house in the 1920 census. The story was, however, rejected by Farnsworth Wright, editor of *Weird Tales*, on the ground that the historical section tended to bog down the narrative pace. This criticism is probably sound, and Lovecraft may have learned from it when he came to write his next story that delved deeply into Providence history—*The Case of Charles Dexter Ward*.

II

The genesis of *Ward* is shrouded in some obscurity, even though there seems a strong likelihood that it grew out of Lovecraft's continued yearning for his native city. He wrote to his aunt Lillian that in late July 1925 he was thinking of writing a "novel or novelette of Salem horrors which I may be able to cast in a sufficiently 'detectivish' mould to sell to Edwin Baird for *Detective Tales*" (cited in Joshi, *I Am Providence* 1.592). The reference is to Edwin Baird, who in his short stint as the first editor of *Weird Tales* (1923-24) had accepted all the stories Lovecraft had sent him. Baird had, however, just rejected "The Shunned House" for *Detective Tales*, but perhaps he had suggested that some other tale involving a detective might be suitable. What Lovecraft did at this juncture was not to write the Salem story, but rather "The Horror at Red Hook" (1-2 August 1925), which does indeed feature a detective (Thomas Malone of the N.Y.P.D.). It is not clear whether Lovecraft actually submitted "The Horror at Red Hook" to Baird, but in any case the story (one of the poorest of Lovecraft's lengthier tales, with a stereotyped plot based on hackneyed magical incantations and laced with ugly racism) was quickly accepted by *Weird Tales*. This period was virtually the only time when Lovecraft experienced any kind of creative spark during his New York stay: he went on to write "He" on August 11 and "In the Vault" on September 18. To be sure, neither of these stories is a masterwork, but "He" probably reflects his sentiments about New York—and, more pertinently, its effect upon his own psyche—as poignantly as any tale, poem, or letter in his surviving body of work.

But what of the Salem idea? It is not clear how concrete an idea it was at this juncture; but in September, Lovecraft read Gertrude Selwyn Kimball's *Providence in Colonial Times* (1912) at the New York Public Library, and this rather dry historical work clearly fired his imagination: his letters to Lillian of the period are filled with the interesting historical tidbits he culled from the treatise. But Lovecraft's growing inability to do meaningful creative work while in the metropolis put any plans for a novel, or even a short story, on indefinite hold.

Finally, in April 1926, apparently through the joint action of Frank Belknap Long and of Lovecraft's aunts, Lovecraft received the invitation he had no doubt hoped for more than a year would come: Lillian asked him to return to Providence. Why Lovecraft did not simply decide on his own to come back to his hometown is not entirely clear; perhaps he felt it would be a sign of disloyalty to his wife Sonia, who was largely supporting him at a time when he had virtually ceased to look for employment. At any rate, Lovecraft jumped at the opportunity, returning home on April 17 and expressing his transcendent euphoria in an imperishable letter to Frank Belknap Long:

> Well—the train sped on, and I experienced silent convulsions of joy in returning step by step to a waking and tri-dimensional life. New Haven—New London—and then quaint Mystic, with its colonial hillside and landlocked cove. Then at last a still subtler magick fill'd the air—nobler roofs and steeples, with the train rushing airily above them on its lofty viaduct—*Westerly*—in His Majesty's Province of RHODE ISLAND & PROVIDENCE-PLANTATIONS! GOD SAVE THE KING!! Intoxication follow'd—Kingston—East Greenwich with its steep Georgian alleys climbing up from the railway—Apponaug and its ancient roofs—Auburn—just outside the city limits—I fumble with bags and wraps in a desperate effort to appear calm—THEN—a delirious marble dome outside the window—a hissing of air brakes—a slackening of speed—surges of ecstasy and dropping of clouds from my eyes and mind—HOME—UNION STATION—PROVIDENCE!!!! (SL 2.46-47)

The printed text does not tell the full story: in Lovecraft's handwritten manuscript of this letter, the final word is an inch high with four underscores. Maurice Lévy is correct in remarking: ". . . this ecstatic return to his native land was in effect a return to the maternal breast. There is something moving in the account he gives of this mythical return to his home, something that betrays a vital, primordial experience" (23). And, of course, any reader can recognize its near-exact parallel when Charles Dexter Ward, returning from three years spent overseas in the pursuit of occult knowledge, takes his own train ride from New York to Providence. It would be difficult to find a parallel in the whole of Lovecraft's work to the quiet simplicity of the concluding sentence of this passage: "It was twilight, and Charles Dexter Ward had come home."

To be sure, Lovecraft's return to Providence—he settled with Lillian into an apartment house at 10 Barnes Street, just north of Brown University—did render uncertain the question of Sonia's role in his life. It is plain that he considered the marriage a failure—or, at any rate, that he regarded himself as unfit to live anywhere outside his native city—and he is probably to be criticized for failing to stand up to his aunts when, at some unspecified later date, they responded with hostility to Sonia's offer to set up a hat shop in Providence. The aunts, still proud of their membership in Providence's social aristocracy, could not "afford" the ignominy of seeing their nephew's wife a tradeswoman in their own city. Sonia, seeing the writing on the wall, eventually filed for divorce.

Lovecraft's return home inspired a burst of fiction-writing such as he had never experienced before and would never experience in future: within a period of six to nine months, he produced 150,000 words of fiction, including such impressive works as "The Call of Cthulhu," "Pickman's Model" (1926), "The Silver Key" (1926), *The Dream-Quest of Unknown Kadath* (1926-27), and "The Colour out of Space" (1927). *Charles Dexter Ward* was the second-to-last component of this sequence, but for now our attention should be turned to the *Dream-Quest*, which, in spite of its superficial Dunsanianism, is in many ways a kind of thematic mirror-image of *Ward*. For what is the upshot of this seemingly unfocused novel, where Randolph Carter wanders all through dreamland in search of his "sunset city"? The baleful god Nyarlathotep speaks poignantly of the matter at the conclusion:

> "For know you, that your gold and marble city of wonder is only the sum of what you have seen and loved in youth. It is the glory of Boston's hillside roofs and western windows aflame with sunset; of the flower-fragrant Common and the great dome on the hill and tangle of gables and chimneys in the violet valley where the many-bridged Charles flows drowsily. These things you saw, Randolph Carter, when your nurse first wheeled you out in the springtime, and they will be the last things you will ever see with eyes of memory and of love. And there is antique Salem with its brooding years, and spectral Marblehead scaling its rocky precipices into past centuries, and the glory of Salem's towers and spires seen afar from Marblehead's pastures across the harbour against the setting sun." (MM 400-401)

Although the very next sentence would seem to have some reference to our current concern—"There is Providence, quaint and lordly on its seven hills over the blue harbour, with terraces of green leading up to steeples and citadels of living antiquity"—we must remember that Randolph Carter is portrayed as a native of Boston, so that his memories of that metropolis would naturally fill his mind and constitute the "sunset city" he so ardently seeks. In any case, what is the purpose of both the *Dream-Quest* and *Charles Dexter Ward?* Is it not to convey the plangent message—a message that Lovecraft had embodied in his own life—that you *can* go home again?

The *Dream-Quest* was completed on 22 January 1927; almost immediately, Lovecraft plunged into another "young novel" (SL 2.100), *The Case of Charles Dexter Ward.* Actually, at the outset he did not regard it as anything more than a novelette: on January 29 he announced that "I am already at work on a new shorter tale" (*Mysteries of Time and Spirit* 21); by February 9 he was on page 56, with an estimated 25 pages more to go (ES 1.68); by February 20 he finally realized what he had got himself into, for he was on page 96 "with much still to be said" (ES 1.71); the last page of the autograph manuscript (page 147) notes that the work was finished on March 1.

The fact, however, that Lovecraft was still talking of the Salem idea just as he was finishing the *Dream-Quest*—". . . sometime I wish to write a novel of more naturalistic setting, in which some hideous threads of witchcraft trail down the centuries against the sombre & memory-haunted background of ancient Salem" (SL 2.99)—leads me to think that the reading of Gertrude Kimball's *Providence in Colonial Times*—as well, of course, as his return to Providence—led to a uniting of the Salem idea with a work about his hometown. Lovecraft makes plain that Joseph Curwen "had fled from Salem to Providence . . . at the beginning of the great witchcraft panic."

The evolution of the work goes back even beyond August 1925. The quotation from Borellus that comprises the epigraph is a translation or paraphrase by Cotton Mather in the *Magnalia Christi Americana* (1702), which Lovecraft owned. Since the epigraph from Lactantius that heads "The Festival" (1923) also comes from the *Magnalia*, perhaps Lovecraft found the Borellus passage at that time also. It is copied down in his commonplace book as entry 87, which David E. Schultz dates conjecturally to April 1923.

In late August 1925 Lovecraft heard an interesting story from Lillian: "So the Halsey house is haunted! Ugh! That's where Wild Tom Halsey kept live terrapins in the cellar—maybe it's their ghosts. Anyway, it's a magnificent old mansion, & a credit to a magnificent old town!" (*Letters from New York* 185). The Thomas Lloyd Halsey house at 140 Prospect Street is the model for Charles Dexter Ward's residence, which Lovecraft numbered 100 Prospect Street—probably deliberately, so that curious readers of his novel wouldn't intrude upon the privacy of the tenants of the Halsey house. Although now broken up into apartments, it is a superb late Georgian structure (c. 1800) fully deserving of Lovecraft's encomium: "His [Ward's] home was a great Georgian mansion atop the well-nigh precipitous hill that rises just east of the river; and from the rear windows of its rambling wings he could look dizzily out over all the clustered spires, domes, roofs, and skyscraper summits of the lower town to the purple hills of the countryside beyond" (MM 113). Lovecraft was presumably never in the Halsey mansion, but he had a clear view of it from 10 Barnes Street; looking northwestward from his aunt's upstairs back window, he could see it distinctly.

As for the house's ghostly legendry, we read the following in the WPA guide to Rhode Island (1937):

> [Halsey] was a famous *bon vivant* in Colonial days, and there is a legend that he kept live terrapins in his cellar. For many years during which the mansion was empty, Negroes in the vicinity were convinced a piano-playing ghost haunted the property. They would not enter the house under any circumstances, and at night always gave it a wide berth. It is also said that a bloodstain on the floor has defied many years of scrubbing. (290)

No doubt these were the sorts of stories Lillian heard in 1925.

Lovecraft began reading *Providence in Colonial Times* at the very end of July 1925. Since he could not check the book out of the New York Public Library but had to read it in the genealogical reading room during library hours, his consumption of it was sporadic, and he only began making headway in it in mid-September. It was at this time that he read of John Merritt as well as of the Rev. John Checkley, "famous as a wit & man of the world" (*Letters from New York* 193), both of whom would later pay visits to Joseph Curwen. Lovecraft's letters for the rest of the month contain much other matter derived from reading the Kimball book, and there is no question but that it helped to solidify his knowledge of colonial Providence so that he could rework it in fiction a year and a half later. Lovecraft, of course, does much more than merely recycle odd bits of history: he mingles history and fiction in an inextricable union, breathing vivid life into the dry facts he had gathered over a lifetime of study of his native region and insidiously inserting the imaginary, the fantastic, and the weird into the known historical record.

There are, of course, more specifically literary influences on the novel. Indeed, it could be said that, all aside from Lovecraft's reading of the Kimball book and his ecstatic return to Providence, he might not have written *Charles Dexter Ward*—or, at any rate, written in the exact manner that he did—had he not just concluded the writing of his seminal treatise on weird fiction, "Supernatural Horror in Literature." This treatise, begun at W. Paul Cook's suggestion in November 1925, was invaluable in both giving Lovecraft a sense of purpose during the latter stages of his New York period and reinvigorating his imagination by an examination of the classics of supernatural literature, from the Gothic novels to his own day. Indeed, *Charles Dexter Ward* can stand as Lovecraft's most notable tribute to old-time Gothicism, even more so than "The Rats in the Walls" (1923). The theme of the quest for eternal life, the evocation of the medieval occultists and alchemists, and the general sense of a horror emerging from the depths of history were central themes in such Gothic novels as William Godwin's *St. Leon* (1799) and Charles Robert Maturin's *Melmoth the Wanderer* (1820); and Lovecraft updated these venerable motifs by transferring them to the relative modernity of the New World and depicting their baleful incursion into the world of his own day. One of the most piquant moments in *Ward*—when Joseph Curwen, posing as Ward, observes that "the creaking of Epenetus Olney's new signboard (the gaudy crown he set up after he took to calling his tavern the Crown Coffee House) was exactly like the first few notes of the new jazz piece all the radios in Pawtuxet were playing" (MM 188)—fuses unwholesome antiquity and brash modernity into an uncanny amalgam.

One specific literary influence may be noted here: Walter de la Mare's novel *The Return* (1910). Lovecraft had first read de la Mare in the summer of 1926 and stated that the British author "can be exceedingly powerful when he chooses" (SL 2.57); of *The Return* he remarks in "Supernatural Horror in Literature": "we see the soul of a dead man reach out of its grave of two centuries and fasten itself upon the flesh of the living, so that even the face of the victim becomes that which had long ago returned to dust" (D 415). In de la Mare's novel, of course, there is actual psychic possession involved, as there is not in *Charles Dexter Ward*; and, although the focus in *The Return* is on the afflicted man's personal trauma—in particular his relations with his wife and daughter—rather than the unnaturalness of his condition, Lovecraft has manifestly adapted the general scenario in his own work.

Richard Ward has noted another important literary influence: M. R. James's "Count Magnus," included in the first of James's story collections, *Ghost-Stories of an Antiquary* (1904). Lovecraft first came upon James only in December 1925 (see *Letters from New York* 253), and he appeared to be particularly taken with "Count Magnus," given the space he devotes to it in "Supernatural Horror in Literature." Richard Ward points out that Count Magnus and Joseph Curwen have numerous similarities: they both have extensive collections of occult books (both real and imaginary); the portraits of both men figure significantly in the plots of the two stories; and, most significantly, both men exercise a baleful influence upon the hapless protagonists who come into contact with them. Richard Ward concludes: "Both characters are found to have left a dark magical legacy with the power to capture the imaginations of those who stumble upon it to the point of absolute obsession. This legacy, through the power of its creator, is able to manifest itself tangibly in the present" (17).

Other, more minor sources can also be noted. Marinus Bicknell Willett's name surely derives from a book that Lillian sent him in November of that year (*Letters from New York* 178):

> Francis Read. *Westminster Street, Providence, as It Was about 1824*. From Drawings Made by Francis Read and Lately Presented by His Daughter, Mrs. Marinus Willett Gardner, to the Rhode Island Historical Society. Providence: Printed for the Society, 1917.

Bicknell is an old Providence name. Thomas William Bicknell, for example, was a well-known historian who wrote a five-volume *History of the State of Rhode Island* (1920), a work that Lovecraft almost certainly read. I am not entirely sure, however, where Lovecraft derived the name Charles Dexter Ward. Ward is a name from Providence colonial history, and in the novel Lovecraft refers to a political dispute between the party backing Samuel Ward and the one backing Stephen Hopkins around 1760. Lovecraft also owned two anthologies of English literature compiled by Charles Dexter Cleveland. Dexter is a prominent family in Providence.

If the source for Ward's name is unclear, the source for the character himself is not. Of course, there are many autobiographical touches in the portraiture of Ward; but many surface details appear to be taken from a person actually living in the Halsey mansion at this time, William Lippitt Mauran (b. 1910). Lovecraft was probably not acquainted with Mauran, but it is highly likely that he observed Mauran on the street and knew of him. Mauran was a sickly child who spent much of his youth as an invalid, being wheeled through the streets in a carriage by a nurse. Indeed, a mention early in the novel that Ward as a young boy was "wheeled . . . in a carriage" in front of the "lovely classic porch of the double-bayed brick building" that was his home may reflect an actual glimpse Lovecraft had of Mauran in the early 1920s, before he went to New York. Moreover, the Mauran family also owned a farmhouse in Pawtuxet, exactly as Curwen is said to have done. Other details of Ward's character also fit Mauran more closely than Lovecraft. One other amusing in-joke is a mention of Manuel Arruda, captain of a Spanish vessel, the *Fortaleza*, which delivers a nameless cargo to Curwen in 1770. Manuel Arruda was actually a Portuguese door-to-door fruit merchant operating on College Hill in the later 1920s![1]

---

1. See McNamara and Joshi. Most of the information in this article is derived from discussions with Mauran's widow, Grace Mauran.

III.

But what, beyond these obscure tips of the hat and in-jokes, is the fundamental message of *The Case of Charles Dexter Ward?* To answer this question, we must first ascertain exactly what Curwen and his cohorts around the world were attempting to do by gathering up these "essential Saltes." Lovecraft makes the matter a trifle too clear in a passage toward the end—a passage that, one hopes, he might have had the good sense to omit in a revised version:

> What these horrible creatures—and Charles Ward as well—were doing or trying to do seemed fairly clear . . . They were robbing the tombs of all the ages, including those of the world's wisest and greatest men, in the hope of recovering from the bygone ashes some vestige of the consciousness and lore which had once animated and informed them. (MM 199)

It is not, indeed, entirely clear how the tapping of human brains—even the "world's wisest and greatest"—would result in some scenario that (as a frantic Ward writes to Willett toward the end) might threaten "all civilisation, all natural law, perhaps even the fate of the solar system and the universe" (MM 181–82). Curwen occasionally speaks in notes and letters about calling up entities from "Outside ye Spheres" (MM 162)—including perhaps Yog-Sothoth, who is first mentioned in this novel—but these hints are so nebulous that not much can be made of them. There are further hints that Curwen died in 1771 not because of the raid by the local citizenry but because he had raised some nameless entity and could not control it. Nevertheless, the basic conception of a Faustian quest for knowledge has led Barton L. St. Armand, one of the acutest commentators on the work, to declare: "The simple moral of *The Case of Charles Dexter Ward* is that it is dangerous to know too much, especially about one's own ancestors" (178).

Well, perhaps it is not so simple as that. By this interpretation, Ward himself becomes the villain of the piece; but surely it is Curwen who is the real villain, for it is he who conceived the idea of ransacking the world's brains for his own (rather unclear) purposes. Ward certainly does pursue knowledge ardently, and he certainly does resurrect Curwen's body; but it is false to say (as St. Armand does) that Curwen "possesses" Ward. There does not appear to be any psychic possession—at least of the obvious sort—here, as there is in "The Tomb" and as there will be again in "The Thing on the Doorstep" (1933). Curwen is *physically* resurrected, and when Ward proves unwilling to assist him in carrying out his plans, Curwen ruthlessly kills him and tries to pass himself off as Ward. And note Ward's defense of his actions in the letter to Willett, specifically the sentence: "I have brought to light a monstrous abnormality, but I did it for the sake of knowledge" (MM 182).

This single utterance comprises Ward's (and Lovecraft's) justification: in the first part of the sentence Ward confesses to moral culpability; but the second part of the sentence is preceded by "but" because Ward (with Lovecraft) sees the pursuit of knowledge as intrinsically good. Sometimes, however, that pursuit simply leads to unfortunate and unforeseen consequences. Ward was perhaps naive in thinking that his resurrection of Curwen would lead to no harm; but, as Willett himself says at the end: ". . . he was never a fiend or even truly a madman, but only an eager, studious, and curious boy whose love of mystery and of the past was his undoing" (MM 230).

Psychic possession of a subtler sort may, nevertheless, be involved in the tale. Curwen, in the 1760s, marries not only because he wishes to repair his reputation, but because he needs a descendant. He seems to know that he will one day die and need to be resurrected by the recovery of his "essential Saltes," so he makes careful arrangements to that effect: he prepares a notebook for "One Who Shal Come After" and leaves sufficient clues as to the location of his remains. It may well be, then, that Curwen exercises psychic possession on Ward so that the latter finds first his effects, then his body, and so brings him back to life. Perhaps it would be more accurate to say that the whole scenario embodies Lovecraft's notions of fate and determinism: Ward seems inevitably compelled to pursue the course he does, and this inevitability adds a measure of poignancy to the horror of the situation.

The Case of Charles Dexter Ward represents one of Lovecraft's few relative triumphs of characterisation. Both Curwen and Ward are vividly realized—the latter largely because Lovecraft drew unaffectedly upon his own deepest emotions in the portrayal. Willett is not so successful, and on occasion he reveals himself to be somewhat pompous and self-important. After solving the case he makes the following ludicrous speech: "I can answer no questions, but I will say that there are different kinds of magic. I have made a great purgation, and those in this house will sleep the better for it" (MM 228). Regrettably, Willett later became the model for the even more pompous librarian Dr. Henry Armitage, the "hero" (in the superficial sense) of "The Dunwich Horror."

But St. Armand is nonetheless right in seeing Providence itself as the principal "character" of the novel. As can be seen from my notes, it requires a lengthy commentary to specify not only all the historical data Lovecraft has unearthed, but the countless autobiographical details he has enmeshed into his narrative. The opening descriptions of Ward as a youth are filled with echoes of Lovecraft's own upbringing, although with provocative changes. For example, a description of "one of the child's first memories"—"the great westward sea of hazy roofs and domes and steeples and far hills which he saw one winter afternoon from that great railed embankment, all violet and mystic against a fevered, apocalyptic sunset of reds and golds and purples and curious greens" (MM 113)—is situated in Prospect Terrace, whereas in letters Lovecraft identifies this mystic vision as occurring on the railway embankment in Auburndale, Massachusetts, around 1892.

It is of interest to note how Willett's complete eradication of Curwen stands in such stark contrast to Malone's obvious failure to eliminate the age-old horror in Red Hook: New York may be the haven of all horror, but Providence must at the end emerge cleansed of any evil taint. This resolution is found in all Lovecraft's tales of Providence, including "The Shunned House" and "The Haunter of the Dark" (1935). In many ways, indeed, *The Case of Charles Dexter Ward* is a refinement of "The Horror at Red Hook." Several features of the plot are borrowed from that earlier story: Curwen's alchemy parallels Robert Suydam's cabbalistic activities; Curwen's attempt to repair his standing in the community with an advantageous marriage echoes Suydam's marriage with Cornelia Gerritsen; Willett as the valiant counterweight to Curwen matches Malone as the adversary of Suydam. Lovecraft has once again reverted to his relatively small store of basic plot elements, and once again transformed a mediocre tale into a masterful one.

The fleeting mentions of Yog-Sothoth point ahead to the extensive use of this cosmic entity in "The Dunwich Horror," written just over a year after *Ward*. Lovecraft had laid down the skeleton of what would come to be called (not by him but by his disciples, especially August Derleth) the Cthulhu Mythos in "The Call of Cthulhu," written in the summer of 1926; in the *Dream-Quest* Lovecraft had made the god Nyarlathotep (introduced in the prose-poem "Nyarlathotep" [1920]) a major character; and in *Ward* there are hints that those "Outside Spheres" are really controlling the action of the petty human puppets who fill the stage. Perhaps, if Lovecraft had ever revised the novel, he would have fleshed out these hints; but his general tendency was not to make extensive rewrites of his tales but simply to write new tales that embodied his broadening conceptions, and with such works as "The Whisperer in Darkness" (1930), *At the Mountains of Madness* (1931), and "The Shadow out of Time" (1934-35) the Cthulhu Mythos is transformed from a scenario of gods and men into a scenario whereby human beings are the hapless and accidental victims of purely natural, if overwhelmingly powerful, races of beings coming from the depths of space.

The Case of Charles Dexter Ward did not see print until 1943, when it was included in the second Lovecraft omnibus from Arkham House, *Beyond the Wall of Sleep*. The text was written in Lovecraft's inimitable longhand on many different types of paper, from the backs of correspondence received to what appear to be pages of a ledger or accounting book. Lovecraft mentioned the novel to various correspondents in the late 1920s and 1930s, always disparagingly; one of these, R. H. Barlow, repeatedly pestered him to let him read and transcribe the text, and Lovecraft finally consented in 1934. Barlow produced a typescript of only 23 pages—probably less than a fifth of the text. This partial typescript did contain some slight revisions by Lovecraft, but it was not followed by August Derleth and Donald Wandrei, who presumably prepared their own typescript for *Beyond the Wall of Sleep*. This typescript no longer survives, but, if gauged by the printed text, it was full of errors, as Derleth and Wandrei's ability to read Lovecraft's crabbed chirography leaves something to be desired. I published a corrected text in the 1985 revised edition of *At the Mountains of Madness and Other Novels*.

It is certainly a pity that Lovecraft made no efforts to prepare *Charles Dexter Ward* for publication, even when book publishers in the 1930s were specifically asking for a novel from his pen; but we are in no position to question Lovecraft's own judgment that the novel was an inferior piece of work, a "cumbrous, creaking bit of self-conscious antiquarianism" (OFF 120). It has certainly now been acknowledged as one of his finest works, and, as I have noted, it emphasizes the message of *The Dream-Quest of Unknown Kadath* all over again: Lovecraft is who he is because of his birth and upbringing as a New England Yankee. The need to root his work in his native soil became more and more clear to him as time went on, and it led to his gradual transformation of all New England into a locus of both wonder and terror.

Works Cited

Joshi, S. T. *I Am Providence: The Life and Times of H. P. Lovecraft*. New York: Hippocampus Press, 2010. 2 vols.

Lévy, Maurice. *Lovecraft: A Study in the Fantastic*. Trans. S. T. Joshi. Detroit: Wayne State University Press, 1988.

Lovecraft, H. P. *Letters from New York*. Edited by S. T. Joshi and David E. Schultz. San Francisco: Night Shade Books, 2005.

Lovecraft, H. P., and Donald Wandrei. *Mysteries of Time and Spirit: The Letters of H. P. Lovecraft and Donald Wandrei*. Edited by S. T. Joshi and David E. Schultz. San Francisco: Night Shade Books, 2002.

McNamara, M. Eileen, and S. T. Joshi. "Who Was the Real Charles Dexter Ward?" *Lovecraft Studies* Nos. 19/20 (Fall 1989): 40–41, 48.

Rhode Island: A Guide to the Smallest State. Boston: Houghton Mifflin, 1937.

St. Armand, Barton L. "Facts in the Case of H. P. Lovecraft." 1972. In S. T. Joshi, ed. *H. P. Lovecraft: Four Decades of Criticism*. Athens: Ohio University Press, 1980. 166–85.

Schultz, David E. "From Microcosm to Macrocosm: The Growth of Lovecraft's Cosmic Vision." In *An Epicure in the Terrible: A Centennial Anthology of Essays in Honor of H. P. Lovecraft*, ed. David E. Schultz and S. T. Joshi. 1991. New York: Hippocampus Press, 2011. 208–29.

Ward, Richard. "In Search of the Dread Ancestor: M. R. James' 'Count Magnus' and Lovecraft's *The Case of Charles Dexter Ward*." *Lovecraft Studies* No. 36 (Spring 1997): 14–17.

Excised Passages from "The Thing on the Doorstep"

In my proposed multi-volume edition of *The Variorum Lovecraft*, which could begin publication as early as next year, I hope to present all the relevant textual variants for all the stories that Lovecraft wrote over his short literary career. One phase of that project may include the printing of passages from handwritten or typed manuscripts (chiefly the former) that were excised as Lovecraft was writing the story or as he performed a subsequent revision of it. One very interesting example, because of the number and relative significance of such excised passages, is "The Thing on the Doorstep."

This tale was written frenetically in a matter of four days (21–24 August 1933, as indicated at the end of the autograph manuscript) in a scribbled pencil draft that was so illegible that, when Lovecraft (unwisely) passed the manuscript on to a "delinquent [revision] client" (*SL* 4.310) for typing, he or she missed some of Lovecraft's section divisions, typing the story in only five sections when it contained seven. Naturally, the typist did not transcribe the excised passages, which were clearly crossed out in pencil. They are printed here for the first time, and they shed interesting light on the development of the story as Lovecraft was writing it.

The first excised passage of any consequence occurs in the middle of the first section of the story, which supplies a potted biography of Edward Derby from his childhood to the time he met Asenath Waite. At the end of the paragraph discussing Derby's "self-reliance and practical affairs" (*DH* 278), we find the following:

> By the time he was 25 Derby was a fairly well-known minor poet and fantaisiste, though his lack of contacts & experience had slowed down his literary growth by making his products derivative & over-bookish. I was perhaps his closest friend, seeing him

The passage breaks off in the manuscript, and Lovecraft resumes with a new paragraph, "Derby's parents . . ." (*DH* 278). The above passage was in fact transferred to a paragraph three paragraphs later, although there Lovecraft adds that Derby was "a prodigiously learned man and a fairly well-known poet

Excised Passages from "The Thing on the Doorstep" 411

and fantaisiste" (*DH* 279). Clearly, Lovecraft wished to add additional biographical detail about Derby, especially in terms of his relations to the narrator, Daniel Upton; it is in the intervening paragraphs that he supplies the key detail that Derby would come to Upton's house and either knock or ring the doorbell in a characteristic manner—"three brisk strokes followed by two more after a pause" (*DH* 278), a detail that plays a crucial role at the end of the story. Lovecraft also adds information about Derby's attendance of Miskatonic University and also about his reading of occult books (the usual litany of the *Necronomicon*, the *Book of Eibon*, and others follows [*DH* 279]); it is no doubt for this reason that he added the detail that Derby was "prodigiously learned," which was missing in the first draft of the passage.

In the middle of Section II occurs another excision. By now Derby has met Asenath and fallen under her sway. In a paragraph in which Upton describes how Derby brought Asenath to his house for a call, the text states that Upton "perceived that their intimacy was beyond entangling" (*DH* 282). There follows this excised passage:

> This rather disturbed me, for the Derbys are old Essex County stock & I did not wish to see any incongruous element enter in. Not only did my daughter's recollections influence me, but I had heard from others that Asenath was in every way an "uninhibited young modern" of the sort that good old families cannot well assimilate.

Not much need be made of this excision, aside from the fact that it reflects Lovecraft's customary disapproval of "mixed" marriages, going well beyond his horror of interracial unions (or "miscegenation") to disapproval of marital unions even of members of different social classes. Lovecraft may have considered the passage redundant, because Asenath's portrayal as an "uninhibited young modern" may have seemed unduly repetitive of an earlier passage in which she is described as a member of the "intelligentsia" (*DH* 281) at Miskatonic.

The next excised passage is of considerably greater significance. It occurs at the very end of Section II, which discusses the new household that Edward and Asenath have established in Arkham, although she has brought along three servants from her home in Innsmouth. At the end of the section Lovecraft writes:

> My first call at Derby's new home was by no means unpleasant. The servants—especially the flat-nosed wench who opened the door—distinctly repelled me; & my wife, who was with me, thought Asenath's expression was vaguely sardonic. Of the conversation I recall only a queer outburst from our hostess, who repeated vehemently that wish to be a man which had so impressed my daughter at school. This was fixed in my mind because of an even queerer & surprisingly tasteless rejoinder of Edward's—a rejoinder which had the aspect

of a sly "dig", & which was cut off by a crushing glance from Asenath. He had murmured 'that some people would give a good deal to be wholly human'—no doubt referring to the anile whispers of grandams about Innsmouth folk.

There is much in this passage that Lovecraft would have found objectionable in the overall context of the story. First, the passage needlessly duplicates an earlier passage in which Upton's daughter—presented as a classmate of Asenath's at the Hall School (*DH* 280), presumably a private secondary school—notes that Asenath's "crowning rage . . . was that she was not a man" (*DH* 281). (Lovecraft has revised that earlier passage so that it is the daughter of a friend, rather than Upton's own daughter, who makes the observation.) More significantly, Lovecraft probably decided that Edward's "rejoinder" would at this stage be uncharacteristic of him, since he had only a few paragraphs earlier emphasised "Edward's weak will" and Asenath's "strong will" (*DH* 282). Moreover, the suggestion that Asenath was not "fully human" would have telegraphed some phases of the climax. Lovecraft was certainly wise in omitting this passage.

At the end of the first paragraph of Section III, a lengthy excision was made. Lovecraft is passing quickly over the next two years of Asenath and Edward's life, recounting that "Occasionally the Derbys would go on long trips—ostensibly to Europe, though Edward sometimes hinted at obscurer destinations" (*DH* 284). At this point, several lines have been erased; then we find the following:

> . . . which professional ethics ought to have held back. He had been summoned one Candlemas to the lonely Crowninshield place; & could not feel easy after what he had seen. Fortunately, it was dead. He had known monstrous births before—but when monstrosity takes certain directions, there are questions one has to ask oneself . . . questions about people, & about the universe itself. Candlemas is nine months after the Witches' Sabbat, & country legend has much to say about it. Were not Innsmouth folk said to keep the Sabbat? Where were the Derbys last May-Eve? Dr. Hathorne allowed that if he were Edward Derby he would leave Asenath while the leaving was good. He was never quite specific, though, until that night at the last when the horror came to my doorstep. Now he will back me up in trying to do what must be done.

The passage appears to discuss a character—Dr. Hathorne, presumably the Derbys' family physician—who has been entirely removed from the narrative. (The name seems to be a clear allusion to John Hathorne, one of the judges in the Salem witch trials; he is mentioned in passing in *The Case of Charles Dexter Ward* [see *MM* 150] and "The Dreams in the Witch House" [*MM* 263].) It appears that we are to understand that Asenath has given birth to a stillborn "monstrosity." Lovecraft must have determined (rightly) that this

Excised Passages from "The Thing on the Doorstep"

development was too sudden in its evocation of weirdness than what the story's narrative pace required at this time. It would have constituted too explicit a turn to horror, so Lovecraft removed it.

Toward the end of Section III another excised passage occurs. Here Lovecraft is discussing how Derby is becoming increasingly alarmed about the strange travels that Asenath compels him to make, and the bizarre "objects" brought back from those expeditions. At the end of a paragraph in which Derby expresses doubt about whether old Ephraim Waite is really dead ("in a spiritual as well as corporal sense" [*DH* 286]), we find the following, after some erasures:

> upstairs—but sometimes she couldn't hold on, & he would find himself suddenly in his own body again in some far off, horrible, & perhaps unknown place. Sometimes she would get hold of him again & sometimes she couldn't. Often he had to find his way home from frightful distances, getting somebody to drive the car after he found it. The worst thing was that she was holding on to him longer & longer at a time. She wanted to be a man—to be fully human—that's why she got hold of him. Some day she would crowd him out & disappear with his body—disappear to become a great magician like her father & leave him stranded in that female shell that wasn't even quite human. Yes, he knew about the Innsmouth blood now. There had been traffick with things from the sea—it was horrible. . . .

Once again, Lovecraft has determined that this passage telegraphs matters in an unsatisfying way. He went on to write a passage about Derby being stranded in Chesuncook, Maine, and having to call Upton to fetch him, since he could not drive his own car. It is only as Upton is driving him back that the above passage—somewhat expanded—becomes incorporated into the narrative (*DH* 288). This leads one to wonder whether Lovecraft, in the course of composing the story, decided to add the Chesuncook passage as a more vivid way of suggesting Asenath's increasing control of Edward's body, rather than having it simply stated bluntly by Edward.

Toward the end of this episode—when Asenath has mentally taken over Edward's body, ousted Upton from the driver's seat (a tricky maneuver at best, one would imagine), and begun to reassure Upton that nothing is really amiss, especially in regard to the relationship between Edward and Asenath—a fascinating excision occurs. Asenath (in Edward's body) tells Upton: "I shall take a rest from now on—you probably won't see me for some time, and you needn't blame Asenath for it" (*DH* 291). Then:

> "Don't be frightened on her account, either—in case I've been unloading any savage nonsense. *She is better protected than you can realise.* I'd be a fool to

harm her, for it would all come back on me sooner or later. And of course I don't wish to harm her. Those spells of mine are just overwrought nerves.["]

What could the "protection" referred to by Asenath be? Is this an anticipation of the climax, where Asenath reveals the power to cast her mind out of her own (dead) body and into that of Edward? If so, Lovecraft again must have concluded that it was too clear a telegraphing of the conclusion, so he removed the passage.

In the early portion of Section V, a final excision occurs. Here Lovecraft is discussing the increasing rumours that the sounds of Asenath sobbing have been heard at the Derbys' house. After the sentence "And then someone complicated matters by whispering that the sobs had once or twice been in a man's voice" (*DH* 293), we find this:

> The tragic culmination came in mid-October. It was Thursday, the night when the three Derby servants went out—always together, & always heading for the same unknown haven in their native Innsmouth. I was waked about three in the morning by a frantic ringing & pounding of the knocker at the front door, & when I slipped on a dressing gown & went down I found Edward [erasure]. It was Edward, & I saw in a flash that his personality was the old one which I had not encountered since the day of his ravings on that terrible ride from Chesuncook. His face was distorted by a mixture of wild emotions in which fright & triumph seemed incongruously to have dominance. I could see

This passage was in part revised into the paragraph that follows, but it seems as if the excised passage was actually meant to initiate the climax of the story. It is possible that Lovecraft was initially planning to have Derby admit at this point that he had killed Asenath (not merely that she had "gone on a long research trip" [*DH* 293]). But Lovecraft must have felt that this would have rushed the conclusion of the story, so he had the "final nightmare" come four months later, just "before Candlemas" (*DH* 298).

The various excised passages in the manuscript of "The Thing on the Doorstep" suggest that Lovecraft, even if he had had a synopsis of the story drawn up (or, indeed, two synopses—one detailing events in order of occurrence, the other in order of narration—as he advises writers to prepare [*CE* 2.176]), realised that changes must be made in the course of a narrative as it is being written. As he states in "Notes on Writing Weird Fiction" (1933), written probably just before he began work on "The Thing on the Doorstep":

> Change incidents and plot whenever the developing process seems to suggest such change, never being bound by any previous design. If the development suddenly reveals new opportunities for dramatic effect or vivid storytelling,

Excised Passages from "The Thing on the Doorstep"

add whatever is thought advantageous—going back and reconciling the early parts to the new plan. Insert and delete whole sections if necessary or desirable, trying different beginnings and endings until the best arrangement is found. But be sure that all references throughout the story are thoroughly reconciled with the final design. Remove all possible superfluities—words, sentences, paragraphs, or whole episodes or elements—observing the usual precautions about the reconciling of all references. (CE 2.176-77)

"The Thing on the Doorstep" is far from being one of Lovecraft's stellar tales, but the very difficulties Lovecraft experienced in its composition, as testified by the numerous passages he excised and reworked, are an exemplification of the fluid and organic manner in which he fashioned a tale so that it would achieve maximum impact.

V. On Lovecraft's Essays, Poetry, and Letters

"History of the *Necronomicon*"

> No weird story can truly produce terror unless it is devised with all the care & verisimilitude of an actual *hoax*.
> —H. P. Lovecraft to Clark Ashton Smith 17 October 1930 (SL 3.193)

That Lovecraft took the above dictum to heart is nowhere more clearly evident than in the intentional hoax called "History of the *Necronomicon*"—a hoax so pervasive and convincing that bibliographers and critics have frequently labelled the piece an "essay," to say nothing of the countless fans who either suspect or, indeed, are certain that the *Necronomicon* actually exists—a misconception not allayed by the four different versions of the *Necronomicon* that have been published, of which one has even reached (horror of horrors) the paperback stage. Some of the producers of these volumes may have known that Lovecraft often toyed with "writing" the *Necronomicon* himself, but few have evidently recalled his remark (in a letter to Jim Blish and William Miller, Jr) that "if anyone were to try to write the *Necronomicon*, it would disappoint all those who have shuddered at cryptic references to it" (*Uncollected Letters* 37). Like a beautiful woman, the *Necronomicon* is best left semi-clothed in mystery.

If the *Necronomicon* is Lovecraft's most celebrated creation, it is by no means his most easily understood. Numerous erroneous views about it—and about the joke-essay "History of the *Necronomicon*" itself—remain, thanks in no small way to the blunders of Lovecraft "scholars" who ought to know better. L. Sprague de Camp recorded that the "essay" was written in 1936—a date derived from the erroneous publication date of 1936 of the pamphlet published by Wilson Shepherd as recorded in all bibliographies from Laney-Evans (1943) to the present. For those who have seen the pamphlet, it ought *a priori* to have been unbelievable how a "Memorial Edition" can predate decease—for Lovecraft, as we know, died in 1937. Hence it is no surprise to informed readers that the "History of the *Necronomicon*" was written as early as 1927: in a letter to Clark Ashton Smith of 27 November 1927 (SL 2.201f.) we read that "I have drawn up some data on the celebrated & unmentionable *Necronomicon* of the mad Arab Abdul Alhazred . . .," a statement followed by a lengthy account of editions and translations of the tome which parallels precisely the information found in the finished article.

To trace the creation of the idea of the *Necronomicon* and analogous occult books in Lovecraft's fiction is beyond the scope of this brief note. Donald R. Burleson has come up with strong evidence that the idea was triggered by Nathaniel Hawthorne, although we must also remember Lovecraft's remark that among the conventional stage-properties of the Gothic novel were "mouldy hidden manuscripts" (*D* 375)—so that it is not surprising that in Lovecraft's most "Gothic" work, *The Case of Charles Dexter Ward*, we find a host of evil books—many real—among which, of course, is the *Necronomicon*. George T. Wetzel's claim that the *Necronomicon* was first alluded to in "The Statement of Randolph Carter" (1919) cannot stand up to scrutiny, for we read there that one particular volume was "written in characters whose like [the narrator] never saw elsewhere" (MM 300)—and the narrator was, as an earlier passage reveals, familiar with Arabic. In any case, the idea of forbidden books first enters Lovecraft's fiction in this tale, and the *Necronomicon* makes its first appearance in "The Hound" (1922), although Alhazred's "unexplainable couplet" is cited in "The Nameless City" (1921). These data alone would cause us to laugh at Lin Carter's belief that the idea for the *Necronomicon* came from Robert W. Chambers's *The King in Yellow* (a work mentioned by Lovecraft himself in his "essay"), since Lovecraft did not read Chambers's work until 1927.

A final misconception has been created by Lovecraft himself; namely, the derivation of the Greek title *Necronomicon* (the Arabic title *Al Azif* was cribbed by Lovecraft from Samuel Henley's notes to Beckford's *Vathek*). Lovecraft cites his derivation of the title: "νεκρός, corpse; νόμος, law; εικών, image = An Image [or Picture] of the Law of the Dead" (SL 5.418). Unfortunately for Lovecraft (who never learned Greek fluently, not having gotten "beyond the first six books of Xenophon" [SL 4.173]), his derivation is almost entirely wrong. George T. Wetzel (who, with William Scott Home, has been futilely speculating on the derivation of *Necronomicon*) keenly pointed out the similarity of the title to the *Astronomica* (or *Astronomicōn*) of Manilius, an astronomical poem in Latin of the first century C.E. A study of the derivation of *Astronomicōn* reveals the proper derivation of *Necronomicon*: νεκρός, corpse; νέμω, to consider; -ικόν, neuter adjectival suffix (= Lat. *-icus*, Engl. *-ical*). Hence the Greek title of the *Necronomicon* translates to: "Book concerning the Dead" (with possible overtones of classification), a rather more prosaic one than Lovecraft's. All this, of course, need not deny that Lovecraft intended his title to mean what he thought it meant....

We have already touched upon the erroneous belief that Wilson Shepherd's pamphlet was printed in 1936. The actual date of publication—late

1937—has been determined by Kenneth W. Faig, Jr, while Shepherd himself has told Dirk W. Mosig that 80 copies of the pamphlet were originally printed. Shepherd's text is not as accurate as it could have been, but those who are scrupulous enough to demand absolute textual cleanliness may resort to the facsimile reprint of Lovecraft's autograph draft of the "essay" printed in *Lovecraft at Last* (1975), pp. 104-5. For others, this charming pamphlet—one of the rarest of Lovecraft's publications—may serve as a memorial to one of the most fertile minds of the century; a mind who created countless images of archaic horror and cosmic dread, not the least of them the image of a crumbling tome whose fading letters—whether in Arabic, Greek, Latin, or English—can summon those very gods who, crushing what they chanced to mould in play, will some day blow Earth's dust away... If such a bleak vision is only implicit in this flippant and tongue-in-cheek article, then it only underscores Lovecraft's bitterly cynical remark: "The world is indeed comic, but the joke is on mankind" (CE 5.54).

Works Cited

Lovecraft, H. P. *Uncollected Letters.* Edited by S. T. Joshi. West Warwick, RI: Necronomicon Press, 1986.

Lovecraft, H. P., and Willis Conover. *Lovecraft at Last.* Arlington, VA: Carrollton-Clark, 1975.

"Supernatural Horror in Literature"

In November 1925, when Lovecraft was living alone at 169 Clinton Street in Brooklyn, he received an offer from his friend W. Paul Cook to write "an article . . . on the element of terror & weirdness in literature"[1] for publication in Cook's legendary amateur journal, the *Recluse*. In this innocent and almost incidental way was born probably one of the most significant—certainly one of the longest—essays ever written by Lovecraft; a work of criticism which even today has no rivals in keenness of historical analysis and in the pithy and penetrating studies of such modern titans of weird fiction as Arthur Machen, Algernon Blackwood, Lord Dunsany, M. R. James, William Hope Hodgson, Ambrose Bierce, and many others. It is a sad fact that most of the better studies of the weird tale—Edith Birkhead's *The Tale of Terror* (1921), Eino Railo's *The Haunted Castle* (1927), Maurice Lévy's *Le Roman "gothique" anglais* (1968)—are solely or largely concerned with the Gothic novels of the late eighteenth and early nineteenth centuries; modern criticism has been unusually slow in exploring the enormous quantities of superb weird fiction written from the middle nineteenth century to the present. But Lovecraft's treatise gains its importance not merely from its discussion of the whole spectrum of horror literature from antiquity to the 1930s, but from the insight it can provide into Lovecraft's own theory and practice of weird writing.

Lovecraft admitted that "I shall take my time about preparing"[2] the treatise, and such proved to be the case. By 1925 he had, of course, read many of the significant works of weird fiction written up to his day, but knew that an extensive course of rereading would be necessary for proper execution of the task. It was, in fact, only in December 1925 that Lovecraft seems first to have come across the work of M. R. James (*Letters from New York* 253), and he had encountered Blackwood's "The Willows"—which he ultimately ranked as the finest weird tale in all literature—only about a year previously (*Letters from New York* 63). Machen he had discovered in 1923 (see *SL* 1.228, 233f.) and Bierce and Dunsany in 1919 (*SL* 1.91f., 2.222).

---

1. HPL to Lillian D. Clark, 11–14 November 1925 (ms., JHL).
2. Ibid.

Once he received the request from Cook, therefore, Lovecraft at once abandoned his desultory reading of weird fiction and undertook a more thorough and systematic course of absorbing the weird classics, doing much work at the New York Public Library and the Brooklyn Public Library. It appears that he began writing the essay very late in 1925: by early January he had already written the first four chapters (on the Gothic school up to and including Maturin's *Melmoth the Wanderer*) and was reading Emily Brontë's *Wuthering Heights* preparatory to writing about it at the end of Chapter V (*SL* 2.36); by March he had written Chapter VII, on Poe;[3] and by the middle of April he had gotten "half through Arthur Machen" (Chapter X) (*Letters from New York* 301). The work was probably finished in essence by May, for at that time Lovecraft remarks that he has not yet read the work of Walter de la Mare—whom he ultimately ranked only just below the "modern masters" (Machen, Blackwood, Dunsany, and James) among living fantaisistes—but that he "really ought to [read him] before giving my article a final form" (*SL* 2.53). This surely means—given Lovecraft's disinclination for using the typewriter—that the article was still in autograph manuscript and that he was merely making random inclusions into the holograph text. Indeed, in early June, when he had read de la Mare, he not only "made space" (*SL* 2.57) for him in the essay, but was adding "paragraphs here & there" (*SL* 2.57-58) as well as continuing random readings. By the middle of October 1926 Lovecraft announces that he has "delayed typing my now finished sketch of weird fiction because of some new source material discovered at the Providence Public Library" (*SL* 2.77). (Lovecraft had returned to Providence from New York in April 1926.) What this new material was we do not know, but it appears that Lovecraft must have prepared the typescript by the end of the year and sent it to Cook. Even this, however, did not end the history of the first publication of "Supernatural Horror in Literature": as late as May 1927, when the essay had already been set in type, Lovecraft continued to make last-minute additions on the proofs—chiefly to take note of the work of F. Marion Crawford (whose "The Upper Berth" alone had been cited in the text theretofore) and Robert W. Chambers (*SL* 2.122, 127). The *Recluse*—only one issue was ever published—came out in August 1927,[4] nearly half of it devoted to Lovecraft's essay.

---

3. HPL to Lillian D. Clark, 5 March 1926 and 6 March 1926 (mss., JHL).

4. *SL* 2.60. This letter is dated July 1926 in *SL*, but this must be an error for July 1927, since the letter mentions the two novels, *The Dream-Quest of Unknown Kadath* and *The Case of Charles Dexter Ward*, written in late 1926 and early 1927, as already complete.

But Lovecraft continued to take notes for additions to his essay for some future republication. A list of "Books to mention in new edition of weird article" survives at the end of his commonplace book, and most of the works on the list—John Buchan's *Witch Wood* (1927), Leonard Cline's *The Dark Chamber* (1927), H. B. Drake's *The Shadowy Thing* (1928), etc.—were in fact discussed in the revised version of the essay. Several items, however, were not discussed; they are as follows (brackets in the text are Lovecraft's):

R. E. Spencer—The Lady Who Came to Stay (1931)

[Hogg—Memoirs of a Justified Sinner?] and others

Blackwood—"Chemical" <from Asquith's Ghost Book [1927]>

"The Undying Thing" by Barry Pain (in Stories in the Dark 1901)

Lovecraft frequently made note in letters of the worthiness—or lack of it—of this or that weird writer for inclusion in his treatise. But the chance for revision did not come until late 1933, when Charles D. Hornig wished to serialise the essay in his fanzine, the *Fantasy Fan*. Lovecraft evidently revised the essay all at once, not piecemeal over the course of the serialisation (October 1933–February 1935); indeed, he seems simply to have sent Hornig an annotated copy of the *Recluse*, with separate typed sheets for the major additions.[5] This is borne out by the nature of the revisions: aside from random revisions in phraseology, there is almost no change in the text save the following additions:

Chapter VI: the small paragraph on H. H. Ewers and part of the concluding paragraph (on Meyrink's *The Golem*);

Chapter VIII: the section beginning with the discussion of Cram's "The Dead Valley" up to that discussing the tales of Edward Lucas White; the last paragraph, on Clark Ashton Smith, is augmented;

Chapter IX: the paragraph on Buchan, much of the long paragraph discussing "the weird short story", and the long section on Hodgson.

Of these, the section on Hodgson was added separately in August 1934[6] (this is an earlier version of the essay later published as "The Weird Work of William

---

5. See *LAL* 86, 97. Cf. also this remark in a letter to J. V. Shea, 8–22 November 1933 (ms., JHL): "[*Etidorhpa* by John Uri Lloyd] just missed inclusion in my article," indicating that the entire revision (or at least the revision of Chapter VIII, where a note on this work would presumably have been included) had already been completed. It is not likely that HPL's remark implies a literary judgment on *Etidorhpa*, i.e., that the novel somehow did not merit inclusion in his article.

6. "I've prepared a note [about Hodgson] to insert in my article at the proper point (near

Hope Hodgson"[7]), while the section on *The Golem* was revised after April 1935, when Lovecraft (who had based his note on the film version) read the actual novel and disconcertedly observed its enormous difference from the film.

The serialisation in the *Fantasy Fan* ended, however, in the middle of Chapter VIII, as the magazine folded in February 1935. In late summer 1936 Willis Conover conceived the idea of reprinting the text in his *Science-Fantasy Correspondent* from the point where it had left off in the *Fantasy Fan*; the project never came to fruition, although in anticipation of it Lovecraft sent to Conover the annotated copy of the *Recluse* which Hornig had returned to him (*LAL* 86, 97) and also prepared a condensation of the first eight chapters of the text for Conover to print prior to resuming the serialisation.[8]

The first publication of the complete revised text of "Supernatural Horror in Literature" was in *The Outsider and Others* (1939), edited by August Derleth. There is some mystery as to which text Derleth used in the preparation of his text: he could not have used the abortive *Fantasy Fan* serialisation, for he fails to include some minor revisions in wording Lovecraft made there. He similarly could not have used Conover's copy of the *Recluse*, for this was still in Conover's possession as late as 1975 (cf. *LAL* 110 and 259). Conover did, however, retype "about half" (*LAL* 213) of the entire essay, incorporating all the changes, and sent the typescript to Lovecraft. Lovecraft acknowledged receiving the text and made a few final corrections (*LAL* 219), but his terminal illness prevented him from returning the typescript to Conover. It is possible that Derleth found this typescript amongst Lovecraft's papers after R. H. Barlow had donated them to the John Hay Library, and so based his text upon it and the *Recluse* appearance. If so, he never returned the typescript to the library, for its whereabouts are now unknown.

Assuming that Derleth printed Lovecraft's additions as he intended them (and we have no authority to doubt it, however reluctant we may be to rely upon Derleth's recension of the text), we must note that Lovecraft did not take very great care in the revision of his essay. The additions are made sporadically with no especial attempt to incorporate the new material into the

---

the end of Ch. IX) & sent it to Hornig." HPL to R. H. Barlow, [22 August 1934] (*OFF* 168). This clearly suggests that an entirely revised text had already been sent to Hornig.

7. "Meanwhile I have already prepared a brief article on the tales of William Hope Hodgson at [Herman C.] Koenig's request—which he will send you in connexion with a biographical article of his own." HPL to Wilson Shepherd, 29 May 1936 (ms., JHL).

8. This condensation, first published in *Weird Tales* 47, No. 2 (Fall 1973): 52–56, was issued separately by Conover as *Supernatural Horror in Literature as Revised in 1936* (Arlington, VA: Carrollton-Clark, 1974), and was also included in *LAL* 147–53.

historic progression of the weird tale, and certainly no systematic or comprehensive revision of the entire text (a task which would presumably have entailed that most horrible of tasks for Lovecraft, retyping) was even considered. It is particularly surprising that the last chapter took no regard of the later fantastic work of Blackwood, Machen (only *The Green Round* [1933], read by Lovecraft very soon after publication [SL 4.397]), and Dunsany (especially such novels as *The King of Elfland's Daughter*, *The Blessing of Pan*, and *The Curse of the Wise Woman*, all of which he read [SL 1.356; 2.277; 4.390; 5.268, 353-54]). It is true that Lovecraft did not much care for the later work of Dunsany, but surely at least a brief summary of this and other work would have been appropriate.

At this point it might be well to discuss in general how complete Lovecraft's treatise is. Critics have not been inclined to agree with Fred Lewis Pattee's dictum that the essay "has omitted nothing important" (207): Peter Penzoldt chided Lovecraft for not even mentioning Oliver Onions and Robert Hichens (63f.), while Jack Sullivan has quite rightly taken Lovecraft to task for his very scanty mention of LeFanu (32). E. F. Bleiler has remarked:

> Lovecraft had an excellent knowledge of Edwardian and contemporary supernatural fiction, but his knowledge of earlier material was limited. What he knew of Gothic fiction he picked up from Edith Birkhead and Montague Summers, and went little beyond them. He was very weak on Victorian literature. He dismisses Le Fanu with a brief comment and seems to have been unaware of the work of Mrs. J. H. Riddell, Mrs. Henry Wood, Mary Braddon, Rhoda Broughton and others. (Letter 814)

This statement contains much that is true, some that is false—Lovecraft did not know of Montague Summers's criticism until relatively late in life—and some that is irrelevant. Lovecraft in fact displays his knowledge of the best Victorian weird writing in his remark that "the Victorians went in strongly for weird fiction—Bulwer-Lytton, Dickens, Wilkie Collins, Harrison Ainsworth, Mrs Oliphant, George W. M. Reynolds, H. Rider Haggard, R. L. Stevenson and countless others turned out reams of it" (SL 4.239), and his omission of the writers cited by Bleiler—none of whom have been at all influential in the history of weird writing—cannot be considered significant. It is true that Lovecraft's readings in the Gothics were none too comprehensive, but it is equally true that most of the several hundred Gothic novels written in the late eighteenth and early nineteenth century fully deserve his label of a "dreary plethora of trash." Lovecraft is certainly to be commended for his brief citations of fantasy in ancient literature (even though some of these were derived from second-hand sources[9]), although I find it a little surprising that

---

9. HPL's citation of Pliny the Younger's letter to Sura derives from Joseph Lewis

he does not cite Greek epic (the various descents into the Underworld by Homer [*Odyssey*, Book XI], Virgil [*Georgics*, Book IV; *Aeneid*, Book VI], Ovid [*Metamorphoses*, Book X—a possible parody of Virgil], and others), Greek and Roman tragedy (especially such things as the grisly conclusion of Euripides' *Medea*[10] and the bloodthirstiness of Seneca's dramas, which led directly to the Elizabethan tragedy cited by Lovecraft), and other random works such as Lucian's *True History* or Catullus 63 (the "Attis" poem), which he must have read.[11] Perhaps he did not wish to give too much emphasis to this very early material, since he was clearly correct in stating that "the typical weird tale of standard literature is a child of the eighteenth century."

One of the most interesting features of the text, from the perspective of our understanding of Lovecraft, is the degree to which Lovecraft attributes to other writers qualities that are manifestly found in his own work. In particular, he points out the "cosmicism"—the central principle in his fiction, involving the suggestion of the vast gulfs of space and time and the consequent triviality of the human race—of many authors whose actual sense of the cosmic was probably very small. Hence *Melmoth the Wanderer* is said to reveal "an understanding of the profoundest sources of actual cosmic fear." Machen is hailed as the best "of living creators of cosmic fear." The word "cosmic" here may be no more than a rhetorical ornament, for as early as 1930 Lovecraft was coming to "suspect the cosmicism of Bierce, [M. R.] James, & even Machen" (*SL* 3.196), while in 1932 he stated bluntly that Machen's "imagination is not cosmic" (*SL* 4.4). Of Dunsany we are told: "His point of view is the most truly cosmic of any held in the literature of any period." But by 1936 Lovecraft had come to revise his estimate: "What I miss in Machen, James, de la Mare, Shiel, & even Blackwood and Poe, is a sense of the *cosmic*. Dunsany ... is the most cosmic of them all, but he gets only a little way" (*SL* 5.341). Most remarkable, however, is his assessment of Poe:

French's *Masterpieces of Mystery* (1920), where the item was included. HPL's mention of Phlegon's "Philinnion and Machates" probably derives from Lacy Collison-Morley's *Greek and Roman Ghost Stories* (1912; rpt. Chicago: Argonaut, 1968).

10. "The horrible death of Glauce and Creon is described exhaustively in the terrible style of which Euripides was such a master. It is sheer Grand Guignol." H. D. F. Kitto, *Greek Tragedy* (1939), ch. 8.

11. Lucian's work was probably an influence upon *The Dream-Quest of Unknown Kadath*, for both works contain an almost identical scene where a galley suddenly leaps into space. For Catullus cf. "The Rats in the Walls" (1923): "The reference to Atys made me shiver, for I had read Catullus and knew something of the hideous rites of the Eastern god, whose worship was so mixed with that of Cybele" (*DH* 37).

> Poe ... perceived the essential impersonality of the real artist; and knew that the function of creative fiction is merely to express and interpret events and sensations as they are, regardless of how they tend or what they prove—good and evil, attractive or repulsive, stimulating or depressing—with the author always acting as a vivid and detached chronicler rather than as a teacher, sympathiser, or vendor of opinion.

Poe scholars may raise their eyebrows at the claim for Poe's "impersonality" and "detachment," although it is surely true that Poe scorned the moral didacticism of the prevailing Victorian temper; but let us recall Lovecraft's statement of his own aesthetic of weird fiction, written in 1927:

> Now all my tales are based on the fundamental premise that common human laws & interests have no validity or significance in the vast cosmos-at-large.... To achieve the essence of real externality [i.e. cosmism], whether of time or space or dimension, one must forget that such things as organic life, good & evil, love & hate, & all such local attributes of a negligible & temporary race called mankind, have any existence at all. (SL 2.150)

It is, however, unjust to think that Lovecraft's analyses are vitiated in this way. In fact, in both his specific comments on individual writers and in his general remarks on the aesthetic foundations of weird literature—the importance of "atmosphere," the cosmic point of view, the superiority of impressions and images over the "mere mechanics of plot"—his essay has stood the test of time and has been little improved upon by subsequent scholarship.

It is, then, easy to second-guess Lovecraft, and to complain of the relative praise given to this or that author;[12] but no one can deny (nor has anyone yet done so) that Lovecraft's work remains, as Bleiler noted, "the finest historical discussion of supernatural fiction" ("Introduction" viii). Jack Sullivan similarly finds that "Lovecraft's essay remains the most empathetic and original study of the genre to date" (5). And Bleiler is correct in emphasising the value of Lovecraft's work as an *historical* study; for—granting any omissions of particular authors or works, important or otherwise—Lovecraft never loses sight of the historical development of the field, and it is precisely in this regard—as well as in its analysis of certain authors whom he read "empathetically" and perceptively—that the essay gains its primary value. The central place given to Poe—as both the summation of the Gothic movement (recall that "MS. Found

---

12. T. O. Mabbott, in his review of *The Outsider and Others* in *American Literature* 12 (1940): 136, remarks that HPL "tends to underrate Stevenson," while both he and Edmund Wilson ("Tales of the Marvellous and the Ridiculous" 46f.) feel that HPL's praise for Dunsany is excessive (Wilson also feels that HPL rated Machen too highly). None of these judgments has been supported by subsequent criticism.

in a Bottle" [1831] was written only eleven years after the publication of *Melmoth*) and as forger of an entirely new tradition in fantastic writing and in short fiction as a whole—is surely a sound historical decision, for all Lovecraft's adulation of Poe. The subsequent history of weird fiction, both in Europe and in America, was, as Lovecraft knew, either an attempt to imitate Poe's psychological realism or to escape from his influence and continue the now enfeebled Gothic tradition. Lovecraft was particularly acute in selecting, from the vast torrents of weird fiction produced in the latter half of the nineteenth and the first decades of the twentieth centuries, the four "modern masters" who, as we now clearly see, have—with the inclusion of Lovecraft himself—shaped contemporary fantastic writing. The fact is still more remarkable when we reflect that three of these four "modern masters" (Machen, Blackwood, and Dunsany) outlived Lovecraft by anywhere from ten to twenty years. M. R. James's last collection of stories, *A Warning to the Curious*, was published in the year Lovecraft began his treatise, so that his analysis of James's work could, chronologically speaking, almost qualify as a book review.

Bleiler has already noted one of the important sources of the essay; and the work is—in spite of Derleth's statements to the contrary (10)—rather embarrassingly reliant in its first five chapters upon Edith Birkhead's *The Tale of Terror* (1921). The fact that Lovecraft had at the time not even read the whole of *Melmoth the Wanderer*, but only those excerpts of it printed in George Saintsbury's *Tales of Mystery* (1891) and Julian Hawthorne's *Lock and Key Library* (1912) (see *SL* 2.36), testifies to his dependence upon other critics for the Gothic tradition. Lovecraft does not, certainly, conceal his debt to Birkhead—he cites her and Saintsbury at the conclusion of chapter IV—but he does not go out of his way to proclaim it, either.[13] The chapter on continental weird fiction seems to be fairly original, and is the more valuable as this body of work is still generally ignored by Anglo-American critics. The Poe chapter was also an early breakthrough in criticism, although the information on Poe's life and background was probably derived from George E. Woodberry's biography of 1885.[14] But it is in the last three chapters—particularly chapter X—that the work gains its chief scholarly value. Here Lovecraft had almost no previous criticism upon which to work—save in the cases of Hawthorne

---

13. HPL did not, incidentally, read Dorothy Scarborough's *The Supernatural in Modern English Fiction* (1917) until March 1932 (see *ES* 2.469). He charitably says that it is "Rather good as far as it goes." He read Eino Railo's *The Haunted Castle: A Study of the Elements of English Romanticism* (1927) only after writing his essay (see *SL* 2.186).

14. See *LL* 942. HPL read the biographies of Hervey Allen and Joseph Wood Krutch after writing his essay.

and Bierce—and it is interesting that these chapters are given over almost entirely to critical analysis rather than to biographical or historical criticism. If we must carp we may say that Lovecraft paradoxically cites too many works rather than too few—works which, while perhaps worthy ventures in their own right, are hardly central to the development of the field: the disproportionately lengthy analysis of Cline's admittedly brilliant *Dark Chamber* (1927) is an example, as are mentions of such exceedingly obscure works as Gorman's *The Place Called Dagon*, Leland Hall's *Sinister House*, the tales of Mrs H. D. Everett (*The Death Mask* [1920]), Drake's *The Shadowy Thing*, and the like.

The general value of Lovecraft's remarks on the nature and function of weird fiction—or, rather, his type of weird fiction—is perhaps beyond the scope of this essay, but some notes can perhaps be added, specifically in reference to their relevance to contemporary horror fiction. Aside from many random but very perspicacious remarks in letters, one of the first occasions in which Lovecraft defended his theory of the weird was in the so-called *In Defence of Dagon* essays, written in 1921 as part of a discussion with the Transatlantic Circulator, an Anglo-American group of amateur journalists who exchanged works in manuscript and commented upon them. Lovecraft sent several of his stories—"Dagon," "The White Ship," "The Nameless City"—through the Circulator, and the generally unfavourable remarks by other members led him to articulate his theory of the weird in terms remarkably similar to those found in the introduction to "Supernatural Horror in Literature." Consider the opening paragraphs:

> In replying to the adverse criticisms of my weird tale "Dagon", I must begin by conceding that all such work is necessarily directed to a very limited section of the public. Fiction falls generally into three major divisions; romantic, realistic, and imaginative. The first is for those who value action and emotion for their own sake; who are interested in striking events which conform to a preconceived artificial pattern. . . .
>
> The second fictional school—the realism which rules the public today—is for those who are intellectual and analytical rather than poetical or emotional. It is scientific and literal, and laughs both at the romanticist and the mythmaker. It has the virtue of being close to life, but has the disadvantage of sinking into the commonplace and the unpleasant at times. Both romanticism and realism have the common quality of dealing almost wholly with the objective world—with things rather than with what things suggest. The poetic element is wanting. Romanticism calls on emotion, realism on pure reason; both ignore the *imagination*, which groups isolated impressions into gorgeous patterns and finds strange relations and associations among the objects of visible and invisible Nature. (CE 5.47)

This very unorthodox division of literature into three categories—romantic, realistic, and imaginative—allows Lovecraft to stress the importance of the last by maintaining that it draws upon the best features of the other two: like romanticism, imaginative fiction bases its appeal on emotions (the emotions of fear, wonder, and terror); from realism it derives the important principle of truth—not truth to fact, as in realism, but truth to human feeling. As a result, Lovecraft comes up with the somewhat startling deduction that "The imaginative writer devotes himself to art in its most essential sense" (CE 5.47).

In defending himself, and his writing, from charges of "unwholesomeness" and immorality (charges still made today against weird fiction), Lovecraft states that the weird, the fantastic, and even the horrible are as deserving of artistic treatment as the wholesome and the ordinary. No realm of human existence can be denied to the artist; everything depends upon the treatment, not the subject matter. Lovecraft cites Wilde's pretty paradox that

> a healthy work of art is one the choice of whose subject is conditioned by the temperament of the artist, and comes directly out of it.... An unhealthy work of art, on the other hand, is a work ... whose subject is deliberately chosen, not because the artist has any pleasure in it, but because he thinks that the public will pay him for it. In fact, the popular novel that the public calls healthy is always a thoroughly unhealthy production; and what the public calls an unhealthy novel is always a beautiful and healthy work of art. (Cited in CE 5.62-63)

In this way Lovecraft neatly justifies his unusual subject-matter while simultaneously condemning the popular best-seller as a product of insincere hackwork. And yet, because Lovecraft realises that weird fiction is necessarily a cultivated taste, he is compelled to note repeatedly that he writes only for the "sensitive"—the select few whose imaginations are sufficiently liberated from the mundanities of daily life to appreciate images, moods, and incidents that do not exist in the world as we know and experience it. This leads to the following amusing declaration, in response to a Circulator member's assertion that Lovecraft's stories would gain a wider following if he wrote about "ordinary people":

> I could not write about "ordinary people" because I am not in the least interested in them. Without interest there can be no art. Man's relations to man do not captivate my fancy. It is man's relation to the cosmos—to the unknown—which alone arouses in me the spark of creative imagination. The humanocentric pose is impossible to me, for I cannot acquire the primitive myopia which magnifies the earth and ignores the background. (CE 5.53)

What Lovecraft is really saying is that his disinclination to write for or about "ordinary people" is derived not only from his own lack of "interest" in them, but from the fact that such people in turn have no particular interest in his imaginative work.

Lovecraft's defence of weird fiction as the literature of pure imagination and as the preserve of a select few is a very compelling one, and we can see how well it justifies the work of such of his contemporaries and successors as Lord Dunsany, E. R. Eddison, Arthur Machen, Clark Ashton Smith, Ramsey Campbell, T. E. D. Klein, and Thomas Ligotti. The bestsellerdom of Stephen King, Clive Barker, and Anne Rice, on the other hand, seem motivated by exactly that sort of "unhealthiness" that Wilde detected in the popular novel, and there can hardly be a doubt as to which group of writers will survive as exponents of genuine literature and which will be banished to the oblivion of superficial, if lucrative, hackdom.

Another area in which Lovecraft's theory of the weird may gain significant contemporary relevance is in his remarks on the aesthetic status of non-supernatural horror—a subgenre that has become very popular of late, under the various terms "psychological suspense," "dark suspense," or "dark mystery." Is this type of fiction—from Bloch's *Psycho* to Thomas Harris's *The Silence of the Lambs*—genuinely a branch of weird fiction? Lovecraft is somewhat ambiguous on the matter, but in the end he decides in the negative. His discussion, in "Supernatural Horror in Literature," of such things as Poe's "The Man of the Crowd" and several of Bierce's non-supernatural tales may suggest that he is not intrinsically opposed to the notion of a weird tale based on "abnormal psychology and monomania" (his designation for a certain group of Poe's tales); but the general tone of his remarks leads one to believe that very few such works could pass his muster. A critical passage in "Supernatural Horror in Literature" attempts to distinguish between the weird and the merely grisly: "This type of fear-literature must not be confounded with a type externally similar but psychologically widely different; the literature of mere physical fear and the mundanely gruesome." This distinction sounds good on paper, but it seems very hard to apply in actual cases. Is there a point at which the "mundanely gruesome" becomes so extreme as to be transmogrified into something else?

Lovecraft bases his view on a somewhat complicated argument as to the effect of the weird upon our emotions. His canonical statement of the weird occurs early in "Supernatural Horror in Literature":

> The true weird tale has something more than secret murder, bloody bones, or a sheeted form clanking chains according to rule. A certain atmosphere of breathless and unexplainable dread of outer, unknown forces must be present; and there must be a hint, expressed with a seriousness and portentousness becoming its subject, of that most terrible conception of the human brain—a malign and

particular suspension or defeat of those fixed laws of Nature which are our only safeguard against the assaults of chaos and the daemons of unplumbed space.

This view—specifically the notion of the violation of natural law—had been evolving for several years, and rested upon the critical formulation that the weird tale must depict phenomena that cannot be explained by science *as currently understood*. As early as 1921, in discussing "tales of a psycho-analytical, telepathic, and hypnotic order", he stated: "Telepathy, the only mythical member of this triad, may some time furnish me with a plot; but the other two are likely to become systematised by science in the course of the next few decades, hence will pass out of the realm of wonder into that of realism" (CE 5.53). He later used this formulation in his celebrated discussion of Faulkner's "A Rose for Emily." This story was included in Dashiell Hammett's *Creeps by Night* (1931), one of the most heterogeneous weird-suspense anthologies ever compiled, containing everything from the cosmic horror of Donald Wandrei's "The Red Brain" to John Collier's *conte cruel*, "Green Thoughts." The volume's appearance led to an illuminating debate between Lovecraft and August Derleth as to whether Faulkner's tale was weird, Derleth apparently averring that it was (we have lost his side of the correspondence) and Lovecraft emphatically affirming the contrary. Lovecraft first gives his opinion of the story itself:

> . . . I'm far from denying the Faulkner yarn a high place as a realistic story. It is a fine piece of work—but is *not weird*. This sort of gruesomeness does *not* suggest anything beyond ordinary physical life & commonplace nature. Necrophily is horrible enough—but only *physically* so, like other repellent abnormalities. It excites loathing—but does not call up anything beyond Nature. We are horrified at Emily as at a cannibal—or as at some practitioner of nameless Sabbat-rites—but we do not feel the stark glimpse or monstrous doubt hinting at subversions of basic natural law. (*ES* 1.403–4)

Derleth did not seem convinced by this, so Lovecraft continues in greater detail:

> Manifestly, this ["A Rose for Emily"] is a dark and horrible thing which *could happen*, whereas the crux of a *weird* tale is something which *could not possibly happen*. If any unexpected advance of physics, chemistry, or biology were to indicate the *possibility* of any phenomena related by the weird tale, that particular set of phenomena would cease to be *weird* in the ultimate sense because it would become surrounded by a different set of emotions. It would no longer represent imaginative liberation, because it would no longer indicate a suspension or violation of the natural laws against whose universal dominance our fancies rebel. (*SL* 3.434)

Lovecraft's argument—fundamental to his view of weird fiction—is persuasive, but I believe it contains a few fallacies that may at least force us to qualify it. It is true enough that the horrible and the gruesome do not by themselves constitute weirdness; it is also true that necrophilia is horrible, but it is not merely "physically" so: the power of Faulkner's tale rests on our perception of the astonishing aberration of Emily's psyche that led her to kill her lover, keep the corpse in her bedroom, and lie next to it for decades, until her own death. I think Lovecraft's bias toward external, cosmic horror and his general lack of interest in human beings (I do not say this pejoratively, as I see nothing wrong with not being interested in human beings) caused him to underrate the degree to which the mysteries of the mind could be nearly as powerful and bizarre as the mysteries of the universe. One must grant, however, that there is no actual "subversion of basic natural laws" in Faulkner's tale—to say that it somehow subverts our norms of "human nature" is to say nothing in particular—and if in the end "A Rose for Emily" remains on the borderland of the weird, then it is closer to that realm than Lovecraft was willing to concede.

But in virtually outlawing the non-supernatural horror tale from the domain of weird fiction—in proclaiming, that is, that only those tales that convey some sense of the anomalous occurrence of that "which *could not possibly happen*"—is Lovecraft not contradicting his own later aesthetic of the weird? The critical passage, written in 1931, is this:

> The time has come when the normal revolt against time, space, and matter must assume a form not overtly incompatible with what is known of reality—when it must be gratified by images forming *supplements* rather than *contradictions* of the visible and mensurable universe. And what, if not a form of *non-supernatural cosmic art*, is to pacify this sense of revolt—as well as gratify the cognate sense of curiosity? (SL 3.295-96)

It is possible that this remark applies more to the technique, rather than to the metaphysics, of weird fiction; in other words, Lovecraft is specifying a methodology of weird writing whereby a background of scientific realism, and an eschewing of scenarios and phenomena which contemporary science has proven demonstrably false (e.g., ghosts, werewolves, vampires, and the like), is maintained. As he wrote in "Notes on Writing Weird Fiction":

> Inconceivable events and conditions have a special handicap to overcome, and this can be accomplished only through the maintenance of a careful realism in every phase of the story *except* that touching on the one given marvel. This marvel must be treated very impressively and deliberately—with a careful emotional "build-up"—else it will seem flat and unconvincing. (CE 2.177)

Even if the utterance is interpreted metaphysically, it should not be understood as signaling Lovecraft's acceptance of the sort of non-supernatural phenomena—necrophilia, cannibalism, gruesome murders—that he had previously disallowed: these would not be representative of "non-supernatural *cosmic* art." Rather, what we find in Lovecraft's own later fiction is an instantiation of this conception by means of what Matthew H. Onderdonk termed the "supernormal": "scientifically conceived gods and associated lore to take the place in literature of the simon-pure supernaturalism and more strictly poetical gods of our past days" (12). What this means is that the various "supernatural" phenomena in Lovecraft's tales no longer defy natural law as such, but only our *conceptions* of natural law. This is made clear in a very carefully written passage in "Notes on Writing Weird Fiction":

> I choose weird stories because they suit my inclinations best—one of my strongest and most persistent wishes being to achieve, momentarily, *the illusion* [my italics] of some strange suspension or violation of the galling limitations of time, space, and natural law which for ever imprison us and frustrate our curiosity about the infinite cosmic spaces beyond the radius of our sight and analysis. (CE 2.175-76)

Lovecraft's later fiction is a systematic working out of this idea.

We seem to have strayed far from "Supernatural Horror in Literature", but in fact Lovecraft's entire theory of weird fiction can be found encapsulated in that essay. It quite literally occupies a central place in his work: it was written at almost the midpoint of his career, a decade on either side of the commencement of his mature fiction-writing ("The Tomb," 1917) and his death in 1937. What is more, it not only allowed him to codify his views on the weird tale, but it seemed to galvanise him creatively: it is surely no accident that, shortly after the bulk of his work on the essay was finished in the summer of 1926, Lovecraft produced a torrent of fiction that included "The Call of Cthulhu" (1926), "Pickman's Model" (1926), "The Silver Key" (1926), *The Dream-Quest of Unknown Kadath* (1926-27), *The Case of Charles Dexter Ward* (1927), and "The Colour out of Space" (1927).

"Supernatural Horror in Literature" also provides important evidence as to literary influences upon Lovecraft's own work. A careful reading of both the well-known and obscure works cited in the essay can reveal much about the sources of Lovecraft's tales: Drake's *The Shadowy Thing* is a clear influence upon "The Thing on the Doorstep"; Gorman's *The Place Called Dagon* may have influenced "The Shadow over Innsmouth" and "The Dreams in the Witch House"; "The Haunter of the Dark" draws upon Hanns Heinz Ewers's "The Spider." Many other such influences could be traced upon further investigation. It hardly need be added that these purely literary influences do not compromise the fundamental originality of Lovecraft's work, for in his later work he transmuted what he borrowed and made it uniquely his own: his days of slavishly imitating Dunsany or Machen were long over.

Lovecraft, then, is certainly at liberty to dismiss his essay, with characteristically exaggerated humility, as "an exceedingly cursory touching of high spots—being based on a criminally desultory reading programme & containing some woefully regrettable omissions—& inclusions" (SL 2.209); but students of his work will find it an inexhaustible mine of information about his life, work, and mind, and students of weird fiction can derive from it valuable insights on the theory and practice of weird fiction. Far from thinking that Lovecraft somehow wasted his time on the writing and revision of this work, we ought instead to be grateful for such a felicitous union of creative and analytical genius.

Works Cited

Bleiler, E. F. "Introduction to the Dover Edition." In *Supernatural Horror in Literature*. New York: Dover, 1973.

———. Letter to the Editor. *Times Literary Supplement* (17 July 1981): 814.

Derleth, August. "Introduction." In *Supernatural Horror in Literature*. New York: Ben Abramson, 1945.

Lovecraft, H. P. *Letters from New York*. Edited by S. T. Joshi and David E. Schultz. San Francisco: Night Shade Books, 2005.

Onderdonk, Matthew H. "The Lord of R'lyeh." 1945. *Lovecraft Studies* No. 7 (Fall 1982): 8–17.

Pattee, Fred Lewis. Review of *Supernatural Horror in Literature*. *American Literature* 18 (May 1946): 175–77. Rpt. in *A Weird Writer in Our Midst: Early Criticism of H. P. Lovecraft*, ed. S. T. Joshi. New York: Hippocampus Press, 2010. 207–9.

Penzoldt, Peter. *The Supernatural in Fiction*. 1952. Extracts in *H. P. Lovecraft: Four Decades of Criticism*, ed. S. T. Joshi. Athens: Ohio University Press, 1980. 63–77.

Sullivan, Jack. *Elegant Nightmares: The English Ghost Story from LeFanu to Blackwood*. Athens: Ohio University Press, 1978.

Wilson, Edmund. "Tales of the Marvellous and the Ridiculous." 1945. In S. T. Joshi, ed. *H. P. Lovecraft: Four Decades of Criticism*. Athens: Ohio University Press, 1980. 46–49.

Two Spurious Lovecraft Poems

Lovecraft scholarship during the past decade has added several lost and previously uncredited items to the Lovecraft corpus—including such significant discoveries as "The Night Ocean," "The Trap," "The Tree on the Hill," and the like. What is not so well known is that a few works hitherto believed to be Lovecraft's have, after further consideration, been removed from his canon. Dirk W. Mosig was largely responsible for the banishing of the "Lovecraft-Derleth posthumous collaborations," and no reputable critic would now employ these items in an analysis of Lovecraft without careful consideration of their sources and genesis. Mosig and I have, respectively, also condemned two minor poems credited to Lovecraft—both, however, included in the Arkham House edition of *Collected Poems* (1963)—as being actually the work of Jonathan E. Hoag. These poems are "Death" and "To the American Flag," both apparently written in 1918.

Mosig first noticed that "Death" was included in the volume, *The Poetical Works of Jonathan E. Hoag* (New York, 1923), edited by Lovecraft; this would certainly have been an odd circumstance if Lovecraft had actually written the poem. Soon afterwards I found that "Death" had been published five years earlier, in the amateur journal the *Silver Clarion* (November 1918). In this appearance, too, the poem is unambiguously attributed to Hoag. Much later I noticed (and am amazed that Mosig did not) that "To the American Flag" is also included in Hoag's *Poetical Works*. No previous periodical appearance has been found, but I have no doubt that such an one exists: it is likely that it appeared in the columns of Hoag's hometown newspaper, the *Troy* [NY] *Times*, where many of Hoag's other poems appeared and where several of Lovecraft's annual birthday tributes to Hoag were also published.

We are thus faced with the following queries: Are the poems actually by Lovecraft, and was their early attribution to Hoag an error? How, if the poems are by Hoag, did they get attributed to Lovecraft? Did Lovecraft revise the poems in question?

The first query can, I think, safely be dispensed with: even if we can accept that John Milton Samples, editor of the *Silver Clarion* and associate of both Lovecraft and Hoag, made some error in listing Hoag as the author of "Death" when he published the poem, it is impossible to imagine that Lovecraft would have included this poem and "To the American Flag" in Hoag's collection of poems if Lovecraft were really the author. Lovecraft, of course, does on occasion note misattributions of his work, as when "Lines on Graduation from the R. I. Hospital's School for Nurses" was attributed to the "traitor" (SL 1.59) John T. Dunn in its publication in the *Tryout* (February 1917); but such a misattribution could scarcely have occurred with Lovecraft himself editing the volume in which the two poems appeared.

The matter of how Lovecraft's name became attached to these two poems is as yet not entirely certain. The poems were reprinted—along with "August," "Phaeton," "Providence," and "Sunset"—in a special memorial issue of the *Californian* (Summer 1937), edited by Hyman Bradofsky. When I questioned Bradofsky on the matter, he informed me that he had published these poems under Lovecraft's name on the recommendation of Rheinhart Kleiner. I have no idea why Kleiner felt that "Death" and "To the American Flag" were by Lovecraft. The other four poems reprinted clearly appeared under Lovecraft's name in all their previous appearances; indeed, "Phaeton" appeared in the *Silver Clarion* only a few months before the appearance of "Death" (August 1918). Lovecraft's letters to Kleiner may contain the missing clue; but, aside from what was published in the *Selected Letters* and collected in the Arkham House Transcripts, I have not had access to these letters.

The final query—the possibility of Lovecraft's revision of the two poems—can be answered in the affirmative, but need not affect greatly our assessment of the poems' ultimate authorship. Lovecraft had become acquainted with Hoag as early as 1917: when Hoag's "Fragments from an Hour of Inspiration" was published in the *Tryout* for July 1917, it was headed by a brief verse "Prologue" by Lovecraft; but this prologue was clearly segregated from Hoag's poem. Lovecraft's first birthday poem to Hoag dates to February 1918 ("To Jonathan E. Hoag, Esq., on His 87th Birthday: February 10, 1918"). It is entirely possible that Lovecraft revised "Death" for its appearance in the *Silver Clarion*; but there is no reason to believe that such revision went beyond minor improvements of rhyme and metre. Lovecraft, indeed, probably performed such revision on all Hoag's poetry as it appeared in his *Poetical Works*. Much later, in 1926, Lovecraft reports ghostwriting an entire poem, "Alone," for Hoag; but such extensive revision may have only been caused by Hoag's extreme old age—he was to die in October 1927 at the age of ninety-six.

To say that "Death" and "To the American Flag" are "un-Lovecraftian" would be to beg the question; there is in fact nothing in these mediocre but competent poems to suggest that they are not Lovecraft's, save alone their publishing history. The sentiments in "Death"—that the pleasures of this world are ample compensation for the myth of immortality—are something

Lovecraft never tired of uttering in his letters and essays; while the argument that Lovecraft would not be patriotic toward America given his Anglophilic tendencies, and hence could not have written "To the American Flag," falls to the ground on several counts: Lovecraft was in fact amply proud of England's and America's victory over Germany in World War I, and he was also entirely capable of expressing insincere sentiments in poetry, as witness his championing of democracy in "Lines on the 25th Anniversary of the *Providence Evening News*" (1917). "Death" is in fact more competent and pleasing than many of Lovecraft's other poems of this period, and it is somewhat regretful that we must relegate it to, at best, the realm of Lovecraft's revisions. No one, however, need regret the banishment of "To the American Flag."

In this whole matter there is still the chance that some passage in Lovecraft's letters to Kleiner will indicate the complete or near-complete Lovecraftian authorship of these poems—for surely Kleiner would not, in 1937, have unearthed these two-decade-old poems and attributed them to Lovecraft for no reason at all. But until such vindication comes, it may be best to segregate "Death" and "To the American Flag" from the genuine Lovecraft corpus.

A Look at Lovecraft's Letters

The publication of the five volumes of Lovecraft's *Selected Letters* (1965-76) could be said to have singlehandedly initiated a newer, deeper trend in Lovecraft studies; for before the 2000 pages of this series emerged, few were aware of the many different sides of Lovecraft the man and writer, and few had any perception to what degree his correspondence in sheer bulk dwarfs the rest of his work—fiction, poetry, essays, revisions—combined. The 930 letters published in the *Selected Letters* were in almost every case abridged—indeed, in one anomalous instance (#484), only the greeting and the closing were printed, and the body of the letter entirely excised—and only a tiny fraction of the surviving correspondence was published. And yet, the editing of these 930 letters took nearly forty years—August Derleth began collecting letters from correspondents almost upon Lovecraft's death in 1937—and the tireless work of three editors, Derleth, Donald Wandrei, and James Turner. The sheer audacity of Arkham House in publishing the letters—initially planned for one volume, then augmented respectively to three and five volumes[1]—may be lost on some of us now, since Lovecraft's greatness as an epistolarian is taken for granted by all scholars and many enthusiasts; yet it must be remembered that no figure in fantasy or science fiction has been accorded this treatment save Poe, Bierce, John W. Campbell, and Philip K. Dick. Arthur Machen's selected letters only appeared in 1988; Robert E. Howard's appeared in two volumes in 1989-91; an interesting volume of correspondence between Lord Dunsany and Arthur C. Clarke was published in 1998; a selection of Clark Ashton Smith's letters has been published, but their interest stems as much from the fact that they were written to Lovecraft as that they were written by Smith; and probably few others in the field deserve to have their letters published. At a time when T. S. Eliot's and W. B. Yeats's letters have yet to be published in a definitive format, five volumes of Lovecraft's letters is a remarkable achievement.

---

1. A supplementary volume of letters and an index were announced in Arkham House catalogues before Derleth's death in 1971, but copyright disputes evidently derailed these plans. I supplied the index in 1980 (Necronomicon Press).

And yet, how infinitesimal is even this amount when compared to the whole of Lovecraft's surviving correspondence, or—even more unthinkable—his total correspondence, surviving and destroyed. How many letters did Lovecraft write? The exact number has been hotly debated and of course can never be truly ascertained. The figure of 100,000 arrived at (probably by sheer speculation) by L. Sprague de Camp seems a bit high. Lovecraft variously gave his daily output of letters at anywhere between 5 and 15; if we assume a middle ground of 8 or 10, we reach some 3500 letters a year; over a twenty-five year period (1912–37) we already reach 87,500 at what is probably a conservative estimate. Of these, it is my belief that no more than 10,000 now survive. We know that such correspondents as Alfred Galpin, Samuel Loveman, and—most tragically for us—his wife Sonia Greene destroyed all or many of their letters from Lovecraft, and many other letters have surely been lost or destroyed by time and carelessness. Now if those 930 letters in the *Selected Letters* were published complete (and the abridgements in some instances have been radical—only three paragraphs of a 46-page letter to J. Vernon Shea were published), they could easily have taken up twice the space they now occupy. This means that every 100 letters of Lovecraft would fill an average (400 pp.) volume. The 10,000 surviving letters would then fill 100 volumes!

But let us descend from these vertiginous figures. As R. Alain Everts has pointed out, most of Lovecraft's letters were not the treatise-length works that have excited our wonder, but were short, one- or two-page letters written on the front and back of a single sheet of paper. And yet, those long letters are clearly in evidence—30, 40, 50, and evidently in at least one instance (#381 of the *Selected Letters*) 70 handwritten pages long. One can only wonder at the reaction of Lovecraft's correspondents at receiving novel-length letters of this sort. How did they answer them? Did they try to do so? Or did they merely imitate some of Lovecraft's characters and lapse into a merciful fit of fainting?

Lovecraft was, curiously enough, at first a very reluctant letter-writer. In 1931 he testified: "In youth I scarcely did any letter-writing—thanking anybody for a present was so much of an ordeal that I would rather have written a two-hundred-fifty-line pastoral or a twenty-page treatise on the rings of Saturn" (*SL* 3.369–70). He declares that it was his cousin Phillips Gamwell (who died in 1916) whose stimulating correspondence urged Lovecraft into the letter-writing habit, but it was his joining the amateur journalism movement in 1914 that really impelled his voluminousness in this regard. As an official of the United Amateur Press Association (at various times Chairman of the Department of Public Criticism, Vice-President, President, and Official Editor) Lovecraft wrote much official correspondence, some of which we would very much like to have. Each year the UAPA selected several important literary figures to be Laureate Judges to select prize-winning stories, articles, and poems published in that year, and at one point Lovecraft notes his intention of writing to the poets Vachel Lindsay and Harriet Monroe to offer them the post (*Uncollected Letters* 25). Whether he did so I do not know, but it would have been one of the only times when Lovecraft came into contact with literary figures outside the narrow worlds of amateurdom and fantasy fiction.

That the bulk of his total correspondence was with amateur writers—or, at least, with associates whom he first met in amateurdom—is easy to see from the enormous number of letters surviving to such figures as Rheinhart Kleiner, Maurice W. Moe, Alfred Galpin, James F. Morton, Frank Belknap Long, and many others. The various round-robin correspondence cycles in which Lovecraft participated—the Kleicomolo, the Gallomo, and others—are too well known to require description. It was tragically short-sighted of Derleth and Wandrei to have failed to publish many of these early letters dealing with Lovecraft's complex and multi-faceted involvement with amateurdom: interested as they were only in his relations with the fantasy field, Derleth and Wandrei did not realise that amateurdom was a lifelong pursuit of Lovecraft's and one that may well have been more important to him—certainly one that shaped more of his attitudes—than the tiny realm of pulp fiction. If Lovecraft had ever corresponded with some of the contemporary giants of weird fiction—he just missed corresponding with Bierce, and felt too diffident to write to Machen, Blackwood, or Dunsany—this emphasis may have had slightly greater justification; but, in truth, his correspondence with such figures as Seabury Quinn, Henry S. Whitehead, or even Derleth himself is of much less significance than that with Moe, Kleiner, Galpin, and Morton.

And yet, it is this amateur correspondence that either has been largely lost or is still unpublished and even unknown. Only recently has a correspondence cycle from Lovecraft to Arthur Harris (the Welsh amateur who issued Lovecraft's first pamphlet, *The Crime of Crimes*, in 1915) come to light; and his letters to Helm C. Spink and Hyman Bradofsky—important amateurs of the 1930s—have recently surfaced. Lovecraft corresponded with almost all important, and many unimportant, amateurs of his day, and many must surely have kept at least some of these letters. If unearthed and published, they would shed valuable light on a crucial period of Lovecraft's life given short shrift in the *Selected Letters*.

Of course, when Lovecraft began publishing his stories in *Weird Tales*, many fans and writers came into contact with him through that magazine: in this way Lovecraft began to correspond with the nineteen-year-old Donald Wandrei, the nineteen-year-old J. Vernon Shea, the eighteen-year-old August Derleth, the fifteen-year-old Robert Bloch, the thirteen-year-old R. H. Barlow, and more established writers like Henry S. Whitehead, E. Hoffmann Price, and Robert E. Howard. Needless to say, many of these correspondents became very important to Lovecraft: Barlow became, at nineteen, his literary executor (perhaps because Lovecraft saw in him the same incandescent brilliance which, a decade earlier, had impressed him in Alfred Galpin; and in this he may not have been far wrong), Derleth and Wandrei his posthumous editors, and Howard a close associate whose own voluminous replies to Lovecraft's letters would lend themselves ideally to combined publication, as has been done with other figures—notably Alexander Pope and Horace Walpole—where both sides of a correspondence cycle survive. In its own way the Lovecraft-Howard correspondence rivals the Pope-Swift correspondence of the early eighteenth century, and would perhaps be of as much importance to fantasy scholars as the latter is to students of the Augustan age.

As Lovecraft became the fountainhead of the fantasy fandom movement of the 1930s, his correspondents in almost every instance were eager youths—Barlow, Duane Rimel, F. Lee Baldwin, Donald A. Wollheim, Kenneth Sterling, W. F. Anger, Willis Conover, and others—who all looked up to him as a mentor and teacher. Lovecraft naturally slipped into this role, for it finally made real his wistful dream of being a "grandpa" surrounded by excited young children. The Grand Old Man had at last found his respectful audience.

And this raises a matter of utmost importance in considering Lovecraft's letters: the varying tones he adopted when dealing with different correspondents. Far from showing Lovecraft to be insincere or hypocritical, this adaptation of tone and matter to the individual reveals the consideration and courtesy ingrained in his behaviour. Nothing could exemplify this aspect of Lovecraft better than the correspondence to Elizabeth Toldridge, a disabled would-be poet[2] in Washington, D.C., with whom he corresponded faithfully for eight years, until his death. Even the voluminous published correspondence to Toldridge does not tell the whole story: only the unabridged, unpublished letters show how carefully and tactfully Lovecraft answered each point raised by his correspondent, tirelessly gave kind and constructive advice on her insipid poetry (much of which, evidently kept by Lovecraft, survives in manuscript in the John Hay Library), acknowledged the newspaper "cuttings" she sent him, and in general adopted a patient and interested tone in all his correspondence to her. Hypocrisy? Hardly: Lovecraft was merely trying to bring a few moments' pleasure into an invalid's drab existence; and the fact

---

2. Actually, as James Turner has pointed out to me, she published two slim books of poetry in the teens, years before ever encountering HPL; but these were probably published at her own expense.

that the correspondence ceased only with his death testifies that Lovecraft must have been successful in his attempt.

Other correspondence cycles reveal analogous shifts in tone: tongue-in-cheek archaism to Rheinhart Kleiner (himself a polished poet adhering to older standards in prose and poetry); ludicrous slang and colloquialism to James F. Morton; playfully horrific greetings to Clark Ashton Smith; studied—perhaps excessive—politeness to Helen Sully (to the point that eventually she became infuriated that Lovecraft continued to address her as "Miss Sully" instead of as "Helen"); and the like. The correspondence differs, of course, in substance as well, depending on the interests of the correspondent: the letters to Derleth are primarily about weird fiction or regional/historical matters, in accordance with Derleth's mainstream literary work; the letters to E. Hoffmann Price are almost solely about weird fiction (and—rather monotonously—about Lovecraft's resolutely non-commercial stance, something Price, as a "professional" writer, found almost incomprehensible); heavily philosophical is the correspondence to Galpin (in his youth as fervent a Nietzschean as Lovecraft), Moe (an idealist who formed the perfect counterweight to Lovecraft the materialist), Morton (an atheist even more extreme than Lovecraft), and, to a degree, with Robert E. Howard: to no one else could Lovecraft have written the lengthy and stalwart defences of civilisation over barbarism than to the creator of Conan. It is not certain that Lovecraft got the better of this argument. The correspondence to Wandrei is also primarily literary, but not restricted narrowly to horror fiction as it is to Derleth and Price; rather, Wandrei, holding many of the same philosophical and literary attitudes as Lovecraft, elicited from his correspondent some very profound statements of his literary theory, and the recent unabridged publication of their illuminating joint correspondence may be the vanguard of several such volumes now in the planning stages.

Two correspondence cycles perhaps stand apart, and may represent the pinnacle of Lovecraft's epistolary art: the letters to Frank Belknap Long and to Clark Ashton Smith. The letters to Smith, of course, also centre primarily on weird fiction; but do so in such a way as to reveal volumes about Lovecraft's aesthetic theory. Lovecraft confided in Smith much more than he did, say, in Derleth: Smith shared Lovecraft's "cosmic" viewpoint, as Lovecraft knew Derleth (the "self-blinded earth-gazer" [SL 3.295]) did not; as a result, Lovecraft had no difficulty communicating his sense of "cosmic outsideness" and "adventurous expectancy" to Smith. But the correspondence to Frank Belknap Long may be the greatest Lovecraft ever wrote: Long and Lovecraft, extremely close friends for fifteen years through many personal meetings, let their hair down completely in their letters, talking about everything from eroticism to cosmicism, amateur affairs to weird fiction, Colonial architecture to aesthetic sincerity to the decline of the West to Greek philosophy to Anglo-Catholicism. The massive letter #466 contains more philosophical substance and rhetorical flourishes than any story or essay he ever wrote, and ought to stand next to "The Colour out of Space" and *At the Mountains of Madness* as one of his towering literary achievements.

It is now, of course, scarcely to be doubted that Lovecraft's letters are great literary works, but Lovecraft was the first to disavow the claim: "Nobody expects anything of a letter, or judges any man's style by one. Even when I write one by hand I pay no attention to rhetorick, but just sail along at a mile-a-minute pace. . . . If you were to analyse the language of this letter you would find it shot all to hell with solecisms and bad rhythms" (*SL* 3.337). This passage tells us many things. When Lovecraft wrote, early in his career, that "my reading of publish'd letters hath largely been confined to those of 18th century British authors" (*SL* 1.88) along with Cicero and Pliny the Younger, he should have added an important qualification: his letters—those written, at any rate, in his prime—are leagues away from the laboured pomposity of Pope's or Johnson's correspondence (the former consciously wrote with the expectation that his letters would one day be published), but resemble instead the easy grace and fluency of Gray or Cowper. And in spite of the "mile-a-minute" rate, there are in fact few solecisms in Lovecraft's letters[3]—and this is one more reason why his letters are one of his greatest accomplishments, for the obvious rapidity with which most of his correspondence was written by no means excludes some dazzling rhetorical strokes: we have the bizarre "stream-of-consciousness" letters (cf., e.g., #454) where Lovecraft free-associates for pages on end; we have devastating destructions of his opponents' arguments, as in the early letter to Moe on the subject that "the Judaeo-Christian mythology is NOT TRUE" (*SL* 1.60f.); unexpected poignancy or eloquence as Lovecraft records important episodes in his life, such as his return to Providence from New York in 1926 ("HOME–UNION STATION–*PROVIDENCE!!!!*"–*SL* 2.47) or the death of Robert E. Howard ("But it is damn hard to realise that there's no longer any REH at Lock Box 313!"–*SL* 5.277). It is certainly not the case that Lovecraft "paid no attention to rhetorick"; rather, that rhetorical instinct—in the best sense of the term, as the ability to express each idea in the language best suited to it—was so imbued in him that it emerged in even the most hastily written epistle.

---

3. Vernon Shea, however, once piqued HPL by pointing out the doubtful usage "three alternatives" in one letter (*SL* 4.99); and there are other solecisms—found also in the stories—such as the use of "data" in the singular (and this from one who was a Latin scholar) and the continual misspelling of "accommodate" (as "accomodate") and "Portuguese" (as "Portugese").

J. Vernon Shea was one of several who suggested that there were many potential essays buried in the letters (see *SL* 4.351), and such is indeed the case. Lovecraft actually did make some attempts to create essays out of letters, but only sporadically and half-heartedly. As I have pointed out elsewhere (see *In Defence of Dagon* and "Lovecraft's Philosophy"), in the 1930s Lovecraft (and/or Barlow) extracted the philosophical portions of the three open letters he had sent through the Transatlantic Circulator in 1921 and assembled them into an independent essay—a somewhat problematical procedure, since much of the "essay" is a polemic directed toward a single opponent whose views cannot always be accurately inferred only from Lovecraft's side of the debate. Posthumously, of course, Lovecraft's letters have been mined for essay-material: "Some Backgrounds of Fairyland" (in *Marginalia*) is part of a letter to Wilfred Talman, as are the two Lovecraft items in *The Occult Lovecraft* (1975); the autobiographical *E'ch-Pi-El Speaks* (1972) is a letter to an unknown correspondent; even the "Observations on Several Parts of America" (1928) began life as a letter to Maurice Moe, but Lovecraft found that his summary of his travels of 1928 would save him the trouble of writing the same thing to many correspondents, so he typed up the letter with few modifications and circulated it as a travelogue. It is, in fact, unfortunate that Lovecraft did not seriously try to market letter-excerpts as essays, for if published in important magazines of the day—*Atlantic*, *Harper's*, *Scribner's*—they might have led to his developing a reputation as a man of letters instead of merely as a pulp fictionist.

Conversely, sometimes Lovecraft's lengthy letters were planned out as carefully as any story or essay. For his "last" letter (dated in the *Selected Letters* to 15 March 1937, but obviously begun earlier, perhaps months earlier) we have been given a brief series of notes and topics to be covered in the letter, and Lovecraft confessed that this was a frequent practice of his; an unpublished document in the John Hay Library entitled "Objections to Orthodox Communism" (1936) is nothing more than the outline of a letter on that subject written to C. L. Moore (19 June 1936; #856). And yet, one of the most exciting things about Lovecraft's longer letters is their almost kaleidoscopic shift from one topic to the other, a shift determined only by the course of the argument or the various points raised by the correspondent. In a magnificent letter to Woodburn Harris (prefaced by the sensible caveat: "WARNING! Don't try to read this all at once!"—*SL* 3.58) Lovecraft proceeds from the collapse of American culture to a comparison of the Greek tragedians and Shakespeare to the growth of the machine-culture to the notion of love to styles of discourse in debates to democracy to the nature of the human psyche, with asides about Joseph Wood Krutch and Havelock Ellis (and this is merely the portion of the letter—obviously abridged—published in the *Selected Letters*).

Indeed, one could cull an entire volume of pithy utterances from the letters; here is an example from Volume 1 alone:

Peace is the ideal of a dying nation. (SL 1.12)

Our philosophy is all childishly *subjective*. (SL 1.24)

Frankly, I cannot conceive how any thoughtful man can really be happy. (SL 1.26)

Truth-hunger is a hunger just as real as food-hunger. (SL 1.45)

Possibly it is better to be near-sighted and orthodox like Mo[e], trusting all to a Divine Providence, R.I. (SL 1.57)

Entity precedes morality. (SL 1.63)

Adulthood is hell. (SL 1.106)

Success is a relative thing—and the victory of a boy at marbles is equal to the victory of an Octavius at Actium when measured by the scale of cosmic infinity. (SL 1.111)

The cosmos is a mindless vortex; a seething ocean of blind forces, in which the greatest joy is unconsciousness and the greatest pain realisation. (SL 1.156)

The one sound power in the world is the power of a hairy muscular right arm! (SL 1.209)

Honestly, my hatred of the human animal mounts by leaps and bounds the more I see of the miserable vermin. (SL 1.211)

A gentleman shouldn't write all his images down for a plebeian rabble to stare at. (SL 1.243)

I no longer really desire anything but oblivion. (SL 1.302-3)

The aeons and the worlds are my sport, and I watch with calm and amused aloofness the anticks of planets and the mutations of the universes. (SL 1.327)

And who can forget the imperishable "What is anything?" (SL 3.83 etc.).

We can learn more about Lovecraft's development as a stylist from reading his letters than from reading either his stories or his poems or his essays; for his letters both document and exemplify the gradual modification—and mastery—of his style in his stories, poems, and essays. We should note that Lovecraft's first published work was a letter to the editor of the *Providence Sunday Journal* (published 3 June 1906) on a point of astronomy. This indicates the dominance of science in Lovecraft's literary output in his early years, when he was writing many more scientific treatises than stories or poems. The shift toward literature came around 1911, and shortly thereafter we see Lovecraft don the ill-fitting cloak of eighteenth-century diction in stories, letters, and poems alike. The verse letter *Ad Criticos* (composed in four "books," only two of which were evidently published) initiated a literary controversy in the *Argosy* and other early pulps, and shows Lovecraft to have mastered the rococo externals—but, alas! not the inner fire or living music—of Dryden's and Pope's great satires (*Ad Criticos* clearly looks back to Dryden's *Mac Flecknoe* and Pope's *Dunciad*), and it is not surprising that much of his prose had also adopted the "ineffably pompous and Johnsonese" style (*SL* 4.360) he was later to condemn in his early story "The Beast in the Cave" (1905). Indeed, throughout much of Lovecraft's early career there is a curious cleavage between his fiction and verse on the one hand, full of eighteenth-century affectations, and his scientific and philosophical works, written in a forceful, direct, uncluttered prose reminiscent of Swift or T. H. Huxley. His early letters mirror the split; in remarking on his literary preferences, he writes in a letter of 1918 (addressed as from "Will's Coffee House/Russell Street, Covent-Garden, London"):

> I like the novels of J. Fenimore Cooper and of N. Hawthorne, and the verse of O. W. Holmes. The critical dissertations of J. R. Lowell likewise gratify my taste.... On second perusal, I find Mr. Emerson not altogether wanting in good sense, tho' I much prefer my older friend Mr. Addison. (*SL* 1.73)

Pure eighteenth century! It is all very clever, but one can never be quite certain whether Lovecraft is in fact writing with tongue in cheek or is somehow actually trying—naively and pitifully—to transport himself psychologically to the eighteenth century. But a few months *earlier* than the above, in a heated controversy about religion, Lovecraft could write the following:

> What am I? What is the nature of the energy about me, and how does it affect me? So far I have seen nothing which could possibly give me the notion that cosmic force is the manifestation of a mind and will like my own infinitely magnified; a potent and purposeful consciousness which deals individually and directly with the miserable denizens of a wretched little flyspeck on the back door of a microscopic universe, and which singles this putrid excrescence out as the one spot whereto to send an onlie-begotten Son, whose mission is to redeem these accursed flyspeck-inhabiting lice which we call human beings—bah!! Pardon the "bah!" I feel several "bahs!", but out of courtesy I only say one. But it is all so very childish. I cannot help taking exception to a philosophy which would force this rubbish down my throat. 'What have I against religion?' That is what I have against it! (*SL* 1.63–64)

This passage is actually much more rhetorically elaborate than the previous one, but it is so in a direct and straightforward manner, with telling colloquialism ("I feel several 'bahs!'"), parody ("onlie-begotten Son"), piquant compounds ("flyspeck-inhabiting lice"), and rhetorical questions. It is as if Lovecraft, when spurred into arguments about issues important to him, sheds his archaism like a cloak and writes with the vigour and force we know from the later fiction.

As the years progress Lovecraft's letters become longer and more involved, filled with lengthy philosophical, historical, and literary disquisitions. But more importantly, the split between his fiction and his essays narrows and finally disappears, so that in a story like "The Shadow out of Time" (1934–35) the bulk of the narrative has the same forceful directness as his letters, except as the climax approaches and Lovecraft gradually begins to modulate the tempo of the story and raise the tone to a higher pitch, introducing emotion-laden words to prepare the reader for the cataclysmic conclusion.

What is even more remarkable is that the eighteenth-century pretence is sloughed off even in his later poetry, and it is here that the letters to Elizabeth Toldridge gain their great importance. She began to correspond with Lovecraft in late 1928, just at the time when he was beginning to rethink his entire theory of poetry prior to writing his late triumphs, "The Ancient Track," "The Outpost," "The East India Brick Row," and *Fungi from Yuggoth*. It was precisely her adherence to older norms in poetry that impelled Lovecraft to clarify his own new poetics:

> As for the archaisms and inversions whose elimination I am advising—I really do not think you will miss them as much as you imagine. Certainly straightforward verse will soon come to 'feel like poetry' to you; since the poetic essence is not a superficial thing of outward trappings, but a deeply seated type of pattern and symbolic vision whose force is all the greater for simple and unbedizened formulation. So much more effective will you find this sincere way of writing, that in time it is the artificial and inverted sort of thing which you will consider ineffective and unpoetic. (SL 3.11–12)

Lovecraft could not more accurately have described what he was trying to do in the *Fungi from Yuggoth*, especially the poignant and autobiographical opening of "Background" (XXX):

> I never can be tied to raw, new things,
> For I first saw the light in an old town,
> Where from my window huddled roofs sloped down
> To a quaint harbour rich with visionings.

It is by now clear that Lovecraft's letters contain a mine of information; and before concluding with some observations on the place of his letters in his work it may be well to adumbrate their manifold importance to Lovecraft studies. Without the letters we would not know of Lovecraft's hand in the overwhelming bulk of his revisions, from C. M. Eddy's "Ashes" to Hazel Heald's "Out of the Aeons"; in recent years it is consultation of unpublished letters that has resulted in the addition of several "new" revisions—"Ashes," Duane Rimel's "The Tree on the Hill" and "The Disinterment," Henry S. Whitehead's "The Trap," R. H. Barlow's "The Night Ocean"—to the Lovecraft corpus. We learn countless details about his writing—dates of stories, poems, and essays; publications of works not otherwise known; sources and origins of works—as well as incalculable details about the particulars of his life. But more important, we learn of Lovecraft's keenness as a thinker—his absorption of ancient philosophy, of the philosophy of Nietzsche and the Social Darwinists, of Spengler's *Decline of the West* and Bertrand Russell's *Our Knowledge of the External World*; his powerful materialist stance—expressed in his letters much more cogently than in essays such as "Idealism and Materialism: A Reflection" (1919)—and the modifications of that stance in the light of Einstein, Planck, and the astrophysicists; his towering condemnations of conventional religion; his aesthetic theory, founded upon Poe and the Decadents and constantly refined into the doctrine of non-commercial "self-expression"; the increasing attention given in his later years to the problems of the world economy and of government, to the point that Lovecraft became a socialist who wished FDR to be yet bolder in his reforms. All these things we would know dimly and perhaps not at all without the letters: the long digressions on the political and economic system of the Old Ones and the Great Race in *At the Mountains of Madness* and "The Shadow out of Time" suddenly make sense, given Lovecraft's later interests; the glancing allusions to Einstein and to "intra-atomic action" in "The Shunned House" and "The Dreams in the Witch House" dimly mirror his reconciliation of materialism with modern indeterminacy; and, more profoundly, the increasingly cosmic scope of his later fiction is an echo of the expansion of his thought from his early absorption in the prettiness of the Queen Anne poets to his later interests in the nature of the world and the universe.

What, then, did Lovecraft's letters mean to him—and what do they mean to us? The first branch of the question is easier to answer than the second, for Lovecraft plainly declared that correspondence was essentially a substitute for conversation. Both early and late in his career he testified to the importance of correspondence to him:

> As to letters, my case is peculiar. I write such things exactly as easily and as rapidly as I would utter the same topics in conversation; indeed, epistolary expression is with me largely replacing conversation, as my condition of nervous prostration becomes more and more acute. I cannot bear to talk much now, and am becoming as silent as the Spectator himself! My loquacity extends itself on paper. (SL 1.52)

As a person of very retired life, I met very few different sorts of people in youth—and was therefore exceedingly narrow and provincial. Later on, when literary activities brought me into touch with widely diverse types by mail—Texans like Robert E. Howard, men in Australia, New Zealand, &c., Westerners, Southerners, Canadians, people in old England, and assorted kinds of folk nearer at hand—I found myself opened up to dozens of points of view which would otherwise never have occurred to me. My understanding and sympathies were enlarged, and many of my social, political, and economic views were modified as a consequence of increased knowledge. Only correspondence could have effected this broadening; for it would have been impossible to have visited all the regions and met all the various types involved, while books can never talk back or discuss. (SL 4.389)

Many critics seem to detect, in this use of correspondence as vicarious conversation, one more indication of Lovecraft's eccentricity, as if he could not conduct a personal relationship except on paper. But with whom could he have discussed such philosophical and literary matters among his known acquaintances in Providence? Surely C. M. Eddy was not as stimulating as Clark Ashton Smith or Robert E. Howard, and Lovecraft's New York period—with the heyday of the Kalem Club and its regular meetings full of variegated discussion—belie the picture of him as tight-lipped recluse. Lovecraft's mind simply required the diverse stimulus of correspondence with all manner of associates, each of very different character and interests.

The only disadvantage in all this was that Lovecraft almost never corresponded with his intellectual equal, so that his own arguments and rebuttals—occasionally superficial or fallacious—can appear triumphs of logical reasoning. It was pitifully easy for Lovecraft to destroy Maurice Moe's or his opponent Wickenden's idealism (the latter in the *In Defence of Dagon* essay-letters); only Clark Ashton Smith, Alfred Galpin, possibly Robert E. Howard, and especially the little-known but brilliant amateur Ernest A. Edkins could hold a candle to Lovecraft in both intellectual capacity and argumentative skill; and with Smith he very rarely disputed. One cannot help wishing that Lovecraft could have corresponded with a true authority in some of the fields—philosophy, Colonial history, general literature—on which he held forth with such apparent authority. Certainly, in his later years when most of his correspondents could have been his sons, he had little trouble dispensing with the occultist leanings of Nils H. Frome, the incredibly erroneous views on sex of Woodburn Harris, or the elementary historical errors of Bernard Austin Dwyer. He might have had a little more trouble with T. E. Hulme's mysticism, and Bertrand Russell might not have been quite as sanguine about Lovecraft's modified late materialism (which involved a fundamental misunderstanding of quantum theory) as Lovecraft himself was.

To the charge—made frequently in recent years—that Lovecraft "wasted his time" writing so many letters we must respond more critically. The charge carries the hidden premise that, since Lovecraft is currently best known for his stories, he should have written more of them and fewer letters. This premise is questionable on several grounds. Lovecraft is certainly well known for his fiction now, but who is to say that that situation will persist in the future? The current literary status of Horace Walpole rests not upon *The Castle of Otranto* or his other fictions (now only of historical importance) but to the thousands of letters he wrote in his career—it is those letters that have been lavishly and painstakingly edited in a landmark 43-volume edition by Yale University Press. Thomas Gray is heralded equally as a poet and as an epistolarian, and William Cowper's letters now considerably outshine his conventional poetry in critical esteem. But even if Lovecraft continues to hold the attention of future generations with his stories (as, indeed, is very likely and entirely justified, for there are complexities and profundities in the fiction that scholars are only now reaching), the claim that Lovecraft "wasted his time" in his correspondence implies that we know better than Lovecraft what Lovecraft should have done with his life. But no one has the right to tell Lovecraft what to do: he led his life to suit himself, not us, and it is very clear that correspondence was very important to him; if he had never written any stories but only letters, it would certainly be our loss, but it would have been his prerogative. In any case, it is by no means certain that Lovecraft would have written more stories even had he curtailed his correspondence, for his fiction-writing was always a sporadic thing dependent upon mood, inspiration, and many other temperamental factors.

The world of Lovecraft's letters is almost inassimilably rich; one can reread the letters indefinitely and find new things each time. The publication of his complete correspondence may be an unrealisable dream, but it is one worth keeping in our minds: the image of hundreds of bound volumes of letters, dwarfing to insignificance the dozen or so volumes of what would be his collected fiction, poetry, and essays, will make us comprehend the full literary and personal achievement of H. P. Lovecraft, the man who lived to write and wrote to live.

Works Cited

Everts, R. Alain. Letter to the Editor. *Fantasy Commentator* 5, No. 3 (Fall 1985): 217.

Lovecraft, H. P. *Uncollected Letters*. Edited by S. T. Joshi. West Warwick, RI: Necronomicon Press, 1986.

Lovecraft's Fantastic Poetry

The judgment on Lovecraft's poetry has been severe. Winfield Townley Scott, although himself only a minor poet—perhaps more minor than Lovecraft—declared, in tones of magisterial doom, that the bulk of Lovecraft's verse is "eighteenth-century rubbish" (Scott 214). If this verdict cannot be overturned, then we must add that most of Lovecraft's early fantastic poetry is "Poesque rubbish." What this means is that Lovecraft, while developing the knack of imitating Poe's metre and rhythm-patterns ably enough, found nothing of his own to say in most of this body of work. And yet, as with so much of Lovecraft's inferior work—and it is perhaps this that distinguishes him from most other writers—it is possible to find things to note and even enjoy in nearly all his fantasy verse.

It is interesting that the first two examples of Lovecraft's fantastic poetry are, at least in part, parodies. "Unda; or, The Bride of the Sea" (1915) is subtitled "A Dull, Dark, Drear, Dactylic Delirium in Sixteen Silly, Senseless, Sickly Stanzas," and tells the histrionic tale of a romantic young swain who falls in love with a sea-nymph (or whatever Unda is supposed to be), loses her when she returns to her native deep, and then himself drowns so that he is now "safe with my Unda, the Bride of the Sea." Lovecraft utters the ostensible moral of the poem in a witty "Epilogue" of tripping heroic couplets:

> Brothers, attend! if cares too sharply vex,
> Gain rest by shunning the destructive sex!

But in fact, it appears that what is really being parodied is the late Romantic ballad with its florid imagery and sexual undercurrent. It is as if Alexander Pope were satirising a poem of Thomas Moore.

Much more may be said of "The Poe-et's Nightmare" (1916), Lovecraft's most significant work of fantastic poetry aside from *Fungi from Yuggoth*. R. Boerem has already written a thoughtful and detailed study of this poem (Boerem, "Nightmare"), and I shall add only a few notes. In the first place, the structure of the poem parallels "Unda," although here we have both a lengthy introductory section and a concluding section in heroic couplets, with a long central portion in pentameter blank verse. I am not sure that this structure is very efficacious; for the comic outer portions tend to subvert the point of the cosmic centrepiece, and yet we know that Lovecraft's real views are embedded in this middle section. By attributing the "nightmare" of Lucullus Languish merely to overeating and excessive reading of Poe, especially in such lines as

> He feels his aching limbs, whose woeful pain
> Informs his soul his body lives again,
> And thanks his stars—or cosmoses—or such—
> That he survives the noxious nightmare's clutch.

the cosmic vistas revealed in the nightmare are made the butt of jest. This is probably why, when in 1936 R. H. Barlow wished to include "The Poe-et's Nightmare" in a proposed collection of Lovecraft's fantastic verse, Lovecraft advised dropping the comic framework (OFF 342). This is in fact what was done when *Weird Tales* published the poem posthumously (July 1952) under the subtitle of the central portion, *Aletheia Phrikodes* (The Frightful Truth).

What I find most interesting about "The Poe-et's Nightmare" is its mere existence. This is really the first instance of Lovecraft's artistic expression of cosmicism, written a year before his resumption of fiction-writing with "Dagon" (itself only marginally cosmic) and a full decade or more before his crystallisation of cosmicism in "The Call of Cthulhu" (1926), *At the Mountains of Madness* (1931), and "The Shadow out of Time" (1934–35). And yet, it would be difficult to find a more concentrated dose of cosmicism than in "The Poe-et's Nightmare":

> Alone in space, I view'd a feeble fleck
> Of silvern light, marking the narrow ken
> Which mortals call the boundless universe.
> On ev'ry side, each as a tiny star,
> Shone more creations, vaster than our own,
> And teeming with unnumber'd forms of life;
> Tho' we as life would recognise it not,
> Being bound to earthy thoughts of human mould.

More important, we learn that this cosmicism is derived not from literature but from philosophy. Such lines as

> . . . whirling ether bore in eddying streams
> The hot, unfinish'd stuff of nascent worlds

make clear the dominant influence on this central section—Lucretius. And although Lucretius, unlike Lovecraft, finds not terror but only awe and wonder and majesty in the contemplation of infinite space, both see in the vastness of the cosmos a refutation of human self-importance. In this sense

"The Poe-et's Nightmare" is a clue to the development of Lovecraft's whole cosmic philosophy. Although he later remarked that he derived much of that philosophy (at least as far as fictional technique is concerned) from Dunsany,[1] the fact that this poem precedes Lovecraft's reading of Dunsany by three years points to the conclusion that his cosmicism was not literarily influenced but taken from his early readings in the atomic philosophy of Democritus, Epicurus, and Lucretius, tempered by nineteenth-century advances in biology, chemistry, and astrophysics. Poe's imagination is—Lovecraft's effusive comments to the contrary notwithstanding—only sporadically cosmic, in such vignettes as "The Conversation of Eiros and Charmion" or the philosophical prose-poem *Eureka*; and in the end Lovecraft found even Dunsany's cosmicism wanting.[2] Lovecraft's cosmicism rested upon a sturdier foundation.

The linkage of horror and philosophy that we find in "The Poe-et's Nightmare" informs many of Lovecraft's other fantastic poems. The Latin motto of the central section of that poem—*Omnia risus et omnia pulvis et omnia nihil* ("All is laughter, all is dust, all is nothing")[3]—underscores the bleak nihilism of the work, while the meaningful subtitle "Aletheia Phrikodes" could serve as the motto for a whole string of Lovecraft's poems of the 1916-19 period. Lucullus Languish finds the truth about the ultimate secrets of the cosmos too hard to bear:

> He bade me brave th' unutterable Thing,
> The final truth of moving entity.
> ...but my soul,
> Clinging to life, fled without aim or knowledge,
> Shrieking in silence thro' the gibbering deeps.

Similarly, in "The Rutted Road" (1917) the narrator, wondering what he will encounter at the end of his journey, concludes:

---

1. It was Dunsany "from whom I got the idea of the artificial pantheon and myth-background represented by 'Cthulhu', 'Yog-Sothoth', 'Yuggoth', etc." "Some Notes on a Nonentity" (1933; CE 5.209-10).

2. "What I miss in Machen, James, Dunsany, de la Mare, Shiel, and even Blackwood and Poe, is a sense of the cosmic" (SL 5.341).

3. Translated into Greek, it served as the epigraph to HPL's hilarious parody "Waste Paper." The motto is HPL's own coinage and is not derived from Juvenal, as Barton Levi St Armand and John H. Stanley believe ("H. P. Lovecraft's *Waste Paper*: A Facsimile and Transcript of the Original Draft," *Books at Brown* 26 [1978]: 41). St Armand and Stanley also assert, without cause, that HPL's Greek translation is "faulty." It is not.

> What lies ahead, my weary soul to greet?
> *Why is it that I do not wish to know?*

But this poem is merely a contrived shudder, for we are not led to believe that the forthcoming vision is of any philosophic relevance. This poem, like many of Lovecraft's, including even the famous "Nemesis" (1917), is deserving of Winfield Townley Scott's censure: "To scare is a slim purpose in poetry" (Scott 215). Merely to send shudders up one's spine is an inadequate motive for writing a poem (or, for that matter, a prose tale); those shudders must have some broader significance. Happily this is the case with several Lovecraft poems, in particular "The Eidolon" (1918). Here the narrator, "at a nameless hour of night," fancies he looks upon a beauteous landscape:

> Fair beyond words the mountain stood,
> Its base encircled by a wood;
> Adown its side a brooklet bright
> Ran dancing in the spectral light,
> Each city that adorn'd its crest
> Seem'd anxious to outvie the rest,
> For carven columns, domes, and fanes
> Gleam'd rich and lovely o'er the plains.

But the daylight shows a grimmer scene:

> The East is hideous with the flare
> Of blood-hued light—a garish glare—
> While ghastly grey the mountain stands,
> The terror of the neighb'ring lands.

Lovecraft is careful to indicate that the horror is more than a spook or a haunted wood:

> Aloft the light of *knowledge* crawls,
> Staining the crumbling city walls
> Thro' which in troops ungainly squirm
> The foetid lizard and the worm.

Repelled by the sight, the narrator asks to see "the living glory—Man!" But an even more loathsome sight greets his eyes:

> Now on the streets the houses spew
> A loathsome pestilence, a crew
> Of things I cannot, dare not name,
> So vile their form, so black their shame.

In its way "The Eidolon" is as nihilistic as "The Poe-et's Nightmare," although lacking its cosmic scope. What is more interesting is the notion that knowledge (here symbolised by the light of day) is in itself a source of horror and tragedy. This same conception is found not only in another fine poem, "Revelation" (1919), but in the celebrated opening of "The Call of Cthulhu," where again the metaphors of light (knowledge) and darkness (ignorance) are at play:

> The most merciful thing in the world, I think, is the inability of the human mind to correlate all its contents. We live on a placid island of ignorance in the midst of *black* seas of infinity, and it was not meant that we should voyage far. . . . some day the piecing together of dissociated knowledge will open up such terrifying vistas of reality, and of our frightful position therein, that we shall either go mad from the revelation or flee the deadly *light* into the peace and safety of a new *dark* age. (DH 125)

The question of why Lovecraft found certain types of knowledge frightful is too large a question to be dealt with here; but it informs his whole aesthetic of horror.

Lovecraft's fantastic poetry virtually comes to an end by 1919; from the period between 1920 and 1928 we find almost no examples, just as we find few works of poetry generally. There are several causes for this: first, it is clear that by 1919 fiction has become his principal aesthetic outlet; second, I believe that Lovecraft's reading of the poetry of Clark Ashton Smith in the summer of 1922 did much to stifle his own poetic output. Here was a poet who, although inspired by Swinburne and George Sterling, was writing fresh, vigorous fantastic poetry of a quality that Lovecraft could never achieve. "Nero," "The Star-Treader," and *The Hashish-Eater* may have done much to show Lovecraft how wooden and mechanical were such of his poems as "Despair" and "The House." It is significant that Lovecraft, the inveterate mimic in poetry, never produced a "Clark Ashton Smith imitation"—he could never have done so. As it is, Poe remained the dominant influence on his early fantastic verse, and it may be amusing to see the lengths to which Lovecraft went to ape Poe, especially in metre.

To take the simplest metre—iambic tetrameter couplets, used by Lovecraft in "The Eidolon," "The Nightmare Lake," "A Cycle of Verse," and "To Zara"—the prototypical example is Poe's early poem "Alone":

> From childhood's hour I have not been
> As others were—I have not seen
> As others saw—I could not bring
> My passions from a common spring—

Compare Lovecraft's "The Eidolon":

> 'Twas at a nameless hour of night
> When fancies in delirious flight
> About the silent sleeper reel
> And thro' his mindless visions steal . . .

The metre used by Lovecraft in "Astrophobos"—

> In the midnight heavens burning
>   Thro' ethereal deeps afar,
> Once I watch'd with restless yearning
>   An alluring, aureate star;
> Ev'ry eye aloft returning,
>   Gleaming nigh the Arctic car.

—and, with modifications, in "Revelation" and "Hallowe'en in a Suburb" (1926) is derived roughly from Poe's "The Haunted Palace":

> In the greenest of our valleys
>   By good angels tenanted,
> Once a fair and stately palace—
>   Radiant palace—reared its head.
> In the monarch Thought's dominion—
>   It stood there!
> Never seraph spread a pinion
>   Over fabric half so fair!

Typically, however, Lovecraft irons out the metrical irregularity in line 6, producing monotony.

Curiously, the metre that strikes us as the most "Poesque" in Lovecraft's work, that used in "Nemesis"—

> Thro' the ghoul-guarded gateways of slumber,
>   Past the wan-moon'd abysses of night,
> I have liv'd o'er my lives without number,
>   I have sounded all things with my sight;
> And I struggle and shriek ere the daybreak, being driven to madness with fright.

and, with modifications, in "The City," "The House," and "Festival" (more commonly known as "Yule Horror"), is, as Lovecraft himself states, "a cross betwixt that of Poe's 'Ulalume' & Swinburne's 'Hertha'" (SL 1.52), although owing much more to the latter than the former; consider that celebrated poem's first stanza:

> I am that which began;
> > Out of me the years roll;
> Out of me God and man;
> > I am equal and Whole;
> God changes, and man, and the form of them bodily; I am the soul.

But it is possible that Swinburne himself adapted this metre from Poe's "Dream-Land":

> By a route obscure and lonely,
> Haunted by ill angels only,
> Where an Eidolon, named Night,
> On a black throne reigns upright,
> I have reached these lands but newly
> From an ultimate dim Thule—
> From a wild weird clime that lieth, sublime,
> > Out of Space—out of Time.

Amusingly, Lovecraft parodied himself in a Christmas greeting, "A Brumalian Wish," in which the debt to "Ulalume" is more evident:

> From the damnable shadows of madness,
> > From the corpse-rotten hollow of Weir,
> Comes a horrible message of gladness,
> > And a ghost-guided poem of cheer—
> And a gloom-spouting pupil of Poe sends the pleasantest wish of the year!

Similarly, "Nathicana"—

> And here in the swirl of the vapours
> I saw the divine Nathicana;
> The garlanded, white Nathicana;
> The slender, black-hair'd Nathicana;
> The sloe-eyed, red-lipp'd Nathicana;
> The silver-voic'd, sweet Nathicana;
> The pale-rob'd, belov'd Nathicana.

is a pungent parody of the ponderous repetition of words and phrases in "Ulalume"—

> The skies they were ashen and sober;
> The leaves they were crisped and sere—
> The leaves they were withering and sere:
> It was night in the lonesome October
> Of my most immemorial year:
> It was hard by the dim lake of Auber,

> In the misty mid region of Weir:—
> It was down by the dank tarn of Auber,
> In the ghoul-haunted woodland of Weir.

"Despair" approximately imitates this metre—

> Thus the living, lone and sobbing,
> In the throes of anguish throbbing,
> With the loathsome Furies robbing
>   Night and noon of peace and rest.
> But beyond the groans and grating
> Of abhorrent Life, is waiting
> Sweet Oblivion, culminating
>   All the years of fruitless quest.

while deriving its message from "For Annie":

> The sickness—the nausea—
> The pitiless pain—
>   Have ceased, with the fever
> That maddened my brain—
>   With the fever called "Living"
> That burned in my brain.

The slight variations in metre and rhythm in Lovecraft's poems cannot conceal their obvious debt to Poe in mood and word-choice. It is clear that Lovecraft read Poe's better-known horrific poems with care, although he fortunately avoided imitating—metrically or otherwise—such of Poe's highly original poems as "The Raven" or "Bells."

The one other detectable influence in Lovecraft's early fantastic poetry is, apparently, Sir Walter Scott, evidently the model for the entirely undistinguished horror-ballad or "tale in rhyme," "Psychopompos" (1918), although there does not seem to be any poem of exactly this type in Scott's poetical works. For much of his life Lovecraft refused to consider "Psychopompos" a poem at all, inserting it in a list of his prose tales (see *LAL* 224).

The remarkable outburst of poetry, most of it fantastic, in late 1929 is a phenomenon parallel to Lovecraft's tremendous surge of fiction-writing in late 1926 and early 1927. But while the cause for the latter—his euphoric return to Providence after two traumatic years in New York—is easy to detect, the cause for the former is more difficult to ascertain. Now that the supposed influence of Edwin Arlington Robinson, suggested independently by Winfield Townley Scott and Edmund Wilson, has been exploded, the matter does not seem attributable to merely literary influences. David E. Schultz has put forward Lovecraft's extensive work on Maurice W. Moe's never-published handbook, *Doorways to Poetry*, but I think this motive must be taken in conjunction with an anomalous hiatus in his fiction-writing. Between the completion of "The Dunwich Horror" in the fall of 1928 and the commencement of "The Whisperer in Darkness" in February 1930, Lovecraft wrote no fiction—except the (admittedly significant) ghost-written novelette "The Mound" (late 1929–early 1930). Even here we note that by the fall of 1929 it had been a full year since Lovecraft had written any fiction at all; perhaps he felt that horrific poetry would help to revive his fictional powers. It was also an appropriate time for him to implement some new theories on poetry-writing: gone was the desire to imitate the eighteenth-century poets, Lovecraft urging instead—both to himself and to his correspondents—a modern idiom shorn of hackneyed inversions and poeticisms. The results are such works as "The Ancient Track," "The Messenger," and *Fungi from Yuggoth*. With the exception of the last, however, the poetry of this period lacks any sort of philosophical underpinning. Although "The Messenger" is as flawless a horrific sonnet as was ever written by Clark Ashton Smith or Donald Wandrei (whose *Sonnets of the Midnight Hours* Lovecraft had read in 1927 [SL 2.186]), it does nothing but very artistically provide a shudder. The same is true of "The Wood"—Donald R. Burleson is fond of citing its imperishable line, "Forests may fall, but not the dusk they shield"—or, less competently, the windy and meaningless "The Outpost."

Even many of the *Fungi from Yuggoth* sonnets have no other intention but to horrify. That they do so very skilfully is a secondary matter. Much has been written about this sonnet cycle, but I wonder how many have noticed that its dominant feature is utter randomness of tone, mood, and import. Unlike Wandrei's *Sonnets of the Midnight Hours*, unified by the fact that they are all derived from Wandrei's dreams and by their narration in the first person, in Lovecraft's sonnet series we have miniature horror stories ("The Well") cheek by jowl with autobiographical vignettes ("Expectancy," "Background"), pensive philosophy ("Continuity"), apocalyptic cosmicism ("Nyarlathotep"), and versified nightmares ("Night-Gaunts"). I assuredly cannot see any "continuity" or "story" in this cycle, as R. Boerem and Ralph E. Vaughan purport to do. The mere idea of continuity seems demolished by Lovecraft's claim that he might "grind out a dozen or so more before I consider the sequence finished" (SL 3.116)—this after having written 33 (or 34) of the 36 sonnets. Recent claims by Dan Clore and Robert H. Waugh that the cycle exhibits some kind of "thematic" unity do not signify much: almost any composite work of this kind can be made to yield some kind of thematic unity, as can Lovecraft's work as a whole. I have already pointed out that, around 1933, Lovecraft attempted to rewrite the *Fungi* into prose, in the fragment called "The Book"; he seems to have got as far as the first three sonnets (which are indeed a continuous narrative), but beyond this his inspiration appears, not surprisingly, to have flagged. Even if we assume that the first three sonnets are a sort of framing device and that the other 33 are vignettes derived from the book the narrator has discovered (it need not be the *Necronomicon*, either here or in the fragment "The Book"), it is difficult to conceive the cycle as an unified whole. It seems more likely that Lovecraft looked upon *Fungi from Yuggoth* as an opportune means of crystallising various conceptions, types of imagery, and fragments of dreams that would otherwise not have found creative expression—an imaginative housecleaning, as it were. The degree to which he embodied items from his commonplace book in the sonnets supports this conclusion; in effect, *Fungi from Yuggoth* could be read as a sort of versified commonplace book.

Of course, the *Fungi* not only resurrect ideas used in previous tales (the sonnet "Nyarlathotep" is very close in conception to the prose-poem of 1920) but also anticipate those used in later tales. Yuggoth is mentioned for the first time here, prior to its extensive use in "The Whisperer in Darkness"; shoggoths are introduced in "Night-Gaunts," although it is not clear whether they are the same entities that appear, a year and a half later, in *At the Mountains of Madness*:

> . . . that foul lake
> Where the puffed shoggoths splash in doubtful sleep.

Still more significantly, Innsmouth (first cited in "Celephaïs" [1920], and evidently set in England) is transferred to New England and made a component of Lovecraft's fictional topography:

> Ten miles from Arkham I had struck the trail
> That rides the cliff-edge over Boynton Beach,
> And hoped that just at sunset I could reach
> The crest that looks on Innsmouth in the vale.

But if the value of *Fungi from Yuggoth* as an adjunct to Lovecraft's fiction is clear, its independent value as poetry is no less so. Even if individual poems are, as Lovecraft himself admitted and as David E. Schultz has proven, "pseudo-sonnets" in the sense that they do not—or, at least, do not consistently—follow the metrical norms of either the Italian or the Shakespearean sonnet form (even with all its possible variants), they are nevertheless Lovecraft's finest poems from the standpoints of metre, word-choice, imagery, and texture. I do not know if there is a more satisfactory example of his poetry than "Continuity":

> There is in certain ancient things a trace
> Of some dim essence—more than form or weight;
> A tenuous aether, indeterminate,

> Yet linked with all the laws of time and space.
> A faint, veiled sign of continuities
> That outward eyes can never quite descry;
> Of locked dimensions harbouring years gone by,
> And out of reach except for hidden keys.
>
> It moves me most when slanting sunbeams glow
> On old farm buildings set against a hill,
> And paint with life the shapes which linger still
> From centuries less a dream than this we know.
> In that strange light I feel I am not far
> From the fixt mass whose sides the ages are.

Much of the power of this sonnet rests upon its reflection of Lovecraft's personal philosophy: we know from the bulk of his other writings how he cherished "old farm buildings set against a hill"—but, far from a harmless antiquarianism, this sentiment becomes a symbol for his aesthetic and spiritual allegiance to "centuries less a dream than this we know." This single line is worth all the "eighteenth-century rubbish" Lovecraft ever wrote, for it shows how he has finally learned to make aesthetic use of his sense of alienation from his time—not by mechanically donning the ill-fitting dress of an archaic poetic idiom, but by skilfully manipulating the language of his own day. In the final line, the faintly archaic "fixt"—emphatically placed after the metrical irregularity of the preceding word—gives the whole sonnet a sense of timeless cosmicism. It is a fitting conclusion to *Fungi from Yuggoth*, that heterogeneous repository of so many of Lovecraft's dreams and fancies.

We need take little notice of Lovecraft's later fantastic verse: "Bouts Rimés" (1934) is a harmless bit of fun, where R. H. Barlow provided the end-rhymes and Lovecraft wrote the rest of the verse to match them; the acrostic to Edgar Allan Poe (1936) and the sonnets to Clark Ashton Smith and Virgil Finlay, perhaps his last creative utterances, written very late in 1936, are pleasing and competent but no more. The entirety of Lovecraft's fantastic poetry can certainly take its place next to that of his friends Frank Belknap Long and Donald Wandrei, although it is cast into the shade not only by that of Clark Ashton Smith but also of the unjustly neglected Samuel Loveman.

In the final analysis, Lovecraft's weird poetry gains its greatest value for the light it sheds on his fiction. More could perhaps be done with the early work, since so much of it was written before Lovecraft's fiction-writing really got underway; and the *Fungi* are inexhaustible sources for details and conceptions found in tales early and late. It is, however, fortunate that Lovecraft ultimately came to the conclusion that he was principally a *"prose realist"* (SL 3.96); for if he had written nothing but poetry he would not be much remembered today, nor deserve to be. This is because he never really found a distinctive voice as a poet. It is true that his early fiction bears—sometimes too strongly—the marks of his reading of Poe, Dunsany, Machen, Blackwood, and others; but in the end Lovecraft's fiction became uniquely his own. This his poetry never did, save fleetingly toward the end. And yet, his poetry refuses to fade away, and commands our attention if only for its skill, precision, and occasionally an unforgettable line, conception, or image.

Works Cited

Boerem, R. "A Lovecraftian Nightmare." In S. T. Joshi, ed. *H. P. Lovecraft: Four Decades of Criticism*. Athens: Ohio University Press, 1980. 217–21.

———. "The Continuity of the *Fungi from Yuggoth*." In S. T. Joshi, ed. *H. P. Lovecraft: Four Decades of Criticism*. Athens: Ohio University Press, 1980. 222–25.

Clore, Dan. "Metonyms of Alterity: A Semiotic Interpretation of *Fungi from Yuggoth*." *Lovecraft Studies* No. 30 (Spring 1994): 21–32.

Schultz, David E. "The Lack of Continuity in *Fungi from Yuggoth*." *Crypt of Cthulhu* No. 20 (Eastertide 1984): 12–16.

Scott, Winfield Townley. "A Parenthesis on Lovecraft as Poet." 1945. In S. T. Joshi, ed. *H. P. Lovecraft: Four Decades of Criticism*. Athens: Ohio University Press, 1980. 211–16.

Vaughan, Ralph E. "The Story in *Fungi from Yuggoth*." *Crypt of Cthulhu* No. 20 (Eastertide 1984): 9–11.

Waugh, Robert H. "The Structural and Thematic Unity of *Fungi from Yuggoth*." *Lovecraft Studies* No. 26 (Spring 1992): 2–14.

Lovecraft, Regner Lodbrog, and Olaus Wormius

Those few fortunate souls who have seen the *Acolyte* for Summer 1944 have presumably observed the editors' note by Francis T. Laney and Samuel D. Russell prefacing the first publication of Lovecraft's curious poem, "Regnar Lodbrug's [sic] Epicedium: (An 8th Century Funeral Song . . . . Translated from Olaus Wormius":

> This interesting item presents to *Acolyte* readers what was to us, at least, an entirely new facet of HPL's writings. Written about 1920, *The Epicedium* is probably one of the very earliest attempts to "translate" a mythical manuscript, and is also notable for the first reference to the redoubtable Olaus Wormius, who later became renowned as a translator and publisher of the diabolic writings of the mad Arab, Abdul Alhazred. The various gaps in the poem are, we assume, deliberate; and probably are meant to convey the idea that only portions of so ancient and battered a vellum could be deciphered. So far as we know, *Regnar Lodbrug's Epicedium* is new to print.

Through no fault of their own, nearly the entirety of this utterance by Laney and Russell is false: 1) "Regner Lodbrog's Epicedium" (to give it its exact title) dates not to 1920 but to 1914; 2) it was not translated from "a mythical manuscript"; and 3) while the poem indeed contains the first reference to Olaus Wormius in Lovecraft, the apparent implication here that Wormius is himself mythical is also false.

The solution to this entire affair begins with a letter by Lovecraft to Maurice W. Moe, dated 17 December 1914:

> I recently tried the "Hiawatha" type of blank verse in translating a curious bit of primitive Teutonic martial poetry which Dr. Blair quotes in his "Critical Dissertation on the Poems of Ossian." This fragment is a funeral song composed in Runes by the old Danish monarch Regner Lodbrok (eighth century A.D.). In the Middle Ages Olaus Wormius made the rather incoherent Latin version which Blair uses. It is in stanzas, each headed by the words "Pugnavimus ensibus." In translating, I end each stanza with a rhyming couplet. (AHT)

This tells us much that we need to know. Hugh Blair (1718–1800), whose landmark *Lectures on Rhetorick and Belles-Lettres* (1784) Lovecraft owned, published *A Critical Dissertation on the Poems of Ossian, the Son of Fingal* in 1763. This work, noted for its defence of the claims by James Macpherson that the poems of "Ossian" were authentic (i.e., were actually written by an ancient Scottish bard rather than fabricated by Macpherson himself), contains a lengthy disquisition on ancient Runic or "Gothic" poetry in general. At one point Blair writes:

> Our present subject leads us to investigate the ancient poetical remains, not so much of the east, or of the Greeks and Romans, as of the northern nations; in order to discover whether the Gothic poetry has any resemblance to the Celtic or Galic, which we are about to consider. Though the Goths, under which name we usually comprehend all the Scandinavian tribes, were a people altogether fierce and martial, and noted, to a proverb, for their ignorance of the liberal arts; yet they too, from the earliest times, had their poets and their songs. Their poets were distinguished by the title of *Scalders*, and their songs were termed *Vyses*. Saxo Grammaticus, a Danish historian of considerable note, who flourished in the thirteenth century, informs us, that very many of these songs, containing the ancient traditionary stories of the country, were found engraven upon rocks, in the old Runic character, several of which he has translated into Latin, and inserted into his history. But his versions are plainly so paraphrastical and forced into such an imitation of the style and the measures of the Roman poets, that one can form no judgment from them of the native spirit of the original. A more curious monument of the true Gothic poetry is preserved by Olaus Wormius, in his book de Literatura Runica. It is an Epicedium, or funeral song, composed by Regner Lodbrog; and translated by Olaus, word for word from the original. This Lodbrog was a king of Denmark, who lived in the eighth century, famous for his wars and victories; and, at the same time, an eminent *Scalder* or poet. It was his misfortune to fall at last into the hands of one of his enemies, by whom he was thrown into prison, and condemned to be destroyed by serpents. In this situation, he solaced himself with rehearsing all the exploits of his life. The poem is divided into twenty-nine stanzas, of ten lines each; and every stanza begins with these words, Pugnavimus ensibus. We have fought with our swords. Olaus's version is in many places so obscure as to be hardly intelligible. I have subjoined the whole below, exactly as he has published it; and shall translate as much as may give the English reader an idea of the spirit and strain of this kind of poetry. (Blair 143–47)

There follows, in a footnote, the entire twenty-nine stanzas of Olaus' Latin translation of Regner Lodbrog's epicedium; in the text Blair translates, in prose, the second through the seventh stanzas (for some reason he omits the first). It is no accident that Lovecraft's own translation from Olaus extends only to these exact seven stanzas.

I now append first Olaus' Latin translation, then Blair's prose translation (I have divided it into paragraphs corresponding to each stanza), then Lovecraft's poetic translation (corrected from the *Acolyte* appearance by consultation with the autograph manuscript):
Olaus Wormius:

1.

Pugnavimus ensibus
Haud post longum tempus
Cum in Gotlandia accessimus
Ad serpentis immensi necem
Tunc impetravimus Thoram
Ex hoc vocarunt me virum
Quod serpentem transfodi
Hirsutam braccam ob illam ceem
Cuspide ictum intuli in colubrum
Fero lucidorum stupendiorum.

2.

Multum juvenis fui quando acquisivimus
Orientem versus in Oreonico freto
Vulnerum amnes avidae serae
Et flavipedi avi
Accepimus ibidem sonuerunt
Ad sublimes galeas
Dura ferra magman escam
Omnis erat oceanus vulnus
Vadavit corvus in sanguine Caesorum.

3.

Alte tulimus tunc lanceas
Quando viginti annos numeravimus
Et celebrem laudem comparavimus passim
Vicimus octo barones
In oriente ante Dimini portum
Aquilae impetravimus tunc sufficientem
Hospitii sumptum in illa strage
Sudor decidit in vulnerum
Oceano perdidit exercitus aetatem.

4.

Pugnae facta copia
Cum Helsingianos postulavimus

Ad aulum Odini
Naves direximus is ostium Vistulae
Mucro potuit tum mordere
Omnis erat vulnus unda
Terra rubefacta Calido
Frendebat gladius in loricas
Gladius findebat Clypeos.

5.

Memini neminem tunc fugisse
Priusquam in navibus
Heraudus in bello caderet
Non findit navibus
Alius baro praestantior
Mare ad portum
In navibus longis post illum
Sic attulit princeps passim
Alacre in bellum cor.

6.

Exercitus abjecit clypeos
Cum hasta volavit
Ardua ad virorum pectora
Momordit Scarforum cautes
Gladius in pugna
Sanguineus erat Clypeus
Antequam Rafno rex caderet
Fluxit ex virorum capitibus
Calidus in loricas sudor.

7.

Habere potuerunt tum corvi
Ante Indiorum insulas
Sufficientem praedam dilaniandam
Acquisivimus feris carnivoris
Plenum prandium unico actu
Difficile erat unius facere mentionem
Oriente sole
Spicula vidi pungere
Propulerunt arcus ex se ferra.

Hugh Blair:

We have fought with our swords. I was young, when, towards the east, in the bay of Oreon, we made torrents of blood flow, to gorge the ravenous beast of prey, and the yellow-footed bird. There resounded the hard steel upon the lofty helmets of men. The whole ocean was one wound. The crow waded in the blood of the slain.

When we had numbered twenty years, we lifted our spears on high, and every where spread our renown. Eight barons we overcame in the east, before the port of Dominum; and plentifully we feasted the eagle in that slaughter. The warm stream of wounds ran into the ocean. The army fell before us.

When we steered our ships into the mouth of the Vistula, we sent the Helsingians to the hall of Odin. Then did the sword bite. The waters were all one wound. The earth was dyed red with the warm stream. The sword rung upon the coats of mail, and clove the bucklers in twain.

None fled on that day, till among his ships Heraudus fell. Than him no braver baron cleaves the sea with a ship; a cheerful heart did he ever bring to the combat.

Then the host threw away their shields, when the uplifted spear flew at the breasts of heroes. The sword bit the Scarfian rocks; bloody was the shield in battle, until Rafno the king was slain. From the heads of warriors the warm sweat streamed down their armour.

The crows around the Indirian islands had an ample prey. It were difficult to single out one among so many deaths. At the rising of the sun I beheld the spears piercing the bodies of foes, and the bows throwing forth their steel-pointed arrows. Loud roared the swords in the plains of Lano.—The virgins long bewailed the slaughter of that morning.

H. P. Lovecraft:

With our swords have we contended!
Come but new to Gothland's shore
For the killing of the serpent
We have gain'd from Thor ( )
( )
From this deed they call me man
Because I have transfix'd the adder:
Shaggy breeches from that slaughter.
( )
I have thrust a spear into the serpent
With metal brighter ( )

With our swords have we contended!

But a youth was I when eastward
In the channel of Oreon
With our foemen's gore in torrents
We the ( ) and wolves delighted;
And the yellow-footed buzzard.
There the harden'd steel resounded
On the high-wrought hostile helmets.
One vast wound was all the ocean
And the hungry raven waded
Searching for its carrion food
Deep in dead men's thick'ning blood.

With our swords have we contended!
Ere two score of years we counted
High we bore our glist'ning lances
Wide we heard our fame and praises.
In the east before the harbour
(Barons eight we overcame;)
We the rav'ning eagle glutted;
Dripping wounds fill'd up the ocean.
Weary of the hopeless fray,
All the host dissolved away.

With our swords have we contended!
When the Vistula we enter'd
With our ships in battle order
We unto the hall of Woden
Sent the bold Helsingian foemen.
Then the sword-points bit in fury;
All the billows turn'd to life-blood
Earthg with streaming gore was crimson'd;
Reeking sword with ringing note
Shields divided; armour smote.

(*With our swords have we contended!*)
(None had fallen on that day)
(Till on his ship Heraudus fell:)
(Than him before no braver baron)
Cleft the sea with ships of battle;
Never after him was chieftain
Lighter hearted in the fighting.

With our swords have we contended!
Now the host flung down their buckles;

> Flying spears tore heroes' bosoms
> Swords on Scarfian rocks were striking.
> Gory was his shield in slaughter
> Till the royal Rafno perish'd.
> Sweat from weary hands and pale
> Trickled down the suits of mail.
>
> *With our swords have we contended!*
> Copious booty had the ravens
> Round about th' Indirian islands,
> In that single day of action
> (One in many deaths was little.   )
> (The rising sun grew bright on spears)
> In the forms of prostrate warrior-men.
> Arrows from their bows ejected;
> (Weapons roared on Lano's plain.   )
> (Long the virgin mourned that slaughter)

In spite of the fact that Blair has failed to translate the first stanza, it can readily be seen that Lovecraft was otherwise much dependent on Blair for his own rendition of this very peculiar Latin; indeed, Lovecraft has also versified the two final sentences in Blair, which actually derive from the first few lines of the eighth stanza of the Latin text. I am not entirely clear what the gaps and parentheses in Lovecraft's text are meant to signify; the gaps may indicate places where he (not surprisingly) cannot make much sense of the Latin and suspects something missing.

While this poem is indeed the first mention of Regner Lodbrog in Lovecraft, it is not the only one. The last four lines of stanza 4, the fourth and fifth lines of stanza 23, and the last four lines of stanza 29 of Olaus' Latin version as printed in Blair are cited as an epigraph to the poem "The Teuton's Battle-Song" (*United Amateur*, February 1916). The poem itself, of course, is written in Lovecraft's usual heroic couplets. I know of no other mention of Regner Lodbrog in any text by Lovecraft.

Olaus Wormius is a different story, and I think we are now in a position to understand why Lovecraft habitually dated him to the thirteenth century when in fact Olaus (Ole Wurm, 1588–1654) is clearly a figure of the seventeenth century. It does not appear as if Lovecraft knew of him other than in this mention by Blair, who never supplies his life dates or even the approximate period in which he wrote. What I believe has happened is that Lovecraft has confused Olaus with Saxo Grammaticus, whom Blair places in the thirteenth century, or merely assumed that Olaus and Saxo were contemporaries. The fact that Lovecraft mentions in the letter to Moe that Olaus flourished in the "Middle Ages" clearly means that he thought Olaus to date to this time, and that his repeated dating of Olaus' purported Latin translation of the *Necronomicon* to 1228 is simply the result of an error, not a deliberate change on Lovecraft's part.

After this poem, Lovecraft cites Olaus in "The Festival" (1923), referring to "the unmentionable *Necronomicon* of the mad Arab Abdul Alhazred, in Olaus Wormius' forbidden Latin translation" (D 211). In "History of the *Necronomicon*" (1927) he writes: "After this [i.e., the banning of the Greek text in 1050] it is only heard of furtively, but (1228) Olaus Wormius made a Latin translation later in the Middle Ages . . ." In "The Dunwich Horror" Lovecraft refers to "the hideous *Necronomicon* of the mad Arab Abdul Alhazred in Olaus Wormius' Latin version, as printed in Spain in the seventeenth century" (*DH* 169); this would be an historically plausible mention had he not already dated Olaus to the thirteenth century.

Wormius himself is an interesting figure in his own right. He was a Danish philologist and historian who did valuable work in the collection of texts and other materials pertaining to his native land. The volume referred to by Blair as *De Literatura Runica* appears to be a work published as *Runir; seu, Danica Literatura Antiquissima, vulgo Gothica Ducta Luci Reddita* (1636) [Runes; or, The Most Ancient Danish Literature, Commonly Called Gothic Poems, Brought to Light]. He also wrote a book on the philosopher's stone—*Liber Aureus Philosophorum* (1625)—but, even though it would make Olaus a more likely candidate for the translator of the *Necronomicon*, I can find no evidence that Lovecraft knew of this work.

All this may seem much ado about nothing, and it probably is; but it is one more small indication of the trouble Lovecraft could get into when he relied upon second-hand erudition. The poem "Regner Lodbrog's Epicedium" is actually a rather striking piece of work, and it is remarkable that it was one of the earliest poems of Lovecraft's mature literary career; had he written more poems of this sort, and not been fatally lured by the swan song of the eighteenth-century heroic couplet, he might have amounted to something as a poet. And if he had done a little more research on Olaus Wormius, he would have saved himself a small but embarrassing error in the otherwise ingenious "history" of his most celebrated mythical tome.

Works Cited

Blair, Hugh. *A Critical Dissertation on the Poems of Ossian, the Son of Fingal.* 1763. Rpt. in *The Poems of Ossian.* Leipzig: Gerhard Fleischer, 1826. Vol. 3.

Lovecraft, H. P. "Regner Lodbrog's Epicedium." A.Ms., JHL, Brown University. T.Ms. (prepared by R. H. Barlow), JHL. Printed in the *Acolyte* 2, No. 3 (Summer 1944): 14–15.

Lovecraft's Essays

Many things have been said about H. P. Lovecraft and his work, but there is one very prominent feature of his writing that receives surprisingly little attention: its rhetorical skill. The term *rhetoric* has long been viewed askance as something a little bogus and meretricious, but its root meaning is simply the artful manipulation of words for purposes of persuasion. In the midst of this postmodern age where the barrenness of Hemingway and Sherwood Anderson has given way to the convoluted esoterism of Thomas Pynchon and the rich lyricism of Gore Vidal, there will perhaps be fewer complaints about Lovecraft's "adjectivitis" and a better appreciation of the density of style and structure that makes the best of his stories something akin to hypnotic incantations. Rhetoric is no doubt present in them, but more in the sense of an all-pervading atmosphere that lightly erases the real and substitutes the fantastic in its place; for rhetoric in its purer form, we need look no further than Lovecraft's many essays.

Lovecraft's earliest writing appears to have been poetry, but stories and essays followed shortly thereafter. Of these juvenile essays not many remain, and we have lost such immortal masterpieces as "Mythology for the Young" (1899) and "An Historical Account of Last Year's War with SPAIN" (1899). But masses of Lovecraft's juvenile scientific journals, notably the *Scientific Gazette* (1899–1904) and the *Rhode Island Journal of Astronomy* (1903–07), survive, and their publication in facsimile would provide much edification and amusement. Science was at the foundation of Lovecraft's entire nonfictional writing—perhaps even his literary work as a whole—for a strain of scientific logic and reasoning is evident even in his literary essays. Part of the problem with his poetry, indeed, is that much of it is similarly intellectual in essence, creating the impression of a rhymed essay. Perhaps Lovecraft thought he was following the eighteenth century in this; perhaps he not only agreed with Matthew Arnold's dictum that Dryden and Pope were "classics of our *prose*" but also found a virtue therein.

The first thing Lovecraft did when he joined amateur journalism in 1914 was to flood amateur papers with poetry and essays; fiction would follow only in 1917, and even then in a trickle until about 1920 or so. This means that for at least six years the bulk of Lovecraft's literary work took the form of verse or of prose nonfiction; and that nonfiction spanned the full spectrum of subject matter, from literary criticism to philosophy to politics to amateur affairs. The majority of Lovecraft's essays were written before 1925, and in all charity must be called apprentice work. Their prime function was in letting him flex his literary muscles, hone his style, and find out by experimentation how best to say what he wanted to say. In the end he determined, wisely, that fiction not only would allow him the greatest creative scope but could even subsume much of the essence of his nonfiction: his philosophy of cosmicism found no more potent expression than in *At the Mountains of Madness*; his late political thought was best encapsulated in "The Shadow out of Time"; it could even be said that he wrote no finer travel essays than "The Colour out of Space" and "The Whisperer in Darkness."

If, then, we must concede that Lovecraft's essays are by and large not intrinsically interesting, they nevertheless form invaluable adjuncts to his fiction. They state what the fiction implies; they clarify what the fiction masks in a haze of imagery and symbolism. Unlike his stories, most of his essays were written for a specific purpose or a specific market—usually the amateur press. It is, in fact, unfortunate and even a little strange that he never attempted to market the best of his later essays to a wider audience: the earnest political tract "Some Repetitions on the Times" (1933) could have found a place in the *Atlantic Monthly* or *Harper's*, while with very slight modification "Cats and Dogs" (1926) would not have been out of place in the *New Yorker*. J. Vernon Shea recommended that Lovecraft abstract some of the elaborate philosophical, political, or literary arguments in his letters and send them to professional magazines; Lovecraft claimed to be struck by the ingenuity of the idea, but never followed it up. Perhaps he feared rejection, or felt that he could never hope to secure even a small foothold in the mainstream of American literature and thought; whatever the reason, Lovecraft's diffidence relegated him and his oftentimes incisive nonfictional work to a position of self-imposed marginality, where its influence extended only to a small band of devoted followers. Lovecraft was a giant in the incredibly tiny realms of amateur journalism and weird fiction, but that is small comfort.

Let us return to the matter of rhetoric. Lovecraft's influences in his nonfiction were as diverse as Cicero, Addison, Johnson, and Macaulay, but this list alone suggests his adherence to the grand, lush "Asianic" style of composition in contrast to the restrained "Attic" style of Thucydides, Caesar, and Swift. The rhetorical flourish is something Lovecraft never abandoned. He was very fond of the epigrammatic opening that purported to utter some broad truth about human beings and the cosmos: "Endless is the credulity of the human mind"; "It is a particular weakness of the modern American press, that it seems unable to use advantageously the language of the nation"; "Extreme literary radicalism is always a rather amusing thing." The rhetorical purpose of this device is clear: it piques the reader's interest, either because such a resounding opening is rather transparently perceived to be a highly idiosyncratic opinion being passed off as an axiom or because the grandeur of it seems far out of keeping with the subject at hand. It allows Lovecraft an entry into his discussion; occasionally, indeed, an entire paragraph is spent in generalization before the actual topic is broached.

It is also clear that Lovecraft later transferred this device to his stories, so that they too open ponderously: "Life is a hideous thing"; "From even the greatest of horrors irony is seldom absent"; "Mystery attracts mystery." The influence of Poe is cited here (recall his "Misery is manifold. The wretchedness of earth is multiform" from "Berenice," the obvious ancestor to "Life is a hideous thing"), but Poe himself derived it from the eighteenth-century essayists and from the eighteenth and nineteenth century's perceived need to counteract the "lies" of fiction by a suitable dose of moralistic philosophising. Lovecraft's early tales follow this tradition: the narrative itself becomes, formally, a mere instantiation of the generalised "truth" uttered at the outset.

The reason why rhetoric plays so central a role in Lovecraft's essays is that so many of them are polemics. In some cases they are aimed at specific individuals ("In a Major Key," "A Reply to *The Lingerer*"); more often they address general issues on which he wishes to take a definite stand, usually in violent opposition to prevailing opinion ("Idealism and Materialism—A Reflection"; "The Vers Libre Epidemic"). Lovecraft felt embattled from many directions: a materialist in an age that was inclining toward idealism and mysticism; a traditionalist in poetry when poets were abandoning metre and rhyme; a militarist at a time when the world wished above all things to avoid another world war. Even when his attitudes modified with the passage of time, he remained at loggerheads with his era: it is amusing to see him, as a Decadent, attacking those lingering old-timers who still saw Tennyson or Browning as the pinnacles of art, when a few years previous he might have been of their number. It is as if Lovecraft consciously wished not to fit into his age: even as a supporter of FDR he departed from him in recommending a limitation rather than an extension of the vote. Lovecraft throve by opposition: all his essays have a certain hectoring undertone, so as to make sure that even the most sympathetic reader is properly convinced of the incontrovertible truth of his position.

It is for this same reason, too, that satire—frequently of a vicious, biting, even malicious sort—so heavily enters these essays. Things that threaten the stability of civilisation must be battled with the strongest tools available. Free verse is particularly hard hit. Practitioners of it reject the intellectual "(an element which they cannot possess to any great degree)"; and Lovecraft's "utterances prior to the summer of 1891 [i.e., prior to the age of one] betray a marked kinship to the vers libre of today." That this latter remark is really of the nature of an unprovoked attack—coming as it does suddenly in the midst of an autobiographical essay—shows his willingness to lash out at his opponents at every turn. Many of his satiric salvos are so effective, of course, because they are supported on the whole by a very keen exercise of logic that can demolish an opponent's argument if the least area of vulnerability is presented. Occasionally it backfires; and Lovecraft's sober statement that Charles D. Isaacson's liberal views on racial prejudice "are too subjective to be impartial" could be a textbook case of Freudian "projection." But generally the satire hits home precisely because it serves as a sort of knockout blow after a merciless logical dissection of the opposing view. In many cases, of course, we are lacking the actual words of the opponent (as with the Mr Wickenden who receives the bulk of Lovecraft's unwontedly mild retorts in *In Defence of Dagon*), but they can usually be inferred well enough. And it has to be admitted, too, that Lovecraft wins the argument so often and so easily because he rarely meets an intellect equal to or surpassing his own.

The best of Lovecraft's essays are, on the whole, his later ones—such exceptions as *In Defence of Dagon* or "A Confession of Unfaith" are too few to make a difference. And we have already suggested the reasons why his essay production declined in his later years: correspondence had largely taken over this function, as had his fiction itself. Several of his better travel essays are, in fact, letters either sent to a single correspondent or typed up to distribute to many associates, so as to save the trouble of explaining the same things to different recipients. But even in his later years the amateur world served as the forum for most of his essays—that is, where the essays had a forum at all. We have already remarked that some of his essays never seem to have been submitted either to amateur or to professional markets; we do not even know why some pieces, like the curious "Some Causes of Self-Immolation," were even written, since they seem to have met no one's eye but their creator's, achieving instant oblivion as soon as the ink was dry.

Lovecraft's essays run the gamut of subject-matter: metaphysics, ethics, aesthetics, weird fiction, literary criticism, politics, travel, amateur journalism, and autobiography. In their totality they reveal the breadth of his intellectual curiosity and the gradual expansion of his intellectual horizon with the passage of time. It cannot be repeated too often that most of these essays were written during a period when Lovecraft was still labouring under serious (and largely self-imposed) handicaps: the handicaps of sequestration, bookishness, dogmatism, self-centeredness, racism, and general intolerance and inflexibility. Lovecraft would not want to be judged or remembered by the great majority of his essays. The few later pieces, from "Cats and Dogs" (1926) to "Some Current Motives and Practices" (1936), provide glimpses—but no more—of a Lovecraft who has at last opened his eyes to the world around him and sloughed off many of the prejudices and affectations that limited his vision. This is the picture we come upon in his later fiction and letters, and it is that picture that he would wish us to remember. Lovecraft has suffered by his own celebrity, which impels the discovery and dissemination of any work, however crude, embarrassing, or simply inferior, that came from his pen; but that celebrity rests upon strong foundations—the genuine merit of his later writing, which every fair-minded reader and critic will use as the yardstick of his achievement. His peripheral and incidental work, with its occasional brilliance of rhetoric, logic, and wit, can only augment, never compromise, that achievement.

I. The Weird Fantaisiste

Lovecraft was distinctive in being both a powerful theoretician and practitioner of the weird tale. Some of his remarks—those, for example, found in his landmark critical essay "Supernatural Horror in Literature" (1925-27)—are nearly definitive and have influenced much subsequent work in the field. Of course, it could be said that his theory of weird fiction was largely an after-the-fact justification of his own brand of cosmic horror, but his pronouncements are no less suggestive for that.

Lovecraft's first utterance of his theory of the weird occurs in the *In Defence of Dagon* essays of 1921. There he makes a highly provocative division of fiction into three branches: romantic (this is "for those who value action and emotion for their own sake; who are interested in striking events which conform to a preconceived artificial pattern"); realistic (this is "for those who are intellectual and analytical rather than poetical or emotional"); and imaginative (this "groups isolated impressions into gorgeous patterns and finds strange relations and associations among the objects of visible and invisible Nature" [CE 5.47]). This tripartite division, unorthodox as it is, is vital to Lovecraft's purpose, for what he is really asserting is that imaginative fiction draws upon the best aspects of both realism and romanticism without the drawbacks of either. In later years Lovecraft was emphatic about the distinction between weird fiction and romanticism, probably because it was and continues to be an assumption of many readers, writers, and critics that the former grew out of the latter in the Gothic novels of the late eighteenth century and was therefore a part of the latter. In a letter to Clark Ashton Smith (November 16, 1926) Lovecraft rebuts this position with vigor:

> As to romanticism and fantasy—I myself dislike the former except in the latter form. To me there is really something 'non-vital' about the overcoloured representation of *what purports to be real life*. . . . There is to me something puerile in devising a sort of conventionalised variant of life, with spurious and artificial thoughts and feelings, and then getting maudlin and excited and effusive over it. But fantasy is something altogether different. Here we have an art based on the imaginative life of the human mind, *frankly recognised as such*; and in its way as natural and scientific—as truly related to natural (even if uncommon and delicate) psychological processes as the starkest of photographic realism. (SL 2.90)

This passage is enormously significant because it underscores what Lovecraft has really been thinking all along but cannot quite bring himself to say: that weird fiction is almost indistinguishable from realism, and indeed *is* a sort of realism (as regards truth to human emotions and to the facts of science) except where the bizarre enters in. Lovecraft found actual realism—the realism, say, of Dreiser—wearisome and admitted to an inability to write it; but his type of weird fiction is realistic because, as he says in "Notes on Writing Weird Fiction," "Inconceivable events and conditions have a special handicap to overcome, and this can be accomplished only through the maintenance of a careful realism in every phase of the story except that touching on the one given marvel" (CE 2.177).

It is important to establish that the sort of "marvel" Lovecraft is conceiving here is not, strictly speaking, "supernatural." That word never appears in his later writing on the subject. When he says in "Notes on Writing Weird Fiction" that "I choose weird stories because they suit my inclination best—one of my strongest and most persistent wishes being to achieve, momentarily, the illusion of some strange suspension or violation of the galling limitations of time, space, and natural law which for ever imprison us and frustrate our curiosity about the infinite cosmic spaces beyond the radius of our sight and analysis" (CE 2.176), he is careful to speak of the "illusion" of defying natural law; the "suspension or violation" pertains merely to the limitations of our own human conceptions of natural law.

Lovecraft, I believe, came dimly to recognise that he was at a watershed in the history of weird fiction: gone was the time when even an aesthetic belief in such stereotyped creations as vampires, werewolves, and ghosts could be maintained for the duration of a tale; these creatures too obviously defy known and incontrovertible natural laws to be anything but preposterous. What remains? Chiefly it is the "great outside"—those vast untapped regions of space where man has not yet probed; as he wrote in a celebrated letter to Frank Belknap Long (27 February 1931): "Reason as we may, we cannot destroy a normal perception of the highly limited and fragmentary nature of our visible world of perception and experience as scaled against the outside abyss of unthinkable galaxies and unplumbed dimensions" (SL 3.294). This leads to a momentous declaration:

> The time has come when the normal revolt against time, space, and matter must assume a form not overtly incompatible with what is known of reality—when it must be gratified by images forming *supplements* rather than *contradictions* of the visible and mensurable universe. And what, if not a form of non-supernatural cosmic art, is to pacify this sense of revolt—as well as gratify the cognate sense of curiosity? (SL 3.295-96)

It can be seen from all this that Lovecraft's mature weird writing is very close to science fiction, and it is not surprising that late in life he seized the opportunity afforded by Hyman Bradofsky's *Californian* to write an essay (almost a polemic) about "interplanetary fiction," an essay that repeats many of the important theoretical statements of his piece on writing weird fiction. It is difficult to gauge the influence of Lovecraft's jeremiad, but shortly after his death the field certainly began to develop greater seriousness and substance, much along the lines Lovecraft here recommends. Fritz Leiber, himself one of the pioneers of literate and aesthetically refined science fiction, has aptly remarked that C. S. Lewis's *Out of the Silent Planet* (1938) seems almost to have been written with Lovecraft's stipulations in mind, especially as regards the sense of wonder attendant on leaving the earth and the nonanthropomorphism of alien entities (see Leiber, "Through Hyperspace" 473).

The curious document known as the commonplace book relates not so much to Lovecraft's theory as to his practice of weird fiction. It is difficult to characterise this work: perhaps Lovecraft's own description, that it "consists of ideas, images, and quotations hastily jotted down for possible future use in weird fiction" (CE 5.219), is the best we can do. Much can be written on Lovecraft's use of this idea-book in his own fiction, and interested readers must consult David E. Schultz's definitive edition and commentary. The dates that Lovecraft has supplied sporadically in the text are somewhat unreliable, and it is clear that he could not recall exactly when certain entries were made. Even the date of 1919, listed by Lovecraft as the commencement of the work, may be in doubt.

For our purposes we can remark on the "images" that the commonplace book contains in such abundance, for they relate to what Lovecraft says toward the end of "Notes on Writing Weird Fiction": "all a wonder story can ever be is *a vivid picture of a certain type of human mood*" (CE 2.177). That mood is to be evoked principally by the manipulation of images; and it becomes obvious upon reading the commonplace book that it was some focal image that gave birth to some of the best of Lovecraft's tales. In many cases, curiously, this image does not in the end occupy a central place in the finished story—the vignette of a man fashioning a bas-relief in his dreams is tossed almost haphazardly into "The Call of Cthulhu"—and yet that image nonetheless served as the nucleus around which the entire narrative was built. The commonplace book can tell us much about the psychology of Lovecraft's process of composition, but we remain bafflingly far from knowing how his mind absorbed the ideas, images, and moods he experienced and metamorphosed them into some of the finest weird fiction of the century. If we knew this, we could all be Lovecrafts.

II. Mechanistic Materialist

Philosophy traditionally contains five broad subdivisions—metaphysics, ethics, epistemology, politics, and aesthetics. Lovecraft dealt vigorously with each of these except epistemology (the theory of knowledge, or how we know what we know), an issue that never concerned him greatly even though it became the dominant strain of twentieth-century philosophical thought in the work of Ludwig Wittgenstein, Bertrand Russell, Gilbert Ryle, and others. Aside from routine admissions of the fallibility of the senses, Lovecraft was confident that we could know enough about ourselves and the universe around us to take reasonably definite stands on the fundamental issues of philosophy.

In this space we cannot hope to give anything like a full account of Lovecraft's philosophy, and perhaps there is no need, as his essays, a layman's views intended for other laymen, are largely self-explanatory. All we wish to do is to provide some background and context.

When Lovecraft declared himself a mechanistic materialist, he was asserting two related positions: first, the universe (and everything in it, including human beings) is a "mechanism," governed by fixed (if in some cases unknown) laws of causality, and is accordingly wholly deterministic (i.e., everything occurs through logical necessity, and there is no such thing as free will); second, there is no substance or essence in the universe not encompassed by the laws of physics, chemistry, and biology—in particular, there is no such thing as an immaterial "soul." Lovecraft was of course aware that the old-time atomistic materialism of Democritus had gone by the board with the division of the atom, and he states that the word *materialism* is now meant in a purely historical sense, not as implying that all entity is material. In effect, materialism is more important for what it denies than for what it affirms, since the denial of "soul" really means a discarding of the entire framework of religion. Lovecraft's is, indeed, one of the most purely secular philosophies ever envisaged.

Let us be clear that very little of Lovecraft's metaphysical thought is original. Most of it was derived from the great physicists and biologists of the later nineteenth century, and two works in particular—Ernst Haeckel's *The Riddle of the Universe* (1899) and Hugh Elliot's *Modern Science and Materialism* (1919)—supplied Lovecraft with nearly all the metaphysical tools he needed. Even his cosmicism—stressing the insignificance of humanity in an aimless and eternal cosmos—is implicit in these works, and Lovecraft simply laid greater emphasis on it. Similarly, his anthropological explanations of the natural origin of religious belief in primitive man—which he calls "the most important of all materialistic arguments" (CE 5.60)—were derived wholly from such works as E. B. Tylor's *Primitive Culture* (1871) and John Fiske's *Myths and Myth-Makers* (1872). Lovecraft also uses the theory of evolution to deny the existence of a human soul; for where along the course of our evolution from apes to human beings did we acquire this mysterious substance?

The affirmation of a mechanistic view of the universe necessitates the denial of teleology—the notion that the cosmos as a whole is evolving toward some goal or other, presumably (as in religious metaphysics) a superior state of existence. Lovecraft is tireless in refuting this point: it is as if he almost welcomes the prospect of the universe's purposelessness.

Conventional mechanistic materialism was dealt some serious blows by twentieth-century advances in astrophysics, notably Einstein's theory of relativity and Planck's quantum theory. Lovecraft's essays do not reveal his attempts to come to terms with these potentially devastating findings as well as his letters do, but it is evident that he grappled as best he could with these issues while still trying to maintain the essence of his creed. The matter is too complex for discussion here, but the interested reader should study two of Lovecraft's letters to Frank Belknap Long (20 February 1929 and 22 November 1930) for his admirable attempt to harmonise mechanistic materialism with modern indeterminacy.

If Lovecraft's metaphysics is relatively unoriginal, his ethics is scarcely less so. The early influence of Schopenhauer and Epicurus can be felt throughout his thought: from Schopenhauer he derived the belief that pain is the predominant attribute of existence, while with Epicurus he maintained that the diminution of this pain is the highest pleasure human beings can achieve. Lovecraft initially claimed to be a moral relativist (one man's meat is another man's poison), but gradually this view gave way to a belief in "tradition" as the "one anchor of fixity" (as he terms it in a letter to Elizabeth Toldridge of 10 June 1929 [SL 2.357]) left to human beings in an aimless cosmos. This position is indefensible philosophically and is perhaps the most extreme example of what might be called Lovecraft's ethical fascism: what was suitable to him should, evidently, be suitable to all. Tradition meant much to Lovecraft, and he therefore finds convoluted sophistical arguments to erect it as the one bulwark against the meaninglessness of existence.

This emphasis on tradition is important, as it lays the groundwork for Lovecraft's entire aesthetic stance, represented by such essays as "Heritage or Modernism: Common Sense in Art Forms" (1935). Art must, in his view, continue to build upon the past: modifications may be made because of evolving worldviews, but a core of tradition must remain. From this perspective Lovecraft feels safe in demolishing the functionalists in architecture, and indeed many of his criticisms are telling. How his general aesthetic position comes into play in the realm of literary criticism is something we shall examine later.

Many of the essays on philosophy had a peculiar genesis, and there are unresolved questions concerning the composition of some of them. "Idealism and Materialism—A Reflection" appeared in the "July 1919" issue of the *National Amateur*; but this issue was much delayed, and in fact contained Lovecraft's story "The Picture in the House" (definitely dated to late 1920), so that the dating of the essay to 1919 is frankly tentative. The three *In Defence of Dagon* essays (the general title is R. H. Barlow's) were written for an Anglo-American correspondence group called the Transatlantic Circulator, where members exchanged stories, poems, and essays in manuscript. Without annotation it is sometimes difficult to follow Lovecraft's argument, as he is replying to comments made on his stories and his general philosophical position by other members; some of these comments still survive, while others (especially the philosophical remarks of the Mr Wickenden whom Lovecraft so takes to task) have perished. Nonetheless, they remain some of Lovecraft's finest essays in their rhetorical brilliance, logical argumentation, and stylistic verve.

"Nietzscheism and Realism" is a series of extracts made by Sonia Greene from Lovecraft's letters to her, so that formal unity is not to be looked for; these extracts are, in fact, uncannily similar to Nietzsche's own aphorisms, although Schopenhauer also looms large as an influence. The title is almost certainly Sonia's. Then there is the bizarre piece called "Some Causes of Self-Immolation" (1931). There is no clue as to why Lovecraft wrote this essay or whether he attempted to secure its publication (it remained in manuscript until after his death); in spite of the flippancy of the title and the comical subtitle and pseudonym, it appears to be a seriously intended investigation of certain psychological phenomena.

It is in Lovecraft's letters that we may more readily and vividly discover the details of his philosophical thought; on the whole his essays are a little heavy and dogmatic, and do not quite display his ongoing quest to clarify and overhaul his philosophy as new evidence emerges or his attitudes change. If Lovecraft is by no stretch of the imagination a great philosopher, he is by all means an interesting one, and he made that philosophy the backbone of his entire literary work. That alone is sufficient reason for studying it.

III. Literary Critic

Lovecraft's literary criticism outside the domain of weird fiction is disappointing at best, and of interest only for the light it sheds on other aspects of his work and thought. Most of his pure literary criticism was written during his amateur period and includes such things as a basic guide to prose grammar and syntax ("Literary Composition"), a skeletonic outline of the principles of verse ("What Belongs in Verse"), and windy "puffs" of leading amateur writers ("The Poetry of Lilian Middleton"), which sound like nothing so much as Poe's effusive reviews of women poets. All this is routine, but other pieces help to trace the surprisingly radical evolution of Lovecraft's critical thought during the last two decades of his life.

In a letter to August Derleth (7 December 1929) Lovecraft made a very important assessment of his aesthetic development: "I can look back . . . at two distinct periods of opinion whose foundations I have successively come to distrust—a period before 1919 or so, when the weight of classic authority unduly influenced me, and another period from 1919 to about 1925, when I placed too high a value on the elements of revolt, florid colour, and emotional extravagance or intensity" (*ES* 234). Classicism and Decadence: these are the two successive phases of Lovecraft's early critical theory. We hardly need evidence of his classicist tendencies; a passage from "The Case for Classicism" (1919) is both a summation and a swan song for this view:

> The literary genius of Greece and Rome, developed under peculiarly favourable circumstances, may fairly be said to have completed the art and science of expression. Unhurried and profound, the classical author achieved a standard of simplicity, moderation, and elegance of taste, which all succeeding time has been powerless to excel or even to equal. (*CE* 2.37)

But if the ancients have said everything worth saying, all the moderns can (and should) do is to imitate them; and Lovecraft, faithful to his principles, did just that, writing masses of poetry under the dominant influence of Dryden and Pope and composing prose derived from the periodical essays of Addison and Johnson. But a classicist in the early part of this century might well have felt embattled; and such things as free verse, simple spelling, and other evils of the day had to be vigorously combated. It is no surprise that the sixth word of "Metrical Regularity" (1915) is "decadence": Lovecraft saw decadence everywhere—in art and architecture as well as in literature—and up to 1919 he was conducting a heroic rearguard battle against it.

Then something strange happens: Lovecraft begins to embrace the "Decadents." These Decadents are, of course, not the ones who practice free verse or simple spelling, but those later nineteenth-century French writers such as

Verlaine and Huysmans, along with such of their English disciples as Pater and Wilde, who are rebelling at the limitations of bourgeois aesthetics and seeking to go beyond them. What seems to have happened to Lovecraft is that during the period 1919-21 he read a number of writers and thinkers who influenced him profoundly—Haeckel, Wilde, Freud—and so belatedly entered the twentieth century. He began to see that his old-time classicism was no longer viable; as he writes in "Rudis Indigestaque Moles" (1923):

> Do our members realise that the progress of science within the last half-century has introduced conceptions of man, the world, and the universe which make hollow and ridiculous an appreciable proportion of all the great literature of the past? Art, to be great, must be founded on human emotions of much strength; such as come from warm instincts and firm beliefs. Science having so greatly altered our view of the universe and the beliefs attendant upon that view, we are now confronted by an important shifting of values in every branch of art where belief is concerned. (CE 2.63)

The advances of modern science (notably psychology, physics, and biology) have made many older aesthetic attitudes untenable; and a selective adoption of Decadence was, for Lovecraft, actually a means for preserving (or, as he might have said, conserving) as much of the past as possible. Some things, of course, would have to go: the didactic principle, so essential to classical aesthetics, was in truth never espoused by Lovecraft and, under the influence of Wilde (see "Ars Gratia Artis"), definitively dispensed with. Even such things as unity and restraint would require modification: "What is art but a matter of impressions, of pictures, emotions, and symmetrical sensations? It must have poignancy and beauty, but nothing else counts. It may or may not have coherence" ("In the Editor's Study" [CE 2.71]). But note how quickly Lovecraft points out that he "is no convert to Dadaism." His Decadence, in effect, was his way of showing his scorn for the outmoded aesthetics of the Victorians while at the same time maintaining a distance from the extreme radicals in prose (Joyce, Stein) and verse (Eliot, cummings) whose work he always considered beyond the pale.

Lovecraft's later literary theory is on the whole found in his letters. He in fact ceases to be interested in literary criticism as such and instead turns his attention to broader questions of aesthetics: How to distinguish good art from bad? What is the purpose of art? What is art's relation to human psychology? Lovecraft's answers to these questions take us beyond the scope of this note, but "What Belongs in Verse" (1935) is worth considering in that it provides a hint of the spectacular metamorphosis in his attitude to poetry. It did not, in fact, take long for him to recognise that his early verse was shallow and insincere; as he writes to Elizabeth Toldridge (8 March 1929):

> In my metrical novitiate I was, alas, a chronic and inveterate mimic; allowing my antiquarian tendencies to get the better of my abstract poetic feeling.... Self-expression as such sank out of sight, and my sole test of excellence was the degree with which I approached the style of Mr. Pope, Dr. Young, Mr. Thomson, Mr. Addison, Mr. Tickell, Mr. Parnell, Dr. Goldsmith, Dr. Johnson, and so on. (SL 2.314–15)

His verse writing, in other words, was an extension of his antiquarianism. As Lovecraft sloughed off his exclusively classicist mode, he began to realise that the verse of today must be expressed in the language of today; more, that certain issues and subjects "belong essentially to the domains of science, history, administration, and philosophy" (CE 2.182), so that a poet must decide not only how to say what he has to say but whether what he has to say is even amenable to verse treatment. Lovecraft practiced what he preached, and his later verse deals with ethereal images and moods whose embodiment could only be poetry, not the philosophical essay or the short story. *Fungi from Yuggoth* redeems all the "eighteenth-century rubbish" he ever wrote.

It is safe to say that Lovecraft's literary criticism will never gain much recognition in its own right. Its value lies rather in helping to chart the wide-ranging evolution of his critical theory and to provide clues as to how that changing critical theory found expression in his creative work. It is hard to imagine the author of "Metrical Regularity" and "The Vers Libre Epidemic" referring in later years to Cabell's *Jurgen* and Joyce's *Ulysses* as "significant contributions to contemporary art" (CE 2.77), but that he did so is, once again, a tribute to the unflagging flexibility and openness of his mind. That Lovecraft could continue to evolve—intellectually, aesthetically, and personally—at an age when most are settling into fossilised complacency is the most admirable thing about him.

IV. Political Theorist

Lovecraft would probably be embarrassed at the reprinting of most of his early political essays: it is well known that his political philosophy experienced—outwardly at any rate—the most spectacular revolution of any aspect of his thought, and late in life he was fond of berating himself for the lack of true insight into political matters he had displayed in youth. In a letter to Jennie K. Plaisier (8 July 1936) he writes:

> I used to be a hide-bound Tory simply for traditional and antiquarian reasons—and because I had never done any real *thinking* on civics and industry and the future. The depression—and its concomitant publicisation of industrial, financial, and governmental problems—jolted me out of my lethargy and led me to reëxamine the facts of history in the light of unsentimental scientific

analysis; and it was not long before I realised what an ass I had been. The liberals at whom I used to laugh were the ones who were right—for they were living in the present while I had been living in the past. They had been using science whilst I had been using romantic antiquarianism. (SL 5.279)

Bearing in mind, then, that nearly all his political essays represent this earlier, unthinking attitude, let us see what can be made of them.

The cardinal tenet of Lovecraft's early political thought is aristocracy in all its forms—political, social, racial, and intellectual—and he stresses one or the other aspect of it as it suits his purpose. In truth, aristocracy is a tenet he retained, with considerable modifications, throughout his life, so that it is misleading to speak of his progress *from* aristocracy to socialism; it would be more accurate to say that he arrived at socialism *through* aristocracy. We already find a paean to aristocracy in "Nietzscheism and Realism" (1922): "I believe in an aristocracy, because I deem it the only agency for the creation of those refinements which make life endurable for the human animal of high organisation" (CE 5.70). No doubt Lovecraft considered himself such an animal, and his ideal governmental system would be designed to foster the comfort of himself and people like him. Self-serving as this appears to be, it is entirely understandable and requires no especial comment. In his earlier years he felt that a frank hereditary or culturally recognised aristocracy would be the only way to ensure such comfort; and it was, ironically, his upper-class disdain of money-grubbing capitalism (something he himself could never adopt, as is seen in his humiliating attempts to take on various commercial occupations in his New York period) that turned him from a pure aristocrat into a socialist aristocrat. Capitalism is the foe to both aristocracy and socialism, and Lovecraft's gradual shift only occurred because of his grudging admission that the old-time aristocracy he longed for—and had actually experienced in his early youth as a member of Providence's social elite—was dead in the mechanised world of the 1920s and 1930s.

There are those who find Lovecraft's whole concept of "fascistic socialism" paradoxical: many political theorists maintain that participatory democracy is an essential component of the sort of moderate socialism Lovecraft was proposing. Lovecraft thought differently, and his socialism would, while distributing economic wealth more equitably to all, restrict political power to the few—that "oligarchy of intelligence" (as he terms it in "Some Repetitions on the Times" [CE 5.93]) that alone, in his mind, is capable of deciding on the highly complex political and economic issues of a mechanised world. Whether this is any different from a sort of old-world benevolent aristocracy is something he never addresses.

Lovecraft's early political essays are not quite as embarrassing as some of his contemporaneous letters, and a few of them actually utter truths that were valid enough in their day. He is right to criticise naive American patriotism in "Revolutionary Mythology" (1918); his hard-headed realism regarding the inevitability of war led him to condemn the League of Nations in "The League" (1919); and he even has some justification for attacking German- and Irish-Americans in "Old England and the 'Hyphen'" (1916), for this essay was written not long after actual plots against the government by these groups were discovered. And Lovecraft is within his rights to denounce alcohol and the hypocrisy of advertising in "More *Chain Lightning*," even though he ultimately came to realise the unworkability of Prohibition. And yet, it is still enormously refreshing to come to "Some Repetitions on the Times" (1933). (This essay was written shortly before the inauguration of Roosevelt, but Lovecraft never seems to have made any effort to prepare it for publication.) It is not simply that this piece states political positions more in line with our own: this would be a superficial, if not contemptible, reason for praising it. Rather, it finally reveals some of the flexibility and insight that Lovecraft was showing in all phases of his thought at this time: he seems at last to know what he is talking about, instead of rattling off dogmatic opinions spawned in the cloistered confines of his reclusive youth.

"The Crime of the Century" (1915), however, raises one issue we have hitherto ignored: racism. I am no longer convinced that we can be very lenient on Lovecraft on this matter. Yes, it is true that many of his time and class thought as he did; but it is also true that the foremost thinkers of his day were shedding these beliefs in light of evidence amassed by biologists, anthropologists, and psychologists. Lovecraft maintained the error of the black's biological and cultural inferiority to the end of his life, even though studies by Franz Boas and W. E. B. Du Bois at the turn of the century had destroyed such a contention; he was always a segregationist, claiming that assimilation of aliens could only occur with racially homogeneous groups and only if the aliens shed the entirety of their heritage and culture and adopted those of the dominant group. And it is a sad fact that his views did not change nearly as much toward the end of his life as some apologists wish us to believe. This is the tragedy of Lovecraft's racism: in this one regard he failed to exhibit that openness to new evidence that he displayed in every other facet of his thought. The mere fact that he was forced to debate the issue so vehemently with his younger correspondents, who had not received the upbringing he had, should have urged him to give his views a careful scrutiny; but nothing of the sort happened.

Lovecraft's entire political thought is only a sort of adjunct to his aesthetics: what he wished was a political system that could ensure the maintenance of a high cultural standard, and it hardly mattered which system it was so long as the desired result was accomplished. That he finally woke up from his dream of hereditary aristocracy and embraced a socialism that could deal with the problems of the modern world is a tribute to his clear-headedness, and that he could infuse such narratives as At the Mountains of Madness and "The Shadow out of Time" with such searching political speculations shows how politics had risen to the forefront of his attention in his later years. In this sense, these two works are at once his most cosmic and his most human stories.

V. Antiquarian Travels

When we read in a 1915 letter that "I have never been outside the three states of Rhode Island, Massachusetts, and Connecticut!" (SL 1.10) we sense behind the feigned humility a disingenuous smugness at having led so circumscribed an existence; by contrast, a 1931 letter listing nineteen states visited suggests not merely greater mobility but a firmer grasp of political, social, and cultural reality through the abandonment of self-conscious sequestration. If anyone still believes the hoary myth of Lovecraft's reclusiveness, his travelogues will certainly be a powerful antidote; but we should beware of falling into the opposite fallacy of assuming that his extensive travels along the eastern seaboard during the last decade of his life suddenly show him to be a worldly-wise, cosmopolitan sophisticate of the Henry James sort. The continuing provinciality of much of Lovecraft's outlook can, if in no other way, be detected by the frequency with which, in these essays, he compares so many different architectural, scenic, and historical features of the lands he is visiting with the corresponding features in New England. It is as if New England in general, and Providence in particular, were the eternal standard or touchstone by which everything else is judged; and, for all the cosmicism of his metaphysics, he knew that his emotional ties were deeply rooted in the soil and culture of New England. Lovecraft may have travelled far, but he always came home.

In those travelogues not designed for publication—represented by "Observations on Several Parts of America" (1928), "Travels in the Provinces of America" (1929), and "An Account of Charleston" (1930)—Lovecraft was free to indulge his every whim. The antiquated style of these pieces is the first thing that strikes us; and yet, they provide emphatic evidence to demolish another silly myth, that of Lovecraft's archaistic "pose." What this position claims is that Lovecraft's archaism was an affectation intended with naive seriousness; and what these travelogues reveal is the tongue-in-cheek humour indicative of his complete awareness of his "affectation" and his adoption of it very largely with playful intent. Lovecraft's general adherence to the standards of the past is not in question; but surely such a sentence as "The chasmal majesty of the enormous gulph was such as to suggest the monstrous scenery of other planets" (CE 4.33) is meant to dynamite its own ponderousness.

Less attractive idiosyncrasies of Lovecraft find their way into these travelogues, notably racism and even occasional snobbery. In so late a work as his Charleston travelogue of 1930 he writes, with evidently a straight face:

> Gentlefolk in Charleston still pursue their ways for pleasure and not for show or profit, and are still decently anxious to keep their names and personal affairs out of the papers. . . . The Charleston dailies are the only ones without a vulgar 'society column' to spy upon the comings and goings of important people. (CE 4.82)

This was written at about the same time Lovecraft was violently attacking these same "important people" for their hopelessly reactionary political and social ideals: "God! The utter ignorance and sappiness of the snivelling, myth-swallowing, church-going stuffed shirts who go about cackling dead slogans and spreading the heraldic tail-feathers that proclaim them self-conscious members of a close corporation of 'best people'!" (SL 5.321). In charity to Lovecraft one can suppose that he feels the Charleston "important people" are actual upholders of an enlightened cultural tradition while the "best people" are not; but all this is really another example of Lovecraft's inability to shed the aristocracy of his upbringing even in his socialist period.

Other portions of these travelogues are more amusing. In speaking of the early colonisation of Virginia Lovecraft writes: "In 1619 wives were sent out for the colonists, and in the same year the first cargo of African blacks arriv'd—proving that troubles never come singly" (CE 4.44). Yes, this is sexist and racist, but it is also funny. More genuinely mirthsome is the hilarious vignette of the slightly crazed German ("No doubt he was a leader in some modern religious or ethical cult" [CE 4.34]) whom Lovecraft encountered on his train ride to the South in 1929; it is still more amusing to reflect that this figure was transmogrified into the mad villain of his revision of Adolphe de Castro's "The Electric Executioner."

A more important relation between Lovecraft's travelogues and his fiction occurs in "Vermont—A First Impression" (1927). It is readily apparent that he used whole passages of this essay in the latter portion of "The Whisperer in Darkness" (1930); but a close comparison shows that the wistful nostalgia of the travelogue becomes in the story something darker and more sinister, as if Nature and antiquity have themselves become an emblem for the transience of man. This is one very obvious way in which Lovecraft's travelogues nurtured his creative imagination; indeed, the travelogues themselves approach fictional technique in their careful selectivity of detail, the narrative drive of their historical disquisitions (how can we not think of "The Shunned House" or *The Case of Charles Dexter Ward*?), and their carefully crafted structure behind a mere appearance of rambling spontaneity.

Two of the travelogues were written to order: "Some Dutch Footprints in New England" (1933) was commissioned by Wilfred B. Talman for *De Halve Maen*, the journal of the Holland Society of New York, and "Homes and Shrines of Poe" (1934) was written for Hyman Bradofsky's *Californian*. "An Account of Charleston" was completed shortly after Lovecraft's first visit to Charleston in 1930; and the wealth of historical, architectural, and topographical detail it contains, as well as its exquisite eighteenth-century prose, is a testimonial to the profound impression Charleston made upon him. Lovecraft frequently averred that the city was second only to Providence in his esteem, and that he would willingly move there were it not for the many ties he had to his native city. In 1936 H. C. Koenig was planning to visit Charleston and asked Lovecraft for a brief guide; Lovecraft unearthed his unpublished essay—written solely for his own satisfaction—and truncated it significantly, watering down the eighteenth-century English and also removing some of the more piquant portions. Koenig published this letter as *Charleston*, but a comparison of the two travelogues reveals the earlier one to be far superior both intrinsically and as a key to Lovecraft's own predilections.

Lovecraft's travels played a significant role in his later life, for aside from stimulating his creativity they provided what joy and expansiveness there was in his restricted and penurious existence. There are those who say he "wasted" much of his life in correspondence and in travels that habitually consumed the entire summer: why could he not have written more fiction? There are many fallacies and injustices in this position, but the worst is the tacit assumption that Lovecraft should have lived his life for our, not his own, benefit. If he had never written any fiction, it would be our loss but his prerogative; if he wished to while away the time writing postcards on a park bench in Charleston, that was entirely his right. Lovecraft in fact led very much the life he wished to lead; and the vitality of his travelogues bespeaks the pleasure he derived from absorbing the antiquities of an entire continent. To have squeezed so much enjoyment from such limited means is something we might all emulate.

VI. Amateur Journalist

The circumstances that led to Lovecraft's entry into amateur journalism in 1914, after six years of virtual hermitry, are now well known: his letters to the editor of the *Argosy* criticising the romantic stories of Fred Jackson; the development of a lively feud, conducted in both prose and verse, between those who sided with Lovecraft and those who opposed him; the invitation by Edward F. Daas to join the United Amateur Press Association (UAPA), and Lovecraft's alacrity in doing so. What is less understood is his abiding fascination with and devotion to the amateur cause: why, in spite of the bitter rivalries, pettinesses, and controversies in which he was involved, in spite of the utter and hopeless mediocrity of most of the writers in the amateur world, did Lovecraft never relinquish his association with amateur journalism even after the full-fledged commencement of his career as a professional weird fictionist? Some of his essays on the subject provide an answer; and few passages in Lovecraft are more poignant than that in "What Amateurdom and I Have Done for Each Other" (1921), where he reveals the invaluable psychological aid amateurdom provided:

> In 1914, when the kindly hand of amateurdom was first extended to me, I was as close to the state of vegetation as any animal well can be.... With the advent of the United I obtained a renewed will to live; a renewed sense of existence as other than a superfluous weight; and found a sphere in which I could feel that my efforts were not wholly futile. For the first time I could imagine that my clumsy gropings after art were a little more than faint cries lost in the unlistening void. (CE 1.273)

There is more to it than this, however. Let us consider another passage, this one from "For What Does the United Stand?" (1920):

> ... the United now aims at the development of its adherents in the direction of purely artistic literary perception and expression.... It aims at the revival of the uncommercial spirit; the real creative thought which modern conditions have done their worst to suppress and eradicate. It seeks to banish mediocrity as a goal and standard; to place before its members the classical and the universal and to draw their minds from the commonplace to the beautiful. (CE 1.254)

Are these not Lovecraft's own literary and political tenets? The repudiation of commercialism and the maintenance of classicism are the cornerstones of Lovecraft's own aesthetic; and it was the nucleus of these values that he claimed to find in amateur letters and strove to foster as best he could. Amateurdom also allowed Lovecraft to fall into his natural role of tutor: when, in "Amateur Journalism: Its Possible Needs and Betterment" (1920), he speaks of the need for the "raising of standards" (CE 1.260), he takes it as axiomatic that he would be one of those who—by reason of his clear eminence in this tiny realm—would lead the way both by example and by precept. There is, accordingly, no need to wonder why Lovecraft so readily accepted so many different official functions in the amateur world: President, Vice-President (in which capacity he wrote the promotional flyer *United Amateur Press Association: Exponent of Amateur Journalism*), Official Editor, and, perhaps most important, Chairman of the Department of Public Criticism, which supplied a forum for the expression of his views on the current state of amateur literature.

The Lovecraft we encounter in his earliest amateur years is not an attractive one. It is not so much the substance of his views—racism, political and literary conservatism, militarism—as the dogmatism, inflexibility, and self-righteous pomposity of their expression that is to be regretted. Amateurdom ultimately freed him from the worst of these traits, but the process was more gradual than we might like to believe: as late as "Lucubrations Lovecraftian" (1921) he is seen still cloaking himself with the aura of infallibility and striking out with astonishing viciousness at his opponents.

Perhaps what amazes us most of all about some of these essays is the seriousness with which Lovecraft takes the petty disputes arising in amateurdom. It is one thing to debate politics and literature with Charles D. Isaacson in "In a Major Key" or ethics with the editors of the *Symphony* in "Symphony and Stress"; but Lovecraft devotes just as much energy refuting Graeme Davis's attacks on the UAPA in "A Reply to *The Lingerer*" or arguing the role of amateur criticism in "Lucubrations Lovecraftian."

One of Lovecraft's first goals upon entering amateur journalism was to attempt to reunite the UAPA after it split into two rival factions in 1912 ("A Matter of Uniteds" [1927] is a eulogy to this hopeless effort); and in many early essays on the subject he seems to have regarded it as tantamount to a civil war. The UAPA essentially collapsed in the mid-1920s, and Lovecraft thereafter turned full attention to the other amateur organisation, the National Amateur Press Association (NAPA), although he had been a member of it since 1917; and as late as 1936, in the broadside *Some Current Motives and Practices*, Lovecraft is attempting to heal rifts and fend off attacks on the NAPA's president, Hyman Bradofsky. Amateur journalism, like fandom, is never-changing, and the puerility of most of its members (a product not merely of youth but of the temperament of those who are a part of it) makes one realise why the word *amateur* has gained such overtones of immaturity, incompetence, and triviality. Lovecraft eventually became aware of all this, but his allegiance to both amateurdom and fandom remained.

But if *Some Current Motives and Practices* at least reveals a more mature Lovecraft in his ability to steer clear of savage retort and in his stalwart defence of a beleaguered associate (and Bradofsky, let us recall, was a Jew), then "Mrs. Miniter—Estimates and Recollections" (1934) shows Lovecraft at his most mellow. It is one of his finest efforts. In truth, the essay says as much about Lovecraft as about Miniter: we not merely learn valuable details of his travels to western Massachusetts and the bits of weird folklore Miniter supplied him, but we see a Lovecraft deeply touched by the loss of an old friend, a Lovecraft who has put aside the silly polemics of prior days to write a tribute that reveals his own humanity and sensitivity. If amateurdom had any role in effecting this monumental change—and clearly it did—then it deserves all the encomia Lovecraft gave to it in the course of a lifetime.

VII. Epistolarian

It is now commonly known that Lovecraft was one of the most prolific letter-writers in the history of literature. Whether he actually wrote 100,000 letters—a sum arrived at somewhat speculatively by L. Sprague de Camp, and which is probably too high—it is the substance, not the number, of his letters that is important. Lovecraft wrote letters from a compulsive need to communicate with like-minded individuals, to argue his philosophical and literary theses, and to enlighten his scattered correspondents on his activities. But he also wrote to cheer the drab life of an invalid, to encourage the mental and emotional development of teenage fans, and to act as benevolent uncle to those needing guidance and reassurance. It is this Lovecraft, perhaps more than the weaver of cosmic horrors, that genuinely deserves our admiration.

Lovecraft's letters were, however, occasionally written for more public purposes, as when he sent letters to the editors of magazines or newspapers to voice his opinions or to correct errors. Given his early immersion in the sciences, it should not be surprising that his first appearance in print should have been a letter to the *Providence Journal* (published in the issue for 3 June 1906) debating a point of astronomy. Another early appearance is his celebrated letter to the *Scientific American* of 16 July 1906, recommending a concerted effort to find new planets in the solar system beyond Neptune. A quarter of a century later Lovecraft would utilise in fiction the new planet that had been discovered by means not entirely dissimilar to those outlined in this letter: Pluto becomes the dark planet Yuggoth in "The Whisperer in Darkness" (1930).

Other letters reveal Lovecraft the debunker of pseudoscience at his best: the hollow-earth theory is destroyed in another letter to the *Journal*, while the hapless astrologer J. F. Hartmann is mercilessly dispensed with in a series of letters and parodies in the Providence *Evening News*, where Lovecraft conducted a monthly astronomy column. In truth, these letters are not so much triumphs of logical thinking as entertaining polemics, while the parodies, written under the pseudonym of Isaac Bickerstaffe, Jun., are obvious but amusing send-ups of astrological jargon.

At the same time that Lovecraft was absorbing science, he was consuming the early pulp magazines with great avidity. In his 1914 letter to the *All-Story Weekly* he announces that he has read "every number of your magazine since . . . January, 1905" (MW 496). The staggering amount of pulp fiction Lovecraft must have read in his teens and twenties should give us pause; and, as the letter indicates, he read not merely the weird contributions but apparently everything in the magazines, from humour to love stories: it was, we should remember, the romances of Fred Jackson that led to Lovecraft's entry into amateur journalism. This letter is one of the few instances where Lovecraft admits to unaffected enjoyment of Edgar Rice Burroughs; in later years he would find such enthusiasm a source of embarrassment and seek to conceal or diminish it.

This early reading of pulp fiction should make us less surprised at his discovery of *Weird Tales* in 1923 and his quick success there, in spite of his avowed amateur status. Lovecraft's cover letter to Edwin Baird accompanying his first submissions seems designed to ensure their rejection; indeed, when printing this letter, Baird appended the comment: "Despite the foregoing, or because of it, we are using some of Mr. Lovecraft's unusual stories. . . ." In later letters to Baird he unwinds, telling of the surprising influence of Sherwood Anderson's *Winesburg, Ohio* on "Arthur Jermyn" and uttering the core of his theory of weird fiction long before he did so in his famous letter to Farnsworth Wright of 5 July 1927. Just as in that letter he spoke of the need to escape convention by adopting an attitude of cosmic amoralism, he here lambastes the common run of weird tales and their "conventional values and motives and perspectives" (MW 509).

But for all Lovecraft's cosmic theorising, in his own emotional makeup he always remained a Providence gentleman. It was because he had a stable and familiar background that he was able to traverse the heavens in fiction; and it was the need to preserve that background that impelled his several-year quest—unsuccessful, as it happened—to save the quaint old warehouses on South Water Street in Providence called the Brick Row. The poem "The East India Brick Row" (1929) is well known, as is the letter of 5 October 1926, where he first takes up the defence of these venerable but decaying structures; a 1929 letter (titled in the manuscript "The Old Brick Row") is virtually his final effort, and one can sense in it the desperation of defending a lost cause.

Lovecraft the grandfatherly tutor appears in his late letter to the young Canadian fan Nils H. Frome. This letter was not intended for publication, but Frome published it in a fan magazine after Lovecraft's death. In steering Frome away from the fallacies of fortune-telling, numerology, and the like, and in recommending a whole shelf of up-to-date works on astronomy, physics, and biology for a proper understanding of man and the cosmos, Lovecraft comes full circle. Science was never far from his thoughts: his philosophy was founded upon it, his tales are infused with it, and his mind never functioned save by its tenets or within its parameters. And yet, as he writes to Frome, it is precisely because he does not believe in the supernatural that he gains such pleasure from it.

As an epistolarian Lovecraft was by turns friend, instructor, and wit. His letters reveal both his literary and his intellectual powers at their widest compass, and it may not be too bold a prediction to assert that one day his letters will equal, and perhaps surpass, his fiction as the quintessence of Lovecraft's literary expression.

VIII. Personal

Lovecraft's avowedly autobiographical writing is scanty and even a little disappointing; his letters are his true autobiography, and they make him one of the most voluminously documented figures in human history. The few brief autobiographical essays he wrote over his twenty-year literary career were all written for specific occasions; "The Brief Autobiography of an Inconsequential Scribbler" (1919) was commissioned by John Milton Samples, editor of the *Silver Clarion*, while "Some Notes on a Nonentity" (1933) was written for William L. Crawford's *Unusual Stories* but never appeared there. Lovecraft remarks in a letter to R. H. Barlow (17 December 1933) that Crawford wished the sketch to be cut down to 900 words, which Lovecraft did (this version has recently been discovered[1]); Lovecraft handed over the original draft to Barlow, who later donated it to the John Hay Library. "Some Notes on a Nonentity" is certainly Lovecraft's most compact and expressive autobiographical piece, but even it provides only tantalising hints where the letters supply copious detail.

The self-image that emerges from these articles is a miracle of conscious artistry: Lovecraft becomes his own greatest fictional character. This is not to say that he utters actual falsehoods about himself; but he practices extreme selectivity. Why does he never mention his marriage in "Some Notes on a Nonentity"? Why, in "The Brief Autobiography" (intended, let us recall, for an amateur audience and written before he had wholeheartedly embarked upon his career as weird fictionist), does he not allude to his voracious reading of the early pulp magazines? The fact is that Lovecraft is very deliberately fashioning an image of himself as classicist, scientist, and philosopher who "looked on man" (as he wrote in "A Confession of Unfaith") "as if from another planet" (CE 5.147). The "Confession" is a charming piece—who can forget the tableau of Lovecraft building altars to Pan, Apollo, and Diana?—and

---

1. See "Notes on a Nonentity," *Lovecraft Annual* No. 4 (2010): 164-65.

we have already remarked of its importance in delineating his early philosophical development; but it is also one more element in his grand self-portrait as the emotionless cosmic spectator.

Some highly peculiar essays might be considered here, chiefly because their interest is frankly more biographical than intrinsic. "Within the Gates" is surely one of the strangest things Lovecraft ever wrote. Delivered at an amateur journalism convention in Boston on 4 July 1921, this short, humorous speech is startling for its mere existence: six weeks earlier Lovecraft was professing nearly suicidal depression at the death of his mother on 24 May 1921. And yet, the best thing that he could have done after this traumatic event was to resume the normal course of his life, and this speech may indicate that he did just that. A few of the jokes are rather good—as when Lovecraft refers to Dante as his "fellow-poet" (CE 1.294)—and it would certainly have been an entertainment to see and hear Lovecraft deliver this light-hearted *jeu d'esprit*. One of those who may have done so was his future wife Sonia Greene, for the two appear to have met for the first time at this convention.

"Commercial Blurbs" (the title is R. H. Barlow's) is a testament to the depths of Lovecraft's despair as a jobless husband alone in New York in 1925. Can anyone imagine Lovecraft as a writer of advertising copy? These articles appear to have been written for a trade magazine in which his associate Arthur Leeds was involved. A passage in his letter to Mrs. F. C. Clark (28 May 1925) seems to allude to them:

> Leeds and I had talked very seriously about the Yesley writing venture; and when I rode down town with Leeds I continued the conversation, getting more and more workable details from his kindly and willing lips. . . . He agreed to shew me the ropes thoroughly, and see that my articles (which need not be signed) received proper sales treatment; and predicted that I ought to stand as good a chance at making money as himself or anybody else who has proved he can do it. And I told him I would tackle the thing—and he means to send me my first assignment in a week or two, when he can get together the leads best suited to me (real estate, largely) and find the right models for imitation among his old magazines. (*Letters from New York* 136)

It is not known whether these sketches were actually published in any trade magazines or catalogues; but it is clear that they did not lead to a position for Lovecraft, as he endured another year of futile job-hunting before returning to Providence, without his wife, in April 1926.

That return, however, indirectly impelled one of Lovecraft's finest essays, "Cats and Dogs." His departure from New York caused his secession from the Blue Pencil Club, an amateur group in which James Ferdinand Morton was at the time a leading figure. This club was to have a debate on the relative merits of cats and dogs, and Lovecraft, unable to attend in person but unwilling to pass up an opportunity for registering his wholesale love of cats, wrote his response so that Morton could read it to the group. As pure rhetoric this essay is very fine—note its tongue-in-cheek humour, its skilful marshaling of facts, the dainty elegance of its style, so like the felidae it is extolling—but its real importance is its covert subject matter: the essay is not about cats, it is about Lovecraft. For Lovecraft claimed to see in cats all those traits he himself shared (or wished to share): emotional aloofness, aristocratic independence, philosophical calm. The essay is metaphysics ("The real lover of cats is one who demands a clearer adjustment to the universe than ordinary household platitudes provide" [CE 5.186]), it is politics ("The dog is a peasant and the cat is a gentleman" [CE 5.187]), it is aesthetics ("In [the cat's] flawless grace and superior self-sufficiency I have seen a symbol of the perfect beauty and bland impersonality of the universe itself" [CE 5.185]); in effect, Lovecraft utilises every philosophical tool at his disposal to defend his love of cats, and conversely that love of cats is seen to entail and imply the whole of his cosmic philosophy. In no other essay did he ever weave together the many and varied strands of his thought so seamlessly as here.

What essays like "Cats and Dogs," and to a lesser extent certain other of his essays, suggest is the degree to which Lovecraft infuses himself in all his work; in this sense everything he wrote is "personal" because it is the outgrowth of a keen mind reflecting upon the varied phenomena of the human and the cosmic realm. Mediocre, routine, or mechanical as many of his essays may be, they are all the distinctive product of a mind that continually and admirably grappled with the complex issues of human existence and strove to make sense of them as best it could. Let us repeat that Lovecraft will never be known purely as an essayist; but his essays are always surprising us by flashes of insight into the life of man or, at the very least, into his own life.

Works Cited

Leiber, Fritz. "Through Hyperspace with Brown Jenkin: Lovecraft's Contribution to Speculative Fiction." (1966.) In Peter Cannon, ed. *Lovecraft Remembered*. Sauk City, WI: Arkham House, 1998. 472–83.

Lovecraft, H. P. *Commonplace Book*. Edited by David E. Schultz. West Warwick, RI: Necronomicon Press, 1987. 2 vols.

———. *Letters from New York*. Edited by S. T. Joshi and David E. Schultz. San Francisco: Night Shade Books, 2005.

VI. On Lovecraft's Legacy and Influence

The Development of Lovecraftian Studies: 1971–1982

In the last year of his life August Derleth wrote what is perhaps his best article on Lovecraft, "H. P. Lovecraft: The Making of a Literary Reputation, 1937-1971"; and although the article was not published until 1977, its importance derives from the fact that Derleth was in the forefront—indeed, was frequently the cause—of Lovecraft's burgeoning posthumous fame and reputation. Derleth's accomplishments in the field of Lovecraftian studies have, since his death in 1971, come under increasing attack. While it is true that he alone of Lovecraft's colleagues had both the diligence and the independent reputation (as, for example, R. H. Barlow did not) to establish Lovecraft, however humbly, in the literary world, certain of his other qualities and actions have not won him respect: his frequently unscrupulous control of Arkham House and of the Lovecraft copyrights; his misconceived attempt to further Lovecraft's fame through his "posthumous collaborations" with Lovecraft; his continual dissemination of dogmatic and highly erroneous views about Lovecraft the man and writer. Derleth's effect upon the development of critical interpretation of Lovecraft's life and work will be considered in a later section, but there can be no question of his success in collecting and publishing Lovecraft's work in book form—although even here his efforts were marred by hasty and slipshod practises that produced serious corruptions in Lovecraft's texts—and his putting Lovecraft upon the literary map. The mere fact that we can now look upon his achievements in so ambiguous a light demonstrates the enormous strides the field of Lovecraftian studies has taken in a mere decade. The work of the Lovecraft scholars of today could hardly have been imagined by Derleth or anyone else even twenty years ago; and there is no need to berate Derleth for his failings when, without his actions, it is likely that modern Lovecraft scholarship would not exist at all in its present state. The work of Derleth was a necessary link in the chain that will lead to Lovecraft's full recognition as a writer of major stature in this century. We all wish that Derleth could have done certain things better; but most of his mistakes have been rectified without great difficulty, while his diligence and zeal will always give him a place in the history of Lovecraftian studies.

VI. ON LOVECRAFT'S LEGACY AND INFLUENCE

I have chosen to write this article for several reasons: firstly, I have myself been involved with the leading trends in Lovecraft criticism since at least 1975; secondly, I feel that we are on the threshold of a new picture of Lovecraft, in which Lovecraft will be seen both as a figure of great popular appeal and of substantial literary and philosophical merit. This period of transition—which, sad to say, almost required August Derleth's death to initiate—is of enormous interest, and all Lovecraft scholars in the forefront of the field are filled with an enthusiasm for their subject which is hard to describe but easy to feel. The nearest parallel is, perhaps, with the classical scholars of the early Renaissance, who realised that they were rediscovering lost works of supreme greatness and brushing from them the cobwebs of misunderstanding which had enshrouded them for centuries. The parallel is instructive in more than one way; for not only were Lovecraft's texts as corrupt as were the great Latin and Greek treatises after centuries of haphazard transmission, but modern scholars are at last probing the depths of Lovecraft's work and thought to a level far beyond that of prior decades, so that he is coming to be regarded not merely as a skilful weaver of tales, but one whose work is almost inexhaustibly rich in substance and texture—work that is not merely superior to other works in the tiny genre of weird fiction, but which need fear no comparison from the greatest products of modern literature. It is only because trained literary scholars are finally exploring Lovecraft's work that he is emerging from the level of mere "fan" criticism to actual recognition in the broader context of contemporary world literature. This process is by no means complete, and I am still overwhelmed at how much there is to do in Lovecraft studies; moreover, Lovecraft's reputation is still by no means as firmly established as it deserves. We are, as I say, in a period of transition; and it is in the hope that the details of this transition may some day be of interest to future scholars that I am writing this account.

I. The Dissemination of Lovecraft's Work

    A. In English

As the decade of the 1970s opened, Arkham House was still alone in the publication of Lovecraft's work in hardcover. It is, in a way, unfortunate that Derleth and Wandrei decided to establish Arkham House at all; for it thereby became a "specialty firm" that eventually accumulated a devoted following of aficionadoes but which was separated from the main trends in the publishing industry at large. One supposes that Derleth could perhaps have tried a bit harder at the start to have Lovecraft published by a major commercial firm—certainly Lovecraft himself had come close to such an achievement in his own lifetime. The publication of all Lovecraft's work by Arkham House has established, as it were, a barrier that is difficult to cross by those who wish for his work a greater and more distinguished access; the many paperback reprints of his work have been singularly ineffective in convincing major hardcover firms to publish Lovecraft—and, of course, Derleth's overprotective policy regarding the Lovecraft copyrights was as much if not more of a deterrent.

But whatever the case, Arkham House opened the decade with a useful—although incomplete and astonishingly corrupt—edition of Lovecraft's "revisions" and collaborations, *The Horror in the Museum and Other Revisions*. The third volume of the monumental *Selected Letters*—the last Lovecraft volume to appear under Derleth's direct supervision—emerged in 1971. This third volume seems by general consent to be regarded as the greatest of the series, not only for its size but for the wealth of brilliant political, literary, and philosophical discussions included in it—including large parts of a 110-page letter to Frank Belknap Long of 27 February 1931. Certainly no other firm but Arkham House could even have contemplated the publication of such a series of letters, before Lovecraft had achieved any status as a serious literary figure. Some day, of course, the letters will have to be re-edited and published in unabridged form; but the series as it stands will be an invaluable research tool for many years.

After Derleth's death a certain confusion seemed to follow at Arkham House, caused partially by the fact that no competent editor was at hand to succeed Derleth and partially by Donald Wandrei's secession from the firm. This latter circumstance has caused great bitterness on all sides and is an issue into which we need not enter; but I have still not been able to ascertain its precise effect upon the editing of the final two volumes of Lovecraft's letters. By around 1975 James Turner succeeded Roderic Meng as managing editor of Arkham House, and he began to undertake the long-overdue task of finishing the *Selected Letters* series. The final two volumes came out in late summer and autumn of 1976 and met with mixed reactions. Wandrei has maintained that Turner merely adopted the selection Wandrei himself had made for the last two volumes; but I cannot imagine that this is correct, since the editorial method in these two volumes seems so much different from that of their predecessors. An overwhelming bulk of the volumes has been given over to Lovecraft's (admittedly brilliant) discussions of the contemporary political and economic scene, and many literary and philosophical discussions found in surviving manuscript letters of this period have been excluded. Now Turner has professed an interest in such political matters as Lovecraft discussed, and it seems a logical inference that this interest dictated his selection of letters. The volumes, although bulky, have not won general recognition, although textually they are far superior to the error-riddled first three volumes.

In catalogues of the period Arkham House announced a supplementary volume of letters (presumably to include letters received too late to be included in the chronological sequence of the series) and an index. These projects were dropped, probably as a consequence of Wandrei's departure from the firm and his launching a suit in connexion with the publication of the letters. When I conceived the idea of compiling an index to the *Selected Letters* in early 1978, I offered it to Arkham House; but Turner replied to me that the project was still being planned for publication. I felt that this was either untrue or that it would take Turner far too long to compile the index, so I went ahead and produced it myself in the summer of 1978; financial difficulties with the Necronomicon Press, however, prevented its appearance until the spring of 1980. Turner also announced in 1976 a *Miscellaneous Writings* of Lovecraft to appear from Arkham House; this project was still alive in 1978, when Turner mentioned it to me in passing. The contents of this volume have never been ascertained, although scholars hypothesised (correctly, I think) that it would contain merely works by Lovecraft previously published in early Arkham House volumes and not as yet reprinted (including many essays and some unreprinted fiction). I suspect that this project has now been effectively dropped; and Dirk W. Mosig suggested to me that the cause may have been the extensive republication of obscure and early Lovecraftiana by Necronomicon Press. This may well be right, although many long essays first published in early Arkham House volumes (e.g., "Travels in the Provinces of America," "Some Causes of Self-Immolation") have never been reprinted. Many important works still lie buried in these Arkham House volumes, and their reprinting would serve a substantial purpose.

Of other hardcover editions the only notable one was *To Quebec and the Stars*, edited by L. Sprague de Camp. This volume was very poorly received and has not sold at all well; but such a negative response is not entirely just. The volume contained a judicious selection of essays (many, however, already reprinted by Necronomicon Press) collected by de Camp in the course of work on his Lovecraft biography; it also contained Lovecraft's longest single work, the previously unpublished travelogue of Quebec (1930–31). Both the essays and the travelogue are valuable, but it may have been better had each been published as a separate volume; for their combination into a single book has made its price prohibitively high. De Camp's critical commentary is not especially notable, although he has taken a certain care in the presentation of the text.[1]

Of *A Winter Wish*, a collection of rare poetry edited by Tom Collins, little

---

1. There are still several hundred transcriptional errors in the Quebec travelogue, but this item is perhaps the most difficult to edit of any in the HPL corpus.

need be said. Collins succeeded in finding a great many poems aside from those included in the unfortunately titled *Collected Poems,* and his research in Lovecraft's amateur publications was notable;[2] unfortunately, Collins was more careless even than Derleth in the presentation of the texts, and hideous omissions and mistranscriptions mar this otherwise valuable book.[3] Much of Lovecraft's poetry is still unpublished or unreprinted, and a volume at least as large as *A Winter Wish* could be filled with such work.

Lovecraft's general popularity can be measured by the fluctuations in the mass-market paperback appearances of his work. Of course, only the fiction has hitherto been widely disseminated, although it may not be long before his essays and letters find similar distribution: Panther Books in England was bold enough to include "Supernatural Horror in Literature" in its edition of *Dagon and Other Macabre Tales,* and it went through three printings by 1973. In 1970, however, Random House began two separate but anomalously overlapping paperback editions of Lovecraft's work, one under the imprint of Beagle Books and the other under the more widely known Ballantine Books imprint. Beagle's first volume, *The Tomb* (December 1970), was in fact identical to the Panther Books volume (1969) of the same name, and eventually eleven volumes of the Beagle Edition of H. P. Lovecraft—a trifle misnamed, since nearly half the volumes consisted of imitations of Lovecraft's work by other hands—appeared by the end of 1971. Coincidentally with this, Lin Carter edited two impressive collections of Lovecraft's "dream-world" tales for his Adult Fantasy series—*The Dream-Quest of Unknown Kadath* (May 1970) and *The Doom That Came to Sarnath* (February 1971)—along with the useful anthology, *The Spawn of Cthulhu* (October 1971). In this extensive campaign of reprinting Lovecraft's work may be added the surprising appearance of *Fungi from Yuggoth and Other Poems* (February 1971; a reprint of *Collected Poems* excluding one poem[4]) from Ballantine, although it was unfortunately not kept in print as were the other volumes. By around 1973, however, the Beagle Books imprint went into abeyance, and the volumes of its series were trans-

---

2. Collins was responsible for the attribution of one poem—"North and South Britons"—to HPL; it was written under a pseudonym in its only publication.

3. See my "Textual Commentary on *A Winter Wish,*" *Miskatonic* 6, No. 2 (February 1978): [11–21]; in augmented form in *Crypt of Cthulhu* 3, No. 4 (Eastertide 1984): 31–45. This review and subsequent remarks upon it by Collins, Mosig, and myself caused great agitation and hostility in HPL studies for some years, although the dispute subsequently died down.

4. The poem excluded, "To the American Flag," has by happenstance been established as spurious, so that its omission was a happy stroke of luck.

ferred to the Ballantine Books imprint, where they continued to be reprinted through 1976. The importance of this wide availability of Lovecraft's work over five or six years can hardly be overestimated, and it can rightly be said that Lovecraft's popular appeal has never been higher before or since; the most notable indication being the celebrated review of the Ballantine volumes by Philip Herrera in *Time* magazine for 11 June 1973. Herrera announced that more than 1,000,000 copies of the paperback editions had been disseminated—a figure that, however startlingly high it may be, must have been obtained from the publishers. We may assume, then, that about 2,000,000 books were printed during the years 1970-1976; but by 1977, sales must have begun to wane, and it was decided to let the entire series drop. The disastrous result was that for several years (roughly 1977 to 1982) Lovecraft disappeared from the bookstores, and his major work could only be obtained in hardcover through Arkham House. Ironically, it was precisely at this time that the emerging scholarly criticism of Lovecraft was bearing fruit through successive volumes devoted to his life and work. I was even once told that Ballantine had let their contract with Arkham House for the paperback rights expire; but if so, they presumably renewed it shortly, and by the middle of 1982 six volumes of Lovecraft's work were again on the stands. These included four from the original Beagle edition (the two volumes of Derleth's "posthumous collaborations" and the two volumes of *Tales of the Cthulhu Mythos* had been allowed mercifully to vanish) and Carter's two collections. The resulting anomalies (particularly in the overlapping of contents) were not pleasant to behold, but at least Lovecraft had returned to the public eye.

Both during and after the initial wave of Beagle/Ballantine reprints, other major paperback publishers tried to capitalise on works by Lovecraft not reprinted by Ballantine. The most notable are the two volumes of the famous Lancer/Zebra/Jove editions of Lovecraft, *The Dunwich Horror* and *The Colour out of Space*. Lancer published *The Dunwich Horror* in December 1963 and followed with *The Colour out of Space* in June 1964. The former received two further printings, the latter three; these must have gone out of print by around 1971 or 1972. Zebra Books then purchased the rights to the two volumes, but issued only *The Colour out of Space* in October 1975. This edition vanished very quickly, although I recall seeing it in a bookstore as late as 1977. In the course of time the paperback division of Harcourt Brace Jovanovich (Jove) obtained the paperback rights to the two volumes and reissued them in April and May of 1978. All know the amusing tale of the Jove *Colour out of Space*, which announced on the cover a preface by Frank Belknap Long but failed to include it; these copies were withdrawn very quickly and a second printing was hastily issued in August 1978 containing the preface. But even these volumes vanished from the shelves almost instantaneously; and it was the more tragic because they surely contained the best of Lovecraft's non-novel-length fiction.

Since at least 1980, when scholars began to notice that the Jove editions would not be reprinted, efforts were undertaken to issue—or, rather, to persuade a major paperback house to issue—an omnibus of Lovecraft's best work. This finally occurred in October 1982, with the appearance of *The Best of H. P. Lovecraft: Bloodcurdling Tales of Horror and the Macabre* from Ballantine. Behind this volume, however, lies a wealth of detail that may shed light on the difficulties involved in getting Lovecraft published in a commercial but non-popular format. As early as 1977 I began giving thought to compiling a *Portable Lovecraft* for Viking Press (now Viking/Penguin), which would contain not only his greatest fiction but also his best essays, poetry, and correspondence. By this time, too, I had virtually completed my preliminary textual work on Lovecraft's fiction and had restored it to a state at least far closer to what Lovecraft intended than the version produced by Derleth. My initial enquiry with Viking produced no results, but in 1980 Marc A. Michaud urged me to try again; we actually compiled a rough list of items to be included in the volume. With the assistance of Marc's brother Paul R. Michaud, we made contact with Viking/Penguin; and, although the idea of a *Portable Lovecraft* was ruled out rather early, the firm was still considering the issuance of a large omnibus volume that would contain nearly all Lovecraft's fiction (perhaps something like the Italian *Opere Complete* [see below]). Ultimately, however, the negotiations fell through. Later, in the summer of 1981, I began separate enquiries with Dutton Paperbacks for a similar omnibus volume. At first Dutton appeared to be interested, and actually requested to see some of Lovecraft's fiction that would be included in such a volume; but their queries eventually confirmed that Ballantine had already negotiated (or re-negotiated) the paperback rights and was planning to reissue their series; hence Dutton was compelled to drop the project. Eventually word got about that Ballantine, in addition to reissuing its six-volume paperback series, was also planning an omnibus of Lovecraft's best work; moreover, Robert Bloch had been selected to write an introduction for the volume. Much confusion ensued at this point, for Bloch was under the impression[5] that Michaud—who was in touch with Lester Del Rey, editor of the fantasy/science-fiction line at Ballantine—was to edit the volume, and that I would provide my corrected texts for printing. Michaud and I had already made a selection for such a volume, but neither of us was contacted in connexion with it. Apparently Bloch had himself made a list of tales for inclusion (very similar to the contents of the Arkham

---

5. See his letter to the editor in *Crypt of Cthulhu* 1, No. 4 (Eastertide 1982): 36.

House *Dunwich Horror and Others*), and this turned out to be the one used for the volume. It was certainly strange that Ballantine did not choose to use the corrected texts for the edition (although some corrections were derived from a superficially corrected fifth printing of *The Dunwich Horror*), since they were so easily available and since the volume was entirely reset in any case; but at least the long-awaited volume had appeared, and in a format not entirely unsuited (save for its lurid subtitle) to the dignity of Lovecraft's work. A *Portable Lovecraft* still remains a worthwhile goal, and I am now giving thought to compiling a collection of Lovecraft's *Selected Essays*; although this latter will almost certainly never reach the mass-market paperback stage.

Of other paperback appearances (aside from the Scholastic Book Services edition of *The Shadow over Innsmouth* [1971], which has been kept in print and which was edited by Lovecraft's correspondent Margaret Sylvester, now Margaret Ronan) all have been from small "specialty firms" within the weird fiction field, hence have added little to Lovecraft's literary stature, although they have made available some rare and obscure works. Several of these volumes— *Hail, Klarkash-Ton!* (1971), a collection of nine postcards from Lovecraft to Clark Ashton Smith assembled by Roy A. Squires; *Medusa: A Portrait* (1975), reprinting Lovecraft's poem of that title; *Antarktos* (1977), a reprint of the sonnet in *Fungi from Yuggoth*; and Squires's reprint of *The Cats of Ulthar* (1979)—were directed specifically toward collectors and contain no notable features save elegant printing and illustration; although Tom Collins's afterword to the *Medusa* pamphlet was enlightening on the origin of that poem. Scarcely more substantial was Gerry de la Ree's publication of an autobiographical letter by Lovecraft under the title *E'ch-Pi-El Speaks* (1972), which said little that we did not know from previously available sources.

On a more scholarly level was the unfortunately titled *Occult Lovecraft* (1975), assembled by Anthony Raven. This pamphlet, although highly criticised, actually contains much useful information, including parts of a letter (or letters) by Lovecraft under the title "The Cosmos and Religion" and "The Incantation from Red Hook" (providing Lovecraft's explanation—sometimes erroneous—of the incantation he included in "The Horror at Red Hook"), memoirs by Frank Belknap Long and Samuel Loveman, and interpretative essays by Raven. We need not have been told by Raven that Lovecraft's knowledge of occultism was superficial—although it might have benefited Philip A. Shreffler had he borne this in mind (see Section II.B of this essay). Finally, note can be made of two facsimile publications: Willis Conover's facsimile (1974) of the T.Ms. of Lovecraft's abridgement of "Supernatural Horror in Literature" in 1936, and R. Alain Everts's facsimile and transcription of an A.Ms. of "The Statement of Randolph Carter." This A.Ms. (although not the original draft) predates the surviving T.Ms. in the John Hay Library, so that some divergences between the standard printed version (deriving ultimately from the T.Ms.) and the A.Ms. as noted by Everts are due to later revision by Lovecraft; otherwise, Everts's introduction is competent and important for being one of the first indications of the severe textual corruption of Lovecraft's fiction.[6]

But the leader of specialty firms in the Lovecraft field since at least 1977 has been Necronomicon Press, founded and edited by Marc A. Michaud. It would, I suppose, be inelegant of me to sing its praises too highly, for I have myself been closely connected with the firm almost since its inception; but Michaud's industriousness and his desire to publish large quantities of Lovecraftiana at the most inexpensive price deserve the highest commendation. The early publications of the firm are embarrasingly crude but still enormously useful, especially *The Conservative* (1976, 1977) and the monumental *Writings in The United Amateur* (1976). The bitter controversy and legal imbroglio resulting from the publication of the first edition of *The Conservative* need not here be explored; but the unavailability of this important body of work will shortly be nullified by a third edition of *The Conservative* edited by me. Michaud's earliest works through 1977 were facsimile reprints of amateur journalism items by and about Lovecraft, and of the later volumes *The Californian* (1977) was the most useful. By the end of 1977 Michaud began to experiment with a reset design, although the earliest specimens were not well conceived: the frivolous *Collapsing Cosmoses* (1977) and the error-riddled *Fungi from Yuggoth* (1977; a new, corrected edition was issued in 1982). Finally Michaud and I collaborated on the first volume of *Uncollected Prose and Poetry* (1978), although at the time we had no idea of compiling any more such volumes. This volume, although also typographically inferior, included many obscure items unearthed by my colleagues and myself in the course of my bibliographic work. The volume's success led to the publication of two further collections (1980, 1982), each in its critical and textual accuracy better than the last, since we always tried to learn from our mistakes. A fourth volume may be forthcoming.

In the meantime, however, Michaud had not abandoned the notion of facsimile publication, and some of his happier later ventures were facsimiles of R. H. Barlow's rare edition of *The Cats of Ulthar* (1977); *Looking Backward*

---

6. Stuart D. Schiff also reprinted in facsimile a late A.Ms. of "The White Ship" in *Whispers* (July 1974). This A.Ms. was copied over (presumably from the surviving T.Ms. in the JHL) by HPL late in his life for Alvin Earl Perry. In addition to a few stenographic errors, it seems to contain a few wilful revisions (although generally only in terms of punctuation) that must be incorporated into any text claiming to be definitive.

(1980; a reprint not of the pamphlet of 1920 but of the magazine appearance of 1944); the useful *Notes and Commonplace Book* (1977); and the very successful *A History of the Necronomicon* (1977, 1977, 1980—the last with an afterword by me). Michaud had also branched into the publication of Lovecraft criticism, both reprinted and original; indeed, it is these volumes (for which see Part III) that have been perhaps of most service to the scholarly field. This enormous activity, which sometimes resulted in the publishing of up to ten books and pamphlets a year (although the pace slowed in 1980–81 due to financial difficulties), has been vital in keeping Lovecraft in the forefront of attention—at least within the weird fiction field—during an otherwise fallow period in publications of Lovecraft's work; and Michaud's efforts have not gone without notice in the wider literary world.[7]

Of other reprints note may be made of R. Alain Everts's reissue of the seven-volume *Lovecraft Collectors Library* in one volume (1979) and, more noticeably, the reprint of the second Ben Abramson edition (1945) of *Supernatural Horror in Literature* by Dover (1973). This latter volume, still in print, also kept Lovecraft's name visible during the five-year absence of the Ballantine paperbacks, and it is still not without use today, although I have since prepared a critical edition of the work with a revised text.

B. In Other Languages

The 1970s was the decade of Lovecraft's most extensive exposure in the foreign press, for only French and, to a lesser degree, German and Spanish translations of Lovecraft's work were copious before 1970. What is more, before 1970 no collections of tales by Lovecraft had appeared in Japanese or the Scandinavian languages, and only two in Dutch; since 1970 all these countries have issued Lovecraft's work extensively in book form. It will perhaps be most convenient to study Lovecraft's foreign diffusion by individual language.

In sheer quantity the Spanish have been far in the lead, and have issued no fewer than sixteen volumes by eight different publishers since 1971; four separate collections were published in 1974 alone. Many of these are merely popular editions equivalent to the American Ballantine or British Panther editions (and these figures do not include translations of the Derleth "posthumous collaborations," in some of which Lovecraft alone is listed as "author"), but some are more notable. In 1971 Rafael Llopis, the leading Spanish Lovecraftian, compiled *Viajes al otro mundo* (Alianza Editorial; 6th ed. 1981), a

---

7. See the notices of his work in the *New York Times Book Review* (9 August 1981) and the *Chicago Tribune* (27 October 1982).

collection of four stories in the "Randolph Carter cycle" (excluding "The Unnamable"), with a highly intelligent and lengthy introduction. Llopis's earlier anthology, *Los mitos de Cthulhu* (Alianza, 1969; 6th ed. 1980), included six Lovecraft tales, among them—surprisingly—"The Doom That Came to Sarnath" and "Out of the Aeons." In 1974 Eduardo Haro Ibars edited another worthy collection, *El sepulcro y otros relatos* (Ediciones Jucar), with another significant introduction. Barral Editores issued in 1974 a two-volume series, *Los horrores de Dunwich* and *La sombra más allá del tiempo*, containing the majority of Lovecraft's lengthier Mythos tales. Finally, Spain followed France and Italy in issuing Lovecraft's revisions in two volumes (Luis de Caralt, 1978).

The important French translations of Lovecraft had begun to appear so early as 1954 and continued through the 1960s, so that by 1970 only a few works remained to be translated. Bernard Da Costa produced an excellent translation (with brief commentary) of "Supernatural Horror in Literature" (Bourgois, 1971), far superior to the Bergier-Truchaud translation of 1969. In 1975 appeared the curious volume *Lettres d'Arkham* (Glenat), edited by Yves Rivière. This book (which Christian Bourgois once described to me as a "petit scandale") consists of tiny excerpts of letters by Lovecraft derived from the first two volumes of the *Selected Letters*; dates of writing and addressees are almost never identified, but instead the excerpts are arranged by subject-matter. This was not the first time Lovecraft's letters had been translated into French (the *L'Herne* Lovecraft issue of 1969 had included some), but it represented—however disreputably—the first book appearance of Lovecraft's letters in translation. Shortly thereafter Francis Lacassin, a leading Lovecraft scholar, undertook to produce a much more distinguished translation, and the first of a projected three-volume series of *Lettres* (Bourgois) emerged in 1978. To this volume—again a selection from the first two volumes of the *Selected Letters*—the highest praise must be given, for it may still be the best annotated edition of Lovecraft produced in any language. Lacassin's notes to the letters are highly intelligent, and the formidable job of translating Lovecraft's idiosyncratic epistolary style was entrusted to the capable hands of the late Jacques Parsons. It is perhaps Parsons's death that has delayed the appearance of the second volume (although I have heard that the first was not, surprisingly, a financial success), which was announced for late 1981. The French had also led the way in translating Lovecraft's revisions in two volumes (Bourgois, 1975), and have been the first to translate Lovecraft's poetry—"The Ancient Track" and "Psychopompos" by France-Marie Watkins (into French verse) and the entire *Fungi from Yuggoth* (into prose) in the journal *Ides . . . et Autres* (1978).

The opening of the 1970s saw the distinguished German hardcover firm of Insel Verlag continuing its translations of Lovecraft's work for its Bibliothek des

Hauses Usher series; five exquisitely produced volumes were issued between 1968 and 1973, and all have been reprinted in paperback by Suhrkamp. Only recently have some of Lovecraft's lesser work appeared in German: *Die Katzen von Ulthar*, ed. Kalju Kirde (Suhrkamp, 1980), including the "dream-world" tales (which, interestingly, were among the first to be translated into French), and *Die Traumfahrt zum unbekannten Kadath* (Stuttgart: Hobbit Press, 1980). Recently Franz Rottensteiner has come to the fore and edited two collections, *In der Gruft and andere makabre Erzählungen* (Suhrkamp, 1982), and *Der Schatten aus der Zeit: Geschichten kosmischen Grauens aus dem Cthulhu-Mythos* (1982), which is one of the very few hardcover editions ever issued by Suhrkamp. The Germans have yet to issue Lovecraft's revisions (although Rottensteiner has just informed me of plans to do so), but—aside from an astonishingly wide representation in anthologies, including not only many translations of Peter Haining's and Michel Parry's anthologies but such distinguished volumes as Manfred Kluge's *Die besten Gespenstergeschichten aus aller Welt* (1976), and Christian Brandstatter's *Phantastica* (1976), which included "The Music of Erich Zann" as part of *Eine Homage für E. T. A. Hoffmann*—plans to issue a 12-volume edition of Lovecraft's letters (presumably a complete translation of the *Selected Letters*) were announced in 1975 by Verlag Claus Neugebauer.[8] Although a prospectus to the project was issued, it ultimately fell through from insufficient finances. It would certainly have been a worthy venture in a land that regards Lovecraft not merely as a consummate literary artist but a significant thinker as well.

Italian book publication of Lovecraft's work has been dominated by two firms, Sugar Editore in Milan and Fanucci Editore in Rome. Sugar had been the prime force in Lovecraft publishing before 1970, and in 1973 it capped its efforts with the massive 939-page *Opere Complete* (rpt. 1978), including nearly all Lovecraft's fiction plus "Supernatural Horror in Literature"; it has, however, recently been revealed that the translation of many items was erroneous, and that frequent abridgements were made in the texts. Without these blemishes this volume would have been a landmark in Lovecraftian publishing history. Fanucci has now taken the lead by issuing Lovecraft's revisions in two volumes, *Nelle spire di Medusa* (1976) and *Sfida dall'infinito* (1976), under the editorship of the leading Italian Lovecraft scholars, Gianfranco de Turris and Sebastiano Fusco.

These volumes are, however, not merely translations of the American *Horror in the Museum and Other Revisions* (as are the corresponding French and

---

8. This firm also announced another volume, *Howard Phillips Lovecraft: Materialen zu seinem Leben and Werk*, ed. Hans Joachim Alpers, for late 1975; but this also never appeared.

Spanish editions), but innovative and imaginative volumes incorporating the most recent advances in Lovecraft criticism (both volumes received much assistance from Dirk W. Mosig); *Sfida dall'infinito* includes such items as "The Challenge from Beyond," "Collapsing Cosmoses," and the first republication of "The Night Ocean," the Lovecraft-Barlow collaboration discovered by Mosig. Also included were memoirs of Lovecraft by E. Hoffmann Price, R. H. Barlow, Wilfred B. Talman, and Kenneth Sterling—so that the volume is rather like some of the Arkham House miscellanies, *Marginalia* or *The Shuttered Room*. Finally, de Turris and Fusco edited *I miti di Cthulhu* (Fanucci, 1975), essentially a translation of Derleth's *Tales of the Cthulhu Mythos* but including much other matter, including the first Italian appearance of letters by Lovecraft. Fanucci was planning several other volumes in the late 1970s—including a collection of Lovecraft's essays (whose appearance would be a real landmark in the foreign press) and a translation of my own *H. P. Lovecraft: Four Decades of Criticism*; but financial difficulties have not allowed them to carry out the plans.

Recent Dutch appearances may be noted, although, as with the French and German, they are merely offering works by Lovecraft not yet available in the language. The three novels were published in separate editions by A. W. Bruna (1972–74), and they were followed by a collection of short stories in 1976, *Het huis in de nevel*.

The 1970s saw the first book appearances of Lovecraft's work in the Scandinavian languages, although some anthology appearances had occurred as early as 1955. In Sweden a collection of short tales appeared in 1973, *Skräckens labyrinter* (Askild & Karnekull), and in 1975 Delta Forlags issued *The Case of Charles Dexter Ward* under the odd title *Gengångaren* ("Ghost Story"). The latter, however, appeared in a distinguished series of fantasy classics, *Skräckens classiker*. Sam J. Lundwall, who edited the former volume, also issued the notable anthology *Den fantastika Romanen: Gotisk Skräkkromantik från Horace Walpole till H. P. Lovecraft* (1973), which reveals how Lovecraft is coming to be regarded as one end of a literary epoch, as Jacques Finné also noted in his anthology, *L'Amerique fantastique de Poe à Lovecraft* (1973). In Norwegian a single volume has appeared, *Tingen på terskelen* (1973), a collection of tales edited by Øyvind Myhre and Einar Engstad.

The most phenomenal foreign response of the decade has been the Japanese; for, although Lovecraft had appeared sporadically in periodicals and anthologies since as early as the late 1940s, no book of his work was issued until the *Lovecraft Kessakushu* (Sodosha) of 1973. This volume included not merely stories and an abridgement of "Supernatural Horror in Literature," but 50 pages of biographical and critical commentary by Katsuo Jinka and Hiroshi Aramata. This was followed by two separate volumes of *Lovecraft Kessakushu* from Sogensha (1974, 1976 [second volume rpt. 1982]), edited respectively by Tadaaki Onishi and Toshiyasu Uno. Between them appeared the remarkable *Lovecraft Zenshu I* (Sodosha, 1975), an exquisite hardbound and slipcased edition including the shorter tales, Leiber's "Literary Copernicus," an autobiographical letter by Lovecraft, and extensive commentary by Aramata. This was the first of a projected five-volume Collection of H. P. Lovecraft's Fiction, being the first of two volumes of short fiction; the next volume to be published, *Lovecraft Zenshu IV* (Sodosha, 1978), is actually the second volume of the longer tales and also contains Leiber's "Through Hyperspace with Brown Jenkin" and commentary by Aramata. This latter volume is especially noteworthy for including reproductions of some of Nicholas Roerich's paintings, alluded to in *At the Mountains of Madness*. These distinguished slipcased editions testify to the high reputation of Lovecraft in Japan—a reputation that may not be forthcoming in his own language for some years.

Some note may in conclusion be made about foreign periodicals that feature Lovecraft's work. Many of these are not much higher than the "fan" level—*Ganymed Horror* and *Weird Fiction Times* (German), *Drab* and *Rigel* (Dutch), *Crypt Horror Tales* and *Genso to Kaiki* (Japanese)—while others correspond to the American science fiction magazines: *Nueva Dimensión* (Spanish) and *Hayakawa's Mystery Magazine* (Japanese). The German *Quarber Merkur*, however, although not professionally published, is a distinguished and scholarly journal that contains frequent reviews of Lovecraft's work. Similar, although on slightly lower a level, is the Italian *Il Re in Giallo*. Since Lovecraft's appearance in *L'Herne* and *Fiction* in the late 1960s, he seems to have dropped out of the French periodical press—probably because nearly all his fiction is now available in book form. It ought finally to be noted that books by Lovecraft regularly receive lengthy reviews in the most prestigious foreign newspapers and magazines—*Süddeutsche Zeitung, Frankfurter Rundschau, Die Zeit, National Zeitung, Die Welt der Literatur* in German; *Fiction, La Quinzaine Litteraire* in French; *G Sera, Il Tempo, Paese Sera, Roma, La Reppublica* in Italian—a far cry from his near-total neglect by American or English periodicals. In general there can be no question but that Lovecraft is far more highly regarded abroad than here—as was startlingly proven by the great International Lovecraft Symposium in Trieste in June 1977—for the simple reason that foreign criticism draws no distinction between great work in weird fiction and great work in other genres of literature. For a great many reasons Americans find it difficult to regard weird fiction as serious literature; and, although the recent burgeoning of fantasy criticism and in particular criticism of Lovecraft may help to change that attitude, it shall be long before the barrier is definitively overcome.

II. Lovecraft Criticism

A. Biographical

After Derleth's *H. P. L.: A Memoir* (1945) few efforts were made to produce a detailed biographical portrait of Lovecraft; instead, Derleth himself continued to add notes here and there ("Addenda to *H. P. L.: A Memoir*" [1949]; *Some Notes on H. P. Lovecraft* [1959; rpt. Necronomicon Press, 1982]), and, more importantly, solicited many memoirs by Lovecraft's surviving colleagues. A lengthy biographical account was produced by Arthur Koki as his M.A. thesis for Columbia, "H. P. Lovecraft: An Introduction to His Life and Writings" (1962), but this significant document was never published and is now of merely historical importance. Koki's view toward his subject was an intelligent and sympathetic one, and there seems to have been nothing standing in the way of publication—at least not from Derleth, who was zealous to protect Lovecraft's character and reputation from detractors. Shortly before his death Derleth was himself contemplating a full-length biography: a volume entitled *H. P. Lovecraft: Notes toward a Biography* was listed as forthcoming from Arkham House in 1970.[9] Parts of this manuscript survive in the August Derleth Papers at the State Historical Society of Wisconsin in Madison, although I have not had a chance to consult it.

But it is highly unlikely that Derleth would have produced a satisfactory result: although his energy and diligence were boundless (so that he would surely have completed the book had he lived), he was not in any sense a scholar and did not have the discipline to sort evidence and do original research. Most of his biographical articles on Lovecraft derive their information from (and in large part are extracts of) Lovecraft's letters to him or to other correspondents—letters that Derleth had at hand for the *Selected Letters* project. He knew nothing of Lovecraft's New England background, had not paid much attention to the 1000 pages of Lovecraft's letters to his aunts during his years (1924-26) in New York, and was certainly no literary critic in spite of such works as "The Weird Tale in English Since 1890" (a blatant plagiarism, in part, of "Supernatural Horror in Literature") and *Writing Fiction*. His busy writing schedule precluded the years of uninterrupted study required to produce a comprehensive biography. Recent scholars have maintained that the greatest flaw in Derleth's biography would have been excessive partiality to

---

9. See *Thirty Years of Arkham House* (1970), 16. In the *Arkham Collector* No. 10 (Summer 1971): 302, Derleth actually announced that the biography would appear in late 1972, although this is probably another example of his typical optimism regarding the punctuality of Arkham House publications.

Lovecraft, but I am no longer certain of this. It is certainly true that Derleth was far from understanding Lovecraft's cosmic viewpoint and philosophical thought in general (but then, I know of no one even now who can claim such understanding), but Derleth's "partiality" was, I think, in general well founded and based upon personal acquaintance (if only through correspondence); and Derleth would surely not have acted as apologist without providing justification: his rebuttal to Colin Wilson's hostile attacks on Lovecraft (a far more "partial" and prejudiced view than Derleth's, and founded on much weaker ground) in *The Strength to Dream* (1961) was intelligently reasoned and restrained (see Derleth, "H. P. Lovecraft and His Work" xix–xx). I am honestly sorry that Derleth did not finish his biography, which would at least have been a step in the right direction.

And yet, as in so many other realms, the production of a full-length biography of Lovecraft had to wait until after Derleth's death. L. Sprague de Camp announced in the preface to his *Lovecraft: A Biography* (1975) that he knew of Derleth's plan for a biography and decided to take up the project himself only upon Derleth's death. De Camp was in many senses more qualified than Derleth to write a biography (although not necessarily a biography of Lovecraft): he was at least a little closer to the ideal of a scholar than Derleth, and, although he too was a prolific and multifaceted writer, made himself spend three full years in the production of his work. But the result is still a "popular" biography in the sense that it was published by a singularly non-scholarly commercial firm (Doubleday) and designed to capitalise on the growing Lovecraft "fan" movement spurred by the Ballantine paperbacks: it is symptomatic that, in the abridged paperback reissue of the biography by Ballantine (August 1976), the notes, bibliography, and index—nearly the only parts of the book useful to scholars—were dropped. And de Camp's highly confusing system of footnoting made it difficult even for trained scholars to tell precisely what the references for the notes were.[10] There is no question that a great deal of scholarly effort was put into the researching and writing of the biography; and although some of the information is erroneous, it is certainly a landmark work and a tribute to de Camp's zeal and diligence. And

---

10. One persistent error that has arisen out of de Camp's footnoting system is the belief that HPL's juvenile poem "On the Creation of Niggers" (1912; unpublished until my edition of *Saturnalia and Other Poems*, 1984), was published in the *Argosy* (see de Camp 95 and 455). This was mentioned by B. L. Bender in his thesis on HPL, although for its appearance in *Lovecraft Studies* (Spring/Fall 1981) I corrected it accordingly. Darrell Schweitzer, also misled on this point, believed—when he reviewed my bibliography in *Science Fiction Review* No. 40 (Fall 1981) 28–that I was actually suppressing the "publication" of the poem in order to whitewash HPL's reputation!

yet, it is my feeling that much of the criticism directed against it is misplaced, and that its real shortcomings have rarely been touched upon.

And criticism it certainly received. It was only to be expected, of course, that many reviewers who knew little of Lovecraft would either praise it (for the volume certainly looks impressive) or would use it as a springboard for condemning Lovecraft as a hack or lunatic. Of the most inept reviews we need only mention those by Christopher Lehmann-Haupt (*New York Times*), Larry McMurtry (*Washington Post*), Ursula Le Guin (*Times Literary Supplement*), and David Sinclair (*London Times*). Of those reviewers who severely criticised de Camp most were either previously acquainted with Lovecraft's work—like Elmer Blistein (*Providence Sunday Journal*), Professor of English at Brown University—or actual Lovecraft scholars—Tom Collins, Fritz Leiber, and especially Dirk W. Mosig. Unfortunately, the reviews of these scholars appeared only in "fan" magazines or science-fiction and fantasy journals, so that their cautionary words have not been heard by the public at large. De Camp, however, felt it worthwhile to rebut some of these attacks, and in *Fantasy Crossroads* he conducted a lengthy debate with Mosig (since Derleth's death Lovecraft's foremost defender)—a debate that now reads rather amusingly, since these illustrious figures would often spend pages merely discussing points of grammatical usage and style.

What, precisely, are the failings of the de Camp biography? Certain points are easily noted: the amateurish literary criticism included in the volume (Barton L. St Armand, when asked what he thought of de Camp's criticism, is said to have replied: "What criticism?"), which went little beyond plot description and easily revealed de Camp's own prejudices for certain facets of Lovecraft's work, as when he compared *The Dream-Quest of Unknown Kadath* to Lewis Carroll's *Alice* books; certain flagrant errors of fact, as when he dated the "History of the *Necronomicon*" (1927) to 1936; or when he hypothesised a lost novelette by Lovecraft (another mistake that has had a curiously long life), which is nothing more than the extant tale "The Mound";[11] and things of this sort. But the principal failing of de Camp's work (as Mosig intermittently hinted) was de Camp himself. De Camp was so different from Lovecraft in character, motivation, and goals that he could never even remotely understand why Lovecraft did the things he did: de Camp was a "professional" writer and could not understand Lovecraft's "amateur" status; he felt that

---

11. Lin Carter announced, at the 5th World Fantasy Convention in October 1979, his intention of "finding" this novelette for his nascent journal *Weird Tales*; and although I tried at the time to tell him his search was misguided, Carter persisted in the delusion. Recent discussions with him, however (December 1982), reveal that he has at last realised the vanity of his quest.

Lovecraft's fondness for the past was a mere affectation; he was strikingly unable to tell when Lovecraft in his letters and essays was joking and when he was being serious. As de Camp announced in his preface, he felt that he himself was, when younger, actually closer in spirit to Lovecraft; as a result, when he saw Lovecraft doing something that de Camp felt had either led him (de Camp) or would have led him into error, he automatically condemned it in Lovecraft. The result is that de Camp actually becomes too emotionally involved in his subject, and also looks upon Lovecraft as "immature" when he does things that de Camp may have done and regretted in his own youth. This frequent wrist-slapping of Lovecraft becomes rapidly tedious; and yet, most critics of de Camp have not realised that it is not the mere passing of value judgments that is to be condemned (for a purely "objective" biography is neither possible nor desired: it is the duty of a biographer to interpret his subject in the manner he feels appropriate), but rather the making of value judgments based upon incorrect perspective and insufficient evidence. It is perfectly right for a biographer to criticise his subject when he sees that subject doing things that hinder his own happiness and ideals; and de Camp actually feels that Lovecraft frequently does this, but I have never been convinced of it.

The startling example of de Camp's misunderstanding of Lovecraft's motives is his condemnation of Lovecraft's "amateur" status: why was Lovecraft, de Camp argues, not more aggressive in the selling of his work? The money thus gained could have relieved his poverty and allowed him wider travel to those antiquarian sites around the Atlantic seaboard he so cherished. Stated in this way, the criticism seems entirely just. But what de Camp overlooks is that Lovecraft's gentlemanly status (not a pose in any sense but a social reality to one born in the reign of Victoria in conservative New England) could not allow him to act as a "tradesman" and hawk his work about like a pedlar; and more, Lovecraft stated that it was the sheer act of writing—of capturing images clamouring within the artist to be expressed—that was the aim and end of writing, and actual publication was a distinctly secondary factor. To most of us nowadays these views sound either disastrously antiquated or intolerably "highbrow"; but we should be aware that opinions of this sort have been held in all civilised ages from Periclean Athens to Augustan Rome to Renaissance Italy to Georgian England. And Lovecraft expresses them with a sincerity impossible to ignore save to those who have already made up their minds to the contrary. It is precisely the abandonment of this arbitrary attitude—this act of judging Lovecraft not on his own terms but on ours—that I have frequently advised.

One of the most vehemently debated subjects raised by the de Camp biography was the issue of Lovecraft's "racism." It was upon this point that Mosig came most strenuously to Lovecraft's defence; but it is not clear whether

Mosig quite understood de Camp's position. Mosig's defence—first embodied in a letter to Frank Belknap Long included in Long's *Howard Phillips Lovecraft: Dreamer on the Nightside* (1975) and later in the article "H. P. Lovecraft: Rabid Racist—or Compassionate Gentleman?"—was based on the following points:

1. Consideration must be taken of the time and place in which Lovecraft lived—the New England of the early decades of the century—since in Lovecraft's day "racist" attitudes were far more prevalent and less objectionable than today;
2. It must be noted that Lovecraft never acted in a racist manner in public, but only recorded his views on paper;
3. Lovecraft's most vehement views on race were expressed in private letters to his aunts never intended for publication;[12]
4. Lovecraft's prime motivation for disliking minorities was that they were helping to destroy the architecture and mores of the past which Lovecraft cherished and felt worth preserving in the name of culture.

Now of these points de Camp was actually aware of the first and alludes to it in passing (see de Camp 90f.); but this did not seem to stop him from making pointlessly extensive quotations and to criticise Lovecraft for his beliefs in a very unhistorical manner. The second point is one to which I give little credence; Mosig wrote: "When did he discriminate, when did he attack, verbally or physically, a member of any minority group? HPL certainly did not behave like a racist in any manner, and it is behavior that counts" (Long 229). But we need not all be Hitlers to be racists; indeed, few racists aside from the Ku Klux Klan ever do take physical action of any sort. And Mosig's emphasis on "behavior" is only a result of his adherence to the psychological school of Behaviourism; and to anyone not agreeing with its tenets behaviour is not "all that counts." The third point is equally irrelevant, and is indeed more damaging to Mosig's case than otherwise: one would assume that Lovecraft is "letting his hair down" and expressing his real feelings to his aunts (who would understand and sympathise with his views) than to other correspondents who had not had the upbringing Lovecraft had. It is simply not true (or at least very unlikely) that Lovecraft merely told his aunts "what they wanted to hear," as Mosig contends. The fourth point is valid enough—it was recognised in a nebulous way even by Derleth (see *Some Notes on H. P. Lovecraft* vi–viii—a really intelligent discussion of the issue)—but is not nearly complete: Lovecraft's views cannot be accounted

---

12. It is to be observed that Derleth published none of the more virulent of these letters to his aunts in the *Selected Letters*, forcing de Camp to unearth them from the archives of the JHL.

for merely in this way, and he felt that he had scientific and philosophical justification for maintaining the inherent inferiority of certain races.

It is this last point upon which de Camp and I conducted a brief debate in the pages of *Outré*, edited by the late J. Vernon Shea.[13] In his biography de Camp had put forward the belief that many of Lovecraft's views about race were derived from H. S. Chamberlain's *Foundations of the Nineteenth Century*; but de Camp could adduce nothing but internal evidence for the claim. Mosig had already questioned its validity, and some time later I suggested a simple alternate source for Lovecraft's views—Nietzsche, especially such works as *Twilight of the Idols*. But I was unable to show at all conclusively that Lovecraft had read Nietzsche much before 1918, at which time his views—or, rather, the scientific and philosophical foundations for them, which was the real issue at hand—had already been solidified. I then observed that Lovecraft cited T. H. Huxley in the early essay "The Crime of the Century" (1915), and am now convinced—although I am not certain de Camp is—that Huxley was the source for his views, especially such books as *Man's Place in Nature* (1894). There is no question, of course, but that Lovecraft's upbringing made him receptive to such views—note the fact that as a boy he had named his cat "Nigger-Man," a perfectly common sort of name at the time—and that other books read earlier than Huxley had provided a nucleus: the early poem "De Triumpho Naturae" (1905) is dedicated to "William Benjamin Smith . . . Author of *The Colour Line: A Brief in Behalf of the Unborn*." But this discovery that the major philosophical source for his views was so respected and brilliant a philosopher as Huxley (and, of course, later Nietzsche—or perhaps misinterpretations of Huxley and Nietzsche, since neither were "racists" in any real sense) may make us wary of passing off Lovecraft's views contemptuously as "pseudo-scientific," as de Camp was wont to do: the fact is that the belief in the natural superiority and inferiority of races was assumed as "proven" by a large segment of the intelligent classes of Lovecraft's day.

And yet, in one way I—as well as Barry L. Bender, the most copious commentator on the subject—have been more "harsh" than even de Camp in the matter of Lovecraft's "racism." Before Bender all critics—de Camp and Mosig included—maintained as a defence of Lovecraft that he discarded many of his attitudes late in life and that his views became more in tune with our own on the subject. Bender boldly challenged this position in his thesis, "Xenophobia in the Life and Work of H. P. Lovecraft" (1980), and produced a crushing weight of evidence that showed that Lovecraft's "racist" stance was as firmly

---

13. See *Outré* No. 11 (October 1978): 79; No. 12 (February 1979): 82-83; No. 13 (May 1979): 79; No. 14 (August 1979): 74-76; No. 15 (October 1979): 58; No. 16 (February 1980): 57-58.

The Development of Lovecraftian Studies, 1971–1982 521

held at the end of his life as before. I had independently arrived at this conclusion myself, and think it is incontrovertible; but whereas Bender in his zeal felt that Lovecraft's views remained almost unchanged (save in such works as "Supernatural Horror in Literature," where Lovecraft gives credit to such things as the Jewish horror tradition), I felt that this was too much a swing in the other direction—there is abundant evidence, I think, to justify the belief that Lovecraft's views were rationalised and systematised as he progressed (see my editorial postscript to Bender), and also shifted in focus from a maintenance of "Aryan supremacy" (although this idea was never dropped) to a desire for the preservation of individual culture (whether Western or Eastern, Catholic or Protestant, French or German or English or Japanese) against a kind of amorphous homogeneity produced by excessive intermixing. This goal of Lovecraft's seems to me entirely defensible—although whether racial segregation is the key to it may not be so certain. My general conclusion is to accept Lovecraft's racial views and not to dismiss them as "unimportant" (see Collins, *Winter Wish* 2), for they are highly important in understanding not merely his overall philosophy but his literary work as well); but, correspondingly, not to criticise or censure Lovecraft for them (as de Camp and Bender tend to do), since they were natural products of his upbringing and were later harmonised into his general political and social philosophy. I further advocate the use of the neutral term "racialism" rather than the pejorative "racism" to designate these views in an historical manner.

But whatever its failings, the de Camp biography had one great effect: it exposed Lovecraft to the public eye and to the main trend of literary criticism. The biography received three hardcover printings from Doubleday, a paperback printing from Ballantine, and a hardcover printing from the New English Library. It garnered reviews—sometimes brief, sometimes very lengthy—in such journals as the *Atlantic Monthly*, the *Magazine of Fantasy and Science Fiction*, the *Chicago Tribune*, *Library Journal*, *New York Times*, *Chicago Daily News*, *Science-Fiction Studies*, *Chicago Sun-Times*, *Publishers Weekly*, and the newspapers previously mentioned. Indeed, as we shall see shortly, 1975 was the year of Lovecraft's highest critical reputation and popular appeal. Two unfortunate results of the widespread fame of de Camp's book must, however, be noted. Firstly, it prevented the publication of another biography (or perhaps a sort of "literary biography") by Prof. James Merritt, which Willis Conover had announced as forthcoming (see *Lovecraft at Last* 262). I have never seen this work or been in touch with Merritt; but I understand that Merritt's volume was actually completed and had been accepted for publication, but upon the emergence of the de Camp biography in early 1975 the publisher decided to cancel it, and it has not apparently found another publisher. The second consequence is simply a generalisation of the first: the appearance of so formidable and so widely disseminated a work has prevented the emergence of any other such work by a trained Lovecraft scholar, and one can only hope that in a few years a demand will arise again (perhaps through the new Ballantine printings) for a more accurate and well-rounded work. I have frequently been urged to undertake such a task; but not merely is my interest in Lovecraft primarily literary and philosophical, but I would probably only be satisfied with producing a very detailed, multi-volume work not intended for popular consumption. There are several other Lovecraft scholars active who would be fully capable of producing a biography, but none seems inclined to do so.

Of one of these scholars—Kenneth W. Faig, Jr—some further words must be said. Faig, along with Dirk W. Mosig (for whom see Section II.B), may well be the most important figure in the transition of Lovecraftian studies from an avocation undertaken by "fans" to a scholarly discipline. Faig revolutionised the field of Lovecraft biography through some remarkably fertile work conducted at Brown University during 1971–72, during which he unearthed an enormous amount of primary data from surviving documents, unpublished letters by Lovecraft, and other sources. Some of this information was disseminated through a spate of articles in the fan press since 1971 (especially such notable monuments as "Howard Phillips Lovecraft: The Early Years, 1890–1914," "The Lovecraft Circle: A Glossary," "Lovecraft's Providence," and the long monograph "R. H. Barlow"), but even these voluminous publications (and several other articles still unpublished) do not do justice to the incalculable but largely silent influence of Faig's work upon the rest of the field. Faig actually produced a large but rather rambling volume filled with his insights, *Lovecraftian Voyages*, but seems never to have made even the effort to secure its publication. Finally, Marc A. Michaud and I decided to put together his work in the form of a small pamphlet, *H. P. Lovecraft: His Life, His Work* (1979). Small as this volume is, it contains a wealth of information not found in books thrice its size. But Faig's real influence was in raising Lovecraft studies to levels of precision and detail never before seen—his example once set, other scholars were compelled to follow suit. Much of Faig's work is now superseded only because other scholars—Mosig, David E. Schultz, Donald R. Burleson, R. Boerem, and myself—have picked up where he left off. There is no question but that de Camp used Faig's *Lovecraftian Voyages* (often with scant acknowledgement) as a factual foundation for large parts of his biography.

Another great but silent figure in Lovecraft studies is R. Alain Everts, who since the early 1960s has made it his task to locate as many of Lovecraft's surviving associates (including his ex-wife Sonia Davis, who died only in 1972) and to interview and collect material from them. The astonishing diligence shown by Everts has, unfortunately, borne little fruit, largely because of several legal disputes that have occupied his time for the last decade. But Everts knows the details of Lovecraft's life perhaps as well as anyone, and—although some of his theories and conjectures are rather peculiar—hopes may still be had of significant biographical research from his pen.

Since Derleth's death we have had few important memoirs from Lovecraft's surviving colleagues, and some of the lesser ones—by H. Warner Munn, Vrest Orton, and Samuel Loveman (his piece in *The Occult Lovecraft*—a bizarre and virulent attack by the aged Loveman, who turned against Lovecraft's memory at the end of his life)—tell us almost nothing new. On an intermediate level are memoirs by Kenneth Sterling ("Caverns Measureless to Man") and Wilfred B. Talman (*The Normal Lovecraft*). Sterling valiantly defends Lovecraft as writer, thinker, and human being, but fails to tell much about his collaboration with Lovecraft, "In the Walls of Eryx" (1936)—a matter upon which Lovecraft's letters tell equally little. Talman tries—and, I think, succeeds—in portraying Lovecraft as far more normal than he is sometimes made to appear, and reprints some previously unavailable work by Lovecraft. But the two most substantial memoirs—Willis Conover's *Lovecraft at Last* and Frank Belknap Long's *Howard Phillips Lovecraft: Dreamer on the Nightside*—require more extensive discussion.

It is these two books, along with the de Camp biography, that made 1975 memorable for Lovecraft studies. Conover's volume—an exquisite monument in book production—also received fairly extensive review, in the *Atlantic Monthly*, the *Providence Sunday Journal*, *Library Journal*, *Algol*, *Whispers*, *Publishers Weekly*, and others—more, perhaps, on Conover's own independent fame than on the subject-matter of the volume, since only the last six months of Lovecraft's life were covered. But these last six months not only saw Lovecraft at the height of his intellectual (though, perhaps due to certain setbacks in the publication of his work, not literary) powers, but presented him as a warm human being in startling contrast to the bumbling and immature racist of de Camp's volume. There is, of course, a certain truth to de Camp's comments that the radical difference in the images of Lovecraft derived from these two volumes stems precisely from the fact that Conover's book covered only this small section of Lovecraft's life while de Camp's covered its whole; but this is only a partial qualification. In the end, however, this book lacks real substance and hard information about Lovecraft; it reminds us of certain ancient biographies—Plutarch's *Julius Caesar*, for example, or the portrait of Tiberius in the early books of Tacitus' *Annals*—where art is placed on a higher level than facts. What we really learn is embodied in Lovecraft's correspondence to Conover, which Conover prints in such a confusing manner (as a simulated conversation between himself and Lovecraft) that it is hard to tell whence these passages derive;

it is fortunate that James Turner reprinted much of Lovecraft's correspondence to Conover in a straightforward format in the fifth volume of the *Selected Letters*. We learn much, of course, about Conover's own publishing venture, *Science-Fantasy Correspondent*, and indirectly about the whole world of fantasy fandom in the 1930s—a subject still not thoroughly explored, at least as regards Lovecraft's involvement in it. And no on, can fail to be affected—even jarred—by the poignant account of Lovecraft's final days and death in the hospital.

Frank Belknap Long's *Dreamer on the Nightside* is rather easier to judge, since its virtues and failings are less concealed by elaborate artistry. The volume was received with almost universal disappointment, and I do not believe this was unjustified. From someone who "exchanged numerous letters with him, and met and talked with him at length at least 500 times," and who candidly declares that "I have always felt that I knew Howard Phillips Lovecraft better than anyone else," we are right to expect far more than the meagre and disjointed recollections, interlaced with sadly inept attempts at literary appreciation (it cannot even be called criticism), which make up this deceptively large volume—the largest single memoir of Lovecraft save Conover's. There were, I believe, two reasons for these deficiencies: first, Long's poor memory in describing events that occurred fifty to sixty years before the time of writing (as when he presents Lovecraft, shortly after he came back to Providence in April 1926, discussing "T. S. Eliot's *The Wasteland* [sic] which had only recently [viz., in November 1922] appeared in *The Dial*"); and secondly, what I have been led to understand was Long's motive in writing the volume. Dirk W. Mosig mentioned to me that Long wrote his volume in direct opposition to the de Camp biography, although it is never mentioned by name. If this is true, then he must have written it upon reading a portion of the manuscript of de Camp's book, since Long's volume was already noted as forthcoming in the Arkham House catalogue of September 1974. In any case, there certainly are signs of haste in its composition, and certain veiled polemics scattered through it—as when he writes that "so many totally false assumptions, half-truths, and even malicious fabrications have circulated about HPL in the past decade that a systematic refutation becomes mandatory"; unfortunately, Long was unable to produce that systematic refutation. But apart from the book's manifest failings—the paucity of information provided here that is not found more elaborately in the *Selected Letters*; the weak efforts to reproduce Lovecraft's exact words on a given occasion; a silly attempt to produce a sort of posthumous interview session between Long and Lovecraft;[14] the unin-

---

14. Such a "posthumous interview" (actually excerpts from letters and other writings by HPL) has been produced by Peter Cannon, and appears in *Twilight Zone* for August 1983.

formative introductory matter where Long tries to provide a general overview of Lovecraft's life that is both inadequate and erroneous in details—there are certain vignettes that stand out: Lovecraft's elaborate, almost ritualistic attempt to select a fountain pen; his strange allergy that produced a swelling in his hand when he touched some Egyptian objects at the Metropolitan Museum; Long's vivid descriptions of Lovecraft's associates, especially the members of the Kalem Club; and other smaller details. But in this light the volume ill compares with W. Paul Cook's imperishable memoir, which remains the best account of Lovecraft ever written by an associate.

In general there has been little advance in biographical study of Lovecraft since the de Camp biography, and scholars have almost exclusively turned their attention to the analysis of his work and thought. This is probably for the better; for once the literary world becomes convinced of Lovecraft's enduring merit as a writer and thinker, then biographical investigation will proceed on its own course. Lovecraft's surviving associates are few—a point emphasised with particular poignancy by the deaths of H. Warner Munn and J. Vernon Shea within a month of each other in early 1981—but it is not likely that they have much more to tell us. What is needed now is an even profounder exploration of Lovecraft's mountainous correspondence, both published and unpublished (particularly the invaluable correspondence to his aunts of 1924-26), a more detailed examination of the precise biographical value of such controversial documents as Sonia Davis's memoir, and a thorough exploration of the political, social, and intellectual currents of Lovecraft's time so that his life and actions can be put into historical perspective. In contrast to critical study, no document can be ignored or dispensed with in the study of Lovecraft's life—his own writings, memoirs by friends, primary documents (wills, birth and death notices, etc.), and the like; and the task of synthesising this enormous hoard of information is a daunting one indeed.

B. Critical

The most fertile and explosive advances in the study of Lovecraft have, in the last ten (and particularly the last five) years, been made in the interpretation of his work and thought. There has, however, been a curious cleavage in the critical assessment of Lovecraft, represented on the one hand by the lingering "Derlethian" tradition that (influenced in part by the de Camp biography) has adhered to traditional means of interpreting Lovecraft purely within the field of weird literature, and generally taking no heed of any body of his work save his fiction, and on the other hand with a bold and energetic tradition that, almost upon Derleth's death, began to challenge his interpretations and to expand its attention toward the whole of Lovecraft's work, from revisions and collaborations to poetry to essays and especially to letters, whose monumental significance in the interpretation of his work (not to say their own literary and philosophical merit) is now definitively established. It is hard to deny that this latter school is decidedly in the forefront of criticism, and that the former—which includes not only certain Lovecraft scholars but nearly all other commentators on Lovecraft in general literary criticism or science-fiction criticism—is merely perpetuating outmoded and on occasion erroneous views about Lovecraft the man and writer. The new trend in criticism has been restricted to a very small number of scholars, and their findings have not as yet received sufficient dissemination to make much of an impress upon criticism in general.

But of the "old" school some words must be said; since, however little it has done to advance actual scholarship, it has at least helped to spread Lovecraft's fame. Lin Carter's *Lovecraft: A Look Behind the "Cthulhu Mythos"* (1972) is the major representative of the "old" school; and amidst its amateurish criticism, casual and "fannish" style, and adoption of serious misconceptions about Lovecraft's work (notably Carter's wholehearted acceptance of Derleth's interpolation of "Elder Gods" into Lovecraft's Mythos—on which see further below) it is now only an historical curiosity. Carter, indeed, mentioned to me that Derleth read about half the book in manuscript before his death, and Carter takes pride in the fact that it was the first book to deal entirely with Lovecraft's work—a remark, however, that must be qualified in two ways: first, more than half the volume is devoted to a survey of "Cthulhu Mythos" tales written after Lovecraft's death by other hands; and secondly, it is not certain whether Maurice Lévy's *Lovecraft ou du fantastique* (1972) appeared earlier or later than Carter's book. Nevertheless, no modern critic need even consult this volume any longer, as it has been totally superseded by later (and, indeed, by some earlier) studies. It is remarkable that Carter, who much earlier in his career did so much sound work in Lovecraft (his substantial if error-sprinkled "H. P. Lovecraft: The Books" is still useful today), produced a volume that is so critically disappointing. But Carter was not a trained critic; nor, unfortunately, are any other members of the "old" school, although some sport Ph.Ds.

Of the three other recent volumes conforming to the Derlethian mode—John Taylor Gatto's Monarch Note on Lovecraft (1977), Philip A. Shreffler's *H. P. Lovecraft Companion* (1977), and Darrell Schweitzer's *Dream Quest of H. P. Lovecraft* (1978)—little need be said. Gatto's book[15] is marred by extreme

---

15. Large portions of this book were articles that, I believe, were written separately before incorporation into the volume: his article on "Lovecraft and the Grotesque Tradition" (ch. 2) was actually published in *Nyctalops* about the time of the emergence of his book, and I have a copy of the manuscript of this article and of his article on "The Whisperer in Darkness" (now part of ch. 5), which Mosig sent to me in 1976.

idiosyncrasy—as when he tries to shew that "The Whisperer in Darkness" is subtly pornographic—and shows a remarkably weak grasp of the hard facts of Lovecraft's life and work.[16] The same may be said of Shreffler's volume, in which the author tries to make Lovecraft an occultist—presumably because the author himself has leanings in this direction. It is, however, symptomatic of how slowly the "new" criticism is reaching the critical public that the first chapter of Shreffler's book—a very superficial account of the "American Horror Tradition" and of Lovecraft's place in it—has been reprinted in Peter B. Messent's *Literature of the Occult* (Prentice-Hall, 1981; Twentieth Century Views), when many dozen better articles on Lovecraft could have been chosen.

Still less attention need be given to certain writers who have chosen to write on Lovecraft in the course of wider studies. Here we see the influence not only of Derleth and de Camp but of Colin Wilson—and not the Wilson of recent years, when he has retracted many of his harsher dicta about Lovecraft, but the early Wilson of the vitriolic *Strength to Dream*. Brian W. Aldiss, in the arrogantly titled *Billion-Year Spree: The True History of Science Fiction* (1973), called Lovecraft's work "ghastly"—curiously echoing Wilson's claim that Lovecraft's style is "atrocious" (preface to *The Philosopher's Stone*). The problem with such judgments is not merely that they are arbitrary and subjective, but that the authors make not even the attempt to defend them, believing apparently that they are uttering self-evident truths. Such feeble amateurishness has been carried to its highest levels in the chapter on Lovecraft in Glen St John Barclay's *Anatomy of Horror* (1978), which revives Wilson's belief that Lovecraft was "sick" and maniacal. Barclay's chapter reads as if he has some personal animus against Lovecraft.

Bridging the gap between the "ancients" and the "moderns" in Lovecraft criticism are two important figures—the great French critic Maurice Lévy and his American follower, Barton L. St Armand. Both these distinguished scholars have produced substantial advances in the literary interpretation of Lovecraft's fiction, but have not had the benefit of modern discoveries into Lovecraft's life and work, since Lévy's work generally preceded the "new" school's activity and St Armand has anomalously chosen to ignore it. Lévy's *Lovecraft ou du fantastique* is a greatly revised version of his Ph.D. thesis for the Sorbonne (1969) and is still arguably the best single volume on Lovecraft; its countless keen interpretations of Lovecraft's work are little marred by a relatively poor grasp of the facts of Lovecraft's life and by his acceptance of Der-

---

16. The celebrated mistake was his recording the date of HPL's death as 17 February 1937 instead of 15 March 1937—an error derived, incredibly, from Philip Herrera's book review in *Time*.

leth's conception of the Mythos. Lévy is the striking example of what a brilliant critic can do when faced merely with an author's extant remains, however encrusted they are by misinterpretation. Lévy did much source study for his volume, and by exploring Lovecraft's nonfictional and (to a lesser degree) his poetic writings anticipated the modern approach. Although Lévy strongly disagreed with many of Lovecraft's philosophical views, he unhesitatingly felt that they were worth exploring as keys to the elucidation of Lovecraft's fiction and poetry. His influence has, regrettably, been restricted merely because few scholars have taken the effort to read his book; I trust that my forthcoming English translation may finally give it the attention it deserves.

But in Barton L. St Armand Lévy found a notable successor. St Armand shares with Lévy a poor understanding of Lovecraft's life[17] and augments it by adopting certain arbitrary and idiosyncratic positions that vitiate much of his work, however suggestive and enlightening in detail it remains. His first major work, the slim *Roots of Horror in the Fiction of H. P. Lovecraft* (1977), was, I understand, virtually finished by 1971; but problems with his publishers delayed its appearance, and in the interim St Armand surprisingly neglected to take regard of the great strides in scholarship made since the book's initial writing (hence St Armand still maintains Derleth's exploded "Elder Gods"). In this book, as in its successor, *H. P. Lovecraft: New England Decadent* (1975; rev. 1979), St Armand exhibits many of his fundamental impressions about Lovecraft; it would not be profitable to examine in detail either of these two rich and powerful works, but some of the author's biases and interpretations may be noted.

First, St Armand wants to see Lovecraft as an "aesthetic schizophrenic" in that he champions rationalism and mechanistic materialism in his life and letters but irrationalism and mysticism in his fiction. I will frankly admit that it is this view that I have been principally intent on refuting; hence I suppose I cannot represent it very fairly. But it strikes me that St Armand's deeming Lovecraft's rationalism a "pose" stems (as he in fact once mentioned to me) from the fact that he finds little interest in Lovecraft's philosophy and cannot see how this philosophy is expressed in the fiction.[18] I shall leave it to the reader to determine whether this is a satisfactory manner of dealing with the evidence. St Armand is, indeed, frequently very selective in his use of evidence and tends to ignore what does not fit into his scheme and conceptions;

---

17. As testified by the first part of his M.A. thesis on HPL (1966).
18. St Armand, in *Roots of Horror* (75), makes the remarkable statement that HPL's "mechanistic materialist universe [was] so safe and rational, and yet so excruciatingly tedious and boring at the same time"—a striking contrast to HPL's remark that "the more we learn about the cosmos, the more bewildering does it appear" (*SL* 4.324).

in his *New England Decadent* volume he tried to establish that Lovecraft was a peculiar combination of French Decadence and New England Puritanism, and cited one passage from a letter that seemed to support his thesis—but he left out certain parts of it that actually controverted (or at least severely qualified) it. All this, however, does not prevent St Armand's work from being supremely interesting and important: in *Roots of Horror* there are fine discussions of details (e.g., his identification and interpretation of some epigraphs that head Lovecraft's tales; his keen study of the symbolism in "The Rats in the Walls"; his perceptive comparisons of Lovecraft and Poe) whether or not one accepts (as I do not) his central thesis. St Armand's work can never be ignored, but because of his incomplete and idiosyncratic assessment of evidence it will always remain in need of supplementation and qualification.

The new trend in criticism, as mentioned, got underway not long after Derleth's death; and the destruction of the Derlethian edifice was begun through an attack upon Derleth's conception of the Lovecraft Mythos. This conception had, indeed, been challenged (or, rather, simply ignored) by such early scholars as Leiber, Wetzel, and Onderdonk, but its effective overthrow is the product of recent years. In essence Derleth's view can be summarised as follows:[19]

1. Lovecraft in his fiction created two sets of extra-terrestrial and godlike forces, the "Elder Gods," or the forces of good, and the "Old Ones," forces of evil, who battled continually over possession of the earth;
2. The expulsion of the Old Ones and their imprisonment in various forms parallels the Christian mythos and the expulsion of Satan from Heaven;
3. The Old Ones can be likened to elementals;
4. Certain of Lovecraft's tales "belong" to the Mythos and others do not; more specifically, Lovecraft's tales can be cleanly segregated into the categories of "Mythos tales," "dream-world" tales, and "New England" tales.

In the course of time every one of these views was attacked, and the foremost Lovecraft scholars do not accept any of them. Initially, however, the debate seemed to centre (or perhaps gained its symbolic significance) over the mere term "Cthulhu Mythos" or "Cthulhu Mythology." It was first noted that Lovecraft never seems to have used the term (although it was only several years later that I ascertained its earliest use by Derleth in the article "H. P. Lovecraft,

---

19. It receives its most succinct expression in the introduction ("H. P. Lovecraft and His Work") to *The Dunwich Horror and Others* (Arkham House, 1963), itself a revised version of chapter 3 of his *H. P. L.: A Memoir* (1945).

Outsider," published in June 1937), and this observation prompted Richard L. Tierney, so early as late 1971, to coin the term "Derleth Mythos." In a letter to the editor of *Nyctalops* for October 1971, Tierney laid the foundations for his later article, "The Derleth Mythos" (1972). In it he questioned the very existence of any Elder Gods in Lovecraft (and no Lovecraft text could be satisfactorily adduced to attest to their existence), and wondered whether there were any such competing entities as Derleth imagined; this established, the resulting parallelism with the Christian mythos fell through.

In order, however, definitively to disprove the Christian parallel, scholars had to come to terms with a celebrated piece of evidence that Derleth had advanced in support of his thesis—the supposed quotation from a Lovecraft letter reading "All my stories, unconnected as they may be, are based on the fundamental lore or legend that this world was inhabited at one time by another race who, in practising black magic, lost their foothold and were expelled, yet live on outside, ever ready to take possession of this earth again." Again Tierney led the way. He actually enquired of Derleth, shortly before his death, the precise citation of this quotation, and—as Dirk W. Mosig reported in his seminal article, "H. P. Lovecraft: Myth-Maker" (1976), which, though merely following up and amplifying Tierney's conclusions, remains the pivotal article in the initiation of the new trend in criticism—Derleth reportedly became angry and refused to supply an answer. The logical inference was that the "quotation" was spurious and invented (though not necessarily in conscious deception) to bolster Derleth's thesis.[20] The spuriousness of this quotation, and its superficial similarity to an authentic utterance by Lovecraft that more closely embodies his literary philosophy—"Now all my tales are based on the fundamental premise that common human laws and interests and emotions have no validity or significance in the vast cosmos-at-large. . . . To achieve the essence of real externality, whether or time or space or dimension, one must forget that such things as organic life, good and evil, love and hate, and all such local attributes of a negligible and temporary race called mankind, have any existence at all" (*SL* 2.150)—was what caused the collapse of the Derlethian interpretation. Mosig then went on to deny that the Old Ones were elementals (how, for example, could Cthulhu be called a "water elemental" when he is *trapped* in

---

20. Subsequent research has established that Derleth found the quotation in a letter addressed to him by Harold S. Farnese, a correspondent of HPL's who claimed to have found it in a HPL letter. But no such quotation appears in any extant correspondence from HPL to Farnese; and Farnese, at the time he wrote his letter to Derleth, did not have his letters from HPL in his possession. It is evident that Farnese unwittingly fabricated the quotation, based on his misunderstanding of a passage in one of HPL's letters to him. See further Schultz, "Origin."

the sunken city of R'lyeh and originated from the stars? and the correspondence of other Old Ones to elementals is even less superficially convincing), and to assert—logically enough in light of the quotation just printed—that Lovecraft's fiction is fundamentally unified philosophically. Mosig, however, could not resist lapsing into the somewhat paradoxical position of choosing those tales that he felt were "central" to his new conception of the Mythos (as Derleth and Lin Carter had done before him), although his list of twelve tales at least cut across the mutually exclusive categories established by Derleth. I now tend to regard this practice as needless save purely for convenience, especially as most commentators until recently ignored the important role of some of Lovecraft's revisions in the development of the Mythos. What is more, Mosig found the term "Cthulhu Mythos" so distasteful that he wished to substitute for it the rather awkward Yog-Sothoth Cycle of Myth. This soubriquet has (perhaps fortunately) not gained acceptance, and—although some scholars (like Robert M. Price and Will Murray) wish to retain the term "Cthulhu Mythos," perhaps largely because the introduction of a new term would be more laborious than it is worth—Donald R. Burleson and I independently arrived (although I did so at the suggestion of Scott Connors) at the term Lovecraft Mythos, which is simple and neutral enough to serve conveniently. David E. Schultz, however, believes that any such concept or term is needless—but this position, although having much justification, seems to be an extreme reaction to the Procrustean categorisations of Derleth.

The next major step was one that was long overdue—the mere assembling of literary and biographical evidence connected with Lovecraft's life and work. It is to this task that I have devoted my major attention. So many tasks had been done inadequately or incompetently that it was merely a matter of care and diligence that led to the production and availability of large amounts of primary data essential for a detailed and comprehensive portrait of Lovecraft. My first chance in this direction came when, in 1976, Kent State University Press gave me the opportunity of compiling a new bibliography of Lovecraft. This project took the bulk of the next four years of my career, and in the process of its compilation I asked for assistance from a world-wide array of scholars. Moreover, I was not content merely to copy information from prior bibliographies, but recompiled every bit of information from original sources and personal examination. The result was that I and my colleagues unearthed hundreds of works by and about Lovecraft hitherto unknown and unrecorded; in particular I completely revised the list of Lovecraft's important early publications in the amateur journals, while Dirk W. Mosig and I produced the first comprehensive list of Lovecraftiana in foreign languages. I was initially intending to include a catalogue of manuscripts, but found that such a listing would prove too bulky in an already bulky volume. I may yet compile such a listing.

The coincident emergence of Necronomicon Press allowed me to issue several important compilational works whose market potential to other firms might have been problematical. Michaud and I first compiled a collection of letters by and about Lovecraft in the letter column of *Weird Tales* magazine (1979), then followed it up with the more significant compilation of a listing of Lovecraft's personal library (1980). This latter volume has cleared up several puzzling details about Lovecraft's use of literary sources in his work and has opened avenues for much more extensive work in literary and philosophical influences upon Lovecraft. My index to the *Selected Letters* has already been noted, and its success has led me to compile another index, this time of proper names in his fiction and poetry.

A second goal of my own work, in part parallel to the desire to provide the necessary source materials for more precise work in Lovecraft studies, has been the repeated attempt to take Lovecraft away from the world of fantasy fandom and to establish him definitively in the broader world of scholarly literary criticism. This was actually my primary goal in compiling what eventually became the anthology *H. P. Lovecraft: Four Decades of Criticism*, begun in 1975. I chose from the start to try to interest a university press in the publication of this volume, and not to relegate it to one of any number of fan presses that would have expressed an interest in the book. In this undertaking I eventually (albeit laboriously) succeeded, although another of my goals for the volume—the depiction of the history of Lovecraft criticism from the 1940s to the present, and not necessarily a selection of what I thought were the best articles on Lovecraft written up to that time—was not always understood by reviewers. Nevertheless, I seem to have succeeded partially in alerting the critical world to Lovecraft's existence—if the surprisingly lengthy review of *Four Decades* by S. S. Prawer in the *Times Literary Supplement* for 19 June 1981 is any indication.

This goal was at the heart of my foundation of *Lovecraft Studies*. As early as 1977 Dirk Mosig, Marc A. Michaud, and I had discussed the establishment of such an outlet for the increasing scholarly output devoted to Lovecraft—output that was increasingly out of place in the "fan" magazines of the fantasy and science fiction field; but our plans at that time came to nothing. It was only in the spring of 1979 that Michaud and I (Mosig by this time having abandoned the field) revived the idea, and in autumn the first issue emerged. Since then it has received increasingly wider notice and is being purchased by an increasing number of university libraries.

Mosig and I were for a time the leaders, first in the battle against the Derlethian view of the Mythos, and then in the establishment of a strong foundation for scholarly work in Lovecraft. Shortly thereafter, however, other scholars joined in and began leading Lovecraft studies into exciting new channels through more comprehensive treatments of the whole body of his work and through innovative angles of interpretation. The most dynamic new force was Donald R. Burleson. Burleson began by doing extensive work in the topographical and historical sources for some of Lovecraft's New England tales; and the results of his tireless journeys across the face of New England were embodied in a brilliant article, "Humour beneath Horror: Some Sources for 'The Dunwich Horror' and 'The Whisperer in Darkness.'" Increased attention to advanced techniques of literary criticism led Burleson to further breakthroughs, especially in the comprehensive treatment of Hawthorne's influence upon Lovecraft and, most excitingly, a complete revision of the standard interpretation of "The Dunwich Horror" through the employment of myth criticism ("The Mythic Hero Archetype in 'The Dunwich Horror'"). In a certain sense Burleson has followed St Armand in the interpretation of Lovecraft in terms of imagery, symbolism, and style, but has done so far more perspicaciously through a comprehensive knowledge of Lovecraft's philosophical thought and its relations to his work. Burleson has now consolidated his thoughts on Lovecraft in a landmark volume, *H. P. Lovecraft: A Critical Study* (Greenwood Press, 1983).

In the more purely philosophical realm certain interesting strides were made by Paul Buhle, in "Dystopia as Utopia" (1976), in which he studied Lovecraft's place in social and intellectual history. Buhle—as any commentator on the philosophical thought of Lovecraft must—built upon the foundations laid by the early work of Matthew H. Onderdonk, a pioneer in this field; and I have myself attempted to elaborate some of Onderdonk's conclusions in certain essays. What is needed now is a comprehensive treatment of Lovecraft's philosophy as such—as I attempted in very brief compass to do in the first chapter of my *H. P. Lovecraft* (Starmont Reader's Guide, 1982); for before the details of his metaphysical, ethical, political, and aesthetic thought are worked out, there shall always be imprecision as to the exact relationship between Lovecraft's work and his thought.

In a slightly different direction, the prolific Robert M. Price has with great success shed light on some aspects of Lovecraft's work from the point of view of his own discipline, the history of religion. In his first article, "Higher Criticism and the *Necronomicon*" (1982), he showed how Lovecraft's mythical tome could be better explicated using the method of "higher criticism" as was applied in the nineteenth century to biblical studies. In a similar vein is a brilliant contribution, "Demythologizing Cthulhu" (1983), examining the Lovecraft Mythos again from the standpoint of mythic and religious criticism. This article may actually cause a revolution in Lovecraft studies, as its clear establishment that Lovecraft himself "demythologised" the gods of his Mythos (i.e., himself intimated in later tales that the gods are merely myths distortedly veiling scientific truths) may force us to revise our notions of the interplay between Lovecraft's philosophy and his fiction. But Price's work is of a very wide-ranging character: at times he has attempted to question certain details of Tierney's and Mosig's destruction of the "Derleth Mythos" ("The Lovecraft-Derleth Connection," 1982), at other times he has explored the details of Lovecraft's fiction—and particularly the Mythos—far more closely than previous commentators. This legacy of precision, handed down by such scholars as Faig and Mosig, can still bear much greater fruit.

The quest for producing a comprehensive understanding of Lovecraft has led in recent years to the resurrection and explication of lesser bodies of his work. In particular, modern scholars of the Lovecraft Mythos, having been forced to examine his revisions and collaborations for details concerning the Mythos, are discovering that these works are either of substantial literary merit ("The Mound," "Out of the Aeons," "The Night Ocean") or are at least full of interesting matter. Correspondingly, increasing attention has been paid to unearthing "lost" or previously unattributed revisions by Lovecraft. Mosig began the trend by discovering "The Night Ocean"; Kenneth W. Faig and I unearthed the Lovecraft-Eddy collaboration "Ashes"; I found Lovecraft's revisory hand in Henry S. Whitehead's "The Trap," while William Fulwiler deduced that Lovecraft had at least a certain hand in the conception of Whitehead's "Bothon"; most recently, Scott Connors, Robert M. Price, and I laboriously discovered the text of Duane W. Rimel's "The Tree on the Hill," which Lovecraft revised. Price also maintained that Rimel's "The Disinterment" was almost entirely ghostwritten by Lovecraft, although Rimel has declared that most of the prose in the story is his own.

Conversely, certain works generally attributed to Lovecraft have, after closer examination, been found to be spurious. The greatest efforts in this regard were again by Mosig, who definitively removed the "Lovecraft-Derleth posthumous collaborations" from consideration, since Lovecraft's hand in them in nearly every instance proved to be of the slightest; this discovery, although receiving a sort of canonisation in my bibliography, has not spread beyond the central core of Lovecraft scholars, and publishers continue to reprint the tales under Lovecraft's lucrative name. Of lesser discoveries can be ranked the discrediting by David E. Schultz, Mosig, and myself of the so-called "Complete Chronology" of tales printed (and in fact fabricated) by Derleth as by Lovecraft; the fragment "The Thing in the Moonlight," which Schultz discovered was compiled by J. Chapman Miske; the two poems, "Death" and "To the American Flag," which Mosig and I, respectively, discovered were written by

Jonathan E. Hoag; and a few other items. Probably few other apocryphal works remain in the Lovecraft corpus, although many more unknown revisions (particularly of works other than fiction) may be found in the coming years.

Lovecraft's poetry has still not garnered the attention it merits, in spite of a few keen commentators. No one (save perhaps the overzealous Mosig) would contend that this is a brilliant or even especially significant body of work, but Lovecraft did consider himself primarily a poet during his early years, and the many influences upon his poetry—from the Greek and Latin poets to the poets of Augustan England and of the later Victorian age—have yet to be noted in any sort of detail. R. Boerem wrote two articles that might perhaps initiate new interest in Lovecraft's poetry, although to date only David E. Schultz has done any further work; but Schultz's forthcoming annotated edition of *Fungi from Yuggoth* should prove to be a landmark. Part of the reason for the ignorance of Lovecraft's poetry has merely been its inaccessibility, in spite of such a volume as *A Winter Wish*; many poems have yet to be rescued from the crumbling and scarce amateur journals of the 1910s and 1920s in which they first appeared.

A similar fate has overtaken Lovecraft's essays, which in sheer bulk dwarf the fiction twice over. Although *To Quebec and the Stars*—the first volume devoted solely to Lovecraft's essays—was an auspicious venture, it has not gained followers save, in a minor way, in my own *Uncollected Prose and Poetry* volumes. A significant body of Lovecraft's nonfiction remains unpublished, and legal disputes may prevent its appearance for some time. Lovecraft's voluminous writings on amateur journalism matters—and the equally voluminous replies by other writers which they inspired—are a fertile and untouched area for anyone wishing definitively to map Lovecraft's long and extensive involvement in amateur letters.

It could well be said that the publication of the *Selected Letters* made the emergence of the new trend of criticism possible, at least in its earlier stages. This series immediately established itself as an indispensable reference tool, and Lovecraft scholars can as easily do without it as Lucretian scholars can do without the extant fragments of Epicurus. As remarked earlier, there are certainly flaws in the editing of these volumes—perhaps the most significant being the abridgement, sometimes extensive, of nearly every one of the 930 letters included in the series. Unfortunately, Lovecraft's complete correspondence may not only require generations of editing but would fill up to 100 volumes; and it will require a bold (not to say unoccupied) editor to undertake or even begin the task. That such a task may be the most urgent (or at least most important) duty in Lovecraft studies can be hinted by the fact that several scholars now regard his correspondence not only as his most important work (certainly from a biographical and philosophical standpoint) but even his most literarily brilliant. The real literary genius of Lovecraft emerges in these letters, written spontaneously and without preparation—letters more full of wit, erudition, and stylistic virtuosity than whole novels or philosophical treatises. Perhaps supplementary volumes of letters can be issued periodically, although again legal squabbles will cause possibly insuperable complications.

In conclusion I should make note of my own work in Lovecraft textual studies, and my corresponding plan to edit Lovecraft's *Collected Works* (excluding correspondence) in 13 volumes. I would never have imagined the need for a new edition of Lovecraft had I not, at the insistence of Dirk W. Mosig and Scott Connors, begun in early 1977 to make random examinations into the textual soundness of Lovecraft's works (especially the fiction) published by Arkham House. To my horror, I discovered that severe corruptions had entered into many of the texts, and that—thanks to the providential preservation of many of Lovecraft's manuscripts by R. H. Barlow—it would be possible to restore them to a form not far different from what Lovecraft had desired. Once the task of correction was begun, however, I saw no point in stopping there; my training in classical textual studies led me to explore the whole textual tradition and transmission of Lovecraft's works, and my coincident work on the Lovecraft bibliography led me to unearth and collect hundreds of lost and forgotten articles and poems by Lovecraft. All my goals in Lovecraft studies—the desire to see Lovecraft gain recognition in the broader world of general literary scholarship; the desire to lay a solid foundation for future Lovecraft work; the need to gain a comprehensive impression of Lovecraft through examination of his entire output—led gradually to my decision to begin the *Collected Works*, which will include a full textual apparatus and extensive critical commentary. A project of this scope cannot be done singly, and I have enlisted the aid of all leading Lovecraft scholars in the edition. Although it has no publisher and not even a projected date for the appearance of the first volume, a preliminary glimpse of it may be provided by David E. Schultz's brilliant forthcoming edition of Lovecraft's *Commonplace Book* (Necronomicon Press). This volume—clearly the best annotated edition of any work by Lovecraft to date—has received the assistance of many scholars; although, of course, the primary work is Schultz's.

My initial discovery of the corruptions in Lovecraft's printed texts caused a certain agitation among scholars and is now even infiltrating the foreign press. Giuseppe Lippi took brief note of my work in a new preface to the Italian *Opere Complete* (1978); and when I announced my findings at the Fifth World Fantasy Convention in autumn 1979, Kalju Kirde approached me with some alarm and asked what should be done about the translation of these corrupt texts. I was, however, unable to provide Kirde with my corrections in time for them to affect his recent German editions of Lovecraft, but I have supplied corrected texts for Franz Rottensteiner's recent edition of Lovecraft's revisions in German. My texts have also served as the basis for Masaki Abe's ten-volume edition of Lovecraft in Japanese, and a new Italian translation of Lovecraft's stories may materialise under the direction of Claudio de Nardi and Gianfranco de Turris. It may perhaps be hoped that the French will undertake to provide new translations of Lovecraft's major work and thus replace the already inadequate Jacques Papy translations of the 1950s.

The state of Lovecraft studies is, therefore, still in an exciting ferment, although the general trend toward precision and all-encompassing assessment remains constant. Enormous tasks loom for the Lovecraft scholars of the future, and in the course of time Lovecraft will take his place with other acknowledged writers of our time. Small indications are already pointing in this direction—the inclusion of Lovecraft in the 15th edition of *Bartlett's Familiar Quotations* (1980); the separate entry on Lovecraft in the 15th edition of the *Encyclopaedia Britannica*; the intelligent and appreciative mentions of Lovecraft in such scholarly works as Jack Sullivan's *Elegant Nightmares: The English Ghost Story from LeFanu to Blackwood* (Ohio University Press, 1978) and R. D. Stock's *The Holy and the Daemonic from Sir Thomas Browne to William Blake* (Princeton University Press, 1982). But such a transformation does not occur instantaneously, and there will still be a sort of "jet-lag" where modern Lovecraft scholars will be probing depths far beyond that imagined by the general literary world. At the moment it appears that the major brunt of advanced Lovecraft studies is being borne by only a handful of scholars; but Lovecraft's increasing critical reputation will, in the course of time, attract new scholars whose united efforts will grant Lovecraft and his work the place it deserves in modern literature and thought. It is not too much to hope that that placement may not be long forthcoming.

Works Cited

Bender, Barry L. "Xenophobia in the Life and Work of H. P. Lovecraft." *Lovecraft Studies* No. 4 (Spring 1981): 22–38; No. 5 (Fall 1981): 10–26 (with editorial postscript by S. T. Joshi, 27–28).

de Camp, L. Sprague. *Lovecraft: A Biography*. Garden City, NY: Doubleday, 1975.

Derleth, August. "H. P. Lovecraft: The Making of a Literary Reputation." *Books at Brown* 25 (1977): 13–25.

———. "H. P. Lovecraft and His Work." In Lovecraft's *The Dunwich Horror and Others*. Sauk City, WI: Arkham House, 1963. ix–xx.

———. *Some Notes on H. P. Lovecraft*. Sauk City, WI: Arkham House, 1959.

Long, Frank Belknap. *Howard Phillips Lovecraft: Dreamer on the Nightside*. Sauk City, WI: Arkham House, 1975.

Lovecraft, H. P. *A Winter Wish*. Ed. Tom Collins. Chapel Hill, NC: Whispers Press, 1977.

Lovecraft, H. P., and Willis Conover. *Lovecraft at Last*. Arlington, VA: Carrollton-Clark, 1975.

St Armand, Barton L. *The Roots of Horror in the Fiction of H. P. Lovecraft*. Elizabethtown, NY: Dragon Press, 1977.

Schultz, David E. "The Origin of Lovecraft's 'Black Magic' Quote." *Crypt of Cthulhu* No. 48 (St John's Eve 1987): 9–13. Rpt. in S. T. Joshi, ed. *Dissecting Cthulhu: Essays on the Cthulhu Mythos*. Lakeland, FL: Miskatonic River Press, 2011. 216–23.

R. H. Barlow and the Recognition of H. P. Lovecraft

When "little Bobby Barlow" began corresponding with Lovecraft in 1931, the master of weird fiction had no idea that his Florida associate was thirteen years old; and certainly no one could have predicted that, six years later, he would be appointed Lovecraft's literary executor and play an influential role in the rescuing of Lovecraft's work from pulp oblivion. Certainly, too, it was far from anyone's mind that R. H. Barlow would then leave the fantasy world and become not merely a poet but one of the most productive Mexican anthropologists of the century. Only Barlow's death by suicide in 1951 has prevented his recognition; but it is certainly now time to take stock of his manifold achievements, and I propose to outline his assistance in assuring Lovecraft's posthumous renown.

When we meet the teenager Barlow in 1931 it is as a rabid reader and—more importantly—collector of fantasy and horror literature. But, right from the beginning, his collecting tended not merely to books and magazines (part of his complete file of *Weird Tales* is now in the John Hay Library of Brown University, as well as his complete file of the *Fantasy Fan* and other journals) but to manuscripts. Presumably he got in touch with Lovecraft through *Weird Tales*; not long afterward he was pestering other pulp giants—Clark Ashton Smith; Robert E. Howard, E. Hoffmann Price—with requests to send their manuscripts to him. Barlow had singular perceptiveness: he did not collect hacks like Edmond Hamilton or Seabury Quinn, but only those writers who—as we can see through hindsight—were genuine artists in the weird tale. Indeed, one wonders what was the reaction of E. Hoffmann Price when he read a letter from the seventeen-year-old Barlow in 1935: "The manuscripts I want are your early ones—seriously written without a commercial market in view. Things like Stranger from Kurdistan—Sullen Jest . . ."[1]

With Lovecraft he exercised no such selectiveness—quite the reverse, for he demanded manuscripts not only of Lovecraft's tales but his poems and es-

---

1. R. H. Barlow to E. Hoffmann Price, 16 June 1935 (ms., JHL). All unpublished letters cited in this essay are in JHL.

says as well. In the early going Barlow merely wanted to read those stories of Lovecraft's that he had not read before—those that were either in manuscript or had been published in early amateur journals. As early as 1932 Barlow was retyping Lovecraft's old manuscripts, which the latter often let get worn and frayed—the extant typescript of "The Doom That Came to Sarnath" was prepared by Barlow in January 1932.[2] By early 1933 Barlow proposed a formal deal to Lovecraft: "Since I would like to make copies of all I lack of your work, I shall be glad to kill two birds with one stone . . . and make you a copy in return for the typescript."[3] In this way the manuscripts and typescripts of many early Lovecraft stories were providentially saved, since Lovecraft was in the habit of destroying manuscripts once a reliable (or, sometimes, even an unreliable) printed copy was at hand. And Lovecraft also presented Barlow with the manuscripts of most of his later stories. Barlow retained to the end the notebook containing Lovecraft's final draft of "The Shadow out of Time"—it was the only manuscript Barlow did not turn over to the John Hay Library upon Lovecraft's death.

One of Barlow's most important functions in this regard was in helping to prepare the text of Lovecraft's first two novels, *The Dream-Quest of Unknown Kadath* and *The Case of Charles Dexter Ward*. In early 1934 Barlow asked Lovecraft to unearth these items and let him read them; Lovecraft was reluctant to comply, remarking acerbically: "'Kadath' is a puerile hash of imitation Dunsany conceptions, while 'Charles Dexter Ward' is a cumbrous, creaking bit of self-conscious antiquarianism" (OFF 120). Lovecraft was in fact quite unwilling to let anyone read these now repudiated works, but Barlow kept pestering him and even suggested that he be allowed to prepare typescripts of the tales. Finally Lovecraft relented and sent off the manuscripts in October 1934. It was at this time that Barlow—in spite of his chronically bad eyesight—prepared partial typescripts of the two novels. In 1940 Barlow, now working with Derleth and Wandrei on the second Lovecraft omnibus, asked the John Hay Library to borrow these manuscripts again so that complete transcripts could be made of them; he returned them to the library in late 1941.[4] Barlow's partial typescript of the *Dream-Quest* was used as the basis of the text printed in *Beyond the Wall of Sleep* (1943); Barlow's partial typescript of *Charles Dexter Ward* should have been used by Arkham House, since it contained handwritten corrections and revisions by Lovecraft. Barlow did not make the complete transcripts: evidently he sent the manuscripts to Derleth, who has testified to

---

2. R. H. Barlow to HPL, 14 January 1932 and 21 January 1932.

3. R. H. Barlow to HPL, 10 February 1933.

4. R. H. Barlow to S. Foster Damon, 13 April 1940 and 31 December 1941.

the difficulty of decoding Lovecraft's hieroglyphics (letter to *Weird Tales*, May 1941; *Weird Writer* 99-100).

But Barlow quickly went from reading and collecting to writing and publishing. I have no intention of studying Barlow's fiction, but we should certainly note in passing how rapid was his progress from the early and embarrassingly crude "Annals of the Jinns" (serialised in the *Fantasy Fan*) to such a tale as "A Dim-Remembered Story" (1936)—written, we must remember, by an eighteen-year-old. Lovecraft's comment on it is not overstatement:

> Holy Yuggoth, but it's a masterpiece! *Magnificent* stuff—it will bear comparison with the best of CAS! Splendid rhythm, poetic imagery, emotional modulations, & atmospheric power. Tsathoggua! But *literature* is certainly your forte, say what you will! . . . You've rung the bell this time! All the cosmic sweep of Wandrei's early work& infinitely more substance. Keep it up! (OFF 351)

One wonders what a mark Barlow would have made in weird fiction had he continued to produce work of this quality. As it is, his anthropological interests became paramount, and even among his slim output of later poetry we have only the so-called "Barlow Tributes" to Lovecraft as reminders of his weird work.

On the publishing side Barlow was no less prolific—at least in plans, if not in results. As a youth Barlow was so brimming with ideas that he had trouble finishing many of them. When Henry S. Whitehead died in late 1932, Barlow conceived the plan of issuing Whitehead's selected letters; he collected letters for years, but the project ultimately came to nothing. He wished to issue a collection of C. L. Moore's tales; he planned a collection of Clark Ashton Smith's poetry, *Incantations*; after Lovecraft's death he seemed to be working with material by Edith Miniter, and was perhaps planning a bibliography of her work. All these ventures, too, came to naught, although *Incantations* may have been the nucleus of what became *Nero and Other Poems*, issued in 1937 by the Futile Press, with which Barlow was connected (see below). But among the most interesting projects were various collections of work by Lovecraft.

In early 1933 Barlow learned of the existence of the unbound sheets for Lovecraft's *Shunned House*, which W. Paul Cook had printed in 1928. Enough letters by both Lovecraft and Barlow exist so that we can trace the history of Barlow's undertaking quite precisely. Lovecraft first announced, evidently in response to a query by Barlow:

> As for my "Shunned House"—it never got as far as the stage of publication, although W. Paul Cook meant to bring it out as a small, thin separate book. When his affairs smashed up in 1930 the text had just been printed—in an edition of 250 (actually 300)—& the unbound sheets now repose at the home of Cook's sister in Sunapee, N. H. (OFF 50)

Barlow replied: "Awfully sorry the *Shunned House* didn't quite get published. Do you suppose he'd let some one else market—perhaps crudely bind—the sheets? It's too bad to let them rot."[5] To which Lovecraft responded: "As for 'The Shunned House'—I fancy Cook would be glad if anybody could market it . . . although I don't believe anybody could" (*OFF* 53). But shortly thereafter a spanner was thrown into the works:

> About "The Shunned House"—I'm surprised that Cook hasn't written you the embarrassing news. After all, he'll be obliged to withdraw his permission for the publishing venture, since he has discovered a previous agreement which he had forgotten when writing you. It seems that a year or two ago he promised to let Walter J. Coates—editor of *Driftwind*—handle the binding & distribution in case any action was decided upon, but in the meanwhile he had forgotten all about the matter. Last month he told Coates, merely as a matter of current news, of his new arrangement with you—whereupon Coates reminded him of the old arrangement & reproached him concerning his forgetfulness! Surely an embarrassing situation! As it is, he feels that—as a matter of honour—he'll have to let Coates handle the job (i.e., in case the edition isn't lost after all!) when the time comes; though he is tremendously sorry to disappoint you after having made the agreement with you in perfect good faith. (*OFF* 60)

But by early 1934 Lovecraft announced:

> Arrangements for Coates' issuing "The Shunned House" have fallen through, so Cook has recalled your own wish to bind & market the thing. Do you still want to bother with this matter? Cook—rather prematurely—says he is asking his sister to forward the unbound edition to you . . . but I'm advising him to wait & see whether you are still in a position to consider the matter. Coates kept delaying & delaying, until at last it became clear that he could do nothing in his desperate financial state. (*OFF* 103)

At this time Lovecraft thought that only 115 of the 300 copies printed by Cook survived;[6] but in May 1935 Cook discovered 150 more copies of the unbound sheets and sent these to Barlow (*OFF* 273). Barlow, however, did little with these copies, binding only about eight.

In late 1935 Samuel Loveman enters the picture. Lovecraft wrote:

> Loveman wants to talk business with you about "The Shunned House". He thinks he can actually make it modestly profitable by handling it in his bookshop [Dauber & Pine] and mentioning it in his catalogue. In order to do this he would need from 6 to 12 complete bound copies to start with, as well

---

5. R. H. Barlow to HPL, 10 February 1933.
6. HPL to Duane W. Rimel, 13 May 1934.

as a guarantee that you could fill orders (i.e., by binding up copies) within a reasonable time of receipt. (OFF 291)

But this too came to nothing, and Lovecraft wrote to Barlow in early 1936 with some impatience: "Loveman has been expecting you to get in touch with him regarding the distribution of the S. H., & felt quite disillusioned at his failure to hear from you" (OFF 319). Barlow and Lovecraft did distribute some unbound sheets in the course of 1935 and 1936, but it remained for Arkham House to bind 150 copies and sell them at $17.50 from 1959 to 1961.

Barlow's other great undertaking was Lovecraft's poetry. In late 1934 he wished to print *Fungi from Yuggoth* as a booklet (OFF 173-74); Lovecraft was happy enough to accede to the plan, although he characteristically told Barlow not to spend too much effort on it. Barlow in fact did nothing seriously with the idea for more than a year, but then suddenly in late 1935 he presented Lovecraft with a specimen page of the first sonnet which he had set and printed on his own press. Lovecraft remarked: "Well, bless my soul! What kind of an enterprise is this which I see under way? Yes—the Fungus is correct, even unto the fi and fl, so far as I can see. Won't have to return the proof. But don't waste too much time on junk like this!" (OFF 304). But Lovecraft was concerned to have the *Fungi* printed as accurately as possible, and he did not evidently trust the typescript Barlow had made of the sonnet series some years before; he had difficulty, however, retrieving the carbon copy of his manuscript that he had lent earlier to Louis Smith, another young disciple who in association with William Frederick Anger had also wished to print the *Fungi*. But then, in 1936, Barlow dropped another bombshell, as Lovecraft records:

> Now about this matter of the Collected Poetical Works of H. P. Lovecraft—I'll consider it when I have a finished copy of Klarkash-Ton's "Incantations" in my hands. One thing at a time! But even then there won't be much to add. Most of my verse was utter tripe, as you'll see when I shew you some of the old-time specimens for fun. I wouldn't have it printed again for the world! "Nemesis," "Recapture," "The Ancient Track," and "The Outpost" are all right for inclusion—& I'll give a verdict on "The Nightmare Lake" when I have time to burrow for it in my files.... I have a lot of other old weird verse—some of which I shall let Wollheim & other kid editors reprint in their magazines—but I don't think I'd want it in a collection. However, I'll see when I exhume it. Of non-weird verse perhaps 3 or 4 items are worth preserving—but they ought not to go in a collection predominantly weird. (OFF 338-39)

It was at this critical time that, evidently on Barlow's suggestion, the *Fungi* took the shape it now holds. The sonnet "Recapture," written in November 1929 before the *Fungi* proper, was originally not part of the series at all; it was apparently at Barlow's suggestion that it was inserted into the *Fungi*. Lovecraft initially placed it at the end, but Barlow recommended that it be placed third to last, before "Evening Star" and "Continuity." Lovecraft came to agree with this arrangement, remarking: "'Recapture' seems somehow more specific & localised in spirit than either of the others named, hence would go better before them—allowing the Fungi to come to a close with more diffusive ideas" (OFF 342).

It was also at this time that Lovecraft sent to Barlow a list of the weird poems he felt worth preserving; of course Lovecraft had early laughed out of court Barlow's grandiose plan to publish Lovecraft's collected poetry. But in July 1936 Barlow and Lovecraft both decided that the *Fungi* should be a separate chapbook and the rest of the fantastic poetry constitute another volume. Why did these projects never materialise? Partially it was—as Lovecraft knew— Barlow's youthful impatience: he no sooner started one project than he became filled with enthusiasm for another. Barlow's family life was, moreover, not entirely stable, and when Barlow moved to Kansas in late 1936 Lovecraft noted: "Glad your present environment shews some indications of stability, & trust you can in course of time transport and reestablish the Dragon Fly Press & Bindery & other typically Cassian institutions in wild western soil" (OFF 392).

Barlow's actual publications seem meagre only when compared to his grand schemes, which came to nothing. There were first his two exquisitely printed issues of the *Dragon Fly*, produced for the National Amateur Press Association, which he had joined at Lovecraft's suggestion. There was Frank Belknap Long's *The Goblin Tower* (1935), on which Lovecraft helped to set type. There was a surprise Christmas present for Lovecraft, *The Cats of Ulthar* (1935). We can get inklings of this project as early as October 1935: Barlow, well aware of Lovecraft's typographical fastidiousness, wished to secure a proper text of the tale, so he slyly asked Lovecraft about the textual accuracy of the *Weird Tales* printing, to which Lovecraft replied (without, clearly, suspecting anything): "About 'The Cats of Ulthar'—I don't recall any particular misprint in WT—either original version or reprinting" (OFF 300).

Of course, we cannot forget the secret printing and distribution of the broadside "The Battle That Ended the Century." There is abundant evidence in Lovecraft's letters that he and Barlow wrote the spoof in the summer of 1934 when Lovecraft was visiting Barlow in Florida, and that Barlow typed and mimeographed it on his press, distributing it to their colleagues after Lovecraft had left Florida: this would make it difficult to attribute the whole thing to Lovecraft. The conspiratorial air in some of Lovecraft's letters to Barlow of this period is very amusing; note this passage, commenting on a letter Lovecraft had received from Frank Long:

Note the signature—Chimesleep Short—which indicates that our spoof has gone out & that he at least thinks I've seen the thing. Keep mum—if you didn't know anything about it, you'd consider it merely a whimsical trick of his own—& if you'd merely seen the circular, you wouldn't think it worth commenting upon. I'm ignoring the matter in my reply. (*OFF* 146)

Two years later, in 1936, Barlow typed and printed another broadside for Lovecraft, "Some Current Motives and Practices," dealing with some heated amateur disputes. After Lovecraft's death Barlow produced two large and impressive issues of *Leaves*, containing much work by the Lovecraft circle, and edited the Futile Press edition of Lovecraft's commonplace book—a remarkably prophetic publication in 1938.

It is difficult to avoid the conclusion that the death of Lovecraft in 1937 significantly curbed Barlow's enthusiasm both as a writer and as a publisher, and that it was this, as much as his later inability to work harmoniously with Derleth and Wandrei, that caused his retreat from fantasy. Nevertheless, in spite of the shock and grief Barlow must have felt at Lovecraft's passing, he faithfully and diligently undertook his appointed task as Lovecraft's literary executor. And it is here that Barlow's great foresight should be most enthusiastically praised; for he unhesitatingly felt that Lovecraft's effects—especially his manuscripts—should be preserved for posterity and future scholarship, and he immediately turned over the bulk of Lovecraft's papers to the John Hay Library, which initially was not very eager to accept them. Barlow also gave to the library Lovecraft's files of *Weird Tales*, filling in any gaps with his own collection; he contacted Lovecraft's associates and urged them to donate their letters from Lovecraft, and many did so. This whole process took several years, as Barlow was moving frequently, from Kansas to San Francisco and then to Mexico; by 1942 he told S. Foster Damon, then curator of the Harris Collection of the John Hay Library, that he was "about clean[ed] out of Lovecraft mss., unless there were some in Kansas City."[7] What is harrowing is the following testimonial made by a young man of twenty-one: "All manuscripts of whatever nature, deposited by me in the Harris Collection (Manuscript Division) at the John Hay Library, are in the event of my death to become the property of that institution." This document is dated March 3, 1939; true, Barlow surely wished to ensure the safety of the manuscripts, but we can only wonder whether this thought alone dictated Barlow's avowal.

In 1946 there arose a peculiar exchange of correspondence between Barlow and the John Hay Library, and Barlow's letter is worth quoting at length to show the shift in his intellectual perspective:

---

7. R. H. Barlow to S. Foster Damon, 4 October 1942.

> It occurs to me that we might be able to make a horse-trade. Obviously, all the Lovecraft material should stay in your hands, together with the manuscripts deposited in 1937 and a collection of books (most of the items mentioned in his study "Supernatural Horror in Literature") which I retain here and which is probably the most complete collection of its sort anywhere. This includes copies from Lovecraft's library, from my own 1935 Florida library, etc.—many presentation copies of Merritt, George Allan England, etc. . . .
>
> If the John Hay Library is interested in rounding out the Lovecraft Collection with some 150 scarce books of weird and fantastic fiction, and acquiring permanent title to all the Lovecraft mss., I think I could be tempted into such a deal by the offer of *printing equipment*. This may sound odd, and you may not even be interested, but I am keenly involved in the native language publications, specifically in a little Nahuati ("Aztec") paper, which I want to sustain by hook or crook, on a regular basis—and the real way to do it is to print it here in my home with the aid of native schoolteachers. Have you any old presses lying around?[8]

The library, surprisingly, did not reject this irregular offer outright: since Barlow had been so exemplary a donor to the library, the librarians seemed to feel bound to make an effort to accommodate even so unusual a request. But in the end it came—as so many of Barlow's undertakings—go nothing:

> Mrs. Hathaway has taken up your letter . . . with me and with Professor Damon and even at this length of time and after various inquiries we still feel reluctant to give the obvious answer—namely, that we have no printing machinery and no particular facilities or know how about getting any.[9]

And there the matter evidently rested.

What Barlow's exact trouble was with Derleth and Wandrei, I have not quite been able to ascertain. I suspect, however, that Derleth may have been offended that *he* had not been appointed Lovecraft's literary executor; and Derleth, although himself only twenty-eight at the time of Lovecraft's death, may have felt that Barlow was merely a nineteen-year-old upstart who could not be trusted with such a momentous task. In any case, the hostility seems entirely to have been on the side of Derleth and Wandrei: the latter reviled Barlow's memory as long as he lived. Barlow certainly lent much assistance to the founders of Arkham House: he arranged to have Lovecraft's annotated copies of *Astounding Stories* sent to Derleth as the basis of the text of *At the Mountains of Madness*, since everyone realised that the printed text was entirely

---

8. R. H. Barlow to Christine Hathaway, 1 June 1946.
9. H. B. Van Hoesen to R. H. Barlow, 9 August 1946.

unreliable;[10] and, as we have seen, he assisted Derleth in the preparation of Lovecraft's two other novels. I very much suspect that Derleth and Wandrei simply pushed Barlow, as it were, out of the way, and Barlow was in no position to fight back—perhaps, by now, he had no wish to do so. Barlow retreated to Mexico and gained more respect and satisfaction as an anthropologist than he ever did in fantasy fandom.

What, then, are Barlow's achievements in the realm of weird fiction? Certainly his own tales are not to be despised, even though they are all essentially juvenilia. But it is neither unfair nor condescending to state that Barlow will be remembered most for his early efforts to put Lovecraft on the literary map. Long before the heyday of Lovecraft scholarship in the 1970s, Barlow recognised the value of Lovecraft's letters; he attempted to rescue his poetry and essays from the oblivion of the amateur press; his preservation of Lovecraft's manuscripts and personal effects—although they were inspired by his inveterate collector's instinct and by his responsibilities as Lovecraft's executor—will be eternally remembered as making possible the ultimate textual restoration of Lovecraft's work from the bunglings of all his editors: he has thus had a posthumous triumph of his own, by helping to make the shoddy Derleth editions obsolete. It is not likely that he could himself have edited Lovecraft much better than August Derleth or Donald Wandrei, had the latter given him the opportunity: his *Commonplace Book* edition is filled with errors, even though it is light-years ahead of the two incredibly corrupt *Commonplace Book* editions prepared by Derleth (in *Beyond the Wall of Sleep* and *The Shuttered Room and Other Pieces*). Still, Barlow saw the value of Lovecraft's lesser work, and sought to preserve it, long before others did.

R. H. Barlow was not merely the consummate fan, hounding the titans of his day for manuscripts and personal information; he was a prophetic and profound scholar in fantasy, and could have done much good work had he not, for reasons still not entirely known, become alienated from the field and retired to Mexico and subsequent fame in an entirely different discipline. Poet, fantaisiste, archaeologist, anthropologist, publisher, collector, editor—all these roles did Barlow fill in less than thirty-three years of existence; what further goals his volatile temper would have undertaken had not suicide intervened, no one can say.

Works Cited

S. T. Joshi, ed. *A Weird Writer in Our Midst: Early Criticism of H. P. Lovecraft.* New York: Hippocampus Press, 2010.

---

10. August Derleth to R. H. Barlow, 21 March [1937].

A Literary Tutelage: Robert Bloch and H. P. Lovecraft

Robert Bloch (1917–1994) has never made any secret of his literary and personal debt to H. P. Lovecraft. Bloch corresponded with Lovecraft for the last four years of the latter's life, and received invaluable assistance and advice from the elder writer in the craft of weird fiction. Only now, however, are we able to probe the details of this literary tutelage, with the nearly simultaneous publication of Lovecraft's *Letters to Robert Bloch* (1993) and an augmented edition of Bloch's collection of Lovecraftian pastiches, *Mysteries of the Worm* (1993). These documents make two things very evident: first, that Bloch—who first wrote to Lovecraft when he was sixteen, had his first story professionally published when he was seventeen, and died at the age of seventy-seven a revered figure in the field, just as Lovecraft had been—quickly evolved into a skilful writer in the Lovecraftian tradition; and second, that this apprentice work is both intrinsically valuable and of consuming interest for its foreshadowing of Bloch's later and more distinguished work in the realm of psychological suspense.

Bloch first came in touch with Lovecraft in April 1933, and his first object was to read as much of Lovecraft's work as he had not previously found in magazines. To this end he asked his correspondent to lend him many tales; Lovecraft did so, supplying a list of all the tales he had written up to that time, several of which were still unpublished. In his very first letter to Bloch, however, Lovecraft himself asked his young correspondent whether he had written any weird work (*L* 7) and, if so, whether he might see samples of it. Bloch took up Lovecraft's offer in late April, sending him two short items, "The Gallows" and another work whose title is unknown.

Lovecraft's response to these pieces of juvenilia (which, along with a good many others Bloch sent to the Providence writer, do not survive) is typical: while praising them, he also gave helpful advice derived from his many years as both a critic and a practitioner of the weird tale:

> It was with the keenest interest & pleasure that I read your two brief horror-sketches; whose rhythm & atmospheric colouring convey a very genuine air of unholy immanence & nameless menace, & which strike me as promising in

the very highest degree. I think you have managed to create a dark tension & apprehension of a sort all too seldom encountered in weird fiction, & believe that your gift for this atmosphere-weaving will serve you in good stead when you attempt longer & more intricately plotted pieces.... Of course, these productions are not free from the earmarks of youth. A critic might complain that the colouring is laid on too thickly—too much overt inculcation of horror as opposed to the *subtle, gradual suggestion of concealed horror* which actually raises fear to its highest pitch. In later work you will probably be less disposed to pile on great numbers of horrific words (an early & scarcely-conquered habit of my own), but will seek rather to select a *few* words—whose precise position in the text, & whose deep associative power, will make them in effect more terrible than any barrage of monstrous adjectives, malign nouns, & unhallowed verbs. (L 10)

This is a litany that Lovecraft would repeat for at least another year; and although it took Bloch a little while to realise the wisdom of this caveat, he finally did so. Indeed, by the 1940s Bloch had already evolved that tightlipped, blandly cynical style which would serve him well in his later crime fiction—fiction that, in its relentless emphasis on the psychology of aberrant individuals, is in many ways more potently horrifying than the adjective-choked supernaturalism of his early work.

And yet, Bloch was clearly fond of this thickly laid-on horror at this stage in his career, as indeed Lovecraft was at a corresponding age and for many years later. One gauge of this tendency was Bloch's relative fondness for the tales of Lovecraft's he was reading at this time. It is understandable that he would express enthusiasm for "The Outsider," "The Hound," and "The Lurking Fear," but remain relatively cool toward At *the Mountains of Madness* and "The Shadow over Innsmouth" (L 20), where Lovecraft was attempting to rein in his adjectives and write with more scientific precision and restrained suggestiveness. Although many of Bloch's own early tales do not survive, "The Laughter of a Ghoul"—read by Lovecraft in June 1933 (L 20) and published in the *Fantasy Fan* for December 1934—seems very representative of them: "Slithering secrets dwelt within the archaic avenues of the vast and sombre forest near my manor in the hills—secrets black and hideous, haunting and unspeakable, such as demonian presences mumble nightly in the aeon-dead abysses beyond the light of stars." What Lovecraft probably liked about work of this kind—even though he also recognised that an overuse of fevered prose resulted in unintended humour—was precisely its "atmosphere-weaving," a quality he (correctly) believed sadly lacking in most of the weird fiction published in the pulps. He continually excoriated the brisk, "cheerful" style of the average pulp product, in which spectacular defiances of natural law were regarded both by the characters and by the author with a bland casualness that is fatal to convincingness. Overcoloured as Bloch's early tales may have been, they at least were attempting to achieve an *emotional preparation* for the supernatural.

A few months later Lovecraft read a story of Bloch's entitled "The Grave." Here Lovecraft's advice was the need for clarity in *motivation*. Why would a grave-robber seek his booty in an ancient graveyard, since the skeletons would all have crumbled to dust? Also, how can a skeleton remain articulated after the flesh has fallen off? How were the tunnels leading from the grave dug? Lovecraft also criticises some psychological implausibilities in one character's behaviour. Bloch manifestly took all these recommendations to heart in the course of time.

Lovecraft read something entitled "The Feast" in late June 1933, remarking that it "forms a very clever union of the macabre & the comic" (L 21). It is not clear whether this is an early version of "The Feast in the Abbey," but Lovecraft in any case read that story in September; indeed, he supplied the title, since Bloch had evidently sent it to Lovecraft without one (L 35). This is, of course, Bloch's first published story in *Weird Tales* (it appeared in the January 1935 issue), although "The Secret in the Tomb" (*Weird Tales*, May 1935) had been accepted earlier, in July 1934 (L 50). Lovecraft read the latter tale as well, although apparently not before its acceptance. He did, however, recommend some minor corrections (L 52), which Bloch seems to have made.

Both these stories evince that fascination with the mythical books of the "Cthulhu Mythos" which would remain constant throughout Bloch's early work. It was in these tales, of course, that Bloch devised Ludvig Prinn's *Mysteries of the Worm*, and Lovecraft mentions other titles that were cited in an earlier draft of "The Secret in the Tomb" but later excised (Mazonides' *Black Spell of Saboth*, Petrus Averonius' *Compendium Daemonum*). In "The Suicide in the Study" (*Weird Tales*, June 1935) we find other such titles as "the Black Rites of mad Luveh-Keraph, priest of Bast, or Comte d'Erlette's ghastly *Cultes des Goules*" (M 19). Luveh-Keraph scarcely requires elucidation, save to note that this coinage appears to be Bloch's invention, not Lovecraft's. Some have thought that Bloch merely abstracted this from one of Lovecraft's letters, which frequently include whimsical signatures of this sort; but in fact Lovecraft uses the "Luveh-Keraph" signature for the first time only in April 1935 (L 65), a month after having read "The Suicide in the Study" (L 61). In other words, he picked up the usage from Bloch's story, as a sort of wry acknowledgement.

There is not much to say about these early tales, save that they may be marginally better than most of the other material appearing in *Weird Tales*. If nothing else, the verve of their adjective-laden prose and lurid incidents is engaging. "The Secret in the Tomb" is a preposterous story about a man who battles a skeleton in his ancestral tomb. "The Feast in the Abbey" (not included in *Mysteries of the Worm*) tells of cannibalism in a mediaeval monastery. "The Suicide in the Study" is perhaps the most interesting of the lot: a reprise of the Jekyll/Hyde theme, it tells of a man who believes that the good and evil sides of every individual are *"co-existent"* (M 20) and seeks to bring up his evil side from the depths of his personality. The story is hampered by a conventional conception of what constitutes good and evil; but the evil side, when it finally emerges, presents a loathsome sight:

> Out of the darkness nightmare came; stark, staring nightmare—a monstrous, hairy figure; huge, grotesque, simian—a hideous travesty of all things human. It was black madness; slavering, mocking madness with little red eyes of wisdom old and evil; leering snout and yellow fangs of grimacing death. It was like a rotting, living skull upon the body of a black ape. It was grisly and wicked, troglodytic and wise. (M 22)

Here evil is pictured as simultaneously subhuman (the Darwinian beast) and somehow superhuman—"wise" and incapable of being controlled by our "good" side.

The early story of Bloch's that has brought him the greatest celebrity for its connexions with Lovecraft is "The Shambler from the Stars" (*Weird Tales*, September 1935). Lovecraft mentions something called "The Shambler in the Night" in a letter of November 1934 (L 55); this may be an early version of the story, although if so it is odd that Lovecraft makes no mention in his letter of its central feature—the fact that Lovecraft himself is a character in the story. We all know the story of how "The Shambler from the Stars" was provisionally accepted by Farnsworth Wright of *Weird Tales*, who felt that Bloch needed to get Lovecraft's permission to kill him off (although Wright had evidently not felt a similar need when, years before, Frank Belknap Long had done the same to Lovecraft in "The Space-Eaters"), so that Lovecraft wrote his whimsical letter to Bloch in late April 1935 authorising him "to portray, murder, annihilate, disintegrate, transfigure, metamorphose, or otherwise manhandle the undersigned in the tale entitled THE SHAMBLER FROM THE STARS" (L 67).

The critical issue about the story is not that it is a "contribution" to the "Cthulhu Mythos" but that, like Long's tale, it makes Lovecraft a character, and accordingly assists in the fostering of the Lovecraft legend—the legend of the gaunt, reclusive delver into occult mysteries. Of course, he is never named, merely identified as a "mystic in New England" who was "a writer of notable brilliance and wide reputation among the discriminating few" (M 26-27). But even more interesting, perhaps, is how *Bloch himself* has become a character in his own story. In its early parts Bloch presents a sort of objective assessment of his own career as a writer up to that point, finding much dissatisfaction in it:

> I wanted to write a real story, not the stereotyped, ephemeral sort of tale I turned out for the magazines, but a real work of art. The creation of such a masterpiece became my ideal. I was not a good writer, but that was not entirely due to my errors in mechanical style. It was, I felt, the fault of my subject matter. Vampires, werewolves, ghouls, mythological monsters—these things constituted material of little merit. Commonplace imagery, ordinary adjectival treatment, and a prosaically anthropocentric point of view were the chief detriments to the production of a really good weird tale. (M 26)

This paragraph could have come directly out of Lovecraft's writings on the subject, such as "Notes on Writing Weird Fiction" (1933). That last comment about point of view seems to derive from a letter by Lovecraft to Bloch in June 1933, in which he remarks how he had once (in the "Eyrie" for March 1924) advised "having a story told from an unconventional & non-human angle," specifically a story "from the ghoul's or werewolf's point of view" (L 21); he goes on to remark that H. Warner Munn had attempted to embody this conception in "The Werewolf of Ponkert," but had botched the job because Munn's "sympathies were still with mankind—whereas I called for sympathies wholly dissociated from mankind & perhaps violently hostile to it" (L 21). This notion is not in fact present in "The Shambler from the Stars," but does find its way into "The Dark Demon."

Lovecraft's avowed sequel to Bloch's story—"The Haunter of the Dark," written in November 1935 and published in *Weird Tales* for December 1936—continues the fusion of the real and the imaginary in its portrayal of character. Here the protagonist, Robert Blake, is said to come (like Bloch) from Milwaukee (the address given in the story—620 East Knapp Street—was in fact Bloch's address), but the apartment he occupies on a visit to Providence is transparently Lovecraft's own dwelling at 66 College Street. Then again, the titles of the stories Blake is said to have written at this time—"The Burrower Beneath," "The Stairs in the Crypt," "Shaggai," "In the Vale of Pnath," and "The Feaster from the Stars" (DH 94)—form an exquisite union of elements found in both Bloch's and Lovecraft's stories. In early March 1935 Lovecraft had wryly remarked on Bloch's success in landing tales with titles like "The ⸺ in the ⸺" (LS 11); he echoes them in the above list, although his own tales very frequently have titles of this sort as well. At the end of "The Haunter of the Dark" Robert Blake is left a glassy-eyed corpse staring through a window—a somewhat more tasteful demise than that of the victim of "The Shambler from the Stars," who ends up torn to pieces by a nameless entity.

For "The Shambler from the Stars" Lovecraft devised the Latin title of *Mysteries of the Worm—De Vermis Mysteriis—*and claimed to have modified the narrator's statement of his ignorance of Latin, "since knowledge of elementary Latin is so universal" (*L* 65). And yet, the narrator's lack of knowledge of Latin is critical to the development of the plot, since it is precisely because he finds a Latin copy of *De Vermis Mysteriis*, which he is unable to read, that he feels the need to seek out his New England correspondent and show him the work. (Bloch's deficiencies in Latin make themselves all too evident in another title he devised, the nonsensical *Daemonolorum*, cited in "The Brood of Bubastis" [*M* 95] and elsewhere.)

"The Dark Demon" (*Weird Tales*, November 1936) is interesting in this context because it again displays Lovecraft as a character and, more important, becomes a parable for his early assistance to Bloch's literary development. Here the narrator testifies that he had come into contact with the writer Edgar Gordon, a "reclusive dreamer" (*M* 62) living in the same town. They develop a warm correspondence and also meet in person: "What Edgar Gordon did for me in the next three years can never adequately be told. His able assistance, friendly criticism and kind encouragement finally succeeded in making a writer of sorts out of me, and after that our mutual interest formed an added bond between us" (*M* 62). Lovecraft does not seem to have read this tale prior to publication (*L* 84), but he warmly commends it; he makes no mention of the above tribute, but no doubt he saw clearly its import and was heartened by it. Although Lovecraft himself is mentioned by name elsewhere in the story (*M* 62), Gordon becomes a transparent Lovecraft figure in his bizarre dreams and the very strange work he begins writing as a result of it: the "stories [were] in first-person, but the narrator was not a *human being*" (*M* 64). Gordon, when pressed by the narrator as to where he is getting his ideas, makes cloudy references to a "Dark One," remarking: "He isn't a destroyer—merely a superior intelligence who wishes to gain mental rapport with human minds, so as to enable certain—ah—exchanges between humanity and Those beyond" (*M* 66). This idea is unquestionably derived from Lovecraft's "The Whisperer in Darkness," in which aliens from the depths of space wish to take the brains of selected human beings on fantastic cosmic voyagings.

The mention of dreams is interesting, since in August 1933 Lovecraft, commenting with amazement on Bloch's claim that he dreamed only twice a year, related a hideous dream in which some mediaeval soldiers attempt to hunt down a monstrous entity but to their horror see it meld insidiously with the body of their leader. Bloch claimed to be working on a story based upon this dream (see *L* 33), but apparently never completed it; it does not survive. He does, however, in "The Dark Demon" echo Lovecraft's scorn of conventional Freudian interpretations of dreams. Bloch's narrator remarks, "Gordon's fantasies were far from the ordinary Freudian sublimation or repression types" (*M* 63); Lovecraft in his letter had written: "I may add that all I know of dreams seems to contradict flatly the 'symbolism' theories of Freud. It may be that others, with less sheer phantasy filling their minds, have dreams of the Freudian sort; but it is very certain that I don't" (L 31).

For all Lovecraft's advice to Bloch, he does not seem to have done much actual revision of Bloch's work, as he did—many times unasked—with other young colleagues. In June 1933 Lovecraft remarks that "I added corrections here & there" to a story entitled "The Madness of Lucian Grey," which was accepted for publication by *Marvel Tales* but was never published and is now non-extant. A blurb in *Marvel Tales* described it as "a weird-fantasy story of an artist who was forced to paint a picture . . . and the frightful thing that came from it" (L 13n), which makes one immediately think of Lovecraft's "Pickman's Model." Lovecraft seems to have done much more extensive work in November 1933 on a story called "The Merman":

> I have read "The Merman" with the keenest interest & pleasure, & am returning it with a few annotations & emendations. . . . My changes—the congested script of which I hope you can read—are of two sorts; simplifications of diffuse language in the interest of more direct & powerful expression, & attempts to make the emotional modulations more vivid, lifelike, & convincing at certain points where the narrative takes definite turns. (L 41)

But unfortunately this tale also does not survive.

If any extant work of Bloch's can be called a Lovecraft revision, it is "Satan's Servants," written in February 1935. Bloch comments that the story came back from Lovecraft "copiously annotated and corrected, together with a lengthy and exhaustive list of suggestions for revision" (S 117), and goes on to say that many of Lovecraft's additions are now undetectable, since they fused so well with his own style:

> From the purely personal standpoint, I was often fascinated during the process of revision by the way in which certain interpolated sentences or phrases of Lovecraft's seemed to dovetail with my own work—for in 1935 I was quite consciously a disciple of what has since come to be known as the "Lovecraft school" of weird fiction. I doubt greatly if even the self-professed "Lovecraft scholar" can pick out his actual verbal contributions to the finished tale; most of the passages which would be identified as "pure Lovecraft" are my work; all of the sentences and bridges he added are of an incidental nature and merely supplement the text. (S 118)

And yet, it is not surprising that the original version of the story was rejected by Farnsworth Wright of *Weird Tales*; his comment as noted by Bloch—"that the plot-structure was too flimsy for the extended length of the narrative" (S 117)—is an accurate assessment of this overly long and unconvincing story.

"Satan's Servants" had initially been dedicated to Lovecraft, and after its rejection Bloch urged Lovecraft to collaborate on its revision; but, aside from whatever additions and corrections he made, Lovecraft bowed out of full-fledged collaboration. He did, however, have much to say on the need for historical accuracy in this tale of seventeenth-century New England, and he had other suggestions as to the pacing of the story. Bloch apparently did some revisions in 1949 for its publication in *Something about Cats*, but the story still labours under its excess verbiage and its rather comical ending: a pious Puritan, facing a mob of hundreds of devil-worshippers in a small Maine town, defeats them all by literally pounding them with a Bible! It is just as well that "Satan's Servants" lay in Bloch's files until resurrected as a literary curiosity.

It is with "The Faceless God" (*Weird Tales*, May 1936) that Bloch begins his twofold fascination with Egypt and with the Lovecraftian "god" Nyarlathotep. One of Bloch's earliest enquiries to Lovecraft was an explanation of some of the invented names and terms that appear in some of his tales. In regard to one such query Lovecraft responds in May 1933: "'Nyarlathotep' is a horrible messenger of the evil gods to earth, who usually appears in human form" (*L* 11–12). Bloch, who in his early days was attempting pictorial art, actually drew a picture of Nyarlathotep, which Lovecraft charitably says "just fits my conception" (*L* 21).

The figure of Nyarlathotep is one of the most intriguing in Lovecraft—perhaps because it was never fully developed or coherently conceived. Nyarlathotep is commonly believed to be a shape-shifter—a view evidently derived from some random passages in *The Dream-Quest of Unknown Kadath*, especially where Nyarlathotep himself refers to "my thousand other forms" (MM 403). One gains the feeling, however, that this was a sort of makeshift excuse for Lovecraft to present Nyarlathotep in so many diverse guises in his work. Bloch could not have read the *Dream-Quest* (it was not typed or circulated in Lovecraft's lifetime), but he uses Nyarlathotep in very much the same way as Lovecraft; indeed, it could be said that Bloch has elaborated the conception more exhaustively than Lovecraft himself did.

It would be of interest to know which of Lovecraft's stories mentioning Nyarlathotep Bloch did in fact read. I see no evidence that he had at this time read the early prose-poem "Nyarlathotep" (1920), which had appeared only in amateur magazines; it is here that the connexion between Nyarlathotep and Egypt is explicitly made, and it is this connexion that Bloch develops. The prose-poem is in fact listed in the list of stories Lovecraft sent to Bloch in April 1933, but it is crossed off; and the subsequent letters do not suggest that Lovecraft ever lent Bloch the story. If Lovecraft had in fact sent the item, one imagines that he would not have had to "define" Nyarlathotep as he did in the letter in May. Nyarlathotep is otherwise very glancingly mentioned in "The Rats in the Walls" (1923), extensively cited in *The Dream-Quest of Unknown Kadath* (1926–27) (which Bloch did not read), and glancingly cited in "The Whisperer in Darkness" (1930) and "The Dreams in the Witch House" (1932).

In fact, Bloch probably derived most of his information on Nyarlathotep from "The Haunter of the Dark," the story Lovecraft wrote in November 1935 and dedicated to Bloch. Toward the end of the tale the character Robert Blake writes in his diary: "What am I afraid of? Is it not an avatar of Nyarlathotep, who in antique and shadowy Khem even took the form of man?" (*DH* 114). Here is the Egyptian connexion that Bloch picked up on. "The Faceless God" tells the story of the attempts of an evil Dr Stugatche[1] to unearth a statue of Nyarlathotep buried in the sands of Egypt, only to meet a fittingly horrible end. I am not clear why Bloch conceived of Nyarlathotep as faceless—a detail that perhaps inadvertently recalls Lovecraft's night-gaunts.

Bloch notes that his Egyptological ("or Egyptillogical") tales were "conscious attempts to move away from Lovecraft's literary turf" (*M* 255). How successful Bloch was, in this early period, in these attempts is debatable. He perhaps had not read—or did not know of Lovecraft's hand in—"Under the Pyramids" (the story published in *Weird Tales* as "Imprisoned with the Pharaohs" and attributed to Harry Houdini), and of course Nyarlathotep's Egyptian connexion had indeed been established by Lovecraft. But such a story as "The Opener of the Way" (*Weird Tales*, October 1936), while still perhaps somewhat Lovecraftian in style, does not employ Lovecraft's pantheon of invented deities but seeks to invest horror in the real gods of Egypt (in this case Anubis). "The Brood of Bubastis" (*Weird Tales*, March 1937) is very similar: aside from insignificant references to *De Vermis Mysteriis*, this tale is nothing but a story of the cat-goddess Bubastis, and involves the ingenious idea of an ancient Egyptian colony in England. Lovecraft read the story about two months before his death, noting: "Your Bubastis story is excellent, despite the dubious light in which it presents my beloved felidae" (*L* 87).

"The Secret of Sebek" (*Weird Tales*, November 1937)—a story probably

---

1. This is the name of the character as given in the *Weird Tales* appearance of the story. Subsequent appearances (beginning with *The Opener of the Way* [1945]) give the name as Carnoti. Stugatche is clearly Bloch's original name for this character, and it is mentioned in several letters by HPL. Bloch remarks of it: "The name comes from a group of imaginary characters who—believe it or not—were invented to serve as players on teams in a card-game called 'Baseball'—the invention of my friends Herb Williams and Harold Gauer.... I later used the name for a central character in my story, 'The Faceless God'" (*L* 70n.205). Perhaps August Derleth advised Bloch to change the name for the book appearance.

written just after Lovecraft's death—is an interesting case. The story is set in New Orleans, and concerns the god Sebek, who has the head of a crocodile and the body of a man. A character sees such a figure in a costume ball and, thinking the man in disguise, attempts to pull off his crocodile mask—only to find that "I felt beneath my fingers, not a mask, but living flesh!" (M 129). The dominant influence on this story appears to be "Through the Gates of the Silver Key," which is likewise set in New Orleans and likewise concludes apocalyptically with a character who pulls off an actual mask from another character (Randolph Carter in the body of the extraterrestrial wizard Zkauba), finding a horribly alien countenance underneath. Again, only some random mentions of invented books make this a "Cthulhu Mythos" story.

"Fane of the Black Pharaoh" (*Weird Tales*, December 1937) is perhaps the most interesting of Bloch's Egyptian tales, both for its intrinsic effectiveness and for its connexions with Lovecraft. This is an entire story about the pharaoh Nephren-Ka. The name had been invented by Lovecraft, and is first cited in the early story "The Outsider" (one of Bloch's favourites): "Now I . . . play by day amongst the catacombs of Nephren-Ka in the sealed and unknown valley of Hadoth by the Nile" (*DH* 52). Lovecraft resurrects him in a single tantalising sentence in "The Haunter of the Dark": "The Pharaoh Nephren-Ka built around it [the Shining Trapezohedron] a temple with a windowless crypt, and did that which caused his name to be stricken from all monuments and records" (*DH* 106). Bloch elaborates upon this sentence, although departing somewhat from it. In "Fane of the Black Pharaoh" Nephren-Ka is rumoured to have been a worshipper of Nyarlathotep, and his "atrocious sacrifices" (M 134) caused him to be deposed. Then, hiding in a secret temple, Nephren-Ka is granted the gift of prophecy by Nyarlathotep and paints an enormous series of pictures of the years and centuries to come. A modern explorer learns just how much truth there is in this old fable.

"The Shadow from the Steeple" (*Weird Tales*, September 1950) simultaneously concludes the trilogy begun with "The Shambler from the Stars" and "The Haunter of the Dark" and is Bloch's final word about Nyarlathotep. As early as December 1936 Lovecraft wrote, ". . . I hope to see 'The Shadow in the Steeple' when you get it written" (*L* 84); this is an early version of the story, as Bloch notes (S 118–19), but for some reason he put it aside for many years before resuming it. The story as we have it was either written or revised around 1950, for it makes mention of Edmund Fiske's "fifteen-year quest" (M 183) to discover the truth about the death of Robert Blake.

As in "The Dark Demon," both Bloch and Lovecraft become characters in the story—the latter explicitly and by name. The narrator notes: "Blake had been a precocious adolescent interested in fantasy-writing, and as such became a member of the 'Lovecraft circle'—a group of writers maintaining correspondence with one another and with the late Howard Phillips Lovecraft, of Providence" (M 180). Later it is said that "another Milwaukee author" (M 181) had written a story about Nephren-Ka entitled "Fane of the Black Pharaoh"! With somewhat questionable taste, Bloch even incorporates Lovecraft's death into the fabric of the plot, noting that Fiske had intended in early 1937 to visit Lovecraft and query him about Blake's death, but that Lovecraft's own passing foiled these plans. Bloch has written on many occasions of the shock he felt at hearing of Lovecraft's death, and the narrator of "The Shadow from the Steeple" remarks that Lovecraft's "unexpected passing plunged Fiske into a period of mental despondency from which he was slow to recover" (M 185); but I still wonder whether it was proper for Bloch to make fictional use of both Lovecraft's life and his demise in this fashion. In any event, it transpires that Dr Dexter—the "superstitious" (*DH* 114) physician who had hurled the Shining Trapezohedron into the river after Blake's death—is Nyarlathotep himself, a clever twist on Lovecraft's premise. The story also effectively incorporates features from the sonnet "Nyarlathotep" from Lovecraft's *Fungi from Yuggoth* (1929-30), which says that ". . . at last from inner Egypt came / The strange dark one to whom the fellahs bowed" and that "wild beasts followed him and licked his hands."

Bloch's Egyptian tales may have been an attempt to escape partially from Lovecraft's influence, but we have seen that they were only indifferently successful in that objective, although many of them are quite successful as stories. Bloch was so steeped in Lovecraft's work at this time that many borrowings may well have been unconscious. Hence something so slight as one character's observation in "The Grinning Ghoul" (*Weird Tales*, June 1936) that there is no dust on the stairs of a crypt (M 57) may be an echo of the similarly dustfree corridors of the ancient city in *At the Mountains of Madness*, swept clean by the passing of a shoggoth. "The Creeper in the Crypt" (*Weird Tales*, July 1937) is set in Arkham and makes clear allusion to Lovecraft's "The Dreams in the Witch House"; but it may also betray the influence of "The Shadow over Innsmouth" (the narrator, after his experiences, seeks aid from the federal government to suppress the horror), and also perhaps of "The Terrible Old Man," as the tale involves a Polish and an Italian criminal who kidnap a man only to undergo a loathsome fate in the cellar of an old house, just as in Lovecraft's story a Pole, a Portuguese, and an Italian seek to rob the Terrible Old Man but meet death at his hands instead.

"The Sorcerer's Jewel" (*Strange Stories*, February 1939) is clearly a variation on "The Haunter of the Dark" and its Shining Trapezohedron. A character refers to a "Star of Sechmet":

> "Very ancient, but not costly. Stolen from the crown of the Lioness-headed Goddess during a Roman invasion of Egypt. It was carried to Rome and placed in the vestal girdle of the High-Priestess of Diana. The barbarians took it, cut the jewel into a round stone. The black centuries swallowed it." (M 155)

This is precisely analogous to the "history" of the Trapezohedron, from remote antiquity to the present, provided by Lovecraft in "The Haunter of the Dark"—and it is in this passage that Lovecraft mentions Nephren-Ka. And, just as Blake, when looking into the Shining Trapezohedron, "saw processions of robed, hooded figures whose outlines were not human, and looked on endless leagues of desert lined with carved, sky-reaching monoliths" (DH 104), so a similar experience befalls a character in "The Sorcerer's Jewel":

> A swirling as of parted mists. A dancing light. The fog was dispersing, and it seemed to be opening up—opening to a view that receded far into the distance.... At first only angles and angles, weaving and shifting in light that was of no color, yet phosphorescent. And out of the angles, a flat black plain that stretched upward, endlessly without horizon.... (M 156–57)

But Bloch's early Lovecraftian tales may be of the greatest interest, at least as far as Bloch's own subsequent career is concerned, for the hints they provide of how he metamorphosed his writing from the florid supernaturalism of his youth to the psychological suspense of his maturity. At first glance, these two modes could not be more different; but in several tales of the late 1930s through the 1950s, Bloch shows how elements from both can be fused to produce a new amalgam.

The first thing Bloch had to do was to gain control of his style. Already by late 1934 Lovecraft is noting that "The tendency toward overcolouring so marked last year is waning rapidly, & your command of effective diction . . . is becoming more & more dependable" (L 55). One of the stories that elicited this comment was "The Grinning Ghoul," and indeed it is one of the first of Bloch's stories that plays on the distinction between psychological and ontological horror. The protagonist is a "moderately successful practising psychiatrist" (M 51), one of whose patients is a professor who admits to having bizarre dreams. Naturally, the psychiatrist initially dispenses with the dreams as mere vagaries, but later learns that they have an all too real source.

Still more remarkable, and one of the finest stories of Bloch's early period, is the uncollected tale "Black Bargain" (*Weird Tales*, May 1942).[2] Here both the Lovecraftian idiom and the customary Lovecraftian setting have been abandoned totally, and the subtle incursion of horror in a very mun-

---

2. I am grateful to Robert M. Price for providing me with the text of this story.

dane environment produces potently chilling effects. A cynical and world-weary pharmacist supplies some odd drugs—aconite, belladonna, and the like—to a down-and-outer who comes into his store clutching a large black book in German black-letter. A few days later the customer returns, but he has been transformed: he is spruced up with new clothes and claims that he has been hired by a local chemical supply house. As the man, Fritz Gulther, and the pharmacist celebrate the former's good fortune at a bar, the pharmacist notices something anomalous about the man's shadow: its movements do not seem to coincide with Gulther's. Thinking himself merely drunk, the pharmacist attempts to put the incident out of his mind.

Gulther then offers the pharmacist a job at the chemical company as his assistant. Going there, the pharmacist finds in Gulther's office the book he had been carrying—it is, of course, *De Vermis Mysteriis*. Eventually he worms the truth out of Gulther: Gulther had uttered an incantation, made a sacrifice, and called up the Devil, who had offered him success on one condition: "'He told me that I'd have only one rival, and that this rival would be a part of myself. It would grow with my success'" (74). Sure enough, Gulther's shadow seems both to be growing and to be subsuming Gulther's own life-force. As Gulther begins to panic, the pharmacist suggests that they prepare a counter-incantation to reverse the effect; but when he returns to Gulther's office with chemicals he has brought from his pharmacy, he finds Gulther transformed:

> I sat. Gulther rested on the desk nonchalantly swinging his legs.
> "All that nervousness, that strain, has disappeared. But before I forget it, I'd like to apologize for telling you that crazy story about sorcery and my obsession. Matter of fact, I'd feel better about the whole thing in the future if you just forget that all this ever happened." (76)

The pharmacist, dazed, agrees, but he knows that something has gone wrong. In fact, the shadow has now totally usurped Gulther.

It is not the use of *De Vermis Mysteriis* that represents the Lovecraftian connexion in this fine, understated tale; instead, it is Gulther's concluding transformation. In effect, the shadow has taken possession of Gulther's body and ousted his own personality—in exactly the same way that, in "The Thing on the Doorstep" (1933), Asenath Waite ousts the personality of her husband Edward Derby from his body and casts it into her own body. The concluding scene in "Black Bargain" is very similar to a scene in Lovecraft's story where Derby's personality is evicted while he is being driven back to Arkham from Maine by the narrator, Daniel Upton. Asenath (in Derby's body) remarks: "'I hope you'll forget my attack back there, Upton. You know what my nerves are, and I guess you can excuse such things'" (*DH* 291).

Several years later Bloch wrote another powerful tale, "The Unspeakable

Betrothal" (*Avon Fantasy Reader*, 1949)—whose title, Bloch has repeatedly insisted, is not his. Here too we encounter a prose style radically different from the adjective-riddled hyperbole of "The Feast in the Abbey," and Bloch effectively experiments with stream-of-consciousness in capturing the visions that plague a young girl both at night and by day:

> But everything kept going round and round, and when Aunt May walked past the bed she seemed to flatten out like a shadow, or one of the things, only she made a loud noise which was really the thunder outside and now she was sleeping really and truly even though she heard the thunder but the thunder wasn't real nothing was real except the things, that was it nothing was real any more but the things. (M 168)

These visions—which convince the girl's family and friends that she is psychologically aberrant—again prove to be based upon reality, and at the end she is transported into space by the entities have infiltrated her mind. Two years prior to the publication of this story, Bloch had written his first non-supernatural novel of psychological horror, *The Scarf* (1947); and the rest of his career would see an alteration between supernaturalism and psychological suspense, with intermittent fusions of the two. "The Unspeakable Betrothal" is such a fusion in its sensitive delineation of a psyche that has been rendered subtly non-human by outside sources. And yet, even here the influence of Lovecraft can be felt. "The Whisperer in Darkness" is very much in evidence in the "deep, buzzing voice" (M 166) that the girl hears, and also at the conclusion when nothing but the girl's face is left, as her body has been spirited away. Lovecraft himself, however, is not given enough credit for mingling supernatural and psychological horror: he did just that in "The Shadow over Innsmouth" and perhaps also in "The Shadow out of Time," and Bloch may well have found suggestive hints in both.

"Notebook Found in a Deserted House" (*Weird Tales*, May 1951) uses somewhat the same stylistic device as "The Unspeakable Betrothal" in its narration by an ill-educated boy rather than a learned omniscient narrator. This story does not feature much psychological analysis, and in its rather grotesque misconstrual of Lovecraft's shoggoth (here interpreted as some sort of tree spirit) it led the way to Ramsey Campbell's similar error in his juvenile story, "The Hollow in the Woods" (in *Ghostly Tales* [1957/58]). But, if nothing else, it shows how a tale of basically Lovecraftian conception can be adapted to a very different idiom. Here, again, however, perhaps Bloch was simply adapting Lovecraft's own extensive use of New England dialect in such tales as "The Picture in the House," "The Dunwich Horror," and "The Shadow over Innsmouth."

"Terror in Cut-Throat Cave" (*Fantastic*, June 1958) is of interest in combining the crime or adventure story with supernaturalism. The basic plot of the tale may have been conceived as early as 1933, for Lovecraft makes mention of one of Bloch's story plots as the "idea of finding a *Thing* in the hold of a long-sunken treasure-ship" (*L* 26). This is, indeed, exactly the core of "Terror in Cut-Throat Cave," although by the time Bloch wrote it he had mastered the tough-guy style he would use to such powerful effect in *The Dead Beat* (1960), and his powers of characterisation render the three main figures crisply—Howard Lane, the jaded writer who seeks a thrill from searching for underwater treasure; Don Hanson, a lumbering giant who has eyes for nothing but money; Dena Drake, Don's mistreated companion, who stays with her brutal lover for lack of any other meaningful goal in her life. I am not certain why this story is in *Mysteries of the Worm*: there is no "Mythos" allusion of any kind in it, and Robert M. Price's suggestion that Hanson is "something of a modern Obed Marsh" (*M* 218) is unconvincing. And yet, there is one fascinating Lovecraftian connexion. Toward the end Lane's mind is taken over by the nameless submerged entity, and he writes: "For already I was a part of it and it was a part of me" (*M* 249). No reader can fail to recall Robert Blake's poignant reflection of the fusion of his own mind with that of Nyarlathotep in "The Haunter of the Dark": "I am it and it is I . . ." (*DH* 115). That one sentence in Bloch's story is enough to reveal his borrowing of a central feature of Lovecraft's tale for his own work.

It would be twenty years before Bloch would write another tale that might conceivably be considered Lovecraftian; but when he did so, he did it with a vengeance. *Strange Eons* (1978) is Bloch's most extended tribute to Lovecraft. No one is likely to think it a masterwork of literature, but it may be among Bloch's more successful later novels and is certainly a delight to the Lovecraftian.

The premise of *Strange Eons* is simple: Lovecraft was writing truth, not fiction. This is, of course, the premise under which many occultist groups function; some asserting, with added implausibility, that Lovecraft himself was unaware of the literal truth of his work. This view was already prevalent among a few in Lovecraft's own lifetime; note his amused comment on the beliefs of the mystical William Lumley: "We [the Lovecraft circle] may *think* we're writing fiction, and may even (absurd thought!) disbelieve what we write, but at bottom we are telling the truth in spite of ourselves—serving unwittingly as mouthpieces of Tsathoggua, Crom, Cthulhu, and other pleasant Outside gentry" (*SL* 4.271).

Bloch actually renders the idea half-believable by the gradualness of his exposition and by his suggestion that Lovecraft was in fact aware of what he was writing and was trying to utter a warning of some kind. The novel opens with an individual discovering a painting that seems strikingly similar to one ascribed to Richard Upton Pickman in "Pickman's Model"; later it is discovered that the painting is in fact by one Richard Upton, who was in touch with Lovecraft and had shown him some spectacular canvases in Boston. As *Strange Eons* progresses, various events seem uncannily to mimic those found in Lovecraft's stories—"The Lurking Fear," "The Statement of Randolph Carter" ("*You fool—Beckman is dead!*" [SE 25]), "The Whisperer in Darkness," and so on.

The focus of the novel is, as might be expected, Nyarlathotep—here embodied in the person of Reverend Nye, a black man who leads the Starry Wisdom sect, seemingly just another of the harmless cults found so bountifully in southern California. But very quickly it becomes clear that Nye and his cult are far from harmless, as character after character dies off after learning too much. Drawing upon the prose-poem "Nyarlathotep," Bloch sees in the figure of Nyarlathotep nothing less than a symbol for—and, indeed, the actual engenderer of—a cataclysmic chaos that could destroy the world and perhaps the universe.

Strange Eons is a grand synthesis of Lovecraftian tales and themes. Bloch fuses elements from the "Cthulhu Mythos" into a convincing unity: Nyarlathotep prepares for the emergence of Cthulhu from the depths of the Pacific; the mind-exchange that Asenath Waite practised in "The Thing on the Doorstep" allows a Starry Wisdom member to deceive an opponent at a critical juncture, just as the mimicry that tricked Wilmarth at the conclusion of "The Whisperer in Darkness" does so at an earlier point in the novel; and the female protagonist serves, like Lavinia Whateley in "The Dunwich Horror," as the unwilling mate in a sexual union with one of the Great Old Ones. Throughout *Strange Eons*, all the characters attempting to thwart Nyarlathotep—including a powerful secret branch of the U.S. government—are themselves thwarted by Nyarlathotep and his minions; and the conclusion offers no reassurance.

The final section of *Strange Eons*, a harrowing account of a severe earthquake that causes the submersion of a large part of California sometime in the near future, is narrated in a hypnotic, quasi-stream-of-consciousness manner that is as potently effective as the most incantatory Lovecraftian prose. Here the resemblance to the prose-poem "Nyarlathotep" is very marked, as all civilisation seems to be cracking at the foundations. It is quite possible that Bloch was thinking not only of the prose-poem but of the passage (which he had already quoted in "The Shadow from the Steeple") in the sonnet "Nyarlathotep" in *Fungi from Yuggoth*:

> Soon from the sea a noxious birth began;
> Forgotten lands with weedy spires of gold;
> The ground was cleft, and mad auroras rolled
> Down on the quaking citadels of man.

> Then, crushing what he chanced to mould in play,
> The idiot Chaos blew Earth's dust away.

That "noxious birth" is, in Bloch's conception, nothing less than the emergence of Cthulhu, and the novel ends grimly and apocalyptically:

> That is not dead which can eternal lie, and the time of strange eons had arrived. The stars were right, the gates were open, the seas swarmed with immortal multitudes and the earth gave up its undead.
> Soon the winged ones from Yuggoth would swoop down from the void and now the Old Ones would return—Azazoth [sic] and Yog-Sothoth, whose priest he [Nyarlathotep] was, would come to lightless Leng and old Kadath in the risen continents which were transformed as he was transformed....
> He rose, and mountains trembled, sinking into the sea.
> Time stopped.
> Death died.
> And Great Cthulhu went forth into the world to begin his eternal reign. (SE 194)

Such a cheerless ending would be unthinkable to many modern weird writers, who feel obligated to restore bourgeois normality at the end regardless of the havoc their monsters have caused; but Bloch is true to Lovecraft's vision here, for he knew that that vision was a bleak one that saw little place for mankind in a boundless universe in which it was an infinitesimal atom. This is what makes *Strange Eons* the true homage that it is.

Bloch learned much from Lovecraft about the craft of writing weird fiction, and he put that knowledge to good use. But while his early "Cthulhu Mythos" stories entertain, while *Strange Eons* is an affectionate tribute, Bloch's real stature as a writer resides in his short stories of the 1940s onward and in such gripping novels—which combine psychological penetration with hardboiled cynicism—as *Psycho* (1959) and *The Dead Beat* (1960). Just as Lovecraft's later work straddles the always nebulous borderline between horror and science fiction, so Bloch's most representative writing effects a union between the horror tale and the mystery or detective story. This is his true contribution to literature, and it will be for that that he will be remembered. But his Lovecraftian works will also occupy a place of honour in his canon, if only because they exemplify the ties of friendship that a respected master established with his enthusiastic pupil. Along with Fritz Leiber, Henry Kuttner, C. L. Moore, and a few others, Robert Bloch more than justified Lovecraft's predictions of his future greatness, and in turn Bloch more than repaid the debt he owed to the twentieth century's leading weird writer.

Works Cited

Bloch, Robert. "Black Bargain." *Weird Tales* 36, No. 5 (May 1942): 66–76. [Rpt. in S. T. Joshi, ed. *American Supernatural Tales*. New York: Penguin, 2007.]

———. *Mysteries of the Worm.* 2nd ed. Edited by Robert M. Price. Oakland, CA: Chaosium, 1993. [Abbreviated in the text as M.]

———. "Satan's Servants." In Lovecraft's *Something about Cats and Other Pieces*. Sauk City, WI: Arkham House, 1949. [Abbreviated in the text as S.]

———. *Strange Eons.* Chapel Hill, NC: Whispers Press, 1978. [Abbreviated in the text as SE.]

Lovecraft, H. P. *Letters to Robert Bloch.* Edited by David E. Schultz and S. T. Joshi. West Warwick, RI: Necronomicon Press, 1993. [Abbreviated in the text as L.]

———. *Letters to Robert Bloch: Supplement.* Edited by David E. Schultz and S. T. Joshi. West Warwick, RI: Necronomicon Press, 1993. [Abbreviated in the text as LS.]

Passing the Torch: H. P. Lovecraft and Fritz Leiber

Fritz Leiber's apparently startling remark that H. P. Lovecraft was "the chiefest influence on my literary development after Shakespeare" (cited in Byfield 11) may perhaps be less puzzling if we interpret the statement absolutely literally; for Leiber's emphasis here may be on the word *development*, and if this is the case, then it suggests that Lovecraft's own work—as well as his brief but intense correspondence with Leiber in 1936-37—provided Leiber with suggestions as to the improvement of the style, plotting, motivation, and conception of his early tales, and that these suggestions held Leiber in good stead throughout the subsequent course of his long and fruitful career. It is a truism that Leiber, perhaps alone of Lovecraft's literary associates, did not imitate Lovecraft either stylistically or thematically—except in the late work, "The Terror from the Depths" (1976), commissioned for a volume of pastiches of Lovecraft's "Cthulhu Mythos"—but instead struck out on his own right from the beginning of his career. This aesthetic independence has been a major reason for the survival of Leiber's work while that of other, more derivative writers has achieved merited oblivion; but that Lovecraft taught Leiber much about the craft of writing is evident both in Leiber's several insightful critical essays on Lovecraft and in his early tales, especially those gathered in his first collection, *Night's Black Agents* (1947).

Leiber (1910-1992) wrote four important essays on Lovecraft. They are: "A Literary Copernicus" (1949); "My Correspondence with Lovecraft" (1958); "The 'Whisperer' Re-examined" (1964); and "Through Hyperspace with Brown Jenkin" (1966). There are some lesser articles—among them "Lovecraft in My Life" (1976) and his contributions to *H. P. Lovecraft: A Symposium* (1963)—but the above four embody Leiber's most significant thought on Lovecraft. Aside from the light they shed on Leiber's own work, they are among the most perspicacious pieces ever written on Lovecraft; many believe that "A Literary Copernicus" may still be the finest single article on Lovecraft to date. All these essays reveal how carefully Leiber had absorbed the essence of Lovecraft's work at a relatively early stage in his career.

"A Literary Copernicus," written for *Something about Cats and Other Pieces*

(1949), is a radical expansion of two earlier articles, "The Works of H. P. Lovecraft: Suggestions for a Critical Appraisal" (1944) and "Some Random Thoughts about Lovecraft's Writings" (1945), both published in the Lovecraftian fanzine, *The Acolyte*. The very core of the article—that Lovecraft was a "literary Copernicus" for reinventing the Gothic tale for modern times—is not only one of the most important utterances made about Lovecraft but is what Leiber himself chiefly derived from Lovecraft's stories and applied to his own work, albeit in a somewhat different way. Consider the opening paragraph of the article:

> Howard Phillips Lovecraft was the Copernicus of the horror story. He shifted the focus of supernatural dread from man and his little world and his gods, to the stars and the black and unplumbed gulfs of intergalactic space. To do this effectively, he created a new kind of horror story and new methods for telling it. (FM 65)

When Leiber goes on to say that Lovecraft "firmly attached the emotion of spectral dread to such concepts as outer space, the rim of the cosmos, alien beings, unsuspected dimensions, and the conceivable universes lying outside our own space-time continuum" (FM 66), he is not only stressing that Lovecraft presented a fusion of the traditional horror tale with the nascent science fiction story, but still more significantly presented a *secular* supernatural tale whereby fear is instilled not by conventional appeals to the devil but to the petrifying notion of the vastness of the cosmos and the insignificance of humanity within it. Leiber delivers a scarcely veiled rebuke to August Derleth, who attempted for decades to maintain that Lovecraft's "Cthulhu Mythos" can somehow be reconciled with standard Christian doctrine: "I believe it is a mistake to regard the beings of the Cthulhu Mythos as sophisticated equivalents of the entities of Christian demonology, or to attempt to divide them into balancing Zoroastrian hierarchies of good and evil" (FM 68). It would take twenty years for this remarkably prescient analysis to be elaborated by such modern Lovecraft scholars as Richard L. Tierney ("The Derleth Mythos," 1972) and Dirk W. Mosig ("H. P. Lovecraft: Myth-Maker," 1976).

Leiber's other articles on Lovecraft are less significant for the study of his own work, but are nonetheless perspicacious. "Through Hyperspace with Brown Jenkin" is perhaps the most impressive, being a trenchant exploration of the notion of time-travel in Lovecraft's fiction. It shows how carefully Leiber read such of Lovecraft's tales as "The Dreams in the Witch House" and "The Shadow out of Time"; and it is no accident that these tales are among those that influenced Leiber the most. "The 'Whisperer' Reexamined" is a sharp criticism of "The Whisperer in Darkness" from the point of view of its deficient characterisation: the protagonist, Albert N. Wilmarth, is too easily "hoodwinked" (FM 82) by the alien entities of the tale.

This leads to a more general criticism of Lovecraft:

> In "Notes on the Writing of Weird Fiction" Lovecraft summed up [his] limitation: "All that a wonder story can ever be is *a vivid picture of a certain type of human mood.*" This aesthetic dictum, while having some technical validity, breathes loneliness and can be very stultifying to the writer's urge to say things about the real world, set down insights into real people, speculate imaginatively, and get closer to his reader than merely sharing "a vague illusion of the strange reality of the unreal." (FM 83)

This criticism is not entirely fair to Lovecraft—who was not interested in the "real world" or in setting down insights into "real people," and whose cosmic perspective was opposed to the vaunting of human beings against the awesome backdrop of the cosmos—but it points to Leiber's own belief that fantasy, horror, and even cosmicism are not incompatible with the portrayal of vital human characters with whom the reader can identify.

In "My Correspondence with Lovecraft" Leiber tells the story of his brief personal involvement with the Providence writer. He had been profoundly moved by reading "The Colour out of Space" in *Amazing Stories* (September 1927) and *At the Mountains of Madness* and "The Shadow out of Time" in 1936 issues of *Astounding Stories*. No doubt he read Lovecraft's other stories in *Weird Tales* as well, but the citation of the above three tales—Lovecraft's most "science-fictional" works—points to their focal influence upon Leiber's early work. Too shy to write to the great master of weird fiction, however, Leiber nonetheless came into contact with Lovecraft when his wife Jonquil wrote to him through *Weird Tales*. For a time Lovecraft was writing separate letters to both Fritz and Jonquil (as well as to Leiber's early collaborator Harry O. Fischer), although the duration of this correspondence was quite brief: perhaps no longer than the period from October 1936 to March 1937, when Lovecraft died at forty-six. Neither Fritz nor Jonquil could know that Lovecraft was already in the final stages of intestinal cancer; and it is poignant to read—given the near-certainty that bad diet was a significant cause of Lovecraft's illness and death—how Leiber and Fischer ruminated "that something must be done to provide Lovecraft with fresh vegetables" (FM 80).

But that brief association was enough to effect some permanent changes in Leiber's work. Leiber had sent the typescript of his novelette, "Adept's Gambit" (rejected by *Weird Tales*), to Lovecraft; in response, Lovecraft on 19 December 1936 wrote a letter of twenty sheets, written on both sides of the page—perhaps 10,000 words in length—commenting in detail on points of style and historical accuracy in the tale, and supplying a copious reading-list of works on Greek and Roman history for any future historical fiction that Leiber might do. Leiber is right to call this lengthy epistle "crazily generous by hard-headed standards," and he goes on to say that it "influenced me permanently toward greater care in the polishing and final preparation of manuscripts" (FM 79).

The version of "Adept's Gambit" published in *Night's Black Agents* is very likely quite different from what Leiber sent to Lovecraft, since Leiber confesses in "Fafhrd and Me" that the novelette went through "three or four recastings and rewritings" (FM 15) after its initial rejections. (One of these versions contained glancing references to Lovecraft's Mythos, and Leiber was probably wise in excising them from the final draft.) Lovecraft's fundamental criticism was that the story exhibited a certain fuzziness in the historical setting. From his remarks it is possible to infer that the tale was more firmly set in the Hellenistic period than the version as we have it, and the ever-scrupulous Lovecraft did not fail to pick up on certain inaccuracies or anachronisms in the portrayal of the period. In the published version we are told that "it was hardly a year since the Seleucids had beaten the Ptolemies out of Tyre" (N 22); other hints of this sort—assuming they were in the version he read—led Lovecraft to conjecture a date of 250 B.C.E. for the tale's action; but a later mention of Alexander the Great (d. 323 B.C.E.) as living "more than a hundred years ago" would give a somewhat later period, say 220 B.C. Interestingly enough, Leiber was conceiving a future tale in which Fafhrd & the Gray Mouser would be reincarnated into the Julio-Claudian age (i.e., the 1st century C.E.) by means of an elixir; it was for this reason that he had asked Lovecraft to supply him a reading-list of works on this period of ancient history.

"Adept's Gambit" does not bear much resemblance to Lovecraft's own work; indeed, in its picaresque narrative, its vivid character portrayals, and its liberal doses of humour and buffoonery it is about as far from the bulk of Lovecraft's dark, brooding, non-humanocentric work as can be imagined. Lovecraft himself was aware of the fact, remarking in his letter that "the style & manner of approach are almost antipodal to my own." He was also at a loss for parallels, citing the possible influence of James Stephens (*The Crock of Gold*), Dunsany (he is perhaps thinking of Dunsany's own picaresque pseudo-historical novels, *The Chronicles of Rodriguez* [1922] and *The Charwoman's Shadow* [1926]), Cabell, and others. There is perhaps an accidental resemblance to Lovecraft's then-unpublished novel, *The Dream-Quest of Unknown Kadath*—Lovecraft remarks on the similarity himself ("This picaresque kind of writing has a strong fascination, & I once attempted it myself . . . in a long novelette")—but of course Leiber could not have actually been influenced by the work. In any event, Lovecraft was highly impressed with the story, addressing his long letter to Leiber (19 December 1936) as from "The Castle of Mist" and signing himself "The Old Man Without a Beard." One remark in the letter is worth citing:

Certainly, you have produced a remarkably fine & distinctive bit of comic fantasy in a vein which is, for all the Cabellian or Beckfordian comparisons, essentially your own. The basic element of allegory, the earthiness & closeness to human nature, & the curious blending of worldly lightness with the strange & the macabre, all harmonise adequately & seem to express a definite mood & personality. The result is an authentic work of art . . . ("Letters" 40)

He adds presciently: "Let us hope that your mental collaboration [with Harry O. Fischer] will give rise to a long sequence of tales about Fafhrd & the Mouser . . ." ("Letters" 43).

If "Adept's Gambit" bears little resemblance to Lovecraft's work, another Fafhrd and Gray Mouser story is so dependent upon Lovecraftian conceptions that it can qualify as a pastiche, although even this tale is considerably more imaginative as a pastiche than other Lovecraft-derived works. "The Sunken Land" (1942) is another relatively early story in which Fafhrd catches a fish in whose mouth is found an object that is both a ring and a key. This object makes Fafhrd think of the legends of a land called Simorgya, whose inhabitants "'were mighty magicians, claiming power over wind and wave and the creatures below. Yet the sea gulped them down for all that'" (N 6). The ship on which Fafhrd and the Mouser are sailing is rammed by another ship, controlled by the evil Lavas Laerk, and after a fight with its crew Fafhrd is taken prisoner and made to serve as an oarsman. Lavas Laerk is seeking to attain the sunken land of Simorgya, and after a time he and his crew seem to do so, coming upon a vast mountain jutting out of the sea. But something seems to be wrong, and Fafhrd is the only one to be aware that "Simorgya had indeed sunk under the sea and only risen up yesterday—or yester-hour" (N 15). Lavas Laerk comes upon the treasure-house of Simorgya and his crew revels in the gold and jewels therein; but from behind a golden door a "strange, undulant blanketlike monster" (N 16) emerges and overwhelms Lavas Laerk's men, while Fafhrd escapes with the help of the Mouser, whose ship has arrived to rescue him. Simorgya then once again falls back into the sea.

This story is an amalgam of at least four different Lovecraft stories, although some of the borrowings are very slight. When the Mouser, seeing the ring for the first time, remarks that he "did not recognize the style" (N 4), we think of the bizarre jewellery of the Innsmouth denizens of "The Shadow over Innsmouth" (1931), which "belonged to some settled technique . . . utterly remote from any—Eastern or Western, ancient or modern—which [the narrator] had ever heard of or seen exemplified" (DH 311). Later, as Lavas Laerk's crew penetrate the treasure-house and note its eerie phosphorescence, we are perhaps meant to recall Lovecraft's early tale, "The Temple" (1920), which involves a German submarine commander who comes upon a similarly phosphorescent temple buried beneath the waves of the Atlantic. And that "blanketlike" monster is perhaps akin to Lovecraft's protoplasmic shoggoth from At the Mountains of Madness (1931).

But clearly the predominant influence on this tale is "The Call of Cthulhu" (1926), Lovecraft's prototypical account of a sunken continent that suddenly rises up from the waves and from which the shapeless monstrosity Cthulhu momentarily emerges to wreak havoc on a hapless crew of Norwegian sailors who come upon it by accident. Indeed, "The Sunken Land" is nothing more than a rewriting of "The Call of Cthulhu," transferring the setting from the real world of the South Pacific to an heroic fantasy realm and including rather more fisticuffs and swordplay than was Lovecraft's wont.

Another early Leiber tale—"Diary in the Snow," first published in *Night's Black Agents*—is less obviously derivative but still owes its very conception to Lovecraft. Here it transpires that a race of extraterrestrial entities, dwelling in a world of bitter cold, discover the existence of Earth and look with envy at its temperateness. As they dwell on a planet enormously distant from earth, mind-exchange with the inhabitants of Earth is the only feasible way to effect their removal from their world; and "Diary in the Snow" is the account of a writer in a remote snowbound cottage who unwittingly serves as the conduit for the creatures' advent to this planet, unaware that the science-fiction tale he is writing is in reality his subconscious mind's warning of how these entities are planning to usurp the human race.

There is, perhaps, no specific Lovecraft story which served as the model for "Diary in the Snow," although the conceptions broached in it are heavily Lovecraftian. The idea of mind-exchange over enormous distances of space brings "The Shadow out of Time" (1934–35) to mind, and this is perhaps the most direct influence. Lovecraft, of course, used mind-exchange in a number of other tales, notably "The Thing on the Doorstep" (1933) and "The Haunter of the Dark" (1935); but only "The Shadow out of Time" involves mind-exchange over vast galactic spaces. Also, the scenario of the writer and his colleague being besieged by alien forces—for after a time they develop a dim awareness of the true state of affairs—recalls "The Whisperer in Darkness" (1930), where Henry Akeley finds himself trapped in his lonely Vermont farmhouse as the fungi from Yuggoth seek to overwhelm him and take his mind on stupendous transcosmic voyages. One very telling tip of the hat to Lovecraft in "Diary in the Snow" is the narrator's description, at the outset, of the anomalous phenomena he notes around him as "a sense of strangeness, a delightful feeling of adventurous expectancy" (N 208). Lovecraft may well have used that latter phrase in a letter to Leiber, for it became a standard coinage in his own aesthetic of the weird: "What has haunted my dreams for nearly forty years is *a strange sense of adventurous expectancy connected with landscape and architecture and sky-effects"* (SL 3.100).

Other early Leiber tales are influenced by Lovecraft in less significant ways; indeed, in some cases the resemblance may be accidental. "The Inheritance" (N) also deals with personality-exchange, and was perhaps influenced by "The Thing on the Doorstep," where a woman with great hypnotic powers displaces the personality of her husband and occupies his body on occasion. "The Man Who Never Grew Young" (N) appears to reflect Lovecraft's fascination with time—recall his celebrated statement that "*Conflict with time* seems to me the most potent and fruitful theme in all human expression" ("Notes on Writing Weird Fiction" [CE 2.176])—in its depiction of a man who somehow travels backward through time. The influence of "The Shadow out of Time"—in which a man's mind, displaced by that of an alien entity, travels back 150,000,000 years into the body of his displacer—may be conjectured, although the parallels are not very precise: Leiber's tale simply involves a man who himself is somehow doubling back upon the time-stream.

The uncollected tale "The Dead Man" (*Weird Tales*, November 1950) betrays—as Stefan Dziemianowicz has pointed out—a peculiar influence of "The Thing on the Doorstep" in its use of a series of three knocks followed by two more as a cue to bring a patient out of a hypnotic trance; Lovecraft used the identical three-and-two pattern as a secret code between two characters in his story.

A reading of *Night's Black Agents* makes clear the central lesson Leiber learned from Lovecraft: the need to update the horror tale to make it relevant to present-day concerns. Lovecraft, of course, did so by fusing horror and science fiction, replacing the fear of vampires, werewolves, and ghosts (all completely outmoded in the light of contemporary science) with that of the boundless cosmos. Antiquarian though he may have been, Lovecraft was keenly aware of such radical and potentially disturbing conceptions as Einsteinian space-time, the quantum theory, and Heisenberg's indeterminacy principle, and utilised them to give a distinctly modern cast to such stale conceptions as the vampire ("The Shunned House") and the witch ("The Dreams in the Witch House"), to say nothing of the possibility of extraterrestrial incursions in such tales as "The Colour out of Space," "The Whisperer in Darkness," *At the Mountains of Madness*, and "The Shadow out of Time."

Leiber went about it in a somewhat different way. In his belief that weird fiction must be made relevant to contemporary audiences by means of vividly realised human characters and realism of setting, Leiber melded supernatural horror with the very real horrors of urbanism ("Smoke Ghost," "The Hound"), crime ("The Automatic Pistol"), and the omnipresent anxiety of living in the modern world ("The Dreams of Albert Moreland"); anticipating in this regard the work of Ramsey Campbell and many other contemporary writers. In a few striking stories ("The Hill and the Hole," "A Bit of the Dark World") Leiber even attempts (successfully) to duplicate Lovecraft's harrowing cosmicism.

"Smoke Ghost" is Leiber's prototypical tale of the horror to be found in the city. The very title suggests a paradoxical union of the antiquated (a ghost) and the modern (smoke from factories). This ghost, however, in the eyes of the protagonist, Mr Wran, is "'a ghost from the world today, with the soot of the factories on its face and the pounding of machinery in its soul'" (N 109). The vista of slum roofs seen by Wran symbolises for him "certain disagreeable aspects of the frustrated, frightened century in which he lived" (N 112). When Wran's son sees the ghost and cries, "Black man, black man" (N 120), we are not to interpret the remark racially but as emblematic of the omnipresent filth—literal and moral—in modern society. We may also think of Leiber's discussion, in "A Literary Copernicus," of Nyarlathotep, who in "The Dreams in the Witch House" appears as the Black Man. In pondering what Nyarlathotep may "mean," Leiber conjectures that one possibility is that "Nyarlathotep stands for man's self-destructive intellectuality, his awful ability to see the universe for what it is and thereby kill in himself all naive and beautiful dreams" (FM 70). This is, to be sure, not exactly what is going on in "Smoke Ghost," but Leiber may still have learned from Lovecraft how to use a symbol something like Nyarlathotep to convey his own views on the state of modern man.

Leiber's "The Hound" exactly mirrors the title of one of Lovecraft's early tales, but this duplication may be accidental, as Leiber's tale appears to owe nothing at all to Lovecraft's lurid and consciously self-parodic story, in which two graverobbers meet their comeuppance when they pilfer the tomb of an old ghoul whose soul is represented by a gigantic hound. Leiber's "The Hound" is grimly potent, but again we are to see in the hound of the tale a symbol for the horrors of urbanism: "this thing . . . was part and parcel of the great sprawling cities and chaotic peoples of the Twentieth Century" (N 187). Later the narrator's friend, speaking of the relentless march of technology, points to the inability of the human spirit to keep pace:

> "Meanwhile, what's happening inside each of us? I'll tell you. All sorts of inhibited emotions are accumulating. Fear is accumulating. Horror is accumulating. A new kind of awe of the mysteries of the universe is accumulating. A psychological environment is forming, along with the physical one. . . . Our culture becomes ripe for infection. . . . our culture suddenly spawns a horde of demons. And, like germs, they have a peculiar affinity for our culture. They're unique. They fit in. You wouldn't find the same kind any other time or place." (N 190-91)

"The Automatic Pistol" is a somewhat slighter but piquant tale that effects a union of the gangster story and the supernatural tale. A criminal's gun is explicitly compared to a witch's familiar (N 133), making us recall perhaps how Lovecraft brought the tale of witchcraft up to date in "The Dreams in the Witch House" by the incorporation of Einsteinian physics. There the rat-like creature Brown Jenkin, the familiar of the witch Keziah Mason, appears in hyperspace as a "polyhedron of unknown colours and rapidly shifting surface angles" (MM 273). In these tales Leiber pioneers the modernisation of the weird tale; but he does so not as Lovecraft did—by attempting to make the supernatural plausible by appeals to advanced science—but by placing it in the frenetic urban milieu that holds so many of us in its tenacious grip. Nevertheless, it is likely that Leiber found in Lovecraft's tales some suggestive hints of how such a modernisation might be effected.

Three tales in *Night's Black Agents* feature the cosmicism and the very intellectualised, philosophical horror that lie at the core of Lovecraft's best work. In "The Dreams of Albert Moreland" the central character dreams that he is playing a chesslike game on some enormous gameboard, convinced that the fate of mankind depends on the outcome. The basic plot is strikingly similar to that of "The Dreams in the Witch House," in particular the tableau where a statuette from Moreland's dream-world is found in his room, a scene identical to one found in Lovecraft's tale, and a confirmation that the "dreams" in both tales bear some harrowing relationship to the "real" world. (Leiber could not know that a further similarity exists in the original title of Lovecraft's story—"The Dreams of Walter Gilman.") When Moreland fancies that "some cosmic beings, neither gods nor men, had created human life long ago as a jest or experiment or artistic form" (N 174), we are clearly meant to recall Lake's conjecture in *At the Mountains of Madness* that the Old Ones had created all earth life as "jest or mistake" (MM 22). But Leiber performs a brilliant union of social commentary and cosmicism by attributing the "omnipresent anxiety" that Moreland sees on "each passing face" as symptomatic of a broader evil:

> For once I seemed able to look behind the mask which every person wears and which is so characteristically pronounced in a congested city, and see what lay behind—the egotistical sensitivity, the smouldering irritation, the thwarted longing, the defeat . . . and, above all, the anxiety, too ill-defined and lacking in definite object to be called fear, but nonetheless infecting every thought and action, and making trivial things terrible. And it seemed to me that social, economic, and physiological factors, even Death and the War, were insufficient to explain such anxiety, and that it was in reality an upswelling from something dubious and horrible in the very constitution of the universe. (N 179)

Later Moreland believes that he is "getting perilously close to the innermost secrets of the universe and finding they were rotten and evil and sardonic" (*N* 182), a common theme in Lovecraft's work.

"The Hill and the Hole" speaks of some anomalous survey readings whereby a hill seems to be a pit, leading the narrator to reflect about "how little most people knew about the actual dimensions and boundaries of the world they lived in" (*N* 159). And later: "Once admit that the dimensions of a thing might not be real . . . and you cut the foundations from under the world" (*N* 165). Lovecraft speaks in "The Call of Cthulhu" of the geometry of R'lyeh being *"all wrong"* (*DH* 143) and of "an angle which was acute, but behaved as if it were obtuse" (*DH* 152), exactly the sort of reversal that we find in Leiber's tale. The fact that a surveyor's instrument confirms the anomalousness of the situation may point to the influence of "The Colour out of Space," where a spectroscope is applied to the meteorite and reveals "shining bands unlike any known colours of the normal spectrum" (*DH* 58). In both cases it is important that the weird phenomena not be discounted as a mere hallucination; and the utilisation of scientific instruments in perfect working order is the best means to suggest that some genuine bizarrerie actually exists.

"A Bit of the Dark World" (1962) is a later story added to the revised (1978) edition of *Night's Black Agents*, probably because Leiber saw it to be thematically similar to the Lovecraftian tales in the volume. There is, of course, a passing reference to "Mountains of Madness near the South Pole" (*N* 246), but the relationship is deeper than this. This tale consists largely of an intellectual discussion of the foundations of fear. Whereas one character speaks of mundane horrors—"'Nazi death camps, brain-washing, Black-Dahlia sex murders, race riots, stuff like that'"—another character counters: "'I'm talking about supernatural horror, which is almost the antithesis of even the worst human violence and cruelty. Hauntings, the suspension of scientific law, the intrusion of the utterly alien, the sense of something listening at the rim of the cosmos or scratching faintly at the other side of the sky'" (*N* 245), a very Lovecraftian formulation. Later a character has a cosmic experience very similar to those of Lovecraft's protagonists:

> I looked up at the heavens. There was no Milky Way yet, but there would be soon, the stars were flashing on so brightly and thickly at this smog-free distance from LA. I saw the Pole Star straight above the dark star-silhouetted summit-crag of the hillside across from me, and the Great Bear and Cassiopeia swinging from it. I felt the bigness of the atmosphere, I got a hint of the stupendous distance between me and the stars, and then—as if my vision could go out in all directions at will, piercing solidity as readily as the dark—I got a lasting, growing, wholly absorbing sense of the universe around me. (*N* 263)

The tale goes on to relate exactly such an "intrusion of the utterly alien," an entity as incomprehensible as the creature (or creatures) in "The Colour out of Space."

Late in life Leiber finally broke down and produced an avowed Lovecraftian pastiche, writing "The Terror from the Depths" when invited by Edward Paul Berglund to contribute to his anthology, *The Disciples of Cthulhu* (1976). The result is an extraordinarily rich and complex novelette that, as Byfield (57-58) has shown, is a model for Leiber's incorporation of the mythic theories of Jung and Joseph Campbell in his later work. On a superficial level, "The Terror from the Depths" can be read as a vast in-joke: it would require a lengthy commentary to pinpoint all the tips of the hat to works by Lovecraft scattered through this story, including something so insignificant as the cry "Merciful Creator!" (*TD* 301), borrowed from "Pickman's Model" (*DH* 22). More interestingly, Leiber has written a loose sequel to some of Lovecraft's most celebrated later tales, especially "The Whisperer in Darkness," whose protagonist Albert N. Wilmarth plays a major role in the story. Wilmarth, amusingly enough, bears a striking physical resemblance to Lovecraft himself. Although Leiber of course never met Lovecraft, he had by this time read enough about Lovecraft's life and mannerisms to capture some of his characteristic behaviour-patterns:

> He [was] . . . a tall young man, cadaverously thin, always moving about with nervous rapidity, his shoulders hunched. He'd had a long jaw and a pale complexion, with dark-circled eyes which gave him a haunted look, as if he were constantly under some great strain to which he never alluded. . . . He'd seemed incredibly well read and had had a lot to do with stimulating and deepening my interest in poetry. (*TD* 290)

The narrator, Georg Reuter Fischer, even remarks to Wilmarth at one point: "'You know, . . . I had the craziest idea—that somehow you and he [Lovecraft] were the same person'" (*TD* 310). Lovecraft himself, indeed, plays a minor role in the tale. Conversely, Fischer (whose first and last names are derived from Leiber's friends Georg Mann and Harry O. Fischer, and whose middle name is Leiber's own) is clearly modelled on Leiber himself, so that the story's scenario—in which Wilmarth acts as a sort of mentor to Fischer in the pursuit of arcane knowledge—echoes Lovecraft's own brief tutorship to the young Leiber.

More than mere imitation, however, "The Terror from the Depths" strives both to recapture some of the textural richness of Lovecraft's best stories and, perhaps, to show that profound portrayals of human character are not incompatible with the general "cosmic" orientation of Lovecraft's work. To put it very crudely, Fischer finds himself simultaneously attracted and repelled by the cosmic forces dwelling under his Southern California home;

and his first-person narrative reveals, entirely unbeknownst to himself, the degree to which these forces have throughout his entire life affected his mind and guided his actions to the final cataclysmic conclusion. Leiber here has drawn from many of Lovecraft's tales: Cthulhu's control of dreams ("The Call of Cthulhu"); the possible attractions of yielding to the non-human ("The Shadow over Innsmouth"); the compelling quest for scientific knowledge in the face of personal danger ("The Whisperer in Darkness," *At the Mountains of Madness*). And yet, the result is a story that features considerably more psychological analysis than Lovecraft ever included in his own work.

Accordingly, "The Terror from the Depths" can on one level be seen as Leiber's attempt to "rewrite" "The Whisperer in Darkness" so that it has more to say about the "real world" and "real people." Recall that one of Leiber's criticisms of Lovecraft's tale is that Wilmarth is presented as excessively gullible—a comment that may point to Leiber's overall dissatisfaction with the portrayal of character in Lovecraft's work generally. The same cannot be said of "The Terror from the Depths," where the slow absorption of both Fischer and Wilmarth into the physical and mental grasp of the cosmic entities is depicted with subtlety and psychological insight. In Lovecraft's tale Wilmarth is also momentarily attracted by the prospect of cosmic insights that might be made available to him: "To shake off the maddening and wearying limitations of time and space and natural law—to be linked with the vast *outside*—to come close to the nighted and abysmal secrets of the infinite and the ultimate—surely such a thing was worth the risk of one's life, soul, and sanity!" (*DH* 243). But in the end he draws back and flees to the safety of the human world. Leiber's scenario shows that the mere option to yield or not to yield to the non-human has become a moot point, since Fischer's mind has long ago been captured by the cosmic beings. What Leiber has done here—and, really, throughout his work—is to break down the simple dichotomy of external horror and internal horror, showing that both can be, and usually are, fused into an enigmatic and chilling union.

It cannot be repeated frequently enough that Fritz Leiber was one of the few writers of the "Lovecraft Circle" to have fully assimilated the Lovecraft influence and gone on to produce vital, original work that reflects his own (not Lovecraft's) themes, concerns, and philosophy. The same cannot be said for the Lovecraftian work of August Derleth, Frank Belknap Long, Brian Lumley, and even Ramsey Campbell. Campbell became an original writer only when he repudiated the Lovecraft influence that dominated his first volume, *The Inhabitant of the Lake* (1964), and went on to write the very different work for which he is now justly acclaimed. Leiber never had to make such a clear break, perhaps because his youthful conceptions were already pointing in a somewhat Lovecraftian direction (especially in the mingling of horror and science fiction), so that he could use Lovecraft's work less as the source of abject imitation than as a spur to his imagination. Leiber never attempted to imitate Lovecraft's distinctive style (save, as an homage, in "The Terror from the Depths"), and instead drew upon fundamental Lovecraftian themes, moods, and aesthetic principles—the impingement of vast extraterrestrial entities upon the earth; the focusing upon a hapless, solitary human being caught in the web of cosmic forces; the intellectual terror of a defiance or subversion of natural law; the need to modernise the weird tale by utilising modern science as a source of terror—as the foundation of his early work. *Night's Black Agents* is a testimonial to how much Leiber has learned from Lovecraft, but many other works could be cited to flesh out the picture.

In the end, however, Leiber remains a writer capable of expressing his own unique vision; the most important lesson he drew from Lovecraft was some clues on how best to express it.

Works Cited

Byfield, Bruce. *Witches of the Mind: A Critical Study of Fritz Leiber.* West Warwick, RI: Necronomicon Press, 1991.

Dziemianowicz, Stefan. "Dead Ringers: The Leiber-Lovecraft Connection." *Crypt of Cthulhu* No. 76 (Hallowmass 1990): 8–13.

Leiber, Fritz. *Fafhrd & Me: A Collection of Essays.* Newark, NJ: Wildside Press, 1990. [Abbreviated in the text as *FM*.]

———. *Night's Black Agents.* 1947. New York: Berkley, 1978. [Abbreviated in the text as *N*.]

———. "The Terror from the Depths." 1976. In *Tales of the Cthulhu Mythos*, ed. August Derleth and James Turner. Rev. ed. Sauk City, WI: Arkham House, 1990. 267–312. [Abbreviated in the text as *TD*.]

Lovecraft, H. P. "Letters to Fritz and Jonquil Leiber." In Benjamin J. S. Szumskyj and S. T. Joshi, ed. *Fritz Leiber and H. P. Lovecraft: Writers of the Dark.* Holicong, PA: Wildside Press, 2003. 11–64.

Mosig, Dirk W. "H. P. Lovecraft: Myth-Maker." 1976. In S. T. Joshi, ed. *H. P. Lovecraft: Four Decades of Criticism.* Athens: Ohio University Press, 1980. 104–12.

Tierney, Richard L. "The Derleth Mythos." In Meade and Penny Frierson, ed. *HPL.* Birmingham, AL: Meade and Penny Frierson, 1972. 53.

Lovecraft at Last

Willis Conover's *Lovecraft at Last* was published on May 15, 1975, in an edition of 1000 numbered and slipcased copies and 2000 unnumbered copies. The nearly simultaneous appearance of L. Sprague de Camp's *Lovecraft: A Biography* and Frank Belknap Long's *Howard Phillips Lovecraft: Dreamer on the Nightside* made 1975 a banner year in the recognition of Lovecraft as a literary figure and as an icon in popular culture. The First World Fantasy Convention, held in October of that year, and largely devoted to Lovecraft, seemed to represent a capstone in Lovecraft's emergence as a figure of international renown.

In 1975, the question "Who is H. P. Lovecraft?" still required an answer, at least as far as the general public was concerned. Having begun his career writing hundreds of essays and poetry for amateur publications, Lovecraft gained a steady following through the pages of the pulp magazine *Weird Tales*, where his short stories of horror and fantasy were recognised widely as literature worthy of a place beside the works that influenced them most—the tales of Edgar Allan Poe. Lovecraft's popularity in *Weird Tales* did not, however, translate to recognition in the mainstream literary world; he himself rightly scorned the pulps as havens of formula-ridden mediocrity and hoped that book publication by an established firm would lend his work the dignity it deserved. But the unworldly Lovecraft's intermittent negotiations with such publishers as Putnam and Knopf proved unsuccessful, and with each rejection came increasingly severe blows to his ever-fragile self-esteem. As he lay dying in the winter of 1936-37, Lovecraft might well have envisioned the ultimate oblivion that would overtake his work, lost in the crumbling pages of dime-store pulps.

What saved that work from obscurity was the devotion of Lovecraft's friends. It is a testament to the power of his personality that Lovecraft could elicit such devotion, even from those who had never met him but were linked only by correspondence. August Derleth and Donald Wandrei expended their own time and resources in founding a publishing company, Arkham House, initially for the sole purpose of preserving Lovecraft's work in hardcover; but Derleth never met him and Wandrei met him only fleetingly in his native Providence, Rhode Island, and on his rare visits to New York in the 1930s. Numerous other friends have testified to the fascination of Lovecraft's personality as conveyed through the sheafs of handwritten letters that he scattered so prodigally to all who wrote to him—friends in the amateur journalism movement, professional colleagues such as Robert E. Howard and E. Hoffmann Price, and, of course, youths such as Willis Conover.

Ironically, in 1975 Conover was largely a mystery man to Lovecraft devotees. Although widely known because of his involvement in the Voice of America and because of his extensive collection of jazz recordings, his brief correspondence with Lovecraft during the last six months of the latter's life was known only to specialists, since the fifth and final volume of Lovecraft's *Selected Letters*, containing brief excerpts from his letters to Conover, did not appear until 1976. It became quickly evident from a reading of *Lovecraft at Last* that Conover was one of those many "kid editors," as Lovecraft called them, who approached the Providence writer in the last decade of his life, seeking guidance and advice. The science fiction, fantasy, and horror pulps had engendered, by the early 1930s, a vigorous "fan" movement that led youngsters (almost all of them were teenage boys) to publish, at their own expense, humble magazines devoted to the fields in question. Lovecraft, as a towering figure in weird fiction, was a magnet for such youths, among whom were Robert H. Barlow, Robert Bloch, Fritz Leiber, Henry Kuttner, Donald A. Wollheim, Charles D. Hornig (founder of the first fanzine, the *Fantasy Fan*, in 1933), and, belatedly, Willis Conover. Not all of these admirers were teenagers—Leiber was twenty-six when he first wrote to Lovecraft in the fall of 1936—nor were they actual editors of fan magazines, but they formed a recognisable cadre of youthful devotees whose relationship with Lovecraft was markedly different from that of his professional colleagues or of his associates in the amateur press. Lovecraft, always given to a playful affectation of extreme old age, now finally had a band of eager "grandsons" who looked to him for great learning, wisdom, and experience, and who hoped to gather whatever jewels might be imbedded in those letters that he wrote for hours daily.

Although Conover never states it explicitly in *Lovecraft at Last*, Lovecraft's sudden death was a severe emotional shock and caused an abrupt dampening of his enthusiasm for weird fiction. His return to Lovecraft, around 1972, came at a highly propitious moment. It was at this time that the devotion of Derleth and Wandrei in keeping Lovecraft in print was paying off: Beagle Books (later absorbed by Ballantine Books) had begun reissuing Lovecraft's work in mass-market paperback editions, and these were so popular that they elicited a full-page review by Philip Herrera in *Time* magazine (11 June 1973). Herrera reported that more than a million copies of those paperback editions had already been sold. Lovecraft was on his way to becoming a fixture in American popular culture. Nevertheless, in his preface Conover exaggerates considerably the extent of Lovecraft's critical esteem in the mid-1970s. Not only was Lovecraft still virtually unknown to the literary and academic communities, but the cottage industry known as "Lovecraft scholarship" was only just beginning, pioneered by Dirk W. Mosig and Kenneth W. Faig, Jr. *Lovecraft at Last*, along with the other two books that emerged in 1975, gave a significant impetus to further work on Lovecraft, revealing a literary figure far more complex than that of mere lurid pulp legend.

In many ways Conover's book is the most impressive of those three books, not least because it fulfilled gloriously its relatively humble aims whereas the other two could be said to have bitten off more than they could chew. De Camp's book was, indeed, the first full-scale biography of Lovecraft—August Derleth's slim *H. P. L.: A Memoir* (1945) could hardly qualify as such—but it was highly controversial in its seeming lack of sympathy with Lovecraft's character and motives, and in its numerous errors of fact and interpretation. Long's book, although not purporting to be a formal biography, disappointed somehow because one expected more from a man who had known Lovecraft for nearly twenty years and who, for a time (especially during Lovecraft's residence in New York from 1924 through 1926), had met him nearly every day. Unfortunate attempts to duplicate Lovecraft's exact words, a focusing on relatively inessential and anecdotal aspects of his life, and other failings quickly caused Long's book to be deprecated. Later, it was learned that the volume had been written in great haste: alarmed at the hostile portrait of Lovecraft that was emerging in de Camp's book (chapters of which Long had read in manuscript), Long felt the need to paint what he believed to be a more honest portrait, resulting in a manuscript that was in need of much revision. Conover, for his part, made no claim that his book was anything but a heartfelt tribute to the friendship that developed between a teenager and an elderly, dying man; and no one could claim that it was anything but impeccable in every regard—in its style, in its substance, and most of all in its production values.

The virtues of *Lovecraft at Last* are too numerous to cite. Perhaps its greatest triumph is the seamless way that it interweaves a multiplicity of documents—letters by Lovecraft and Conover; articles on Lovecraft from contemporary fan magazines; manuscripts, autographs, book reviews, and photographs—into a smooth-flowing narrative that fulfills Conover's wish to present the illusion of a conversation between himself and his revered mentor. In a sense, the book can almost be considered a hypertext: at one moment we come upon a casual mention of F. Lee Baldwin's article on Lovecraft in *Fantasy Magazine*, and the next moment we are presented with that article itself; discussions of the cover art in *Weird Tales* leads, by a turn of the page, to an example of that art; and so on. Conover spared no expense in his scrupulous reproduction of these documents, including the smallest features of Lovecraft's own handwritten letters.

In light of these virtues, the few blemishes in *Lovecraft at Last* can easily be overlooked. Conover's unfortunate attempt to cast doubt on the likelihood that Lovecraft's father died of syphilis has been contradicted by the medical evidence, which shows almost conclusively that Winfield Scott Lovecraft did indeed die of tertiary neurosyphilis in 1898. (At the same time, it is equally certain that Lovecraft himself was not congenitally syphilitic, as a Wasserman test taken a few days before his own death confirms.) There are a small number of mistranscriptions of Lovecraft's epistolary prose, none affecting any significant point. Other features of the book that may make us alternately smile or wince have to do with what can only be termed Conover's recklessly courageous exposure of his own teenage callowness. His continual joking in regard to the mythical "gods" of Lovecraft's pseudomythology impel the ever-courteous Lovecraft—always careful to reply point-by-point to his correspondents' missives—to engage in such sophomoric humour himself.

In some ways it is unfair to compare *Lovecraft at Last* with de Camp's *Lovecraft: A Biography*. It may well be argued that Conover presents only a tiny fraction of Lovecraft's life whereas de Camp presents the whole of it; but Conover's portrayal can stand as a microcosm of Lovecraft at his best. Anyone who has read the whole of Lovecraft's *Selected Letters* can attest to the remarkable manner in which he transformed himself, literarily and personally, over the course of fewer than three decades. The early Lovecraft—crabbed, dogmatic, overbookish, and, let it be honestly stated, not without his share of political and social prejudices—metamorphosed gradually into the genial, generous, broad-minded, and expansive individual that we know from his last decade; and Conover provides an unforgettable snapshot of the final stage of that change, when Lovecraft faced the added obstacles of increasing poverty and increasing illness with a good-natured stoicism that doubles our admiration for his strength of character. And the grim conclusion—in which Lovecraft suddenly reveals his terminal illness by feeble pencil marks on a postcard sent by Conover, followed by his aunt Annie Gamwell's shocking report of Lovecraft's death—brings the book to a close with all the startling abruptness of a Shakespearean tragedy.

The entire fantasy and science-fiction community hailed *Lovecraft at Last* upon its appearance; even de Camp wrote a positive review of it in the fanzine *Amra* (October 1975). It did not, however, receive as much attention in the mainstream press as it deserved. Aside from routine reviews in *Publishers Weekly* and *Library Journal*, all we have is a brief notice by Phoebe Adams in the *Atlantic Monthly* (July 1975), who remarked that the book "is, if not a full self-portrait by Lovecraft, certainly an attractive and enlightening self-sketch." Yet, *Lovecraft at Last* set the stage for much of the work that followed. With the appearance of the last two volumes of *Selected Letters* the next year, the tools that were necessary for a more profound study of Lovecraft's life and work were now available. It is true that a number of the forthcoming works that Conover lists in his bibliography—including his own book of "new discoveries"—never appeared; but other hands were not slow to take up the task of interpreting Lovecraft for a new generation. I can remember my own first reading of *Lovecraft at Last* as an inexperienced eighteen-year-old ensconced in the hushed reading room of the John Hay Library at Brown University, and it was not much later that my establishment of the academic journal *Lovecraft Studies*, the publication of my critical anthology *H. P. Lovecraft: Four Decades of Criticism* (1980), my bibliography of Lovecraft (1981), and my preparation of corrected texts of Lovecraft's work with Arkham House in the mid-1980s laid the groundwork for such works as Donald R. Burleson's *H. P. Lovecraft: A Critical Study* (1983) and *Lovecraft: Disturbing the Universe* (1990); Peter Cannon's monograph for Twayne Publishers (1989); the critical anthology *An Epicure in the Terrible* (1991), edited by David E. Schultz and myself; and numerous other works. Not the least of these were a flurry of small volumes of work by and about Lovecraft published by Necronomicon Press, including my own full-scale biography, *H. P. Lovecraft: A Life* (1996), in which I attempted to present a portrait of Lovecraft more in consonance with Conover's view than with de Camp's. All this activity culminated in the H. P. Lovecraft Centennial Conference at Brown University in 1990, a fitting pendant to the World Fantasy Convention of fifteen years earlier.

But is *Lovecraft at Last* merely a work for Lovecraft aficionados? Can someone who knows little about Lovecraft gain anything from this book? It may take a considerable exercise of the imagination for someone in my position to adopt the attitude of a neophyte, but I think the effort is worth making. Suppose, then, that I were a person who had heard only vaguely of Lovecraft—perhaps I had unwisely seen some of the wretched film adaptations of his work, or even been compelled to read a story or two of his in a college course. I see a book entitled *Lovecraft at Last*. The title is deliberately ambiguous: as I read the book I see that I am not only encountering the real Lovecraft at long last, but a Lovecraft in the last stages of a tragically shortened life, who nevertheless continued writing to the bitter end like one of his own harried narrators. I see Lovecraft befriending a boy thirty years his junior, treating him as a near-equal, informing him on all manner of arcane subjects from alchemy to eighteenth-century orthography; but most of all I see the plangently human story of a boy who needs a mentor and a man who needs to play the role of mentor, and that it is this mutual dependency that maintains the relationship between the two until one of them is quite literally at death's door. I see a Lovecraft who, although forced by necessity to publish his work in crude pulp magazines, never yielded in his aesthetic integrity, determined to write what he wished and in the manner he wanted whether he was paid for it or not. And not infrequently I find that Lovecraft's comments retain their validity to the present day, as when he notes that "virtually all so-called weird films are simply infantile nonsense." Best of all, I see, if not exactly a comprehensive biography, at least the tantalising fragments of a biography—more, an autobiography in Lovecraft's own words, as he looks back upon a full life of four and a half decades. And I conclude that, poverty-stricken though he may have been, and plagued at the end by painful illness, Lovecraft led a life we may all envy: a life whose salient incidents were not external, but instead focused, with an almost fathomless exclusivity, on the development of mind and imagination. And I am thankful to Willis Conover for sharing with me that brief, but special, relationship he had with one of the most interesting men of our time.

The Cthulhu Mythos

It is one of the many paradoxes of the Cthulhu Mythos that its development over most of the past seventy-five years owes less to its creator, H. P. Lovecraft, than to his colleague and self-styled disciple, August Derleth (1909–1971). It was, indeed, Derleth who gave it its name, and it was Derleth who was chiefly responsible for nurturing its growth in a particular direction, both by encouraging certain writers and by discouraging others. That Derleth took the Mythos in directions Lovecraft would almost certainly not have approved is now widely accepted; what directions Lovecraft himself would have taken if he had lived longer is largely a matter of conjecture.

Exactly why the Cthulhu Mythos has been so widely imitated, not only by the many writers with whom Lovecraft was acquainted in his lifetime but by dozens, perhaps hundreds, of writers after his death, many of whom have little connexion with the intricate network of friends, colleagues, and disciples that developed during and after his lifetime, is a perhaps unanswerable question. Chris Jarocha-Ernst, in *A Cthulhu Mythos Bibliography and Concordance* (1999), lists 2,631 works of the Cthulhu Mythos written up to the time of its publication. This number is perhaps a bit inflated, since it includes more than 100 letters by Lovecraft in which Mythos names of various sorts are mentioned, often in passing; but the figure is still impressive. Commonly drawn parallels with the equally well-developed mythos of Sherlock Holmes do not seem particularly helpful, given the wide difference in genre orientation, and given also that the detective story much more readily lends itself to formulaic imitation than the horror tale. Lovecraft's own colleagues, Clark Ashton Smith and Robert E. Howard, would appear to have fashioned equally compelling myth-cycles, the first in his fantastic realms of Zothique, Averoigne, and Hyperborea, and the other in his popular tales of King Kull, Solomon Kane, and Conan the Cimmerian; but, although Conan has enjoyed wide dissemination in films, comic books, and other media, relatively few other writers have produced actual imitations.

The Cthulhu Mythos is, accordingly, an unusual icon of supernatural literature because it is so centrally derived from the work of a single author. Unlike such icons as the ghost or the vampire, whose roots in folklore reach into the earliest origins of human society, the Mythos is a uniquely intellectualised, even philosophical icon that could not have emerged except at a critical moment in Western history, when conventional religious belief was being threatened by radical discoveries in the sciences, which were painting a picture of the universe as a spatially and temporally infinite realm where the achievements, and even the very existence, of the human race were merely fleeting accidents. In a real sense, the Cthulhu Mythos could only have been fashioned by one who had understood, or at any rate absorbed, Einstein, Darwin, and Freud. Lovecraft himself referred to his creation as an "artificial mythology" (SL 3.66), but, as we shall see, David E. Schultz may be more on target when he refers to the Mythos as an "antimythology" ("Microcosm" 222)—for, in truth, the Mythos subverts the goals and purposes for which actual religions or mythologies function.

The Lovecraft Mythos

In Lovecraft's hands, the "typical" Mythos tale, if there really is such a thing, depicts the incursion of immensely powerful forces from the depths of space—labelled as "gods" by the human beings who either combat them or seek to gain a sliver of reflected power by worshipping them—to various remote corners of the earth. Knowledge—of a sort—about these "gods" can be found in various books of occult lore, themselves so rare that extant copies of them can be numbered on the fingers of one hand. Accordingly, the central icon of the Mythos can be seen to consist of several subsidiary icons, of which four can be concretely identified: (1) a vitally realised but largely imaginary New England topography; (2) an ever-growing library of occult books, both ancient and modern (and, in consequence, a band of scholars who seek out these texts, either to carry out the spells and incantations contained in them or to combat them); (3) the "gods," their human followers, and their monstrous "minions" or acolytes; and (4) a sense of the cosmic, both spatial and temporal, that often links the Mythos more firmly with science fiction than with the supernatural. How Lovecraft came to fuse these four elements into his most representative Mythos tales requires not only an understanding of the course of Lovecraft's two-decade career as a fiction writer, but a grasp of the philosophical thought that underlies it.

The Cthulhu Mythos, as envisioned by Lovecraft, was an expression of his deepest philosophical convictions. Growing up in a conventionally religious household in Providence, Rhode Island, the precocious Lovecraft quickly shed his religious belief and, by successive absorption of Greco-Roman literature and thought and the sciences of chemistry and astronomy, became an atheist and materialist who saw in science the ultimate arbiter of truth; but at the same time he recognised that science did not, and perhaps could not, fully explicate the universe, so that a permanent reservoir of mystery would remain. What is more, as both an appreciator of art and a creative artist, he understood that scientific truth could not provide emotional satisfaction; that could come only from art and from other sources such as close ties to one's family and one's race, and to the topographical and historical milieu that the accidents of one's birth and upbringing had provided.

Lovecraft lived in a time of intellectual ferment. His prodigious self-taught learning in the sciences had made him a master of such disciplines as chemistry, biology, geology, astronomy, and anthropology; but much of this learning, derived from such nineteenth-century titans as Darwin, Thomas Henry Huxley, Ernst Haeckel (*The Riddle of the Universe*, 1899), Edward Burnett Tylor (*Primitive Culture*, 1871), and Sir James George Frazer (*The Golden Bough*, 1890f.), had to undergo painful revision as the twentieth century introduced new conceptions that threatened to modify, and perhaps overthrow, the rather cocksure materialism of the nineteenth—especially such things as Einstein's theory of relativity, Max Planck's quantum theory, and Werner Heisenberg's indeterminacy principle. The Cthulhu Mythos is, in a very real sense, a reflection of Lovecraft's awareness of the uncertainty of knowledge in his own time, but at the same time it is a subtle rebuke to those who saw in that uncertainty an excuse to return to the credulous and outmoded myths of religion.

A littérateur as much as a scientist, Lovecraft read voraciously, both in his chosen field of supernatural fiction and in general literature. Much of his early fiction is imitative—of Edgar Allan Poe, whom he read at the age of eight; of Lord Dunsany, the Irish fantaisiste whose works he enthusiastically embraced in 1919; of Arthur Machen, whose dark tales of the "little people" in secret corners of the world fired his imagination; and of Algernon Blackwood, whose cosmic vision was scarcely less intense than Lovecraft's own—and it would take a full decade for Lovecraft to assimilate these and other influences so that he could write tales that were, while still indebted in certain elements to his predecessors, nonetheless fully his own.

The first tale of Lovecraft's maturity, "The Tomb" (1917), already begins the etching of the history and topography of New England that would be one of his great strengths as a writer, and that makes him, no less than Nathaniel Hawthorne or Sarah Orne Jewett, an authentic local color writer. Lovecraft was aware that New England offered, in the otherwise brashly new United States, a depth of history that could otherwise be found only in the Old World. Just as the Gothic novels of the late eighteenth and early nineteenth centuries drew upon the depths of mediaeval ignorance and superstition as the haven for their incursions of horror into a rational age, so did the seventeenth century in New England—typified by religious fanaticism, witchcraft fears, and ever-present terror of the untenanted wilderness beyond the limited zones of settled civilization—represent a kind of American dark age from which all horrors could emerge. "The Terrible Old Man" (1920), brief as it is, is significant not merely in its citation of the first of Lovecraft's imaginary New England towns, Kingsport, but in its suggestion that sorcery can unnaturally prolong a person's life well beyond the norm—a theme that resonates in many of the Mythos tales.

In "The Terrible Old Man," however, Kingsport is largely a product of Lovecraft's imagination. Two years later he first visited the town of Marblehead, Massachusetts, and was captivated by the seeming completeness of its preservation of a colonial past. Not long thereafter he wrote "The Festival," in which Kingsport is now identified with Marblehead. The story is an important precursor to the Mythos not only in its clear evocation of a New England weighted with age-old horrors, but in its depiction of a hideous hybrid race of creatures—"They were not altogether crows, nor moles, nor buzzards, nor ants, nor vampire bats, nor decomposed human beings; but something I cannot and must not recall" (*D* 215)—that anticipate several of the subsidiary Mythos entities. In later years Lovecraft would admit that his other mythical cities were based very loosely upon real places. Arkham—first cited in "The Picture in the House" (1920)—was derived from Salem (although Salem had, at this time, no university to match the imaginary Miskatonic University). Dunwich, vividly realised in "The Dunwich Horror" (1928), was based upon a trip Lovecraft took to a remote south-central Massachusetts area containing the towns of Wilbraham, Hampden, and Monson. Innsmouth, the decaying seaport in "The Shadow over Innsmouth" (1931), was based on several trips made to Newburyport, Massachusetts, a town whose genteel decline into seediness has now been strikingly reversed. Lovecraft was perhaps a bit cavalier in stating so frequently in letters that his imaginary towns were based on single real towns in New England; in reality, his visits throughout the region—to the coastal towns of Gloucester and Rockport, Massachusetts; to the rural stretches of Vermont in 1927 and 1928, depicted so poignantly in "The Whisperer in Darkness" (1930); or to such towns as Foster, Greenwich, and Providence in his native state of Rhode Island—coloured the smallest touches of landscape description throughout his work.

The icon of the occult book is first found in "The Statement of Randolph Carter" (1919), not otherwise considered a Mythos tale. Here we find a learned scholar who has come upon what his friend, the narrator, calls a "fiend-inspired book . . . written in characters whose like I never saw elsewhere" (MM 300). This description makes it clear that this book cannot be the celebrated *Necronomicon* of the mad Arab Abdul Alhazred; that tome was first cited in "The

Hound" (1922), although the author and his "unexplainable couplet" ("That is not dead which can eternal lie, / And with strange aeons even death may die") were first mentioned in "The Nameless City" (1921). Lovecraft himself did not create many more imaginary tomes, but very quickly his colleagues fashioned an entire library of them: the *Liber Ivonis* or *Book of Eibon* (invented by Clark Ashton Smith); *Cultes des Goules* by the Comte d'Erlette (not invented by Derleth, as its author's name might suggest, but by Robert Bloch); *Nameless Cults* by von Junzt (the German title of which, *Unaussprechlichen Kulten*, was devised by a group effort by several of Lovecraft's colleagues); *Mysteries of the Worm* by Ludvig Prinn (invented by Bloch; Lovecraft devised the Latin title, *De Vermis Mysteriis*); and so on. Lovecraft lent his imprimatur—after a fashion—to these titles by citing them in his own stories along with the *Necronomicon*, and he made the game more entertaining by citing genuine works of occult lore (the *Demonolatreia* of Remigius) or of scholarship (*The Witch-Cult in Western Europe* by Margaret A. Murray) that could well have been imaginary, and that were in fact taken to be imaginary by several generations of readers.

We should not be surprised that so bookish a man as Lovecraft—who, as a child, absorbed in secret the eighteenth-century books found in the attic of his home in Providence—should come to find such power in the written word. While he himself only scorned conventional occultism and found actual occult treatises dull and unimaginative, his imaginary books suggest that words can have a direct impact upon human and cosmic existence, through the efficacy of spells and incantations—just as, in his own life, several key books directly inspired both his fiction and his evolving philosophy.

What has, however, not been widely recognised is that Lovecraft's own conception of the *Necronomicon* and other invented tomes changed quite radically over the years, and from tale to tale. As Robert M. Price has shown, the *Necronomicon* can be variously seen as a grimoire (a book "containing recipes and prescriptions for spells"), a demonology ("a guidebook to heretical beliefs, to be used in suppressing them"), and a scripture ("Genres in the Lovecraftian Library" 14-15); it can be seen from this that the purposes to which the *Necronomicon* and other titles are put vary widely from one story to the next, and in some cases it is not clear whether the *Necronomicon* is actually advocating the return of the "gods" it describes or warning readers against them.

Some, perhaps much, of this ambiguity may have to do with the fact that those "gods" themselves undergo radical change throughout the last decade of Lovecraft's life, when his most representative fiction was written. Although the first "god" invented (or, in this case, adapted) by Lovecraft was the ancient Philistine god Dagon in "Dagon" (1917), it was only in "The Call of Cthulhu" (1926) that the Cthulhu Mythos, as such, can (retroactively) be said to have come into genuine existence; for it was only here that all the four subsidiary icons—topography, occult lore, gods, and cosmicism—are first conjoined into a coherent whole. In this mesmerising tale, a professor unearths evidence that a race of extraterrestrial entities, led by a creature called Cthulhu, came to earth from the depths of space millions of years ago, building a geometrically bizarre city called R'lyeh. A sculptor fashions a statue of Cthulhu in his dreams; later the professor's nephew, the story's narrator, describes the object: "If I say that my somewhat extravagant imagination yielded simultaneous pictures of an octopus, a dragon, and a human creature, I shall not be unfaithful to the spirit of the thing" (*DH* 127). R'lyeh sank under the sea, somewhere in the South Pacific; but a cult member captured in Louisiana testifies to the core of his beliefs:

> They worshipped, so they said, the Great Old Ones who lived ages before there were any men, and who came to the young world out of the sky. Those Old Ones were gone now, inside the earth and under the sea; but their dead bodies had told their secrets in dreams to the first men, who formed a cult which had never died. This was that cult, and the prisoners said that it had always existed and always would exist, hidden in distant wastes and dark places all over the world until the time when the great priest Cthulhu, from his dark house in the mighty city of R'lyeh under the waters, should rise and bring the earth again beneath its sway. Some day he would call, when the stars were ready, and the secret cult would always be waiting to liberate him. (*DH* 139)

R'lyeh does rise—not because "the stars are ready," but as the result of an earthquake (an actual event that occurred on February 28, 1925); some hapless sailors witness the event and actually catch a glimpse of Cthulhu: "A mountain walked or stumbled" (*DH* 152). But R'lyeh falls back into the ocean, taking Cthulhu with it. The world is safe—for now.

It is difficult to convey in short compass the extraordinarily complex texture of "The Call of Cthulhu," with its multiple shiftings of perspective and its suggestion of a horror that threatens not only our tiny planet but the entire universe. The story was too imaginatively advanced for Farnsworth Wright, editor of the pulp magazine *Weird Tales*, where most of Lovecraft's stories up to this point had appeared; he rejected it when it was first submitted to him. But, in the summer of 1927, at the urging of Donald Wandrei, Wright asked to see the story again, and Lovecraft accompanied it with an important letter outlining his literary principles:

> Now all my tales are based on the fundamental premise that common human laws and interests and emotions have no validity or significance in the vast cosmos-at-large. To me there is nothing but puerility in a tale in which the human form—and the local human passions and conditions and standards—

are depicted as native to other worlds or other universes. To achieve the essence of real externality, whether of time or space or dimension, one must forget that such things as organic life, good and evil, love and hate, and all such local attributes of a negligible and temporary race called mankind, have any existence at all. Only the human scenes and characters must have human qualities. These must be handled with unsparing *realism*, (not catch-penny *romanticism*) but when we cross the line to the boundless and hideous unknown—the shadow-haunted Outside—we must remember to leave our humanity and terrestrialism at the threshold. (SL 2.150)

There may be some exaggeration here: it is difficult to see that *all* Lovecraft's stories up to this point had exemplified the principles he outlines. The element of cosmicism—which we now recognise as his signature conception—is evident only in a small number of tales, notably "Dagon" (in which a hideous aquatic entity emerges from the depths of the Pacific after a land mass has suddenly arisen—a clear anticipation of "The Call of Cthulhu"), "Beyond the Wall of Sleep" (in which an ignorant denizen of Catskill mountains is psychically possessed by a cosmic entity from outer space), and a very few others. In any event, Lovecraft appears to be fashioning a manifesto for the kind of fiction he wished to write in the future, and by and large he fulfilled it in the tales of his final decade of writing.

By the time "The Call of Cthulhu" was resubmitted to (and accepted by) *Weird Tales*, Lovecraft had already written a tale that perhaps exemplifies his cosmic perspective better than any other single work. "The Colour out of Space" (1927) is not generally considered a tale of the Cthulhu Mythos, because it does not cite any of the cosmic entities that have become its chief defining trait, but in its suggestions of stupendous cosmicism, in its sensitive etching of a haunted New England landscape, and in its overall artistry, it may stand preeminent in Lovecraft's oeuvre. Here a hapless farmer "west of Arkham" (*DH* 53) finds his life changed when a meteorite lands on his property. It exhibits extraordinarily bizarre chemical characteristics (Lovecraft's early enthusiasm for chemistry is put to good use here), and it would appear that some entity or entities were embedded in the meteor and have now escaped, subtly corrupting both the landscape and the human beings who occupy it. Plants turn grey and brittle, and the farmer and his family also decay, mentally, psychologically, and finally physically. In a riveting climactic scene, the entities shoot back into space from the well where they have apparently been dwelling.

Here again a summary or synopsis utterly fails to convey the subtlety of the tale. In fact, we know neither the physical nor—more importantly—the psychological properties of the entities involved. We do not know whether they are material or otherwise, or whether they are actuated by hate, fear, malice, self-preservation, or any other of the traits conventionally attributed to human beings. It is in this tale, preeminently, that Lovecraft has dispensed with "such things as organic life, good and evil, love and hate, and all such local attributes of a negligible and temporary race called mankind." Even Cthulhu is once described as "ravening for delight" (*DH* 152), which suggests a quasi-human psychology of hatred and revenge; but of the entities in "The Colour out of Space," no such emotion can be attributed.

Lovecraft unfortunately regresses in his next major tale, "The Dunwich Horror" (1928). Largely an evocation of the rural region of central Massachusetts that he visited in the summer of 1928 in the company of an old friend, Edith Miniter, this tale reads almost like a parody of itself—or a parody of the hundreds of unimaginative Cthulhu Mythos tales that would be written in its wake. A librarian of Miskatonic University, Henry Armitage, is highly suspicious of a clan of farmers named Whateley, living in Dunwich, especially when one of them, Wilbur, the child of Lavinia Whateley, attempts to steal the *Necronomicon* from the library after Armitage refuses him permission to borrow the rare book. Wilbur dies in the attempt, and his body, which virtually disintegrates upon death, shows that "he had taken somewhat after his unknown father" (*DH* 176). But worse is to come: some strange creature is ravaging the countryside around Dunwich. Armitage—after spending days deciphering an encrypted diary by Wilbur—ascertains that Wilbur had envisioned "some plan for the extirpation of the entire human race by some terrible elder race of beings from another dimension" (*DH* 185). Whateley's death had forestalled the plan, but clearly some entity that he had evidently called out of space was on the loose and must be stopped. So Armitage and two colleagues, muttering spells at the creature, manage to send it back into space. Only at the end do we learn that the creature was Wilbur's twin brother, the spawn of Lavinia Whateley and the cosmic entity Yog-Sothoth.

"The Dunwich Horror," in some sense, made the rest of the Cthulhu Mythos—at least as envisioned by August Derleth and his successors—possible in its naive portrayal of a good-vs.-evil scenario in which human beings and their fate are at the centre of the picture. Armitage delivers a number of self-important lectures on the subject, concluding that "We have no business calling in such things from outside, and only very wicked people and very wicked cults ever try to" (*DH* 197). One would like to think—and it has been so argued—that this story was meant as a deliberate parody and that Armitage is to be taken as a kind of pompous buffoon, but Lovecraft confessed in a letter that during the writing of the story, "[I] found myself psychologically identifying myself with one of the characters (an aged scholar who finally combats the menace) toward the end" (*ES* 1.158). Donald R. Burleson ("The Mythic Hero

Archetype in 'The Dunwich Horror'") makes the valid point that a lengthy quotation from the *Necronomicon* early in the story—"Man rules now where they [the Old Ones] ruled once; They shall soon rule where man rules now" (*DH* 170)—suggests that Armitage's "victory" is a fleeting and ineffectual one, to be overturned by the ultimate triumph of the Old Ones; but the final impression of the story does leave a strong suggestion that human beings can at least hold the Old Ones in check for a time. Clearly, this story does not embody the moral neutrality that Lovecraft felt such cosmic narratives ought to have.

"The Dunwich Horror" is the only tale that puts the entity Yog-Sothoth at centre stage. First cited in passing in *The Case of Charles Dexter Ward* (1927), this creature is never actually seen in the tale, and we can only gain some idea of his physical attributes by the fleeting glimpse of his offspring as revealed at the end of the story, and effectively conveyed in the ignorant patois of a Dunwich denizen:

> "Bigger'n a barn . . . all made o' squirmin' ropes . . . hull thing sort o' shaped like a hen's egg bigger'n anything, with dozens o' legs like hogsheads that haff shut up when they step . . . nothin' solid a baout it—all like jelly, an' made o' sep'rit wrigglin' ropes pushed clost together . . . great bulgin' eyes all over it . . . ten or twenty maouths or trunks a-stickin' aout all long the sides, big as stovepipes, an' all a-tossin' an' openin' an' shuttin . . . all grey, with kinder blue or purple rings . . ." (*DH* 194)

As with Cthulhu, one can only appreciate the richness of Lovecraft's imagination in fashioning an entity so different from the ghosts and vampires and werewolves of conventional supernatural fiction.

With "The Whisperer in Darkness" (1930) things are a bit better. A wondrous evocation of the landscape of rural Vermont, this substantial narrative richly exemplifies the documentary style that has been so widely used in other Cthulhu Mythos tales. Virtually an epistolary tale, "The Whisperer in Darkness" tells, by the exchange of letters between a professor at Miskatonic, Albert N. Wilmarth, and an intelligent but rustic denizen of Vermont, Henry Wentworth Akeley, how the floods that had devastated New England in November 1927 (a real event) washed down strange creatures—"a sort of huge, light-red crab with many pairs of legs and with two great bat-like wings in the middle of the back" (*DH* 211)—from the remote hills where they apparently dwelt. Akeley concludes that these creatures come from another planet—very likely the planet Yuggoth, on the rim of the solar system (to be equated with the recently discovered Pluto)—and that they have come here to mine a certain substance they cannot find on their native planet. Akeley calls them the "fungi from Yuggoth," because their physical constitution appears to be a mix of what would conventionally be considered animal and plant characteristics. They are capable of tremendous intellectual and scientific feats, notably the science of surgery; in fact, they have fashioned a way to extract the brain of any living creature, preserve it in a canister, and take it on cosmic voyagings throughout the universe.

It is at this point that Wilmarth—and perhaps Lovecraft—begin to draw back in apprehension. In the essay "Notes on Writing Weird Fiction" (1933), Lovecraft stated that one of his chief goals was to "achieve, momentarily, the illusion of some strange suspension or violation of the galling limitations of time, space, and natural law which for ever imprison us and frustrate our curiosity about the infinite cosmic spaces beyond the radius of our sight and analysis" (CE 2.175–76). This is exactly what Wilmarth says at one point as he imagines what it might be like to go on disembodied voyages through space: "To shake off the maddening and wearying limitations of time and space and natural law—to be linked with the vast outside—to come close to the nighted and abysmal secrets of the infinite and the ultimate—surely such a thing was worth the risk of one's life, soul, and sanity!" (*DH* 243). But in fact Wilmarth becomes horrified at the prospect, especially when he learns (or suspects) that his friend Akeley has been replaced by one of the fungi—or perhaps by the leader of the fungi, the shape-shifting cosmic entity Nyarlathotep.

The figure of Nyarlathotep is perhaps the most interesting—at any rate, the most exhaustively developed—of any of the "gods" of the Cthulhu Mythos as created by Lovecraft. First appearing as a mysterious, pharaoh-like creature in the prose poem "Nyarlathotep" (1920), he returns in vivid form in the dreamland fantasy *The Dream-Quest of Unknown Kadath* (1926–27), as the archenemy of Randolph Carter, who searches throughout dreamland for the "sunset city" that haunts his dreams. In "The Whisperer in Darkness" he is avowedly worshipped by the fungi from Yuggoth, who state that "To Nyarlathotep, Mighty Messenger, must all things be told. And He shall put on the semblance of man, the waxen mask and the robe that hides, and come down from the world of Seven Suns to mock" (*DH* 226). Nyarlathotep will make one more vivid appearance in a Lovecraft story.

By this time Lovecraft himself was aware that he was fashioning something new and innovative. Even though he never devised the term "Cthulhu Mythos," he was becoming gradually cognisant that his tales were building upon one another and developing some kind of pseudomythological framework. Many commentators have been puzzled by Lovecraft's comment, in the autobiographical sketch "Some Notes on a Nonentity" (1933), that it was Lord Dunsany "from whom I got the idea of the artificial pantheon and myth-background represented by 'Cthulhu', 'Yog-Sothoth', 'Yuggoth', etc." (CE 5.209–10), but the influence of Dunsany, when properly understood, was critical. Dunsany's early books of short stories, *The Gods of Pegāna* (1905) and

Time and the Gods (1906), established an entire cosmogony of gods, demigods, and worshippers, all set in the imaginary realm of Pegāna. Pegāna is not, as is often believed, a dreamworld; there is in fact some suggestion that it is set in the distant past of the real world. But clearly we are dealing with a land quite remote from the present day. The gods of this realm are by no means as terrifying in appearance or in action as Lovecraft's; they are, to be sure, powerful, imposing, and occasionally vengeful, but they are on the whole remote, interfering in human affairs only when some lowly human being develops sufficient hubris to challenge the gods and their prerogatives.

Lovecraft produced a dozen or more blatant imitations of Dunsany during the period 1919–21, but relatively few of these dealt with the kind of gods that populate the Pegāna pantheon. Only one, "The Other Gods" (1921)—a classic tale of hubris where Barzai the Wise seeks to climb Mount Hatheg-Kla and catch a glimpse of the gods of earth, only to learn that these "mild" gods are in fact protected by "other" gods far more powerful and baleful than they, and who exact suitable vengeance on Barzai (*D* 131)—can be said to duplicate the Dunsany mythos. Lovecraft's great innovation was to remove these cosmic but remote entities from the never-never-land of fantasy and thrust them boldly into the real world, making also a genre shift from pure fantasy to supernatural horror. The Nyarlathotep in the dreamland fantasy *The Dream-Quest of Unknown Kadath*, while intimidating, can nonetheless be dealt with, even reasoned with; and in the end Carter bamboozles him and returns to the "sunset city" he sought (which proves to be his memories of the very real New England landscape of his boyhood). In "The Call of Cthulhu" and other Mythos tales, the "gods" are much less easily handled, and rarely can humanity score even a partial victory over them.

The Later Lovecraft Mythos

While he was writing "The Dunwich Horror" Lovecraft noted that it was part of the "Arkham cycle" (*SL* 2.246). This is one of the first indications that Lovecraft was becoming gradually aware of the internal coherence of his Mythos. While it is abundantly clear that he did not plan the Mythos in advance, and in fact rarely felt bound by the data of previous tales in effecting innovations to the Mythos in later tales, it is perhaps only a slight exaggeration to say, as George T. Wetzel has done, that Lovecraft's "Mythos stories should actually be considered not as separate works but rather the different chapters of a very lengthy novel" (79). Lovecraft himself flippantly referred to his myth-cycle as "Cthulhuism & Yog-Sothothery" (*ES* 1.336). In a more significant passage in a long letter to Frank Belknap Long, written in February 1931, Lovecraft wrote as follows:

> I really agree that 'Yog-Sothoth' is a basically immature conception, & unfitted for really serious literature.... But I consider the use of actual folk-myths as even more childish than the use of new artificial myths, since in employing the former one is forced to retain many blatant puerilities & contradictions of experience which could be subtilised or smoothed over if the supernaturalism were modelled to order for the given case. The only permanently artistic use of Yog-Sothothery, I think, is in symbolic or associative phantasy of the frankly poetic type; in which fixed dream-patterns of the natural organism are given an embodiment & crystallisation.... But there is another phase of cosmic phantasy (which may or may not include frank Yog-Sothothery) whose foundations appear to me as better grounded than those of ordinary oneiroscopy; personal limitation regarding the *sense of outsideness*. I refer to the aesthetic crystallisation of that burning & inextinguishable feeling of mixed wonder & oppression which the sensitive imagination experiences upon scaling itself & its restrictions against the vast & provocative abyss of the unknown. (SL 3.293-94)

This passage is not easy to interpret. What Lovecraft appears to mean by the first phase of cosmic fantasy ("symbolic or associative phantasy of the frankly poetic type") is the Dunsanian Pegāna pantheon, where the gods are manifestly symbols for various phenomena in the human world. The second phase of cosmic fantasy seems to be what Lovecraft believes himself to be writing. This discussion occurred in the course of a debate, inspired by Joseph Wood Krutch's *The Modern Temper* (1929), regarding the validity of art in an age of science. Krutch had maintained that many previous artistic attitudes—specifically romanticism—were now outmoded because, after the work of Darwin, Freud, and others, the sources of romanticism were too clearly understood to be based upon false perspectives to be usable in serious art. Lovecraft himself was wrestling with the validity of conventional supernatural fiction in an age that had banished the ghost, vampire, werewolf, and other standard entities to the dustbin of intellectual history. What could be done? His answer was Yog-Sothothery, or the expansion of the scope of supernaturalism to the unknown cosmos, where scientific disproof would be more difficult:

> The time has come when the normal revolt against time, space, & matter must assume a form not overtly incompatible with what is known of reality—when it must be gratified by images forming *supplements* rather than *contradictions* of the visible & mensurable universe. And what, if not a form of *non-supernatural cosmic art*, is to pacify this sense of revolt—as well as gratify the cognate sense of curiosity? (SL 2.295-96)

In other words, supernatural fiction had to become more like science fiction (a genre officially begun with the establishment of *Amazing Stories* in 1926), so that it could retain credence in a sceptical world. The entities in "The Colour out of Space" (a tale published in *Amazing Stories*) came from such remote depths of space that the laws of matter that we know in our corner of the universe apparently did not apply to them; so, too, apparently, with Cthulhu, who has the unique ability to recombine disparate parts of himself.

Lovecraft's letter to Long was written at the time he was writing one of his most significant stories, the short novel *At the Mountains of Madness* (1931). Here a radical revision of the Mythos occurs. An expedition to the Antarctic finds evidence of large barrel-shaped entities conforming to no known species in the earth's history. The narrator, William Dyer, and his colleague, Danforth, discover that these entities—apparently corresponding to what the *Necronomicon* calls the "Old Ones"—had come from the depths of space and established cities all over the earth millions of years ago, including an immense city in the Antarctic. The Old Ones had fashioned slaves out of protoplasm called shoggoths to do the manual labor of building these titanic cities, but over the course of time the shoggoths had developed semi-stable brains and waged intermittent wars of rebellion against their masters; it would seem that in one such rebellion they had triumphed. This would all be bad enough, but Dyer and Danforth learn—by interpreting the extensive historical bas-reliefs in the Old Ones' cities—that the Old Ones had created all earth life, including "a shambling primitive mammal, used sometimes for food and sometimes as an amusing buffoon by the land dwellers, whose vaguely simian and human foreshadowings were unmistakable" (MM 65). This delightful touch of misanthropy—this attribution of a degrading or contemptible origin of our species—only underscores the "indifferentism" that Lovecraft professed as central to his philosophy:

> I am not a *pessimist* but an *indifferentist*—that is, I don't make the mistake of thinking that the resultant of the natural forces surrounding and governing organic life will have any connexion with the wishes or tastes of any part of that organic life-process. Pessimists are just as illogical as optimists; insomuch as both envisage the aims of mankind as unified, and as having a direct relationship (either of frustration or of fulfilment) to the inevitable flow of terrestrial motivation and events. That is—both schools retain in a vestigial way the primitive concept of a conscious teleology—of a cosmos which gives a damn one way or the other about the especial wants and ultimate welfare of mosquitoes, rats, lice, dogs, men, horses, pterodactyls, trees, fungi, dodos, or other forms of biological energy. (SL 3.39)

This dovetails nicely with the programmatic intention, expressed in the "Call of Cthulhu" letter, to avoid the "local attributes of a negligible and temporary race called mankind" when writing cosmic horror fiction.

What *At the Mountains of Madness* makes clear, as Robert M. Price has pointed out, is that Lovecraft was undertaking a systematic course of "demythologising" his "gods" so that they become nothing more than extraterrestrials. In fact, as Price notes, this demythologising had been going on all along, but it only becomes explicit with this novel. What this also means is that the various human cults who had worshipped these "gods" and sought to foster their return to earthly dominance—and this would include Alhazred of the *Necronomicon* and other authors of occult lore—are grotesquely mistaken as to the true nature of these entities, who really care little about humanity or the earth at large, and whose occasionally catastrophic encounters with human beings are tantamount to our casual encounters with an ant-hill on the sidewalk. It is true that Lovecraft is not always quite as thorough in embodying this "indifferentism" in his stories—as we have seen, "The Dunwich Horror" paints a very different picture, and even in "The Whisperer in Darkness" the fungi from Yuggoth wage somewhat comical gun battles with the doggedly struggling Akeley—but Lovecraft's principle is now clear, and *At the Mountains of Madness* exemplifies it brilliantly.

From this tale to "The Shadow over Innsmouth" (1931) would appear to be an immense leap from the cosmic to the mundane; but powerful elements of cosmicism are nonetheless present under the surface. Here the decaying Massachusetts port of Innsmouth is seen by a lonely protagonist, Robert Olmstead (never named in the story but named in Lovecraft's story notes), to be the gateway to an immense undersea world populated by the Deep Ones, hybrid entities that are the hideous result of miscegenation between alien fish-frogs and the human inhabitants of the town. Their characteristic fishy expression—branded by locals as "the Innsmouth look"—is a harbinger for a much more profound physiological and psychological change that will render them virtually immortal and able to dwell forever in their undersea cities. In a stunning climax, Olmstead discovers that, through heredity, he is himself related to the Deep Ones; in a pungent parody of the Twenty-third Psalm, he overcomes his horror of them and maintains that he and a cousin "shall swim out to that brooding reef in the sea and dive down through black abysses to Cyclopean and many-columned Y'ha-nthlei, and in that lair of the Deep Ones we shall dwell amidst wonder and glory forever" (*DH* 367). Here again it is difficult to capture in a synopsis the all-pervasive atmosphere of claustrophobic gloom and decay that Lovecraft has fashioned through his richly evocative prose.

The rest of Lovecraft's fiction-writing career, marred by a lack of self-confidence and a sense of frustration with the course of his work, is somewhat uneven. "The Dreams in the Witch House" (1932) is an overwritten and predictable story in which the witch Keziah Mason, living in a peculiarly angled house in Arkham, seeks to transport her victims to "the mindless entity Azathoth, which rules all time and space from a curiously environed black throne at the centre of Chaos" (MM 282). Azathoth—first cited in a fragment, "Azathoth" (1922), and then in *The Dream-Quest of Unknown Kadath* and other tales—appears to be the chief "god" of Lovecraft's pantheon, but the above description suggests that he is nothing more than a symbol for the mysteries of an unknown universe. Nyarlathotep figures in this story as a variant of the "black man" of the traditional witch cult. "The Thing on the Doorstep" (1933) is another disappointing story in which Asenath Waite, a woman from Innsmouth, is able to exchange her mind with that of her husband, the weak-willed Edward Derby, even after Derby has killed her. Aside from the setting in Arkham, there is relatively little in this story to connect it with the Mythos, although at one point Derby suggests that the shoggoths are in league with the Deep Ones.

Much more must be said of "The Shadow out of Time" (1934-35). Just as *At the Mountains of Madness* suggested the immense vortices of space, so does this novella etch the incalculable gulfs of time whereby all human history is merely a minuscule point amid the endless stretches of infinity. A professor of Miskatonic, Nathaniel Wingate Peaslee, suffers amnesia for five full years. When he returns to his own self, he has recurring dreams that his body had been captured by the mind of a species called the Great Race. This species had "conquered the secret of time" (*The Shadow out of Time* 48) by its ability to thrust its minds forward and backward in time and space, possessing the bodies of any creatures it came upon and forcing the extruded minds to occupy the bodies of their displacers. At the time of Peaslee's "amnesia," the Great Race was occupying the bodies of a race of large cone-shaped beings in the Australia of 150,000,000 years ago. In the body of his mental captor, Peaslee was compelled to write the history of his own time for the Great Race's archives. This is the substance of Peaslee's dreams; but those dreams become hideous reality when an archaeological expedition to Australia uncovers traces of the Great Race's city, now largely destroyed and submerged under the sands. In a mad rush through the city one night, Peaslee comes upon what he most fears: the history he had written 150,000,000 years ago.

Lovecraft's final original tale, "The Haunter of the Dark" (1935), is a lesser work but still compelling in its depiction of an "avatar of Nyarlathotep" (*DH* 114) that, while trapped in a darkened belfry tower in a Providence church, manages to establish psychic contact—and ultimately psychic union—with a harried writer, Robert Blake. When it escapes from its confinement and is winging its way to Blake, it and Blake are simultaneously killed by a bolt of lightning. Chiefly an evocation of Lovecraft's affection for his native city, "The Haunter of the Dark" is a compact and satisfying tale, and by no means an unfitting end to his "artificial mythology."

The Derleth Mythos

At this point it is imperative to examine the early development of the Cthulhu Mythos by Lovecraft's friends and colleagues, during and just after his lifetime. The first "addition" to the Mythos was Frank Belknap Long's story "The Space-Eaters" (*Weird Tales*, July 1928). This rather ungainly tale—obviously autobiographical in its postulation of two protagonists, named Frank and Howard, battling mysterious entities that are eating their way through space—is related to the Mythos only in regard to its epigraph from "John Dee's *Necronomicon*" and in its purported suggestions of the cosmic. Lovecraft would later cite Dee as the English translator of the *Necronomicon* in one of his own stories as well as in his "History of the *Necronomicon*" (MW 52–53), a tongue-in-cheek account of the writing and dissemination of the dread volume. Long then wrote "The Hounds of Tindalos" (*Weird Tales*, March 1929), which introduces those curious canines who move through the angles of space to harass hapless dreamers. Long's short novel *The Horror from the Hills* (*Weird Tales*, January–February and March 1931) may be his most significant contribution to the Cthulhu Mythos, in spite of the fact that he incorporated directly into the story a lengthy passage from a Lovecraft letter of 1927 recounting a bizarre dream of horrors in the ancient Roman province of Hispania (Spain). Here we are introduced to the baleful entity Chaugnar Faugn, the elephant god of Tsang. At one point a character engages in a fascinating discourse regarding the morality of Chaugnar:

> "Don't imagine for a moment that Chaugnar is a beneficent god. In the West you have evolved certain amiabilities of intercourse, to which you presumptuously attach cosmic significance, such as truth, kindliness, generosity, forbearance and honor, and you quaintly imagine that a god who is beyond good and evil and hence unnameable to your 'ethics' can not be omnipotent.
>
> "But how do you know that there are any beneficent laws in the universe, that the cosmos is friendly to man? Even in the mundane sphere of planetary life there is nothing to sustain such an hypothesis." (22)

This is reasonably close to Lovecraft's "indifferentism"—not surprisingly from one who largely shared Lovecraft's religious scepticism.

Long's addition to the growing bibliography of Mythos books was picked up by Robert E. Howard, who invented von Junzt's *Nameless Cults* as well as Justin Geoffrey, a mad poet who died in Hungary. These elements are cited in Howard's "The Black Stone" (*Weird Tales*, November 1931), but it is not entirely clear whether they were so cited as an homage to Lovecraft; indeed, they became incorporated into the Cthulhu Mythos only because Lovecraft, in turn, cited them in his own stories. A more interesting case along the same lines is that of Clark Ashton Smith. In "The Tale of Satampra Zeiros" (*Weird*

Tales, November 1931), Smith invented the toad-god Tsathoggua. But because this story, written in late 1929, was initially rejected by Weird Tales, Lovecraft got the credit for the first citation of Tsathoggua in print in "The Whisperer in Darkness." A few years later, noting how many other writers had cited his creation, Smith made the pregnant comment: "It would seem that I am starting a mythology" (letter to August Derleth, December 24, 1932; ms., JHL). This suggests that Smith conceived himself to be working independently of Lovecraft in fashioning gods, books (The Book of Eibon), and other elements that would later be co-opted into the Mythos only by virtue of Lovecraft's citing them in his own stories. Lovecraft, indeed, made a game of citing others' "contributions" to his myth-cycle in "The Whisperer in Darkness," when he rattles them off in bewildering fashion:

> I found myself faced by names and terms that I had heard elsewhere in the most hideous of connexions—Yuggoth, Great Cthulhu, Tsathoggua, Yog-Sothoth, R'lyeh, Nyarlathotep, Azathoth, Hastur, Yian, Leng, the Lake of Hali, Bethmoora, the Yellow Sign, L'mur-Kathulos, Bran, and the Magnum Innominandum—and was drawn back through nameless aeons and inconceivable dimensions to worlds of elder, outer entity at which the crazed author of the Necronomicon had only guessed in the vaguest way. (DH 223)

Here Lovecraft is not only paying his own homage to Smith's, Howard's, and other colleagues' "additions," but tipping the hat to such predecessors as Dunsany (Bethmoora), Robert W. Chambers (the Yellow Sign), Bierce (Hastur, the Lake of Hali), and others. Lovecraft repeatedly received queries from fans and writers regarding the reality of his pantheon and of the occult books cited in his tales; several fans wished Lovecraft to write the Necronomicon himself.

It was, however, August Derleth who, from as early as 1931, became fascinated, even obsessed, with the Mythos and, especially after Lovecraft's death, took it in directions that Lovecraft would emphatically not have approved. The exact degree of Derleth's culpability in so doing is debatable, but we can see that he made three central contentions in regard to the Mythos, all of which are plainly false: (1) that the "gods" of the Mythos are elementals; (2) that the "gods" can be differentiated between a beneficent group of "Elder Gods," who are on the side of humanity, and a group of evil and maleficent "Old Ones," who seek to destroy humanity; and (3) that the Mythos as a whole is philosophically akin to Christianity.

Exactly how Derleth came to this interpretation is difficult to fathom; perhaps more difficult to fathom is how so many other writers and critics blandly accepted his disfigurement of the Mythos as a sound interpretation of Lovecraft's writing. Derleth became fascinated with elementals (entities that embody the four elements of earth, air, fire, and water) through his reading of Algernon Blackwood, whose powerful tale "The Wendigo" can be seen as a depiction of an air elemental. In "H. P. Lovecraft and His Work" (1963) he maintained that Cthulhu was a water elemental and that Nyarlathotep was an earth elemental. This is already problematical, especially since Cthulhu is said to have come from the stars and is *imprisoned* under water, making it unlikely that that is his natural element. But Derleth was faced with the awkwardness of dealing with such gods as Azathoth and Yog-Sothoth, who do not seem to be elementals in any sense, and with the fact that there are no gods in Lovecraft corresponding to air and fire elementals, forcing Derleth himself to invent Hastur (mentioned only in passing in the above passage in "The Whisperer in Darkness" and derived from random mentions in Ambrose Bierce and Robert W. Chambers) as an air elemental and Cthugha, "corresponding to the fire elemental Lovecraft failed to provide" (xiv). But if Lovecraft was working steadily on the Cthulhu Mythos for the last decade of his life, and if he envisioned his "gods" as elementals, how could he have committed the gaffe of "failing" to provide two of the four elementals?

Still worse is Derleth's fashioning of benign "Elder Gods" out of whole cloth. They exist nowhere in Lovecraft, and the motive for their invention by Derleth appears to be merely to shield himself from the bleak, amoral cosmic vision at the heart of Lovecraft's work. A devoutly religious man, Derleth could apparently not face the atheistic purport of Lovecraft's "artificial mythology," and so he deliberately distorted it so that it more closely corresponded with his own worldview. To bolster his interpretation of the Mythos, Derleth produced the following passage that he claimed to derive from a Lovecraft letter:

> All my stories, unconnected as they may be, are based on the fundamental lore or legend that this world was inhabited at one time by another race who, in practising black magic, lost their foothold and were expelled, yet live on outside ever ready to take possession of this earth again. ("H. P. Lovecraft and His Work" xiii)

In spite of its superficial resemblance to Lovecraft's "Now all my stories . . ." quotation, the import of this passage is antipodally different. In his later years, as scepticism regarding Derleth's interpretation of the Mythos began to develop, he was asked to produce the original of this passage; he reportedly became angry and refused. As David E. Schultz has pointed out, this is not because Derleth literally fabricated the quotation; it was that he had obtained it from a letter by a brief correspondent of Lovecraft, Harold S. Farnese, who sent this passage to Derleth and claimed that it was a paraphrase of a Lovecraft letter; in fact, Farnese had made up the passage himself (see Schultz,

"The Origin of Lovecraft's 'Black Magic' Quote"). In any case, this passage was the cornerstone of the Cthulhu Mythos for decades.

The central points in what has come to be called "the Derleth Mythos" were apparently embodied in the first draft of Derleth's "The Return of Hastur," written in 1931 and sent to Lovecraft. At this time Derleth proposed to Lovecraft the name "The Mythology of Hastur," but Lovecraft demurred, recognising that Hastur (which Lovecraft may not even have envisioned as an entity, much less as a "god" and a "half-brother to Cthulhu," as Derleth imagined) was a relatively minor element in his mythology. After Lovecraft's death, Derleth coined the term "Cthulhu mythology" (first in the article "H. P. Lovecraft, Outsider"), later modified to Cthulhu Mythos. Derleth also cited a letter written by Lovecraft after *Weird Tales* had rejected "The Return of Hastur"—"I *like* to have others use my Azathoths & Nyarlathoteps—& in return I shall use Klarkash-Ton's Tsathoggua, your monk Clithanus, & Howard's Bran"—as constituting Lovecraft's "permission" for Derleth to elaborate the Mythos; but he should have paid greater attention to the previous sentence: "The more these synthetic daemons are mutually written up by different authors, the better they become as general background-material" (*ES* 1.353). For Lovecraft never wrote a story "about" the Cthulhu Mythos; all these mythological elements were indeed "background-material" for tales that had strong philosophical and aesthetic underpinnings. What Derleth and his followers did was to write tales in which the whole point—if indeed there is a point—is merely the expounding of the Cthulhu Mythos. As such, these tales are philosophically vacuous; they are merely stories.

"The Return of Hastur," as published (*Weird Tales*, March 1939), expounds the entirety of the Derleth Mythos:

> . . . its beings are of two natures, and two only: the Old or Ancient Ones, the Elder Gods, of cosmic good, and those of cosmic evil, bearing many names, and themselves of different groups, as if associated with the elements and yet transcending them: for there are the Water Beings, hidden in the depths; those of Air that are the primal lurkers beyond time; those of Earth, horrible animate survivals of distant eons. Incredible ages ago, the Old Ones banished from the cosmic places all the Evil Ones, imprisoning them in many places; but in time these Evil Ones spawned hellish minions who set about preparing for their return to greatness. (*The Mask of Cthulhu* 11)

There is considerable confusion of terminology here, for in later stories Derleth referred to the "Old Ones" as the "evil" gods. How exactly any entities can represent "cosmic" good and evil, since these conceptions are so bound to human society, is not easy to answer. But the end result of this distortion is that most of the writers of the Cthulhu Mythos unwittingly ended up imitating Derleth rather than Lovecraft.

Derleth is culpable, not so much on the grounds of departing from Lovecraft's conception of the Mythos, as in attributing his own interpretation of the Mythos to Lovecraft, as he did repeatedly in introductions to collections of Lovecraft tales, and in his misconceived "posthumous collaborations" with Lovecraft (now collected in *The Watchers out of Time and Others*), in which he chose random plot germs from Lovecraft's commonplace book and fashioned whole stories (most of them Mythos tales) from them and deemed them works "by H. P. Lovecraft and August Derleth." (Some unscrupulous publishers have reprinted these stories and left Derleth's name off of them altogether.) But the true heinousness of Derleth's misinterpretation is the imaginative impoverishment it entails: in nearly all the Mythos stories that he himself wrote, and in a substantial number of those written by others, a basic scenario is repeated over and over again: "minions" of the Old Ones seek to return the gods to power over earth, but are foiled at the last moment by valiant protectors of humanity. This stale idea quickly led to the devolution of the Mythos into a hackneyed formulism, and it is not surprising that such critics as Edmund Wilson and Damon Knight condemned both Lovecraft and his followers for poor writing and for imaginative sterility.

A few writers, including some of Lovecraft's closest colleagues, held out. Whether we are to regard Donald Wandrei's *Dead Titans, Waken!* (written in 1929–31 and published many years later in a revised form as *The Web of Easter Island*) as a contribution to the Mythos is debatable: it mentions no actual god or book from Lovecraft's stories. But in its documentary style, in its learned protagonist—Carter E. Graham, "curator of the Ludbury Museum of Archaeology and Anthropology" (14)—in its suggestion that disparate events are interconnected pieces of a broader horrific tableau (reminiscent of "The Call of Cthulhu"), and especially in its hints of cosmic menace, it is very much in the spirit of Lovecraft.

Robert Bloch benefited from having corresponded with Lovecraft for the last four years of the latter's life, so that his early writings reveal a dynamism and originality far beyond what one might expect. He effected a coup when he wrote "The Shambler from the Stars" (*Weird Tales*, September 1935), in which an unnamed figure manifestly based upon Lovecraft (he is a writer, he lives in Providence, and so forth) appears—and in fact is killed at the end of the tale. It was this piquant tale that inspired Lovecraft to respond with "The Haunter of the Dark," in which Robert Blake is killed off. Only many years later did Bloch complete the trilogy by writing "The Shadow from the Steeple" (*Weird Tales*, September 1950). In another story, "The Dark Demon"

(*Weird Tales*, November 1936), a character named Edgar Gordon is another transparent stand-in for Lovecraft.

It was with "The Faceless God" (*Weird Tales*, May 1936) that Bloch began his decades-long fascination with the icon of Nyarlathotep. Bloch retains the Egyptian background of Nyarlathotep in this story and in several others, notably "Fane of the Black Pharaoh" (*Weird Tales*, December 1937), in which a pharaoh named Nephren-Ka (a name randomly cited in Lovecraft's "The Outsider" [1921]) is said to be a worshipper of Nyarlathotep. But Bloch's most noteworthy use of Nyarlathotep occurred decades later, as we shall see.

Still more imaginative are the contributions of Fritz Leiber, a late correspondent of Lovecraft who clearly learned the master's lessons well. The first draft of Leiber's novella, "Adept's Gambit," read and appreciated by Lovecraft, made mention of some elements of the Mythos, but the published version excised them. Other stories in Leiber's first collection, *Night's Black Agents* (1947), reveal strong Lovecraftian influence—but just as strongly do they reveal a thorough assimilation of that influence in tales that remain Leiber's own. Consider "The Sunken Land" (1942), which speaks of a sunken continent, Simorgya, that has just risen out of the sea, exactly as in "The Call of Cthulhu." "Diary in the Snow" deftly uses the theme of interplanetary mind-exchange as expounded in "The Shadow out of Time," while "The Dreams of Albert Moreland" strikingly echoes one element in "The Dreams in the Witch House" (a physical object from the dreamworld is brought back by the dreamer into the waking world) while retaining powerful originality of conception in other regards.

But the dominant figure in the Cthulhu Mythos in the generation after Lovecraft's death was August Derleth—understandably so, as he was Lovecraft's publisher (he had formed the publishing firm of Arkham House solely in order to issue Lovecraft's works in hardcover, although he subsequently published much other supernatural work by leading writers of the period) and self-styled interpreter. Derleth wrote sixteen "posthumous collaborations" with Lovecraft, including the novel *The Lurker at the Threshold* (1945), two collections of Cthulhu Mythos tales, *The Mask of Cthulhu* (1958) and *The Trail of Cthulhu* (1962), and edited the landmark anthology *Tales of the Cthulhu Mythos* (1969). His collected Mythos tales have now been issued, appropriately enough, under the title *In Lovecraft's Shadow* (1999).

What Derleth—and many others who followed in his, rather than in Lovecraft's, wake—failed to realise was the aesthetic futility of merely mimicking Lovecraft's dense and at times flamboyant prose style and rewriting the plots of Lovecraft's own stories. Where Derleth and others did strike out in new directions, they generally did so blunderingly. Several of Lovecraft's stories were apparently great favourites of Derleth's, and he repeatedly effected only the slightest variations upon them: "The Whippoorwills in the Hills" is a slight rewrite of "The Dunwich Horror"; "The Sandwin Compact" and "The Watcher from the Sky" echo "The Shadow over Innsmouth"; "The Gorge Beyond Salapunco" is heavily reliant on "The Call of Cthulhu." Derleth repeatedly made the mistake of setting his tales in New England (a region he did not know well) out of a belief that Mythos tales must originate in this locale. His one meritorious Mythos story, "The Dweller in Darkness" (*Weird Tales*, November 1944), is wisely set in Derleth's native Wisconsin, and the topographical atmosphere is impressively convincing. Although marred by Derleth's misinterpretation of the Mythos—Elder Gods, elementals, and the like— the tale, in spite of its heavy debt to "The Whisperer in Darkness," effectively makes use of the Nyarlathotep icon.

One interesting case is C. Hall Thompson, who was not a member of the "Lovecraft circle" but who wrote an impressive novella, "Spawn of the Green Abyss" (*Weird Tales*, November 1946). Set in the town of Kalesmouth, in New Jersey, the story is a clever variant of "The Shadow over Innsmouth" in its portrayal of a man, Lazarus Heath, who stumbles upon an undersea city whose architecture was "all wrong" (a deft borrowing from "The Call of Cthulhu"), mates with the empress of the city, bears a child, and returns with it to his home. The child, Cassandra, herself appears to mate with the god Yoth Kala. All this sounds like lurid pulp trash, but the prose is skilful and the characterisation surprisingly sensitive—a weak point with many Cthulhu Mythos tales, by Lovecraft and others. Derleth was reportedly incensed by this "outsider" making use of the Mythos, and he demanded that Thompson write no more such stories.

The Modern Mythos

By the 1960s, especially with the republication of Lovecraft's stories by Arkham House after a period when they were out of print, a new generation of Lovecraftians seemed ready to take the Mythos into new directions. One surprising contribution was from James Wade, a musical composer who wrote the novella "The Deep Ones" (*Tales of the Cthulhu Mythos*). Although using a modified version of the "Derleth Mythos," Wade produced a richly textured work set in hippie-filled California that relies somewhat on "The Shadow over Innsmouth" and "The Call of Cthulhu" but retains originality. Also surprising was Colin Wilson, the British novelist and critic who wrote harshly of Lovecraft in *The Strength to Dream* (1961), a book that so angered Derleth that he dared Wilson to write his own Cthulhu Mythos story. Wilson complied with at least two works. The novella "The Return of the Lloigor" (*Tales of the Cthulhu*

Mythos) is impressive but ultimately disappointing, as it depicts entities called the Lloigor (invented by Derleth) who have come from the stars and descended into the earth, but who from time to time erupt with destructive results. Wilson has returned to Lovecraftian roots by creating an explicitly philosophical horror: the Lloigor are the universe's greatest pessimists:

> . . . the Lloigor, although infinitely more powerful than men, were also aware that optimism would be absurd in this universe. Their minds were a unity, not compartmentalised, like ours. There was no distinction in them between conscious, subconscious and superconscious mind. So they saw things clearly all the time, without the possibility of averting the mind from the truth, or forgetting. . . . The Lloigor *lived* their pessimism. (227-28)

What makes this conception interesting is that it is exactly the kind of conception that would terrify Wilson, whose own philosophy of life and society is based upon an optimistic belief in humanity's infinite intellectual and psychological progress. Just as Lovecraft's tales depict what to him was most cataclysmically frightening—a perception that the materialism of modern science may be a misconstrual of the true nature of the universe—so Wilson has here drawn upon *his* fears (not Lovecraft's) as the basis of a tale, using Cthulhu Mythos elements only as a framework and springboard. The development of the idea in "The Return of the Lloigor" is sketchy, however.

Very different is Wilson's novel *The Mind Parasites* (1967). Set in the near future—the year 2007—it tells the tale of a band of archaeologists who discover the remains of an ancient city two miles underground in Turkey, far antedating any known human civilisation; journalists name it Kadath. This discovery is in fact a red herring to distract humanity from the invasion of nebulous entities named mind parasites, who are attacking the intelligent and creative members of the species. The protagonist, Gilbert Austin, presents a fascinating case that the mind parasites have been at work since at least the early nineteenth century—for it was exactly at that time when a deep strain of pessimism, misanthropy, and neurosis appears to have entered into the aesthetic and cultural products of Western civilisation. This extraordinarily clever premise allows Wilson to write a thrilling and fast-paced novel, even though nearly all the "action" occurs within the characters' minds. Here again Wilson has produced a genuinely original contribution to the Cthulhu Mythos: not content merely to rewrite one of Lovecraft's own stories, and disdaining the attempt to imitate Lovecraft's style, he has utilised Lovecraftian elements as the basis for a novel whose conception and execution derive strictly from his own aesthetic and philosophical concerns. Wilson's two sequels to this novel—*The Philosopher's Stone* (1971) and *The Space Vampires* (1976)—owe much less to Lovecraft and are rather less compelling.

Another British writer, Ramsey Campbell, would do somewhat similar things with the Mythos, even though in a less explicitly philosophical way. Fascinated with Lovecraft from childhood, he produced a collection of Mythos stories, *The Inhabitant of the Lake and Less Welcome Tenants* (1964), published by Arkham House when he was eighteen. Derleth had read drafts of several of these tales years earlier and made one important suggestion to Campbell: do not set the stories in New England (where Campbell had never been), but in your native England. Campbell did exactly that, and therefore utilised the Lovecraftian icon of topography to depict a haunted England centred upon several fictitious cities—Brichester, Temphill, Goatswood—in the Severn Valley. The tales in *The Inhabitant of the Lake* are hardly worth discussing, even though they are written with a verve and enthusiasm that sets them apart from many other such imitations. Very shortly after he completed the volume, however, Campbell began developing his own distinctive voice, and in *Demons by Daylight* (1973) he almost single-handedly ushered in a new mode of weird fiction—crisply written in contemporary prose, sexually explicit, with the supernatural phenomena delineated with subtlety and ambiguity, and serving as metaphors for modern-day social and political concerns. He did not entirely abandon the Lovecraftian idiom, however, and in "Cold Print" (*Tales of the Cthulhu Mythos*) and "The Franklyn Paragraphs" (*Demons by Daylight*) he effected two of the most ingenious riffs on the "forbidden book" icon. "Cold Print" transfers the idea into the realm of violent pornography, as a seedy individual comes to Brichester—now manifestly an echo of Campbell's native Liverpool—to find the sadistic pornography he seeks, but finds something much more ominous when he stumbles upon a copy of the *Revelations of Glaaki*. "The Franklyn Paragraphs" is a masterful adaptation of Lovecraft's "documentary style," in which letters, newspaper articles, telegrams, and the like are cited to augment the tale's verisimilitude. The writer Errol Undercliffe has come upon a rare volume, Roland Franklyn's *We Pass from View*, but is horrified to discover that Franklyn's soul has been trapped in the book, so that the words on the page rewrite themselves as Franklyn cries out for help. Campbell went on to write a few other Lovecraftian tales, and also edited the anthology *New Tales of the Cthulhu Mythos* (1980).

Far less impressive is the work of Brian Lumley, who has accepted the "Derleth Mythos" wholesale and, in his prolific writings, taken it to extremes of absurdity and bathos that even Derleth would have been unable to imagine. An early novel, *Beneath the Moors* (1974), introduces the novelty of tying the Lovecraftian dreamworld (from *The Dream-Quest of Unknown Kadath* and other stories) into the Cthulhu Mythos. Here a professor discovers the ancient city of Lh-yib, the sister city of Ib (from Lovecraft's "The Doom That

Came to Sarnath"), which worshipped the lizard-god Bokrug. Lumley, however, commits the gaffe of bringing Bokrug on stage and having it give a sober lecture to the professor as to the origin of his race.

With *The Burrowers Beneath* (1974), Lumley begins a six-book cycle that featured members of what he calls the Wilmarth Foundation, who are devoted to the gallant mission of protecting humanity from the evil machinations of the Old Ones. These creatures are collectively referred to as the CCD (Cthulhu Cycle Deities), and Lumley uncritically makes much use of star-shaped soapstone objects (cited by Lovecraft in *At the Mountains of Madness*, although their purport is never clarified) as talismans to protect its bearer from attack by the Old Ones. This dubious invention of Derleth's is taken to grotesque extremes by Lumley. There is scarcely any reason to examine in detail the plots of the remaining novels—*The Transition of Titus Crow* (1975), *The Clock of Dreams* (1978), *Spawn of the Winds* (1978), *In the Moons of Borea* (1979), and *Elysia: The Coming of Cthulhu* (1989)—save to note that Lumley has unsuccessfully attempted to render the essentially intellectual conceptions of Lovecraft's Mythos into action-adventure tales in which human beings, Elder Gods, Old Ones (including such entities as Ithaqua and Nyarlathotep), and lesser creatures all do battle with one another. *The Clock of Dreams* makes such heavy use of the dreamworld of *The Dream-Quest of Unknown Kadath* as to be a virtual rewrite of it. Mercifully, Lumley has now abandoned the Cthulhu Mythos to write equally preposterous science fiction vampire novels.

In recent years much has been made of Fred Chappell's novel *Dagon* (1968). Written by a distinguished mainstream novelist and poet who had little or no connexion with the Lovecraft circle or the Lovecraft fan movement, this extraordinarily grim chronicle of a scholar's gradual degradation through sexual obsession in rural North Carolina certainly draws upon Mythos elements: the scholarly protagonist (he is writing a treatise on *Remnant Pagan Forces in American Puritanism*), the occasional citation of the god Dagon (seen here as a symbol for unbridled sex), and the evocation of horrors latent in a backwoods locale. Whether this novel constitutes a true "contribution" to the Cthulhu Mythos, or should be deemed merely "influenced" by the Mythos will have to be determined by the individual reader.

With the death of August Derleth in 1971, interesting things began to happen. First, a new generation of scholars began examining Lovecraft's life and work with greater care and scholarly attention; among them, Richard L. Tierney ("The Derleth Mythos") and Dirk W. Mosig ("H. P. Lovecraft: Myth-Maker") systematically demolished the Derlethian conception of the Mythos and explicated Lovecraft's own bleak cosmic vision. In the course of time, this scholarly work achieved its result in more cogent and sophisticated utilisations of the Mythos and its various icons. An early example was Karl Edward Wagner's masterful tale "Sticks" (*Whispers*, March 1974), an homage to the artist Lee Brown Coye, who illustrated several Lovecraft editions from Arkham House in the 1960s. Making use of the stick-lattice figures that Coye made his signature, "Sticks" speaks of these figures as glyphs designed to summon the Great Old Ones. Less successful is Stephen King's "Jerusalem's Lot" (in King's *Night Shift*, 1978), which, although deft in its use of the documentary style and of the occult tome *De Vermis Mysteriis*, fundamentally boils down to a story about a giant worm. The influence of "The Haunter of the Dark" is evident throughout the tale.

One of the most curious developments in recent Mythos fiction is that Lovecraft himself has become a leading icon. The traditional view of Lovecraft as an "eccentric recluse" closeting himself away in his Providence garret, only venturing out at night, beset by phobias and neuroses, and writing down his bizarre conceptions for an unappreciative public—is itself largely a myth, but that has not stopped it from becoming a powerful incentive to the creation of both historical and supernatural tales. We have seen that such of Lovecraft's colleagues as Frank Belknap Long and Robert Bloch already made use of Lovecraft-figures in tales written in Lovecraft's lifetime. Derleth and others frequently cited Lovecraft by name in their Mythos tales, as a writer who thought he was writing fiction about the Old Ones but was in fact unwittingly revealing the truth about them.

The use of Lovecraft as an icon divides between those who depict him as an historical figure and those who incorporate him in manifestly fictional, and usually supernatural, escapades. In the first camp the most notable proponent is Peter Cannon, a leading Lovecraft scholar who in such deft works as *Pulptime* (1984)—about Lovecraft, Frank Belknap Long, and other members of the "Lovecraft circle" teaming up with an aged Sherlock Holmes—and, even more impressively, *The Lovecraft Chronicles* (2004)—a kind of alternate-world fantasy in which Lovecraft becomes a successful writer, moves for a time to England, then returns in his old age to Providence—has drawn upon his exhaustive knowledge of the facts of Lovecraft's life and work to paint a convincing picture of the writer and his milieu. Less successful is Richard A. Lupoff's *Lovecraft's Book* (1985), which implausibly has Lovecraft becoming unwittingly involved with American Nazis in the early 1930s. A revised version, restoring cuts made to the original edition, has been published as *Marblehead* (2007). As for the second camp, we have an unfortunate example in Gahan Wilson's "H. P. L." (in *Lovecraft's Legacy*, edited by Robert E. Weinberg and Martin H. Greenberg [1990]), in which a dying Lovecraft appeals to his own gods and is saved from death by cancer, and later is carried off to heaven in the arms or tentacles of one of the deities he has invoked. But this mediocre tale is a masterwork as compared to *Shadows Bend*, by David Barbour and Richard Raleigh (2000), a ludicrous narrative of Lovecraft and Robert E. Howard in New Mexico.

In the 1970s and 1980s some veteran writers made sterling contributions. Fritz Leiber wrote the substantial novella "The Terror from the Depths" for Edward Paul Berglund's *The Disciples of Cthulhu* (1976). A loose sequel to "The Whisperer in Darkness," it depicts the elderly Albert N. Wilmarth—who bears striking similarities to Lovecraft himself—seeking to save his friend George Reuter Fischer (who shares several traits of Leiber's personality) from becoming enmeshed in the cosmic forces that dwell underneath his southern California home. Leiber, while drawing upon several of Lovecraft's tales, provides a degree of psychological analysis that Lovecraft never included in his own work. Robert Bloch's novel *Strange Eons* (1978) is a grand synthesis of Lovecraftian themes and conceptions, centreing around the figure of the Reverend Nye (in reality Nyarlathotep) to engender the destruction of the world and perhaps the universe. Fred Chappell, in "The Adder" (in *More Shapes Than One*, 1991), ingeniously develops the forbidden book icon by depicting the *Necronomicon* as capable of rewriting the texts of other works by merely coming into physical contact with them.

A dynamic new voice in weird fiction is Thomas Ligotti, who burst on the scene with the scintillating collection *Songs of a Dead Dreamer* (1986). Ligotti has occasionally adopted the Lovecraftian idiom in tales that expound his own nightmarish vision while adhering to central Lovecraftian conceptions. "The Last Feast of Harlequin" (*Magazine of Fantasy and Science Fiction*, April 1990) is dedicated to Lovecraft and is clearly indebted to "The Festival" and "The Shadow over Innsmouth." "Vastarien" is a searching exploration of the forbidden book theme, while "Nethescurial" is an extraordinary subtle—perhaps even unconscious—adaptation of "The Call of Cthulhu." Like Lovecraft's tale, it is divided into three sections, and it tells of the existence of a mysterious island named Nethescurial as the haven of "an absolute evil whose reality is mitigated only by our blindness to it" (*Grimscribe* 75).

T. E. D. Klein shares, with Ligotti and Campbell, preeminence in artistic weird fiction, and his one Mythos contribution, "Black Man with a Horn" (*New Tales of the Cthulhu Mythos*), shares with his other work a deftness of prose style, a subtlety in the build-up of a horrific climax, and a deep understanding of the psychological effects of horror. Here a distant member of the "Lovecraft circle" (clearly modelled upon Frank Belknap Long, with whom Klein was well acquainted) stumbles upon evidence that Lovecraftian horrors are true. Behind this simple scenario is a sense of the overwhelming effects of the realisation that horror lurks behind the placid surface of everyday life. Veteran horror wrier F. Paul Wilson has skilfully transferred the icon of haunted New England to the pine barrens region of New Jersey in "The Barrens" (*Lovecraft's Legacy*).

Other writers having little connexion with the core Lovecraft circle or its later disciples have also produced meritorious work. Almost unclassifiable is *Résumé with Monsters* by William Browning Spencer (1995), a long and complex novel whose plot is difficult to summarise. Its protagonist, Philip Kenan, thinks he is cursed by the Old Ones. Initially we are led to believe that this is a purely psychological dilemma, the result of indoctrination by his father, a passionate Lovecraft reader; but gradually we learn that Philip's concerns are all too real. Lively, pungently written in a modern idiom, and full of piquant plot twists, the novel is one of the most imaginative treatments of the Cthulhu Mythos ever written. This could certainly not be said for Joseph S. Pulver, Sr's *Nightmare's Disciple* (1999), which seeks to fuse the serial-killer novel with the Mythos, with grotesque and at times bathetic results. Appallingly prolix, the novel seeks to cite nearly every single Mythos name or entity ever devised, and wearies the reader with surfeit. W. H. Pugmire, gifted with a richly evocative prose style, has produced noteworthy short specimens in such works as *Dreams of Lovecraftian Horror* (1999) and *The Fungal Stain* (2006). And mention must be made of Ann K. Schwader's *The Worms Remember* (2001), which deftly renders the Cthulhu Mythos into verse, following Lovecraft's own example in his sonnet cycle *Fungi from Yuggoth* (1929–30).

The Cthulhu Mythos, with its potential for flamboyance and extravagance, has always been potentially the object of parody and even derision. As early as 1940, the science fiction writer Arthur C. Clarke produced the harmlessly amusing "At the Mountains of Murkiness," poking fun at Lovecraft's dense prose style—this in spite of the fact that such of his novels as *Childhood's End* (1953) and *2001: A Space Odyssey* (1968) could be said to utilise the Lovecraftian idea (expressed in "The Shadow out of Time") that human development has been fostered by intervention by a more advanced alien race. Specific parodies of the Mythos include such items as Peter Cannon's gorgeous *Scream for Jeeves* (1994), in which P. G. Wodehouse's Bertie Wooster and his butler Jeeves become involved in Lovecraftian adventures, and Mark McLaughlin's *Shoggoth Cacciatore and Other Eldritch Entrees* (2000), whose title speaks for itself. Some of the actual "scholarship" on the Mythos—whether it be such popular tracts as Lin Carter's *Lovecraft: A Look Behind the Cthulhu Mythos* (1972) or the more rigorous *The Necronomicon Files* by Daniel Harms and John Wisdom Gonce III (1998) or Harms's *Encyclopedia Cthulhuiana* (1994)—have their elements of parody, but also contain much useful information.

The Mythos in the Media

In the past several decades the central icons of the Cthulhu Mythos have seeped into the media, with interesting if mixed results. Adaptations of Lovecraft's stories into film have been almost uniformly unsuccessful; representative is *The Dunwich Horror* (1970), in which the Old Ones are depicted as hippies dancing in a drug-delirium. More successful is *The Curse* (1987), in which the haunted New England of "The Colour out of Space" is transported effectively to the rural South. Of Stuart Gordon's self-parodic "Reanimator" films it is difficult to speak without a smile. *Re-Animator* (1985) and *Bride of Re-Animator* (1991) are certainly delightful send-ups of Mythos conventions as well as the conventions of schlock horror films; Gordon's more serious *Dagon* (2001)—in reality an adaptation of "The Shadow over Innsmouth"—has moments of atmospheric effectiveness. In reality, films that do not purport to adapt a specific Lovecraft story have been far more successful than the actual Lovecraft adaptations. Consider Peter Weir's masterful *The Last Wave* (1977), a film that brilliantly utilises such Mythos icons as ancient gods dwelling under the earth, their influence on human beings through dreams, and the like. Set in Australia, the film comprises a magnificent, if loose, adaptation of "The Shadow out of Time," although Weir has never explicitly identified Lovecraft as a source. John Carpenter has frequently acknowledged his admiration for Lovecraft, and his *The Thing* (1982) borrows heavily from *At the Mountains of Madness*. His more recent *In the Mouth of Madness* (1994) features a character who combines the traits of Stephen King and Lovecraft, with predictable shambling underground horrors making an appearance. More distinctive is the HBO television film *Cast a Deadly Spell* (1991), which, during production, was called *Lovecraft*. Set in an alternate-world Los Angeles, it ingeniously combines the Mythos with hard-boiled detection in its portrayal of a tough private eye, H. Phil Lovecraft, on the hunt for the Old Ones. While not directly based on a specific Lovecraft story, it captures the essence of the Cthulhu Mythos surprisingly well.

In 1982 Chaosium introduced the "Call of Cthulhu" role-playing game, and has subsequently issued dozens of guidebooks and supplements to it. Set in the 1920s, the game involves, among other piquant details, the need for characters to preserve "sanity points" in order to shield themselves from the cosmic horrors surrounding them. Chaosium has also issued a popular Mythos card game.

The Cthulhu Mythos remains a popular venue in literature and the media. Since the 1980s Robert M. Price has been a kind of August Derleth redivivus in publishing a dozen or more anthologies of Cthulhu Mythos tales by writers old and new, and other editors such as James Turner (*Cthulhu 2000*

[1995]; *Eternal Lovecraft* [1998]), Stephen Jones (*Shadows over Innsmouth* [1994]; *Weird Shadows over Innsmouth* [2005]), and John Pelan and Benjamin Adams (*The Children of Cthulhu* [2002]) continue to issue anthologies of Mythos tales, good, fair, and middling.

While the Cthulhu Mythos is largely a literary phenomenon, there is some evidence that it is seeping out into wider realms of media and society. Every so often one hears of teenagers or other individuals committing criminal acts under the inspiration of the *Necronomicon*. (Matters have not been helped by the fact that at least four books have been issued that purport to be the *Necronomicon*; most of these are obvious parodies, but one takes itself quite seriously as an occult sourcebook.) Jason Colavito has recently made a bold argument for an even broader incursion of the Mythos into pop culture. He presents convincing evidence that such proponents of the theory of extraterrestrial visitation as Erich von Däniken and Graham Hancock were directly or indirectly inspired by Lovecraft's tales, interpreting their fictional premises of alien manipulation of human minds as actually occurring. If this is so, then the Cthulhu Mythos has entered the popular consciousness far more profoundly and disturbingly than its self-deprecating creator could ever have imagined.

Works Cited

Burleson, Donald R. "The Mythic Hero Archetype in 'The Dunwich Horror.'" *Lovecraft Studies* No. 4 (Spring 1981): 3–9.

Colavito, Jason. *The Cult of Alien Gods: H. P. Lovecraft and Extraterrestrial Pop Culture*. Amherst, NY: Prometheus Books, 2005.

Derleth, August. "H. P. Lovecraft and His Work." In Lovecraft's *The Dunwich Horror and Others*. Sauk City, WI: Arkham House, 1963. ix–xx.

———. *The Mask of Cthulhu*. 1958. New York: Ballantine, 1971.

Ligotti, Thomas. *Grimscribe: His Lives and Works*. New York: Carroll & Graf, 1991.

Long, Frank Belknap. *The Horror from the Hills*. 1931. In Long's *Odd Science Ficion*. New York: Belmont, 1964.

Price, Robert M. "Demythologizing Cthulhu." *Lovecraft Studies* No. 8 (Spring 1984): 3–9, 24.

———. "Genres in the Lovecraftian Library." *Crypt of Cthulhu* No. 3 (Candlemas 1982): 14–17.

Schultz, David E. "From Microcosm to Macrocosm: The Growth of Lovecraft's Cosmic Vision." In David E. Schultz and S. T. Joshi, ed. *An Epicure in the Terrible: A Centennial Anthology of Essays in Honor of H. P. Lovecraft*. 1991. New York: Hippocampus Press, 2011. 208–29.

———. "The Origin of Lovecraft's 'Black Magic' Quote." *Crypt of Cthulhu* No. 48 (St. John's Eve 1987): 9–13. Rpt. in S. T. Joshi, ed. *Dissecting Cthulhu: Essays on the Cthulhu Mythos*. Lakeland, FL: Miskatonic River Press, 2011. 216–23.

Wandrei, Donald. *The Web of Easter Island*. Sauk City, WI: Arkham House, 1948.

Wetzel, George T. "The Cthulhu Mythos: A Study." 1955/1972. In S. T. Joshi, ed. *H. P. Lovecraft: Four Decades of Criticism*. Athens: Ohio University Press, 1980. 79–95.

Wilson, Colin. "The Return of the Lloigor." 1969. In *Tales of the Cthulhu Mythos, Volume 2*, ed. August Derleth. New York: Ballantine Books, 1971. 205–69.

The Recognition of H. P. Lovecraft, 1937–2013

[*Transcript of a speech given at the First Baptist Church, Providence, R.I., 22 August 2013, to kick off the NecronomiCon convention.*]

What I hope to address here briefly, if possible, is: How did Lovecraft get to be world-famous? He certainly wasn't world-famous in his time. Here was a man who did not publish a single book of his stories in his lifetime. On five different occasions, publishers approached him, or he approached a publisher, about a collection; every time, those negotiations failed for one reason or another. At the very end of his life, only one story appeared as a separate book, *The Shadow over Innsmouth*, and it was poorly printed, full of typographical errors, and distributed only in a few hundred copies. I do not doubt that Lovecraft, as he lay dying in his hospital bed at Jane Brown Memorial Hospital, not far from here, in the early morning hours of March 15, 1937, was envisioning the ultimate oblivion that would overtake his work, lost as it was in those crumbling pulp magazines that were already disintegrating to dust—*Weird Tales, Astounding Stories, Amazing Stories*—let alone his essays and poetry and letters, some of which had never been published. It would be no surprise if he thought that his work would simply fade away with his own body.

But his survival, at least in the short term, was a result of the great devotion of his friends. Robert Barlow, his literary executor, only nineteen years old, took a long bus ride from Kansas to Providence to go through his papers after his death, and donated the bulk of them to the John Hay Library—an act of incredible foresight, because those papers laid the foundation for later scholarship that would raise him to world stature.

August Derleth and Donald Wandrei spent their own money, and their time and effort, to start the publishing company Arkham House for the specific purpose of publishing Lovecraft's stories in hardcover. And those editions were well received at the start, although I think some book reviewers looked upon them more as a tribute to friendship than for their purely literary worth. Weird fiction at that time was not highly regarded as a literary form; most mainstream critics did not believe that you could write literature of horror and the supernatural. Indeed, in 1945, then the so-called dean of American critics—the leading literary critic in this country—decided to review some of Lovecraft's works, and his judgment was not favourable. He said, in a book review published in the *New Yorker:* "The only real horror in most of these fictions is the horror of bad taste and bad art."

Well, that doesn't sound very good! Mr. Wilson may have thought he would bury Lovecraft, but Lovecraft refused to be buried. The first paperback editions of Lovecraft's work came out right around that time. They may not have been distributed widely, but they set the stage for his later renaissance. The 1950s were actually a rather lean period for Lovecraft's work in general; Arkham House was going through some tough times and could not keep Lovecraft's work in print. They themselves only published a few titles in that whole decade. But interesting things were happening overseas. The first editions of Lovecraft in England appeared in the early 1950s. A few years later, more surprisingly, Lovecraft was first translated into foreign languages—first in France in 1954, then in Spain in 1957. The French, as they had done a century before with Poe, hailed Lovecraft as an exemplary writer of what they called *le fantastique*. The French had no prejudice against horror fiction as a literary genre, and so they championed Lovecraft. German and Italian translations followed soon thereafter.

In the early 1960s Arkham House was able to reprint Lovecraft's fiction in three substantial volumes and keep those volumes in print. The revenue for those editions actually came from those early film adaptations of Lovecraft. We remember them all—*The Haunted Palace, Die, Monster, Die!, The Shuttered Room*. They're campy and perhaps a little crude, but they gave some money to Arkham House, and they started planting the seeds of Lovecraft's later emergence as a figure of popular culture.

Indeed, as the 1960s and '70s advanced, a very strange thing happened: horror fiction suddenly became a best-selling phenomenon. Ira Levin published *Rosemary's Baby* in 1967; William Peter Blatty published *The Exorcist* in 1971; the early novels of Stephen King started publication in the early 1970s. Lovecraft rode the wave of that popularity. Those Arkham House editions were reprinted by Lancer Books, and then by Ballantine Books, and sold over a million copies over the next several years. So Lovecraft was becoming firmly implanted in popular consciousness—indeed, to such an extent that *Time* magazine took notice of Lovecraft in a lengthy review in its June 11, 1973 issue.

But popularity is one thing; critical esteem is a very different thing. Literary history is littered with the corpses of popular writers who then faded from the scene—and deserved to fade: their popularity was a transient phenomenon, subject to time and whim. Would Lovecraft meet that same fate? Perhaps not.

What happened in the 1970s was that, shortly after August Derleth's death in 1971, a new crop of Lovecraft scholars emerged, taking Lovecraft much more seriously than had been done in the past, studying him more searchingly and with greater analytical skill—critics like Dirk W. Mosig, Kenneth W. Faig, Jr., David E. Schultz, Barton L. St Armand (a professor at Brown), Peter Cannon. Their work was in a sense showcased at one of the great events this city has held—the First World Fantasy Convention, held in 1975, theoretically to celebrate the entire realm of weird fiction, but with a significant Lovecraft component. There were many individuals—from Mosig to Fritz Leiber to Robert Bloch to Frank Belknap Long—who all came to celebrate Lovecraft's legacy.

This was about the time when I emerged on the scene in a very tentative manner. As a teenager I had read Lovecraft in my public library in Muncie, Indiana, and I knew I had to study this curious Providence writer. I knew I had to come here to absorb the influence of Lovecraft, to get a sense of what he meant as a writer and as a thinker. Luckily, I was accepted at Brown in 1976 and spent the next six years there, doing as much work as I possibly could while still attending classes. I did a significant amount of work, including a bibliography, and I spent years correcting Lovecraft's texts; they had been printed with many errors in previous editions. These texts were printed by Arkham House in the 1980s. They gained a bit of attention, but Lovecraft was still very far from achieving renown as a leading writer in world literature.

However, around that time other scholars emerged—Steven J. Mariconda, Robert M. Price with his very lively magazine *Crypt of Cthulhu*, Will Murray, Robert H. Waugh. The work of these scholars was commemorated in another great event that took place here—the H. P. Lovecraft Centennial Conference in 1990, held at Brown and featuring many scholars from around the world who came to speak on a very hot August weekend. And at the end of that event we had the unveiling of the H. P. Lovecraft Memorial Plaque on the grounds of the John Hay Library.

I think a lot of us at that time felt that that was the acme of Lovecraft's recognition. A major university had sponsored a good academic convention, and he was a hugely popular writer. But more things were to come. I spent several years writing a full-length biography of Lovecraft, and it was published in 1996 by Necronomicon Press, then the leading small-press publisher of Lovecraftiana, run by Marc A. Michaud, who had done incredible work for the last several decades. That book got some good reviews, most notably by Joyce Carol Oates in the *New York Review of Books*, and she called Lovecraft the "King of Weird"! That was very different from what Edmund Wilson had said fifty years before. Now we're getting somewhere!

A few years later, Penguin asked me to compile the first of three volumes of Lovecraft's stories in annotated editions for Penguin Classics; so at least in the eyes of the Penguin editors, Lovecraft was a classic. And I'm sure that those editions helped to inspire the Library of America to issue its edition of Lovecraft in 2005. And that, I think, represents the ultimate canonisation of Mr. H. P. Lovecraft. He had arrived; he was in the canon of American literature, right there with Poe and Hawthorne and Melville and Henry James and Willa Cather and Edith Wharton. He had made it.

More things happened around that time. A whole new crop of imaginative writers emerged who drew inspiration from Lovecraft. Unlike many writers in the past, who had merely imitated the flamboyant externals of Lovecraft's work, these looked deeper, more searchingly, into the essence of Lovecraft's cosmic vision, his sense of a humanity alone in the universe and facing a bleak future of ultimate oblivion. Today, such as Caitlín Kiernan, Laird Barron, W. H. Pugmire, Joseph S. Pulver, Sr., Jason V Brock, Lois Gresh, Cody Goodfellow, and many others are here, and they will be speaking about what it means to write in the Lovecraftian literary tradition.

And, even more surprisingly, Lovecraft has become a media figure. I mentioned those early film adaptations; crude as they were, they laid the groundwork for better things to come. For the last twenty years or so, there has been an annual H. P. Lovecraft Film Festival in Portland, Oregon, run mostly by Andrew Migliore and now taken over by others, and it has featured filmmakers from around the world showing films short and long. We have filmmakers who have come here this weekend to discuss the very difficult art of translating Lovecraft's words into images. But there's more than that. Lovecraft has been on television; he has been adapted for comic books, role-playing games, interactive video games, rock music, classical music, and many other media.

Lovecraft has continued to expand around the world. Those early translations in Europe have given way to still newer editions. Lovecraft is now in Russian, Estonian, Turkish, Serbo-Croatian, Bengali, Chinese, Japanese, modern Greek. Truly, Lovecraft belongs to the world.

And yet, in the most fundamental sense, he remains a uniquely American, a uniquely Rhode Island phenomenon. Let us remember what is written on his tombstone at Swan Point Cemetery, not far from here: "I am Providence." What a wealth of meaning lies in those simple words; how profoundly they speak of Lovecraft's attachment to this city—its architecture, its topography, its history (now stretching back almost four hundred years), its people. Lovecraft travelled up and down the Eastern Seaboard, from Quebec to Key West, but he always came back to Providence. It was not merely his home; it was his haven, his sanctuary. It was the only place he felt he truly belonged, the only place he felt he could be the man and the writer he wished to be. And so it is fitting that we have come from the four corners of the earth to celebrate his life and legacy.

I have to believe that he would be pleased.

Sources

I. Biographical Studies

"Lovecraft and *Weird Tales*." Introduction to *H. P. Lovecraft in "The Eyrie."* West Warwick, RI: Necronomicon Press, 1979.

"Further Notes on Lovecraft and Music." *Romantist* 4-5 (1980/81): 47-49.

"Lovecraft's Library." Introduction to *Lovecraft's Library: A Catalogue.* West Warwick, RI: Necronomicon Press, 1980.

"Lovecraft's Revisions: How Much of Them Did He Write?" *Crypt of Cthulhu* No. 11 (Candlemas 1983): 3-14.

"Lovecraft and His Wife." Introduction to *The Private Life of H. P. Lovecraft* by Sonia H. Davis. West Warwick, RI: Necronomicon Press, 1985.

"Lovecraft and the Films of His Day." *Crypt of Cthulhu* No. 77 (Eastertide 1991): 8-10.

"The Rationale of Lovecraft's Pseudonyms." *Crypt of Cthulhu* No. 80 (Eastertide 1992): 15-24, 29.

"Lovecraft and the Munsey Magazines." Introduction to *H. P. Lovecraft in the Argosy: Collected Correspondence from the Munsey Magazines.* West Warwick, RI: Necronomicon Press, 1994.

"Barbarism and Civilisation: Robert E. Howard and H. P. Lovecraft in Their Correspondence." *Studies in the Fantastic* No. 1 (Summer 2008): 95-124.

II. Philosophical Studies

"The Political and Economic Thought of H. P. Lovecraft." *Miskatonic* 6, No. 4 (February 1979): [20-24].

"'Reality' and Knowledge: Some Notes on Lovecraft's Aesthetic." *Lovecraft Studies* No. 3 (Fall 1980): 17-27.

"*In Defence of Dagon* and Lovecraft's Philosophy." Introduction to *In Defence of Dagon.* West Warwick, RI: Necronomicon Press, 1985.

"Lovecraft's Alien Civilisations: A Political Interpretation." *Crypt of Cthulhu* No. 32 (St John's Eve 1985): 8-24, 31 (abridged). Rev. ed. in *Selected Papers on Lovecraft.* West Warwick, RI: Necronomicon Press, 1989.

"Lovecraft and a World in Transition." *Mage* (Winter 1985): 23–32.

"Lovecraft and the 'Big Issue.'" *Providence Sunday Journal Magazine* (5 August 1990): 14.

"H. P. Lovecraft: The Fiction of Materialism." In Douglas Robillard, ed. *American Supernatural Fiction: From Edith Wharton to the Weird Tales Writers*. New York: Garland, 1996. 141–66.

"Lovecraft on Religion." Introduction to Lovecraft's *Against Religion*. New York: Sporting Gentleman, 2010.

"Time, Space, and Natural Law: Science and Pseudo-Science in Lovecraft." *Lovecraft Annual* 4 (2010): 171–201.

III. Thematic and Textual Studies

"Autobiography in Lovecraft." *Lovecraft Studies* No. 1 (Fall 1979): 7–19.

"Lovecraft's Other Planets." *Crypt of Cthulhu* No. 4 (Eastertide 1982): 3–11 (abridged). Rev. ed. in *Selected Papers on Lovecraft*. West Warwick, RI: Necronomicon Press, 1989.

"Textual Problems in Lovecraft." *Lovecraft Studies* No. 6 (Spring 1982): 18–32.

"The Structure of Lovecraft's Longer Narratives." *Crypt of Cthulhu* No. 37 (Candlemas 1986): 3–17.

"The Dream World and the Real World in Lovecraft." *Crypt of Cthulhu* No. 15 (Lammas 1983): 4–15.

"Topical References in Lovecraft." *Extrapolation* 25, No. 3 (Fall 1984): 247–65.

"Humour and Satire in Lovecraft." *Crypt of Cthulhu* No. 61 (Yuletide 1988): 3–13.

"A Guide to the Lovecraft Fiction Manuscripts at the John Hay Library." *Lovecraft Studies* No. 16 (Spring 1988): 24–33; No. 17 (Fall 1988): 14–20.

IV. Studies of Individual Works

"Who Wrote 'The Mound'?" *Nyctalops* No. 14 (March 1978): 41–42. Rev. ed. *Crypt of Cthulhu* No. 11 (Candlemas 1983): 27–29, 38.

"On 'The Book.'" *Nyctalops* 3, No. 4 (April 1983): 9–13.

"On 'Polaris.'" *Crypt of Cthulhu* No. 15 (Lammas 1983): 22–26.

"On 'The Tree on the Hill.'" *Crypt of Cthulhu* No. 17 (Hallowmass 1983): 6–9.

"Lovecraft and the *Regnum Congo*." *Crypt of Cthulhu* No. 28 (Yuletide 1984): 13–17.

"The Sources for 'From Beyond.'" *Crypt of Cthulhu* No. 38 (Eastertide 1986): 15–19.

"On 'The Descendant.'" *Crypt of Cthulhu* No. 53 (Candlemas 1988): 10-11.
"What Happens in 'Arthur Jermyn.'" *Crypt of Cthulhu* No. 75 (Michaelmas 1990): 27-28.
"'The Tree' and Ancient History." *Nyctalops* 4, No. 1 (April 1991): 68-71.
"Lovecraft and Dunsany's *Chronicles of Rodriguez.*" *Crypt of Cthulhu* No. 82 (Hallowmass 1992): 3-6.
"Some Sources for 'The Mound' and *At the Mountains of Madness.*" In *Primal Sources: Essays on H. P. Lovecraft.* New York: Hippocampus Press, 2003.
"*The Case of Charles Dexter Ward.*" Introduction to *The Case of Charles Dexter Ward.* Tampa, FL: University of Tampa Press, 2009.
"Excised Passages from 'The Thing on the Doorstep.'" *Lovecraft Annual* 4 (2013): 171-77.

V. On Lovecraft's Essays, Poetry, and Letters

"'History of the *Necronomicon.*'" Afterword to *A History of the Necronomicon.* West Warwick, RI: Necronomicon Press, 1980.
"'Supernatural Horror in Literature.'" *Fantasy Commentator* 5, No. 3 (Fall 1985): 194-204.
"Two Spurious Lovecraft Poems." *Crypt of Cthulhu* No. 20 (Eastertide 1984): 25-26.
"A Look at Lovecraft's Letters." *Crypt of Cthulhu* No. 46 (Eastertide 1987): 3-12.
"A Look at Lovecraft's Fantastic Poetry." *Aklo* (Summer 1991): 20-30.
"Lovecraft, Regner Lodbrog, and Olaus Wormius." *Crypt of Cthulhu* No. 89 (Eastertide 1995): 3-7.
"Lovecraft's Essays." Introduction and section introductions to Lovecraft's *Miscellaneous Writings.* Sauk City, WI: Arkham House, 1995.

VI. On Lovecraft's Legacy and Influence

"The Development of Lovecraftian Studies, 1971-1982." *Lovecraft Studies* No. 8 (Spring 1984): 32-36 (Part I.B; as "Lovecraft in the Foreign Press, 1971-1982"); No. 9 (Fall 1984): 62-71 (Part I.A); No. 10 (Spring 1985): 18-28 (Part II.A); No. 11 (Fall 1985): 54-65 (Part II.B).
"R. H. Barlow and the Recognition of Lovecraft." *Crypt of Cthulhu* No. 60 (Hallowmass 1988): 45-51, 32.
"The Lovecraft Centennial Conference: Concluding Address." *Books at Brown* 37-39 (1991-92): 149-55.
"A Literary Tutelage: Robert Bloch and H. P. Lovecraft." *Studies in Weird Fiction* No. 16 (Winter 1995): 13-25.

"Passing the Torch: H. P. Lovecraft's Influence on Fritz Leiber." *Studies in Weird Fiction* No. 24 (Winter 1999): 17–25.

"*Lovecraft at Last*." Foreword to *Lovecraft at Last* by H. P. Lovecraft and Willis Conover. New York: Da Capo Press, 2002.

"The Cthulhu Mythos." In *Icons of Horror and the Supernatural*, ed. S. T. Joshi. Westport, CT: Greenwood Press, 2006. 97–128 (Vol. 1).

"The Recognition of H. P. Lovecraft, 1937–2013." Speech delivered at the First Baptist Church, 22 August 2013.

Index

À Rebours (Huysmans) 295
Abe, Masaki 537
Abraham, Margaret 57
"Account of Charleston, An" 488, 489, 490
Ackerman, Forrest J 312
Acolyte 248, 465, 567
Acton, Lord 101
"Ad Criticos" 67-68, 448
Adams, Benjamin 614
Adams, Henry 147
Adams, Phoebe 582
"Adder, The" (Chappell) 611
Addison, Joseph 14, 23, 55, 59, 154, 483
"Adept's Gambit" (Leiber) 568-70, 605
Adler, Alfred 300
Aeneid (Virgil) 247, 378, 379
Aeschylus 380
Age of Fable, The (Bulfinch) 192
Akley, Bert G. 229
Albert (King of Belgium) 293
"Alchemist, The" 54, 193, 269
Aldiss, Brian W. 527
"Aletheia Phrikodes" 454, 455
Alexander the Great 569
Alfredo 56, 227
Alhazred, Abdul 174, 189, 275, 281, 286, 419, 420, 465, 472, 588-89, 598
"Alienation" 237, 348, 350
All-Story 62, 63, 69-70
All-Story Cavalier 63, 64, 65, 69, 494
"Alone" (Poe) 457
"Amateur Journalism: Its Possible Needs and Betterment" 491
Amazing Stories 71, 250, 568, 596-97
"American to Mother England, An" 58
Amerique fantastique de Poe à Lovecraft, L' (Finné) 513
Amra 582

Anabasis (Xenophon) 378
Anatomy of Horror (Barclay) 527
"Ancient Track, The" 461, 511, 543
Anderson, Sherwood 153, 494
Anger, William Frederick 543
"Annals of the Jinns" (Barlow) 541
Antarktos 508
Apollonius Rhodius 378
Appleton, Lawrence (pseud. of HPL) 56
Arabian Nights 28, 161, 183
Aramata, Hiroshi 513, 514
Argonauts, The 378
Argosy 62, 63, 64, 65, 66, 68, 69, 70, 71, 490, 516n10
Aristotle 99, 101
Arkham House 243, 246-47, 248, 249, 251-52, 255, 322-39, 407, 437, 440, 501, 502-4, 506, 507-8, 513, 524, 536, 540, 543, 546, 579, 583, 605, 610, 616, 617, 618
Arnold, Matthew 473
Arruda, Manuel 404
"Ars Gratia Artis" 484
"Ashes" (Lovecraft-Eddy) 33, 450, 534
Asquith, Lady Cynthia 424
Astounding Stories 151, 177, 207, 250, 253-55, 256-57, 305, 323, 332, 546, 568
Astronomica (Manilius) 420
"Astrophobos" 458
At the Mountains of Madness 29, 514; aesthetics of, 207, 208, 454, 474, 597-98; autobiography in, 221; and Robert Bloch, 549, 558; and dream world, 278, 280, 281, 286-87; humour and satire in, 294, 313, 314-15; influences on, 390-92; and Fritz Leiber, 568, 571, 572, 574, 577; and Brian Lumley, 609; politics in, 104, 122-35, 137, 138-39, 140-41, 149, 450, 488;

625

rejection of, 14, 347–48; and science, 107, 112, 113, 158–59, 171, 172, 174, 189, 204, 232, 238, 305–6; shoggoths in, 462; structure of, 264–65, 266, 268, 270–71, 272; style of, 154, 245; textual history of, 251, 255–56, 257, 323, 332, 546; and "The Tree on the Hill," 359; topical references in, 292

At the Mountains of Madness and Other Novels 252, 408

"At the Mountains of Murkiness" (Clarke) 612

Atlantic Monthlyi 582

Atlantis: The Antediluvian World (Donnelly) 373

"Autobiography in Lovecraft" (Joshi) 8

"Automatic Executioner, The" (de Castro) 35

"Automatic Pistol, The" (Leiber) 574

"Azathoth" (novel fragment) 259, 279, 283, 295–96, 323, 372

"Azathoth" (sonnet) 350

Azif, Al (Alhazred) 420

Bach, Johann Sebastian 22, 24, 25

"Background" 449, 461

Bailey, John Eglinton 366

Baird, Edwin 19, 165, 398, 494

Balderston, John 52

Baldwin, F. Lee 581

"Ballade of Patrick von Flynn, Ye" 53, 60

Barbour, David 611

Barclay, Glen St John 527

Barlow, R. H.: and Zealia Bishop, 36, 343, 344–45, 346; HPL's collaborations with, 41–42, 43, 233, 313, 314, 339, 450, 463, 513; and HPL's death, 20, 616; as HPL's editor, 243n2, 454, 501, 509; HPL's letters to, 37, 443, 495; and HPL's manuscripts, 244, 247, 249, 251, 256, 324, 325, 326, 327, 328, 329, 330, 331, 332, 335, 336, 337–38, 347, 372, 408, 425, 482, 496, 536, 616; on HPL's pseudonyms, 53, 55, 69; and HPL's reputation, 539–47, 616–17; and Duane W. Rimel, 40

"Barlow Tributes, The" (Barlow) 541

"Barrens, The" (Wilson) 612

Bartlett's Familiar Quotations 537

Bat, The (film) 50

"Battle That Ende the Century, The" (Lovecraft-Barlow) 41, 43, 308, 312, 313, 544–45

Baudelaire, Charles 29, 84, 295

Beagle Edition of H. P. Lovecraft 505

"Beast in the Cave, The" 193, 196–97, 248, 448

Beckford, William 420, 570

Beethoven, Ludwig van 26

"Bells" (Poe) 460

"Bells, The" 348

Bender, Barry Leon 516n10, 520–21

Beneath the Moors (Lumley) 608

Bennett, F. V. 66–67, 68, 70, 72

Benson, E. F. 106

"Berenice" (Poe) 220, 222, 475

Bergier, Jacques 19, 20, 511

Berglund, Edward Paul 576

Berkeley, George 301

Berkeley Square (film) 52

Best of H. P. Lovecraft: Bloodcurdling Tales of Horror and the Macabre, The 507

Best Supernatural Stories of H. P. Lovecraft, The 243n1

Besten Gespenstergeschichten aus aller Welt, Die (Kluge) 512

"Bethmoora" (Dunsany) 276

Beware After Dark! (Harré) 29, 252, 324

"Beyond the Wall of Sleep" 107, 108, 109, 126, 139, 155, 178–79, 204, 209, 233, 261, 272, 299, 316, 323–24, 591

Beyond the Wall of Sleep 251, 345, 407, 408, 547

Bickerstaffe, Isaac, Jr (pseud. of HPL) 53, 54, 55, 493

Bicknell, Thomas William 404

Bierce, Ambrose 63, 225, 243, 273, 319, 320, 422, 427, 430, 432, 601, 602

Billion Year Spree (Aldiss) 527

Birkhead, Edith 422, 426, 429

Birth of a Nation, The (film) 50

Bishop, Jeremy (pseud. of HPL) 56

Bishop, Zealia 29, 36–37, 44, 45, 61, 338, 343–36, 388

"Bit of the Dark World, A" (Leiber) 575–76

"Black Bargain" (Bloch) 559–60

Black Cat 62
"Black Man with a Horn" (Klein) 611-12
"Black Stone, The" (Howard) 227, 600
Blackwood, Algernon 63, 264, 422, 424, 426, 427, 587, 602
Blair, Alexander Ferguson (pseud. of HPL) 56
Blair, Hugh 465-72
Blatty, William Peter 617
Bleiler, E. F. 426, 428, 429
Bloch, Robert 9, 99, 289, 297, 313, 432, 507, 548-65, 589, 604-5, 610, 611
Boaz, Franz 212, 487
Boerem, R. 60, 349, 453, 461, 535
"Boiling Point, The" 312
Bolingbroke, Henry St John, Viscount 312
"Book, The" (fragment) 324, 347-51, 360, 372, 374, 461-62
"Book, The" (sonnet) 349
Book of Dzyan, The 358
Book of Eibon 411, 589, 601
Book of the Damned, The (Fort) 299, 373
Borellus (Pierre Borel) 401
Boswell, James 23-24
"Bothon" (Whitehead) 37
"Bouts Rimés" (Lovecraft-Barlow) 463
Bradofsky, Hyman 42, 438, 442, 479, 490, 492
Brandstatter, Christian 512
"Brief Autobiography of an Inconsequential Scribbler, The" 495
"Britannia Victura" 58
Brontë, Emily 423
"Brood of Bubastis, The" (Bloch) 553, 556
Brown, A. H. 117
"Brumalian Wish, A" 459
Buhle, Paul 533
Bulfinch, Thomas 192
Bullen, John Ravenor 115, 116, 117, 119
Burke, Rusty 96
Burleson, Donald R. 7, 8, 175, 229, 267n3, 378, 420, 461, 531, 533, 583, 592-93
Burroughs, Edgar Rice 64-65, 196
Burrowers Beneath, The (Lumley) 609
Byfield, Bruce 576
Byrd, Richard E. 253, 305

C., E. F. W. 66-67
Cabell, James Branch 153, 485, 569, 570
Cabinet of Dr. Caligari, The (film) 51
Californian 42, 339, 438, 479, 490
Californian, The (book) 509
"Call of Cthulhu, The": and Cthulhu Mythos, 589-91, 595, 597, 606; and Fritz Leiber, 571, 575, 577, 605; and Thomas Ligotti, 611; origin of, 480; philosophy of, 172, 174, 179-80, 316, 375, 454, 457; religion in, 134, 188, 189; and science, 107, 109, 110, 113, 170, 171, 172, 196, 204-5, 208, 215, 239, 394; structure of, 261, 263-64, 267-68, 270, 271-72, 273; style of, 150; textual history of, 250, 252, 324; topical references in, 290, 298; and "The Tree on the Hill," 360; and *Weird Tales*, 14, 160
Callaghan, Gavin 8
Campbell, Joseph 576
Campbell, Ramsey 561, 572, 577, 608
Cannon, Peter 7, 8, 583, 610, 612
"Canterville Ghost, The" (Wilde) 319
Carpenter, John 613
Carroll, Lewis 517
Carter, Lin 420, 505, 506, 517n11, 526, 531, 612
"Case for Classicism, The" 153, 483
Case of Charles Dexter Ward, The 348, 358, 393-409, 513; autobiography in, 220-21; characters in, 110-11, 175; and colonial history, 30, 306, 412, 490; and Cthulhu Mythos, 420, 593; and dream world, 275, 286; humour in, 309-10, 313; structure of, 260, 268, 269-70, 272; textual history of, 246-47, 249, 324-25, 326, 540; themes in, 205-6, 209-10; topical references in, 291-92, 293, 296
Cast a Deadly Spell (film) 613
Castle of Otranto, The (Walpole) 452
"Cats, The" 33
"Cats and Dogs" 55, 247, 474, 477, 496-97
"Cats of Ulthar, The" 112, 278, 318
Cats of Ulthar, The 509, 544
Cavalier 63

"Celephaïs" 155, 223–24, 226, 259, 279, 280, 283, 294, 295, 311, 325, 348, 462
"Challenge from Beyond, The" (Lovecraft et al.) 42, 337, 513
Chamberlain, Houston Stewart 520
Chambers, Robert W. 63, 420, 423, 601, 602
Chaosium 613
Chaplin, Charlie 49
Chappell, Fred 609, 611
Charleston 490
Charwoman's Shadow, The (Dunsany) 569
Checkley, John 402
"Chemical" (Blackwood) 424
Chopin, Frédéric 25
"Christmas" 59
Chronicle of Nath (Yergler) 358
Chronicles of Rodriguez, The (Dunsany) 383–87, 569
Churchward, Colonel James 299
Citadel of Fear (Stevens) 69
"City, The" 458
Clansman, The (Dixon) 50
Clark, Lillian D. 397, 398, 399, 400, 401, 404, 496
Clarke, Arthur C. 440, 612
Classics and Contemporaries (Joshi) 9
Cleopatra (film) 52
Cleveland, Charles Dexter 404
Cline, Leonard 430
Clock of Dreams, The (Lumley) 609
Clore, Dan 461
Coates, Walter J. 542
Cobb, Irvin S. 64
Cockcroft, T. G. L. 252
Colavito, Jason 614
Colbert, Claudette 52
"Cold Print" (Campbell) 608
Coleridge, Samuel Taylor 183, 192
"Collapsing Cosmoses" (Lovecraft-Barlow) 42, 43, 308, 312, 336, 513
Collapsing Cosmoses 509
Collected Poems 437, 505
Collins, Tom 56, 504–5, 508
"Colloquy of Monos and Una, The" (Poe) 353, 354
Color Line, The (Smith) 146, 211, 520
"Colour out of Space, The" 113, 150, 154, 171, 174–75, 204, 205, 262, 292–93, 297, 313, 317, 357, 370, 474, 568, 572, 575, 591–92, 596–97, 613
Colour out of Space, The 506
"Comment" 57
"Commercial Blurbs" 496
Commonplace Book 243n2, 358, 424, 536, 545, 547
"Complete Chronology" (spurious) 534
"Composite Story." See "Challenge from Beyond, The"
"Confession of Unfaith, A" 161, 164, 183, 194, 476, 495–96
Conger, Alice 73
Connors, Scott 531, 534, 536
Conover, Willis 425, 508, 521, 523–24, 579–84
"Conqueror Worm, The" (Poe) 354
Conservative 53, 115, 296, 321
Conservative, The (book) 509
"Continuity" 461, 462–63, 544
"Convention, The" 55
"Conversation of Eiros and Charmion, The" (Poe) 353, 455
Cook, W. Paul 47, 48, 54, 179, 249, 252, 333, 334, 394, 402, 422, 423, 525, 541–
"Cool Air" 221, 325
Corbett, Jim 87, 88
Corelli, Archangelo 25–26
"Correction for Lovecraft" 68
"Count Magnus" (James) 273, 403–4
"Courtyard, The" 348
Cowper, William 452
Coye, Lee Brown 610
Cram, Ralph Adams 424
Crane, Hart 224
Crawford, F. Marion 423
Crawford, William L. 333, 495
"Crawling Chaos, The" (Lovecraft-Jackson) 31–32, 54, 295
Crean, T. P. 67
"Creeper in the Crypt, The" (Bloch) 558
Creeps by Night (Hammett) 29, 433
Crime of Crimes, The 442
"Crime of the Century, The" 211–12, 289, 487, 520
Critical Dissertation on the Poems of Ossian, A (Blair) 465–72
Crofts, Anna Helen 32, 59

Crowley, James Laurence 58
Crypt Horror Tales 514
Crypt of Cthulhu 618
Cthulhu Mythos 18-19, 35, 75, 113-14, 173-75, 188-89, 204, 393, 407, 526, 529-31, 534, 550, 551, 562, 563, 564, 566, 567, 569, 585-614
Cthulhu Mythos Bibliography and Concordance, A (Jarocha-Ernst) 585
Cultes des Goules (d'Erlette) 589
Cummings, Ray 16, 65
Currey, L. W. 333
Curse, The (film) 613
Curse of Race Prejudice, The (Morton) 212
Curse of the Wise Woman, The (Dunsany) 294, 383, 395
"Curse of Yig, The" (Lovecraft-Bishop) 19, 36, 45
Curse of Yig, The 345
"Cycle of Verse, A" 61, 457

Da Costa, Bernard 511
Daas, Edward F. 72, 491
Dadaism 484
Daemonolatreia (Remigius) 589
"Dagon" 107, 118, 150, 170, 199, 204, 261, 290-91, 393, 394, 430, 454, 589, 591
Dagon (Chappell) 609
Dagon (film) 613
Dagon and Other Macabre Tales 251, 505
Dalton, John 161
"Damned Thing, The" (Bierce) 273
Damon, S. Foster 545
Däniken, Erich von 614
Dante Alighieri 496
Dark Chamber, The (Cline) 430
"Dark Demon, The" (Bloch) 552, 553-54, 557, 604-5
Dark Tower, The (Lewis) 240
Darwin, Charles 121, 161, 184, 194, 294, 320, 377, 587, 596
David Garrick (film) 51
Davis, Graeme 492
Davis, Robert H. 63
Davis, Sonia. See Greene, Sonia H.
De Bry, Brothers 363-65
de Camp, L. Sprague 8, 20, 32, 115, 251, 264, 318, 324, 419, 441, 493, 504, 516-20, 521, 523, 524, 525, 527, 579, 581, 582, 583
de Castro, Adolphe 35-36, 41, 44, 489
de la Mare, Walter 403, 423
de la Ree, Gerry 508
De Mille, James 388-90, 392
De Nardi, Claudio 537
De Rerum Natura (Lucretius) 120
de Turris, Gianfranco 512, 537
De Vermis Mysteriis (Prinn) 552-53, 560, 589
"De Triumpho Naturae" 145, 146, 211, 520
Dead Beat, The (Bloch) 562, 564
"Dead Bookworm, The" 56
"Dead Man, The" (Leiber) 572
Dead Titans, Waken! (Wandrei) 604
"Dead Valley, The" (Cram) 424
"Deaf, Dumb and Blind" (Lovecraft-Eddy) 34
"Death" (Hoag) 437-39, 534
"Death Diary" 41
"Death of Halpin Frayser, The" (Bierce) 273
Death Ship, The (Russell) 390
Decline of the West, The (Spengler) 138, 148, 450
Dee, John 600
"Deep Ones, The" (Wade) 606
DeMille, Cecil B. 52
Democritus 120, 161, 367, 380, 455, 480
Demons by Daylight (Campbell) 608
Dempsey, Jack 81, 82
Derleth, August: and R. H. Barlow, 540, 545, 546-47; and Cthulhu Mythos, 18-19, 188, 407, 513, 526, 527-28, 529-31, 534, 567, 609, 613; on HPL, 22, 54, 226, 347n1, 372, 429, 501, 515-16, 517, 519, 525, 581; as HPL's editor, 243, 246, 249, 251-52, 255, 322, 323, 324, 325, 326-27, 329-30, 332, 333, 338, 339, 407, 425, 505, 507; HPL's letters to, 51, 229, 433, 442, 444, 483; and HPL's recognition, 501-2, 579, 580, 616; and HPL's revisions, 31, 37, 38, 345-46; and "posthumous collaborations," 437, 506, 510, 604; and *Weird Tales*, 19, 20

"Derleth Mythos, The" (Tierney) 530, 567, 609
d'Erlette, Comte 589
Descartes, René 367-68
"Descendant, The" 299, 325, 372-74
Description of the Town of Quebeck, A 504
"Despair" 457, 460
Detective Tales 398
"Diary in the Snow" (Leiber) 571-72, 605
"Diary of Alonzo Typer, The" (Lovecraft-Lumley) 19, 43, 44, 45, 337, 358
"Dim-Remembered Story, A" (Barlow) 42, 541
Dionysius II (Tyrant of Syracuse) 380, 381
"Discarded Draught: 'The Shadow over Innsmouth'" 332
Disciples of Cthulhu, The (Berglund) 576
"Disinterment, The" (Lovecraft-Rimel) 41, 357, 361, 450, 534
Dixon, Thomas, Jr 50
Dixon, Wheeler Winston 157
Don Rodriguez (Dunsany). *See Chronicles of Rodriguez, The*
Donnelly, Ignatius 373
"Doom That Came to Sarnath, The" 251, 277-78, 326, 375, 511, 540, 608-9
Doom That Came to Sarnath, The 505
Doorways to Poetry (Moe) 152, 461
Doré, Gustave 183
Douglas, Drake 264
Dowe, Jennie E. T. 59
Doyle, Sir Arthur Conan 51
Drab 514
Dracula (film) 50
Dragon Fly 544
Drake, H. B. 430, 435
"Dream-Land" (Poe) 459
Dream Quest of H. P. Lovecraft, The (Schweitzer) 526
Dream-Quest of Unknown Kadath, The: autobiography in, 227; and Robert Bloch, 555-56; and Cthulhu Mythos, 594, 595, 599; L. Sprague de Camp on, 517; dream world in, 275, 276, 277, 278, 279, 280-86, 287-88; and Lord Dunsany, 155, 228; humour in, 309, 310-11; and Fritz Leiber, 569; and Brian Lumley, 608, 609; structure of, 259; style of, 154, 247; textual history of, 246, 249, 326, 540; themes in, 224, 372, 400-401, 408; writing of, 150, 226, 251, 260, 348
Dream-Quest of Unknown Kadath, The (collection) 505
Dreamer's Tales, A (Dunsany) 383, 385
"Dreams in the Witch House, The": and Robert Bloch, 556, 558; and Cthulhu Mythos, 598-99, 605; dreams in, 107; humour in, 313; influences on, 435; and Fritz Leiber, 567, 572, 573, 574; and Salem witch trials, 512; and science, 108, 111, 114, 214, 302, 303, 304, 359-60, 370, 450; structure of, 260-61, 271, 272-73; style of, 154, 180, 246; textual history of, 249, 250, 252, 326-37
"Dreams of Albert Moreland, The" (Leiber) 574-75, 605
"Dreams of Yith" (Rimel) 40, 234
Dreiser, Theodore 478
Dryden, John 24, 153, 448, 473, 483
Du Bois, W. E. B. 487
du Maurier, George 50
Dunciad (Pope) 60, 67, 448
Dunn, John T. 438
Dunsany, Lord: and Arthur C. Clarke, 440; and dream world, 276; influence on HPL, 32, 63, 111-12, 150, 155, 174, 187, 228-29, 275, 277, 280, 281, 282, 286, 287, 294, 319, 352-56, 378, 383-87, 395, 400, 455, 587, 594-95, 596; and Fritz Leiber, 569; HPL on, 165, 179, 373, 395, 422, 426, 427; and Edgar Allan Poe, 352-54; and Duane W. Rimel, 40
"Dunwich Horror, The": and *The Case of Charles Dexter Ward*, 175-76, 406, 407; and cryptography, 366; and Cthulhu Mythos, 188, 472, 563, 592-93, 595, 606; dialect in, 395; and dream world, 275; humour in, 317, 318; interpretations of, 533, 598; and HPL's revisions, 39-40; and racism, 212; and science, 204, 205-6, 208; setting of, 151, 171, 588; structure of, 262, 264, 265, 271; style of, 180, 245; textual his-

tory of, 252, 257, 327; and *Weird Tales*, 14, 17–18; writing of, 388, 461
Dunwich Horror, The 506
Dunwich Horror, The (film) 613
Dunwich Horror and Others, The 243n1, 252, 508
"Dweller, The" 348
"Dweller in Darkness, The" (Derleth) 606
Dwyer, Bernard Austin 18, 323, 347, 451
Dyalhis, Nictzin 84
Dziemianowicz, Stefan 572

"East India Brick Row, The" 494
E'ch-Pi-El Speaks 446, 508
Eddington, Arthur S. 241
Eddy, C. M., Jr 33–34, 39, 44, 297, 329, 450, 451, 534
Edkins, Ernest A. 451
Edward VII (King of England) 294
"Eidolon, The" 456–57, 458
Einstein, Albert 105, 120, 148, 166–67, 185, 186, 191, 202–3, 238–39, 300–302, 303, 481, 587
"Elder Pharos, The" 348
"Electric Executioner, The" (Lovecraft-de Castro) 35, 36, 489
Elegant Nightmares (Sullivan) 537
Eliot, T. S. 55, 57, 119, 144, 148, 153, 187, 296
Elliot, Hugh 120, 162, 166, 201, 368–70, 371, 481
Ellsworth, Lincoln 305
Encyclopaedia Britannica 298, 366
Encyclopedia Cthulhuiana (Harms) 612
Encyclopedia of Occultism (Spence) 299
"End of the Jackson War, The" 68
Epicure in the Terrible, An (Schultz-Joshi) 583
Epicurus 120, 121, 161, 165, 379, 455, 481, 535
Erik Dorn (Hecht) 153, 296, 320
Etidorhpa (Lloyd) 424n5
Eureka (Poe) 455
Euripides 267, 427
"Evening Star" 544
Everts, R. Alain 7, 252n11, 334, 441, 508–9, 510, 522–23
"Evil Clergyman, The" 347
Evolution of the Weird Tale, The (Joshi) 8

Ewers, Hanns Heinz 424, 435
"Ex Oblivione" 53, 59
Exorcist, The (Blatty) 617
"Expectancy" 461

"Faceless God, The" (Bloch) 555–56, 605
"Facts concerning the Late Arthur Jermyn and His Family" 109, 110, 113, 153, 195, 197, 212, 269, 293, 327, 375–77, 494
"Fafhrd and Me" (Leiber) 569
Faig, Kenneth W., Jr. 421, 522, 534, 581
Fairbanks, Douglas 49
"Fall of the House of Usher, The" (Poe) 150, 198, 352, 354
Fanciful Tales 250–51, 330
"Fane of the Black Pharaoh" (Bloch) 557, 558, 605
Fantastika Romanen, Den (Lundwall) 513
Fantasy Crossroads 517
Fantasy Fan 251, 252, 299, 312, 323–24, 328, 331, 424–25, 539
Fantasy Magazine 337, 581
Fantazius Mallare (Hecht) 320
Farnese, Harold S. 17, 530n20, 602
Farsaci, Larry 69
Faulkner, William 158, 170, 433
"Feast in the Abbey, The" (Bloch) 550–51, 561
"Festival" 458
"Festival, The" 151, 200, 245, 327–28, 396, 401, 472, 588, 611
Fiction 514
Finlay, Virgil 463
Finné, Jacques 513
"First Law, The" (Jackson) 65–66
Fischer, Harry O. 568, 576
"Fishhead" (Cobb) 64
Fiske, John 121, 161, 184, 481
Fitzgerald, F. Scott 157
"For Annie" (Poe) 460
"For What Does the United Stand?" 491
Fort, Charles 299, 373
Foundations of the Nineteenth Century (Chamberlain) 520
"Four O'Clock" (Greene) 33
"Fragments from an Hour of Inspiration" 438

Frankenstein (film) 50
Franklin, Benjamin 310
"Franklyn Paragraphs, The" (Campbell) 608
Frazer, Sir James George 121, 161, 184, 587
Freud, Sigmund 139, 194, 299-300, 596
"From Beyond" 106-7, 110, 201-2, 252-53, 299, 328, 367-71, 395
"From the Sea" (Rimel) 41
Frome, Nils H. 451, 494-95
Frozen Pirate, the (Russell) 193, 390-92
Fulwiler, William 37, 134, 311n4
Fungi from Yuggoth 120, 151, 234, 236, 237, 344, 348-51, 372, 449, 461-63, 508, 509, 511, 535, 543-44, 558, 563-64, 612
Fungi from Yuggoth and Other Poems 505
Fusco, Sebastiano 512

"Gallows, The" (Bloch) 548
Galpin, Alfred 25, 54, 56, 57, 59, 60, 224, 227, 252, 441, 443, 444
Gamwell, Annie E. Phillips 397, 582
Gamwell, Phillips 441
Ganymed Horror 514
Gardner, Mrs. Marinus Willett 404
Garth, Sir Samuel 56
Gatto, John Taylor 526-27
"Gaudeamus" 220
Gengångaren 513
Genso to Kaiki 514
Ghost Book, The (Asquith) 424
"Ghost-Eater, The" (Lovecraft-Eddy) 33
Gibbon, Edward 88
Goblin Tower, The (Long) 544
Gods if Pegāna, The (Dunsany) 594
Godwin, William 403
Golden Atom 69
Golden Bough, The (Frazer) 121, 161, 184, 587
Golem, The (Meyrink) 50, 424, 425
Gonce, John Wisdom, III 612
Good Anaesthetic, A 193
Goodenough, Arthur 229
"George Beyond Salapunco, The" (Derleth) 606
Gordon, Stuart 613
Gorgias 367

Gorman, Herbert 430, 435
Grant, Madison 212
"Grave, The" (Bloch) 550
Gray, Thomas 452
"Great God Pan, The" (Machen) 273
"Green Meadow, The" (Lovecraft-Jackson) 31-32, 45, 54
Greene, Sonia H. 33, 46-48, 147, 222, 225, 396-98, 400, 441, 496, 522
Grey, Zane 65
Griffith, D. W. 50
Grimm, Brothers 161, 183, 192
"Grinning Ghoul, The" (Bloch) 558, 559
Guest, Edgar A. 64, 84

"H. P. L." (Wilson) 610
H. P. L.: A Memoir (Derleth) 515, 581
H. P. Lovecraft: A Critical Study (Burleson) 8, 533, 583
H. P. Lovecraft: A Life (Joshi) 7, 583, 618
H. P. Lovecraft: A Symposium 566
"H. P. Lovecraft: An Introduction to His Life and Writings" (Koki) 515
H. P. Lovecraft: Four Decades of Criticism (Joshi) 7, 8, 513, 532, 583
H. P. Lovecraft: His Life, His Work (Faig) 522
"H. P. Lovecraft: Myth-Maker" (Mosig) 530, 567, 609
H. P. Lovecraft: New England Decadent (St Armand) 528-29
H. P. Lovecraft: Notes toward a Biography (Derleth) 515
"H. P. Lovecraft: Rabid Racist—or Compassionate Gentleman?" (Mosig) 519
"H. P. Lovecraft: The Books" (Carter) 526
H. P. Lovecraft: The Decline of the West (Joshi) 7, 8, 195n1
"H. P. Lovecraft: The Making of a Literary Reputatuion, 1937-1971" (Derleth) 243n1, 501
"H. P. Lovecraft and His Work" (Derleth) 602
H. P. Lovecraft Centennial Conference 8, 583, 618
H. P. Lovecraft Companion, The (Shreffler) 526
H. P. Lovecraft Film Festival 619

"H. P. Lovecraft, Outsider" (Derleth) 529-30, 603
Haeckel, Ernst 120, 162, 184, 210, 239, 300, 320, 371, 480-81, 587
Hail, Klarkash-Ton! 508
Haining, Peter 512
Hall, Leland 430
"Hallowe'en in a Suburb" 458
Halve Maen, De 490
Hamilton, Edmond 15, 16, 65
Hammett, Dashiell 29, 433
Hancock, Graham 614
Handel, George Frideric 23-25, 392
Harding, Warren G. 150, 290, 306
Harms, Daniel 612
Harré, T. Everett 29, 252, 324
Harris, Arthur 442
Harris, Thomas 432
Harris, Woodburn 446, 451
Hartmann, J. F. 55, 239, 493
Hathaway, Christine 546
Haunted Castle, The (Railo) 422, 429n13
"Haunted Palace, The" (Poe) 353-54, 458
"Haunter of the Dark, The" 234, 237, 253, 268, 272, 313, 317-18, 348, 359, 435, 552, 556, 557, 558-59, 562, 571, 599, 604, 610
Hawthorne, Julian 429
Hawthorne, Nathaniel 420, 429, 587
Hayakawa's Mystery Magazine 514
"He" 222-23, 298, 328, 383, 385-86, 387, 398-99
Heald, Hazel 19, 38-40, 249, 335, 450
Hearn, Lafcadio 295
Hecht, Ben 296, 320
Heisenberg, Werner Karl 168, 304, 587
Hellenica (Xenophon) 378
Hemingway, Ernest 154, 289
Henley, Samuel 420
"Herbert West—Reanimator" 111, 210, 220, 221, 258, 262-63, 291, 294, 300, 311, 328
"Heritage or Modernism: Common Sense in Art Forms" 119-20, 141, 482
Hermes Trismegistos 358
Herne, L' 511, 514
Herrera, Philip 506, 580
"Hertha" (Swinburne) 458
Hichens, Robert 426

"Hill and the Hole, The" (Leiber) 575
Hill of Dreams, The (Machen) 223, 373
Hippocampus Press 8
"Historical Account of Last Year's War with SPAIN, An" 473
"History of the *Necronomicon*" 329, 419-21, 472, 517, 600
History of the Necronomicon, A 510
Hitler, Adolf 155
Hoag, Jonathan E. 60, 437-39, 534-35
"Hoard of the Wizard-Beast, The" (Lovecraft-Barlow) 41
Hodgson, William Hope 390, 424-25
Hogg, James 424
Hollick-Kenyon, Herbert 305
"Hollow in the Woods, The" (Campbell) 561
Holy and the Daemonic from Sir Thomas Browne to William Blake, The (Stock) 537
Home, William Scott 365, 420
Home Brew 198, 328, 330
Homer 427
"Homes and Shrines of Poe" 490
Hopkins, Stephen 404
Hornig, Charles D. 424, 425
"Horror at Martin's Beach, The" (Lovecraft-Greene) 33
"Horror at Red Hook, The" 14, 17, 212-13, 223, 225, 227, 261-62, 266, 298, 309, 329, 366, 398, 407, 508
Horror from the Hills, The (Long) 600
"Horror in the Burying-Ground, The" (Lovecraft-Heald) 39-40
"Horror in the Museum, The" (Lovecraft-Heald) 19, 39
Horror in the Museum and Other Revisions, The 243n1, 346, 503, 512
Horrores de Dunwich, Los 511
Houdini, Harry 31, 34
"Hound, The" 17, 34, 151, 178, 225n6, 281, 295, 311-12, 329, 420, 549, 573, 589
"Hound, The" (Leiber) 573
"Hounds of Tindalos, The" (Long) 301-2, 600
"House, The" 61, 398, 457, 458
House of the Seven Gables, The (Hawthorne) 150, 205
Howard, I. M. 73

Howard, L. Phillips (pseud. of HPL) 55
Howard, Robert E. 16, 20, 73-96, 227, 440, 443, 444, 445, 451, 585, 601, 603, 611
"Howard P. Lovecraft's Fiction" (Cook) 54
Howard Phillips Lovecraft: Dreamer on the Nightside (Long) 519, 523, 524-25, 579, 581
Huis in de nevel, Het 513
Hulme, T. E. 451
Hume, David 184
Huxley, Aldous 187, 320
Huxley, Thomas Henry 120, 121, 146, 161, 184, 194, 211-12, 320, 362-65, 520, 587
Huysmans, Joris-Karl 295, 484
"Hylas and Myrra—A Tale" 56
"Hypnos" 105, 107, 108, 110, 167, 297, 300-301

I Am Providence: The Life and Times of H. P. Lovecraft (Joshi) 7
Ibars, Eduardo Haro 511
"Ibid" 308
Ibsen, Henrik 18
"Idealism and Materialism: A Reflection" 120, 300, 450, 475, 482
Ides . . . et Autres 511
"Idle Days on the Yann" (Dunsany) 276, 277, 354
Image-Maker of Thebes, The (film) 49-50
"Imp of the Perverse, The" (Poe) 226
Imparcial, El (pseud. of HPL) 54-55
"In a Major Key" 475, 492
In Defence of Dagon 115-21, 162, 344, 430, 446, 451, 476, 477, 482
In der Gruft und andere makabre Erzählungen 512
In Lovecraft's Shadow (Derleth) 605
In the Confessional and the Following (de Castro) 35
"In the Editor's Study" 484
In the Mouth of Madness (film) 613
"In the Vault" 320, 329-30, 398
"In the Walls of Eryx" (Lovecraft-Sterling) 43, 122, 124-25, 131, 134, 233-34, 312-13, 337, 361, 523
Incantations (Smith) 541, 543

Inhabitant of the Lake, The (Campbell) 577, 608
"Inheritance, The" (Leiber) 572
"Inspiration" 53
International Lovecraft Symposium (Trieste) 514
"Introduction, The" 57
Invisible Man, The (film) 50-51
Isaacson, Charles D. 476, 492

Jackson, Fred 65-68, 70, 71, 490, 494
Jackson, Winifred Virginia 31-32, 54, 58
James, Henry 488
James, M. R. 63, 273, 403-4, 422, 427, 429
James, William 355
"January" 59
Jarocha-Ernst, Chris 585
Jeans, Sir James 239
"Jerusalem's Lot" (King) 610
Jewett, Sarah Orne 587
Jinka, Katsuo 513
Johnson, Samuel 25, 27, 51, 57, 154, 301, 483
Joly, John 306
Jones, John J. (pseud. of HPL) 56
Jones, Stephen 614
Joyce, James 485
Jung, Carl Gustav 300
Junzt, Friedrich von 189, 589, 600
Jurgen (Cabell) 153, 485
Juvenal (D. Junius Juvenalis) 313, 315

Kalem Club 398, 451
Kant, Immanuel 368
Katzen von Ulthar, Die 512
Keats, John 59, 154
Keffer, Willametta 53, 54
"Key, The" 349
Kimball, Gertrude Selwyn 399, 401, 402
King, Stephen 610, 613, 617
King in Yellow, The (Chambers) 420
Kingdom of Evil, The (Hecht) 320
Kipling, Rudyard 116, 295
Kirde, Kalju 512, 536-37
Klein, T. E. D. 611-12
Kleiner, Rheinhart 60, 151, 221n2, 225n6, 312, 320, 438, 439, 444
Kline, Otis Adelbert 41
Kluge, Manfred 512

Knight, Damon 604
Koenig, H. C. 312, 490
Koki, Arthur S. 334, 515
Krutch, Joseph Wood 208, 320, 596
Ku Klux Klan 50, 99, 146, 519

Là-Bas (Huysmans) 295
Lacassin, Francis 511
Lactantius (L. Caecilius Firmianus Lactantius) 401
Lady Who Came to Stay, The (Spencer) 424
"Laeta; a Lament" 58
Laney, Francis T. 465
Lang, Andrew 28
Lang, Fritz 51
Laplace, Pierre Simon, marquis de 161
"Last Feast of Harlequin, The" (Ligotti) 611
"Last Test, The" (Lovecraft-de Castro) 19, 35, 36
Last Wave, The (film) 613
"Laughter of a Ghoul, The" (Bloch) 549
Lauterbach, Edward S. 257n17
Le Fanu, J. Sheridan 426
"League, The" 487
Leaves 324, 325, 336, 545
Lectures on Rhetorick and Belles-Lettres (Blair) 466
Leeds, Arthur 496
Leiber, Fritz 9, 122, 137, 169, 191, 214, 238, 304, 314, 479, 514, 566-78, 580, 605, 611
Leiber, Jonquil 568
Letters to Robert Bloch 548
Lettres 511
Lettres d'Arkham 511
Leucippus 120, 161
Levin, Ira 617
Lévy, Maurice 46, 142, 219, 273, 284, 399, 422, 526, 527-28
Lewis, C. S. 240, 479
Lewis, Sinclair 157
Liber Aureus Philosophicus (Wormius) 472
Life of Jesus (Renan) 187
Life of Johnson (Boswell) 24
"Life's Mystery" 55
"Ligeia" (Poe) 150, 352, 354
Ligotti, Thomas 611
Lindsay, Vachel 442

"Lines on Graduation from the R. I. Hospital's School for Nurses" 438
"Lines on the 25th Anniversary of the *Providence Evening News*" 439
Lippi, Giuseppe 536
"Literary Composition" 483
"Literary Copernicus, A" (Leiber) 514, 566-67, 573
Literature of the Occult (Messent) 527
Littlewit, Humphry (pseud. of HPL) 57-58
Llopis, Rafael 510-11
Lloyd, John Uri 424n5
Lock and Key Library, The (Hawthorne) 429
Locker-Lampson, Frederick 151
Long, Frank Belknap 20, 60, 207, 224, 228, 247, 301-2, 337, 338, 343-46, 399, 444-45, 463, 478, 481, 503, 506, 508, 519, 523, 524-25, 544-45, 551, 579, 581, 595, 600, 610, 611
Looking Backward 509-10
Lopes, Duarte 363-64
"Lord of Illusion, The" (Price) 38, 338
Lost World, The (film) 51
Lovecraft, H. P.: aesthetics of, 105-14, 116-20, 152-55, 160, 214-16, 294-97, 430-35, 477-80, 483-85, 590-91; and amateur journalism, 490-93; and autobiography, 219-31, 495-97; cosmicism of, 157-59, 171-72, 454-55; on culture, 76-90; on films, 49-52; letters by, 73-96, 308, 440-52, 493-95; marriage of, 46-48, 396-98; and Munsey magazines, 62-72; and music, 22-26; philosophy of, 120-21, 161-78, 320-21, 367-71, 480-82, 587; poetry of, 151-52, 347-51, 437-39, 453-64, 465-72, 543-44; political views of, 91-95, 99-104, 122-43, 147-49, 485-88; pseudonyms of, 53-61; and racism, 75-76, 145-47, 211-14, 375-77; and religion, 182-90; reputation of, 501-14, 539-47, 579-80, 616-20; as revisionist, 31-45, 343-46, 357-61; and science, 191-210, 232-41, 297-306; scholarship on, 7-9, 515-37, 580-84; style of, 178-80, 244-46, 473-77; travels of, 488-90; on weird fiction,

422-30; and *Weird Tales*, 13-21; and World War I, 290-91
Lovecraft, Sarah Susan Phillips 182, 224, 396, 496
Lovecraft, Winfield Scott 182, 582
Lovecraft: A Biography (de Camp) 8, 516-20, 521, 579, 581, 582
Lovecraft: A Look Behind the "Cthulhu Mythos" (Carter) 526, 612
Lovecraft: Disturbing the Universe (Burleson) 583
Lovecraft Annual 8
Lovecraft at Last (Lovecraft-Conover) 421, 523-24, 579-84
Lovecraft Chronicles, The (Cannon) 610
Lovecraft Collectors Library 510
"Lovecraft in My Life" (Leiber) 566
Lovecraft kessakushu 513
Lovecraft ou du fantastique (Lévy) 526, 527-28
Lovecraft Studies 8, 532, 583
Lovecraft zenshu 514
Lovecraft's Book (Lupoff) 610
Lovecraftian Voyages (Faig) 522
"Loved Dead, The" (Lovecraft-Eddy) 33-34, 291, 297
Loveman, Samuel 224, 225, 228, 312, 333, 383, 441, 508, 523, 542-43
Lowndes, Robert A. W. 20
Lucian of Samosata 311
Lucretius (T. Lucretius Carus) 120, 379, 455, 535
"Lucubrations Lovecraftian" 147, 321, 492
Lumley, Brian 608-9
Lumley, William 19, 43, 337, 562
Lundwall, Sam J. 513
Lupoff, Richard A. 610
Lurker at the Threshold, The (Derleth) 330, 605
"Lurking Fear, The" 17, 108, 139, 198-99, 212, 258, 262, 263, 268-69, 330, 375, 549

Mabbott, T. O. 116, 428n12
Mac Flecknoe (Dryden) 448
McCarthy, Joe 16
Macauley, George W. 57
McGeoch, Verna 60
McGrew, Donald Francis 65

Machen, Arthur 63, 200, 223, 273, 373, 422, 423, 426, 427, 440, 587
McIlwraith, Dorothy 19, 20
Mackie, J. L. 168
McLaughlin, Mark 612
Macleod, Fiona 74
"Madness of Lucian Gray, The" (Bloch) 554
Maeterlinck, Maurice 116
Magnalia Christi Americana (Mather) 401
Mainwaring, Archibald 56-57
Mainwaring, Arthur 56
"Man of Stone, The" (Lovecraft-Heald) 38
"Man of the Crowd, The" (Poe) 432
"Man Who Never Grew Young, The" (Leiber) 572
Man's Place in Nature and Other Anthropological Essays (Huxley) 362, 520
Manilius (M. Manilius) 420
Mann, Georg 576
Marblehead (Lupoff) 610
Marginalia 248, 372, 446, 513
Mariconda, Steven J. 7, 178
Marvel Tales 325, 326, 554
Marx, Karl 102, 128
Mask of Cthulhu, The (Derleth) 605
Mather, Cotton 401
"Matter of Uniteds, A" 492
Maturin, Charles Robert 266, 271, 403, 423
Mauran, William Lippitt 404
Mausolus 381
Medea (Euripides) 267, 427
Meditations on First Philosophy (Descartes) 368
"Medusa: A Portrait" 56
Medusa: A Portrait 508
"Medusa's Coil" (Lovecraft-Bishop) 36-37, 44-45, 127, 247-48, 265, 269, 295, 337-38, 376
Melmoth the Wanderer (Maturin) 266, 271, 403, 423, 427, 429
Memoirs of a Justified Sinner (Hogg) 424
"Memory" 353
Mendelssohn, Felix 24
Meng, Roderic 503
"Merman, The" (Bloch) 554
Merritt, A. 69-70
Merritt, James 521

Merritt, John 402
"Messenger, The" 461
Messent, Peter B. 527
"Metal Chamber, The" (Rimel) 361
Metamorphoses (Ovid) 378
Metcalf, T. N. 63, 68-69
"Metrical Regularity" 483, 485
Metropolis (film) 51
Meyrink, Gustav 50, 424
Michaud, Marc A. 7, 8, 50n2, 507, 509-10, 532, 618
Michaud, Paul R. 507
Michelangelo 87
Middleton, Lilian 54
Migliore, Andrew 619
"Million Years After, A" (Roof) 392
Milman, H. H. 88
Milton, John 190
Mind Parasites, The (Wilson) 607
Miniter, Edith 492-93, 541
Miscellaneous Writings 504
Miske, J. Chapman 534
Miti di Cthulhu, I (de Turris-Fusco) 513
Mitos de Cthulhu, Los 511
Modern Science and Materialism (Elliot) 162, 166, 201, 368-70, 371, 481
Modern Temper, The (Krutch) 208, 596
Modern Weird Tale, The (Joshi) 8
Moe, Maurice W. 60, 152, 194, 225-26, 355-56, 444, 445, 446, 451, 460-61, 465
"Monody on the Late King Alcohol" 60
Monroe, Harriet 442
Monteverdi, Claudio 25
"Moon-Bog, The" 277, 278, 294
"Moon of Skulls, The" (Howard) 74
"Moon Pool, The" (Merritt) 69-70
Moore, C. L. 446, 541
Moore, Thomas 354, 453
"More *Chain-Lightning*" 292, 487
Morton, James F. 54, 212, 444, 496-97
Mosig, Dirk W. 7, 8, 34, 42, 43, 109, 221, 352, 421, 437, 504, 513, 517-19, 520, 522, 524, 530-31, 532, 534, 535, 536, 567, 581, 609
"Mound, The" (Lovecraft-Bishop) 36, 37, 44, 45, 122-35, 138, 141-42, 149, 239, 247, 266, 268, 269, 270, 271, 287, 291, 294, 312, 338, 343-46, 388-89, 461, 517

Mozart, Wolfgang Amadeus 22-23, 25
"Mrs. Miniter—Estimates and Recollections" 492-93
"MS. Found in a Bottle" (Poe) 428-29
Mulock, Mrs 28
Munday, John 116-17, 118
Munn, H. Warner 14, 15, 523, 525, 552
Munsey magazines 62-72
Munsey's Magazine 62, 68
Murray, Margaret A. 200, 298, 589
Murray, Will 7, 40, 531
"Music of Erich Zann, The" 14, 383, 512
Mussolini, Benito 148
"My Correspondence with Lovecraft" (Leiber) 566, 568
"My Favourite Character" 151
Myhre, Øyvind 513
"Myrrha and Strephon" 56
Mysteries of the Worm (Bloch) 548, 551, 562
"Mystery of Murdon Grange, The" 354
"Mythology for the Young" 473
Myths and Myth-Makers (Fiske) 121, 161, 184, 481

"Nameless City, The" 199-200, 204, 250-51, 272, 277, 330, 354, 372, 420, 589
Nameless Cults (Junzt) 589, 600
Narrative of Arthur Gordon Pym, The (Poe) 392
"Nathicana" 56, 459
National Amateur 331, 336, 482
National Amateur Press Association 55, 394, 397, 492, 544
Natural History of Religion, The (Hume) 184
Nauck, Mrs. Wilhelm 223
Necronomicon (Alhazred) 16, 18, 17, 189, 275, 281, 287, 358, 366, 374, 411, 419-21, 472, 588-89, 592, 593, 598, 600, 601, 614
Necronomicon Files, The (Harms-Gonce) 612
Necronomicon Press 8, 504, 509-10, 532, 583, 618
Nelle spire di Medusa 512
Nelson, Dale J. 164
"Nemesis" 456, 458, 543

Nero and Other Poems (Smith) 541
"Nethescurial" (Ligotti) 611
"New-England Fallen" 145
New Lands (Fort) 299, 373
New Lovecraft Collector 9
New Tales of the Cthulhu Mythos (Campbell) 608
New York Review of Books 618
New York Times 305
New Yorker 474, 617
Nietzsche, Friedrich 120, 147, 166, 194, 212, 444, 450, 482, 520
"Nietzscheism and Realism" 164, 482, 486
"Night-Gaunts" 348, 461, 462
"Night Ocean, The" (Lovecraft-Barlow) 42, 44, 450, 513, 534
Night's Black Agents (Leiber) 566, 569, 571, 572, 574, 575, 578
"Nightmare Lake, The" 457, 543
Nightmare's Disciple (Pulver) 612
"Notebook Found in a Deserted House" (Bloch) 561
Notes and Commonplace Book, The 510
"Notes on a Nonentity" 495n1
"Notes on Writing Weird Fiction" 105, 162, 180, 196, 272, 394, 414–15, 434–35, 478, 479, 552, 568, 594
"Novel of the Black Seal" (Machen) 273
Nueva Dimensión 514
Nyctalops 530
"Nyarlathotep" (prose-poem) 32, 52, 204, 407, 555, 563
"Nyarlathotep" (sonnet) 348, 461, 462, 558, 563–64

Oates, Joyce Carol 618–19
"Objections to Orthodox Communism" 446
"Observations on Several Parts of America" 247, 446, 488, 504
Occult Lovecraft, The 446, 508, 523
"October" 59
"Ode to a Grecian Urn" (Keats) 59
"Ode to Selene or Diana" 56
Odyssey (Homer) 182, 259, 378
"Of Evil Sorceries done in New-England of Daemons in No Humane Shape" 330
"Old Brick Row, The" 494

"Old Christmas" 59, 119
"Old England and the Hyphen" 487
"Omnipresent Philistine, The" 153, 321
"On a Grecian Colonnade in a Park" 59
"On Mr. L. Phillips Howard's Profound Poem Entitled 'Life's Mystery'" 55
On Not-Being (Gorgias) 367
"On Religion" 57, 59
"On the Creation of Niggers" 516n10
"On the Methods and Results of Ethnology" (Huxley) 362
"On the Natural History of the Man-like Apes" (Huxley) 362–63
Onderdonk, Matthew H. 119, 317, 371, 435, 533
O'Neil, N. J. 75
Onions, Oliver 426
Onishi, Tadaaki 514
"Opener of the Way, The" (Bloch) 556
Opere complete 507, 512, 536
O'Reilly, Michael Ormonde (pseud. of HPL) 56
Orton, Vrest 523
Ossian (James Macpherson) 466
"Other Gods, The" 34, 111, 221n2, 249, 251, 259, 278, 280, 281, 282, 287, 311, 330–31, 595
"Our Apology to E. M. W." (Russell) 68
Our Knowledge of the External World (Russell) 371, 450
"Out of the Aeons" (Lovecraft-Heald) 39, 45, 237–38, 290, 299, 450, 511
Out of the Silent Planet (Lewis) 479
"Outpost, The" 461, 543
Outré 520
"Outsider, The" 17, 18, 178, 221–22, 289, 549, 557, 605
Outsider and Others, The 243n1, 252, 255, 425
Ovid (P. Ovidius Naso) 27, 56, 378, 427
O-Wash-Ta-Nong 57
Owen, Olive G. 60

Paget-Lowe, Henry (pseud. of HPL) 54, 57, 58–59, 60
Pain, Barry 424
Paley, William 88
Papy, Jacques 537
Parmenides 367
Parry, Michel 512

Parsons, Jacques 511
Passing of the Great Race, The (Grant) 212
Passions of the Soul, The (Descartes) 368
Pater, Walter 484
Pattee, Fred Lewis 426
Pawtuxet Valley Gleaner 193
"Peace Advocate, The" 57-58
Peirce, Earl 20
Pelan, John 614
"Pensive Swain, The" 57
Penzoldt, Peter 258, 426
Perry, Alvin Earl 249n9
"Perverted Poesie or Modern Metre" 57
Petaja, Emil 239, 305
"Phaeton" 438
Phantastica (Brandstatter) 512
Phantom of the Opera, The (film) 51
Phillips, Edwin E. 334
Phillips, Ward (pseud. of HPL) 54, 58, 59, 60, 330
Philosopher 252
Philosopher's Stone, The (Wilson) 607
"Phoenix on the Sword, The" (Howard) 76
"Pickman's Model" 223, 259, 275, 284, 292, 297, 331, 554, 562-63, 576
"Picture in the House, The" 33, 155, 198, 249-50, 318, 331, 353, 362-66, 395, 482, 588
Picture of Dorian Gray, The (Wilde) 296
Pigafetta, Filippo 362-65
Pine Cones 299, 323
Place Called Dagon, The (Gorman) 430, 435
Plaisier, Jennie K. 485
Planck, Max 185, 302-3, 481, 587
Plato 368
Pnakotic Manuscripts 277, 278, 281, 285, 287
Poe, Edgar Allan 63, 150, 154, 155, 157, 161, 178, 192, 226, 263, 273, 291, 297, 308, 352-56, 365-66, 392, 393, 423, 427-29, 432, 453, 454, 455, 457, 458-60, 475, 483, 529, 587, 617
"Poe-et's Nightmare, The" 107, 110, 453-55, 457
"Poem of Ulysses, The" 22n1, 149, 378
Poemata Minora, Volume II 56

Poetical Works of Jonathan E. Hoag, The (Hoag) 437-38
"Poetry and the Gods" (Lovecraft-Crofts) 32, 59, 295
"Poetry of Lilian Middleton, The" 483
"Polaris" 252, 276-77, 279, 352-56
Politics (Aristotle) 101
Pope, Alexander 25, 60, 67, 443, 448, 453, 473, 483
Popular Magazine 62
Portable Lovecraft 507, 508
Prawer, S. S. 532
"Premature Burial, The" (Poe) 226, 365
Price, E. Hoffmann 15, 17, 38, 230, 237, 249, 250, 331, 338-39, 358, 444, 513, 539
Price, Robert M. 7, 40, 41, 383, 531, 533-34, 589, 597-98, 613
Primitive Culture (Tylor) 121, 161, 184, 298, 481, 587
Prinn, Ludvig 550, 589
Private Life of H. P. Lovecraft, The (Davis) 46
[Providence] *Evening News* 493
Providence in Colonial Times (Kimball) 399, 401, 402
"Providence in 2000 A.D." 145
Providence Journal 317, 493
Providence Sunday Journal 315, 447
[Providence] *Tribune* 193
Pryke, Reginald A. 13
Psycho (Bloch) 432, 564
"Psychopompos" 116, 460, 511
Pugmire, W. H. 612
Pulver, Joseph S., Sr 612
Purcell, Henry 24
"Pursuit" 349

Quarber Merkur 514
"Quest of Iranon, The" 14, 112, 221n2, 249, 278-79, 310, 332
Quinn, Seabury 15, 16
Railo, Eino 422, 429n13
Rajala, J.-M. 8
Raleigh, Richard 611
Raleigh, Richard (pseud. of HPL) 56
"Rats in the Walls, The" 74, 140, 150, 151, 154, 197-98, 252, 258-59, 269, 289-90, 295, 297, 298, 306, 373-74, 403, 529, 556

Raven, Anthony 508
"Raven, The" (Poe) 460
Re in Giallo, Il 514
Read, Francis 404
"'Reality' and Knowledge" (Joshi) 8, 132, 371
"Recapture" 151, 152, 543-44
Recluse 422, 425
"Recognition" 236
"Regner Lodbrog's Epicedium" 465-72
Regnum Congo (Pigafetta) 362-65
"Remarkable Document, A" 292
Remigius (Nicholas Remy) 589
"Reminiscence of Dr. Samuel Johnson, A" 53, 57, 149, 308, 318
"Renaissance of Manhood, The" 291
Renan, Ernest 187
"Reply to *The Lingerer*, A" 475, 492
Résumé with Monsters (Spencer) 612
Return, The (de la Mare) 403
"Return of Hastur, The" (Derleth) 18, 603
"Return of the Lloigor, The" (Wilson) 606-7
"Revelation" 457, 458
"Revolutionary Mythology" 487
Reynolds, B. M. 18-19
Rhode Island Journal of Astronomy 62, 193, 473
Riddle of the Universe, The (Haeckel) 162, 210, 239, 300, 371, 480-81, 587
Rigel 514
Rime of the Ancient Mariner, The (Coleridge) 183, 192
Rimel, Duane W. 40-41, 42, 234, 335, 357-61, 450, 534
Rise and Fall of the Cthulhu Mythos, The (Joshi) 7, 9
Rising Tide of Color Against White World-Supremacy, The (Stoddard) 212
Rivière, Yves 511
Robertson, T. W. 51
Robinson, Edwin Arlington 151, 460
Roerich, Nicholas 514
Roman "gothique" anglais, Le (Lévy) 422
Roof, Katharine Metcalf 392
Roosevelt, Franklin Delano 129, 450, 475, 487
Roosevelt, Theodore 144

Roots of Horror in the Fiction of H. P. Lovecraft, The (St Armand) 528-29
"Rose for Emily, A" (Faulkner) 170, 433-34
Rosemary's Baby (Levin) 617
Ross, James Clark 390
Rottensteiner, Franz 512, 537
Rowley, Ames Dorrance (pseud. of HPL) 56, 58
"Rudis Indigestaque Moles" 484
Runir (Wormius) 472
Russell, Bertrand 166, 168, 194, 303, 320, 371, 450, 451-52
Russell, John 67, 68, 70, 71, 72
Russell, Robert Leonard 19, 20
Russell, Samuel D. 465
Russell, W. Clark 193, 390-92
"Rutted Road, The" 455-56

"Sacrifice to Science, A" (de Castro) 35
St Armand, Barton L. 138, 405, 406, 517, 527, 528-29
St. Leon (Godwin) 403
Saintsbury, George 429
Samples, John Milton 57, 437, 495
"Sandwin Compact, The" (Derleth) 606
Santayana, George 168, 300, 320
"Satan's Servants" (Bloch) 554-55
Sater, Elsye Tash 116, 118
Saxo Grammaticus 471
Scaliger, Julius Caesar 315
Scarborough, Dorothy 429n13
Scarf, The (Bloch) 561
Schatzen aus der Zeit, Der 512
Schiff, Stuart D. 336
Schliemann, Heinrich 298
Schopenhauer, Arthur 164-65, 166, 320, 481, 482
Schultz, David E. 7, 8, 392, 394, 401, 460, 462, 479, 531, 534, 535, 536, 583, 586, 602
Schwader, Ann K. 612
Schwartz, Julius 323
Schweitzer, Darrell 52, 516n10, 526
Science-Fantasy Correspondent 425, 524
Scientific American 235, 493
Scientific Gazette 193, 473
Scot 326
Scott, Sir Walter 460

Index 641

Scott, Winfield Townley 151, 453, 456, 460
Scream for Jeeves (Cannon) 612
Seasons, The (Thomson) 145
"Secret in the Tomb, The" (Bloch) 550
"Secret of Sebek, The" (Bloch) 556-57
Selected Letters 73, 246-47, 438, 440-41, 442, 446, 503-4, 511, 512, 515, 524, 532, 535, 580, 582, 583
Selected Letters (Howard) 73
Seneca the Younger (L. Annaeus Seneca) 427
Senf, C. C. 13
Sepulcro y otros relatos, El 511
Service, Robert W. 84
Sfida dall'infinito 512, 513
"Shadow—A Parable" (Poe) 353, 354
"Shadow from the Steeple, The" (Bloch) 557-58, 563, 604
"Shadow out of Time, The": adaptations of, 613; autobiography in, 222; and R. H. Barlow, 540; and Robert Bloch, 561; cosmicism in, 159, 177-78, 454, 599; humour and satire in, 294, 313, 316-17; influences on, 52, 193; and knowledge, 108, 112, 114, 136, 137, 138-39, 140-41, 143, 149; and Fritz Leiber, 567, 568, 571, 572, 605; politics in, 101, 104, 122-33, 450, 474, 488; and racism, 212; and Duane W. Rimel, 361; and science, 204, 207, 208-9, 210; and science fiction, 151, 207, 232, 233, 234-35, 239-40; setting of, 171; structure of, 264, 265, 268, 270, 271, 272-73; style of, 449; textual history of, 249, 254, 256-57, 332; themes in, 173, 612; writing of, 348, 351
"Shadow over Innsmouth, The": adaptations of, 613; autobiography in, 219-20, 227, 229-30; and Robert Bloch, 549; and Cthulhu Mythos, 606, 611; dialect in, 395; influences on, 435; and Fritz Leiber, 570, 577; and HPL's poetry, 348; and knowledge, 108; politics in, 122-27, 130-31, 134, 137, 138, 139-40, 142; and racism, 145-46, 211, 213-14; and science, 151, 394; setting of, 588; structure of, 264, 271; textual history of, 332-33;
themes in, 159, 172, 173, 375, 598; topical references in, 292, 293, 294; writing of, 351
Shadow over Innsmouth, The 508, 616
Shadows Bend (Barbour-Raleigh) 611
Shadowy Thing, The (Drake) 430, 435
Shakespeare, William 17, 18, 60, 566
"Shambler from the Stars, The" (Bloch) 313, 551-52, 557, 604
Shea, J. Vernon 7, 126, 136, 441, 445n3, 446, 474, 520, 525
Shelley, Mary 50
Shepherd, Wilson 329, 419, 420-21
Shiel, M. P. 427
Shoggoth Cacciatore and Other Eldritch Entrees (McLaughlin) 612
Shreffler, Philip A. 508, 526, 527
"Shunned House, The" 61, 150, 151, 169, 173, 200-201, 202, 203, 268, 269, 272, 302, 303, 333, 371, 396, 398, 450, 490, 572
Shunned House, The 252, 541-43
Shuttered Room and Other Pieces, The 513, 547
"Silence—A Fable" (Poe) 353
Silence of the Lambs, The (Harris) 432
Silver Clarion 57, 437, 438, 495
"Silver Key, The" 14, 158, 226, 228, 241, 252, 262, 280, 294, 296, 314, 319-20, 333
Sime, Sidney H. 295
"Sin-Eater, The" (Macleod) 74
Sinister House (Hall) 430
Sitter, Willem de 303-4
Skräkens labyrinter 513
"Skull-Face" (Howard) 75
"Slaying of the Monster, The" (Lovecraft-Barlow) 41
Smith, Charles W. ("Tryout") 59
Smith, Clark Ashton 20, 73, 152, 227, 246, 253, 295, 298, 320n6, 323, 347n1, 358, 388, 419, 424, 440, 444, 451, 457, 461, 463, 477, 541, 543, 585, 589, 600-601, 603
Smith, Louis 543
Smith, Paul S. 19
Smith, Tevis Clyde 75, 79
Smith, William Benjamin 146, 211, 520
"Smoke Ghost" (Leiber) 573

Softly, Edward (pseud. of HPL) 56, 58, 59
Sombra más allá del tiempo, La 511
"Some Backgrounds of Fairyland" 446
"Some Causes of Self-Immolation" 368, 476, 482, 504
Some Current Motives and Practices 477, 492, 545
"Some Dutch Footprints in New England" 490
"Some Notes on a Nonentity" 495, 594
"Some Notes on Interplanetary Fiction" 124, 173, 308, 479
"Some Repetitions on the Times" 100, 101, 102, 122, 127, 128, 129, 130-31, 474, 486, 487
Something about Cats and Other Pieces 555, 566-67
Songs of a Dead Dreamer (Ligotti) 611
Sonnets of the Midnight Hours (Wandrei) 152, 461
"Sorcerer's Jewel, The" (Bloch) 558-59
"Sorcery of Aphlar, The" (Rimel) 40
"Space-Eaters, The" (Long) 551, 600
Space Vampires, The (Wilson) 607
Spawn of Cthulhu, The (Carter) 505
"Spawn of the Green Abyss" (Thompson) 606
Spence, Lewis 299
Spencer, R. E. 424
Spencer, William Browning 612
Spengler, Oswald 138, 148, 290, 450
"Spider, The" (Ewers) 435
Spink, Helm C. 442
Squires, Roy A. 333, 508
"Star-Winds" 234, 236
"Statement of Randolph Carter, The" 150, 225, 226, 252, 334, 348, 420, 508-9, 588
Stephens, James 569
Sterling, George 227, 457
Sterling, Kenneth 20, 43, 234, 337, 513, 523
Stevens, Francis 69, 70
Stewart, J. H., Jr 18
"Sticks" (Wagner) 610
Stock, R. D. 537
Stoddard, Lothrop 212
Stoic philosophy 135
Strange Eons (Bloch) 562-64, 611

"Strange High House in the Mist, The" 18, 228, 282, 315, 334, 348, 360, 383, 384-85, 387
Strange Manuscript Found in a Copper Cylinder, A (De Mille) 388-90, 392
"Street, The" 145
Strength to Dream, The (Wilson) 516, 527, 606
Studies in Pessimism (Schopenhauer) 164
"Suicide in the Study, The" (Bloch) 550
Sullivan, Jack 428, 537
Sully, Helen V. 444
Summers, Montague 426
"Summer Sunset and Evening, A" 57, 58
"Sunken Land, The" (Leiber) 570-71, 605
"Supernatural Horror in Literature" 30, 64, 72, 117, 179, 191, 263, 366, 402-3, 422-36, 477, 505, 508, 511, 512, 513, 515, 521, 546
Supernatural Horror in Literature 510
Supernatural in Fiction, The (Penzoldt) 258
Supernatural in Modern English Fiction, The (Scarborough) 429n13
"Sweet Ermengarde" 308, 334
Swift, Augustus T. 69-70
Swift, Jonathan 55, 443
Swinburne, Algernon Charles 154, 457, 458, 459
Sylvester, Margaret 508
"Symphony and Stress" 492

"Tale of Satampra Zeiros, The" (Smith) 388, 600-601
Tale of Terror, The (Birkhead) 422, 429
Tales (Library of America) 182
Tales of Magic and Mystery 325
Tales of Mystery (Saintsbury) 429
Tales of the Cthulhu Mythos (Derleth) 506, 513, 605
Tales of War (Dunsany) 386
Talman, Wilfred B. 34, 446, 490, 513, 523
Tartini, Giuseppe 25
Tatler 59
Taylor, Frank Bursley 305-6
"Temple, The" 155, 199, 204, 291, 311, 570-71

Tennyson, Alfred, Lord 144
Terhune, Albert Payson 63, 65
"Terrible Old Man, The" 198, 318, 334, 558, 588
"Terror from the Depths, The" (Leiber) 566, 576-77, 578, 611
"Terror in Cut-Throat Cave" (Bloch) 561-62
"Teuton's Battle-Song, The" 471
Theobald, Lewis, Jun. (pseud. of HPL) 53, 54, 55, 57, 58, 59-60
Thing, The (film) 613
"Thing in the Moonlight, The" (spurious) 534
"Thing on the Doorstep, The" 114, 179, 210, 221, 224-25, 227-28, 249, 266, 267, 270, 335, 348, 410-15, 435, 560, 563, 571, 572, 599
Thompson, C. Hall 606
Thomson, Christine Campbell 29
Thomson, James 145
"Through Hyperspace with Brown Jenkin" (Leiber) 514, 566, 567
"Through the Gates of the Silver Key" (Lovecraft-Price) 38, 43, 44, 59, 137, 226-27, 234, 237, 239, 240-41, 262, 266, 277, 286, 287, 299, 338-39, 358, 557
Tierney, Richard L. 124, 238-39, 530, 534, 609
"'Till A' the Seas'" (Lovecraft-Barlow) 41-42, 233, 314, 339
Time 506, 580, 617
Time and the Gods (Dunsany) 595
Times Literary Supplement 532
Tingen på terskelen 513
"To a Dreamer" 326
"To a Youth" 56
"To Charlie of the Comics" 49
"To Jonathan E. Hoag, Esq." 438
"To Maj.-Gen. Omar Bundy, U.S.A." 58
"To Mr. Terhune, on His Historical Fiction" 63
"To Pan" 56
To Quebec and the Stars 504, 535
"To the American Flag" (Hoag) 437-39, 534
"To the Eighth of November" 57
"To the Old Pagan Religion" 56, 58
"To Zara" 457

Toldridge, Elizabeth 343, 443-44, 449, 481, 484
"Tomb, The" 54, 150, 151, 178, 220, 222, 252, 261, 291, 297, 354, 393, 394, 435, 587
Tomb and Other Tales, The 505
Tombaugh, C. W. 304
Toynbee, Arnold 148
Trail of Cthulhu, The (Derleth) 605
Transatlantic Circulator 115-21, 319, 344, 381, 430-31, 446, 482
"Transition of Juan Romero, The" 196, 335
"Trans-Neptunian Planets" 235
"Trap, The" (Lovecraft-Whitehead) 37, 300, 450, 534
Traumfahrt von unbekannten Kadath, Die 512
"Travels in the Provinces of America" 35, 488
"Tree, The" 112, 275, 278, 335, 378-82
"Tree on the Hill, The" (Lovecraft-Rimel) 40, 357-61, 450, 534
Tremaine, F. Orlin 253-54, 255
Trilby (du Maurier) 50
"Trip of Theobald, The" 55
Troy Times 437
Truchaud, François 511
True History (Lucian) 311
True Supernatural Stories 331
"Truth about Mars, The" 233
Tryout 53, 55, 56, 57-58, 329-30, 334, 335, 379, 438
Turner, James 440, 443, 503-4, 524, 613
"Two Black Bottles" (Lovecraft-Talman) 34
Tylor, Edward Burnett 121, 161, 184, 298, 481, 587

"Ulalume" (Poe) 458-60
Ulysses (Joyce) 153, 485
Unaussprechlichen Kulten (Junzt) 189, 589
Uncollected Prose and Poetry 509, 535
"Unda, or, The Bride of the Sea" 57, 58, 453
"Under the Pyramids" (Lovecraft-Houdini) 31, 34, 45, 248, 252, 261, 354, 556
"Undying Thing, The" (Pain) 424

Unhappy Far-Off Things (Dunsany) 386
United Amateur 59, 249, 333, 336
United Amateur Press Association 54, 72, 394, 441-42, 491
United Amateur Press Association: Exponent of Amateur Journalism 492
"Unknown, The" 53, 58
"Unnamable, The" 225-26, 297, 317, 511
Uno, Toshiyasu 514
"Unspeakable Betrothal, The" (Bloch) 560-61
Unusual Stories 495
Unutterable Horror: A History of Supernatural Fiction (Joshi) 8
"Upper Berth, The" (Crawford) 423

Vagrant 54, 248, 252, 325
"Vastarien" (Ligotti) 611
Vathek (Beckford) 259, 420
Vaughan, Ralph E. 461
Verlaine, Paul 484
"Vermont—A First Impression" 229, 489
Verne, Jules 193
"Vers Libre Epidemic, The" 475, 485
Viajes al otro mundo 510-11
Virgil (P. Vergilius Maro) 247, 379, 427
Vivaldi, Antonio 24, 25, 26
Voltaire (François-Marie Arouet) 184
"Volunteer, The" 58
Voyages of Capt. Ross, R.N., The 390

Wade, James 606
Wagner, Karl Edward 610
Wagner, Richard 24, 25
Walpole, Horace 452
Wanderings in Roman Britain (Weigall) 373
Wandrei, Donald 152, 243, 246-47, 249, 251-52, 255, 323, 324, 325, 327, 331, 332, 333, 408, 440, 442, 443, 444, 461, 463, 502, 503-4, 540, 545, 546-47, 579, 580, 590, 604, 616
Ward, Richard 403-4
Ward, Samuel 404
Warning to the Curious, A (James) 429
Wasso, J. 17
Waste Land, The (Eliot) 55, 144, 296
"Waste Paper" 56, 57, 296, 297

"Watcher from the Sky, The" (Derleth) 606
Watchers out of Time and Others, The (Derleth) 604
Watkins, France-Marie 511
Waugh, Evelyn 244n3, 320
Waugh, Robert H. 8, 461
Web of Easter Island, The (Wandrei) 604
Wegener, Alfred Lothar 306
Weigall, Arthur 373
Weir, Peter 613
"Weird &c. Items in Library of H. P. Lovecraft" 28
Weird Fiction Times 514
Weird Tale, The (Joshi) 8, 377
"Weird Tale in English Since 1890, The" (Derleth) 515
Weird Tales 13-21; and R. H. Barlow, 539, 544, 545; and Robert Bloch, 550, 552, 554; and August Derleth, 603; and Fritz Leiber, 568; HPL on, 71, 176, 581; HPL's letters in, 494, 532, 552; HPL's poetry in, 454; HPL's possible editorship of, 397; HPL's reading of, 302, 392, 494; HPL's revisions in, 35, 36, 38, 39, 45, 247, 297, 337, 338, 339, 345, 358, 556; HPL's stories in, 74, 166, 309, 313, 398, 442-43, 544, 579, 591; and HPL's textual history, 248, 250, 252, 253, 324, 325, 326, 327-28, 329-30, 331, 332, 333, 334-35, 336; rejections by, 344, 347-48, 590; and Clark Ashton Smith, 601
"Weird Work of William Hope Hodgson, The" 424-25
Weiss, Henry George 20
"Well, The" 461
Wellman, Manly Wade 18
Wells, H. G. 116
"Wendigo, The" (Blackwood) 602
"Werewolf of Ponkert, The" (Munn) 552
Wesley, W. H. 365
West, Nathanael 320
Wetzel, George T. 53, 56, 284n5, 299, 420, 595
"What Amateurdom and I Have Done for Each Other" 491
"What Belongs in Verse" 483, 484

"What the Moon Brings" 251, 336
"Whippoorwills in the Hills, The" (Derleth) 606
"Whisperer in Darkness, The": autobiography in, 219, 229; and Robert Bloch, 553, 556, 561, 563; and Cthulhu Mythos, 593-94, 598, 601, 602, 606; humour in, 317; interpretations of, 527; and Fritz Leiber, 567-68, 571, 572, 576-77, 611; and HPL's poetry, 462; politics in, 122-27, 130, 134, 135-36, 137; and Duane W. Rimel, 358, 359; and science, 107, 108, 114, 151, 170, 204, 205, 206-7, 232, 233, 236-37, 238; setting of, 171, 293, 474, 489, 588; structure of, 262, 266, 267, 269-70; style of, 245, 246, 257; textual history of, 252, 336; themes in, 173, 176; topical references in, 298-99, 301-2, 304-5; writing of, 388, 461
"'Whisperer' Re-examined, The" (Leiber) 566, 567-68
Whispers 336
White, Edward Lucas 424
White, Matthew, Jr 63, 66
White Fire (Bullen) 115
"White Ship, The" 117, 119, 249, 259-60, 277, 304, 311, 319, 333, 336, 352
Whitehead, Henry S. 20, 37-38, 450, 534, 541
Whitman, Walt 119
Wickenden, Mr 120-21, 163, 451, 482
Wilcox, Joseph V. 19
Wilde, Oscar 117-18, 178, 229-30, 296, 319, 353, 431, 484
Williams, Roger 393

Willie, Albert Frederick (pseud. of HPL and Alfred Galpin) 56
"Willows, The" (Blackwood) 264, 422
Wilson, Colin 516, 527, 606-7
Wilson, Edmund 17, 151, 178, 241, 428n12, 460, 604, 617, 619
Wilson, F. Paul 612
Wilson, Gahan 610
Winesburg, Ohio (Anderson) 153, 494
"Winged Death" (Lovecraft-Heald) 19, 39
Winter Wish, A 56, 504-5, 535
"Wisdom" 57
Witch-Cult in Western Europe, The (Murray) 200, 298, 589
"Within the Gates" 496
Wodehouse, P. G. 612
Wollheim, Donald A. 16, 253, 543
Wolverine 54, 327, 330
"Wood, The" 461
Woodberry, George E. 429
Wormius, Olaus (Ole Wurm) 465-72
Wright, Farnsworth 14, 15, 16, 19, 35, 43, 74, 76, 250, 312, 319, 344, 347n1, 494, 551, 554, 590
Wright, Harold Bell 64
Writing Fiction (Derleth) 515
Writings in The United Amateur 509
Wuthering Heights (Brontë) 423

"Xenophobia in the Life and Work of H. P. Lovecraft" (Bender) 520-21
Xenophon 378, 420

"Year Off, A" 151
Yeats, W. B. 154
Young, S. Hall 57

Zoilus (pseud. of HPL) 54, 55
Zorn, Ray H. 69

www.ingramcontent.com/pod-product-compliance
Lightning Source LLC
Chambersburg PA
CBHW071429300426
44114CB00013B/1360